NEW CENTURY BIBLE COMMENTARY

Old Testament General Editor
RONALD E. CLEMENTS

Proverbs

THE NEW CENTURY BIBLE COMMENTARIES

EXODUS (J. P. Hyatt)
DEUTERONOMY (A. D. H. Mayes)
JOSHUA, JUDGES, RUTH (John Gray)
1 AND 2 KINGS Volumes 1 and 2 (Gwilym H. Jones)
1 AND 2 CHRONICLES (H. G. Williamson)
EZRA, NEHEMIAH, AND ESTHER (D. J. Clines)
JOB (H. H. Rowley)
PSALMS, Volumes 1 and 2 (A. A. Anderson)
ECCLESIASTES (R. N. Whybray)
THE SONG OF SONGS (John G. Snaith)
ISAIAH 1–39 (R. E. Clements)
ISAIAH 40–66 (R. N. Whybray)
JEREMIAH (Douglas Rawlinson Jones)
LAMENTATIONS (Iain W. Provan)
EZEKIEL (John W. Wevers)
HOSEA (G. I. Davies)
HAGGAI, ZECHARIAH AND MALACHI (Paul Redditt)
THE GOSPEL OF MATTHEW (David Hill)
THE GOSPEL OF MARK (Hugh Anderson)
THE GOSPEL OF LUKE (E. Earle Ellis)
THE GOSPEL OF JOHN (Barnabas Lindars)
THE ACTS OF THE APOSTLES (William Neil)
ROMANS, Second Edition (Matthew Black)
1 AND 2 CORINTHIANS (F. F. Bruce)
GALATIANS (Donald Guthrie)
EPHESIANS (C. Leslie Mitton)
PHILIPPIANS (Ralph P. Martin)
COLOSSIANS AND PHILEMON (Ralph P. Martin)
1 AND 2 THESSALONIANS (I. Howard Marshall)
PASTORAL EPISTLES (A. T. Hanson)
HEBREWS (R. McL. Wilson)
1 PETER (Ernest Best)
JAMES, JUDE, AND 2 PETER (E. M. Sidebottom)
JOHANNINE EPISTLES (K. Grayson)
THE BOOK OF REVELATION (G. R. Beasley-Murray)

Other titles are in preparation

NEW CENTURY BIBLE COMMENTARY

Based on the Revised Standard Version

PROVERBS

R. N. WHYBRAY

Marshall Pickering
An Imprint of HarperCollins*Publishers*

WILLIAM B. EERDMANS PUBLISHING COMPANY, GRAND RAPIDS

Marshall Pickering is an Imprint of
HarperCollins*Religious*
Part of HarperCollins*Publishers*
77–85 Fulham Palace Road, London W6 8JB

First published in Great Britain
in 1994 by Marshall Pickering
and in the United States by Wm. B. Eerdmans Publishing Co.,
255 Jefferson Ave., S.E., Grand Rapids, Michigan 49503.

1 3 5 7 9 10 8 6 4 2

A catalogue record for this book is
available from the British Library

Marshall Pickering ISBN 0-551-02831-9
Eerdmans ISBN 0-8028-0787-9

Photoset in Great Britain by
Rowland Phototypesetting Ltd
Bury St Edmunds, Suffolk
Printed in the United States of America
for Marshall Pickering and Wm. B. Eerdmans

CONTENTS

PREFACE

This commentary is concerned primarily with the elucidation of the Hebrew text of Proverbs (MT). The Septuagint (LXX) often has a substantially different text, with additions and omissions as well as variants. Many of these represent a deliberate departure from the Hebrew text which lay before the translators. They will be noted here only where it can be argued that they do in fact represent a variant Hebrew text or a different vocalization, and so may help to elucidate or correct MT.

In the discussions of textual and philological matters, references to the notes provided in *BHS* will be generally avoided as they represent the views and preferences of a single scholar, Professor Johannes Fichtner (1902–1962), and reflect the scholarship of that time. They are too brief to be really useful and can be misleading. In this commentary some attempt is made to explain why certain emendations and revocalizations are accepted or seriously considered. Considerations of space make it impossible to deal with all the proposals that have been made; many of these, however, are to be found in works noted in the bibliography.

The common practice of making frequent cross-references to passages in the literatures of other ancient Near Eastern peoples has not been followed in this commentary. That Proverbs has many themes and modes of speech in common with other wisdom literatures is so well known as to need no detailed demonstration. Only a few instances of particularly close resemblances between Proverbs and passages from those literatures will be noted here. The drawing of parallels between Proverbs and Ecclesiasticus has similarly been eschewed except when these are especially illuminating.

I regret that the commentary by A. Meinhold (*Die Sprüche* [Zürcher Bibelkommentare], Zurich: Theologischer Verlag, 1991) did not come into my hands until my own commentary was completed.

My thanks are due to my wife Mary and to my stepdaughters Catherine and Elizabeth for discussions of the meaning of particular proverbs and for assistance with the arrangement of the bibliography.

Ely, July 1992 R. N. Whybray

ABBREVIATIONS

AB	*The Anchor Bible*, Garden City, New York
ANET	*Ancient Near Eastern Texts Relating to the Old Testament*, ed. J. B. Pritchard, Princeton, 1969^3
AO	*Der Alte Orient*, Leipzig
AOAT	*Alter Orient und Altes Testament*, Kevelaer
ATD	*Das Alte Testament Deutsch*, Göttingen
ATANT	*Abhandlungen Zur Theologie des Alten und Neuen Testaments*
BASOR	*Bulletin of the American Schools of Oriental Research*, Baltimore
BAT	*Die Botschaft des Alten Testaments*, Stuttgart
BETL	*Bibliotheca Ephemeridum Theologicarum Lovaniensium*
BHS	*Biblia Hebraica Stuttgartensia*, ed. K. Elliger and W. Rudolph, Stuttgart, 1977
Bib.	*Biblica*, Rome
BKAT	*Biblischer Kommentar, Altes Testament*, Neukirchen
BOT	*De Boeken van het Oude Testament*, Roermond
BWANT	*Beiträge zur Wissenschaft vom Alten und Neuen Testament*, Stuttgart
BZAW	*Beihefte zur Zeitschrift für die Alttestamentliche Wissenschaft*, Berlin
CBC	*Cambridge Bible Commentary on the New English Bible*, Cambridge
CBQ	*Catholic Biblical Quarterly*, Washington, DC
CC	*Communicator's Commentary, Old Testament*, Dallas
CTJ	*Calvin Theological Journal*, Grand Rapids
DOTT	*Documents From Old Testament Times*, ed. D. W. Thomas, London, 1958
DSB	*The Daily Study Bible*, Edinburgh and Philadelphia
EB	*Etudes Bibliques*, Paris
ET	English Translation
ET	*The Expository Times*, Edinburgh
ETL	*Ephemerides Theologicae Lovanienses*
FOTL	*The Forms of the Old Testament Literature*, Grand Rapids

GK	*Gesenius' Hebrew Grammar*, ed. E. Kautzsch, revised by A. E. Cowley, Oxford, 1910
HAT	*Handbuch zum Alten Testament*, Tübingen
HBK	*Herder's Bibelkommentar*, Freiburg
HKAT	*Handkommentar zum Alten Testament*, Göttingen
HSAT	*Die Heilige Schrift des Alten Testaments*, Bonn
HUCA	*Hebrew Union College Annual*, Cincinnati
ICC	*International Critical Commentary*, Edinburgh
Int.	*Interpretation*, Richmond, Virginia
JAOS	*Journal of the American Oriental Society*, Baltimore
JB	*Jerusalem Bible*
JBL	*Journal of Biblical Literature*, Philadelphia
JEA	*Journal of Egyptian Archaeology*, London
JNES	*Journal of Near Eastern Studies*, Chicago
JNWSL	*Journal of Northwest Semitic Languages*, Leiden
JQR	*Jewish Quarterly Review*, London
JSOT	*Journal for the Study of the Old Testament*, Sheffield
JSS	*Journal of Semitic Studies*, Manchester, Oxford
JTS	*Journal of Theological Studies*, Oxford
KB^2	*Lexicon in Veteris Testamenti Libros*, ed. L. Koehler and W. Baumgartner, 2nd edn 1953
KB^3	*Hebräisches und Aramäisches Lexikon zum Alten Testament*, ed. L. Koehler and W. Baumgartner, 3rd edn revised by J. J. Stamm, Leiden, 1967-
KEH	*Kurzgefasstes Exegetisches Handbuch zum Alten Testament*, Leipzig
KHC	*Kurzer Hand-Commentar zum Alten Testament*, Tübingen
LBBC	*Layman's Bible Books Commentary*, Nashville
LUÅ	*Lunds Universitets Årsskrift*
LXX	*Septuagint (Greek Version)*
MT	*The Masoretic Text of the Hebrew Bible*
NEB	*New English Bible*
NS	New Series
NZSTh	*Neue Zeitschrift für Systematische Theologie und Religionsphilosophie*, Berlin
OBO	*Orbis Biblicus et Orientalis*, Freiburg, Switzerland
OED	*Oxford English Dictionary*
OLZ	*Orientalische Literaturzeitung*, Berlin
OTL	Old Testament Library, London and Philadelphia
OTM	*Old Testament Message*, Dublin

OTS	*Oudtestamentische Studiën*, Leiden
Pesh.	Peshitta (Syriac Version)
RB	*Revue Biblique*, Paris
REB	*Revised English Bible*
RES	*Revue des Etudes Sémitiques*, Paris
RHPR	*Revue d'Histoire et de Philosophie Religieuses*, Strasbourg
SAT	*Die Schriften des Alten Testaments*, Göttingen
SB	*La Sainte Bible*, ed. L. Pirot, Paris
SBJ	*La Sainte Bible de Jérusalem*, Paris
SBT	*Studies in Biblical Theology*, London
SDB	*Supplément au Dictionnaire de la Bible*, ed. H. Cazelles and A. Feuillet, Paris
SEÅ	*Svensk Exegetisk Årsbok*, Lund
SHAW	*Sitzungsberichte der Heidelberger Akademie der Wissenschaften*, Heidelberg
SJT	*Scottish Journal of Theology*, Edinburgh
SKK	*Stuttgarter Kleiner Kommentar*, Stuttgart
SPAW	*Sitzungsberichte der Preussischen Akademie der Wissenschaften*, Berlin
StANT	*Studien zum Alten und Neuen Testament*, Munich
Suppl.	Supplement(s)
Symm.	Symmachus
Targ.	Targum
TBC	Torch Bible Commentaries, London
TDNT	*Theological Dictionary of the New Testament*, Grand Rapids
TDOT	*Theological Dictionary of the Old Testament*, Grand Rapids
THAT	*Theologisches Handwörterbuch zum Alten Testament*, Munich and Zurich
ThWAT	*Theologisches Wörterbuch zum Alten Testament*, Stuttgart
TLZ	*Theologische Literaturzeitung*, Leipzig
TOTC	*Tyndale Old Testament Commentaries*, London
TynB	*Tyndale Bulletin*, London
TZ	*Theologische Zeitschrift*, Basel
UF	*Ugarit-Forschung*, Kevelaer/Neukirchen
VT	*Vetus Testamentum*, Leiden
Vulg.	Vulgate
WC	Westminster Commentaries, London
WMANT	Wissenschaftliche Monographien zum Alten Testament, Neukirchen
WO	*Die Welt des Orients*, Göttingen

ZÄS	*Zeitschrift für Ägyptische Sprache und Altertumskunde*, Berlin
ZAW	*Zeitschrift für die Alttestamentliche Wissenschaft*, Berlin
ZThK	*Zeitschrift für Theologie und Kirche*, Tübingen

SELECT BIBLIOGRAPHY

COMMENTARIES *(cited in the text by author's name only)*

Aitken, K. T., *Proverbs* (*DSB*), 1986.

Alden, R. L., *Proverbs*, Grand Rapids, Michigan, 1983.

Barucq, A., *Le Livre des Proverbes* (Sources Bibliques), 1964.

Cohen, A., *Proverbs. Hebrew Text and English Translation with Introduction and Commentary*, London and Bournemouth, 1952.

Cox, D., *Proverbs with an Introduction to Sapiential Books* (*OTM*), 1982.

Delitzsch, F., *Salomonisches Spruchbuch*, Leipzig, 1873, repr. Basel, 1985.

Duesberg, H. and Auvray, P., *Le Livre des Proverbes* (*SBJ*), Paris, 2nd edn, 1957.

Frankenberg, W., *Die Sprüche, übersetzt und erklärt* (HBK), 1898.

Gemser, B., *Sprüche Salomos* (*HAT*), 2nd edn, 1963.

Greenstone, J. H., *Proverbs With Commentary*, Philadelphia, 1950.

Hamp, V., *Das Buch der Sprüche* (*EB*), 1949.

Hitzig, F., *Die Sprüche Salomos übersetzt*, Zurich, 1858.

Hubbard, D. A., *Proverbs* (CC), 1989.

Johnson, L. D., *Proverbs, Ecclesiastes, Song of Solomon* (*LBBC*), 1982.

Jones, E., *Proverbs and Ecclesiastes* (TBC), 1961.

Kidner, D., *The Proverbs. An Introduction and Commentary* (TOTC), 1964.

Lamparter, R. J., *Das Buch der Weisheit: Prediger und Sprüche* (*BAT*), 2nd edn 1959.

Lang, B., *Anweisungen gegen die Torheit. Sprichwörter – Jesus Sirach* (*SKK*), 1973.

McKane, W., *Proverbs: A New Approach* (OTL), 2nd edn 1977.

Nowack, W., *Die Sprüche Salomos* (*KEH*), 1883.

Oesterley, W. O. E., *Proverbs* (WC), 1929.

van der Ploeg, J., *Spreuken* (*BOT*), 1952.

Plöger, O., *Sprüche Salomos (Proverbia)* (*BKAT*), 1984.

Renard, H., *Le Livre des Proverbes* (*SB*), 1946.

Ringgren, H., *Sprüche Salomos* (*ATD*), 2nd edn 1967.
Schneider, H., *Die Sprüche Salomos, Das Buch des Predigers, Das Hohelied* (*HBK*), 1962.
Scott, R. B. Y., *Proverbs. Ecclesiastes* (*AB*), 1965.
Toy, C. H., *Proverbs* (ICC), 1899.
Volz, P., *Hiob und Weisheit* (*Das Buch Hiob, Sprüche und Jesus Sirach, Prediger*) (*SAT*), 1921.
Whybray, R. N., *The Book of Proverbs* (*CBC*), 1972.
Wiesmann, H., *Das Buch der Sprüche* (*HSAT*), 1923.
Wildeboer, G., *Die Sprüche* (*KHC*), 1897.

OTHER WORKS *(cited by author's name only)*

Bühlmann, W., *Vom rechten Reden und Schweigen. Studien zu Proverbien 10–31* (*OBO* 12), Freiburg, Switzerland and Göttingen, 1976.
Dahood, M., *Proverbs and Northwest Semitic Philology*, Rome, 1963.
Van der Weiden, W. A., *Le Livre des Proverbes. Notes philologiques* (*Biblica et Orientalia* 23), Rome, 1970.

OTHER STUDIES

Ackroyd, P. R., "The Meaning of Hebrew *dôr* Considered", *JSS* 13 (1968), pp. 3–10.
Ahlström, G. W., "The House of Wisdom", *SEÅ* 44 (1979), pp. 74–6.
Albright, W. F., "A New Hebrew Word for 'Glass' in Proverbs 26:23", *BASOR* 98 (1945), pp. 24–5.
—— "Some Canaanite-Phoenician Sources of Hebrew Wisdom", *VT* Suppl. 3, 1955, pp. 1–15.
Aletti, J.-N., "Séduction et parole en Proverbes i–ix", *VT* 27 (1977), pp. 129–44.
Alt, A., "Zur literarische Analyse des Amenemope", *VT* Suppl. 3, 1955, pp. 16–25.
Amsler, S., "La Sagesse de la femme", *La Sagesse de l'Ancien Testament*, ed. M. Gilbert (BETL 51), 1979, pp. 112–16.
Andrew, M. E., "Variety of Expression in Proverbs 23:29–35", *VT* 28 (1978), pp. 102–3.
Anthes, R., *Lebensregeln und Lebensweisheit der alten Ägypter* (*AO* 32/2), 1933.

Audet, J.-P., "Origines comparées de la double tradition de la loi et de la sagesse dans le proche-orient ancien" (*International Congress of Orientalists*), Moscow, 1960, vol. 1, pp. 352–7.

Auvray, P., "Sur le sens du mot *'ayin* en Ez. 1:18 et 10:12", *VT* 4 (1954), pp. 1–6.

Barr, J., "*b'rṣ – molis*: Prov. 11:31, 1 Pet. 4:18", *JSS* 20 (1975), pp. 149–64.

—— "Why? in Biblical Hebrew", *JTS* NS 36 (1985), pp. 1–33

Barucq, A., "Proverbes (Livre des)" *SDB* 8, 1972, cols 1395–1476.

Bauckmann, E. G., "Die Proverbien und die Sprüche des Jesus Sirach", *ZAW* 72 (1960), pp. 33–63.

Bauer, J.-B., "Encore une fois Proverbes 8:22", *VT* 8 (1958), pp. 91–2.

Bauer-Kayatz, C., *Einführung in die alttestamentliche Weisheit* (Biblische Studien, 55), Neukirchen, 1969.

Becker, J., *Gottesfurcht im Alten Testament* (Analecta Biblica, 25), Rome, 1965.

Berger, P.-R., "Zum Huren bereit bis hin zu einem Rundlaib Brot. Prov. 6:26", *ZAW* 99 (1987), pp. 98–106.

Bertram, G., "Praeparatio evangelica in der Septuaginta", *VT* 7 (1957), pp. 225–49.

Bewer, J. A., "Two Suggestions on Prov. 30:31 and Zech. 9:16", *JBL* 67 (1948), pp. 61–2.

Bjørndalen, A. J., "'Form' und 'Inhalt' des motivierenden Mahnspruches", *ZAW* 82 (1970), pp. 347–61.

Blenkinsopp, J., *Wisdom and Law in the Old Testament. The Ordering of Life in Israel and Early Judaism*, Oxford, 1983.

Blocher, H., "The Fear of the Lord is the 'Principle' of Wisdom", *TynB* 28 (1977), pp. 3–28.

De Boer, P. A. H., "The Counsellor", *VT* Suppl. 3, 1955, pp. 42–51

—— "Yhwh as Epithet Expressing the Superlative", *VT* 24 (1974), pp. 233–5.

Boström, G., *Paronomasi i den äldre hebreiska Maschallitteraturen* (*LUÅ* N. F. Avd. 1, Bd 23, Nr 8), Lund, 1928.

—— *Proverbiastudien. Die Weisheit und das fremde Weib in Spr. 1–9* (*LUÅ* N. F. Avd. 1, Bd 30, Nr 3), Lund, 1935.

Boström, L., *The God of the Sages. The Portrayal of God in the Book of Proverbs* (Coniectanea Biblica, OT Series 29), Stockholm, 1990.

Brin, G., "The Significance of the Form *mah-ṭṭôb*", *VT* 38 (1988), pp. 462–5.
Brockelmann, C., *Hebräische Syntax*, Neukirchen, 1956.
Brockington, L. H., *The Hebrew Text of the Old Testament. The Readings Adopted by the Translators of the New English Bible*, Oxford, Cambridge, 1973.
Brunner, H., *Altägyptische Weisheit. Lehren für das Leben*, Zurich and Munich, 1988.
—— "Gerechtigkeit als Fundament des Thrones", *VT* 8 (1958), pp. 420–8.
Bryce, G. E. "Another Wisdom-'Book' in Proverbs", *JBL* 91 (1972), pp. 145–57.
—— *A Legacy of Wisdom. The Egyptian Contribution to the Wisdom of Israel*, Lewisburg and London, 1979.
—— "Omen-Wisdom in Ancient Israel", *JBL* 94 (1975), pp. 19–37.
Buchanan, G. W., "Midrashim pré-tannaïtes. A propos de Prov., 1–9", *RB* 72 (1965), pp. 227–39.
De Buck, A., "Het religieus Karakter der oudste egyptische Wijsheid", *Nieuw Theologisch Tijdschrift* 21 (1932), pp. 322–49.
Bühlmann, W. and Scherer, K., *Stilfiguren der Bibel* (Biblische Beiträge, 10), Freiburg, Switzerland, 1973.
Camp, C. V., *Wisdom and the Feminine in the Book of Proverbs*, Sheffield, 1985.
—— "Wise and Strange: An Interpretation of the Female Imagery in Proverbs in Light of Trickster Mythology", *Semeia* 42 (1988), pp. 14–36.
—— "Woman Wisdom as Root Metaphor: A Theological Consideration" (*JSOT* Suppl. Series 58), Sheffield, 1987, pp. 45–76.
Cathcart, K. J. "Proverbs 30:4 and Ugaritic ḪPN, 'Garment'", *CBQ* 32 (1970), pp. 418–20.
Cazelles, H., "Les débuts de la sagesse en Israël", *Les sagesses du proche-orient ancien, Colloque de Strasbourg 17–19 mai 1962*, Paris, 1963, pp. 27–40.
—— "L'enfantement de la Sagesse en Prov., 8", *Sacra Pagina* I, Paris, 1959, pp. 511–15.
—— Review of G. R. Driver, *Canaanite Myths and Legends*, *VT* 7 (1957), pp. 420–30.

Clifford, R. J., "Proverbs 9: A Suggested Ugaritic Parallel", *VT* 25 (1975), pp. 298–306.
Cody, A., "Notes on Proverbs 22:21 and 22:23b", *Bib* 61 (1980), pp. 418–26.
Cohen, J. M., "An Unrecognized Connotation of *nšq peh* with Special Reference to Three Biblical Occurrences", *VT* 32 (1982), pp. 416–24.
Collins, J. J., "Proverbial Wisdom and the Yahwist Vision", *Semeia* 17 (1980), pp. 1–17.
Conrad, J., "Die innere Gliederung der Proverbien", *ZAW* 79 (1967), pp. 67–76.
Couroyer, B., "Une coutume égyptienne? Proverbes, 17:20", *RB* 57 (1950), pp. 331–5.
—— "L'origine égyptienne de la Sagesse d'Amenemope", *RB* 70 (1963), pp. 208–24.
—— "La tablette du coeur", *RB* 90 (1983), pp. 416–34.
Crenshaw, J. L., "Education in Ancient Israel", *JBL* 104 (1985), pp. 601–15.
—— "Questions, dictons et épreuves impossibles", *La Sagesse de l'Ancien Testament*, ed. M. Gilbert (*BETL* 41), Gembloux/ Paris, 1979, pp. 96–111.
—— "Murphy's Axiom: Every Gnomic Saying Needs a Balancing Corrective", *The Listening Heart. Essays. . . in Honour of R. E. Murphy*, ed. K. G. Hoglund *et al.* (*JSOT* Suppl. Series 58), Sheffield, 1987, pp. 1–17.
—— *Old Testament Wisdom: An Introduction*, Atlanta, 1981.
—— "Prolegomena", *Studies in Ancient Israelite Wisdom*, ed. J. L. Crenshaw, New York, 1976, pp. 1–60.
—— "Wisdom and Authority: Sapiential Rhetoric and its Warrants" (*VT* Suppl. 32), 1981, pp. 10–29.
Crook, M. B., "The Marriageable Maiden of Prov. 31:10–31", *JNES* 13 (1954), pp. 137–40.
Dahood, M., "The Archaic Genitive Ending in Proverbs 31:6", *Bib.* 56 (1975), p. 241.
—— "Congruity of Metaphors" (*VT* Suppl. 16), 1967, pp. 40–49.
—— "The hapax *ḥārak* in Proverbs 12:27", *Bib.* 63 (1982), pp. 60–62.
—— "Honey That Drips. Notes on Proverbs 5:2–3", *Bib.* 54 (1973), pp. 565–6.
—— "Immortality in Proverbs 12:28", *Bib.* 42 (1961), pp. 176–81.

—— "To Pawn One's Cloak", *Bib.* 42 (1961), pp. 359–66.
—— "Philological Observations on Five Biblical Texts", *Bib.* 63 (1982), pp. 390–4.
—— "Proverbs 8:22–31: Translation and Commentary", *CBQ* 30 (1968), pp. 512–21.
Daiches, S., "Note on the Word *ḥṣbh* in Proverbs 9:1", *ET* 55 (1943–4), p. 277.
Daube, D., "A Quartet of Beasties in the Book of Proverbs", *JTS* NS 36 (1985), pp. 380–6.
Davies, E. W., "The Meaning of *qesem* in Prov. 16:10", *Bib.* 61 (1980), pp. 554–6.
Dawes, S. B., "*'ănāwâ* in Translation and Tradition", *VT* 41 (1991), pp. 38–48.
Derousseaux, L., *La crainte de Dieu dans l'Ancien Testament* (Lectio Divina 63), Paris, 1970.
Dion, H.-M., "Le genre littéraire sumérien de l''hymne à soi-même' et quelques passages du Deutéro-Isaïe", *RB* 74 (1967), pp. 215–34.
Doll, P., *Menschenschöpfung und Weltschöpfung in der alttestamentlichen Weisheit* (Stuttgarter Bibel-Studien 117), Stuttgart, 1985.
Donald, T., "The Semantic Field of 'Folly' in Proverbs, Job, Psalms, and Ecclesiastes", *VT* 13 (1963), pp. 285–92.
Donner, H., "Die religionsgeschichtliche Ursprünge von Prov. Sal. 8", *ZÄS* 82 (1957), pp. 8–18.
Dressler, H. H. P., "The Lesson of Proverbs 26:23", *Ascribe to the Lord. Biblical and Other Studies in Memory of Peter C. Craigie* (*JSOT* Suppl. Series 67), Sheffield, 1988, pp. 117–25.
Drioton, E., "Le Livre des Proverbes et la Sagesse d'Aménémopé", *BETL* 12–13, 1959, pp. 229–41.
—— "Sur la Sagesse d'Aménémopé", *Mélanges Bibliques rédigés en l'honneur de André Robert*, Paris, 1957, pp. 254–80.
Driver, G. R., "Ecclesiasticus: A New Fragment of the Hebrew Text", *ET* 49 (1937–8), pp. 37–9.
—— "Hebrew Notes", *VT* 1 (1951), pp. 241–50.
—— "Hebrew Notes on Prophets and Proverbs", *JTS* 41 (1940), pp. 162–75.
—— "Hebrew Roots and Words", *WO* 1 (1941), pp. 406–15.
—— "L'interprétation du texte masorétique à la lumière de la lexicographie hébraïque", *ETL* 26 (1950), pp. 337–53.
—— "Notes on the Psalms", *JTS* 36 (1935), pp. 147–56.

—— "On *ḥēmāh* 'hot anger, fury' and also 'fiery wine'", *TZ* 14 (1958), pp. 133–5.
—— "Problems and Solutions", *VT* 4 (1954), pp. 225–45.
—— "Problems in the Hebrew Text of Proverbs", *Bib.* 32 (1951), pp. 173–97.
—— "Problems in Proverbs", *ZAW* 50 (1932), pp. 141–8.
—— "Proverbs 19:26", *TZ* 11 (1955), pp. 372–4.
—— "Some Hebrew Verbs, Nouns and Pronouns", *JTS* 30 (1929), pp. 371–8.
—— "Some Hebrew Words", *JTS* 29 (1927–8), pp. 390–6.
—— "Studies in the Vocabulary of the Old Testament IV", *JTS* 33 (1931–2), pp. 38–47.
—— "Studies in the Vocabulary of the Old Testament VI", *JTS* 34 (1933), pp. 375–85.
Driver, S. R., *A Treatise on the Use of the Tenses in Hebrew*, Oxford, 1892.
Dubarle, A.-M., "Où en est l'étude de la littérature sapientiale?", *De Mari à Qumrân. Hommage à Mgr J. Coppens I*, Gembloux and Paris, 1969, pp. 246–58.
Duesberg, H. and Franken, I., *Les scribes inspirés*, 2nd edn, Maredsous, 1966.
Dunand, M. "La maison de la Sagesse", *Bulletin du Musée de Beyrouth* 4 (1940), pp. 69–84.
Eissfeldt, O., *Der Maschal im Alten Testament* (*BZAW* 24), 1913.
Eitan, I., "A Contribution to Isaiah Exegesis (Notes, and Short Notes, in Biblical Philology)", *HUCA* 12 (1937), pp. 55–88.
Emerton, J. A., "The Interpretation of Proverbs 21:28", *ZAW* 100 Suppl. (1988), pp. 161–70.
—— "The Meaning of Proverbs 13:2", *JTS* NS 35 (1984), pp. 91–5.
—— "A Note on the Hebrew Text of Proverbs 1:22–23", *JTS* NS 19 (1968), pp. 609–14.
—— "A Note on Proverbs 2:18", *JTS* NS 30 (1979), pp. 153–8.
—— "A Note on Proverbs 12:26", *ZAW* 76 (1964), pp. 191–3.
—— "Notes on Some Passages of the Book of Proverbs", *JTS* NS 20 (1969), pp. 202–20.
Engnell, I., "'Knowledge' and 'life' in the Creation Story", *VT* Suppl. 3, 1955, pp. 103–19.
Erman, A., "Eine ägyptische Quelle der 'Sprüche Salomos'", *SPAW* 15 (1924), pp. 86–93.

Fohrer, G., "Sophia" (*TDNT* 7, pp. 476–96), *Studies in Ancient Israelite Wisdom*, ed. by J. L. Crenshaw, New York, 1976, pp. 63–83.
—— "Die Weisheit im Alten Testament" (*BZAW* 115), 1969, pp. 242–74.
Fontaine, C., "Proverb Performance in the Hebrew Bible", *JSOT* 32 (1985), pp. 87–103.
Fox, M. V., "Aspects of the Religion of the Book of Proverbs", *HUCA* 39 (1968), pp. 55–69.
Franklyn, P., "The Sayings of Agur in Proverbs 30: Piety or Scepticism?", *ZAW* 95 (1983), pp. 238–52.
Franzmann, M., "The Wheel in Proverbs 20:26 and Ode of Solomon 23:11–16", *VT* 41 (1991), pp. 121–3.
Garrett, D. A., "Votive Prostitution Again: A Comparison of Proverbs 7:13–14 and 21:28–29", *JBL* 109 (1990), pp. 681–2.
Gaster, T. H., "Old Testament Notes", *VT* 4 (1954), pp. 73–9.
Gemser, B., "The Spiritual Structure of Biblical Aphoristic Literature", *Adhuc Loquitur. Collected Essays of Dr B. Gemser*, Leiden, 1968, pp. 138–49. *Studies in Ancient Israelite Wisdom*, ed. by J. L. Crenshaw, New York, 1976, pp. 208–19.
Gerleman, G., *Studies in the Septuagint 3: Proverbs* (LUÅ N. F. Avd. 1, Bd 52, Nr 3), Lund, 1956.
—— "Das übervolle Mass", *VT* 28 (1978), pp. 151–64.
Gerstenberger, E., *Wesen und Herkunft des 'apodiktischen Rechts'* (WMANT 20), Neukirchen, 1965.
Gese, H., *Lehre und Wirklichkeit in der alten Weisheit. Studien zu den Sprüchen Salomos und zu dem Buche Hiob*, Tübingen, 1958.
Gibson, J. C. L., *Canaanite Myths and Legends*, 2nd edn, Edinburgh, 1978.
Gilbert, M., "Le discours de la Sagesse en Proverbes, 8. Structure et cohérence", *La Sagesse de l'Ancien Testament* ed. M. Gilbert (*BETL* 51), 1979, pp. 202–18.
—— "Le discours menaçant de Sagesse en Proverbes 1:20–33", *Storia e tradizioni di Israele. Scritti in onore di J. Alberto Soggin*, Brescia, 1991, pp. 99–119.
Glück, J. J., "Proverbs xxx 15a", *VT* 14 (1964), pp. 367–70.
Goldingay, J. E., "Proverbs v and ix", *RB* 84 (1977), pp. 80–93.
Golka, F. W., "Die Flecken des Leoparden. Biblische und afrikanische Weisheit im Sprichwort", *Schöpfung und Befreiung*.

Für Claus Westermann zum 80. Geburtstag, Stuttgart, 1989, pp. 149–65.
—— "Die israelitische Weisheitsschule oder 'des Kaisers neue Kleider'", *VT* 33 (1983), pp. 257–71.
—— "Die Königs- und Hofsprüche und der Ursprung der Israelitischen Weisheit", *VT* 36 (1986), pp. 13–36.
Greenfield, J. C., "The Seven Pillars of Wisdom (Prov. 9:1), a Mistranslation", *JQR* 76 (1985–6), pp. 13–20.
Gressmann, H., "Die neugefundene Lehre des Amen-em-ope und die vorexilische Spruchdichtung Israels", *ZAW* 42 (1924), pp. 272–96.
Grollenberg, L. H., "A propos de Prov. 8:6 et 17:27", *RB* 59 (1952), pp. 40–43.
Grumach, I., *Untersuchungen zur Lebenslehre des Amenope* (Münchener Ägyptologische Studien 23), Munich, 1972.
Habel, N., "The Symbolism of Wisdom in Proverbs 1–9", *Int.* 26 (1972), pp. 131–56.
Haran, M., "The Graded Numerical Sequence and the Phenomenon of 'Automatism' in Biblical Poetry", *VT* Suppl. 22, 1972, pp. 238–67.
Hedley, R. L., "Proverbs 2:17", *JTS* 31 (1930), pp. 395–7.
Herbig, R., "Aphrodite Parakyptusa (Die Frau im Fenster)", *OLZ* 30 (1927), cols 917–22.
Hermisson, H.-J., "Observations on the Creation Theology in Wisdom", *Israelite Wisdom: Theological and Literary Essays in Honor of Samuel Terrien*, Missoula, 1978, pp. 43–57.
—— *Studien zur israelitischen Spruchweisheit* (WMANT 28), Neukirchen, 1968.
Hildebrandt, T., "Proverbial Pairs: Compositional Units in Proverbs 10–29", *JBL* 107 (1988), pp. 207–24.
Hoftijzer, J., "Notes sur une épitaphe en écriture néopunique", *VT* 11 (1961), pp. 344–8.
Hoglund, K. G., "The Fool and the Wise in Dialogue", *The Listening Heart. Essays in Wisdom and the Psalms in Honour of Roland E. Murphy* (*JSOT* Suppl Series 58), Sheffield, 1987, pp. 161–80.
Humbert, P., "Les adjectifs 'Zâr' et 'Nokrî' et la 'Femme Etrangère' des proverbes bibliques", *Mélanges Syriens offerts a M. René Dussaud* I, 1939, pp. 259–66, *Opuscules d'un hébraïsant*, Neuchâtel, 1958, pp. 111–18.

—— "La 'femme étrangère' du Livre des Proverbes", *RES* 4 (1937), pp. 49–64.
—— "Le mot biblique *'ebyôn*", *RHPR* 32 (1952), pp. 1–6, *Opuscules d'un hébraïsant*, Neuchâtel, 1958, pp. 187–92.
—— " 'Qânâ' en hébreu biblique", *Festschrift für Alfred Bertholet*, Tübingen, 1950, pp. 259–66, *Opuscules d'un hébraïsant*, Neuchâtel, 1958, pp. 166–74.
—— *Recherches sur les sources égyptiennes de la littérature sapientiale d'Israël*, Neuchâtel, 1929.
—— "Le substantif *tō'ēbā* et le verbe *t'b* dans l'Ancien Testament", *ZAW* 72 (1960), pp. 217–37.
Humphreys, W. L., "The Motif of the Wise Courtier in the Book of Proverbs", *Israelite Wisdom. Theological and Literary Essays in Honor of Samuel Terrien*, Missoula, 1978, pp. 177–90.
Irwin, W. A., "Where Shall Wisdom be Found?", *JBL* 29 (1961), pp. 133–42.
Irwin, W. H., "The Metaphor in Prov. 11:30", *Bib.* 65 (1984), pp. 97–100.
Jacob, E., "Sagesse et Alphabet. A propos de Prov. 31:10–31", *Hommages à André Dupont-Sommer*, Paris, 1971, pp. 287–95.
Jenni, E., "*śn'* hassen", *THAT* II, 1976, cols 835–7.
Jirku, A., "Das n. pr. Lemuel (Prov. 31:1) und der Gott Lim", *ZAW* 66 (1954), p. 151.
Johnson, A. R., "Māšāl" (*VT* Suppl. 3, 1955, pp. 162–9).
Jongeling, B., "La particule *raq*", *OTS* 18, 1973, pp. 97–107.
Kaiser, O., "Der Mensch unter dem Schicksal", *NZSTh* 14 (1972), pp. 1–28, BZAW 161, 1985, pp. 63–90.
Kayatz, C., *Studien zu Proverbien 1–9* (WMANT 22), Neukirchen, 1966.
Keel, O., *Die Weisheit spielt vor Gott. Ein ikonographischer Beitrag zur Deutung des* m^{e}saḥăqät in *Sprüche 8, 30f.*, Freiburg, Switzerland and Göttingen, 1974.
Keller, C.-A., "Zum sogenannten Vergeltungsglauben im Proverbienbuch", *Beiträge zur Alttestamentlichen Theologie, Festschrift für Walther Zimmerli*, Göttingen, 1977, pp. 223–38.
Koch, K., "Gibt es ein Vergeltungsdogma im Alten Testament?", *ZThK* 52 (1955), pp. 1–42, *Um das Prinzip der Vergeltung in Religion und Recht des Alten Testaments*, Darmstadt, 1972, pp. 130–81. ET "Is There a Doctrine of Retribution in the

Old Testament?", *Theodicy in the Old Testament*, ed. J. L. Crenshaw, Philadelphia, 1983, pp. 57–87.
Kopf, L., "Arabische Etymologien und Parallelen zum Bibelwörterbuch", *VT* 9 (1959), pp. 247–87
Kovacs, B. W., "Is There a Class-Ethic in Proverbs?", *Essays in Old Testament Ethics. J. Philip Hyatt in Memoriam*, New York, 1974, pp. 171–89.
Kraft, C. F., "Poetic Structure and Meaning in Proverbs 8:22–31", *JBL* 72 (1953), pp. vii–viii.
Kramer, S. N., "'Man and his God'. A Sumerian Variation on the 'Job' Motif", *VT* Suppl 3, 1955, pp. 170–82.
Krispenz, J., *Spruchkompositionen im Buch Proverbia*, Frankfurt, 1989.
Kruger, P. A., "Promiscuity or Marriage Fidelity? A Note on Prov. 5:15–18", *JNWSL* 13 (1987), pp. 61–8.
Kruse, H., "Die 'dialektische Negation' als semitisches Idiom", *VT* 4 (1954), pp. 385–400.
Labuschagne, C.J., "The Emphasizing Particle *gam* and its Connotations", *Studia Biblica et Semitica T. C. Vriezen. . . Dedicata*, Wageningen, 1966, pp. 193–203.
Lang, B., *Frau Weisheit. Deutung einer biblischen Gestalt*, Düsseldorf, 1975.
—— "Schule und Unterricht im alten Israel", *La sagesse de l'Ancien Testament*, ed. M. Gilbert, *BETL* 51, 1979, pp. 186–201.
—— "Die sieben Säulen der Weisheit (Sprüche 9:1) im Licht israelitischer Architektur", *VT* 33 (1983), pp. 488–91.
—— "Vorläufer von Speiseis in Bibel und Orient. Eine Untersuchung von Spr. 25:13", *Mélanges bibliques et orientaux en l'honneur de M. Henri Cazelles* (AOAT 212), Kevelaer, Neukirchen, 1981, pp. 219–32.
—— *Die weisheitliche Lehrrede. Eine Untersuchung von Sprüche 1–7* (Stuttgarter Bibel-Studien 54), Stuttgart, 1972.
—— *Wisdom and the Book of Proverbs. An Israelite Goddess Redefined*, New York, 1986.
Lemaire, A., *Les écoles et la formation de la Bible dans l'ancien Israël*, Freiburg, Switzerland and Göttingen, 1981.
—— "Sagesse et écoles", *VT* 34 (1984), pp. 270–81.
Lichtenstein, M. H., "Chiasm and Symmetry in Proverbs 31", *CBQ* 44 (1982), pp. 202–11.
Lichtheim, M., *Late Egyptian Wisdom Literature in the International*

Context. A Study of Demotic Instructions (OBO 52), Freiburg, Switzerland and Göttingen, 1983.

Lipiński, E., "Peninna, Iti'el et l'Athlète", *VT* 17 (1967), pp. 68–75.

—— "Les 'voyantes des rois' en Prov. 31:3", *VT* 23 (1973), p. 246.

Loewenstamm, S. E., "Remarks on Proverbs 17:12 and 20:27", *VT* 37 (1987), pp. 221–4.

Loretz, O., "*'jš mgn* in Proverbia 6:11 und 24:34", *UF* 6 (1974), pp. 476–7.

—— "Il meglio della sapienza è il timore di Jahwè (Prov. 1:7)", *Bibbia e Oriente* (Geneva) 2 (1960), pp. 210–11.

—— "Text und Neudeutung in Spr. 8:22–31", *UF* 7 (1985), pp. 577–9.

Lyons, E. L., "A Note on Proverbs 31:10–31" (*JSOT* Suppl. Series 58), Sheffield, 1987, pp. 237–45.

McCreesh, T. P., *Biblical Sound and Sense. Poetic Sound Patterns in Proverbs 10–29* (*JSOT* Suppl. Series, 128), Sheffield, 1991.

—— "Wisdom as Wife: Proverbs 31:10–31", *RB* 92 (1985), pp. 25–46.

McKane, W., "Functions of Language and Objectives of Discourse According to Proverbs, 10–30", *La Sagesse de l'Ancien Testament*, ed. M. Gilbert, *BETL* 51, 1979, pp. 166–85.

—— *Prophets and Wise Men* (*SBT* 44), London, 1965.

McKenzie, J. L. "Reflections on Wisdom", *JBL* 86 (1967), pp. 1–9.

Macintosh, A. A., "A Note on Proverbs 25:27", *VT* 20 (1970), pp. 112–14.

Mack, B. L., "Wisdom Myth and Mythology. An Essay in Understanding a Theological Tradition", *Int.* 24 (1970), pp. 46–60.

Malchow, B. V. "A Manual for Future Monarchs", *CBQ* 47 (1985), pp. 238–45.

—— "Social Justice in the Wisdom Literature", *Biblical Theology Bulletin* 12 (1982), pp. 120–4.

Meinhold, A., "Gott und Mensch in Proverbien 3", *VT* 37 (1987), pp. 468–77.

—— "Vierfaches: Strukturprinzip und Häufigkeitsfigur in Prov. 1–9", *Biblische Notizen* 33 (1986), pp. 53–79.

Miller, P. D., "Apotropaic Imagery in Proverbs 6:20–22", *JNES* 29 (1970), pp. 129–30.

Morenz, S., "Feurige Kohlen auf dem Haupt", *TLZ* 78 (1953), pp. 187–92.
Mulder, M. J., "Die Partikel *kēn* im Alten Testament", *OTS* 21, 1981, pp. 201–27.
Müller, H.-P., "Der Begriff 'Rätsel' im Alten Testament (*ḥīdāh*)", *VT* 20 (1970), pp. 465–89.
—— "Die weisheitliche Lehrerzählung im Alten Testament und seiner Umwelt", *WO* 9 (1977), pp. 77–98.
Murphy, R. E., "Assumptions and Problems in Old Testament Wisdom Research", *CBQ* 29 (1967), pp. 102–12.
—— "The Faces of Wisdom in the Book of Proverbs", *Mélanges bibliques et orientaux en l'honneur de M. Henri Cazelles* (*AOAT* 212), Kevelaer and Neukirchen, 1981, pp. 337–45.
—— "Form Criticism and Wisdom Literature", *CBQ* 31 (1969), pp. 475–83.
—— "Hebrew Wisdom", *JAOS* 101 (1981), pp. 21–34.
—— "The Interpretation of Old Testament Wisdom Literature", *Int.* 23 (1969), pp. 289–301.
—— "The Kerygma of the Book of Proverbs", *Int.* 20 (1966), pp. 3–14.
—— "Proverbs 22:1–9", *Int.* 41 (1987), pp. 398–402.
—— "Wisdom and Creation", *JBL* 104 (1985), pp. 3–11.
—— "Wisdom and Eros in Proverbs 1–9", *CBQ* 50 (1988), pp. 600–603.
—— "Wisdom and Yahwism", *No Famine in the Land. Studies in Honor of John L. McKenzie*, ed. by J. W. Flanagan and A. W. Robinson, Missoula, 1975, pp. 117–26.
—— *Wisdom Literature: Job, Proverbs, Ruth, Canticles, Ecclesiastes, Esther* (*FOTL* 13), Grand Rapids, 1981.
—— "Wisdom Theses", *Wisdom and Knowledge. Festschrift for Joseph Papin* II, Villanova, 1976, pp. 187–200.
—— "Wisdom-Theses and Hypotheses", *Israelite Wisdom: Theological and Literary Essays in Honor of Samuel Terrien*, ed. by J. G. Gammie *et al.*, Missoula, 1978, pp. 35–42.
Naré, L., *Proverbes salomoniens et proverbes mossi. Etude comparative à partir d'une nouvelle analyse de Pr. 25–29*, Frankfurt, 1986.
Nel, P. J., "Authority in the Wisdom Admonitions", *ZAW* 93 (1981), pp. 418–26.
—— "The Concept 'Father' in the Wisdom Literature of the Ancient Near East", *JNWSL* 5 (1977), pp. 53–66.

—— "The Genres of Biblical Wisdom Literature", *JNWSL* 9 (1981), pp. 129–42.

—— *The Structure and Ethos in the Wisdom Admonitions in Proverbs* (*BZAW* 158), 1982.

Niccacci, A., "Proverbi 22:17–23:11", *Studii Biblici Franciscani Liber Annuus* 29 (1979), pp. 42–72.

North, F. S., "The Four Insatiables", *VT* 15 (1965), pp. 281–2.

O'Connell, R. H., "Proverbs 7:16–19: A Case of Fatal Deception in a 'Woman and the Window' Type-Scene", *VT* 41 (1991), pp. 235–41.

Oesterley, W. O. E., *The Wisdom of Egypt and the Old Testament in the Light of the Newly Discovered "Teaching of Amen-em-ope"*, London, 1927.

Olmo Lete, G. del, "Note sobre Prov. 30:19", *Bib.* 67 (1986), pp. 68–74.

Paul, S. M., "Unrecognized Biblical Legal Idioms in the Light of Comparative Akkadian Expressions", *RB* 86 (1979), pp. 231–9.

Perdue, L. G., "Liminality as a Social Setting for Wisdom Literature", *ZAW* 93 (1981), pp. 114–26.

—— *Wisdom and Cult. A Critical Analysis of the Views of Cult in the Wisdom Literatures of Israel and the Ancient Near East*, Missoula, 1977.

Pleins, J. D., "Poverty in the Social World of the Wise", *JSOT* 37 (1987), pp. 61–78.

Van der Ploeg, J. P. M., "Proverbs 25:23", *VT* 3 (1953), pp. 189–91.

Plöger, O., "Zur Auslegung der Sentenzensammlungen des Proverbienbuches", *Probleme biblischer Theologie. Gerhard von Rad zum 70. Geburtstag*, ed. H. W. Wolff, Munich, 1971, pp. 402–16.

Porteous, N. W., "Royal Wisdom", *VT* Suppl. 3, 1955, pp. 247–61.

Preuss, H. D., *Einführung in die alttestamentliche Weisheitsliteratur*, Stuttgart, 1987.

—— "Das Gottesbild der ältesten Weisheit Israels", *VT* Suppl. 23, 1972, pp. 117–45.

von Rad, G., *Theologie des Alten Testaments* I, Munich, 1957. ET *Old Testament Theology* I, Edinburgh, 1962.

—— *Weisheit in Israel*, Neukirchen, 1970. ET *Wisdom in Israel*, London, 1972.

Ramaroson, L., "'Charbons ardents' 'sur la tête' ou 'pour le feu'?", *Bib.* 51 (1970), pp. 230–34.
Reider, J., "Etymological Studies in Biblical Hebrew", *VT* 2 (1952), pp. 113–30.
—— "Etymological Studies in Biblical Hebrew (II)", *VT* 4 (1954), pp. 276–95.
Reitzenstein, R., *Das mandäische Buch des Herrn der Grosse und die Evangelienüberlieferung* (*SHAW*), Heidelberg, 1919.
—— *Zwei religionsgeschichtliche Fragen nach ungedrückten griechischen Texten der Strassburger Bibliothek*, Strassburg, 1901.
Renfroe, F., "The Effect of Redaction on the Structure of Prov. 1:1–6", *ZAW* 101 (1989), pp. 290–93.
Richardson, H. N., "Some Notes on *lîṣ* and its Derivatives", *VT* 5 (1955), pp. 163–79.
Richter, W., *Recht und Ethos. Versuch einer Ortung des weisheitlichen Mahnspruches* (*StANT* 15), Munich, 1966.
Ringgren, H., *Word and Wisdom. Studies in the Hypostatization of Divine Qualities and Functions in the Ancient Near East*, Uppsala, 1947.
Robert, A., "Les attaches littéraires bibliques de Proverbes 1–9", *RB* 43 (1934), pp. 42–68, 172–204, 374–84.
—— "Le Yahwisme de Prov. 10:1–22:16", *Mémorial Lagrange*, Paris, 1940, pp. 163–82.
Römheld, D., *Wege der Weisheit. Die Lehren Amenemopes und Proverbien 22:17–24:22* (BZAW 184), 1989.
Roth, W. M. W., *Numerical Sayings in the Old Testament*, *VT* Suppl. 13, 1965.
—— "The Numerical Sequence 10/10+1 in the Old Testament", *VT* 12 (1962), pp. 300–311.
Ruffle, J., "The Teaching of Amenemope and its Connection with the Book of Proverbs", *TynB* 28 (1977), pp. 29–68.
Rüger, H. P., "Die gestaffelten Zahlensprüche des Alten Testaments und aram. Achikar 92", *VT* 31 (1981), pp. 229–32.
—— "Zum Text von Prv. 31:30", *WO* 5/1 (1969), pp. 96–9.
Sauer, G., *Die Sprüche Agurs. Untersuchungen zur Herkunft, Verbreitung und Bedeutūng einer biblischer Stilform unter besonderer Berücksichtigung von Proverbia c. 30* (*BWANT* 84), Stuttgart, 1963.
Savignac, J. de, "Interprétation de Proverbes 8:22–32", *VT* Suppl. 17, 1969, pp. 196–203.
—— "Note sur le sens du verset 8:22 des Proverbes", *VT* 4 (1954), pp. 429–32.

—— "La sagesse en Proverbes 8:22–31", *VT* 12 (1962), pp. 211–15.
Schmid, H. H., *Wesen und Geschichte der Weisheit* (*BZAW* 101), 1966.
Scott, R. B. Y., "Folk Proverbs of the Ancient Near East", *Transactions of the Royal Society of Canada* 15 (1961), pp. 47–56, *Studies in Ancient Israelite Wisdom*, ed. by J. L. Crenshaw, New York, 1976, pp. 417–26.
—— "Solomon and the Beginnings of Wisdom in Israel", *VT* Suppl. 3, 1955, pp. 262–79.
—— *The Way of Wisdom in the Old Testament*, New York, 1971.
—— "Wisdom in Creation: the *'āmôn* of Proverbs viii:30", *VT* 10 (1960), pp. 213–23.
—— "Wise and Foolish, Righteous and Wicked. Studies in the Religion of Ancient Israel", *VT* Suppl. 23, 1972, pp. 146–65.
Seeligmann, I. L., "Voraussetzungen der Midraschexegese", *VT* Suppl. 1, 1953, pp. 150–81.
Sheppard, G. T., *Wisdom as a Hermeneutical Construct. A Study in the Sapientilizing of the Old Testament* (*BZAW* 151), 1980.
Shupak, N., "The 'Sitz im Leben' of Proverbs in the Light of Biblical and Egyptian Wisdom Literature", *RB* 94 (1987), pp. 98–119.
Skehan, P. W., "Proverbs 5:15–19 and 6:20–24" (*Studies in Israelite Poetry and Wisdom*, CBQ Monograph Series 1), 1971, pp. 1–8.
—— "The Seven Columns of Wisdom's House in Proverbs 1–9" (*Studies in Israelite Poetry and Wisdom, CBQ Monograph Series* 1), 1971, pp. 9–14.
—— "A Single Editor for the Whole Book of Proverbs" (*Studies in Israelite Poetry and Wisdom, CBQ Monograph Series* 1), 1971, pp. 15–26 (revised version of *CBQ* 10 [1948], pp. 115–30.
—— "Structures in Poems on Wisdom: Proverbs 8 and Sirach 24", *CBQ* 41 (1979), pp. 365–79.
—— "Wisdom's House", *CBQ* 29 (1967), pp. 162–80, *Studies in Israelite Poetry and Wisdom, CBQ Monograph Series* 1, 1971, pp. 27–45.
Skladny, U., *Die ältesten Spruchsammlungen in Israel*, Göttingen, 1962.
Smith, N. G., "Family Ethics in the Wisdom Literature", *Int.* 4 (1950), pp. 453–7.
Snell, D. C., "The Most Obscure Verse in Proverbs: Proverbs 26:10", *VT* 41 (1991), pp. 350–56.

—— "'Taking Souls' in Proverbs 11:30", *VT* 33 (1983), pp. 362–5.
—— "The Wheel in Proverbs 20:26", *VT* 39 (1989), pp. 503–7.
Snijders, L. A., "The Meaning of *zâr* in the Old Testament. An Exegetical Study" (OTS 10, 1954), Leiden, pp. 1–154.
Von Soden, W., "Kränkung, nicht Schläge in Sprüche 20:30", *ZAW* 102 (1990), pp. 120–2.
Steiert, F.-J., *Die Weisheit Israels – ein Fremdkörper im Alten Testament? Eine Untersuchung zum Buch der Sprüche auf dem Hintergrund der ägyptischen Weisheitslehren* (Freiburger Theologische Studien 143), Freiburg, 1990.
Story, C. J. K., "The Book of Proverbs and Northwest Semitic Literature", *JBL* 64 (1945), pp. 319–37.
Thomas, D. W., "*'ēw* in Proverbs 31:4", *VT* 12 (1962), pp. 499–500.
—— "The Meaning of *ḥaṭṭā't* in Proverbs 10:16", *JTS* NS 15 (1964), pp. 295–6.
—— "A Note on *bal-yādᵉ'*āh in Proverbs 9:13", *JTS* NS 4 (1953), pp. 23–4.
—— "A Note on *da'ath* in Proverbs 22:12", *JTS* NS 14 (1963), pp. 93–4
—— "A Note on *l' td'* in Proverbs 5:6", *JTS* 37 (1936), pp. 59–60
—— "A Note on *līqqahat* in Proverbs 30:17", *JTS* 42 (1941), pp. 154–5
—— "Notes on Some Passages in the Book of Proverbs", *JTS* 38 (1937), pp. 400–405.
—— "Notes on Some Passages in the Book of Proverbs", *VT* 15 (1965), pp. 271–9
—— "The Root *yd'* in Hebrew", *JTS* 35 (1934), pp. 298–306, 409–12.
—— "The Root *šnh* = *saniya* in Hebrew, II", *ZAW* 55 (1937), pp. 174–6
—— "Textual and Philological Notes on Some Passages in the Book of Proverbs", *VT* Suppl. 3, 1955, pp. 280–92.
Thompson, J. M., *The Form and Function of Proverbs in Ancient Israel*, The Hague and Paris, 1974.
Torrey, C. C., "Proverbs, Chapter 30", *JBL* 73 (1954), pp. 93–6.
Tournay, R., "Relectures bibliques concernant la vie future et l'angélologie", *RB* 69 (1962), pp. 481–505.
Trible, P., "Wisdom Builds a Poem: The Architecture of Proverbs 1:20–33", *JBL* 94 (1975), pp. 509–18.

Tsevat, M., "Some Biblical Notes", *HUCA* 24 (1952–53), pp. 107–14.
Tsumura. D. T., "The Vetitive Particle and the Poetic Structure of Proverbs 31:4", *Annual of the Japanese Biblical Institute* 4 (1978), pp. 23–31.
Van Leeuwen, R. C., *Context and Meaning in Proverbs 25–27*, Atlanta, 1988.
—— "Proverbs xxv:27 Once Again", *VT* 36 (1986), pp. 105–14.
—— "Proverbs 30:21–23 and the Biblical World Upside Down", *JBL* 105 (1986), pp. 599–610.
Vattioni, F., "Ancora il vento di nord dei Proverbi 25:23", *Bib.* 46 (1965), pp. 213–16.
—— "La casa della sagezza (Prov. 9:1; 14:1)", *Augustinianum* 7 (1967), pp. 349–51.
—— "La giustizia nel commercio secondo Prov. 16:11", *Augustinianum* 6 (1966), pp. 106–12.
—— "Note sul libro dei Proverbi", *Augustinianum* 9 (1969), pp. 124–33.
—— "Proverbes, 30:15–16", *RB* 72 (1965), pp. 515–19.
—— "Sagezza e Creazione in Prov. 3:19–20", *Augustinianum* 6 (1966), pp. 102–5, 324–5.
—— "La 'straniera' nel libro dei Proverbi", *Augustinianum* 7 (1967), pp. 352–7.
Vawter, B., "Prov. 8:22: Wisdom and Creation", *JBL* 99 (1980), pp. 205–16.
Vermes, G., "'The Torah is a Light'", *VT* 8 (1958), pp. 436–8.
Vriezen, T. C., "The Edomite Deity Qaus", OTS 14, 1965, Leiden, pp. 330–53.
Wallis, G., "Zu den Spruchsammlungen Prov. 10:1–22, 16 und 25–29", *TLZ* 85 (1960), cols 147–8.
Watson, W. G. E., *Classical Hebrew Poetry. A Guide to its Techniques* (*JSOT* Suppl. Series 26), Sheffield, 1984.
Van der Weiden, W. A., "Prov. 14:32b 'Mais le juste a confiance quand il meurt'", *VT* 20 (1970), pp. 339–50.
Weinfeld, M., "'You will find favour . . . in the sight of God and man' (Proverbs 3:4) – the History of an Idea", *Eretz Israel* 16 (1982), pp. 93–9.
Westermann, C., "Weisheit im Sprichwort", *Schalom. Studien zu Glaube und Geschichte Israels, Alfred Jepsen zum 70. Geburtstag*,

Stuttgart, 1971, pp. 73–85, *Forschung am Alten Testament. Gesammelte Studien II*, Munich, 1974, pp. 149–61.
—— *Wurzeln der Weisheit. Die ältesten Sprüche Israels und anderer Völker*, Göttingen, 1990.
Whybray, R. N., *The Intellectual Tradition in the Old Testament* (*BZAW* 135), 1974.
—— "Proverbs 8:22–31 and its Supposed Prototypes", *VT* 15 (1965), pp. 504–14.
—— "Slippery Words IV: Wisdom", *ET* 89 (1977–8), pp. 359–62.
—— "The Social World of the Wisdom Writers", *The World of Ancient Israel*, ed. by R. E. Clements, Cambridge, 1989, pp. 227–50.
—— "Some Literary Problems in Proverbs 1–9", *VT* 16 (1966), pp. 482–96.
—— *Wealth and Poverty in the Book of Proverbs* (*JSOT* Suppl. Series 99), Sheffield, 1990.
—— *Wisdom in Proverbs. The Concept of Wisdom in Proverbs 1–9* (SBT 45), London, 1965.
—— "Yahweh-Sayings and their Contexts in Proverbs, 10:1–22:16", *La sagesse de l'Ancien Testament*, ed. by M. Gilbert (*BETL* 51), Leuven, 1979, pp. 153–65.
Williams, J. G., "The Power of Form: A Study of Biblical Proverbs", *Semeia* 17 (1980), pp. 35–58.
—— *Those Who Ponder Proverbs. Aphoristic Thinking and Biblical Literature*, Sheffield, 1981.
Williams, R. J., "The Alleged Semitic Original of the *Wisdom of Amenope*", *JEA* 47 (1961), pp. 100–6.
Wilson, F. M., "Sacred or Profane? The Yahwistic Redaction of Proverbs Reconsidered" (*JSOT* Suppl. Series 58), Sheffield, 1987, pp. 313–34.
Wolters, A., "Nature and Grace in the Interpretation of Proverbs 31:10–31", *CTJ* 19 (1984), pp. 153–66.
—— "Proverbs 31:10–31 as Heroic Hymn: A Form-Critical Analysis", *VT* 38 (1988), pp. 446–57.
—— '*Ṣôpiyyâ* (Prov. 31:27) as Hymnic Participle and Play on *Sophia*, *JBL* 104 (1985), pp. 577–87.
Yee, G. A. "An Analysis of Prov. 8:22–31 According to Style and Structure", *ZAW* 94 (1982), pp. 58–66.
—— " 'I have Perfumed my Bed with Myrrh': The Foreign

Woman (*'iššāh zārāh*) in Proverbs 1–9", *JSOT* 43 (1989), pp. 53–68.
Zimmerli, W., "Ort und Grenze der Weisheit im Rahmen der alttestamentlichen Theologie", *Les sagesses du proche orient ancien*, Paris, 1963, pp. 121–37. ET "The Place and Limit of the Wisdom in the Framework of the Old Testament Theology", *SJT* 17 (1964), pp. 146–58.
—— "Zur Struktur der alttestamentlichen Weisheit", *ZAW* 51 (1933), pp. 177–204. ET "Concerning the Structure of Old Testament Wisdom", *Studies in Ancient Israelite Wisdom*, ed. J. L. Crenshaw, New York, 1976, pp. 175–207.
Zimmern, H., "Die babylonische Göttin im Fenster", *OLZ* 31 (1928), cols 1–3.
Zolli, "Prov. 12:37", *Bib.* 23 (1942), pp. 165–9.

INTRODUCTION
to
Proverbs

A. TITLE AND PLACE IN THE CANON

The title "Proverbs" is an ancient one, attested by the Septuagint's *paroimiai* (in some MSS, *paroimiai Solōmōntos*, "proverbs of Solomon"). This corresponds to the Hebrew title *mišlê š^elōmōh* abbreviated simply to *mišlê* in modern Hebrew bibles. This title is, as with some other books of the Hebrew Bible, simply a repetition of the first words of the book. However, some early Christian writers refer to the book as "Wisdom" or "All-virtuous Wisdom" or the like. These titles, which were also applied to Ecclesiasticus (Ben Sira) and to the Wisdom of Solomon, may go back to an original Hebrew title. The Talmud also speaks of the "Book of Wisdom" (*sēper ḥokmāh*). Such titles are descriptive of the theme or contents of the book. The title in modern English translations is either "The Proverbs" (*AV*, *RV*, *RSV*, *JB*) or simply "Proverbs" (*NEB*, *REB*).

In the Hebrew canon Proverbs is found in the third division known as the Writings (*k^etûbîm*), and always forms part of a distinct group together with Psalms and Job, though these have not always followed the same order. These three books are distinguished in MT by a "poetical" system of accents different from that of the other Old Testament books. The Hebrew order in MT is Psalms, Job, Proverbs; that of modern English bibles Job, Psalms, Proverbs.

B. PROVERBS AS A BOOK OF WISDOM

To call Proverbs a "book of wisdom" is fully justified. The word "wisdom" (*ḥokmāh* in Hebrew) occurs thirty-nine times and the adjective "wise" (*ḥākām*) forty-seven times in these thirty-one chapters; and they are found in almost every section of the book. The book's main theme is that this quality of wisdom is the goal to which all ought to aspire, and that it is – except, perhaps, for a few incorrigibles – attainable by all, a conviction succinctly expressed in the Preface to the whole book (1:1–6).

As will be demonstrated in the introductions to the various

sections of the book, the word *ḥokmāh* is used in proverbs in several distinct senses; nevertheless, a common thread of meaning runs through them all. Elsewhere in the Old Testament *ḥokmāh* means something like "skill": practical knowledge in any sphere, from that of the artisan to that of the politician. But in Proverbs *ḥokmāh* is always *life*-skill: the ability of the individual to conduct his life in the best possible way and to the best possible effect. Its range of meanings is clarified by other nouns with which it is closely and frequently associated in the book, especially *bînāh* and *tᵉbûnāh*, "understanding", and *da'at*, "knowledge". But it should be noted that it is also paired with honesty (*yōšer*, 4:11) and the fear of Yahweh (9:10).

No distinction is made in Proverbs between the pursuit of happiness and prosperity on the one hand and attachment to moral virtues and religious faith and practice on the other: wisdom embraces both. Morality and religion are presented as essential features of the pursuit of wisdom because they lead to prosperity; but they achieve this because they are in themselves intrinsically good and desirable. This unitary view of life, in which there is no awareness of the modern distinction between "religious" and "secular", is not confined to Proverbs but is characteristic of the Old Testament as a whole and indeed of much of the thought of the peoples of the ancient Near East.

That wisdom is universally attainable is particularly stressed in Proverbs in the numerous passages in which the blessings in store for the wise (*ḥākām*) are dramatically contrasted with the dire fate which will befall the fool (*kᵉsîl*, *'ᵉwîl*). The purpose of these antitheses is clear: it is to point out to the listener or reader that he has the opportunity to *choose* between a course of life which will lead to happiness and prosperity and one which will lead to ruin.

Proverbs, then, is in its present form a book whose purpose is to persuade the reader to acquire wisdom. But the book itself tells us little about the source of this teaching or its context within the life of ancient Israel. It has certain affinities with two other Old Testament books: Job and Ecclesiastes, which have also been designated "wisdom books"; all three books have the same characteristic, that they make no allusion to Israel, to the events of Israel's history or to the actions of God in that history. Although in Proverbs God is throughout referred to by the name Yahweh, which was exclusive to Israel, and there is no mention of other gods, there is no suggestion here of a national consciousness. The reader, who is addressed almost exclusively as an individual, might, it seems, be of any nationality.

These facts call forth a host of questions about the sources of this concern with "wisdom" and the context or contexts in which the book was composed. What was the position of the authors in Israelite society? What was the reason for their concern to make the observations and to give the advice of which the book consists? To whom was the book addressed? What was the basis of the authority which the authors implicitly or explicity claim to possess? And at what stage or stages in Israel's history were they active? All these questions have been exhaustively discussed, but no consensus has been reached. The principal theories will be briefly considered here in anticipation of more detailed discussions below.

The theories about the authorship of the material in Proverbs can be divided *grosso modo* into two main categories: those which understand the book – or parts of it – as having its origins in native Israelite, "popular" proverbs and aphorisms, and those who see it as being from the first a purely "literary" work, the product of an "upper class" of highly educated officials or scribes who from the time of the early monarchy onwards assimilated and adapted a sophisticated literary "wisdom tradition" common to the ancient Near Eastern world. These two views are not, however, as completely contradictory as they may seem, for two reasons. First, it is clear that the material in Proverbs is not all of the same kind. Both textual evidence (the headings in 1:1; 10:1; 22:17; 24:23; 25:1; 30:1; 31:1) and the evidence of different styles and points of view show that the book is a compilation from a number of originally different works each of which has its own character. It is therefore possible that some parts may have their origin in a purely Israelite "wisdom", while others were from the first written compositions by learned scribes. Secondly, it is possible that the whole book has been edited and revised by learned scribes who have imposed their own point of view on material which was originally of a more "popular" kind.

The answers to the other questions set out in the last paragraph but one naturally depend on the answers to the question about authorship. The "popular" material, if that is what it is (mainly the short proverbs of which 10:1–22:16 and 25–9 almost entirely consist) may be the result of the collection at a later stage of numerous proverbs which circulated orally among ordinary people. Many of these may go back to pre-literary and pre-monarchical times. Some scholars (notably Audet and Gerstenberger) believe that some at least of these proverbs are not simply examples of popular lore like the popular proverbs of modern English and other traditional usage, but that they were backed up by a distinct authority in the sense that they were intended, under the direction of heads of clans, to regulate the behaviour of the clan society which preceded the formation of an Israelite state with its national legal system. Their assembly into collections may have been due to a desire on the part of later scribes to form a written corpus of Israelite traditional wisdom which was in danger of being forgotten.

On the other hand, chapters 1–9, 22:17–24:22 and possibly 24:23–34, whose style is in the main quite different from that of the short proverbs, are clearly educational in character and seem to be designed to instruct the young, possibly in institutional "schools" perhaps originally connected with the royal court, more probably in the more informal setting of instruction given by fathers to sons in hereditary scribal families. The authority behind this instruction would be that of father or teacher. This would, then, be "upper-class" material. Much of it has a "family relationship" with extant educational works from other countries, notably from Egypt; and some scholars detect the direct influence on it of such foreign literature. Von Rad in particular propounded the theory that the literary wisdom literature of Israel had its origins in the time of Solomon when, according to him, the newly established Israelite court was particularly open to foreign, especially Egyptian, influence – a circumstance which led to Solomon's reputation for wisdom (1 Kg. 4:29–34 [Heb. 5:9–14]) which is reflected in the attribution to him of parts of Proverbs (1:1; 10:1; 25:1). The heading in 25:1 would point to further such activity in the reign of Hezekiah.

The question of the dating of the composition of Proverbs is a complex one. The majority of scholars now believe that the book contains a good deal of material originating in the period of the Israelite monarchy, and possibly in the earlier part of that period. But if the theories of "popular" or of "clan" origin of parts of the book are correct, much may be considerably older than that. On the other hand, it is also universally believed, mainly on the basis of the development of ideas in the book, that Proverbs *in its present form* cannot be earlier than the early post-exilic period. The book shows no sign, however, of the emphasis on the Mosaic Law which developed during the latter part of that period as exemplified in the early second century Ecclesiasticus (Ben Sira).

It must be stressed, finally, that none of the theories alluded to above is susceptible of actual proof, and that some of the questions remain completely open. There is a sense in which Proverbs is "timeless". Much of its teaching is relevant to almost any age, and there is a sense in which dating is irrelevant. It may be noted that some of the comparable literature of ancient Egypt continued to be read and copied for three thousand years, presumably because of its continued relevance. On the other hand, it is of importance for the purpose of interpretation of the text to attempt to assess the social background of the different parts of the book and also to attempt to detect any development of thought which may have taken place over the period of its composition. This will be attempted below mainly on the basis of the internal evidence of the material itself.

C. RELATIONSHIP TO ISRAEL'S RELIGIOUS TRADITIONS

It used frequently to be maintained that the "wisdom" of Proverbs has little or nothing to do with the religion of Israel: it was an alien concept introduced from outside Israel, and it long remained exclusive to a small educated élite at first closely connected with the royal court, which, though nominally Yahwist in belief, had evolved a mode of thought quite different from that of the rest of the nation. This "wisdom" was often described as "secular", and was thought to have provided the basis for a ruthless *Realpolitik* practised by the Israelite kings and their advisers. Although later, with the addition of more "religious proverbs" to the older ones, and of chapters 1–9 – generally believed to be the latest additions to the book – Proverbs acquired a more "theological" character, foreign influences continued to inspire the mode of thought of its authors; and it was not until the time of Ben Sira, the author of Ecclesiasticus in the second century BC that Israelite wisdom became fully integrated with traditional Israelite religious beliefs. This understanding of the situation consequently represented Proverbs as a *corpus alienum* within the Old Testament, impossible to fit into a comprehensive Old

Testament theology and of little interest to the student of Israelite religion.

This view of the matter, though still maintained in its main features by a few scholars (notably Preuss) is no longer generally accepted. It is now widely recognized that it rests both on an inadequate understanding of Israel's religion and on a somewhat inaccurate picture of the nature of the Egyptian Instructions and of the circumstances of their composition.

To take the second of these points first, the association between Egyptian wisdom literature itself and both school and court is now perceived to be much less close than was once supposed. As Hellmut Brunner points out in his *Altägyptische Weisheit* (1988), the extant Egyptian Instructions from the time of the New Kingdom onwards – i.e., from about the fifteenth century BC – make no reference to the king or the royal court, and are certainly not intended as advice to courtiers or officials. Nor were they composed in or for the use of schools, although subsequently they became and long remained standard school texts. They were composed by fathers for their sons. Although the words "father" and "son" in Egyptian could be used in an extended rather than a literal sense to mean teacher and pupil, in several of the Instructions the son who is the recipient of the teaching is specifically named or otherwise identified; and at least in the New Kingdom and later Instructions there is no reason to take these references other than literally. Such Instructions, then, seem to have originated as private communications. This does not tell us anything directly about the origins of the various sections of Proverbs, where no comparable headings are now extant, and whose editors have simply attributed the main sections to Solomon or to "the wise"; but these facts render theories of a court or school origin for Proverbs extremely fragile, and, incidentally, suggest that the words "my son" and "a/your father" which occur frequently in the book may well reflect instruction actually carried on within the family.

Two further considerations suggest that blanket theories of Egyptian influence on Proverbs need to be modified. The first is concerned with style and form: those parts of Proverbs generally held to be the oldest – 10:1–22:16 and 25–9 – consist of collections of short proverbs, a literary form which is almost entirely absent from Egyptian wisdom literature, which is written almost exclusively in the quite different form of the longer "Instruction". On the other hand, the short proverb form is more characteristic of Mesopotamian wisdom literature, although only in a few cases is there any indication of a possibility of direct borrowing from the latter.

The second consideration concerns the theory of a court origin for Proverbs. It is obvious that this, even if it has some validity, can only apply to parts of Proverbs composed before the fall of the Judaean monarchy in 587 BC. The later sections of the book, even if their authors were influenced by foreign models, cannot have been composed at a royal court which no longer existed or for schools attached to such an institution; and some other social background must be sought for them.

Modern study of Egyptian wisdom literature has also, by implication, challenged the theory that the older substratum of Proverbs was "secular", and that "religious" notions were added to it only later. It has been conclusively shown that it is incorrect to label any of the Egyptian wisdom literature as "secular" (De Buck, Anthes, and, more recently, Brunner). It is true that the later Egyptian Instructions, notably that of *Amenemope* (now dated c. 1100 BC), express a deeply held personal, interior religion which is absent from the earlier ones; but it is now universally recognized that the teaching of the earlier Instructions also is based on the fundamentally "religious" concept of *maat*, which may variously – though only approximately – be rendered by "order", "truth", "justice" and the like, which was not just an abstract principle but was accorded divine status. This literature thus gives no support to the idea of an originally "secular" concept of wisdom. The question is now therefore not whether the older wisdom in Proverbs was secular, but whether the religion of Proverbs was dependent on a foreign religious system such as that of Egypt, or whether it was fundamentally of Israelite origin.

To return to the first point: the view that the teaching of Proverbs is alien to Israel's religious traditions is based on an unduly narrow definition of the religion of Israel ("Yahwism"). Von Rad's view that "in principle Israel's faith is grounded in a theology of history. It regards itself as based upon historical acts" (*Old Testament Theology*, 1962, vol. 1, p. 106) was for long the dominant one, even though he himself later considerably modified this view (*Wisdom in Israel*, 1972, pp. 289–96). He asserted, further, that "Even where this reference to divine acts in history is not immediately apparent, as for example in some of the Psalms, it is, however, present by implication"! Since the "wisdom teaching" of the older parts of Proverbs is based entirely on unaided empirical human experience, it "ought not to be at all considered in relation to the central content of Israel's faith and cult" (*Theology*, vol. 1, p. 435).

This definition of the religion of Israel has now more and more been revealed as inadequate. It ignores or treats as irrelevant an important element of Israelite faith – the relationship of the individual Israelite to his God, and the expression of that relationship in his daily life.

The Israelite's religion was hardly restricted to his presence at the annual festivals and the public recitation of a "creed" recounting the historical events through which Yahweh had created and delivered the nation. Besides this corporate aspect of Yahwism there was the sense of an abiding divine presence (Westermann, Terrien), expressed, among its other manifestations, by the personal names given to newborn infants, which incorporate the name Yahweh in various forms and testify in a variety of ways to a confidence in Yahweh's care for the individual. Some aspects of this personal faith are of course to be found in the Psalter, in the psalms of the individual, in which, as stated earlier, von Rad gratuitously found implied references to the history of the salvation of the nation (*Heilsgeschichte*). In Proverbs this kind of individual piety rarely appears on the surface (though see 30:7–9); but there is a strong sense of life lived under the divine blessing for the "righteous". It was in the down-to-earth everyday life of which Proverbs speaks that the ordinary Israelite felt the presence of God.

Further, the total absence from Proverbs of reference to the *Heilsgeschichte* should not be taken as an indication that its authors were unaware of it, or that they ignored it. It cannot be too strongly emphasized that Proverbs is an entirely different kind of book from the other Old Testament books: indeed, that it is unique. It served an entirely different purpose. It is addressed to the individual and to his personal concerns. There is nothing here which is contradictory to the public affirmations of salvation-faith found elsewhere in the Old Testament, and there is no reason to suppose that that historic faith was not taken for granted by its authors.

It has been argued that Proverbs differs from the rest of the Old Testament in its doctrine of God. This view presupposes that there is an entirely consistent doctrine of God throughout the pages of the Old Testament, which is manifestly not the case. But setting aside this consideration, it has been argued that the God of Proverbs, even though he is always referred to by his name Yahweh, lacks most of the characteristics of the God of Israel: that he is perceived only as the One who presides over a system of rewards and punishments which is self-operative and grounded in the very nature of things, simply setting his seal, as it were, on it (Koch). This view rests mainly on the fact that in many of the proverbs in 10:1–22:16 and 25–9 the operation of the principle of retribution, in which persons are rewarded or penalized according to what they deserve, is stated without reference to God. This conclusion, however, is not necessarily correct. A number of proverbs make it clear that Yahweh, far from being a mere rubber stamp, is perceived as fundamentally unknowable and as frequently intervening to frustrate human expectations; that human knowledge is limited. While it is possible that these proverbs are later "religious" additions to an earlier, less "religious" substratum, this cannot be demonstrated, and there is a danger of circular argumentation here. Moreover, such a concept of God is not that of the later Egyptian Instructions, on which Proverbs is often held to be based. It remains more probable that in those proverbs which do not specifically mention Yahweh as the arbiter of human destiny there is nevertheless an unspoken assumption that when "blessings" and their opposites are spoken of, it is he who dispenses them. The picture of Yahweh which then emerges is, then, of a God who rewards and punishes in accordance with the principles of justice, but who nevertheless remains free and inscrutable in his decisions. This picture is fully in accordance with traditional Old Testament teaching, even though the *Heilsgeschichte* element, only peripheral to the concerns of daily living, is absent.

It has been said, and with some justification, that the wisdom theology of the Old Testament is primarily a theology of creation: that is, that God is seen as active in the world primarily as Creator (rather than as Redeemer). Once again it was above all von Rad in his *Old Testament Theology* who asserted that this doctrine of creation was a latecomer to Israelite religious thought and an alien one imported from outside: a doctrine which gives the Old Testament wisdom literature, including Proverbs, an entirely different approach to reality from that of traditional Israelite beliefs, in that it leads to an anthropocentric rather than a theocentric attitude. The emphasis, it is alleged, is on man's attempt to discover the structure of the created world and so, as far as possible, to master it. Later, attempts were made to integrate the doctrine of creation into the Israelite religious tradition; but in as far as wisdom thought and the historical tradition of the redeeming God constituted two totally different modes of thought, wisdom remained *sui generis* a theological outsider. It is now increasingly realized that this is an exaggeration. Although the wisdom teaching of Proverbs undoubtedly acquired its special form partly from influences from outside Israel, it is impossible to believe that in its early period Israel was unique among the peoples of the ancient Near East in having no concept of a creator-god; and in fact there is evidence in some of the oldest Old Testament texts that it did have such a concept, and that – for example, in Gen. 2 – man and his wellbeing are central to that concept, as in Proverbs.

We are justified in concluding from the above considerations that, while Proverbs has much in common with a wider wisdom thought and literature which flourished throughout the ancient Near Eastern world, its teaching should be seen as complementary to that of the historical Israelite religious tradition rather than as opposed to it. It reflects and illustrates an aspect of the Yahwism of individual Israelites about which we should otherwise know little, and has its own contribution to make to our knowledge of that religion.

D. THE FORMS OF SPEECH EMPLOYED IN THE BOOK

Three sections of the book are entitled "proverbs of Solomon" (1:1; 10:1; 25:1). The first of these headings may be intended to refer to the whole book, or at least as far as chapter 29. The Hebrew word here translated by "proverb" is *māšāl*. However, this word tells us very little about the literary forms in which the book is couched. *māšāl* occurs fairly frequently in the other books of the Old Testament, where it has a wide distribution. But it is there used in a variety of senses some of which appear to have little in common. These include short popular proverbs or sayings, prophetic oracles (Num. 23–4), speeches or discourses (Job 27:1; 29:1), psalms (Ps. 78:2), taunts or mocking songs (Isa. 14:4) and parables (Ezek. 17:2). Some of the utterances so designated are very short while others are of considerable length. So also in Proverbs: the material which follows the headings in 10:1 and 25:1 consists of short proverbs, while that which follows 1:1 (chapters 1–9) consists almost entirely of much longer poems. The only common feature of the *māšāl* as it is understood in Proverbs is that it is an utterance proper only to the "wise": in the mouths of fools it is ludicrously inappropriate (26:7, 9).

Formally, Proverbs has one unifying characteristic: it is written entirely in poetry. Quite apart from the technical differences between prose and poetical styles, there is a profound difference between prose and poetry in the ways in which they convey their message to the audience or the reader, which cannot be discussed in detail here. Suffice it to say that in general poetry makes up in allusiveness what it lacks in precision. The poetical saying or proverb, for example, is frequently "open-ended" in that it is deliberately formulated in such a way as to permit a variety of interpretations and applications which go beyond its "literal" meaning but which are equally legitimate and which make it relevant to different circumstances and different ages. This characteristic must be kept in mind in the attempt to interpret Proverbs, both the short proverbs and the longer poems.

The reason why the authors of Proverbs chose the poetical form is not easy to determine; but it probably has something to do with the nature of the authority to which the authors lay claim. For the giving of precise instruction and the laying down of moral and religious rules, the prose style would seem to be perfectly suited; and it was the prose form which was selected by the compilers of the law codes of the Old Testament, and of the Deuteronomic "sermons" found in the opening chapters of Deuteronomy and in the Book of Jeremiah. Moreover, these had the backing of the authority of Moses in the one case and Jeremiah in the other. It may also be that the authority of the wisdom instruction and the wisdom proverb depend less on logic and argument than on persuasion through the actual forms of the language which they use: the persuasive power lay in the sound of the words themselves and in the pictures which they created in the mind of the listener. In this sense these were "powerful words". (It may be noted that this kind of "power" has been linked by some scholars to one of the etymologies proposed for the word *māšāl*, that it is related to the verb *māšal*, "to rule".)

A further possible reason for the use of the poetical form in

Proverbs is its mnemonic value. Poetry is easier to memorize than prose; and it is probable that both the short proverbs and the longer "instructions" were intended to be memorized – the former in order to secure their transmission through succeeding generations, and the latter as an educational method, to impress their teaching on the young mind. For the same reason, much of the wisdom literature of the ancient Near East is in poetical form.

"'Wisdom literature' is not a form-critical term; it is merely a term of convenience to designate the books of Proverbs, Job and Ecclesiastes, and among the Apocrypha, Ben Sira and the Wisdom of Solomon. It has been adopted also by Egyptologists and cuneiform specialists to designate a variety of extrabiblical literature that is similar to the biblical works" (Murphy, *FOTL*, p. 3). Within Proverbs alone, the diversity of forms is quite obvious. The two main types occurring in the book are the short proverb (sometimes called the "sentence" – hence the term "sentence literature") and the instruction. The former is mainly represented in 10:1–22:16 and 25–29; the latter in chapters 1–9, in 22:17–24:23 and in 31:1–9. Several other forms also occur, notably the "wisdom speech" – that is, a speech placed in the mouth of a figure called "Wisdom", represented as a woman (1:20–33; 8;. 9:1–6) –; the "example story", in which a teacher uses a (supposed) account of his own personal experience to teach a lesson (7:6–27; 24: 30–34); the prayer (30:7–9); the acrostic poem (30:10–31). Some of these categories, especially the "sentence literature", can be divided into clearly distinguished sub-categories. These will be discussed below in the introductions to those sections of the book.

The origins and settings of the sentence and instruction forms will also be discussed in the sectional introductions. Here it is necessary only to consider what relationship, if any, exists between these two genres. One thing that is now clear is that the latter is not a "development" from the former. At one time it was generally believed that in the case of the wisdom literature as also of other types of Old Testament literature, the length and degree of organization of a composition reflected the degree of cultural development of the author: early compositions belonged to a relatively simple cultural level, while longer and more complex compositions showed a development in ability to formulate more complex thoughts and to express them in literary form. This opinion has been shown to be erroneous, both in respect of the Old Testament and in terms of the history of human cultural development generally; and indeed, when for example we compare the prolixity of an epic like Beowulf with a witty epigram of the eighteenth century, it is somewhat surprising that this should not have been recognized from the first. Certainly the length of a literary composition is, taken by itself, no criterion of literary skill: to say much in a few well-chosen words may be a sign of the most sophisticated artistry, though equally a short, plain saying may be the product of almost any stage of culture.

In fact, although links between the sentence type and the longer wisdom composition are not lacking, in that an author of the latter type not infrequently finds it useful to incorporate examples of the former into his own work, the two are quite distinct forms of expression, and existed contemporaneously in ancient Israel as well as in the literature of other ancient peoples. For example, in the case of Egyptian literature, where relative dating is easier to determine than in the case of Proverbs, it is noteworthy that of two works which are probably the latest of the so-called "Instructions" and not far apart in time of composition, one, *Papyrus Insinger*, perhaps composed c. 300 BC, is "an organized work" of some eight hundred lines divided into twenty-five chapters each with its own theme and each provided with its own heading (Lichtheim, p. 109), while the *Instruction of Ankhsheshonqy*, probably of an only slightly earlier date, though it was in intention an "Instruction", belonged to "an anthologizing type of wisdom, in which individual precepts were loosely strung together in shorter or longer sequences and without an overall order, though some rudiments of organization may have been present" (Lichtheim, p. 21). Consisting in fact of a mixture of "individual precepts and proverbs", *Ankhsheshonqy* thus has features reminiscent of the "sentence-literature" of the Book of Proverbs.

E. THE STRUCTURE OF THE BOOK

In as far as Proverbs may be said to have a structural – as distinct from a thematic – unity, this is due to a final editor who has imposed his stamp on his collection of originally disparate works. Each of those earlier works may well have had its own history of composition and redaction, but these do not concern us at this point. It is reasonable to suppose that one of the purposes of the final editor was to make a compendium of the whole corpus of Israel's wisdom literature with which he was familiar, or at least of such works as he deemed worthy of inclusion. The question to be asked here is whether it is possible to discover why he arranged it in this particular order.

The seven headings which now divide the book into sections give some indication of the editor's plan, irrespective of whether he himself composed all or some of these headings. In view of Solomon's reputation for wisdom, and in particular of the statement in 1 Kg 4:32 (Heb. 5:12) that he "spoke three thousand proverbs", it is not surprising that the first two sections of the book are claimed as "proverbs of Solomon" (1:1; 10:1). There follow two headings introducing "words of wise men" (22:17; 24:23), the second of which links these two sections with the phrase "These *also* are from the wise". The next heading (25:1) rather surprisingly reverts to a claim of Solomonic authorship ("These also are proverbs of Solomon"); but the reference there to the subsequent editorial work of the "men of Hezekiah" may suggest that this section does not have quite the same stamp of Solomonic authority as the first two sections of the book. This may account for its not being placed next to them. The final two headings (30:1 and 31:1) state clearly that the sections which follow (though this does not necessarily apply to the whole of these chapters) are the work of non-Israelites, one Agur and one King Lemuel – the latter derived from his mother's teaching. The appending of these two sections may be connected in some way with the reference to foreign wise men in 1 Kg. 4:30–31 (Heb. 5:10–11), which recognizes the value of some foreign wisdom though it regards it as inferior to that of Solomon, and perhaps even suggests that Solomon's wisdom provided a model which was imitated abroad. Although the editor of proverbs deemed these works to be worthy of inclusion, he placed them at the end, after the works composed by Israelite wise men.

Besides such considerations, however, there are indications that the arrangement of the book had some deeper purpose. This purpose is evident in the placing of the first section, particularly of the opening verses, and probably also in the choice and placing of the final section.

As has already been suggested, 1:1–7 reads like a preface, not merely to chapters 1–9, but to the whole book. To the heading in v. 1 there is loosely attached a series of assertions (vv. 2–6) that these proverbs will confer on those who attend to them a comprehensive set of intellectual and moral qualities. Finally in v. 7, which has been described as a "motto" summing up the teaching of the whole book, the true source and foundation of the "knowledge" and wisdom so offered is identified: it is the "fear of Yahweh"; and only fools will despise it. How much, if any, of these seven verses is the work of the final editor himself is not certain; but in using them as the preface he has set the tone for the whole book. The reader, as he reads on, will now see every reference to the wise and to wisdom through the editorial spectacles; and, however mundane and even trivial some parts of the book may appear, he will see all its teaching as directed towards the formation of the complete person, both wise and pious: wise because pious, and pious because wise.

The placing of the remainder of chapters 1–9 immediately after the preface serves to add further emphasis to the promises there made and to clothe them, as it were, with flesh and blood. In their present form these chapters serve both to elevate the character of the wisdom teacher who, it will be assumed by the reader, is responsible for everything which follows, and, at the same time, in impressive and mysterious, quasi-mythical language, to stress the intimate relationship of wisdom with God, its attractiveness to the learner, and the indispensability of its acquisition.

It has been suggested with some plausibility that the final section of the book (31:10–31) corresponds to the first section, thus forming an "envelope" within which the rest of the book is contained. Although this section has no heading, its literary form – that of an "alphabetic acrostic" – shows that it is distinct from the preceding section. It is a description of the "good" or ideal wife; but whatever may have been its original purpose, it has been remarked that this "wife" has some of the characteristics of that other female figure, the personified Wisdom of chapters 1–9. (We may note the "marital" language of 4: 5–9.) At the very least, she is clearly a supreme example of wise behaviour as taught throughout the book; she is also one who "speaks wisdom" and teaches it (v. 26); and she is praised as "a woman who fears Yahweh" (v. 30). That Proverbs, which elsewhere has little to say about women – and some of that little far from complimentary! – should conclude with such a eulogy is surprising, unless the editor who arranged the book in this way wished to give a final reminder to the reader of the compelling qualities of "Lady Wisdom".

A quite different theory of the unity and structure of Proverbs was proposed by P. W. Skehan and has enjoyed a certain amount of favour. According to Skehan, the master key to the book is to be found in the statement in 9:1 that

Wisdom has built her house;
she has hewn her seven pillars.

This "house of Wisdom" is, he claims, none other than the Book of Proverbs itself, a building which has the appearance and dimensions of Solomon's Temple. The compiler of the book arranged his material in a series of columns of varying length so that the work had the shape and relative dimensions of that building: first its front elevation (1–9), then the side elevation of the nave (10:1–22:16) and finally the side and rear elevations of the inner sanctuary (22:17–31:31). This elaborate theory is supported by various calculations based on the numerical values of the letters of the Hebrew alphabet. Thus the words "Solomon", "David" and "Israel" in 1:1 when added together give a total of 930, which is almost exactly the number of the units in the book.

A theory of this kind is always difficult to disprove; but the burden of proof lies upon its proponent. Skehan himself admits that there is no evidence of the use of these devices in any other Old Testament book; he also admits that some adjustments to the text are required to make it fit the theory. Further, the "architectural" arrangement of the text in columns of specific lengths which Skehan supposes to have been visible in the compiler's own original autograph must have soon been forgotten and obliterated by copyists, since there is no trace of it either in any Hebrew manuscript or in the earliest Versions, nor any reference to it in any ancient authority.

F. TEXT AND VERSIONS

The Hebrew text (MT) of some parts of Proverbs is fairly free of problems; but in other parts, especially in the case of the individual proverbs in the "sentence literature", there are numerous obscurities which may simply be due to the presence of otherwise unknown words – particularly to be found in poetical works; compare especially Job – whose meaning is not, moreover, easily determined from the immediate context, which frequently does not exceed the compass of a single, brief proverb. Hence the immense volume of attempts by modern scholars to wrestle with the text, of which a sample will be found in the commentary which follows. Many of the more obvious obscurities, however, appear to be due to careless copying; in some cases the restoration of the text has so far remained a completely insoluble problem.

Of the ancient Versions, the Greek Septuagint (*LXX*) is by far the most important for the correction of the Hebrew, but it can only be used with great caution. It is longer than *MT*, having some 130 additional lines, though there are also some omissions. Some of the additional material may go back to a Hebrew *Vorlage* which lay before the translators; but this did not necessarily constitute part of the text of Proverbs as originally written; other "pluses" were evidently first composed in Greek. Some of the variants are probably due to a misunderstanding of the Hebrew by the translator, to a desire to present an idiomatic translation, or to corruption within the *LXX* text itself. The various *LXX* manuscripts sometimes show inner-Greek variants. Many of the additions and variants are due to a tendency to modify the teaching of the book by spiritualizing or moralizing what seemed to the translator to be unacceptable, or to produce an "up-to-date", topical version for the Hellenistic reader. For details, reference may be made to the introduction to McKane's commentary (pp. 33–47), where some 140 variants are listed and an attempt is made to classify these and to suggest which of them may help to restore the original Hebrew text.

The other ancient Versions are of relatively minor importance for the establishment of the text of Proverbs. The Syriac and Coptic Versions were translated from the Greek. Jerome's (Latin) Vulgate is basically a fairly faithful rendering of the Hebrew, but also shows some influence from the Greek.

G. OUTLINE OF CONTENTS

1–9	"Proverbs of Solomon"
1:1–7	Preface
1:8–19	First instruction: avoidance of evil company
1:20–33	Speech by Wisdom
2:1–22	Second instruction: avoidance of the "strange woman"
3:1–12	Third instruction: behaviour towards God
3:13–18	The praise of Wisdom

3:19–20	Wisdom and creation
3:21–35	Fourth instruction: behaviour towards neighbours
4:1–9	Fifth instruction: the importance of traditional wisdom
4:10–19	Sixth instruction: avoidance of evil company
4:20–27	Seventh instruction: the importance of vigilance
5:1–23	Eighth instruction: avoidance of the "strange woman"
6:1–19	Admonitions and warnings
6:20–35	Ninth instruction: avoidance of the "strange woman"
7:1–27	Tenth instruction: avoidance of the "strange woman"
8:1–36	Speech by Wisdom
9:1–18	Wisdom and Folly
10:1–22:16	"Proverbs of Solomon" A collection of short proverbs
22:17–24:22	"Sayings of wise men" A series of instructions
24:23–34	More "sayings of wise men" Proverbs, admonitions and an example story
25–29	More "proverbs of Solomon" transcribed by the men of Hezekiah
30:1–4	"Words of Agur"
30:5–33	Miscellaneous sayings, a prayer, and numerical proverbs
31:1–9	"Words of King Lemuel" An instruction
31:10–31	A poem in praise of the "good wife" An acrostic poem

COMMENTARY ON PROVERBS

"PROVERBS OF SOLOMON"
1–9

These chapters consist mainly of two kinds of material: a series of ten Instructions given by a father to his son, and two speeches by "Wisdom" depicted as a female figure. The whole is preceded by a general Preface, and concludes with a "diptych" contrasting in vivid terms what Wisdom and "the woman Folly" have to offer to those whom they invite to their "houses": life and death respectively. (See the Outline of Contents.)

The *series of Instructions* (1:8–7:27) is not consecutive but is interrupted by three insertions: the first speech by Wisdom (1:20–33); two consecutive short sections referring to Wisdom in the third person (3:13–20); and a miscellaneous collection of admonitions and warnings (6:1–19). Thus the two speeches by Wisdom are also not consecutive but are widely separated, the first occurring after the first Instruction (1:20–33) and the second at the conclusion of the series of Instructions (8:1–36). Several of the Instructions have, in addition, undergone considerable expansion. (See Whybray, *Wisdom in Proverbs*). However, while there thus seems to be some lack of logical arrangement in detail, the section has a certain unity in that the first eight chapters can be seen as a detailed exposition of the theme of the Preface, especially of 1:7, while the final "diptych" (9:1-6, 13–18) gives vivid expression to the theme of wisdom versus folly which is the keynote of the whole section, forming an impressive conclusion to what may at one time have been a self-contained composition.

The Instructions all have a close "family relationship". This is particularly obvious when one compares their introductory words. In every case the word "my son" – in one instance, "sons" – occurs as either the first or the second word; and the first two lines – or in some cases four – of each Instruction consist of a strong affirmation about the importance of the Instruction for the conduct of the pupil's life. It is remarkable – and no satisfactory explanation has been found for this – that although in every case the language used is similar, it is never quite identical: a remarkable number of synonyms is used, and often the same words occur in slightly different combinations. Thus the father refers to his teaching in a variety of ways, speaking of his instruction (*mûsār*), his teaching (*tôrāh*), his wisdom (*ḥokmāh*), his commands (*miṣwôt*), or simply his words (*ᵃmārîm*, *d^ebārîm*), while the pupil is enjoined to "hear" them (*šāma'*), to pay attention to them (*hiqšîb*), not to forget them or reject them, and, in a variety of expressions, to "treasure them in his heart" and so on. The varieties of wording seem endless; yet the basic meaning is always the same. There is greater variety in the main body of the Instruction, and there is a variety of themes; but a constant feature is the contrast drawn between the blessings and advantages which will be conferred on those who heed and obey the Instruction and the dire fate of those who do not.

If each of these ten passages dealt with a different subject, it might be possible to see them as a single Instruction divided, like some of the Egyptian Instructions, into ten "chapters" – though even so, the fact that each is provided with a fairly elaborate introduction covering the same ground would seem to militate against this. But the fact that no fewer than four of them have exactly the same theme – the avoidance of the "strange woman" – seems to rule out entirely the possibility that they might be a single composition. Yet the strong resemblance between them, which – especially in the case of those concerning the "strange woman" – amounts sometimes to identical phraseology, suggests that there must be some kind of link between them. Unity of authorship is less probable than two other explanations: either that some are conscious imitations of others, or that they are all examples of a common "instructional" literary genre current in Israel, at which, so to speak, various writers "tried their hand", sometimes rather slavishly. This last is perhaps the most probable explanation. The reason for their having been editorially combined into a single work may be that the editor wished to form a comprehensive collection of Instructions known to him, or that he hoped that repetition would drive home the teaching more effectively.

There can be no doubt that the main purpose of the Instructions is the education of young men. This is shown quite clearly by their general tone, by the address to "sons", and by the fact that two topics – the avoidance of evil company and the avoidance of immoral women – account for no fewer than six of them. It is also clear that the pupils belonged to the upper class of urban society. The Instructions obviously presuppose the ability to read and write. There are no references to agricultural or other manual labour. Wealth appears to be taken for granted; and – in complete contrast with the sentence literature of 10:1–22:16 and 25–29 – there are no references at all to poverty or the poor: not even a recommendation to help or pity the poor, or to refrain from oppressing them. The main concern of these Instructions is with the happiness and success of the pupil as he will go through life.

Yet, as has already been suggested, it would be wrong to class these Instructions as "secular". In the wisdom literature, both of Israel and of Egypt, it is always taken for granted that no happiness or success in life can be obtained if duties towards God (or the gods) are neglected, or if one's moral conduct is displeasing to God. At the same time, there is reason to suppose that at least some of the references to Yahweh in these Instructions have been added to make this fact explicit. In fact such "theologizing" was not carried out very thoroughly. Six of the ten Instructions (1:8–19; 4:1–9; 4:10–19; 4:20–27; 6:20–35; 7:1–27) contain no references to God at all, while some at least of the references to Yahweh in the others give the impression of having been added to a text which makes excellent sense without them.

The question of the relationship of these chapters to the "instruction" literature of ancient Egypt has been studied by Kayatz. She pointed to similarities between the two bodies of literature with regard to their literary form, especially with reference to 1:1–7, though she also noted differences of form best explained as due to a distinct Israelite tradition. In other respects also she noted quite significant differences. Of these perhaps the most important is that in the Egyptian Instructions neither the standard word for "wisdom" nor any comparable term plays a significant role. Nor is there any notion there which may be compared with the equation of wisdom with the fear of Yahweh which occurs in 1:7 and also in the "theological" verses 1:29 and 2:5. Lesser differences include the expression "my son", which is rare in the Egyptian examples, the references in Proverbs to the role of the mother as co-teacher with the father, which Kayatz believes may indicate a family background rather than that of the school, and the frequency of exhortations to "hear", generally associated with admonitions to strive after wisdom, which appear in the Egyptian Instructions only in the Prologues. The Instructions in Prov. 1–9 are also much shorter than the Egyptian ones. Kayatz's conclusion that, though not directly dependent on Egyptian Instructions, those in Proverbs 1–9 were considerably influenced by the Egyptian literary tradition may be correct, although parallel development from a common Near Eastern matrix, which would probably also account for the few Instructions from Mesopotamia which have come down to us, should also be borne in mind as a possibility.

The *two speeches by Wisdom* (1:20–33 and 8:1–36) are without parallel in the Old Testament. According to Kayatz, their genre is derived from the Egyptian genre of the self-praising speech by a god or goddess. Kayatz lists the characteristics which are common to both: address, demand, self-praise, promise of life or protection to adherents. But Wisdom is not a goddess; and even Kayatz fails to detect Egyptian influence, other than the "I-form", in 1:20–33, where there are very clear connections with purely Israelite forms of speech, notably the prophetic oracle.

Although it may not be possible to explain the origin of this personified Wisdom (see below), traces of its earlier development are to be found elsewhere in the Old Testament. The personification of abstract qualities (for example, of love, faithfulness, justice and peace in Ps. 85:10–11 [Heb. 11–12]), whether it is merely a poetical device or whether mythological notions lie behind it, is fairly common in the poetical books. In the wisdom literature, wisdom is often represented as something infinitely valuable to be sought and obtained at all costs (Job 28, especially vv. 15–19; Prov. 3:15). In one of the Instructions in Prov. 1–9 (4:5–9) the teacher, in an attempt to make this pursuit more attractive to the pupil, goes further and uses imagery in which wisdom is presented not as a precious object but in the form of a marriageable girl who, somewhat like the "good wife" of 31:10–31, will when married support and protect her husband and enhance his reputation and status. (The fact that wisdom is a feminine noun [*ḥokmāh*] in Hebrew was particularly favourable to the use of this imagery.)

In a sense, the picture of Wisdom in chapters 1 and 8 as a woman speaking in public places to the passers-by and calling to them to accept the gifts which she has to offer may be seen simply as a rather spectacular extension of this imagery; but this is not a sufficient explanation of this new and startling phenomenon: it is clear that some further influences have come into play here. One of these is to be found in the motif of the so-called "strange woman" against whom the pupil is warned in the Instructions in chapters 2, 5, 6 and 7. These Instructions depict the danger to the young man of falling into the clutches of immoral women; the pursuit of Wisdom is presented as the infinitely rewarding alternative. That this is so is already clear in 6:22–6, and it is further elaborated in chapter 9, where the "strange woman" motif has blossomed into the "Woman Folly", whose invitation and the consequence of accepting it – death – are starkly contrasted with Wisdom's invitation and its consequence – life.

Even this, however, does not account for much of what Wisdom claims for herself in chapters 1 and 8, in particular 8:22–31, where she asserts that she was created by Yahweh before the creation of the world, that she was present during his acts of creation, and that she is beloved by him. In one sense this passage may be regarded as a "theological" statement which makes it clear that Wisdom is no independent figure or goddess, but that her existence and her influence over mankind are wholly derived from him. But the resemblance of the imagery employed here to that of various Near Eastern mythological literature cannot be ignored.

The extent of this influence, however, and also its origin, have been variously assessed. Some scholars maintain that the figure of Wisdom can be explained without the need to posit a substantial mythological influence. For example, von Rad saw its development as a literary phenomenon which was the result of theological reflection: the figure was not the personification of a divine attribute; rather, it stands for the concept of the nature of reality – the "meaning" or "secret" of life which God has placed in the universe as a mediator between himself and the created world. Fox took a similar view. Camp (1988) regarded personified Wisdom as a "poetic device" intended to emphasize the importance of women and the central place of the family in post-exilic Judaism.

These views do not necessarily conflict with the findings of those scholars who have pointed to features in the portrayal of Wisdom in these chapters which appear to be derived from non-Israelite mythologies. Unfortunately there is no unanimity on this question. Only a few examples can be given here of such theories. Albright, on the basis of the strange form *ḥokmôt* – rather than the usual Hebrew *ḥokmāh* in 9:1 – and of some somewhat obscure Ugaritic texts, postulated the existence of a Canaanite-Phoenician goddess with that name. Others, notably Boström, saw the "Queen of Heaven", the Babylonian Ištar-Astarte, as a source. Kayatz argued for the influence of the Egyptian *maat*. Recently Lang (1986) has put forward a theory which accepts the existence of mythological features in the picture of personified Wisdom while regarding them as of purely Israelite origin: the Wisdom speeches in these chapters were originally composed in praise of an Israelite goddess called Wisdom who was the daughter of El and was worshipped side by side with him in a polytheistic pre-exilic Israel. In the text as it now stands, however, she has been "demythologized" and subordinated to Yahweh.

In fact, all the proponents of mythological influence agree on some kind of "demythologization" of the figure of Wisdom. Whatever remnants of polytheism may be detected in these chapters, there is no question that the text in its present form is monotheistic. Wisdom is completely subordinate to Yahweh. But the question remains whether she was thought of as an actual, living being – the word "hypostasis" is sometimes used in this connection (e.g. by Ringgren) – existing in the divine realm (something like an angelic being in Yahweh's entourage) or whether her representation as such a being is a purely poetical conceit. There is no certainty on this point, and it has been suggested that the distinction between the two may have been beyond the comprehension of the author and his original readers.

Nor is there any agreement about the purpose or function of the figure as conceived by the author. It has already been suggested that it may originally have been created to direct the attention of the young pupil of the Instructions away from the temptations of the flesh; but this hardly accounts for all the features of the Wisdom speeches. Two more profound "theological" purposes have been suggested: that it is intended to act as a kind of "bridge" between God and man at a time when the concern of a transcendent God for his creatures was being questioned (Crenshaw, 1981; Fox), or as a means of bridging another gap, that between the wisdom tradition and traditional Yahwism, by emphasizing that all human wisdom comes from Yahweh (Whybray, 1965). In any case, the incorporation of the two Wisdom speeches of chapters 1 and 8, together with the "diptych" of chapter 9, into this section of the book suggests that these chapters were intended to form part of the teaching given to the young pupil addressed in the Instructions.

Date. There is no agreement among scholars about even the approximate date of these chapters. The view that because they consist mainly of relatively long units in contrast with the short proverbs of 10:1–22:16 and 25–9 they must come from a later period has now been shown to be erroneous. The long form is not a development from the short. The short proverb or "sentence" and the longer Instruction belong to quite different genres (see especially McKane), which could therefore have been employed contemporaneously, as was in fact the case with the non-Israelite wisdom literature. The Instruction form was used in Egypt from the third millennium BC onwards. As far at least as form is concerned, the Wisdom speeches in these chapters also could have been composed at a relatively early time.

Until fairly recently, however, it was generally believed that chapters 1–9 are entirely post-exilic compositions. This view has now been challenged by several scholars. Kayatz, who believes that – apart from the personification of Wisdom in chapters 1 and 8 – the theological gap between 1–9 and the sentence literature of Proverbs has been overstated, places these chapters in the period of the early monarchy. McKane, who follows von Rad in regarding the reign of Solomon as the period when Egyptian wisdom was introduced into Israel through the medium of schools established by that king for the training of an élite class of officials, suggested that the Instruction genre in Israel went back to that time, and that the examples in Prov. 1–9 could consequently have been composed at any time after that, though the Wisdom speeches represent a somewhat later development. Lang, as has already been stated, regards even the Wisdom speeches as having originated in a pre-exilic, polytheistic period, though they were subsequently re-edited and "demythologized" after the Exile.

In the Instructions in these chapters there is in fact almost no internal evidence pointing to any particular period. If they were composed in connection with the service of the Israelite state, there is nothing to indicate this: there are no references there to officials or their training or to the royal court, and the word "king" does not occur there at all. (The reference to Solomon in 1:1 is hardly part of the Instructions themselves, and in fact the only other reference to kings in the whole of chapters 1–9 occurs in 8:15, which speaks in general terms of "kings" and "rulers" deriving their powers from Wisdom.) However, this "negative evidence" is obviously not conclusive.

The main argument for a post-exilic date for these chapters is theological. But the situation is complicated by the possibility that the texts in their present form are the result of a "theological" editing of earlier compositions less overtly theological. In fact, it is extremely unlikely that they are the result of a single act of composition. But the dating of the various stages of composition remains quite uncertain.

THE PREFACE
1:1–7

Verses 1–6, consisting of an attribution of authorship and a statement about the purpose of the teaching which will follow and its value to the reader, have often been compared with the opening sections of Egyptian Instructions, especially with that of the *Instruction of Amenemope* (*ANET*, p. 421; *DOTT*, p. 175). While there is undoubtedly a similarity with the latter sufficient to indicate a "family relationship", there is little similarity of detail. Both prefaces, though in entirely different terms, claim that the teaching will act as a guide to the attentive reader and show him how to live his life successfully, and there is a similarity of grammatical form in that infinitives are used in both texts to list the various benefits conferred on the reader by the teacher (in Prov. 1:2–4, 6 there are six of these, but they have not been rendered as such in *RSV*); but there the resemblance ends. Whereas the Egyptian text is addressed specifically to the aspiring government official, promising to show him how to deal with "elders" and "courtiers" and how to carry out specific duties of his profession, these matters are entirely lacking in the Hebrew text. The latter is not addressed to members of any particular social class or to aspirants to any particular profession, but is apparently of quite general application: it states that the simple or inexperienced, the youth and also the experienced wise man and man of understanding will alike profit by the teaching which will be given. Only v. 6, which promises the ability to understand a **proverb** and a **figure**, **the words of the wise and their riddles**, makes a more specific claim, but that claim has no parallel in the Egyptian text. Some of the other Egyptian Instructions (see Brunner, 1988) begin in somewhat similar ways, but their resemblance to Prov. 1:1–6 is even less striking.

Since the Instructions which follow are a collection of originally separate compositions, it is probable that the Preface was added by an editor, either when that collection was formed or when the whole book of Proverbs attained its present form. This may account for the apparent difference between it and the Instructions as regards the persons addressed: whereas the Instructions are addressed to young men of a particular social class, the Preface envisages a much wider readership.

It is also probable that the Preface was not composed in a single act of composition but has received various additions to an original text, which may have consisted of vv. 1–4, (6). The title or heading (v. 1) is integrally related to vv. 2–4, 6 in that the infinitives with which each of those verses begins cannot stand alone: they are syntactically dependent on v. 1. V. 5, however, breaks the syntactical sequence in that it is couched not in infinitive clauses but in jussive clauses. It gives notice that the book as a whole was written not only for the young, but that it contains teaching from which even the experienced and wise adult can profit. But v. 6 also may be an addition. Whereas the previous verses speak in quite general terms of the value of the teaching, this verse refers quite specifically to a particular skill of a literary nature: the ability to understand obscure sayings. The words **proverb** (*māšāl*), **figure** (*m^e lîṣāh*) and **riddles** (*ḥîdôt*) may refer to different kinds of sayings which occur later in the book. The **words of the wise** (plural, *ḥ^a kāmîm*) may refer to the sections so entitled in 22:17 and 24:23. V. 7, the only verse of the Preface in which Yahweh is mentioned, also appears to be an addition tacked on to the end of the Preface. It is a reminder that the **beginning** of all **knowledge**, **wisdom** and **instruction** is reverence for Yahweh the God of Israel, to ignore which is sheer folly. Wisdom is not simply a human faculty but comes from God. (See also on 9:10.)

A remarkable feature of these verses is the way in which words of similar meaning have been piled up. Thus in vv. 2–5 it is claimed that the teaching which follows will enable the reader to acquire **wisdom** (*ḥokmāh*), **instruction** (*mûsār*), **insight** or understanding (*bînāh*), **wise dealing** or intelligence (*haśkēl*), **prudence** or shrewdness (*'ormāh*), **knowledge** (*da'at*), **discretion** (*m^e zimmāh*), **learning** (*leqaḥ*) and **skill** (*taḥbūlôt*). These words are not synonyms, though the precise distinctions between some of them are not clear. It would be profitless to attempt to understand them as each expressing a different aspect of the teaching. The intention of the author was no doubt to dazzle the reader-pupil with an impressive display of the inexhaustible range of accomplishments to be obtained by giving attention to these "proverbs".

1. On the meaning of **proverb** (*māšāl*) and the attribution to **Solomon** see the Introduction.

2. instruction: this word (*mûsār*) occurs more frequently in Proverbs than in the whole of the rest of the Old Testament. It is particularly frequent in chs. 1–9 and must be regarded as one of the key words of these chapters. It always denotes some form of correction or discipline exercised by one in command – whether God, a father or human teacher, or "Wisdom" – over those in his charge – Israel, the nations, a son or pupil – and often has the meaning of rebuke or, more strongly, punishment: compare, for example, the reference to "the rod of *mûsār*" in Prov. 22:15 and the contrast drawn between *mûsār* and "sparing the rod" in 13:24. But in Prov. 1–9 and frequently elsewhere in Proverbs it has the milder sense of education or teaching. Hence here it is paralleled with **wisdom** and **words of insight** as something which the pupil is urged to "hear" (v. 5) and take to heart. In this verse it is not specified whether the teacher is the human instructor, "Wisdom" or God; but the contents of the instruction are clearly to be found in the book which follows. **words of insight** (*'imrê bînāh*): that is, words which will lead the pupil to gain understanding.

3. wise dealing: this word (*haśkēl*) is the infinitive absolute of the hiphil of the verb *śkl* used as a noun (*GK* 113e). Elsewhere (Job 34:35; Jer. 3:15; Dan. 1:17) it is paralleled with "knowledge" (*da'at*). But the verb *śkl* – and this is true also of *da'at* (v. 4) – does not simply denote the acquisition of facts: it carries the implication of an intelligent assessment of situations which can lead to practical decisions: hence "insight" may be an appropriate translation. The phrase *mûsar haśkēl* (**instruction in wise dealing**), then, refers to the training of the perceptive and intellectual faculties. *REB* paraphrases it as "well-instructed intelligence"; *JB* as "an enlightened state of mind".

righteousness, justice, and **equity**: these purely moral qualities are different in kind from all the other abstract qualities listed in these verses, and it has been suggested that they are a later addition to the text. However, the line is integral to the poetical structure, and to remove it would involve a re-ordering of the sequence of lines, which is hardly justified. The three terms occur together again in 2:9. Probably their purpose is to indicate in non-wisdom terms the way in which *haśkēl*, "insight", is to be exercised. The first two – *ṣedeq* and *mišpāṭ* – often appear in conjunction in the Old Testament as summing up the kind of conduct towards others which God requires of his people. The third, *mêšārîm* (cognate with *yāšār*, "upright, honest"), is frequently used in the Old Testament of giving honest or fair decisions; elsewhere in Proverbs (8:6; 23:16) it is used of speaking the truth or speaking what is right.

4. that . . . may be given: as in vv. 2a, 3ab, 6, this phrase is expressed in the Hebrew simply by an infinitive: "for knowing . . . for understanding . . . for receiving . . . for giving . . ." etc. The gifts offered here to **the simple** and **the youth** are in themselves morally neutral, but regarded as essential for success in life. **prudence** (*'ormāh*) signifies shrewdness; like the cognate adjective *'ārûm* it is sometimes used in a bad sense of cunning or treachery (cf. Gen. 3:1), but in Proverbs almost always in a morally neutral sense; the adjective is several times contrasted with "foolish" or "simple". In 8:5, 12 *'ormāh* is one of the gifts offered by Wisdom. **knowledge** (*da'at*) is also frequently associated with wisdom. *mᵉzimmāh* (**discretion**), like *'ormāh*, has both a neutral and a negative sense, but in Proverbs almost always simply denotes an ability to form practical plans (except in 12:2 and 24:8 [*RSV* "evil devices" and "mischief"]). *pᵉtā'yim* (**the simple** – on the spelling of this word see *GK* 93x) denotes an inexperienced person prone to foolish and so disastrous behaviour, but who is still open to persuasion or to the fruits of experience and so may acquire wisdom (cf. 1:22; 21:11).

5. the wise man also may . . . : the Hebrew has the jussive: "let the wise man . . .". *RSV* has added **also**, which is not represented in the Hebrew, in order to make a better connection with the preceding verse – though the dash which it has inserted after v. 4 is an indication that v. 5 breaks the syntactical sequence. The idea expressed in this verse is also found in 9:9. Both verses contain the identical phrase **and increase in learning**, and it has been suggested by some commentators that v. 5 is a gloss inspired by 9:9. The intention was to point out that the acquisition of wisdom does not end with the attainment of adulthood, but is a lifelong process: there is always more to learn, even for those who are accounted "wise". **wise man** (*ḥākām*), paralleled with **man of understanding**, is here clearly used in a non-technical sense.

learning (*leqaḥ*): the use of this word, derived from *lāqaḥ*, "to receive", together with **hear**, recalls the tradition of oral teaching in which the teacher hands on to the pupil what he himself has learned from his own teachers (cf. 4:1–9). Even written Instructions such as those which follow were no doubt used in oral teaching. **skill**: this rare word, *taḥbūlôt* (it occurs only five times in Proverbs and once in Job) has its origin in a metaphor taken from navigation (LXX here renders it by *kubernēsis*, "steering, pilotage"). It is related to *ḥebel*, "cord, rope" and to *ḥōbēl*, "sailor" (as one who pulls on ropes). It thus means "guidance" or the ability to steer one's course successfully through life. McKane renders the phrase by "learn the ropes". A similar metaphor occurs frequently in the Egyptian Instructions.

6. The syntactical series broken off in v. 4 is here resumed, although the content is somewhat different. This verse seems to be concerned, at least partly, with *understanding* certain forms of the teaching whose meaning is not immediately apparent, rather than simply with its *reception*. The meaning of one of the terms used, however, is uncertain. *m^e^lîṣāh* (**figure**) has been generally thought to be derived from the root *lyṣ*, and so to be cognate with the noun *lēṣ*. This noun, which occurs freely in Proverbs, is rendered by *RSV* by "scoffer". *m^e^lîṣāh* in its only other occurrence in the Old Testament (Hab. 2:6) has the meaning "taunt, mockery". But this meaning is hardly appropriate here, unless, as has been suggested, the underlying meaning of *lēṣ* is "one whose speech is tortuous". Another meaning of the root is represented by the hiphil participle of the verb *lîṣ* (*mēlîṣ*), "interpreter"; but it is difficult to derive from this a meaning for *m^e^lîṣāh* such as "a saying needing interpretation", which would fit the context here in Prov. 1:6. An alternative suggestion (Richardson, 1955, p. 178) is that *m^e^lîṣāh* is derived not from *lyṣ* but from *mālaṣ*, "to be smooth, slippery": if that is so, here it could mean "a slippery saying" or "an allusive saying", that is, one whose meaning is elusive. But there is no certainty about this. The view that it denotes a saying needing interpretation may be supported by its parallelism with *ḥîdōt*, **riddles**, at the end of the verse.

But the connection of these two terms with the other two terms, **proverb** (*māšāl*) and **the words of the wise** is not clear. In particular, *māšāl* may also be intended to imply an obscure saying, or it may be intended as a *contrast* with *m^e^lîṣāh*: the teaching will enable the reader or pupil to understand *not only* plain sayings but also obscure ones. A further point which may be made about this verse is that the use of the word **proverb** here is an indication that this verse is not original to the Preface, as "The proverbs of Solomon (v. 1) for understanding a proverb" (v. 6) is a tautology.

Neither *mᵉlîṣāh* nor *ḥîdāh* occurs again in Proverbs, and it is difficult to say whether any particular passages or verses in the book would have been so described. The view that the "numerical proverbs" in ch. 30 are based on riddles is probably unfounded (Roth, Sauer). *ḥîdāh* is used in the Old Testament for a variety of types of saying; the common element seems to be the notion of speech whose meaning does not lie on the surface but is hidden or mysterious (compare, for example, Samson's riddles in Jg. 14:12–19 and the Queen of Sheba's "hard questions" in 1 Kg. 10:1–3; 2 Chr. 9:1–2) and which can only be understood by a keen-witted person.

7. Gemser and Plöger regard this verse as connected with vv. 8–9 rather than as the final verse of, or an addendum to, the Preface. But a comparison of vv. 8–9 with the introductions to the other Instructions in these chapters, especially 4:1–2 and 6:20–23, where there are verbal similarities, shows that v. 8 marks a new beginning.

The fear of the Lord is the beginning (*rē' šît*) **of knowledge**: this line is found, with some variations, elsewhere. Prov. 9:10a has "the beginning (*tᵉḥillat*) of *wisdom*, and also reverses the order; Prov. 15:33 has ". . . is *instruction* in wisdom"; Job 28:28 has simply "*is* wisdom"; Sir. 1:14, probably citing Prov. 1:7, has "the beginning of wisdom" (this is identical with the LXX version of Prov. 1:7a). All these variants have "wisdom" rather than "knowledge". But the Hebrew text of 1:7a is probably original, since it is unlikely that **knowledge** should have been substituted for "wisdom". Each of these variants has a second line which is different, and different also from Prov. 1:7b. These facts suggest that the sentence "The fear of the Lord is the beginning of knowledge/wisdom" was an independent aphorism which various authors cited and expanded each in his own way. The LXX has in fact expanded the two lines of the verse into four.

The fact that 9:10a virtually repeats 1:7a may suggest that these two lines were at some stage intended to mark the beginning and end of a section of the book which included almost the whole of what is now chs. 1–9 (the technical term for this device is "inclusio").

This first line is a nominal (non-verbal) sentence in which one of two clauses defines or qualifies the meaning of the other. But which is the subject and which the predicate? In other words, does the line define **the fear of the Lord** in terms of knowledge, or knowledge in terms of the fear of the Lord? Grammatically either alternative is a possibility: in nominal sentences the subject normally comes first, but if it is desired to emphasize the predicate, the order may be reversed (*GK* 141 l). The question is important if one is to understand what the author had in mind here. Gemser is no doubt right in arguing that in addressing an Israelite readership or audience (the use of **the Lord** rather than "God" here and throughout the book is significant) it was *knowledge* which the author thought it necessary to commend in terms of Yahwism rather than the opposite.

the fear of the Lord: "fear" in such contexts as this means reverence rather than terror. To be a "fearer of Yahweh" is to be devoted to the exclusive service of Yahweh (see, for example, 1 Kg. 18:3, 12), or, in modern terms, to be a "Yahwist". In Proverbs, where the phrase "the fear of Yahweh" occurs more frequently than in any other Old Testament book, it is the ethical aspect of the service of Yahweh which is most prominent (in 8:13 it is defined as "hatred of evil"). It will have its reward in the gift of "life" – that is, a long and successful life (10:27; 14:27; 19:23). Here, as elsewhere in the book, it is closely associated with knowledge or wisdom: that is, it is asserted that true wisdom consists in obedience to the standard of behaviour required by Yahweh of his people; hence to **despise wisdom** – that is, to reject the conduct recommended in the chapters which follow – is the mark of **fools**.

The line does not, however, *equate* knowledge with the fear of Yahweh; rather, it is with the fear of Yahweh that **knowledge** (and so true wisdom) *begins*: in other words, there is no other to way set about acquiring it. *rē'šît* (**beginning**) in the Old Testament denotes what is first, either in time ("beginning") or in quality ("best", "best part", "best feature"). There is little or no evidence that it can mean "essence" or "sum", as some commentators have proposed. Here **beginning** makes the best sense.

fools (*'ewîlîm*): in Proverbs there are three words usually translated by "fool" or "foolish": *'ewîl*, *kᵉsîl* and *nābāl*. No clear distinction between them can be discerned. All are frequently contrasted with the "wise man". The fool seals his own fate by his behaviour. 27:22 considers the *'ewîl* to be incorrigible; in this he differs from the "simple" person (v. 4), who may be open to salutary advice.

FIRST INSTRUCTION
AVOIDANCE OF EVIL COMPANY
1:8–19

In this Instruction the young man is warned against joining vicious gangs intent on robbery with violence. Since such warnings are needed in every society including our own, there is no reason not to understand it literally. As befits the Instruction form, the pupil is addressed predominantly in the imperative. It is also characteristic that the teacher's warnings are supported with motive-clauses introduced by *kî*, "for, because" (vv. 9, 16, 17).

This is a well-constructed and effective work. After an introduction (vv. 8–9) the teacher states his theme briefly and in general terms (v. 10) and then fills it out with a vivid picture of the way in which the pupil may be persuaded to join in the activities of a gang (vv. 11–14). In vv. 15–16 he repeats his warning, emphasizing once again the wickedness of such a gang's operation; and finally in vv. 17–19 he bluntly describes the dreadful consequences which will befall its participants.

8. It is not certain whether the terms **son** and **father** in these Instructions are to be taken literally or whether they have the more impersonal meaning of "pupil" and "teacher". But the reference to the **mother's teaching** side by side with that of the father, which is not found either in the Egyptian Instructions or in what remains of the Babylonian ones, makes a family setting plausible. Mothers are mentioned with perhaps unusual frequency in Proverbs in conjunction with references to fathers and in a way which may reflect the importance given in Israel to family life. Apart from this verse there are two other clear references to mothers as teachers. 6:20 is almost identical with 1:8 (the only differences are that the former has "keep" instead of **hear** and "command" instead of **instruction**); and in 31:1 the instruction of Lemuel is attributed to the mother alone. The fact that the Instruction of Lemuel is of foreign, probably Edomite or Arabian, origin may suggest that this role of mothers as teachers represents a different tradition from that of Egypt and Mesopotamia. This co-operation between mother and father in the education of their children is clearly not to be explained simply in terms of the obvious role of mothers in bringing up *very young* children, while the father was responsible for later more serious education. The use of the word *tôrāh* (**teaching**) of the mother's activity probably precludes this interpretation, and the recipient is clearly not a very young child.

It should be noted that, unlike the others (4:20–27 is an exception) this Instruction does not develop the idea of Wisdom in personified or quasi-personified terms and also contains no reference to God. Although it would be wrong to speak of its tone as "secular" for reasons given above, the author regards the education provided by father and mother as in itself a sufficient guide to right behaviour and a safe passage through life.

9. These metaphors express the idea of the great value of the parents' teaching. Their implications are made more explicit in their further development in 3:21–4, where it is said that "sound wisdom and discretion", if they are the pupil's constant companions, will be not only "adornment (*ḥēn*) for your neck" but also "life for your soul", and will guarantee that "you will walk on your way securely". In 4:7–9 it is a personified Wisdom who will confer honour on the pupil, placing on his head a "fair garland" (the same phrase as here) and "a beautiful crown". These passages have often been compared with the Introduction to *Amenemope*; but there the metaphor is used quite differently: the words of the teacher are not external ornaments, but are to be put "in thy heart" and "in the casket of thy belly". Ornaments such as are mentioned here were worn by men as well as women: see especially Exod. 32:2; Num. 31:50.

a fair garland (*liwyat ḥēn*): *liwyāh*, which occurs in the Old Testament only here and in 4:9, was probably a kind of plaited wreath or crown signifying a status of honour. The noun *ḥēn* (**fair**), used here with an adjectival function, means "beauty, grace", with regard to women, especially in Proverbs (cf. 31:30, where it is described as "deceitful" or "deceptive"!); but its other meaning of "honour, esteem" is probably also implied here. **pendants**: that is, a necklace or perhaps a "chain of honour" (*REB*). The word occurs only in the plural. Thomas (*VT* 15 [1965], p. 271), in view of LXX's "a chain of gold" and of the shortness of this line, suggested that a word ("of gold") has dropped out after **pendants**; but this is purely speculative.

10–11. V. 10b is metrically unusually short and v. 11 unusually long. It has been suggested that the omission of **do not consent** would help to solve the metrical problem (Gemser); but such an emendation would spoil the effect made by this sharp warning. Plöger rightly warns against such conjectural alterations of the text.

It is true that the phrase is missing from *LXX*; but *LXX*'s translation is too free to be a reliable guide to the Hebrew.

10. My son (*bᵉnî*): this word, although it – or the plural *bānîm*, "sons", in 4:1 – appears at the beginning of each of these Instructions as either the first or the second word, also occurs in the course of several of them for particular reasons. In this Instruction it occurs in such a position twice: here and in 1:15. It usually precedes an imperative (1:10, 15; 3:11; 5:7; 7:24 *bānîm*). It is used to resume the teacher's admonitions after a description of the situation envisaged (1:15; 5:7; 7:24); to resume after a digression (5:20, resuming the warning against the "strange woman"); or to introduce a new item in a series of admonitions (3:11). The fact that it is not accompanied by the elaborate formula characteristic of an introductory preface indicates its incidental function. **consent**: this word (*tōbē̆*) is an unusual form of the jussive qal of *'ābāh*, "to be willing, consent" (*GK* 68h, 75hh). Many *MSS* have the normal form *t'bh*. The suggestion that it should be pointed as *tābō'* ("go") as in some *MSS* (see *BHS* and compare Barucq) is improbable.

11. lie in wait for blood: the meaning of this elliptical phrase is clarified in v. 16: "they make haste *to shed* blood". Gemser accepts an older proposal to emend **blood** (*dām*) to *tām*, "the blameless (man)" (cf., e.g., Job 1:8). This would admittedly make a better parallel with **the innocent** in the second line; but would be an unnecessary and speculative emendation, especially improbable in view of the corresponding phrase in v. 18a, where "blood" is clearly the correct reading. **wantonly** (*ḥinnām*): Oesterley regarded this word as "meaningless" in the context and proposed its omission. But in fact it is essential, as it provides a clue to what is going on in these verses. In their attempt to persuade the young man to join their gang, the first attraction which these "sinners" offer is violence *for its own sake*: this is what they propose first, robbery apparently being a secondary consideration. Like some modern muggers, they *take pleasure* in attacking the innocent **wantonly** – that is, without any reason, indiscriminately.

12. Like Sheol let us swallow (*bāla'*) **them alive** (*ḥayyîm*): this rather overstated simile is reminiscent of the account of the fates of Korah, Dathan and Abiram in Num. 16, especially v. 30: "If . . . the ground opens its mouth and swallows (*bāla'*) them up, . . . and they go down (*yārad*) alive (*ḥayîm*) into Sheol". (Cf. also the fate of Pharaoh's army in Exod. 15:12.) In other passages Sheol is conceived as a monster with a large mouth and an insatiable appetite which swallows its victims (Isa. 5:14; Hab. 2:5; cf. Prov. 27:20; 30:16). In Isa. 28:15 and Hab. 2:5 death (*māwet*) is similarly pictured in personal or quasi-personal terms. Behind this imagery stands the Canaanite mythology represented in the texts from Ugarit: in the myth of Baal and Mot, Baal "goes down into the throat of divine Mot" – that is, of Mot (Death), son of El – and so dies (Gibson, p. 68). Here in Prov. 1:12 the boast of the gang that they will not only kill their victims but swallow them alive is hyperbole intended to convey total extermination. In the second line, **like those who go down** (*yārad*) **to the Pit** reiterates the sense of the first, again using the familiar imagery. **Pit** (*bôr*) is a synonym for Sheol occurring frequently in Old Testament poetry, often in the same phrase as here, *yôr^edê bôr*, meaning the dead.

13. all: meaning "all kinds of" (cf. Gen. 24:10; Lev. 19:23; Neh. 13:16). **our houses**: the speakers are not vagabonds or outcasts, but citizens of the town. They are proposing to raid the houses of fellow-citizens not to steal out of necessity but to take away **precious goods** to embellish their own houses. **spoil**: "plunder" would be a more appropriate translation.

14. throw in your lot among us (literally, "your lot you shall cast in our midst" (*gôrāl^ekā tappîl b^etôkēnû*). In English this phrase, though presumably derived from this verse, has a somewhat different meaning: "to throw in one's lot" with someone is "to associate oneself with the fortunes" of that person or persons (*OED*). In biblical Hebrew the casting of a lot (*hippîl gôrāl*) always signifies, quite literally, the use of this means to select someone to receive a particular thing: land, a stolen piece of clothing, a housing privilege, specific duties, or blame for a disaster. It is never used metaphorically (though *gôrāl* by itself can mean "fate" or "portion in life" assigned to a person by God). Here in 1:14, then, this first line is not just a general invitation to join the gang and share in its risks and rewards, but, quite specifically, a promise or statement that the proceeds of the proposed robberies will not be kept by individual members of the gang, but will be distributed "fairly", like the distribution of territory ("lots") by Joshua or of booty acquired in war, by the casting of lots. That this is the correct interpretation is made clear by the second line: the loot will be counted as property common to the gang and gathered into **one purse** before being distributed to individuals.

15. The teacher now resumes the warning which he gave in v. 10 rather more fully before giving his reasons in the verses which follow. **My son** is lacking in the LXX; but it gives additional solemnity to the warning, and there is no justification for its omission.

16. This verse is virtually identical with Isa. 59:7a, and there can be no doubt that one is copied from the other. Here in Prov. 1:16, however, it is entirely lacking in the best MSS of LXX, and this may suggest that it is a gloss – that is, that it has been inserted into the text by a copyist who thought a quotation from Isa. 59:7 appropriate in this context. In support of this view it has been argued that, although ostensibly offering an argument in support of the teacher's appeal (**for**), it adds nothing to what has already been said, and also breaks the connection between v. 15 and a more relevant motive-clause in v. 17 (though see below on the problems of v. 17!). There is a clearly intentional verbal link between vv. 15 and 16 (**foot/feet**) – and also, more remotely, between vv. 11 and 16 (**to shed blood**) – , but this could be either an indication of an original continuity or, on the other hand, could account for the interpolation as due to an association of words in the mind of the interpolator between the Proverbs passage and the Isaiah text. If the verse is simply an *author*'s citation of an older text, the borrowing could have been in either direction, the dates of both passages being unknown.

17. This is an exceptionally difficult verse, and the commentators are divided about its meaning. There is admittedly general agreement that this is a reference to fowling: to snaring birds with a **net**. But even at this surface level the meaning is not clear, since the word *ḥinnām* (**in vain**) can be interpreted in two different ways: it may mean that even if the birds see the net they are too stupid to understand that it is a trap, or that it is pointless to let the birds see the net spread, as they *will* know what is happening and will *avoid* the trap. The next, but related, problem is to understand how this illustration is related to the matter in hand. In v. 15 the teacher has warned the pupil not to allow himself to be persuaded the join the gang of ruffians, and in vv. 18–19 he gives his reason: the murderers will themselves eventually suffer the same fate as their victims. The question is whether the **bird** of v. 17 stands for the victims or for their murderers. The most plausible interpretation of v. 17 in this context is the first of those outlined above: it is the murderers who, even though they must know – according to generally received wisdom – that "sinners" come to a bad end, go ahead and, like the stupid birds, are caught (so Toy, Barucq, McKane, Plöger).

spread: there is some doubt whether this can be a correct translation of *m^e zōrāh*, the pual participle feminine of *zārāh*, which elsewhere means "to scatter". Since a net cannot be "scattered", Thomas (1955, pp. 281–2), following Rashi and Ibn Ezra, took it to mean "strewn (with seed)", the seed being used as bait to catch the birds. But on the grounds that this supposes an otherwise unattested extension of meaning for this verb, two other suggestions have been made. Driver (*Bib.* 32 [1951], p. 173) proposed that the word should be repointed as either *mūzārāh*, the hophal participle of *zwr*, or *m^e zūrāh*, the qal passive participle of *māzar*, either of which, he argued, could yield the meaning "drawn together" (of the net). Fortunately the general sense of the verse is unaffected. Most commentators and modern translations accept the translation "spread".

bird: the Hebrew has *ba'al kānāp*, literally "possessor of wings", "winged creature". This poetical phrase occurs in only one other place in the Old Testament: Ec. 10:20.

18. The murderers are like the birds of v. 17: they cannot, through their greed and lust for blood, help themselves, but will fall unawares into the trap which waits for them. There is a fine irony here, expressed through the use of the same words – **lie in wait**, **ambush** – as in v. 11, but with an unexpected consequence: **for their own blood**, **for their own lives**. This is an example of the traditional belief that sinners will not only be punished, but that they will be punished in a way which precisely corresponds to their deeds. Though this is not stated, it must be presumed that the agent of the punishment is Yahweh.

19. The Instruction closes with a proverb-like generalized statement about the fate of those who commit deeds of violence, characteristically introduced by *kēn*, "so" (here **Such**). Plöger, commenting on the passage as a whole, observes that in illustrating this axiom in the preceding verses (11–18) the teacher has deliberately cited an extreme and probably very rare example in order to make his warning more impressive; but violent gangs are in fact by no means as rare a phenomenon in most societies as he supposes. **who get gain by violence**: this phrase (*bōṣēa' bāṣa'*) may have a double meaning: the verb *bāṣa'* can mean "cut off (life)" (Job 27:8; Isa. 38:12). The same point would then be made as in v. 18: in cutting off the lives of their victims these men destroy their own lives.

the ways (*'orḥôt*): many commentators emend to *'aḥ^a rīt*, "the end", pointing out that in Job 8:13a, which is very similar to this line, LXX has *ta eschata*, "the end", where again the Hebrew has *'orḥōt* (in the consonantal text this would involve only the transposition of two adjacent letters). The meaning would then be "Such is the *fate* of all who get gain by violence". This would obviously make good sense; however, "ways" is not an impossible reading: the idea that these men have *taken a road* which will lead to death is a perfectly Hebraic one. **its possessors** (*b*ᵉ*'ālâw*): perhaps better, "those who are addicted to it". For this meaning of *ba'al* compare, e.g., *ba'al nepeš*, "given to appetite", that is, "greedy", in 23:2. **takes away the life** (*nepeš yiqqāḥ*): the same phrase in the sense of "kill, put to death" occurs also in 1 Kg. 19:10, 14; Ps. 31:13 (Heb. 14); Jon. 4:3.

SPEECH BY WISDOM
1:20–33

On these speeches by Wisdom and on the figure of Wisdom in general see the Introduction, pp. 26–28.

This is a well-constructed poem (Trible, 1975, pp. 509–18 discerns in it a chiasmic pattern) in three parts. The first, vv. 20–23, is introductory: Wisdom is introduced as a public speaker (vv. 20–21) and then begins her speech, addressing the "simple ones" who are passing by, challenging their lack of sense (v. 22) and summoning them to hear what she has to say (v. 23). The main body of her message (vv. 24–31) comprises two condemnations of those who ignore her advice. These are couched in a style reminiscent of the denunciations of the pre-exilic prophets, each consisting of an accusation and an announcement of judgement. Presumably in order to impress her hearers with the gravity of their predicament, Wisdom condemns them, using the perfect tense, as if they have already rejected her teaching and so come under inescapable judgement. The first of these denunciations (vv. 24–7) is, as one would expect, addressed to the listeners – presumably the "simple" of v. 22a – in the second person ("you"); but the second (vv. 28–31) suddenly switches to the third person ("they"). (This sudden switch has never been satisfactorily explained: see below.) The speech concludes (vv. 32–3) with a general summing-up of the fate of those condemned (v. 32; cf. v. 19) followed by a corresponding promise to those who pay attention to Wisdom (v. 33).

One of the most striking characteristics of Wisdom's speech here is that she makes claims for herself which are elsewhere made only by, or for, God. Whereas in the preaching of prophets like Jeremiah and in the homiletic passages of Deuteronomy it is obedience or disobedience to God's commands which will determine the fate of his people for good or evil, here it is the reception or rejection of *Wisdom*'s teaching which will bring either security or disaster (vv. 29–33). Even some of the language used by Wisdom about herself is the same as that used elsewhere of God. This is especially apparent in vv. 23 and 28. In v. 28 **they will call upon me**, **but I will not answer** and **they will seek me diligently but will not find me** echo many passages in the Psalms and prophets which speak of calling upon and seeking God. In v. 23 two words in particular belong to the prophetic tradition, though these have been obscured in *RSV*'s translation. The Hebrew verb rendered there by **Give heed** is *šûb*, "to return", frequently used in the prophetical books in appeals to "return" to God in repentance; and **I will pour out my thoughts** is, in the Hebrew, "I will pour out my spirit (*rûaḥ*)" (but see below).

V. 29b, the only reference to God in the poem, comes as a surprise in a passage in which otherwise Wisdom speaks exclusively about herself ("I", "my" and "me" occur no fewer than sixteen times in twelve verses) and in a strongly authoritative vein. This verse may be a later addition to the text. Lang's view that the poem was originally a self-praising speech by an Israelite goddess is, however, unduly speculative. Nevertheless Wisdom's quasi-divine claims here require an explanation. It may be that she is to be understood as in some way Yahweh's intermediary, speaking in his name, though this also remains a speculation. But whatever may have been the reason for presenting the voice of wisdom or common sense in such personal terms, in the present context Wisdom may be seen here as the antithesis of the "sinners" of the preceding Instruction: she makes her counter-appeal to the pupil, in the very streets in which he is tempted to listen to their persuasive voices, and so adds weight to the father's own appeal in vv. 8–10.

20–21. Respectable Israelite women did not normally frequent public places; and in particular, a woman shouting to passers-by was liable to be misunderstood. Like the women of the town, Wisdom too has something to offer to the men of the city which can only be communicated in this way, and which is offered in opposition to what the "sinners" have to offer in vv. 11–14 (compare also the "diptych" of 9:1–6, 13–18, where she has to compete with "Folly"). Moreover, by making her appeal in public she reaches the widest possible audience, and also asserts her relevance to the mundane reality of the market place. Lang's view that the poem has a "classroom setting" with Wisdom representing a teacher with his school in the open air is attractive, but presupposes a knowledge of ancient Israelite education which we do not possess. However, Wisdom here *is* a teacher in the sense that what she has to offer is, like that of the father in vv. 8–19, advice to the young (**counsel**, v. 25; **knowledge**, v. 29; **reproof**, vv. 23, 25, 30). The ideas of womanly persuasion and sound teaching are combined in the figure of Wisdom presented in this poem.

20. Wisdom: here the Hebrew has not the usual *ḥokmāh* but the apparently plural form *ḥọkmôt*. This form occurs only here and in 9:1; 24:7 and Ps. 49:3 (Heb. 4). Two main types of explanation have been given of it. That it is not plural in meaning is clear from the fact that it is construed throughout the passage with singular (feminine) verbs: there is no doubt that, as elsewhere where the singular noun *ḥokmāh* is used (e.g. in a similar context in 8:1) it is the single figure of Wisdom that is meant. The majority of commentators regard *ḥokmôt* as an intensive plural form emphasizing the honourable or pre-eminent status of Wisdom or the amplitude of the gifts which she confers (see *GK* 124e for other examples). Albright (*VT* Suppl 3, 1955, p. 8), Scott, Gemser and Dahood, however, regard it as a rare singular form of a Phoenician type. This view is not universally accepted (McKane and Plöger are undecided).

cries aloud: this form (*tārōnnāh*) is also unusual. It has been explained as a cohortative or as a rare emphatic form of the qal imperfect feminine of *rnn*, comparable with the Arabic *modus energicus*, a form which Dahood claimed to have been current in Ugaritic. Another possibility is to point it as *tirneh*, the qal imperfect of *rānāh* which occurs elsewhere only in Job 39:23 of the rattling of armour, but which might conceivably be used of a piercing human voice. **in the street**: Israelite towns were innocent of town planning. The meaning is "outside", "in the open air". **in the markets**: better, "in the public places" such as the open space inside the city gates where people assembled to conduct business (compare v. 21b).

21. walls: *RSV* has here emended Hebrew *hōmiyyôt* to *ḥōmôt*, following LXX. But the change of *ḥ* to *h* is not easy to explain, and the Hebrew text is probably correct. *hōmiyyôt* (on the form see *GK* 75v) is the qal feminine plural participle of *hāmāh*, "to make a noise, be tumultuous"; in the singular it is used in Isa. 22:2 of the city of Jerusalem. Here in Prov. 1:21 it is apparently used as a noun, meaning thronged or noisy places in the city, such as **the entrance of the city gates** with which it is paralleled in the second line. (*REB* has "the bustling streets"). If there is no reference to **walls** here, **on the top of** (*bᵉrō'š*) clearly does not refer to height. Similar phrases occur in Isa. 51:20 and Lam. 2:19 (*bᵉrō'š kol-ḥûṣôt*), rendered by "at every street corner" in *REB*, and in Ezek. 16:25 (*kol-rō'š derek*), *REB* "at the top of every street", *rō'š* having the sense of "beginning, entrance". **city**: this line is very full; Gemser suggests the omission of this word as an unnecessary gloss.

22. simple ones: see on 1:4. **will you love**: for different views on the unusual form see *GK* 63m and Meyer, *VT* 7 (1957), p. 140, n. 1.

How long will scoffers . . . knowledge?: there is a sudden change here from the second person (**O simple ones**) to the third person. V. 23 reverts to the second person. This, together with the fact that the verse is unusually long (three lines) has suggested the possibility that this is an interpolation or that these lines have been misplaced. *REB*, following *NEB*, transposes them to follow v. 27. It should be noted that this second **How long** in *RSV* has no equivalent in the Hebrew: it has been added in an attempt to conceal the difficulty. **scoffers** (*lēṣîm*); **scoffing** (*lāṣôn*): there is no agreement about the meaning of this root (*lyṣ*), which is particularly frequent in Proverbs, where it occurs almost twenty times, but apparently with somewhat different connotations. **delight in**: Hebrew *ḥāmᵉdû lāhem. lāhem*, literally "with regard to themselves," is an "ethic dative" (*GK* 119s), hardly translatable in English. **fools**: this word (*kᵉsîl*) is by far the most common word for "fool" in Proverbs, occurring forty-nine times, almost as frequently as its opposite *ḥākām* (wise).

23. If the last two lines of v. 22 did not originally stand here, its first line (**How long . . . simple?**) needs a second line to complete the couplet. This could be provided by the first line of v. 23 (**Give heed to my reproof**), leaving the rest of v. 23 to form another couplet.

Give heed: in the Hebrew this is not an imperative but an imperfect (*tāšûbû*, literally "you shall return". Emerton (*JTS* 19 [1968], pp. 609–14) suggests that an initial word *mātay*, "when . . . ?", has been omitted by homoioteleuton: that is, because the scribe was confused by the similarity of the words *pᵉtî*, the last word of v. 22a, and *mātay*, in the consonantal text (*pty* and *mty* in the unpointed text). V. 23a would then have originally read "*When* will you return . . . ?" Others, however, regard the line as a conditional phrase, "*If* you will return . . ." (on the construction see *GK* 159b–d), or transpose *hinnēh* (**behold**) from the second line, rendering it as "If" (Driver, *Bib*. 32 [1951], p. 174) with the same result.

I will pour out my thoughts: the word here translated by **thoughts** is *rûaḥ*, which in the majority of instances is correctly rendered by "spirit". Some commentators (Ringgren, McKane, Plöger; also *REB*) so translate it here. If this is the meaning it is a further indication of the close relationship between Wisdom and Yahweh, whose prerogative Wisdom appears here to exercise (cf. Isa. 44:3, where however, a different verb is used, and Isa. 11:2, where the spirit of wisdom is an aspect of the Spirit of Yahweh), going beyond even the prophets' claim to speak on Yahweh's behalf (so Kayatz [1966], p. 127). But this interpretation is probably mistaken. The verb here translated **pour out** (*nb*ʿ hiphil) is regularly used of verbal communication of a person's mind or thoughts (e.g. Ps. 94:4, "They pour out their arrogant words"; Prov. 15:2, "the mouths of fools pour out folly"; Prov. 15:28, "the mouth of the wicked pours out evil things"). Here in Prov. 1:23 *rûaḥ* is paralleled by **words**: and since *rûaḥ* can mean "mind" or "thought" (see R. N. Whybray, *The Heavenly Counsellor in Isaiah xl:13–14*, Cambridge, 1971, pp. 10–13) *RSV*'s **pour out my thoughts** makes the best sense.

24–33. There is a dramatic sequence here. **How long** in v. 22 assumes that the hearers have up to now rejected Wisdom. She offers them another chance (v. 23), and then, presumably after a pause during which **no one has heeded** (v. 24), issues her prediction of the inevitable consequence. But this is not quite like a prophetic judgement scene: Wisdom is not the agent of the calamity but a scornful observer of it (vv. 26–8). Moreover, in its wider context this section is rhetorical, part of the technique of persuasion rather than condemnation, since at the end of the speech (v. 33) an escape route is still open for the person **who listens** to Wisdom. Lang sees vv. 24–6 as "the words of an angry teacher".

24. This verse – and also v. 28 – is reminiscent of Isa. 65:1–2, which is the beginning of a judgement speech of Yahweh. But the similarities are not sufficiently close to suggest that there is a direct relationship between the two passages. Such language is conceivable in a variety of circumstances.

26. also: here and in many other passages this translation of the particle *gam* is incorrect. Here it should be rendered by "on my part" (see Labuschagne, 1966, pp. 193–203, especially p. 198, n. 1). **laugh**, **mock**: these verbs are used of Yahweh's reaction to those who attack him or his adherents (Ps. 2:4; 59:8 [Heb. 9]; cf. also 37:13). This – to us – unpleasant practice was evidently a normal expression of confidence in one's own superior strength and immunity from harm or defeat – compare the "good wife" who "laughs at the time to come" (31:25). Here, however, the mockery suggests pique at being ignored. The harsh tone of these verses is, however, intended to frighten the listeners into mending their ways.

27. Like verse 23, this verse is unusually long, and some commentators regard the third line (**when distress and anguish come upon you**) as a redundant addition merely repeating the previous line in other words.

28. call, **answer**: in v. 24 it was Wisdom who called (*qārā'*), but she was ignored. Now the tables will be turned: those who ignored her will in turn call or cry out (*qārā'*) to her for help, and it will be *she* who **will not answer** *them*. This language calls to mind a similarly double aspect of the relationship between Yahweh and his people: on the one hand Yahweh, speaking through his prophets, calls his people to turn from their evil ways, but they do not answer, and so bring disaster on themselves (Jer. 35:17); while on the other hand, distressed persons, especially in many of the Psalms, call *to* Yahweh for help. In most cases these passages express confidence that he will answer, or appeal to him to do so; but as with Wisdom in 1:28, it is envisaged that he might refuse to do so: in Ps. 22:2 (Heb. 3) the psalmist complains, "O my God, I cry . . . but you do not answer".

seek, **find**: this language also recalls an aspect of the relationship between God and his people, although other words (*dāraš*, *bqš* piel) are used for "seek" than that which is employed here (*šḥr* piel). In Dt. 4:29; Jer. 29:13 Yahweh promises to be found by his people when they seek him in times of distress; but in Hos. 5:6 (cf. Am. 8:12) he warns his sinful people in oracles of judgement that though they may seek him they will not find him, because he has withdrawn his presence from them.

All the third person plural verbs in this verse are in the emphatic form in *-ûn* (see *GK* 47m, 60e).

29. the fear of the Lord: see on 1:7.

31. eat the fruit of their way: that is, suffer the consequences of their way of life. Compare similar expressions in Prov. 18:21; Isa. 3:10. **be sated**: a similar metaphor (cf. Prov. 25:16; Ps. 88:3 [Heb. 4]). The principle is the same as in Gal. 6:7: "Whatever a man sows, that shall he also reap".

32. simple: see on 1:4. **turning away**: elsewhere in the Old Testament this word (*m^{e}šûbāh*) always denotes apostasy from Yahweh. **are killed, destroys**: one's attitude towards wisdom, like one's attitude towards Yahweh, is not just a desirable option but a matter of life and death.

33. evil: here as frequently this word (*rā'āh*) is not used in an ethical sense but means harm or misfortune such as is to be the lot of those who ignore Wisdom's teaching according to the previous verses.

SECOND INSTRUCTION
AVOIDANCE OF THE "STRANGE WOMAN"
2:1–22

Although this is not apparent from *RSV*, this chapter in Hebrew consists of a single sentence of great complexity. Shorn of its embellishments, its basic grammatical structure consists of a conditional sentence (**if**, v. 1, **then**, v. 5) followed by two types of explicatory or qualificatory clause: an infinitive construction defining more precisely the contents of the preceding apodosis (**delivering you**, v. 12) and a final clause indicating the desired outcome (*l^{e}ma'an*, "so that ... may", *RSV* **So you will**, v. 20). This already complex structure is given even greater complexity in two respects: first by the doubling or even tripling of the basic clauses (**if** three times, vv. 1, 3, 4; **then** twice, vv. 5, 9; two infinitive constructions [*l^{e}haṣṣîl^{e}kā*, **delivering you**, both in v. 12 and also in v. 16, where *RSV* has **You will be saved**]); and by the addition of further doubly subordinate clauses, both causal (**for**, vv. 6, 10, 18, 21) and relative (expressed by participles but with the sense of **who**, vv. 13, 14, 17); and so on. There is also much repetition in the chapter: in vv. 2–11 wisdom and its equivalents are mentioned twelve times; and in vv. 12–22 words for "path" occur nine times. There is a constant wearisome repetition of the same thoughts.

As an example of teaching method this cumbersome discourse lacks both precision and compactness; it gives the impression that successive layers have been added to an originally much shorter and crisper Instruction of which 5:1–6 might be taken as a model. In view of the syntactical structure the addition of new lines would have been a simple process, and conversely, much of the chapter could be omitted without mutilating the syntactical coherence. For example, vv. 1, 9, 16–19 alone would constitute a well-constructed and satisfactory composition (see Whybray, 1966, pp. 486–92).

The nub of the original Instruction – that is, the description of the disastrous behaviour against which the pupil is warned – is clearly to be found in vv. 16–19. These verses, with their vivid picture of the **loose woman** who lures the young man to her house which is really the anteroom to **death** and **the shades** (v. 18) contain the only concrete and precise statements in the chapter. It is true that grammatically they are parallel with vv. 12–15, in which another set of villians appear: **men of perverted speech**; but these are described in the same generalizing and moralizing style as much of the rest of the chapter, and are very shadowy characters compared with the "loose woman". Moreover, it is unlikely that the original Instruction had a double theme, since in all the other Instructions in these chapters which deal with the theme of sexual temptations and the loose woman (5:1ff.; 6:20ff.; 7:1ff.) there is no competing theme.

If it is correct to say that this chapter is an expansion of an originally much shorter Instruction, an analysis of its contents may provide the clue to the reasons for such an expansion. It begins (v. 1), like the first Instruction (1:8) with an appeal to the pupil to pay serious attention to the teacher's words. But in v. 2 this teaching is equated with Wisdom; and vv. 2–4 and 9–15 expatiate on the benefits that will be conferred on those who follow Wisdom's teaching. Inserted into this section about Wisdom is a passage (vv. 5–8) which introduces Yahweh: it begins (vv. 5–6) by stressing that it is he who is the source of wisdom, and then expatiates on the benefits of listening to *his* teaching (**his mouth**, v. 6). In other words, the teaching of the human teacher, which in the first Instruction is presented as the sole and sufficient authority, is here first identified with a partly personified Wisdom (**will come into your heart**, **will watch over you**, vv. 10, 11); and then this Wisdom is stated to be Yahweh's own wisdom which comes from his mouth (v. 6) as his gift. A similar process of identification of Wisdom with the fear of Yahweh may have taken place in 1:29.

Thus in this chapter no fewer than three persons are presented as offering advice and guidance to the pupil, and in quite similar terms: the human teacher, Wisdom, and Yahweh. Clearly, as in 1:8–19, it is the human teacher who is the speaker throughout the chapter. But in contrast to 1:8–19, where he alone is said to offer efficacious advice, his claim here in v. 1 has been used in order to introduce successively two further concepts: that of Wisdom as the source of true instruction (cf. 1:20–33), and that of Yahweh as the authority with which Wisdom speaks. The original Instruction may have consisted of an initial appeal by the teacher (vv. 1, 9 – cf. 1:8, but here in the form of a conditional sentence rather than of an imperative), a specific warning (vv. 16–19 – cf. 1:10–18), and possibly a general conclusion (vv. 20–22 – cf. 1:19). (See Whybray, 1966, pp. 486–92.)

1. my commandments: elsewhere in the Old Testament this word (*miṣwāh*) refers to the Law of Moses; but in Proverbs, where it occurs most frequently in these chapters (3:1; 4:4; 6:20; 7:1, 2) it refers to the **words** of the parent or teacher, indicating his position of authority over the young pupil.

2–3. understanding (*tᵉbûnāh*), **insight** (*bînāh*): these are simply synonyms of wisdom. The love of pleonasm has even led the author to use **understanding** twice.

2. and inclining your heart: literally, "(and if) you incline your heart" – taking up the **if** of v. 1. **heart** (*lēb*): better, "mind".

3. yes, if (*kî 'im*); *kî* here, as often, simply gives emphasis to the words which follow, **seek it**, **search for it**. The singular **it** (or, "she") shows that **understanding** and **insight** are not regarded by the author as distinct entities, but are simply other words for wisdom. **Cry out/raise your voice for**: better, "to". The pupil is to try to make contact with wisdom by calling out to her.

5–8. There are close parallels between these verses, which are concerned with **the Lord**, and vv. 9–11, which are concerned solely with **wisdom**. Both begin with the words **then you will understand** (*'āz tābîn*), the object of the verb being **the fear of the Lord**

in v. 5 and **righteousness and justice** in v. 9; in both cases the initial assertion (vv. 5, 9) is followed by a motive clause beginning with *kî*, **for**, vv. 6, 10) stating, in the first case that **the Lord gives wisdom** and, in the other, **wisdom will come into your heart**; in both passages (vv. 8, 11) the two verbs *nāṣar* (**guard**) and *šāmar* (*RSV* "preserve" and "watch over") occur in parallel, though in the reverse order, the subject being in the first case **the Lord** and in the second **discretion** and **understanding**, which are synonyms of wisdom; and finally the words *da 'aṭ*, **knowledge** (vv. 6, 10), *tᵉbûnāh*, **understanding** (vv. 6, 11) and *mišpāṭ* (vv. 8, 9) occur in both passages among the gifts of Yahweh and Wisdom respectively.

These similarities are too great to be unintentional. Whoever was responsible for the text in its present form clearly intended to draw a parallel between the benefits conferred by Wisdom on the one hand and Yahweh on the other. But if both passages are the work of the same author it is strange that having made the relationship between them clear already in v. 6 he should then speak in vv. 10–11 of Wisdom alone as conferring these gifts. There is, then, some reason to suppose that vv. 5–8 are a "theological" addition to a text which originally spoke only of Wisdom.

5. the fear of the Lord: see on 1:7.

6. the Lord gives wisdom: the placing of **the Lord** at the beginning of the sentence in the Hebrew instead of in its normal position following the verb gives it a strong emphasis. The pupil is now told that only God can give what the pupil is told to seek to attain in attending to the teacher and in searching for Wisdom.

7. Read Qere's *yiṣpōn* rather than Kethib's *wᵉṣāpan*. The meaning is the same. **sound wisdom**: not *ḥokmāh*, but *tûšiyyāh*. This word, which apart from Mic. 6:9 and Isa. 28:29 occurs only in Job and Proverbs probably means something like "practical ability". **he is a shield**: the Hebrew has simply "a shield". In view of the deficient syntax, van der Weiden (pp. 26–7) derives the word (*māgēn*) from the root *mgn* which occurs as a verb in 4:9, and renders it by "a gift", seeing it as a second object of **he stores up**; but this is probably simply a case of ellipsis and so correctly translated by *RSV*.

8. guarding: an infinitive used gerundially (GK 114 o). Emendation (see Dahood, pp. 26–7; van der Weiden, pp. 7–8) is not necessary. **his saints**: read *ḥᵃsîdâw* with Qere. A better translation would be "those who are loyal to him" (*REB* "his loyal servants").

9–11. On the relationship of these verses to vv. 5–8 see above.

9. righteousness and justice and equity: these three terms occur together also in 1:3. Several commentators, however, have questioned the text of the second line. **every good path** seems to be only loosely connected with the preceding words; and various suggestions have been made to read a verb here in place of *mêšārîm* (**equity**): either a participle (*m^e^šammēr*, "keeping (to)", *m^e^'aššēr*, "making straight", *m^e^yaššēr*, "making smooth") or an imperfect (*tišmōr*, "you will keep (to)", *te^e^šar*, "you will step forward (on)". MT, however, is not impossible.

10. heart (*lēb*): see on v. 2. The imagery may be conventional: compare *Amenemope* I 3:11–14 (*ANET*, p. 421). **soul** (*nepeš*): the seat of the emotions.

11. will guard you (*tinṣ^e^rekkā*): on the form see *GK* 66f.

12–15. See the comments above on these verses. They consist entirely of colourless generalities compared with the description of the "loose woman" of vv. 16–19 or of the criminal gang of 1:11–14.

12. the way: the metaphor of the two roads as alternative ways of life, the one leading to safety and the other to destruction, is particularly frequent in Proverbs, where its use is characterized by the occurrence of a variety of synonyms for road or path. In 1:15, 19, 31 it has already been used of wicked behaviour. Here (2:12–15) – where its reiteration is in keeping with the generalized style of the passage – there is a contrast intended with the path taken by those who accept Yahweh's gift of wisdom (vv. 7–9). **of evil**: or, "of the evildoer". **men of perverted speech**: literally, "the man who speaks *tahpūkôt*". This word, which is virtually peculiar to Proverbs (Dt. 32:20 is the only other occurrence in the Old Testament), is cognate with the verb *hāpak*, "to overturn, overthrow"; it often, as here, denotes wickedness in general, but particularly with regard to the use of speech to achieve evil ends.

14. This verse reveals stylistic poverty not only by repeating the word *tahpūkôt* (**perverseness**) already used in v. 12, but also by the double use of **evil** (*ra'*). There is no justification for emendation as proposed by some commentators.

16–19. At first sight these verses seem quite straightforward: only an attachment to Wisdom who will set the pupil on the right paths (vv. 8–11) can save the pupil from the temptation to associate with immoral women (**the loose woman**, **the adventuress**), an association which will lead him irrevocably away from **the paths**

of life – that is, to his **death**. This warning is parallel to the warning in vv. 12–15 about associating with **men of perverted speech** who also **forsake the paths of righteousness**. (What is meant by **death** here is not made clear; but it is contrasted with the "life" offered by Wisdom.) In other words, this is a plain warning to the young man about the consequences of sexual immorality, which was a stock theme of ancient Near Eastern, especially Egyptian, Instructions.

However, there are clearly overtones here which are mainly absent from the non-Israelite Instructions. Lang (1972, pp. 87–8) drew attention to the fact that in these chapters there are no fewer than four prominent female figures: Wisdom, the "woman Folly" (9:13–18), the immoral woman depicted here and in three other Instructions, and the flesh-and-blood wife – present or future – to whom the pupil is urged to remain faithful (5:15–20). This is no coincidence: throughout these chapters analogies are drawn and contrasts made which in various ways link all these figures together. This suggests that in the passage here under consideration the figure of the immoral woman represents more than a purely carnal temptation, though that remains the primary meaning. If chapter 2 is taken as a whole, the woman of vv. 16–19 undoubtedly stands in some degree as the antithesis of wisdom, and **her smooth words** (v. 16) with which she entices the young man anticipate the persuasive speech of the "woman Folly" in 9:16–17, which in turn echoes the call of Wisdom in 9:4–6.

Overtones of a somewhat different kind have been discerned by some commentators. This is, as has been pointed out, not an isolated passage, but requires to be interpreted in conjunction with 5:3ff.; 6:24ff and 7:5ff. Each of these passages contains a similar warning against associating with immoral women, and all four passages are to a considerable extent parallel, even in the language employed: **loose woman** (*'iššāh zārāh*) and **adventuress** (*nokriyyāh*) occur again in parallelism in 7:5, a verse which is almost identical with 2:16; and the woman in question is referred to as *zārāh* also in 5:3 (cf. 5:17, 20) and as *nokriyyāh* in 6:24. All these passages refer to her seductive speech, and all refer to the fatal or at least disastrous consequences of association with her. The discussion has therefore necessarily taken into account evidence from all four passages.

Boström (1935) proposed a cultic interpretation. He understood the woman in question to be not an Israelite but a foreigner who attempted to lure the Israelite young man into participation in fertility rites associated with the Babylonian/Canaanite goddess Ishtar/ Astarte. The main evidence for this thesis as far as 2:16–19 is concerned is to be found in the use of the words *zārāh* and *nokriyyāh* to describe the woman, the reference in v. 17 to **her God** rather than "Yahweh" as elsewhere in the book, and the reference to death in vv. 18–19. More recent scholars, however (notably Humbert, 1939 and Snijders, 1954) have demonstrated the improbability of Boströms thesis, though some recent commentators (Gemser, Ringgren, McKane) have retained some features of it.

Whether the kind of sexual cult presupposed by Boström ever existed is now regarded as doubtful. Apart from this, it is by no means certain that the words *zār* and *nokrî* have an ethnic connotation here. Certainly both words frequently mean "foreign", that is, not Israelite. But they are both ambiguous. *zār* frequently denotes simply what is outside one's own possession or social group, especially outside one's family or tribe. In the priestly legislation in the Pentateuch, for example, *'îš zār* means a man who is not a member of a priestly family. In Job 19:27; Prov. 14:10; 27:2 *zār* simply means "another (person)", i.e., not oneself. Somewhat similarly *nokrî* can mean no more than "unknown, unfamiliar". Thus although the woman in question may be a foreigner, she could also be simply a prostitute from outside the city (there is a similar ambiguity in Egyptian Instructions on the same theme, especially the *Instruction of Ani*, 3:13 ff. [*ANET*, p. 420]. But a comparison with the more detailed account of the woman in 7:5–23 suggests a simpler explanation. There there is a reference (vv. 19–20) to the absence of the husband, which suggests that after all the woman is simply an adulteress (we may compare *Ani*: "a woman whose husband is far away"). *'iššāh zārāh* would then mean "the wife of another man", and *nokriyyāh* would further designate her as a woman belonging to another family (cf. Gen. 31:15) and therefore to be avoided. (This down-to-earth interpretation does not, however, conflict with what has been said above about the overtones which imply that she is the counterpart of Wisdom, who herself is not without mythological overtones.) On the other points raised above, namely the meaning of **the covenant of her God** in v. 17 and the references to death in vv. 18–19 see the comments on those verses below.

17. the companion of her youth: the most natural interpretation of this phrase is that it refers to the woman's husband – cf. Mal. 2:14, which speaks of the "wife of your youth" and "your companion" (though here a different word is used). **covenant**: the same verse in Malachi also refers to marriage as a covenant to which Yahweh is witness. Less probable is the view that the verse refers to the woman's acting contrary to her early upbringing (*'allûp*, **companion**, here means "fatherly teaching" according to McKane) and abandoning her status as a member of the covenanted people of Israel rather than specifically to her abandoning her husband and renouncing her marriage vows. The phrase **the covenant of her God** (*bᵉrît *ᵉlōhehā*) could be better rendered as "her sacred (or 'solemn') covenant": the **her** qualifies **covenant** rather than **God** (*GK* 135n); and *ᵉlōhîm* (**God**) here could be understood primarily as an expression of the superlative emphasizing the solemn nature of the marriage covenant (so van der Ploeg), though also retaining something of its original sense (see Thomas, *VT* 3, 1953, pp. 210–19). If this interpretation is correct, the argument that **her God** must refer to a foreign deity loses its force.

18–19. The general theme of these verses occurs again, though in different forms, in 5:5; 7:27; 9:18. Here the pupil is warned, in highly charged metaphors intended to make a deep impression on him in a way comparable to the "hell-fire sermon" of later times, that to enter the house of the adulteress irrevocably leads to death. "Death" is to be understood here as the antithesis of the "life" regularly offered by Wisdom in these chapters, for example in 3:16–18, which comprises such things as long life, riches, honour, prosperity. The pupil must choose to pay attention to Wisdom or to reject her; and if he once chooses the latter course there can be no going back. The adulteress, like the "woman Folly" in 9:13–18, stands for all that is morally evil (in the final form of this chapter this is equated with the rejection of the "fear of Yahweh", v. 5); and those who choose evil will pay the penalty in a short and miserable life which is a kind of death.

18. As in 7:27 and 9:18, the adulteress's house is dramatically represented as itself part of the abode of the dead, or at least a kind of antechamber to it. **her house sinks down to death**: there is a grammatical problem here in that **house** (*bayit*) is a masculine noun whereas the verb (*šāḥāh*) as accentuated in MT is feminine (the feminine third person perfect singular of *šûaḥ*). Of the many attempts to solve this problem, Emerton's proposal to repoint the word as *šūḥāh*, "pit" (1979, pp. 153–8; cf. Prov. 22:14; 23:27) is perhaps the most plausible. The line would then read "her house is *a pit* (leading) to death". **the shades** (*r^epā'îm*): that is, the dead, conceived as gathered in Sheol – cf. 9:18; 21:16; Isa. 14:9 etc.

19. The concept of dying as a journey to the nether world from which there is no return is frequently found in Babylonian literature, and this verse is particularly reminiscent of a passage in the Babylonian *Descent of Ishtar to the Nether World*, when the goddess is said to go down to "the Land of no Return . . . , to the house which none leave who have entered it, to the road from which there is no way back", (*ANET*, p. 107), a passage which is almost verbally identical with a passage in the *Epic of Gilgamesh* (*ANET*, p. 87). This imagery, which is also found in Greek mythology, was probably current over a wide area.

20–22. These verses are only very loosely connected with what precedes. The first two words of v. 20, *l^ema'an tēlēk*, do not mean **So you will walk** (result) but "in order that you may walk" (purpose or intention). This does not follow syntactically or in sense from v. 19, but hangs in the air. Toy supposed that v. 20 has been misplaced from after v. 9, but there is no evidence for this. Moreover, the generalities expressed in vv. 20–22 detract from and weaken the dramatic effect of v. 19, which makes an excellent climax. These verses are quite different from 1:19 and 1:32–3, which are more closely related to their contexts. They appear to comprise two separate additions to the original Instruction. Vv. 21–2 has its own distinctive character and style, being an impersonal comment in the third person plural, and having a close resemblance to the sentence literature and to certain moralizing psalms, especially to Ps. 37:28b-29, as well as to Deuteronomic theology (see below).

21–22. the land (*'ereṣ*) referred to here cannot be other than the land of Canaan which was regarded throughout the Old Testament as the land promised and then given by Yahweh to Israel. The teaching that their continued possession of it is conditional on obedience to the law of Yahweh while disobedience will entail its loss is constantly stressed in Deuteronomy; it also occurs almost as a refrain in Ps. 37 (vv. 3, 9, 11, 22, 29), where it is addressed to individuals as distinct from **the wicked** (especially in vv. 9 & 22, where they will be **cut off** from it). The same assertion is made in Prov. 10:30. This is a reinterpretation of the preceding teaching in terms of Yahwistic orthodoxy.

22. will be rooted out: the verb (*nāsaḥ*) is used in Dt. 28:63 in the passive (niphal) in a threat by Yahweh to remove Israel from the land if it is disobedient. Here also a passive sense is required, but the form (*yissᵉḥû*) is active (qal). It has been suggested that this is an impersonal use of the verb, and that the line should be translated by "they (impersonal) will root out the treacherous". But in view of the parallel verb **will be cut off** it is probably preferable to repoint the verb as *yussᵉḥû* (pual).

THIRD INSTRUCTION
BEHAVIOUR TOWARDS GOD
3:1–12

In this Instruction there is no direct mention of the need to acquire wisdom. After an introduction in which the teacher stresses the importance of paying attention to his teaching (vv. 1–4, cf. 1:8–9; 2:1), that teaching, as regards behaviour towards God, is set out in the form of three positive admonitions. The first two of these (vv. 5–6 and 7–8) are similar in contents: indeed, **do not rely on your own insight** in the first and **Be not wise in your own eyes** in the second are indistinguishable in meaning. The advice is very general. The third admonition (vv. 9–10) is more specific: it counsels the pupil to be careful to pay his sacrificial dues to Yahweh. All three admonitions are similar in form: a statement of what is required, expressed in imperatives and jussives, is followed by a promise of reward. It is probable that it was the certainty here expressed about the operation of a principle of automatic reward which prompted the addition of the fourth admonition (vv. 11–12). Here there is no mention of rewards, but of Yahweh's **discipline** and **reproof**. The author of these verses was aware of the problem raised by cases where expected reward was absent. His solution is that **the Lord reproves him whom he loves**: in other words, that suffering or misfortune may be educative in intention. This admonition is not about human behaviour towards God but about human reaction to God's actions.

The lack of reference to wisdom in this Instruction is no doubt the reason for the subsequent addition of vv. 13–20, which may, however, have originally existed separately. As in chapter 2 where two additional layers have been added to the original Instruction, the first associating Wisdom with the teacher's words (vv. 2–4, 10–11) and the second associating Wisdom with God (vv. 5–9), so also here; but in this case the additions have been made at the end of the Instruction rather than inserted into it at the end of the introduction.

The impression given by the first Instruction (1:8–19) that the pupil addressed is well-to-do is further confirmed here. Vv. 9–10, presumably laying down rules for the pupil's future adult life, speak of "your wealth" (*hôneka̅*, *RSV* **your substance**), **your produce**, **your barns**, **your vats**. Material wealth is to the fore here, and there is no reference to generosity towards the poor. If, as other passages in these chapters suggest, the setting is an urban one, the pupil's family may be substantial landowners who do not necessarily live on their land.

1–4. A number of commentators have noted similarities between these verses and some passages in Deuteronomy, a book which, like the Instructions in Prov. 1–9, is educational in intention, Yahweh – through the medium of Moses – being the teacher and the nation of Israel the pupil. In Dt. 6:1–15 it is promised that if Israel keeps Yahweh's commandments (*miṣwôt*, v. 2) it will be rewarded with a long life (*he*ʾ*rîk yāmîm*, v. 2) and with prosperity. Israel, addressed like the pupil in Proverbs in the masculine singular, is to keep Yahweh's words in their heart (*ʿal-lᵉbābekā*, v. 6), to teach them to its children (*bānîm*, v. 7), to bind them (*qāṣar*) as a sign on its hands and forehead (v. 8) and to write them (*kātab*, v. 9) on the doorposts of its house. It is also warned not to forget (*šākaḥ*) Yahweh (v. 12), for if it does it will be destroyed (v. 15). There are, in addition, many references in Deuteronomy to Yahweh's law (*tôrāh*) and to the tablets (*lūḥôt*, plural of *lûaḥ*; *RSV* "tables") of the Ten Commandments given to Moses, which are described in 9:9, 11 as "the tablets of stone, the tablets of the covenant".

In Prov. 3:1–4 the teacher employs much of the same language in referring to his own instruction: he speaks of his teaching (*tôrāh*) and commandments (*miṣwōt*, v. 1) which must not be forgotten (*šāk-aḥ*), but which if they are heeded will give his "son" (*bēn*) a long life (*ʾōrek yāmîm*) and wellbeing (v. 2). They are to be bound (*qāṣar*) round the neck (3bc – on 3a see below) and written (*kātab*) on the tablet of the heart (*ʿal-lûaḥ libbekā*).

What significance, if any, is there in these coincidences of language? Some of them, like the use of *lûaḥ*, which has quite different referents in the two passages, may be dismissed as purely fortuitous; others can no doubt be explained as showing no more than the existence of a common vocabulary of education. Some of the expressions referred to above occur in other Instructions in these chapters and can be to some extent paralleled, as McKane pointed out, with language used in Egyptian Instructions. Nevertheless the concentration of parallels with Deuteronomy in this short passage is too striking to be totally ignored, though the claims of Robert (1934) for a close dependence of these chapters as a whole on Deuteronomy seem overstated. It may be that the influence, if such it is, operated in the opposite direction. Dt. 8:5 may provide support for this view: "Know in your heart that, as a man disciplines his son, Yahweh your God disciplines you". This suggests that the author of the homiletic introductory chapters of Deuteronomy may have used the already existent language of family education in order to emphasize the mandatory nature of the law of Yahweh, the rewards of obedience to it and the dire consequences of disobedience. Precisely the same idea is to be found in vv. 11–12 of this chapter, though this, as has been suggested above, is a later addition to the original Instruction.

1. teaching (*tôrāh*); **commandments** (*miṣwôt*): see on 1:8 and 2:1. These two words reappear in the introductions to subsequent Instructions, together with others (*mûsār*, "instruction"; *d^ebārîm*, "words"; *^a^mārîm*, also "words") in combinations which show that they are all interchangeable (cf. 1:8; 2:1; 3:1; 4:1; 4:20; 5:1; 6:20; 7:1–2). They occur mainly in parallel pairs, not always in the same order. The verbs which govern them are also interchangeable: hear, receive, treasure up, keep, be attentive, incline the ear, and the negatives "do not reject", "do not forsake", "do not forget".

2. Literally, "for length of days and years of life and wellbeing (*šalôm*) will they add (or, 'increase') to you". It has been suggested that a distinction is made here between **length of days** and **years of life** in that, while the former simply denotes a long life, in the latter the word **life** (*ḥayyîm*), refers, as frequently in the wisdom literature and especially in Proverbs, to the quality of life. But the same expression is used in 4:10, where this does not seem to be the case. *šālôm*, however, does denote a state of unalloyed happiness and contentment, free from anxiety (cf. 3:17).

3. This verse differs from the rest of the passage in that it consists of three lines rather than the usual two. The third line (**write them on the tablet of your heart**) is identical with 7:3b, and is lacking in LXX^B. Many commentators, therefore, have regarded it as a gloss introduced from 7:3. However, there is good reason to suppose that it is the first line (**Let not loyalty and faithfulness forsake you**) which is the added line. Elsewhere in these Instructions (6:21; 7:3; cf. 1:9; 3:22) it is the father's (or parents') teachings which are to be bound or written on the heart. It is therefore probable that the **them** of lines two and three here originally referred not to loyalty and faithfulness but to the father's teachings of v. 1. V. 3a interrupts the flow of discourse, which otherwise follows the same pattern as in the Instructions mentioned above. V. 3a may have skilfully been added in order to associate the father's teaching with virtues characteristic of Yahwism: the double phrase **loyalty and faithfulness** (*ḥesed weᵉmet*), which in 16:6 is paralleled with the fear of Yahweh, is a standard expression which describes the relationship between Yahweh and his people, both collectively and individually.

bind them about your neck: in Dt. 6:8; 11:18 it is enjoined on the Israelites that they should bind Yahweh's words on their hands and foreheads. This was probably intended as a metaphor for keeping them constantly in mind, though later Judaism took it literally in the custom of wearing phylacteries. Whether there is an echo of Deuteronomy here or whether this was simply a current metaphor like that in the following line is not clear. **write them on the tablet of your heart**: Jer. 31:33 uses a similar metaphor. It is also found in *Amenemope*, where the reader is told, with regard to the teachings which follow, "to put them in your heart is beneficial" (I 3:11).

4. So you will find: the Hebrew here has the imperative. On this use of the imperative see *GK* 110f. **good repute** (*śēkel-ṭôb*): *RSV*mg. indicates an emendation of *śēkel* to *šēm*, "name, reputation", as is proposed by some commentaries. The usual meaning of *śēkel* is "insight, understanding", which hardly fits the context. However, no emendation is necessary. Insight or competence and the success which normally followed it were closely linked in the Hebrew mind, a fact which is illustrated by the cognate verb *hiśkîl*, which means both "to have insight" and "to be successful". *śēkel* here should probably be rendered by "success", or, in view of the context, by "approval" (so Gemser, McKane, Plöger). **in the sight of God and man**: the use of the word **God** (*ᵉlōhîm*) rather than the usual "Yahweh" favoured by Proverbs has no theological implication. This is probably a set phrase (cf. Lk. 2:52), an example of merismus, in which polar opposites are cited to indicate totality. The meaning is thus "in the sight of all".

5–8. In these twin admonitions (vv. 5–6, 7–8) the pupil is admonished to **Trust in the Lord with all your heart** (v. 5a) and to **fear the Lord**, **and turn away from evil** (v. 7b). Such wholehearted reliance on Yahweh and fulfilment of his moral requirements, it is promised, will lead to wholly beneficial and desirable consequences (vv. 6b, 8). Each admonition is accompanied by a warning against adopting what is presumably the contrary attitude: trust in one's own competence (v. 5b) and – what is virtually the same thing – confidence in one's own wisdom (v. 7b). These, one may presume, will lead to disaster. But there is a difference between them and the recipes for disaster discouraged in the previous two Instructions: there it was criminal or immoral conduct of a concrete kind; here it is an attitude of mind, which is held to be incompatible with a proper attitude towards God.

McKane sees in these verses an attack on traditional wisdom teaching and an exhortation to substitute the moral teaching of Yahwism for it. But traditional wisdom teaching itself deprecates precisely the kind of self-confidence warned against here. It is again and again emphasized in these Instructions that the conduct of the pupil is to be based not on self-confidence but on strict observance of the father's rules. These are sometimes equated with wisdom, which is to be sought for by the pupil and which, when attained, will form the character of its possessor: he will become "wise". But this wisdom is not the same as being "wise in one's own eyes" (cf. 26:5, 12, 16; 28:11, where also this phrase is used). The need for humility about one's own attainments in this sphere is frequently stressed in the sentence literature, for example in 11:2 ("When pride comes, then comes disgrace, but with the humble is wisdom") and 12:15 ("The way of a fool is right in his own eyes, but a wise man listens to advice"). Although in Isa. 5:21 those who are "wise in their own eyes" are listed among those who have "rejected the law of the Lord of hosts" (v. 24), no such harsh condemnation is intended here. This is simply a statement that submission to the *moral* demands of Yahweh is one essential element in the conduct of the young man who wishes to be successful and prosperous, no more and no less than submission to his *cultic* demands (set out in vv. 9–10), and that such submission is inconsistent with pride in one's ability to manage one's own affairs single-handed. No *specific* moral advice is given here: **turn away from evil** (v. 7b) is too general to constitute a specific line of conduct peculiar to Yahwism.

5. insight (*bînāh*): McKane argues that this word, which is elsewhere always used in a positive sense, has here been given a new meaning: it is "a sinful *hubris* which is incompatible with trust in Yahweh". But this is to overstate the case. At most the word is simply used here ironically of a *supposed* insight: compare Isa. 29, where it is first used (v. 14) contemptuously of those who unjustifiably claim it for themselves, but then, in v. 24, in a positive sense.

6. acknowledge him (*dā'ēhû*, literally "know him", from *yāda'*, "to know"). In the Old Testament the "knowledge" of God includes obedience to his will. Van der Weiden (p. 31) suggested the possibility that *dā'ēhû* here is derived from a recently postulated verb *dā'āh*, "to seek"; but the usual derivation makes excellent sense. **make straight**: better, "make smooth" (compare Isa. 40:3; 45:13).

8. The reward for following the father's advice is expressed in terms of bodily health; but probably it is the wellbeing of the whole person which is meant and not only physical health. *RSV*'s **flesh** presupposes an emendation of the Hebrew *šōr* to *bāśār* or possibly to *šᵉ'ēr*; but this is unnecessary. *šōr*, which occurs in the Old Testament only here and in Ezek. 16:4; Ca. 7:3, means "navel"; but there is reason to suppose that it can also mean "strength, health" (Driver, *Bib.* 32 [1951], p. 175). *šiqqûy* (**refreshment**), literally "drink", here means "medicine". **bones**: that is, the bodily frame or the body as a whole (cf. 16:24).

9–10. This is the only passage in Proverbs in which sacrificial offerings such as are prescribed in the laws of the Pentateuch are positively enjoined. This may simply mean that the cult was a sphere of activity which did not normally fall within the scope of interest of Israel's wisdom teachers. But the reason for its recommendation here is clear. This is the most blatant expression in the Old Testament of the principle of *do ut des* – the offering of gifts to God solely in order to elicit material rewards from him (Plöger; Perdue [1977], pp. 144–6). It goes well beyond the general understanding in Israel that Yahweh was pleased with sacrifice (if offered in sincerity and with pure motives) and would show his pleasure in blessing. This passage confirms the view that in vv. 5–8 also the motive for the admonition to acknowledge Yahweh and submit to his demands was to obtain success and happiness in life rather than a pious desire to serve him.

9. Honour: this verb (*kibbēd*) here means to make sacrificial offerings as in Isa. 43:23; Dan. 11:38. **with your substance**: literally, "of all your wealth". The particle *min* – (**with**) is partitive: the offerer brought a *part* of his produce to Yahweh. **first fruits**: as prescribed in the Pentateuchal legislation (Exod. 23:19; 34:26; Dt. 26:1–11; Lev. 23:10–14 and elsewhere). **produce**: that is, agricultural produce.

10. plenty (*śāba'*): elsewhere in the Old Testament this word is used only adverbially; hence it has been suggested that it should be emended to *šeber*, "corn", which would make a suitable parallel for **wine** (*tîrôš*). But the discovery of a Phoenician parallel has made it possible that *śāba'* itself should be understood as meaning "corn" here.

11–12. On these verses as an addition to the Instruction see on vv. 1–12 above. This is the only passage in Proverbs which attempts an explanation of the apparent failure of God to give the expected reward to those who faithfully serve him. Vv. 6 and 8 have, even though rather crudely, stated the traditional view, which is constantly reiterated in the book, that such rewards can be taken for granted; these verses, on the contrary, express the awareness that this is not always borne out by experience, and offer a solution based on the analogy of the **discipline**, or punishment, meted out by human fathers (*mûsār*, "discipline", in that context, may imply corporal punishment, as in 19:18; 23:13). In the passages in Proverbs which advise the father to exercise such "discipline" (19:18; 23:13; 29:17) there is no suggestion that the child has done anything which *deserves* punishment: punishment is, rather, seen as a necessary feature of the educational process which helps to form the child's character, and so is a sign of the father's love. (The same view appears frequently in Egyptian literature.) So here: the Lord's discipline and reproof are not seen as punishment for disobedience, but as meted out simply for the good of the recipient.

The problem to which these verses attempt a solution is one which is frequently raised elsewhere in the Old Testament, especially in the Book of Job and in some of the psalms of lamentation; and various solutions are proposed there. The solution offered here is also found elsewhere, the most striking parallel to these verses being Job 5:17–18, whose wording is so similar that some commentators have suggested that one passage influenced the other, although there is no agreement about the chronological priority. But it is also found in such works as Ps. 119, especially vv. 71 and 75. The view that it is derived from Deuteronomic theology seems hardly justified: passages like 2 Sam. 7:14–16 and Ps. 89:30–33 (Heb. 31–34) are concerned with God's keeping his promises to a *sinful* person or people, which is quite a different matter. As McKane points out, only Dt. 8:5 in the Deuteronomic literature is sufficiently close to Prov. 3:11–12 to justify the theory of a direct relationship, and this may well be a case where Deuteronomy has been influenced by wisdom thought rather than the contrary (see M. Weinfeld, *Deuteronomy and the Deuteronomic School*, Oxford, 1972, pp. 260ff.; 316, and compare the late Egyptian Instruction *Papyrus Insinger*, 20:13: "Whatever hardship may come, give yourself into the hand of God").

11. be weary: better, "recoil from" (so *REB*) or "take amiss" (*qûṣ*, "to loathe"). In other words, misfortunes should not be attributed to God's malignancy (as did Job) but should be accepted as part of his mysterious educational purpose.

12. as a father (*ûkᵉ'āb*): LXX has a verb here; and the very similar passage in Job (5:18) has *yak'īb*, "he inflicts pain". Emendation to a form of this verb – e.g. the piel *(wᵉ)kē'ēb*, yielding the line "and he inflicts suffering on the son in whom he delights" – would be syntactically an improvement, and would still preserve the "father-son" analogy. However, MT may be correct.

THE PRAISE OF WISDOM
3:13–18

This poem is quite different in style from the preceding Instruction. It is a hymn in praise of Wisdom, and is to that extent similar to hymns in praise of various goddesses from the ancient Near East. It differs, however, from the *self*-praising speeches by Wisdom in 1:20–33 and 8:1–36 in that it is couched in the third person, and in that respect it resembles the poem about Wisdom in Job 28. It would seem that it once existed as a separate composition: it is complete in itself and self-sufficient; it begins with the word *'ašrê*, **Happy (is)**, which often marks the beginning of a religious poem (so Pss. 1:1; 32:1; 41:1 [Heb. 2]; 112:1; 119:1; 128:1; on its meaning see H. Cazelles, *TDOT* 1, pp. 445–8); and its conclusion is marked by the repetition of **happy** (*mᵉ'uššār*) (cognate with *'ašrê*) in its final word. It is wholly concerned with Wisdom and makes no mention of God.

There is good reason to believe that this wisdom poem has been placed here for the same reason as the additions to the second Instruction (2:2–4, 10–11): that is, to equate Wisdom with the words of the teacher with which the preceding Instruction begins (3:1–2), a procedure which is particularly appropriate in that it portrays Wisdom as having in her possession and so able to offer to those who **find** her, among other things, two specific gifts which the teacher has himself already offered to the pupil: **long life** (*'ōrek yāmîm*, v. 16, rendered by *RSV* in v. 2 by "length of days"), and **peace** (*šālôm*, v. 17), rendered by *RSV* in v. 2 as "welfare").

As in 1:20ff. and 8:1ff. Wisdom appears here to be thought of in personal terms (v. 16), yet at the same time as an object, to be acquired at all costs (as in 2:4). This ambiguity runs through much of these chapters, and suggests that, despite the mythological allusions, we are dealing here with what is basically poetical imagery. The two types of imagery do not necessarily go together: it is noteworthy that in Job 28, the only comparable passage in the Old Testament (apart from Ben Sira), the personal representation is lacking. Most of the epithets applied to Wisdom in 3:13–18 are applied to her also elsewhere in these chapters (1:28; 2:4; 4:13; 8:1, 10, 11, 18, 19, 35), but some are applied to the words of the teacher (3:2, 22; 4:22; 6:23). The motif of Wisdom as infinitely precious (vv. 14–15) occurs also in Job 28:15–19. Since there is no reason to suppose a direct connection between Job 28 and Prov. 1–9, this motif at least was probably conventional hyperbole – compare 31:10, where the "good wife" is similarly described as "far more precious than jewels".

13. the man: the repetition of *'ādām* in the two halves of the verse is surprising. Some commentators suggest that *'îš* or **nôš* would be more satisfactory in the second case, especially as LXX uses two different words; but there is no justification for rewriting the Hebrew text.

No distinction is intended between **wisdom** (*ḥokmāh*) and **understanding** (*tᵉbûnāh*) here: they are regarded as one in the verses which follow. The variation is for stylistic reasons.

14. gain (*saḥar*), **profit** (*tᵉbû'āh*): it is clear from v. 16 (**riches**) that, as in the preceding Instruction (v. 10), it is *material* advantages that the author has in mind. In other words, it is more advantageous to put the acquisition of wisdom first as an immediate goal rather than **silver** or **gold**, because in the end it will bring even greater and more durable material rewards.

15. jewels: rather, "(red) corals", regarded as extremely valuable. Read *pᵉnînîm* with Qere and the Versions rather than Kethib's *pᵉniyyîm* (cf. 8:11, which is almost identical with this verse). **nothing you desire** (*ḥᵃpāṣekā*): the **you** is surprising as the rest of the poem has no address in the second person. 8:11 has simply *ḥᵃpāṣîm*, "desirable things" (despite *RSV*'s rendering!). This may be a reference to jewellery: cf. *'abnê ḥēpeṣ*, "precious stones", in Isa. 54:12.

16. Wisdom is here clearly personified. Kayatz, (1966, pp. 105–106) has pointed out a remarkable similarity between what is said of her in this verse and Egyptian pictorial representations of the goddess Maat in which she is shown as holding precisely the symbols of life and riches and honour in her hands.

18. a tree of life: this expression (*'ēṣ ḥayyîm*) occurs also in 11:30; 13:12; 15:4, where it is not associated in any way with wisdom but is simply one of many expressions used in the sentence literature denoting a happy outcome in life. It has been widely believed to be a metaphor ultimately derived from a mythological concept attested in Mesopotamian literature and art of a sacred tree whose fruit would confer immortality, a concept possibly reflected in the tree of life in Gen. 2:9; 3:22, 24. However, it is by no means certain that "tree of life" is the correct meaning here. Since *'ēṣ* in biblical Hebrew does not always mean "tree" but is frequently used in the sense of "wood" or a wooden object, and in some passages refers to a stick or staff (2 Sam. 21:19; 23:7; 2 Kg. 6:6; Ezek. 37:16), and since the verbs **lay hold of** or grasp (*heḥᵉzîq*) and **hold . . . fast** (*tāmak*) are not readily associated with trees and, moreover, there is no mention here of the fruit, "*staff* of life" may well be the meaning of the expression here (see Whybray, *Wisdom in Proverbs*, p. 87, note 2).

are called happy (*mᵉ'uššār*): better, "are made happy". There is a slight difference of nuance between this pual participle and the interjection *'ašrê*, "Happy are . . ." of v. 13. It is fortunate to *find* Wisdom because she will then confer a *state* of good fortune on those who, having found her, hold on to her. There is no need to emend this word, which is in the singular, to a plural (*BHS*): see *GK* 145 l.

WISDOM AND CREATION
3:19–20

There is reason to suppose that these verses were originally independent of what precedes them. After a passage (vv. 13–18) in which Wisdom has held centre stage and its possession by the individual has been so strongly presented, without any reference to God, as offering full satisfaction of all conceivable desires and ambitions, v. 19 changes the subject completely: it is Yahweh (the fact is emphasized by the placing of his name at the very beginning, before the verb) who now holds centre stage, with Wisdom taking the inferior role as no more than the instrument of his action. The theme has also suddenly changed: we are transported, without previous warning, to the creation of the world, a theme which at first sight has no immediate relevance to what has just been said. The introduction of this new theme can only be accounted for if it is seen as intended to define, as the previous poem had not done, the *status* of this apparently omnipotent and generous Wisdom. Vv. 19–20 state, or imply, that this status has both its negative and positive sides: on the one hand, Wisdom is from the very beginning inferior to and dependent on Yahweh, a tool in his hands, so that, by implication, her gifts are not hers but his: she is an intermediary between God and mankind. On the other hand, she is superior to mankind, having existed before the world was created; and Yahweh guarantees the authority which she derives from him. Thus viewed in the context of vv. 13–18 Wisdom appears to be personified; but taken by themselves vv. 19–20 by no means necessarily imply personification, any more than Yahweh's *hand*, which is stated to have founded the universe in Isa. 48:13.

These verses may be a fragment of a longer poem praising Yahweh as Creator (compare Isa. 40:12–17) placed here not primarily as a statement of Yahweh's creative actions but in order to assert that the wisdom eulogized in vv. 13–18 is *Yahweh's* wisdom. The theme is more fully expressed in 8:22–31.

19. by wisdom (*b^eḥokmāh*); that is, *by means of* his wisdom. **founded the earth**; **established the heavens**: the two verbs (*yāsad*, *kônēn*), especially the former, belong to the standard terminology found elsewhere – especially in Second Isaiah and the Psalms – in descriptions of Yahweh's creative activity. This activity is expressed in terms of the generally accepted cosmology of the time (cf. Gen. 1:6–8).

20. It is not clear why these particular aspects of the creation of the world should be singled out (contrast the fuller description in 8:24–9), though the reference to **the deeps** and **the clouds** is appropriate after "the earth" and "the heavens" in v. 19. It may be that a longer poem has been curtailed. **broke forth** (*bāqa'*, niphal): this word is used in Gen. 7:11 of the flooding of the earth by the "fountains of the great deep", together with the opening of the windows of heaven, at the Deluge. But here it is clearly used of the emergence of spring water to fertilize the earth together with the equally gentle fertilization by **the dew** from above.

FOURTH INSTRUCTION
BEHAVIOUR TOWARDS NEIGHBOURS
3:21–35

There is a widespread agreement among commentators that this passage is not an original unit. Several commentators (among them Toy, McKane and Plöger) divide it into two separate pieces, vv. 21–6 and 27–35, with a possible further division between vv. 30 and 31. Both form and content, however, suggest a quite different analysis. Vv. 21–4 are easily recognizable as an introduction, comparable to 1:8–9; 2:1, 9; 3:1–4 and similar introductions in subsequent Instructions, in which the father commends his teaching to his son. Vv. 25–32 comprise a series of six (negative) admonitions expressed in the jussive preceded by *'al*, "Do not". This form – introduction followed by specific admonition – is the regular form of the Instructions in these chapters. Some of them (e.g. 1:19) but not all end with a general comment usually referring in the third person to the fate of the wicked or foolish in contrast with that of the righteous or wise, a comment which appears in some cases to have been expanded in various ways with material of a similar kind.

From this analysis it appears – contrary to the view of some commentators, who regard these as later additions – that the main content of the Instruction, after the introduction, is to be found in the admonitions. However, the first of these, vv. 25–6, is quite different from the others. It is closely related in theme to that of the introduction rather than to what follows; it differs from the other admonitions in being provided with a motive-clause (v. 26); and it was probably added in order to introduce a reference to Yahweh, which is otherwise missing from this Instruction. V. 32 is a similar motive-clause, added in this case to the last of the original admonitions. The original form of the Instruction thus probably consisted of introduction (vv. 21–4) followed by five admonitions (vv. 27–31).

21. *RSV* and some other modern versions – e.g. *REB* – have reversed the order of the lines of this verse. In the Hebrew text the phrase **let them not escape**, preceding **sound wisdom and discretion**, has no clear antecedent unless, as some commentators hold, it refers to the "wisdom" and "understanding" of v. 13; but this would be improbable in view of the large gap between the two verses, even if it were accepted that both verses belonged to a single composition. If an accidental transposition of the two lines in the process of transmission is accepted, **them** refers naturally to **sound wisdom and discretion**, and the whole verse makes good sense.

This Instruction differs from all the others in that the father does not refer specifically to his own teaching. Nevertheless, this seems to be implied. The word **discretion** (*m^e^zimmāh*) is associated with the father's words in 5:2; the admonition **let them not escape from your sight** is repeated almost word for word in 4:21 with a similar reference; and the imagery of v. 22 is similarly applied in 1:9 and 6:21.

sound wisdom: the word is *tûšiyyāh* as in 2:7. **let them not escape** (*'al-yālūzû*): this verb, which is in the qal, is found in the hiphil (*yallîzû*) in the similar 4:21. **escape** (in the sense of "depart") is a not entirely satisfactory meaning for this verb; it has been suggested that this is a different verb cognate with Arabic *lādha* (Gemser). However this may be, the general meaning is clear.

22. life: compare 4:22. **soul**: *nepeš* here refers to human vitality, which can ebb and flow according to circumstances. McKane renders *w^e^yihyû ḥayyîm l^e^napš^e^kā* (**and they will be life for your soul**) by "that they may increase your vitality". *REB* has "They will be a charm hung about your neck". It is true that *nepeš* can mean "neck" or "throat", which would give a suitable parallel for *garg^e^rōtekā*, **your neck**; but the translation of *ḥayyîm* (**life**) by "a charm" is dubious. *ḥēn* (**adornment**), however, whose usual meaning is "grace" or "favour", may mean something like this: compare 17:8, where *'eben ḥēn*, "a stone of *ḥēn*", is something which brings success.

24. If you sit down: the Hebrew text has "if you lie down" (*'im-tiškab*). *RSV*, together with many commentators and translators, has here followed LXX, assuming a scribal error in MT consisting of the accidental addition of one letter (so *tškb*) for *tšb*, "you sit". This emendation, if correct, would avoid the unlikely repetition of the same verb in the two halves of the verse and, with v. 23, make an appropriate triad: walk, sit, sleep (cf. Dt. 6:7; 11:19). Plöger, however, retains the Hebrew text, taking the verb *šākab* on its second occurrence as meaning "to sleep". This is a rather forced interpretation. **be afraid**: this verb (*pāḥad*) denotes extreme fear or terror (compare the noun *paḥad* in v. 25).

25–26. These verses form a kind of appendix to vv. 21–4, but one which is somewhat at variance with their message. In v. 25 **panic** (*paḥad*) clearly picks up the verb (*pāḥad*) of v. 24a; but since the pupil or reader has already been assured that constant attention to "sound wisdom and discretion" will infallibly preserve him from such fear, this additional admonition is redundant. Then in v. 26 Yahweh is suddenly and belatedly introduced as providing an alternative reason for confidence, with no attempt to indicate that he is in any way connected with the above "sound wisdom". He does not reappear in any of the subsequent admonitions, but only at the end (vv. 32–4).

25. sudden panic: this is probably correct, although some commentators repoint *pit'ōm* (sudden) as *pᵉtā'yîm*, "fools, simpletons" (so, e.g., *REB*). **ruin of the wicked**: LXX takes this as a subjective genitive, that is, as meaning ruin *caused by* the wicked. But *RSV* is probably correct: the **panic** in question would then be fear of being counted among the wicked and so suffering their fate.

26. the Lord: the position of this word at the beginning of the sentence in Hebrew emphasizes the subject. **your confidence** (*bᵉkislekā*): this may be the correct translation, in which case the *bēth* which stands at the beginning of the word is the so-called "*bēth* essentiae", which defines the way in which someone (or something) – here Yahweh – shows himself (*GK* 119 h,i). But Dahood, followed by *REB*, sees *kesel* here as a word meaning "flank" on the basis of Ugaritic *ksl*, and translates the word by "at your side". **from being caught**: literally, "from the *leked*". This word, which occurs only here, may mean a snare or trap. The corresponding verb *lākad* means to capture (people or animals). The metaphor is similar to that in v. 23b: as often in the wisdom books, life is pictured as a journey on foot attended by various dangers.

27. to whom it is due (*mibbᵉʿālâw*): this is probably the correct translation, and it is accepted by most commentators. Others, however, have argued that since *baʿal* elsewhere in the Old Testament means "possessor", it cannot denote a person who receives something from another person (so *RSV*mg. has "its owners"). But since "its owners" does not make acceptable sense, a number of emendations have been proposed. On the other hand, it has been pointed out that in Akkadian the phrase *bēl ḫubulli* means "creditor", that is, someone to whom something is due. If *RSV* is correct, it still remains unclear what is meant by persons to whom something is due – that is, who are entitled to something. Partly on the basis of LXX's "the poor", some have interpreted the verse as a simple recommendation to beneficence. But LXX's rendering may be based on a different text; and this would in any case be a strange mode of speech. The solution may lie in the word *ṭôb* (**good**), which may mean material wealth or "goods", as in 12:14; 13:2 and elsewhere. If that is so, the verse may refer to a practice of delaying payment for goods or repayment of loans, which is here condemned. V. **28** is closely linked with this verse and is little more than an echo of it.

29. plan: the reference is to premeditated and malicious crime. The admonition is general: it may refer to such things as spreading malicious rumours or making unfounded accusations against a neighbour (*rēaʿ*), that is, against a fellow-member of the community. The second line emphasizes the serious nature of the offence as a breach of communal solidarity. Two contrasting scenes are here vividly portrayed with a minimum of words: we see clearly the scheming villian and his unsuspecting neighbour who is the intended victim.

30. Do not contend: the behaviour condemned in this verse may be regarded as an example of that referred to in v. 29. *rîb* (**contend**; the normal form of the jussive would be *tārēb*) implies a deliberate dispute – often ending in the lawcourt – rather than a sudden flash of temper: "pick a quarrel" might be an appropriate rendering. **a man** (*'ādām*): this term (often used in Proverbs of individuals rather than collectively) has a wider range than *rēaʿ*, "neighbour", but it is doubtful whether any distinction is intended here. Warnings against quarrels and disputes as disruptive of society form a frequent theme in the wisdom literatures of the ancient Near East.

31. This final admonition is a general warning against the temptation of thinking that crime pays. *ḥāmās* (**violence**) often means physical brutality, but may refer simply to wickedness in general. **choose**: that is, decide (to follow his example). The sense is quite satisfactory, and a proposed emendation of *tibḥar* to *titḥar*, "be indignant at", based on LXX and a comparison with 24:19 and Ps. 37:1, is improbable (see Plöger).

32. On this verse see above on vv. 21–35. It has the form of an independent antithetical proverb of a generalizing kind such as is found in abundance in the sentence literature of Proverbs, especially 10:1–22:16. Those chapters also abound in proverbs which declare that certain persons or actions are an abomination (*tô'ēbāh*) to Yahweh; this verse is particularly close to 11:20 and 15:9. The **perverse man** (*nālôz*), here contrasted with the upright (*yᵉšārîm*), is the person who is morally crooked or "not straight" (cf. 2:15; 14:2). **the upright are in his confidence**: literally, "his *sôd* is with the upright". *sôd* denotes an intimate and confidential relationship, sometimes involving secret discussion of policy (15:22) and thus a position of trust. In Jer. 23:18, 22 Yahweh's *sôd* is the heavenly council into which the true prophet is admitted, and at which Yahweh reveals his message (cf. Am. 3:7). Thus the state of closeness to God referred to in this proverb is the exact opposite of what is designated as Yahweh's *tô'ēbāh* (**abomination**), that is, that which God loathes and cannot endure. (See further on 6:16.)

33–35. These are further antithetical proverbs of the same type as v. 32. This lengthy epilogue is unlikely to have been part of the original Instruction. Vv. 33–4 are linked together by a common subject, but there is no progression of thought from one to the other. They were probably originally separate proverbs. LXX repeats "the Lord" at the beginning of v. 34.

33. abode: this word, *nāweh*, properly refers to a shepherd's hut; but here it is apparently used simply as a variant of *bēt*, **house**, without distinction of meaning.

34. Toward the scorners (*'im-lallēṣîm*): *RSV*, following *BHS* and many commentators, is based here on an emendation of the phrase to *'im-lēṣîm*, "*with* the scorners". Ps. 18:25–6 (Heb. 26–7), which is similar to this verse, uses *'im* in the same way. Driver (*Bib.* 32 [1951], p. 176) retains MT, translating the line by "Though he treats the arrogant arrogantly"; but this involves a somewhat unusual meaning for *'im* and the understanding of *l^{e}* as governing the direct object (an Aramaism).

On the meaning of the verb *lîṣ* (**is scornful**) and the noun *lēṣ* see on 1:22. However the line is rendered it expresses the principle of exact retribution or repayment in kind. **the humble**: Kethib has *^{ca}niyyîm*, Qere *^{ca}nāwîm*, a confusion which occurs elsewhere, especially in the Psalms. Whether these are different words, *'ānî* meaning "poor" and *'ānāw* "humble" is disputed; but the contrast with *lēṣîm* makes it clear that, although elsewhere in Proverbs *'aniyyīm/^{ca}nāwīm* means "the poor", here it means "the humble".

35. The change of theme from wicked and righteous and scorners and humble to **wise** and **fools** is an indication that this verse was not originally attached to vv. 33–4. **get disgrace** (*mērîm qālôn*): although the general sense of this line is clear, the meaning of *mērîm* is not, and there is no agreement among the commentators about it. As *RSV*mg. points out, *mērîm* as the hiphil participle *singular* of *rûm*, "to be high", would mean "exalts". Thomas (*VT* Suppl. 3 [1955], pp. 282–3), followed by McKane, defends *MT* and renders the word by "enhance, increase", rather improbably suggesting that the singular form – which would otherwise have to be emended to the plural – may qualify as a "distributive singular" (see *GK* 135 l. Plöger, referring to Hos. 4:7, "I will change their honour into disgrace", takes it to be the hiphil participle plural of *mûr*, "to exchange". Driver (*Bib.* 32 [1951], p. 177) cites Ps. 109:18, "He clothed himself with cursing as with a cloak (*k^{e}maddô*)" and emends *mērîm* to *maddām*: "disgrace will be their garment".

FIFTH INSTRUCTION
THE IMPORTANCE OF TRADITIONAL WISDOM
4:1–9

The text of this Instruction is somewhat in disarray. In an attempt to improve the sense, *RSV*, following some commentators, has rearranged the three lines of v. 5, moving the first line of the Hebrew text (**Get wisdom; get insight**) to the end of the verse. The reason for this is that this line belongs in sense to the verses which follow, which are concerned with wisdom, rather than with v. 4, which is concerned with the importance of the words of the human "father", and that in their position in *MT* they interrupt what is being said about that. But the difficulties of the text go further than this, and other rearrangements, and some omissions, have been proposed. V. 7, for example, looks like the beginning of a section about wisdom rather than its continuation; and the "Get wisdom; get insight" of v. 5 is oddly repeated there. The original text may have been shorter: *LXX*^{B} omits **and live** from the end of v. 4 and also "Get wisdom; get insight" from v. 5; it also omits v. 7 altogether. It makes no mention of wisdom at all; but this also can hardly be the original text, since much of what follows is inappropriate if spoken simply about the teacher's instruction. Other *MSS* of *LXX* have further substantial variations. McKane remarks that the text is "not stable"; and it is probably impossible to restore an "original" text here.

Apart from its textual problems, this Instruction has some peculiar characteristics. It contains no specific admonitions at all; rather, it corresponds in its entirety to the *introductions* to the other Instructions in chapters 1–9, after which it abruptly ends. It may be a fragment of a longer piece, lacking the whole of the original body of the Instruction. But this "introduction" is disproportionately long, and has probably been expanded. The first part (vv. 1–5, excluding the misplaced interpolated reference to Wisdom) is a recommendation by the "father" of his own teaching backed up by a reminiscence of his own education, while the remainder (vv. 6–9) commends the acquisition of a personified Wisdom who has special gifts to bestow on the pupil. But whereas in the other Instructions (e.g. 2:1.) there is an attempt to identify or at least to relate the two, here no such attempt has been made: the section on Wisdom seems, as far as the text can be relied on, to be an independent and self-contained piece.

A unique characteristic of this Instruction is the father's reminiscence of his own education (vv. 3–5; it is not clear whether the quotation of the instruction received by the pupil's father actually extends to the end of the Instruction or not). It closely resembles some Egyptian texts, notably the *Kemit*, a school text from the Egyptian Middle Kingdom. It should also be noted that this Instruction, like the majority of those in these chapters (the others are I, VI, VII, IX, X), makes no mention of God at all.

1–2. The introduction is similar to that of other Instructions in these chapters, especially 1:8; 3:1; 4:10, 20; 5:1.

1. Hear, O sons: elsewhere in the introductions to these Instructions the pupil is addressed in the singular ("my son"). The plural form is, however, also found in 5:7 and 7:24; but those two verses appear to be interpolations and not original to the Instructions in which they appear, which otherwise keep to the singular. It has been argued that the use of the plural shows that the "father" here – and presumably, therefore, in the other Instructions – must be a "professional" teacher in a "school". Against this are not only the reference to the two parents in the reminiscence in v. 3, but also the specific allusion to the mother's *teaching* in 1:8 and 6:20 (see above on 1:8). It has been suggested that *bānîm*, **sons**, is a mistake for *b^enî* ("my son"); but this would not account for the fact that the *whole* of vv. 1–2 is expressed in the plural. *BHS* proposes a wholesale emendation of these verses to read the singular; but there is no justification for this whatever. Since these ten Instructions are probably not the work of a single author, there is nothing surprising about this particular variation. There is no reason why a father should not have had more than one son needing instruction. There is also probably no significance in the choice of *'āb*, "a father" instead of the "your father" of the other Instructions.

2. precepts (*leqaḥ*): see on 1:5 (*RSV* "learning").

3. a son with my father (*bēn . . . l^e'ābî*): literally, "a son to my father". The meaning is "when I was in the same position with regard to my father as you now are to me". The *lamedh* probably has the sense of "under the authority of". **tender** (*rak*): that is, "of tender age" (Toy). **the only one** (*yāḥîd*): LXX has "beloved". This could be a translation of *yādîd*, though elsewhere (e.g. Gen. 22:2) LXX also renders *yāḥîd* by "beloved". But there is probably an implication here that this was an especially beloved child. The point of the verse is that his education began early: it is never too soon, is the implication, to inculcate sound principles. **in the sight of** (*lip-^enê*): this probably means "under the care of" (cf. Gen. 17:18; Hos. 6:2).

4. he taught me: that is, he then *began* to teach the child. **and live**: the imperative is used here to give an assurance: "and you will live" (*GK* 110 f). On the meaning of "living" in the wisdom literature see the note on "life" in 3:2. The whole phrase from **keep my commandments** occurs again in 7:2. Compare the Egyptian *Kemit*: "My father likewise taught me useful writings which had come down to him. . . . I then found that people praised me, after I became wise, after my eyes were opened".

5. Get wisdom: the verb employed here (*qānāh*) can mean either "get, acquire" or "buy". There is a reference in 17:16 to a fool who has the money (*m*ᵉ*ḥîr*) with which he hopes to "buy" wisdom, and 23:23 refers to "buying" truth (and perhaps also wisdom) and to "selling" it (*mākar*). It has been supposed, especially on the basis of 17:16, that there were teachers in Israel who taught for a fee; but this is disputed. In this verse (and v. 7) there is no reason to suppose that the verb means more than simply "acquire" – that is, by undergoing instruction. **insight**: as elsewhere (e.g. 2:2–3) this is treated as a synonym of wisdom.

6–9. In these verses Wisdom, referred to in the third person, is personified in a way similar to her self-presentation in 1:20–35 and chapter 8.

6. keep; **guard**: compare 2:11–12, where the implication of this activity is more fully explained. **love her**: to "love wisdom" does not necessarily mean more than to apply oneself wholeheartedly to its acquisition (12:1; 29:3). But here the context shows that the phrase is used, metaphorically, of the love of a person. In 8:17 personified Wisdom speaks of a *reciprocal* love between herself and those who seek her out. Kayatz (pp. 99–102) remarks that the Egyptians could speak of "loving" the goddess *Maat*, which meant recognition of her authority; but she points out that as a reciprocal relationship this seems to have been confined to kings. There seems to be no need to suppose an Egyptian influence here.

7. *REB*, following LXX, omits this verse altogether (see above on 4:1–9). The first line presents considerable difficulty, and there is no agreement among the commentators about its syntax. A literal translation would be "The beginning/essence of wisdom get wisdom". Some commentators regard this as impossible Hebrew and unintelligible. Gemser, Barucq and Plöger, with some hesitation, translate roughly as *RSV*, which joins the two halves with **is this**; van der Weiden similarly, except that he renders *rē'šît* by "essence". Ringgren takes the first two words (*rē'šît ḥokmāh*) as a nominal sentence: "Wisdom is the noblest thing" (*cf. AV*, *RV* "Wisdom is the principal thing"), adding "therefore . . .". MacKane, somewhat similarly, prefers "wisdom comes first". **whatever you get**: better, "at the price (even) of all your possessions" (*qinyān*).

8. Prize her highly: this form (*silsēl*, pilpel of *sālal*), is found only here, and its meaning is uncertain. Since the qal *sālal* means "to lift up, take up", it may mean exalt, esteem highly"; but "Exalt her and she will exalt (t^e^rômēm) you" is perhaps somewhat odd. Others have suggested that *silsēl* means "gather up" in the sense of "embrace" (compare *sal*, "basket" into which things are gathered). This would make a good parallel with "embrace" (*ḥbq*) in the second line. This verse, then, would provide the best evidence for the view that Wisdom is here regarded as a bride or lover. However, McKane and Plöger point out that in v. 9 her actions appear to be those of a patroness conferring honours on a protégé rather than of a loved one.

9. a fair garland: compare 1:9, where it is the parents' teaching which is said to "crown" the pupil. **she will bestow on you** (*t^e^mag-g^e^nekkā*): this verb, *mgn* (piel), is unconnected with *māgēn*, "shield", which occurs in 2:7. In the other two passages in which it occurs (Gen. 14:20; Hos. 11:8) it is equivalent to *nātan*, "give". On the construction with a double accusative see *GK* 117ff.

a beautiful crown (*^a^ṭeret tip'eret*): the wearing of a crown was not confined to kings. A bridegroom could be crowned at his wedding (Ca. 3:11), and crowns may have been worn on other festal occasions (Isa. 28:1) or as ornaments signifying honourable status (Ezek. 16:12; Lam 5:16). The word was also used, as here, metaphorically (e.g. Prov. 12:4; 14:24; 16:31; 17:6). In Isa. 62:3 the identical phrase "a beautiful crown" is used in a passage predicting Zion's future restoration to honour.

SIXTH INSTRUCTION
AVOIDANCE OF EVIL COMPANY
4:10–19

This Instruction might be called "The Two Ways". The representation of life as a journey is a frequent theme of these Instructions (compare, e.g., 1:15, 19; 2:7–9, 12–15, 18–19; 3:6, 23). This seems to have been a standard topos of the wisdom literature, as it has been in much subsequent moral teaching: compare, e.g. Ps. 1). In this Instruction it is all-pervasive and gives unity to the whole passage. It affirms human freedom to make a choice about the conduct of one's life, and sets out the inevitable consequences of these two "ways of life", that of righteousness and that of wickedness. There is apparently no middle way, and no possibility of changing course is mentioned: it seems to be taken for granted that the choice once made stamps the character indelibly. A strong pressure is thus put on the pupil to choose now, and to choose rightly and wisely.

The Instruction appears to have undergone almost no subsequent expansion: the only intrusive verse, which breaks the flow of discourse, is v. 13. The word "wisdom" occurs only once (v. 11), and as in 5:1, where the teacher speaks of "my wisdom", wisdom here simply describes the content of the teaching: contrast the elaborate development and personification in 2:2 ff. (On the question whether **instruction** (*mûsār*) is personified in the intrusive v. 13 see below.) There is also no mention of God in the Instruction. The passage falls into three parts: vv. 10–12 form the introduction and vv. 14–15 the main section or admonition, followed by motive clauses in vv. 16–17, and 19+ 18 (the order of these verses has been accidentally reversed) forms a general conclusion.

10. that the years . . . many: compare 3:2. The same claim is made of Wisdom in 3:16; 9:11.

11. I have taught you; I have led you: the perfect tenses here refer not to past completed actions but to actions already begun but envisaged as intended to continue (*GK* 106g,i) and should be rendered in English by the present tense or even (as by *REB* – compare *GK* 106n) by the future. **I have taught you**: Driver (*VT* 1 [1951], pp. 249–50) distinguished this verb (*yrh*, hiphil) from that meaning "teach", on the basis of Akkadian and Ugaritic cognates, and suggested the rendering "I have made you walk", that is, "I (shall) guide you". This would make a suitable parallel to **I have led you**. **paths of uprightness**: McKane prefers "straight paths" (compare the "crooked paths" of 2:15). Whether correct or not, this proposal does not alter the general sense.

13. On this verse see on 4:10–19 above. Its isolation from its present context makes its interpretation problematic. **instruction**: this word (*mûsār*) is construed as masculine at every other occurrence in the Old Testament. It would be possible to repoint *niṣṣᵉrēhā* (**guard her**) with a masculine suffix (*niṣṣᵉrēhū*) – a defective spelling which occurs occasionally (*GK.* 7c) and may be the solution to a similar anomaly in 12:25 – and to accept the testimony of one MS which reads "he" (*hû'*) instead of **she** (*hî'*). Alternatively it has been suggested, hardly plausibly, that "the personified *mûsār* has here been approximated to the personified *ḥokmāh*" (McKane). (In 8:35 Wisdom claims that "he who finds me finds life".) Apart from the grammatical question, which may perhaps be put down as simply an unexplained anomaly, an attempt has been made to relate the verse to v. 10 by emending to *mûsārî*, "*my* instruction" (compare "a father's instruction" in 4:1); but if this is the case it has been misplaced.

16–17. The description of the character of the wicked in these verses is much less specific than that of 1:11–12. The exaggerated imagery is intended to emphasize as strongly as possible that choosing the wrong road inevitably leads to a total deterioration of character. The description is calculated to strike horror into the pupil even before he reaches the dénouement in v. 19.

16. they cannot sleep: on the defective spelling of the verb (*yšn*) see *GK* 69q. Van der Weiden pointed out that the imagery is that of wild animals which cannot sleep until they have found their prey and satisfied their hunger: compare Ps. 59:15 (Heb. 16).

17. This could mean that the wicked literally live on what they have stolen (compare 20:17); but it is more likely that this is a metaphorical way of saying that for such people wrongdoing is as natural as eating and drinking: compare Job 15:16; 34:7 and the English phrase "it was meat and drink to him".

18–19. Most commentators transpose these two verses, partly because this avoids a double change of subject from the wicked to the righteous and back again, and partly because the particle *wᵉ* (**But**) at the beginning of v. 18 is difficult to understand (even if rendered, as it could be, by "and") following v. 17 but appropriate after v. 19. The two verses together form a concise statement of the teaching about the "two ways". The metaphors of **light** and **darkness** signifying happiness, prosperity and life on the one hand and misery, defeat and death on the other, are frequent in poetic speech in general and often occur in the Old Testament. Here the imagery is effectively used in connection with two journeys, the one beginning at dawn with the prospect of increasing light – and so safety – as it proceeds, and the other undertaken in pitch darkness and inevitably ending in disaster.

18. which shines brighter and brighter: literally, "going and shining". On this idiom see *GK* 113u. **until full day**: literally, "until the day is established" (Driver, *JTS* 35 [1934], p. 381). It would be preferable to repoint the construct form *nᵉkôn* as a verb (*nākôn*, niphal of *kûn*).

SEVENTH INSTRUCTION
THE IMPORTANCE OF VIGILANCE
4:20–27

Like 4:10–19, this Instruction is expressed in very general terms; but it differs from it in that it is concerned not simply with external actions but with the inner disposition from which external action springs, and which determines the whole direction of one's life (v. 23).

There is no sign that this Instruction has undergone expansion. There is no mention of God or of wisdom: the words of the human teacher are sufficient in themselves to confer **life** and **healing** on those who take them to heart (v. 22). The structure is simple: vv. 20–22 form the conventional introduction, and vv. 23–7 the contents of the teaching, consisting of five admonitions. There is no general conclusion such as is found in several of the other Instructions. LXX adds such a conclusion consisting of two additional distichs, but this is clearly not original: indeed, it contains a misinterpretation of v. 27 (see below). The absence of a general conclusion confirms the view that this was originally an independent Instruction: if, as some commentators maintain, chapter 4 in its entirety once formed a single unit, the lack of such a conclusion would be strange, especially since one has already been provided earlier in the chapter (vv. 18–19).

The words **heart** (v. 23), mouth (*peh*, *RSV* **speech**, v. 24), lips (*śᵉpātayim*, *RSV* **talk**, v. 24), **eyes** (v. 25), foot (*RSV* **feet**, v. 26) link the admonitions together into a unity. A similar chain enumerating parts of the body, but with a quite different purpose, occurs in Ps. 115:5–7 (mouth, eyes, ears, nose, hands, feet).

20. All the words in this verse recur in the introductions to other Instructions in this series, often in similar combinations.

21. Let them not escape: this is the same verb as in 3:21, but here – uniquely – in the hiphil. The meaning is probably the same: see *GK* 53d, e. **keep them within your heart**: compare 3:3. The word **heart** (here, for some reason, *lēbāb*, elsewhere in this and other Instructions *lēb*) here signifies the mind. McKane suggests that the phrase is a recommendation to learn the teacher's words by heart as a guide to future conduct. Compare the use of "heart" in v. 23.

22. life: compare Wisdom's claim in 8:35a. "Life" here clearly includes physical health as well as material prosperity. **to him who finds them**: the Hebrew has "to those who find them", which conflicts with the singular "his flesh". This may be simply a minor slip either by the author or by an early copyist. The point is that the pupil is very fortunate in having "found" teaching which is universally efficacious. **flesh** (*bāśār*) is sometimes interpreted here as meaning "the whole being" (so *REB*). This may be so; but the claim elsewhere in these Instructions that the teacher's words will confer "length of days and years of life" on the pupil (3:2) shows that the usual meaning "body" would not be inappropriate. **healing**: this word here probably simply means "health": compare 16:24.

23–27. These admonitions should be interpreted in terms of the general tenor of these Instructions. They do not advocate morality for its own sake but as a means to the attainment of the practical goals of success and happiness, as is indicated by the words **the springs of life** (v. 23, compare v. 22) and **all your ways will be sure** (v. 26). This attitude is in keeping with that of much of the ancient Near Eastern wisdom literature.

23. with all vigilance (*mikkol-mišmār*): a better translation would be "more than (*min-*) anything which needs to be guarded". ("*with* all vigilance" would require the reading *b^{e}kol-*, which may underlie the reading of the LXX.) Although elsewhere in the Old Testament *mišmār* denotes the action of guarding rather than an object to be guarded, the resemblance to a line from the Aramaic *Aḥiqar* suggests the latter: "More than anything that needs to be guarded, guard your mouth" (line 98, *ANET*, p. 428b). There the word *mnṭrh* (cognate with Hebrew *nāṭar*, a synonym of *šāmar*) has that meaning (C.-F. Jean and J. Hoftijzer, *Dictionnaire des Inscriptions Sémitiques de l'Ouest*. Leiden, 1965, p. 159). The reason why it is necessary to "guard" the heart, that is, to protect it from wrong thoughts, above all else is that **from it flow the springs** (literally, "the outgoings" (*tôṣ^{e}'ôt*) of life, that is, the influences which can lead to "life". **heart** (*lēb*) is here the inner man or self (compare, e.g., 1 Sam. 16:7).

24. crooked speech: literally, "crookedness of mouth". **devious talk**: literally, "lips of deviousness". Speech was regarded in the wisdom literatures both of the Old Testament and of the ancient Near East as revealing the inner thoughts (the "heart") of a person; and dishonest speech (lies, deceit, perjured testimony, etc.) was universally abhorred.

25. This admonition is related to the verses which follow, which, like 4:14–19, employ the metaphor of a journey to the course of human life. The advice to look straight ahead has nothing to do with the "guardianship of the eyes" of Christian moral teaching, but is concerned with the need to look where one is going in order not to stumble on the way. **gaze**: literally, "eyelids", used simply as a variant for "eyes", McKane prefers to render by "glances". **be straight**: on the form of the verb see *GK* 70b.

26. Take heed to: this is probably the correct rendering. This verb (*pls*, piel) occurs only six times in the Old Testament, and in every case except one has a word meaning "path, road" as its object. In Proverbs it occurs again in 5:6 and 5:21. This translation is based on Driver (1935, pp. 150–1), who, followed by Ringgren, McKane and Plöger, connects it with the Accadian *palāsū*, "to look at, scrutinize". Others, however, connecting it with Accadian *palāšu'*, "to bore, break through", render it by "make level, make smooth", taking it to refer to the construction or preparation of a highway such as is mentioned in Isa. 40:3–4 (so Delitzsch, Wildeboer, Toy, Oesterley, Barucq; *KB*[3] is uncertain). **all your ways will be sure**: literally, "will be firm" (niphal of *kûn*) – that is, you will (as a result of picking your way carefully) have firm ground under your feet.

27. Do not swerve (*nāṭāh*) **to the right or to the left**: this expression occurs in Num. 20:17, where it is used in the literal sense of not straying from a road. The Deuteronomic literature employs a similar expression, but always with a different verb (*sûr*), once in a literal sense (Dt. 2:27) and frequently metaphorically, mainly of disobedience to the Law of Moses (e.g. Dt. 5:32–3; 28:14; Jos. 1:7). There is thus no reason, with Robert (1934, pp. 61–2) to suspect Deuteronomic influence here (see McKane).

The purpose of the two couplets appended by LXX at the end of the chapter (see above on 4:20–27) was to associate God with these admonitions; but they clearly misinterpret v. 27 by asserting that "God knows the ways on the right hand, but those on the left are crooked".

EIGHTH INSTRUCTION
AVOIDANCE OF THE "STRANGE WOMAN"
5:1–23

This chapter, through the expansion of an original, fairly brief Instruction, has become a kind of repository for miscellaneous matter concerned with marital fidelity and the folly of adultery. The theme of the "loose woman" who may try to seduce the inexperienced young man (compare 2:16–19; 6:24–5; 7:5, 24–7) is abandoned after v. 8 except for a brief reference in v. 20. What follows is characterized by differences of style, language and point of view, and itself lacks unity. Vv. 9–14 are a discourse not about seduction by an adulteress but about the fate of the adulterer, that is, of the unfaithful married man who courts disgrace and condemnation by the *qāhāl* and the *'ēdāh* (v. 14, *RSV* **the assembled congregation**), that is, the meetings of the assembled citizens – a national reference never found elsewhere in Proverbs and at variance with the "universal" character of these Instructions. Vv. 15–20 are also addressed to the married man, exhorting him to marital fidelity. Vv. 21–3 form a general conclusion similar to those which conclude some of the other Instructions and introducing God into a chapter which otherwise makes no reference to him.

Few commentators have seriously discussed the question of the literary unity of the chapter (Delitzsch, Renard). But a comparison with the other Instructions having the same theme (2:1ff.; 6:20ff.; 7:1ff.) reveals an underlying common pattern of introduction (vv. 1–2); main section with warning and admonition (vv. 3–6, 8); and general conclusion (vv. 21–3). The original Instruction thus seems to have consisted of vv. 1–6, 8 and possibly part of vv. 21–3 (see below). To this, however, it is necessary to make an addition. Whereas in all the other Instructions with this theme the introduction is followed by a verse (2:16; 6:24; 7:5) which introduces the theme in a couplet asserting that the instruction about to be given (the teacher's words, wisdom, or the like) will save or protect the pupil from the "strange woman", here there is no such verse, and there is consequently an abrupt transition between verses 2 and 3 from introduction to main theme. The theme is not in fact properly introduced; and it is probable that a couplet similar to that found in the comparable Instructions has been accidentally omitted.

The only other problematic verse in the Instruction so reconstructed is v. 7, which interrupts the connection between the description of the death-dealing consequences of association with the "loose woman" (vv. 4–6) and the main admonition in v. 8 and should therefore be considered as an intrusion (see below).

1. This verse closely resembles 2:2 except for the personal forms "*my* wisdom", "*my* understanding", which are unique in these Instructions. However, in 2:2 and similar verses **wisdom**, **under-**

standing and the like are virtually identified with the words of the teacher ("my words", "my commandments", 2:1). There is therefore no justification, with Toy and others, to emend to the simple forms "wisdom" and "understanding". Wisdom is not elsewhere mentioned in this Instruction (this is also the case with God, unless v. 21 is its original conclusion). This use of the word "wisdom" as descriptive of the words of a wise teacher may have contributed to its subsequent personification.

2. Many commentators have regarded the text of this verse as corrupt, and have proposed various emendations, some drastic. However, McKane and Plöger, together with *REB*, have found no difficulty here and have translated the verse in a way similar to that of *RSV*. **that you may keep**: the Hebrew has the infinitive construct *lišmōr*, which here has an explicatory or defining sense: "in keeping" (*GK* 114d, o, r) and does not require a suffix (**you**), although this is found in other cases (2:2; 6:24; 7:5). **discretion** (*m^e^zimmôt*): see on 1:4. On the use of the plural form see *GK* 124e. The line is unusually short; but this fact hardly justifies emendation to bring it into line with 2:11, in which *m^e^zimmāh* is the subject and not the object of the clause. **guard knowledge**: the meaning is that the pupil should be careful with his speech and not betray the knowledge or wisdom which he has gained from his instruction. On the sequence of the infinitive construct followed by a finite verb in this verse see *GK* 114r. On the possibility of the accidental omission of a couplet following this verse see on 5:1–23 above and on v. 3 below.

3–6. Compare 2:16–19; 6:24–5, 32; 7:5, 25–7.

3. LXX, whose text is otherwise inferior to MT, nevertheless perhaps preserves here a trace of the missing couplet (see above): "Give no heed to a worthless woman who for a season pleases thy palate". **a loose woman**: on the meaning of *zārāh* see on 2:16–19. **drip honey**: the same expression occurs in Ca. 4:11 in a poem in which the lover describes the effect on him of the charms of his beloved. It no doubt formed part of the regular language of love. The young man here is similarly enticed, but with disastrous results (v. 4). The **honey** in question (the usual word is *d^e^baš*) is that eaten straight from the honeycomb. **speech**: literally, "palate" (*ḥēk*). The word occurs again as a parallel to **lips** in 8:7.

4. but in the end she is: literally, "but her end (*'aḥ^a^rît*) is". The "end" is not the fate of the woman but of the young man, further described in v. 5. **wormwood** (*laʿ^a nāh*): the plant *Artemisia Absinthium* (vermouth), the bitter taste of whose leaves and buds was, and is, proverbial. **two-edged**: Hebrew *piyyôt*, elsewhere *pîpiyyôt*, plural of *peh*, "mouth" (see *GK* 96). So "a sword with edges" (rather than with only one).

5. Compare 2:18–19; 7:26–7. The imagery of **death** and **the path to Sheol** must be understood in relation to their opposite, **the path of** (that is, "to") life in v. 6, and of the meaning of "life" generally in these Instructions (see on 2:18–19). **follow the path to**: literally, "grasp" (*tāmak*). *REB* has "lead(s) straight to"; but this would be a somewhat unusual extension of the meaning of this verb. Dahood (*Psalms 1–50*, *AB*, 1966, p. 89 on Ps. 16:5) and van der Weiden postulate a verb *yāmak*, "to fall, sink", which would give a good parallel to **go down to**; but this further requires the existence in Hebrew of a conjugation with "infixed *t*" found in Ugaritic and some other Semitic languages, and so is doubly uncertain.

6. This verse presents a number of problems. The verbs *tᵉpallēs* (**she does not take heed to**) and *lō' tēdāʿ* (**she does not know it**), taken as third person singular feminine by *RSV* and the majority of translations, could equally well be second person singular masculine and so addressed to the young man: "lest *you* take heed . . . ; her ways are unsteady, but *you* do not know it". Gemser and Ringgren take this view, and McKane and Plöger regard it as a possibility.

Two further points require discussion. First, as the text stands, **does not** is hardly a satisfactory translation of *pen-*, which normally means "lest, so that not . . .". Most commentators emend this particle to *bal-* or *lō'-*, "not", supposedly following the Versions, but without adequate justification. Gemser, citing Driver, *TZ* 14 (1958), p. 134, attempts to solve the problem by regarding the first line as logically following, not preceding, the second (a so-called "post-positive" construction): "so that you should not recognize the path of life, her tracks are unsteady (and) you do not notice it".

Secondly, however, in the appendix to the second edition of his commentary Gemser has taken a different view of *lō' tēdāʿ*, reverting to the common view that it is third singular feminine, but, following Thomas (*JTS* 36 [1935], p. 411; 37 [1936], pp. 59–60), taking this verb (*yādaʿ*) as unrelated to *yādaʿ* = "to know" and as cognate with an Arabic verb *waduʿa* meaning "to be quiet, still" and translating the phrase by "she it not still", that is, "she is unsteady". So also McKane. This theory, however, has been challenged (Johnstone,

VT 41 [1991], pp. 49–62; Emerton, *VT* 41 [1991], pp. 145–63). On *tᵉpallēs* (**take heed to**) see on 4:26.

7. On this verse see 5:1–23 above. There is no justification for following LXX in emending the plurals **sons**, **listen** and **do not depart** to the singular. See on 4:1. Apart from the change of number, the intrusive character of the verse is shown by the fact that it breaks the sequence of vv. 6 and 8. As the text stands, the **her** of v. 8 has no proximate antecedent. The verse should probably be regarded as a gloss intended to emphasize and draw attention to the admonition which begins in v. 8. On *wᵉʿattā* (**And now**) followed by the imperative of *šāmaʿ* (**listen to**) see Brongers, *VT* 15 [1965], pp. 194–5, 199. **depart from** (*sûr min-*): that is, ignore or forget.

9–14. Although these verses are attached to the preceding sentence by the conjunction **lest** (*pen-*), there is here no further reference to the adulteress or "loose woman". The situation depicted is quite different: whereas in vv. 3–6, 8 only the woman and her own house are mentioned and adultery is to be avoided because it brings "death" in the general sense of what follows from setting out on the wrong road, a course which will eventually but inevitably lead to the loss of the possibility of achieving happiness and wellbeing (compare 4:10–19), here the adulterer's fate is portrayed in quite concrete and immediate terms: he will encounter the implacable hatred of his paramour's family, who will seek, not his life – there is no mention of death, literal or figurative – but – though he apparently will save himself in time v. 14 – his financial and social ruin.

9. The meaning of this verse is disputed. *RSV*'s translation is typical of a number of modern versions; but it is unclear what situation is envisaged. *hôd* (**honour**) normally means splendour or majesty; it has been taken by some interpreters to refer here to manly vigour, but this extension of its meaning is uncertain. It is also not clear in what sense the adulterer's "years" (*šᵉnōtekā*, **your years**) might be given to the merciless or cruel person. Thomas (*ZAW* 55 [1937], p. 174–6; cf. *VT* Suppl. 3, 1955, p. 286, n. 8) and Driver (*ET* 49 [1937–8], p. 38) postulate a distinct verb *šānāh* on the basis of Arabic and Aramaic which would give the meaning "your dignity" (compare *BHS*). But this picture of loss of honour and dignity is hardly convincing in its imprecision, and, as will be seen, does not fit the context of vv. 9–14 as a whole, particularly v. 14. (The view of Scott and van der Weiden that **the merciless** (*ʾazkārî*) refers to death, which was the punishment for adultery according to

Lev. 20:10 and Ezek. 16:40, is also implausible in view of v. 14.)

In view of the general context it is more probable (so Wildeboer, Toy, Gemser) that the verse refers to a situation in which the adulterer is financially ruined by the outraged husband or family of his partner (**others**; **the merciless** – the second of these terms may, however, refer to the usurer and his clutches). The loss of *hôd* (**honour** or dignity) would follow from his loss of wealth (compare again v. 14) – though *BHS*, following Syr. and Targ., suggests emendation to *ḥayil*, wealth (compare Gemser). (It may also be noted that for **your years** LXX has *son bion*, which can mean "your wealth, livelihood".)

10. This verse adds a little precision to the picture painted in v. 9. It confirms the interpretation of that verse given above. The **strangers** (*zārîm*) and **alien** (*nokrî*) may be members of the woman's family (see on 2:16) who, by whatever means, take their revenge by ruining the man (they are referred to in v. 9 simply as "others" (*'aḥērîm*). *kōaḥ* (*RSV* **strength**) should be rendered, as in *RSV*mg, by "wealth" (cf. Job 6:22). **to the house of**: literally "(are) in the house of". This may be a reference to a state of slavery to which the now impoverished man is reduced.

11. at the end of your life (*be'aḥarîtekā*): this is an improbable translation. Although this expression can refer to death or the approach to death (as perhaps in v. 4), there is no reason to suppose that here it means more than "afterwards" – that is (compare 19:20; 23:32; 25:8; 29:21), when the results of the young man's folly show themselves in terms of destitution and hunger. **and . . . you groan** (*wenāhamtā*): this verb is used in Isa. 5:29–30 of the roaring of a hungry lion. LXX and Syr. have "repent", a translation presumably based on *niḥam* rather than *nāham*; but this is improbable. The second line describes the state of starvation to which the young man has been reduced, and which provokes his cry of despair. **are consumed**: that is, have wasted away.

14. utter ruin: the phrase (*bekol-rā'*), literally "in every (kind of) evil", is imprecise. The only thing which is certain is that this final fate which would have almost (*kime'aṭ*, *RSV* **on the point of**), but not quite, overtaken the young man would have overtaken him openly and in public (**in the assembled congregation**). It is unlikely that it refers to capital punishment (see on v. 9), since if this were the case it would certainly have been stated more clearly as a deterrent. Oesterley and Ringgren think of physical punishment (compare 6:33); McKane of denunciation by the husband and a demand for damages. Others surmise that the reference is to ostracism by the community. Since it is not clear what is referred to, it is difficult to understand why the young man's fate is qualified by *kimᵉʿaṭ*, "almost". Possibly his words in vv. 12–14 are to be taken as a confession of his faults by which he succeeds in being let off with a caution; but this would seem to weaken the force of the threat.

the assembled congregation: the Hebrew uses two nouns: the phrase is *bᵉtôk qāhāl wᵉʿēdāh*, literally, "in the midst of the *qāhāl* and the *ʿēdāh*". The two terms are virtually synonymous, and this is probably a hendiadys. Although certain definite functions are ascribed to these assemblies in the post-exilic literature, no precise indication of function is given here. The terms may simply be used to denote any general gathering of the local community.

15–20. These verses, addressed to a married man on the subject of marital fidelity, are in a style quite different from what precedes. They are expressed in the imagery of love-poetry reminiscent of the Song of Songs (see below for details). However, v. 20, with its return to plain language and to the theme of the enticements of the *zārāh*, **loose woman** and *nokriyyāh*, **adventuress**, may be an editorial addition made in order to link vv. 9–19 to the original Instruction of vv. 1–8.

15. Drink water from your own cistern: in Isa. 36:16 this expression is used in a literal sense as part of an idyllic picture of peaceful domestic life in which ordinary people could enjoy their domestic amenities without interference. The **cistern** (*bôr*) was used for preserving a supply of rain-water. This may be a quotation of a popular maxim (Scott). But the second line shows that the meaning here is figurative. The **well** (*bᵉʾēr*) which provides flowing water (*nōzᵉlîm*, from *nāzal* "to flow" – that is, from a spring –) is a metaphor for sexual pleasure as in the very similar expression in Ca. 4:15, where the beloved is described as "a well of living water" (*bᵉʾēr mayim ḥayyîm*) and as "flowing streams" (*nōzᵉlîm*). The emphasis here is of course on the suffixes (**your own**): the husband is urged to confine his sexual gratification to intercourse with his own wife.

16. This verse is difficult for more than one reason, and can be interpreted in three quite different ways. Two of the difficulties are textual and syntactical. *RSV* renders it as a question. If this is correct, the question is equivalent to a negative admonition: such a thing ought *not* to occur. There is, however, no indication in the

Hebrew text that this is a question. The most obvious rendering would be as a positive statement: "Your springs *will* be . . .", though it is true that the interrogative particle *hª*- is not absolutely necessary, provided that it is clear from the context that a question is intended (*GK* 150a). On the other hand, some commentators, on the basis of LXX, hold that this was originally a *negative* sentence from which a negative particle (*pen*-, "lest" or *lō'*, "not") has been accidentally omitted.

The main problem, however, is the meaning of **your springs** (*ma'yᵉnōtékā) and (your)* **streams of water** (*palᵉgê-māyim*). These expressions are clearly a continuation of the sexual imagery begun in v. 15. But in v. 15 this imagery is applied to the *woman*; and some commentators (Gemser, Scott, Plöger) take the verse as referring to adultery not by the husband but by the *wife*, perhaps provoked by the husband's prior adultery. This view receives some support from the fact that in Ca. 4:15 (and also in 4:12) it is the *woman*, not the man, who is described not only as a "well of living water" (cf. Prov. 5:15) but also as a *ma'yān*. The more common view, however, is that springs and streams refer to the male semen, **scattered abroad** by the husband in intercourse with other women than his wife. (In both of these interpretations **abroad** and **in the streets** are taken to mean "outside the marital relationship".) A third, less probable, view is that the verse is a straightforward affirmative sentence: if the husband has intercourse only with his wife he will have numerous progeny who will be a public blessing to him (Snijders, Ringgren). In view of the context the most probable interpretation is that v. 16 is an interrogative sentence equivalent to a negative, and is part of the warning against adultery committed by the husband.

17. This verse suffers from the same ambiguity as v. 16, of which it is the continuation. If the reference is to the wife's adultery, **strangers** (*zārîm*, masculine) might refer to other men belonging to the same community (**with you**), who would thus have infringed the husband's rights over his wife. If on the other hand it is the husband who is the adulterer, *zārîm* may refer to the husband and family of the other women, who would presumably acquire rights over children who might be born of the union, while the natural father would have no such rights: he would have "scattered his seed abroad" and so deprived himself of an heir.

18. Whatever may be the correct interpretation of vv. 16–17, this verse is concerned with the behaviour of the husband. The sexual imagery is continued with yet another water metaphor: the husband's **fountain** (*māqôr*), that is, spring or well, will be **blessed**: this may be a reference to the bearing of legitimate children, though it may simply denote sexual enjoyment, as does the second line. *śāmēaḥ min-* (**rejoice in**) as in Ec. 2:10 means "to take pleasure *from*". **the wife of your youth**: this may be a deliberate reference to the similar expression in 2:17, where the abandonment of the "companion of youth" characterizes the "loose woman".

19. This verse contains three lines, an unusual but not unknown poetical form. The first line (**a lovely hind, a graceful doe**) should probably be taken with verse 18; but it contains no verb, is only loosely attached to its context and can only be construed as in apposition to "the wife of your youth" in v. 18 (or to the feminine verbs in v. 19). It is also not clear how it can be said of wives in general that they are **lovely** or **graceful** (on the form of these expressions, *'ayyelet ᵃhābîm* and *yaᵃlat ḥēn*, see *GK* 128p). The line may be a gloss – perhaps a quotation of a phrase from a current love-song. The proposal to extend it into a couplet by adding a line from the somewhat divergent LXX text (see *BHS* and *REB*) is unnecesssary. The language seems to be that of love-poetry: *'ayyālāh/'ayyelet* (**hind** or female deer) occurs in an erotic context in Ca. 2:7; 3:5, and in the same book the masculine *'ayyāl*, "stag", occurs as an epithet of the lover (2:9, 17; 8:14).

affection: the Hebrew has the plural of *dad*, "breast", a rare word which occurs elsewhere in the Old Testament only in Ezek. 23 (vv. 3, 8, 21). *RSV* appears to have accepted repointing to *dōd*, "love" on the basis of LXX, following some commentators. **fill . . . you with delight**: in Hebrew there is only one word here, literally "saturate, drench" (*rāwāh*, piel) and so "satisfy, sate" (cf. Jer. 31:14). **be infatuated**: literally, "you will be infatuated". The verb (*šāgāh*) means "go astray", sometimes with the implication of drunkenness. However, Driver (*WO* I, 1941, p. 410) postulated another verb *šāgāh* on the basis of an Arabic verb, giving the meaning "you will be wrapped".

At the end of this verse *NEB* adds a verse transposed from 6:22, partly because 6:22 fits awkwardly into its context in MT (see below) and partly on the grounds that LXX at 5:19 supposedly retains some fragments of 6:22. This has been rejected by *REB*. LXX is hardly reliable here, and the arguments for the transposition (on which see Skehan, 1971, pp. 1–8) are insufficient.

20. On the verse as a whole see on 5:15–20 above, and on **be infatuated** see on v. 19.

21–23. These verses are of a generalizing and moralistic character which marks them out from what precedes. One or more of them may have formed the conclusion of the original Instruction, which otherwise lacks a definite conclusion, but this is not certain. They themselves are not a literary unit. V. 21 was probably originally a detached proverb similar to those in the sentence literature (compare 15:3; 22:12). The introduction of a reference to Yahweh at the end of a chapter in which there has been no reference to him at all suggests a subsequent attempt at a Yahwistic interpretation of the whole.

21. watches (*m^e^pallēs*): on this verb see on 4:26. There and in 5:6 to "watch one's path" means to be careful where one walks, that is, behaves; here the same verb is used of Yahweh, who watches or scrutinizes the **paths** walked by human beings, with the implication that he will reward or punish them accordingly. This notion of an all-seeing God occurs frequently in the wisdom literatures of both Egypt and Israel. Although the verse in its present place purports to provide a motive or reason (**For**) for the avoidance of adultery, it is in itself a statement applicable to men (*'îš*) in general.

22. The iniquities . . . ensnare him: literally, "his iniquities ensnare him, the wicked". The construction is unusual. Many commentators regard **the wicked** as a gloss. If this is so, there is no antecedent for "his" and "him", since the "man" of v. 21 is a general term with no implication of wickedness. The construction (an anticipatory suffix, **him**) is not, however, entirely unknown (*GK* 60a, 131m). On the other hand the form **ensnare him** (*yilk^e^dūnô*) is anomalous, and the text may be corrupt (see the discussion in van der Weiden). In any case the verse can hardly have orginally been a continuation of v. 21.

The words **iniquities** (*^a^wônôt*) and **sin** (*ḥaṭṭā't*) are specifically religious terms which do not occur elsewhere in chapters 1–9, though the latter occurs five times in the sentence literature and the former (in the singular) once. This is an additional reason for supposing this verse to be a subsequent addition to the original Instruction.

23. This verse is clearly not the continuation of the preceding verse, since the theme has changed from that of wickedness to that of folly. In v. 22 the wicked person will be ensnared by his sin; the person in question here will perish through his **folly**. This theme is a reversion to that of the original Instruction (compare vv. 1–2); but it cannot have formed its conclusion because of the change from second person to third.

discipline: that is, *mûsār*, which is identified with "life" in 4:13.
he is lost (*yišgeh*): this verb, which occurs also in v. 19, normally means "to go astray". LXX here takes this to mean "to perish".

ADMONITIONS AND WARNINGS
6:1–19

The material in these verses differs both in form and substance from that by which it is surrounded. It is practical wisdom in the form of warnings of a very concrete and down-to-earth kind and consists of four quite independent pieces: vv. 1–5 on the inadvisability of standing security for others; vv. 6–11 on the disastrous consequences of indolence; vv. 12–15 on the fate of the mischief-maker; and vv. 16–19 on Yahweh's detestation of various sins against society. Most of these themes are to be found elsewhere in various parts of the book.

The four sections differ in form as well as theme. Vv. 1–5 are an Instruction, but one which differs markedly from those which form the bulk of chapters 1–9. Vv. 6–11 belong to a type of wisdom saying (compare parts of chapter 30) which comments on human character and behaviour by drawing analogies from animal behaviour. Vv. 12–15 convey a warning by means of a character-sketch. Vv. 16–19, again like much of the material in chapter 30, is a numerical proverb.

It is not clear why this material should have been placed here between two Instructions. It may perhaps be regarded as a continuation of the immediately preceding miscellaneous collection of wisdom sayings in 5:21–3. Whether it once existed as an independent collection before its insertion here is uncertain. If so, the fact that it begins with an Instruction and thus may have been held to be appropriate for inclusion in chapters 1–9 may have some bearing on its present position. It has also been suggested that the verb *lākad*, which occurs in v. 2 and also in 5:22 (**snared**, **ensnare**) may have served as a linking catchword.

1–5. *On the folly of standing security.* The opening word of this passage, **My son** (*b^e nî*), marks it out as an Instruction. But in contrast to the other Instructions in these chapters there is no introduction emphasizing the importance of the "father"'s words. The form is also different: it begins with a hypothetical situation expressed by a chain of conditional clauses (**if**, vv. 1 and 2) and proceeds to a series of imperatives prescribing urgent action which the person addressed must take in order to extricate himself from such a situation. There is no generalizing conclusion, and there is no mention either of God or of wisdom.

There are some uncertainties about the details of the situation envisaged (see below), but its general character is clear enough. The verb *'ārab* (**become surety**, v. 1) means to give a guarantee (to "go bail") to a creditor on behalf of another person, and the phrase *tāqa' kap*, literally, "to strike hands", in this context – though in this sense it occurs only in this book – must denote a ceremony connected with this. (*RSV* renders it by **have given your pledge**). Other passages in Proverbs on the same theme (11:15; 17:18; 20:16; 22:26–7; 27:13) help to some extent to fill out the picture. In particular, 22:27 shows that the pledge in question is a financial one: if the person on whose half the guarantee has been made defaults or is unable to pay, the amount pledged will become due. To give such guarantees in a moment of pity or generosity, therefore, is folly (17:18). It puts the guarantor into the power of the creditor (6:3), who may then seek to recoup his losses by distraining his goods (22:27) or even enslaving him or his family (compare 2 Kg 4:1–7). Throughout Proverbs the likelihood of such a disaster is thought to be so great that, although *giving* to the poor out of one's resources is strongly encouraged in several passages in the sentence literature, standing surety is equally forcefully and unconditionally condemned as an act of folly. Ben Sira's advice (Sir. 29:14–20) is rather different: to help one's neighbour in this way is the act of a good man, though one should first make sure that one has the means to pay if the demand is made. There is nothing in the laws of the Old Testament which deals with this matter.

1. The precise nature of the transaction is obscured by some ambiguities in the text: the meaning of the particle *l^e* in the phrase rendered by *RSV* as **for your neighbour**; the meaning of *zār* (*RSV* **stranger**); and the question whether *zār* and *rēa'* (**neighbour**) are the same person or not. With regard to the first point, the giving of a guarantee in someone's favour is elsewhere expressed by the verb *'ārab* with the accusative (*'ārab zār*, 11:15; 20:16; 27:13) and not as here by *'ārab l^e*. Consequently Wildeboer, Plöger and others hold that *l^e* in the first line of the verse means not "for" but "to": that is, the **neighbour** is not the debtor but the creditor, *to whom* the guarantee is made, while in the second line the undertaking is made *for*, that is, on behalf of, the debtor (here called *zār*: see on 2:16 for the meaning of this word in Proverbs). According to this interpretation, then, *l^e* has two quite different meanings within the same verse. Other commentators regard this interpretation as unnecessarily complicated: they maintain that *l^e* means "for, on behalf of" in both cases, and that the **neighbour** and **stranger** are the same person: the debtor. See also on v. 3.

More important is the question of the meaning of *zār* here. Boström (pp. 53ff.), whose thesis is that the feminine *zārāh* (2:16 and parallels) is a foreign woman, renders the masculine here also by "foreigner": he sees this passage as a warning against commercial transactions with foreigners, which are to be avoided. Unfortunately we are not well informed about what McKane calls "the complicated credit arrangements of commerce" in ancient Israel, and there is nothing in the text to support Boström's view. It is more probable that *zār* means an Israelite not of one's own family (though Snijders, pp. 86–7, thinks it means an "outsider" from Israelite society), and that the situation envisaged is a non-commercial one in which an impulsive act of private generosity may entail serious consequences for the guarantor.

2. if: not expressed in the Hebrew. All the four clauses in vv. 1–2 are parallel conditional clauses governed by the single *'im* (**if**) in v. 1. **snared in**; **caught in**: better, "snared/caught *by*". The guarantor is bound by his promise and finds himself unable to withdraw. **in the utterance of your lips**; **in the words of your mouth**: the Hebrew has the same phrase in both lines: "by the words of your mouth" (*b^e'imrê pîkā*). Such exact repetition is unusual in parallel lines, but emendation is probably not justified (see van der Weiden and Watson, 1984, pp. 42–3). Pesh. varies the expressions, but does not necessarily represent a variant Hebrew text.

3. and save yourself (*w^{e}hinnāṣēl*): the line is unusually long. This word occurs again in v. 5, and Toy, followed by Oesterley, proposed its omission here. **neighbour** (*rēa'*): the second occurrence of this word in the verse makes it probable that the person in question is the debtor, although both he and the creditor have the power to ruin the guarantor, the former by defaulting on his debt and the latter by demanding that the sum guaranteed be produced in case of the debtor's default. (On the spelling of the word on its second occurrence see *GK* 93ss.)

hasten (*hitrappēs*): the meaning of this word is uncertain. The verb *rāpas* (or *rāpaś*) in the qal means "stamp" or "tread down"; it has therefore been supposed by some that the hithpael imperative here means "humble yourself" (literally, "crush yourself"). However, Driver (*JTS* 30 [1929], pp. 374–5) argued that it means "exert yourself" (comparing Akkadian *ana ripsi*, "at once, urgently"). Vulg.'s *festina*, "hasten", conveys a similar idea. LXX's "do not faint" (fail) may represent a variant reading *'al-titrappeh* (hithpael of *rāpāh*). **importune**: literally, "storm at" (*rāhab*). The text does not suggest how this is to be done if the debtor is genuinely unable to pay his debt. The implication is perhaps simply that it would be extremely foolish to allow such a situation to arise.

4. your eyelids (*'ap'appekā*): see on 4:25, where *RSV* renders this word by "gaze".

5. from the hunter: this translation is based on a plausible emendation of the Hebrew text, which has simply "from the hand" (*miyyād*). Van der Weiden's suggestion that *yad* can mean the operative part of a snare, based on Ps. 141:9, is improbable. Several of the Versions have "snare", and there is therefore some ground for emendation to some such word as *paḥ*, "trap, snare" (less probably *māṣôd*, "net") or, as *RSV*, *ṣayyād*, **hunter**. This last suggestion involves only the replacement of a single consonant, and provides a good parallel for **fowler**. Almost all the commentators accept some such emendation.

6–11. *The disastrous consequences of indolence.* This is a theme which appears frequently in the sentence literature of Proverbs. This extended passage on the subject may be compared to the little story with a moral in 24:30–34. Animal fables were popular in Mesopotamia, and there are a number of extant examples from Sumerian literature. This passage, however, is not a fable, in which animals assume human characteristics, but stems from perceptive observation of actual animal habits. In the Old Testament the notion that one can learn lessons from animals appears several times, notably in Job 12:7; Isa. 1:3; Jer. 8:7. Solomon's wise sayings included animal sayings (1 Kg 4:33 [Heb. 5:13]), though no details are given.

Among the creatures whose habits were believed to be in some sense models for human behaviour were *ants*. In the Amarna Letters there is a Canaanite example which, however, fastens on a different characteristic of the behaviour of ants from that described here (*ANET*, p. 486). In Proverbs there is one other reference to ants (the only other one in the Old Testament): 30:25, "The ants are a people not strong, yet they provide their food in the summer". It is striking that the second line of this verse is almost verbally identical with 6:8a. The saying in 30:25 is part of a numerical proverb which has assembled examples of creatures which are small, yet wise. 6:6–8 also proposes the ant as a model of wisdom in its foresight and activity in securing its food supply for the winter, but makes its behaviour more directly relevant to its purpose by stressing that it acts on its own initiative and without the need for supervision rather than by a reference to its weakness and small size. The moral, expressed in vv. 9–11 is plain.

6. sluggard (*'āṣēl*): see on 10:26. **consider**: literally, "see, observe". **and be wise**: that is, "and you will become wise" (*GK* 110f).

7. chief, **officer**: these words (*qāṣîn, šōṭēr*) are here used in a general sense of persons in authority.

8. summer, **harvest**: no contrast is intended here. These were seasons when it was essential both to gather "summer fruit" (especially grapes) and to harvest the grain (compare 10:5).

At the end of this verse LXX adds a paragraph about the bee, whose wisdom is equally shown by its diligence, and which is also useful to mankind. This addition is peculiar to LXX.

10–11. These verses are virtually identical (see on **like a vagabond**) with 24:33–4, where they constitute the "moral" of a little story. This perhaps suggests that they are a proverbial saying which has been worked up in different ways.

10. A little: the tone is ironical. In view of the plural nouns (*šēnôt* and *tᵉnûmôt*) "a few" would be a better translation of this word in the first two occurrences of it in the verse. **folding of the hands**: this was presumably a common expression: compare Ec. 4:5. **to rest**: literally, "to lie down"; this is an extended meaning – compare Job 30:17; Ec. 2:23.

11. like a vagabond (*kimᵉhallēk*, piel participle of *hālak*, "to go, walk"). 24:34 in the parallel passage has the hithpael *mithallēk*. Plöger takes this word as a participle qualifying **will come**: "und schon ist schnell deine Armut da" = "and your poverty has already quickly come"; but most commentaries take it as a participle used as a noun: a vagabond or vagrant (Barucq, Scott) or a highwayman (Toy, Gemser, Ringgren).

an armed man: literally, "a man of (with?) a shield" (*'îš māgēn*). Unfortunately this expression also is of doubtful meaning and so does not assist the interpretation of *kimᵉhallēk*, with which it is parallel. Some commentators take the same view as *RSV*; but the phrase is unique and somewhat odd. Others follow either Driver or Albright. The former (*JTS* 33 [1932], p. 44; 34 [1933], p. 383) takes it to mean a bold or impudent man, connecting it with Arabic *mājīn*; *KB*³ accepts this. The latter (1955, pp. 9–10) interprets it as meaning "beggar", on the basis of Ugaritic *mgn*, "to beg, entreat". The general meaning of the verse is, however, clear: the lazy person will find himself confronted with destitution, which will come upon him without his being aware of its approach.

12–15. *The fate of the mischief-maker.* This description of the worthless person or wicked man whose aim is to cause trouble may be compared with 16:27–30 and Sir. 27:22–4. There is no ostensible motive for his conduct: all that he does springs from deep-seated corruption. This is an elaborate extension, perhaps in the spirit of the numerical proverb (compare vv. 16–19), of the simple statement that the wicked will come to a bad end, such as is made frequently in the sentence literature of Proverbs, e.g. 11:18, 21; 12:7.

12. A worthless person (*'ādām bᵉliyya'al*): on this meaning of *'ādām* see on 3.30. A more common phrase is *'îš bᵉliyya'al* (cf. Prov. 16:27). The precise derivation of *bᵉliyya'al* is uncertain, but its usage elsewhere in the Old Testament suggests that here it denotes depravity or wickedness rather than merely worthlessness. It is appropriately paralleled with *'îš 'āwen* (**a wicked man**). If the pointing of *'ādām* is correct (but see Driver, *Canaanite Myths and Legends*, Edinburgh, 1956, p. 135, n. 6), *bᵉliyya'al* is in apposition to *'ādām* (see *GK*. 131 c), its literal meaning thus being "a man *who is* wickedness".

crooked speech: see on 4:24.

12b–14. If the text is in order (see below on v. 13), these verses list six examples of the behaviour of the wicked man, all except the last expressed in participial clauses. They begin with his misuse of parts of the body and then proceed to the **heart** (v. 14a) or inner self (see 4:23) of which these are the external agents and reach their climax with what appears to be a concrete statement of the nature of the **evil** which he **devises**: he is **continually sowing discord**.

13. The significance of these actions is not clear. **winks with his eyes**: Ps. 35:19; Prov. 10:10; 16:30 contain similar expressions which refer to hostile or malevolent actions, but shed no further light on their purpose. **scrapes**: this translation is uncertain. This verb (*mālal*), if it is to be distinguished from *mālal* "to speak", occurs only here in the Old Testament, and its use in later Hebrew does not entirely justify this rendering. Plöger and others render it by "speaks", that is, "makes a sign". **points**: the hiphil of *yrh* (here the participle *mōreh*) usually means "teach"; but here probably "point" or "point out". The verse thus refers to three movements of the body made with **eyes**, **feet** and **finger**. This "sinister sign language" (McKane) may be connected with malevolent magic, or may be a means of conveying secret information to a confederate. The verse remains obscure. It may be significant that the passage makes good sense without it, although it is present in all the Versions.

14. *RSV*'s rendering of the first line is hardly possible. There is slight manuscript evidence that **evil** may be superfluous (see Toy, Gemser, McKane). If it is omitted, *tahpūkôt* (*RSV* **perverted**) may be taken as the object of the verb and the line rendered "devises mischief (on this word see on 2:12) in his heart continually". **sowing**: literally, "letting loose". **discord**: Kethib and Qere have alternative forms of this word.

15. calamity: literally, "his calamity".

16–19. *A numerical proverb.* This passage has affinities with vv. 12–15 which no doubt account for the juxtaposition of the two passages here. Like vv. 12–15 it lists a number of unpleasant human traits; it associates these with parts of the body; and in its final item (v. 19b) it verbally echoes, in the phrase **sows discord**, the final item in the earlier list (v. 14b). However, it differs from v. 12–15 in two main respects: rather than describing the fate of such persons in impersonal terms as in v. 15, it denounces them as particularly hateful to Yahweh; and it is cast in the form of the "numerical proverb".

Characteristic of the numerical proverb is that it does not merely set out a list of items side by side without overtly specifying their common features, but in a (usually) introductory statement specifies that these are linked by such a common feature (here that they are hateful to Yahweh) and states how many such items there are. This type of saying is not restricted to the Old Testament, but is found among a variety of peoples including the Babylonians, Indians, Arabs and Greeks, and also occurs in post-biblical Jewish literature. (See Roth, 1965). Such lists are believed to constitute early attempts to understand the principles of order in the universe, including human nature and society, by classification and enumeration. Other numerical sayings in Proverbs are 30:7–9, 11–14, 15c–16, 18–19, 21–3, 24–8, 29–31 (30: 11–14, however, lacks the introductory statement). It has been supposed that the origin of the numerical saying is to be found in the posing of riddles, in which persons were asked to guess which things within a specified number had a particular common feature; but this is purely speculative and is not now generally accepted.

Another feature of this proverb, which is also found in some of the numerical proverbs in chapter 30 (vv. 15, 18, 21, 29) is that of the so-called "graded numerical saying" in which not one but two different numerals occur in parallelism, the first being one less than the actual number of items in the list (see Roth, 1962, pp. 300–311). This device, also known as "the numerical sequence x/x + 1", is not peculiar to the numerical proverb but also occurs in a variety of different types of literature in the Old Testament, the most familiar examples being found in Am. 1:3, 6, 9, 11, 13; 2:1, 4, 6. It also occurs in Ecclesiasticus and in Sumerian, Akkadian and Ugaritic texts. Its function is probably purely rhetorical: it heightens tension and also assists poetical parallelism, avoiding the repetition of the same word in parallel lines. The view that it denotes an indefinite number (e.g. "six or seven") is improbable in view of the fact that here as in other examples the second numeral corresponds exactly to the number of things in the list which follows.

16. abomination: this word (*tôʿēbāh*) here connotes not something which is of itself evil, but an attitude of intense hatred towards something: thus in 13:19b and 29:27b it is used of *virtuous* conduct as being hateful to fools or to the wicked. Conduct which is an abomination to Yahweh includes idolatry and cultic or ritual offences, but also ethical ones. It destroys the possibility of a positive relationship with Yahweh (cf. 3:32). Hence lists were compiled (e.g. in Pss. 15 and 24) of Yahweh's ethical requirements for approaching him in the temple. These could be expressed either positively or negatively. Job 31 is an example of such a list, consisting mainly of ethical items, placed in the context of a private communication with

God. Prov. 6:16–19, which covers much of the same ground as the other lists, may be assumed to have been composed for the purpose of ethical instruction. In intention it is comparable to the legal prohibitions of the Decalogue.

17. haughty eyes (*'ênayim rāmôt*): literally, "high – i.e. elevated – eyes", a sign of pride (cf. Ps. 18:2, 28 [Heb. 28, 29]; 131:1). In Isa. 2:11 this attitude is condemned as directed against God, but here it probably refers to arrogance towards other persons. The expression occurs again in Prov. 30:13 in a similar list. **a lying tongue** (*l^eš*ôn *šāqer*): literally, "a tongue of falsehood." See on 4:24 and compare 6:12. Since *šeqer* is repeated in v. 19 (*RSV* **false**), it is clear that this list is not intended to be a systematic or comprehensive catalogue of persons abominated by Yahweh. It is a miscellaneous collection. Lying is put on a par with murder in this verse because, as v. 19 shows, its effects, as in the case of false testimony, can be murderous – as in the "trial" of Naboth (1 Kg. 21). V. 19 in fact mentions two examples of malicious lying which would come under the more general heading of a "lying tongue".

18. This verse does not specify particular actions but is concerned with the **heart**, the inner, hidden organ from which spring all particular actions (compare v. 14), and with the **feet**, often referred to elsewhere in these chapters as part of the imagery of the journey through life but also seen as the agency by means of which a person "proceeds" to put his plans into action. So the verse as a whole speaks of actions first decided on and then carried out. LXX lacks **to run**, and this is omitted by some commentators as superfluous and as overloading the metrical line. But compare 1:16.

19. If the word *yāpîaḥ* (*RSV* **breathes out**) is in fact a verb, the order of the words in the first line is very unusual: verb, object, subject. Such inversion does, however, occasionally occur (*GK* 142f). Gemser, however, suggested that here and in 12:17 and 14:5 *yāpîaḥ* may be a noun, equivalent in meaning to *'ēd*, **witness**. The line would then consist of two phrases, each meaning "a lying/false witness". But no Hebrew noun *yāpîaḥ* is otherwise attested, and Gemser's proposal hardly improves the sense. It should be noted that 6:19a is identical with 14:5b. See also on 19:5.

NINTH INSTRUCTION
AVOIDANCE OF THE "STRANGE WOMAN"
6:20–35

Like chapter 5, this section consists of an Instruction to which further material on the general theme of the folly of adultery has been added. The usual address by the teacher to the pupil ends with v. 25; in the remainder, the adulterer is always referred to in the third person. In vv. 26–8 words and expressions denoting both the woman and the man are used which occur nowhere else in these Instructions: *'iššāh zōnāh*, "prostitute" (*RSV* **harlot**) and *'ēšet 'îš*, "married woman" (v. 26; *RSV* **adulteress** [!]); *'îš*, "a man", that is, "any man" (vv. 27, 28; *RSV* **a man** and **one** respectively). The question form used here is also a device not found elsewhere in the Instructions, as also is the imagery. Vv. 29–31, 33–5 use the threat of concrete forms of punishment including the wronged husband's revenge as deterrents from adultery, whereas in the Instructions the fate of the adulterer is described in general terms such as deterioration of character and "death".

A comparison with the original form of other Instructions suggests that this Instruction originally consisted of vv. 20–22, 24–5. V. 23 was not part of the original Instruction but consists of a gloss followed by what appears to be an originally separate comment (see below). It is possible that some small part of vv. 26–35 formed an original conclusion to the Instruction (compare 1:19; 4:18–19); if so, this may have been v. 32, which asserts that the adulterer **destroys himself**, a fate comparable to the "death" of the other Instructions.

Vv. 26–35 themselves appear not to have been a single literary unit but rather to be a series of unconnected additions. Several verses present difficulties of interpretation.

20–22. This introduction is characteristic of the series. With v. 20 compare 1:8 and, in part, 2:1–2; 3:1, 21; 4:1; 5:1; 7:1–2. With v. 21 compare 3:3 and also 1:9; 3:22. With v. 22 compare 3:23–4; 4:12.

21–22. It has often been pointed out that there are striking similarities between these verses and two passages in Deuteronomy. (6:6–8 and 11:18–19). All three passages use similar though not entirely identical, imagery in enjoining unremitting attention and obedience to teaching just given or about to be given: parental teaching in the case of Proverbs and the Law of Moses in Deuteronomy. They all employ language in which the **heart** is the repository of the teaching, and in this connection they all use the verb *qāšar*, **bind**, as a metaphor, though with reference to different parts of the body (Proverbs, **upon your heart**; Deuteronomy, "on your hand"); and they all stress that the teaching in question must be borne in mind at all times, using the identical grammatical form (Prov. 6:22 **when you walk**; **when you lie down**; **when you awake**; Dt. 6:7 and 11:19 similarly "when you sit / walk / lie down / rise"). In other respects, however, there are important differences between the Proverbs and Deuteronomic passages. It is generally admitted that there is some connection between them; but there is no agreement about the directness of the influence, nor, supposing it to be a direct one, on its direction. McKane speaks of the Proverbs passage as "a free adaptation of Dt. 6:7 or 11:19", while Weinfeld (*Deuteronomy and the Deuteronomic School*, 1972, pp. 299–302) sees Deuteronomy as having here, as elsewhere, "employed modes of expression and imagery taken from the sapiential sphere", adapting the latter in the service of its distinctive concept of the nature of the Law. One of the difficulties to be faced in attempts to solve the problem is that neither the passage in Proverbs nor that in Deuteronomy can be securely dated. One may perhaps cautiously speak of a *convergence* of wisdom and Deuteronomistic teaching at this point.

22. In the Hebrew text all the verbs are in the singular ("she/it will . . ."). In LXX they are all plural; but LXX here has certainly attempted to "improve" the text. On the proposal (*NEB* but not *REB*) to transpose the verse to follow 5:19, where the antecedent would be the wife, see on that verse. Some commentators (e.g. Plöger) consider that the singular verbs show that the author was thinking of the parental teaching of v. 20 as constituting a singular whole; but this does not explain the change from plural to singular between vv. 21 and 22. Perhaps a more plausible explanation is that a line has been omitted similar to 7:4a ("Say to wisdom, 'You are my sister'"). This would account for the unusual three-line verse in the present text, since the restoration of such a line would make two complete couplets. It would also account for the otherwise odd personification or semi-personification in the verse (**will talk with you**), which would be more appropriate to wisdom than to the parental teaching.

when you awake: on this unusual construction (the "hypothetical perfect") see *GK* 159h and S.R. Driver, *Tenses*, section 154 and note 2.

23. The first line of this verse, which interrupts the normal passage from the introduction to the main body of the Instruction, is a gloss defining the meaning of the words **commandment** (*miṣwāh*) and **teaching** (*tôrāh*) used in v. 20, but in a sense not intended by the author of the Instruction. In the Instructions these two words always refer to parental teaching (1:8; 2:1; 3:1; 4:2, 4; 7:1, 2). Here they are defined as **a lamp** (*nēr*) and **a light** (*'ôr*) respectively. *nēr* and *'ôr* are frequently used figuratively, especially in the wisdom literature, sometimes as a parallel pair (Job 18:6; 29:3; Prov. 13:9), to denote success and wellbeing. But they are never used, either separately or together, in these Instructions in this sense, or in connection with the parental teaching. On the other hand, *'ôr* is frequently used in the Old Testament as a figure denoting the salvation bestowed by God (e.g. Isa. 51:4 – in connection with *tôrāh*; Ps. 43:3; compare Ps. 19:8 [Heb. 9] where Yahweh's *commandments* [*miṣwôt*] "enlighten the eyes"), and it was on this basis that the Targums and other early Jewish writings interpreted "light" as meaning the Law of Moses in a number of other biblical texts (see Vermes, 1958, pp. 436–8). Although God is not specifically mentioned in Prov. 6:23, the strong resemblance of the first line to Ps. 119:105, where in a psalm entirely devoted to the praise of the Law, the psalmist speaks of Yahweh's word – that is, Law – as a *nēr* and an *'ōr*, makes it probable that this gloss, inserted at the end of the introductory section of the Instruction as a kind of "footnote", had the Law in mind and reinterpreted v. 20 in this sense. McKane, although he does not regard the verse as a later addition to the Instruction, concludes that "figures of speech which are redolent of the piety inspired by the Law have been imported" into it. The second line of the verse is expressed in terms reminiscent of the language of the Instructions, but can also be seen as an expansion of the first (so Plöger).

24–25. These verses constitute the admonition or main body of the original Instruction. Much of the language is the same as or similar to that of the corresponding passages in other Instructions. **to preserve you** reappears in 7:5; **adventuress** (*nokriyyāh*) in 2:16 and 7:5. **smooth words**, that is, seductive speech, are echoed in slightly different ways but using the same root (*ḥlq*) in all the three comparable Instructions (2:16; 5:3; 7:5). The phrase **the evil**

woman (*'ēšet rā'*) has no counterpart in the other Instructions, but the fact that it is paralleled by *nokriyyāh* has suggested to some commentators that it should be emended to *'iššāh zārāh* ("the loose woman"), making a pair which is found in 2:16 and 7:5 (see below).

24. the evil woman (*'ēšet rā'*), literally, "woman of evil": this phrase does not occur elsewhere in the old Testament, but compare "men of evil" in 28:5. McKane accepts this reading, but the majority of commentators repoint to *'ešet rēa'*, literally "the wife of a neighbour", that is, a married woman, as in v. 29. This is supported by LXX, which clearly read the same consonants as here. Toy, however, followed by *BHS*, emended the phrase to *'iššāh zārāh* (compare 7:5a which would then be identical with this line). This may be correct in view of the parallelism with *nokriyyāh* in the second line (see also above on 6:20–35).

from the smooth tongue of . . . : *lāšôn* (**tongue**) is in the absolute state in MT, and a literal translation of the line would therefore be "from the smoothness of the strange/foreign tongue". But most commentators and *BHS* repoint to the construct *l^ešôn*. LXX, however, has "of a strange tongue".

25. her eyelashes (*'ap'appehā*): this may be a reference to the seductive devices employed by the woman; but see on 4:25.

26. This verse was described by Driver (*VT* 4 [1954], p. 243) as "a proverb which no one has yet explained". However, most commentators agree that it makes a contrast between the demands made by the common prostitute (*'iššāh zōnāh*, *RSV* **harlot**) and by the **adulteress** (the Hebrew has *'ēšet* 'îš, literally "a woman who has a husband") on men who have sexual relations with them: the former's fee is low (**a loaf of bread**), whereas the adulteress seeks far more (whether of a monetary or other kind).

The first line has no verb; but *RSV*'s explanatory addition of **may be hired** almost certainly expresses the intended meaning, whether *b^e'ad* (**for**) is in fact a preposition or whether it is a noun meaning "price" or "exchange" (so Driver). The Versions have nouns here meaning "price".

The second line is more difficult because the meaning of *nepeš y^eqārāh* (*RSV* **a man's very life**, literally "a precious life") is disputed. *nepeš* has many meanings including "soul", "person" and "life". However, Driver argues that it sometimes means "abundance", and that since *yāqār* (this word is not directly translated by *RSV*) means "precious", the phrase should be rendered by "costly abundance":

that is, the adulteress, unlike the prostitute who is satisfied with a little bread, demands a life of luxury from her lover. Thomas (*VT* Suppl. 3, 1955, pp. 283–4) renders *nepeš yᵉqārāh* by "a weighty person": that is, she will only accept a wealthy man as her lover. Both Driver's and Thomas's interpretations agree in seeing here a contrast between the prostitute's modest demand and the excessive cost of a liaison with a married woman, who may ruin her lover by her excessive demands.

The verse is, then, a warning about the folly of adultery; the main problem is whether the penalty which it envisages is merely financial – as in vv. 31, 35 – or death. The latter interpretation, which is favoured by *RSV*, is perhaps the less probable in view of the strangeness of the expression *nepeš yᵉqārāh* in this connection. **stalks**: this verb (*ṣûd*) means "to hunt", and is sometimes used metaphorically of persecution. It may be significant that Ezekiel (13:18, 20) also refers to "hunting souls", using the same verb though in a different mode (*ṣôdēd nᵉpāšôt*), as a magical practice. But it is not clear whether this practice was intended to gain control over other persons or to bring about their deaths. The Ezekiel passage therefore does not solve the main problem of the verse.

The language and style of this verse are quite different from those of the preceding verses and of the comparable Instructions in these chapters (see above on 6:20–35).

27–29. These verses give a quite different reason for avoiding adultery from that given in v. 26: the adulterer will not **go unpunished** (v. 29). What kind of punishment is envisaged is not stated: it may be divine punishment, legal or other punishment by the community, or punishment at the hands of the wronged husband, as in vv. 33–5 (see below). The play on words in v. 27 – *'îš . . . 'ēš* (**a man . . . fire**) – is reminiscent of *'ēšet 'îš*, "a woman who has a husband", in v. 26, and this similarity of sound may account for the present position of these verses. The questions in vv. 27 and 28, a form which does not occur in the Instructions, are also an indication that the passage is not part of the original Instruction. The questions themselves are examples of what Crenshaw (1979, pp. 96–111, especially 100–105) has called "impossible questions": they specify absurdly foolish and fatal actions universally recognized as such, which are then equated with the dangerous folly of committing adultery.

29. (**none . . .**) **will go unpunished** (*yinnāqeh*): literally, "will be held innocent". This phrase occurs frequently in the sentence literature of Proverbs (11:21; 16:5; 17:5; 19:5, 9; 28:20). In each case some form of wicked behaviour is named, and the verse expresses certainty that its perpetrator will not escape punishment; but neither the form which the punishment will take nor the identity of the agent of punishment is specified, with one exception: in 16:5 it is strongly implied that Yahweh himself will execute the punishment. It is reasonable to suppose that this is the case also in the other verses that are worded in exactly the same way, including this verse (6:29).

30–31. Although the interpretation of this passage is difficult and much disputed, v. 31 makes it clear that what is envisaged here is not divine punishment, as probably in v. 29, but human punishment. This is in fact a new theme: adultery and its consequences are now compared and contrasted implicitly – or explicitly if v. 32 belongs to this pericope – with the professional thief (*gannāb*) and what happens to him when he is caught. But the nature of the argument is obscure, and no commentator has succeeded in elucidating it satisfactorily.

In the Hebrew text v. 30 is ostensibly not a question but a statement: "Men *do not* despise". If this is indeed the meaning, the connection between it and v. 31 is difficult to understand: the thief who steals because he is hungry is *not* despised by others, yet if he is caught he will be severely punished, presumably by the same people, who form the community in which he lives (translating *wᵉnimṣā'*, *RSV* **And if he is caught**, adversatively: "*Yet* if he is caught" – an equally possible translation). This has been taken as an implied *a fortiori* argument: if thieves are punished when caught even if they have the excuse of hunger, how much more severely will the adulterer be punished, who has no excuse! But this does not explain the statement in v. 30 that such thieves are not despised. An alternative interpretation would be that a theft committed by a desperate man, which runs the risk of apprehension and punishment, is committed through necessity, not folly, whereas the adulterer's equally hazardous theft of another man's wife has neither excuse nor necessity and is simply stupid. Neither of these interpretations is really satisfactory, partly because there is nothing elsewhere in the Old Testament to suggest that theft was ever condoned in ancient Israel.

The main alternative, accepted by many commentators and modern translations including *RSV*, is to understand v. 30 as a *question* expressed without an interrogative particle (see *GK* 150a) which has the force of a positive statement: "Do not men despise . . . ?" = "Men *do* despise . . .". According to this interpretation the thief is *both* despised by his fellows *and*, if caught, also severely punished; even more so, it is implied, will the adulterer be. McKane and Plöger seek to strengthen this argument by taking *kî yirʿāb* (**when he is hungry**) as meaning "*even if* he is hungry": hunger is no excuse. (It may be remarked that there is probably a hidden allusion here to the adulterer in the words *to satisfy his appetite when he is hungry*: this is precisely the motive of the adulterer who "steals" someone else's wife because he cannot control his sexual appetite.) However, it is doubtful whether v. 30 can in fact be rendered as a question. As the list of examples in *GK* shows, questions not preceded by an interrogative particle in the Old Testament normally occur in direct speech, are quite short, and in their contexts present no problem of ambiguity. None of these conditions is present here. (See also on 5:16 above.)

There is a further difficulty in these verses: in v. 30 the thief is impelled by desperate hunger, yet in v. 31 he has his own **house** in which he stores his wealth (*kol-hôn bêtô*, "all the wealth (*RSV* **goods**) of his house"! This discrepancy may perhaps suggest that v. 30 is a gloss, and that v. 31 refers directly to the adulterer and is the continuation of v. 29. All these difficulties suggest that the text of these verses may be in serious disorder.

31. sevenfold: no such penalty for theft is to be found in the laws of the Old Testament. There the penalty is two, four or five times according to the circumstances (Exod. 22:1–4, 7 [Heb. 21:37; 22:1–3, 6]). No sufficient explanation has been found for this discrepancy; it has been suggested that the word indicates perfect restitution (compare Ps. 79:12), but this is unlikely. Perhaps the passage reflects a quite different custom of which nothing is otherwise known. The reference is unlikely to be to adultery, for which the prescribed penalty was death (Lev. 20:10; Dt 22:22), to which, however, there is no reference (in a literal sense) in Proverbs.

32–35. There are indications that these verses also are of miscellaneous origin. V. 32 is expressed in very general terms and bears the marks of an independent proverb of a type frequently found in the sentence literature. More specifically, the term *ḥᵃsar-lēb*, **has no sense** (literally, "lacking in heart"; see on 2:2; 4:21, 23), equivalent to "fool", is used regularly there, and one such proverb (12:11) uses it in precisely the same way as here: "he who follows worthless pursuits has no sense". As has been suggested, the verse may have been the conclusion of the original Instruction, or, less probably, it may have been attached to vv. 30–31. In either case, v. 33 may well be a later addition to it, expanding it in concrete terms. (It has also been suggested that v. 32 is an interpolation breaking the connection between vv. 31 and 33.) V. 34 may also have originally been a detached proverb to which again a more concrete exposition has been given in v. 35. It should be noted that in v. 35 there is a sudden change from the impersonality of the third person to the address of the second (**you**), and that vv. 34–5 partly reiterate, partly contradict, what has already been said in earlier verses.

32. The Hebrew of the second line (*mašḥît napšô hû' ya^{ca}śennāh*) is unusual. Plöger translates: "he who (wishes to) destroy his life, let him do so". Others have noted a quite separate problem: many recent commentators, on the grounds that **he who does it** (or "let him do so") makes a somewhat feeble parallel, have followed Kopf (1959, pp. 270–71) and Dahood respectively in postulating a second verb *'āśāh* quite distinct from *'āśāh* "to do, make", rendering *ya^{ca}śennāh* either by "sleeps with her" (on the basis of an Arabic root) or "abuses her" (on the basis of an Ugaritic one) compare *REB*). Plöger, however, finds the usual translation satisfactory.

33. Wounds and dishonour: the former presumably at the hands of the husband; the latter, of the community.

34. For jealousy makes a man furious: literally, "jealousy (is) a man's anger". Most recent commentators, however, follow Driver (*Bib.* 32 [1951], p. 177) in reversing the order of the consonants of *ḥ^{a}mat* ("the anger of") and repointing it, giving *tāḥēm*, "inflames": "jealousy inflames a man".

35. gifts: that is, bribes (*šōḥad*). The legal penalty for adultery was death according to the laws of the Pentateuch (see on v. 31 above). It is curious that here (and in vv. 31, 33) much more lenient customs seem to be presupposed, though it has been suggested that what is alluded to here is an attempt to avoid otherwise inevitable trial and execution by making offers of compensation and large bribes to the husband, on whose complaint an action would otherwise be brought.

TENTH INSTRUCTION
AVOIDANCE OF THE "STRANGE WOMAN"
7:1–27

The character, structure and approximate length of the original Instructions in these chapters are now familiar to the reader. With these in mind it is not difficult to discern that this chapter mainly consists of two elements: a relatively short Instruction into which has been inserted a moral tale. Each is complete in itself. The original Instruction consisted of vv. 1–3, 5, 25–7. With its introduction (vv. 1–3) and its single admonition (vv. 5, 25–7) which includes its own warning and needs no generalized and impersonal conclusion, it has a particularly strong resemblance to the Second Instruction (2:1, 9, 16–19) – on this and on the whole chapter see Whybray, 1966, pp. 482–6.

Vv. 6–23 are a vivid and polished moral story having its own introduction, development and conclusion. Its theme and evident purpose show that it comes from the same circles as the Instructions, but there are many indications that it was originally an independent poem. The expression **dressed as a harlot** (v. 10; compare 6:26) shows that the woman in this story is not the same as the **loose woman** and **adventuress** of v. 5: **harlot** (*zônāh*) never occurs in the original Instructions. It is also clear that v. 25, which resumes the Instruction, originally immediately followed v. 5, like 6:24 and 25 which these two verses closely resemble. In its present position v. 25 has no antecedent, since the woman there referred to (**her**) cannot be the woman of vv. 6–23, who is a character in the teacher's story and not the woman against whom the pupil is directly warned in v. 5.

In fact vv. 6–23 constitute a very great expansion of the theme of the Instructions about adultery which is full of fascinating and vivid details marking it out as a very different kind of composition. The description of the woman's character, dress and methods of seduction occupy six verses (18–23); her seductive speech, only briefly mentioned in v. 5 and in its parallels in other Instructions, is here quoted at length (vv. 14–20). There is a description of the furnishings of her bedroom (vv. 16–17); her husband, his business and his absence on a journey are referred to (vv. 19–20), as also is the reaction of the young man and his fate, described in striking imagery (vv. 22–23).

Two verses remain to be accounted for: 4 and 24. V. 24 is virtually identical with 5:7, which, as has been seen, is an intrusion into that Instruction whose purpose is not entirely clear. The purpose of 7:24, however, is quite transparent. It is a somewhat crude device intended to mark the resumption of the thread of discourse which was broken off by the insertion of vv. 6–23 between vv. 5 and 25, and to create a smooth transition from v. 23 to v. 25. On v. 4, which interrupts the continuity between vv. 3 and 5, see below.

1–3. Although there are small variations in detail, there is here once again a very close verbal similarity between these verses and the introductions to other Instructions in this series, and some exact verbal repetitions. V. 1b is identical with 2:1b, v. 2a with 4:4c, and v. 3b with 3:3c. **keep** (*šāmar*), used twice here (vv. 1a, 2a) with **my words** and **my commandments** respectively as its object, is found in 4:21; **my words** (*ᵃmāray*, v. 1a) in 2:1; 4:20; *tôrāh*, teaching, in 1:8; 4:2; 6:20; **commandment(s)** (*miṣwāh, miṣwôt*) in 2:1; 6:20. Many of these terms are clearly used interchangeably. Some of these coincidences and similarities may be due to editorial assimilation of one passage to another or may be the work of glossators drawing attention to comparable passages. But this was evidently the technical vocabulary of education, which provided a stock of terms available for selection by individual teachers and offered the possibility, within strict limits, of stylistic variety.

2. as the apple of your eye: as the context suggests, and as the other occurrences (Dt. 32:10; Ps. 17:8) confirm, this phrase denotes something especially precious, a meaning which has passed into some European languages including English. In a literal sense the "apple" of the eye is the pupil. *'îšôn* is a diminutive form of *'îš*, "a man": one's image reflected in the eye of another person was seen as a "little man" looking out.

3. bind them on your fingers: the corresponding verse in 3:3 has "about your neck". On a possible connection with Dt. 6:8; 11:18, which have "on your hand", see on 6:21. The **fingers** are obviously a place where one might wear a ring or possibly a protective amulet. But, like the neck (1:9; 3:3, 22; 6:21) they are a part of the body where ornaments would be constantly seen and so could be a reminder of something: they would not "depart from the eyes" (4:21). This is thus another figure expressing the importance of never forgetting the teacher's counsels. On **the tablet of your heart** see on 3;3; and compare Jer. 31:33.

4. This is the only reference to Wisdom in this chapter; it should also be noted that God is not mentioned in it at all. Unlike the additions to chapter 2 (vv. 2ff.) which introduce Wisdom as identical with or parallel to the teacher's words, it is a brief intervention which remains undeveloped. The remainder of the chapter, including the poem of vv. 6–23, is the personal instruction of a human teacher. The purpose of the addition was probably to contrast a personified Wisdom with the "loose woman" of v. 5, and, as in 9:1–6, 13–18, to stress that a choice has to be made between the two. (See also the introduction to 7:1–27.)

sister: in Song of Songs (as also elsewhere in the ancient Near East) this word signifies the beloved; in Ca. 4:9, 10, 12; 5:1 it is linked with "bride". This may be the meaning here (see on 4:8), though *mōdāʿ* (**intimate friend**) seems to suggest a lesser relationship: it is cognate with *yādaʿ*, "to know", and appears in its only other occurrence in the Old Testament (Ruth 2:1) to mean "relative", probably as one likely to be an intimate confidant.

5. This verse is identical with 2:16 apart from the first word, where the latter has "to save you" (*lᵉhaṣṣîlᵉkā, RSV* "You will be saved"). Compare also 6:24.

6–7. The person who speaks here and in the following verses may be presumed to be a teacher of young men similar to those who speak in the Instructions. He tells a story supposedly based on his own observation ending with an implied moral (vv. 22–3). This is a standard teaching device in the wisdom literature: compare Prov. 4:3–5; 24:30–34; Ps. 37:35–6; Job 5:3–5.

There is, however, a striking difference between vv. 6–7 in the Hebrew text and in LXX. In the latter, which is otherwise broadly though not entirely in line with the Hebrew, the verbs are in the third person feminine: "For *she* looks out (*parakuptousa*) from a window . . . at one whom *she* may see . . .", etc. "She" is thus the woman of v. 5, and it is she ("the woman") who then meets the young man in the street (v. 10). Boström (1935, pp. 120–127) regarded LXX as the original text of these verses, and went on to interpret the details of the following verses in this light. This is one of the most important texts which he uses to support the view that throughout these chapters of Proverbs the "strange woman" is a foreigner who lures the Israelite young man to participate with her in a sexual fertility rite such as is supposed to have been widespread in a number of parts of the ancient Near East, and which was represented iconographically by a woman (or the goddess of love, Ištar-Astarte) looking from a window: the so-called "Aphrodite Parakuptousa"; for details of the evidence see Boström, Herbig and Zimmern. Albright (1955, p. 10), in view of the representation of this scene in Phoenician ivories, one of which was found in Samaria, took Prov. 7:6–7 as an example of "Canaanite-Phoenician" influence on Proverbs.

Boström's theory as a whole has not been generally accepted (see on 2:16–19 above), though several commentators have accepted the possibility that the "woman at the window" theme, apparently alluded to in LXX, may have been in the mind of the author of the Hebrew text, but that if this were so he used the imagery in an indirect way, rendering it "harmless" (Ringgren; cf. McKane, Plöger). But they point out that the Hebrew text makes perfectly good sense as it stands.

6. For (*kî*) is an addition to the text, linking vv. 6–23 with vv. 1–5.

7. Gemser, following Steuernagel, suggested that the metre and parallelism of this verse could be improved by transferring **a young man** (*naʿar*) to the first line: "And I saw a young man among the simple ones; one without sense among the youths". **the simple**: see on 1:4. **without sense**: see on 6:32.

8. her corner (*pinnāh*): the form is anomalous: "her corner" in Hebrew would normally be *pinnātāh*. A slight change of pointing would give *pinnāh*, "*a* corner" (so LXX; *KB*³). Compare v. 12, where the woman lies in wait "at *every* corner". **her house**: "her" refers by anticipation to the "woman . . . dressed as a harlot" who is directly introduced in v. 10 in such a way that she cannot be the same as the "loose woman" of v. 5.

9. time: in MT the word (*ʾîšôn*) is the same as that which means the pupil of the eye in v. 2. Here it has been taken to mean "middle"; but this does not agree with "twilight". Most recent commentators and translations, together with *KB*³ and *BHS*, emend the word to **ʾĕšûn*, rendering it by "time" (that is, in this context, the moment when it grows dark). In the Old Testament this word occurs only in the qere of Prov. 20:20, but both word and meaning receive support from the cognate languages (see *KB*³).

10. And lo: this particle (*wᵉhinnēh*) is used as a device to call attention to a new action in the course of a narrative, adding vividness to the scene. **wily of heart**: literally, "guarded in heart" (*nᵉṣūrat lēb*), that is, she is a woman who is by nature secretive (see Driver,

VT 1 [1951], p. 250). The meaning may be that she conceals her activities from her husband (vv. 19–20). It can hardly mean that she conceals the fate that she has in store for the young man (vv. 22–3), as that is obviously not how she sees it.

11. The meaning of the two adjectives in the first line is not entirely clear. *hōmiyyāh* (*RSV* **loud**) is the feminine participle qal of *hāmāh*, one of the meanings of which is "to be in turmoil" (1 Kg. 1:41; Isa. 22:2; Ps. 42; 5, 11 [Heb. 6, 12]). It may thus mean "unstable" (*REB* "flighty"), though "noisy" is a possible translation (see on 1:21 above). *sōrāret* (**wayward**): the usual meaning of *sārar*, of which this is a participle, is "to be rebellious, stubborn"; but Driver (*ZAW* 50 [1932], pp. 141–2) pointed out that Akkadian *sarāru* can mean "to be unstable" (*REB* "inconstant"). This interpretation has been accepted by several recent commentaries and translations including *RSV*. "Unstable" and "inconstant" both fit well with the second line which speaks of the woman's restlessness. On the convention that respectable women do not loiter in the streets but **stay at home** see on 1:20–21 above.

12. street, market: see on 1:20 above.

13. with impudent face: literally, "she hardens her face". Compare a similar expression in 21:29. *REB*'s "brazenly" renders the sense well.

14–15. sacrifices (*zibᵉḥê šᵉlāmîm*): that is, the so-called "peace offerings" or "communion sacrifice" (see de Vaux, *Ancient Israel*, London, 1961, pp. 417–18), prescribed in Lev. 7:11–17. Part of the victim was offered to Yahweh, while the rest was eaten by the offerer together with others (compare 1 Sam. 9:11–13). It was, however, laid down that it must be eaten on either the same day or, if the sacrifice was made in payment of **vows**, by the following day (Lev. 7:16–17). The implication of these verses is, then, that the woman invites the young man to her house on the pretext that she needs him to share the feast with her (compare 17:1, where *zᵉbāḥîm* clearly refers to such a feast (*RSV* "feasting").

There is, however, a problem here. In vv. 16–18 the woman also makes it plain that her real motive is a sexual one. Boström (1935, pp. 104ff.) saw great significance in this collocation of cult with sexual intercourse: the woman is a foreigner who lures the young man to participate in a foreign, sexual cult. McKane and Plöger both regard Boström's view as plausible, though not decisive. The alternative view is that the woman's sole purpose is seduction, and that her reference to her having fulfilled her vows is simply an additional device holding out the further prospect of a good dinner. The weak point of Boström's theory – which is part of his general hypothesis of the "strange woman" of these chapters as a foreigner (see on 2:16–19 above) – is that the sacrifice offered by the woman is clearly referred to as the distinctively Israelite "communion sacrifice". This suggests that the woman is simply an Israelite who seizes the opportunity of the absence of her husband to commit adultery, and that no reference to a "sexual cult" is intended.

16–17. Several of the items mentioned in these verses are of uncertain meaning; but they are clearly items of luxury. **coverings** (*marbaddîm*): the only other occurrence of this word in the Old Testament is in 31:22, where it refers to articles of domestic use made by the mistress of a well-equipped household. **I have decked**: this verb (*rābad*) is from the same root as *marbaddîm*; it occurs only here in the Old Testament, but means "to join together, patch" in post-biblical Hebrew. **Coloured spreads** (*ḥ*ª*ṭūbôt*): this word also is unique in the Old Testament. Syria and Arabic cognates perhaps suggest that it refers to items of coloured material. *'ēṭûn* may mean **linen** in view of its Egyptian provenance, but the usual word for linen is *šēš*. **I have perfumed** (*naptî*): literally, "I have sprinkled". **myrrh** and **aloes** are aromatic gums obtained respectively from an Arabian shrub and an East Indian tree; **cinnamon**, now used as a spice, is the aromatic inner bark of a Ceylonese tree. All three perfumes have erotic associations in the Song of Songs; they occur together in the same verse in Ca. 4:14. The fact that they are all imported goods suggests considerable wealth.

18. Two words for **love** are used in this verse: *dōdîm* and *'ªhābîm*. Toy pointed out that both are used only in a sexual sense, although *'āhab*, "to love" and *'hābāh*, "love", have a much wider connotation.

19–20. This description of the activities of the woman's husband has led some commentators to conclude that he – and hence probably also his wife – was a foreigner resident in Israel who, as a merchant, travelled abroad to purchase foreign luxuries such as those mentioned in vv. 16–17. This is to read too much into the text. **a long journey** (*derek mērāḥôq*) is not necessarily a journey outside the borders of Israel. There are relatively few references to trade and commerce in the Old Testament, and it is clear that foreign trade seems to have been largely in the hands of foreigners (the word for merchant, *k*ᵉ*na*ʿª*nî*, originally meant a Canaanite), but internal trade was certainly not wholly so. The view that the woman's husband was a foreigner depends largely on the erroneous assumption that the woman in this passage is identical with the *'iššāh zārāh* of v. 5, and that *'iššāh zārāh* means a foreign woman (see on 2:16–19).

19. my husband: literally, "the man" (*hā'îš*). This expression – used rather than the normal *'îšî* – may suggest contempt or estrangement on the part of the wife.

20. money: literally, "silver", not necessarily in the form of minted coinage, which would imply a fairly late date for this passage. **at full moon** (*l^{e}yôm hakkēse'*): the word *kese'* for the full moon occurs in only one other passage in the Old Testament (Ps. 81:3 [Heb. 4] – the spelling there is slightly different) and is probably a late word in Hebrew. Ps. 81:3, however, refers to it as "the day of our feast" (*yôm ḥaggēnû*). It was clearly either Passover or Tabernacles, each of which was celebrated on the fourteenth and fifteenth day of the month, that is, at full moon (Lev. 23:5–6, 34; Num. 28:16–17; 29:12; Ezek. 45:21, 25). The expected date of the husband's return may be connected with the feast, or the woman may simply be dating it in this way.

21. seductive speech (*leqaḥ*): this word can denote either the giving or receiving of persuasive communication (compare 1:5 with 4:2). Here, as in 16:21, 23 it means "persuasive speech". **persuades**: literally, "turns", that is, influences.

22. All at once (*pit'ōm*): several commentators emend this word, on the basis of LXX, to *petî* (see on 1:4) or its plural: "(like) a simpleton" or "(in the manner of) simpletons". But this is difficult syntactically, and the Hebrew is quite satisfactory: after listening for some time, the young man suddenly makes up his mind (so McKane, Plöger).

or as a stag is caught fast: this translation is based on a conjectural emendation. The Hebrew has *ūk^e'ekes 'el-mûsar '^{e}wîl*. The only other occurrence of *'ekes* in the Old Testament is in Isa. 3:18, where it may mean "anklet"; the older commentaries have thus taken it here to mean "fetter". But even if this is correct, "and like a fetter to punishment the fool" is hardly possible (though Gerleman, 1956, pp. 32–3, followed by Plöger, making only the slight emendation of *k^e'ekes* to *b^e'ekes*, renders the line by "and [as] a fool [goes] to punishment in fetters"). LXX and Vulg. go their own way, and it is difficult to know whether they had different Hebrew texts before them or were attempting to correct an apparently meaningless text. But they were probably correct in seeing that some kind of animal going to its fate would make a better parallel with the previous line than a reference to the "fool" (LXX has "dog"; Vulg. "lamb"). *RSV's* **stag** is plausible, reading *'ayyāl* for **wîl*, "fool". But it is probably not possible to restore the text. Among the numerous suggestions which have been made, Driver's emendation (*VT* 1 [1951], p. 241), accepted by McKane and others, remains close to MT: *kᵉ'akkēs 'el-môsēr 'ayyāl*, "like a stag skipping into the noose" – postulating the meaning "skip" for *'ks* on the basis of an Arabic verb. This verb, with apparently a similar sense, has since been found in the Qumran literature (*Discoveries in the Judaean Desert* 4, Oxford, 1965, pp. 86, 88).

23. If both the second and third lines of v. 22 are similes concerning animals (see above), the third simile (**as a bird rushes into a snare**) would most naturally immediately follow the first two. Toy and McKane accordingly suppose that the order of the lines in this verse has been reversed and that this line should come first. However, they differ about the order of the other two lines. Plöger's rearrangement of the lines is different again. Whatever may be the original order, **he does not know that it will cost him his life** makes an effective conclusion to the poem. It is also clear that, **he does not know** refers – as in *RSV* – to the young man and not to the bird, as *ṣippôr* (**bird**) is normally a feminine noun. In what sense his seduction will cost him his life is not stated; but see on 2:16–19 above.

entrails: literally, "liver".

24. On this verse see on 7:1–27 above.

25. Here the original Instruction broken off in v. 5 is resumed. The woman here is thus the "loose woman" of that verse, not the adulteress of vv. 6–23. **turn aside**: this verb (*śāṭāh*) is used also in 4:15 in a warning not to "walk in the way of evil men". On the form see *GK* 75k.

26–27. These verses are strongly reminiscent of 2:18–19 and 5:5–6, both in theme and vocabulary. Compare **Her house is the way to Sheol** with 5:5b and also with 9:18b; **going down to the chambers of death** with 2:18a and 5:5a. But there is a new feature here. In v. 26 the woman is represented as a murderess. It is possible that there are echoes here of mythological themes; in the present context this statement is in any case not intended to be taken literally. McKane thinks of the Canaanite god Mot ("Death") who opens his mouth and swallows up his victims; if this is so, the woman must presumably be a kind of demonic accomplice, but there is no hint of this in the text. Plöger sees a possible echo of the figure of the Sumerian goddess Inanna or her Babylonian counterpart Ishtar (one might add, closer at hand, the goddess Anat of the Ugaritic texts), who were goddesses both of love and war, of each of whom it could be said that **many a victim she has laid low**. Certainly the imagery of this verse is extremely striking and may have a mythical background, though the situation envisaged cannot be fitted exactly to any known myth. Here, where it is used of a (hypothetical) flesh and blood woman, its function is evidently to emphasize as strongly as possible the dire consequences of consorting with an adulteress. It would, however, be wrong to take it as implying – even though figuratively – that the woman deliberately sets out to destroy the young men whom she seduces; rather, it is she whose **house is the way to Sheol** that is, who has already advanced too far towards her destruction for her to turn back, so that she inevitably drags down with her all those who share in her immoral life (see on 5:6 above, which may mean that the woman is unaware of her fatal condition).

26. many a victim (*rabbîm ḥ^a^lālîm*): better, "many are those slain (whom)". **a mighty host** (*^ca^ṣūmîm*): this word (*'āṣûm*) can mean either "mighty" or "numerous". The latter meaning is preferable in view of the parallelism.

27. the chambers of death (*ḥad^e^rê-māwet*): the world of the dead (Sheol) is here conceived as a house consisting of many rooms (compare Ezek. 32:20–32), to which the woman's house is the entrance. Van der Weiden interprets the phrase as referring to the palace of Mot, the Canaanite god of death.

SPEECH BY WISDOM
8:1–36

See the comments on chapters 1–9. This second speech by Wisdom has much in common with the first (1:20–33) but there are also important differences. The description of the setting (8:1–3) is very similar to 1:20–21. Each speech begins with an address to the "simple ones" and the "foolish" and an appeal to heed Wisdom's teaching (8:4–6a; 1:22–23a). But in place of the denunciation of those who have failed to do so in 1:24–31 the second speech continues with a catalogue of Wisdom's virtues and of the gifts which she is able to bestow on those who do heed her (8:6b-21); and this is followed by a unique passage in which Wisdom asserts her primordial origins (8:22–31). Both chapters, however, end with contrasts drawn between the fates of the two types of person (8:32–6; 1:32–3).

The claims that Wisdom makes for herself in 8:6–21 are not set out in a way which would satisfy modern ideas of logic; but they are far more wide-reaching than anything which Wisdom claims for herself in chapter 1. Whereas in chapter 1 she appears principally as a teacher reminiscent of the human teacher of the Instructions, whose advice and admonitions are of the utmost importance to the conduct of the life of the individual and can only be ignored at his peril, in this second speech she claims to be the source not only of all human wealth and prosperity (8:18, 21) but also of all political power (8:15, 16). In 8:22–31 she goes much further even than this: speaking in cosmic terms, she claims that she is a supernatural being enjoying a special relationship with God which had been established even prior to his creation of the world, at which she was herself present as a witness if not as a collaborator (see below).

There can be no doubt that this self-portrait by a personified Wisdom cannot be fully explained as a purely imaginative literary treatment of an abstract mental or moral attribute. There are undoubtedly mythological echoes here, far more striking than in chapter 1. The more prominent of these will be pointed out in the detailed commentary. (For a general survey of the question see on chapters 1–9 above.)

One general characteristic of Wisdom's speech in vv. 4–36 should be noted at this point. This is that, while Wisdom's purpose is to persuade her hearers to devote themselves to her, the means which she employs to that end take the form of a lengthy self-recommendation in which she boasts of her power and authority and of the gifts which she is able to bestow. In other words, this is a speech by a supernatural being in praise of herself. It is reminiscent of a widespread literary genre attested in Egyptian, Sumerian, Babylonian and other Near Eastern religious texts in which a divinity, frequently a goddess (Maat, Isis, Astarte/Ishtar and many others) praises herself (see Boström. [1935], pp. 172–3; Kayatz [1966], pp. 77–98; Lang [1986], pp. 56 ff.). In the Old Testament too Yahweh occasionally speaks in praise of himself (notably in Isa. 42:8–9; 44:24–8; 45:5–7), but the contents of his speeches are quite unlike those of Wisdom's speech here. It seems probable that some of the imagery of self-praise in Prov. 8 has been shaped by literary conventions derived from polytheism; but, whatever polytheistic connections this text may have had in an earlier form, the chapter *in its present form* is monotheistic: Wisdom is intended to be understood as an attribute or heavenly servant of the sole God Yahweh to whom he has delegated certain powers with regard to his relations with mankind. (On this concept see Whybray, *The Heavenly Counsellor in Isaiah xi 13–14*, Cambridge, 1971.)

This chapter has no doubt been placed here in order to present Wisdom as the alternative to the "loose woman" of the preceding Instructions and the woman of 7:6–23. While these women encounter the "simple" young men at night in secret in the streets and invite them to their house (7:6ff.), using deceitful words to promise them "love" which will in fact turn to "death", Wisdom appears in daylight in the crowded streets and other prominent places in the city, also to address the "simple", and in *truthful* words (vv. 6–9) also offers them love (vv. 17, 36) which, if they regularly frequent her house (v. 34), will lead to "life" (v. 35). This alternative choice is presented even more explicitly in chapter 9.

The chapter in its present form consists of four parts, of which the first three are of approximately equal length and the fourth shorter: vv. 1–11, 12–21, 22–31, 32–6. The first is an account of Wisdom's appearance in the public places of the city and of her attempt to gain a hearing by addressing those who are gathered there, assuring them of the value and importance of what she has to say. The second part, marked out by the initial words **I, wisdom**, enlarges on her preliminary statement, and the third (**The Lord created me** . . .), presents, as it were, Wisdom's credentials. The first words of the final section (**And now, my sons** . . .) mark the conclusion of the whole argument, repeating the appeal to accept Wisdom's teaching and presenting the alternative of "life" and "death" to the audience.

There is reason to suppose that the chapter is of composite origin. It has often been observed that the third section (vv. 22–31) is a self-contained poem with its own literary form and having no thematic links with the other sections. If it were omitted, the rest of

Wisdom's speech would constitute a self-contained unit with a satisfactory logical structure: Wisdom commends herself to her audience as honest, truthful, immensely influential and an invaluable companion and adviser (vv. 5–21), and then concludes her speech by offering all these qualities to those who are ready to listen to her and to devote themselves to her (vv. 32–6). Although the claims which she makes are more far-reaching than those made by her or on her behalf in the preceding chapters, there is no essential difference between them and what has been stated earlier. But vv. 22–31 are quite unparalleled, unless – as is probable – they can be regarded as a kind of baroque development of the simple statement made in 3:19 that "The Lord by wisdom founded the earth". There is accordingly good reason to suppose that they have been inserted into an earlier poem (compare 1:29; 2:5–8; 3:19–20, 32–4) in order to make it clear that the Wisdom who makes these claims is not an independent figure but is Yahweh's own wisdom.

In the remainder of the chapter Wisdom is of course the central figure, but there are two brief references to Yahweh in vv. 13a and 35b. As will be indicated below, there is reason to suppose that they also are interpolations. Both occur in contexts where it appears that some disarrangement of the text has taken place, and where the reference to Yahweh interrupts the flow of Wisdom's discourse. It may therefore be suggested that that these two lines have been inserted into the original speech for the same reason that occasioned the interpolation of vv. 22–31.

1–3. This scene is similar in many ways to that depicted in 1:20–21. Several terms, **call** (*tiqrā'*), **raises her voice** (*tittēn qôlāh*), **cries aloud** (*tārōnnāh*), **gates** (*š^e'ārîm*), occur in both passages, and there are also equivalent or at least analogous terms: in 1:20–21 Wisdom is found "in the street; in the markets", "on the top of the walls" (or of the noisy streets) and "at the entrance of the city gates", while in 8:1–3 she takes her stand **on the heights beside the way**, at the crossroads (*RSV* **in the paths** – see below), **beside the gates in front of the town** and **at the entrance of the portals**. All these are prominent public places in the city from which Wisdom can be seen and heard by a crowd of people.

It is possible that the two texts have influenced one another. On the other hand there are notable differences between them which suggest separate authorship. The word for **wisdom** in 8:1 is the normal *ḥokmāh*, not the rare *ḥokmôt* of 1:20. In 8:1 but not in 1:20

wisdom is paralleled with **understanding** (*tᵉbûnāh*) as in 2:2; 3:13, 19; 5:1. The word for city (*RSV* **town**) in 8:3 is the rare *qeret*, which occurs only four other times in the Old Testament – three times in Proverbs (9:3, 14; 11:11) and once in Job (29:7) – whereas in 1:21 it is the usual *ʿîr*. But *qeret* is also found in Phoenician and Ugaritic. Albright (1955, pp. 8–9) took both *ḥokmōt* and *qeret* to be examples of Canaanite influence, of which he found many others throughout Proverbs, but especially in chapters 8–9.

1. The negative question form (*hᵃlōʾ*, **Does not . . . ?**) has the effect of a strong positive assertion (*GK* 150d): the call by Wisdom (cf. 1:24) is contrasted with the invitations of the "loose woman" and the woman of 7:6–23.

2. On the heights: literally, "On the top of the high places"; compare 9:3. **in the paths** (*bêt nᵉtîbôt*): rather, "at the crossroads" (literally, "between the paths"). For examples of this meaning of *bêt*, which is not the same word as *bayit* (*bēt*) "house", see 2 Kg. 11:15; Ezek. 41:9.

3. the town (*qeret*): see above on 8:1–3. **the entrance of the portals** (*mᵉbôʾ pᵉtāḥîm*): another way of saying **beside the gates**. *petaḥ* is the space through which one enters (or gateway) rather than the gates themselves. A literal translation would be "at the going in of the entrance". **cries aloud**: see on 1:20 for the form.

4–5. In v. 4 Wisdom appeals to all men without distinction; in v. 5 her call is specifically, as in 1:22, to the simple and the fools. This apparent discrepancy recalls 1:4–5, where in the general introduction to these chapters the statement that these "proverbs" are intended for the simple and the youths is glossed by a comment that the wise may also profit from them. 8:4 and 5 may stand in the same kind of relationship, the former verse adapting what was originally teaching for the young to a wider audience.

4. O men: this (*ʾîšîm*) is an unusual plural of *ʾîš* which occurs only in two other Old Testament passages (Isa. 53:3; Ps. 141:4) but is the regular plural in Phoenician.

5. The first line of this verse is similar to 1:4a; see the comment on that verse. **pay attention**: the Hebrew has *hābînû lēb*. The first of these words, more frequently meaning "understand", could mean "pay attention" by itself; but the second word, *lēb*, is difficult to interpret in this context. McKane's argument (compare also Toy) that since it can mean mental capacity it may be considered as the equivalent of *ʿormāh* (**prudence**) in the first line (he translates the phrase by "discern what acumen is") is unconvincing. Gemser and other commentators, on the basis of LXX, emend *hābînû* to *hākînû*: "set your heart aright".

6. noble things (*n^e gîdîm*): in view of the parallelism this word should probably be emended to *n^e gādîm* with the sense of "that which is right" (Grollenberg, 1952, pp. 40–43, followed by McKane and Plöger).

7–9. Throughout this chapter Wisdom's teaching is concerned with ethical behaviour. It should also be noted that the terms *ᵉmet* (**truth**) and *ṣedeq* (**righteous**) are both frequently used in the Old Testament of God and of those who conform their conduct to his standards.

7. wickedness is an abomination to my lips (*tô'ᵃbat ś^e pātay reša'*): "abomination to the lips" is an odd expression. LXX's "false lips are an abomination before me" may represent the original Hebrew text: there is an analogous line in 12:22 (compare also 16:13); see *BHS*. **abomination**: see on 6:16.

8. righteous (*b^e ṣedeq*): on this construction with *b^e* see on 3:26 above.

9. straight (*n^e kōḥîm*), **right** (*y^e šārîm*): these terms often have an ethical sense; but here they probably mean "plain" and "straightforward": in other words, the intelligent (*mēbîn*, **him who understands**) and those who have already attained some degree of knowledge (*mōṣ^e 'ê dā'at*, **those who find knowledge**; compare 1:5) will have no difficulty in understanding Wisdom's teaching.

10–11. This kind of comparison was a commonplace of the wisdom literature: compare 2:4; 3:14–15; 16:16; 20:15; Job 28:15–19. Its occurrence in Prov. 16:16 and 20:15 suggests that it originated in proverbial form and was then elaborated in more consciously literary works. Its most elaborate form is found in Job 28:15–19, where no fewer than thirteen valuable materials are enumerated for comparison with wisdom. Here in Prov. 8 it occurs twice, in vv. 10–11 and v. 19. On the thought behind it see on 3:14.

10. my instruction: some commentators omit the suffix "my" in view of the parallel word **knowledge** and in conformity with the Versions (see *BHS*); but this is not certain. **instead of**: better, "rather than" (see H. Kruse, 1954, pp. 385–400, especially pp. 389, 391). On the construction (*w^e 'al*) see *GK* 152g.

11. This verse, which refers to Wisdom in the third person, can hardly be part of her own speech. It (and possibly also v. 10, if the above proposed emendation is correct) is presumably a gloss. It is almost identical with 3:15.

12. dwell in prudence (*šākantî ʿormāh* – on the construction see *GK* 117bb –) hardly makes sense, and the commonly accepted repointing of *šākantî* to *šᵉkentî*, rendered by "(am) neighbour to . . .", taking the final *yodh* as an archaic case-ending – but see *GK* 90n – is hardly more satisfactory. Perhaps the most probable solution is to repoint the word as piel (*šikkantî*), whose usual meaning would be "I cause to dwell" but which sometimes conveys the idea of causing (someone) to possess (e.g. Dt. 12:11 and other passages in Deuteronomy). So *REB* "I bestow". Targ. and Pesh. here have "I create"; but this would involve a major and otherwise unsupported emendation.

I find (*'emṣā*): Gemser, Ringgren and Plöger interpret this word as meaning "I have in my power" or "I have at my disposal"; but this meaning is not otherwise found in biblical Hebrew. If the word were repointed as a hiphil (*'amṣī'*) it would mean "I cause to find": so *REB*, "I show the way to . . .". *mᵉzimmôt* (**discretion**): see on 1:4.

13. Almost all the commentators regard the first line of this verse, which comprises three lines rather than the usual two, as a later addition, possibly a scribal gloss; and some regard the whole verse as similarly suspect, since it interrupts the catalogue of attributes claimed by Wisdom in vv. 12 and 14. However this may be, the first line is certainly totally unrelated to the context and can hardly be part of Wisdom's speech about herself (see on 8:1–36 above). Its theme is a commonplace of the wisdom literature, as is shown by the similar verses 10:27 and 16:6.

perverted speech: see on 2:12.

14–16. Here Wisdom makes the claim that she is the indispensable authority which governs all political power.

The similarity between these verses and two other passages, Isa. 11:2 and Job 12:13, has often been pointed out. In Isa. 11:2 "the Spirit of the Lord . . . , the spirit of wisdom and understanding (*bînāh*), the spirit of counsel and might (*'ēṣāh ûgᵉbûrāh*), the spirit of knowledge (*daʿat*) and the fear of the Lord" are the attributes of the future ideal Israelite king, bestowed on him by God; in Job 12:13 it is God himself to whom are attributed wisdom, might (*gᵉbûrāh*), counsel and understanding (*'ēṣāh ûtᵉbûnāh*). Here in Prov. 8:14 it is Wisdom who claims to possess counsel (*'ēṣāh*) and sound wisdom (*tûšiyyāh*), insight (*bînāh*) and strength (*gᵉbûrāh*). This employment of identical or equivalent terms in all three passages can hardly be entirely coincidental. It appears from the passages in Job and Isaiah that these were terms applied in the wisdom tradition to God, but also, in a secondary sense, to kings who ruled in his name. In Prov. 8:14–15, however, it is Wisdom who claims, in similar terms, to be the source of all political authority and power.

Robert (1934, p. 187), Ringgren and others explain the connection between the passages in Isaiah and Proverbs by assuming that Prov. 8:14 is dependent on Isa. 11:2; the former presents wisdom in "messianic" terms. Cazelles (1959, pp. 511–5) regards Wisdom here as a kind of substitute for the historical Davidic dynasty but as having an extended authority which includes cosmic and universal dimensions.

But the notion of a direct dependence of Prov. 8:14 on Isa. 11:2 is attended by difficulties. Gilbert (1979, p. 208) points out that the chronological priority of the latter passage is not certain; McKane notes that Isa. 11:2 speaks of the *spirit* of wisdom, a phrase which has a totally different resonance from the personal assertiveness of Wisdom in Prov. 8:14–15 and shows that the two passages are theologically far apart. It is more probable that they have borrowed from current tradition quite independently. In Prov. 8:14 Wisdom makes use of the traditional terminology in order to claim for herself qualities otherwise attributable to God, whereas Isa. 11:2 employs it for a quite different purpose: in connection with the "royal ideology" according to which the king is God's vice-gerent, responsible for the maintenance of order in the world (see Porteous, 1955, pp. 247–61).

14. counsel (*'ēṣāh*): in her first speech (1:25, 30), Wisdom speaks only of the value of her advice in guiding the lives of individuals. But this word is used frequently of the political and military advice given to kings (e.g. 2 Sam. 17:7; 1 Kg. 1:12; cf. Prov. 20:18), and this is clearly its meaning in the present context. *tûšiyyāh* (**sound wisdom**) is ability in practical affairs; *bînāh* (**insight**) is intelligence in general; but *gᵉbûrāh* (**strength**) is regularly used of the political or military power of kings, sometimes in close association with *'ēṣāh* (2 Kg. 18:20; Isa. 11:2; 36:5).

I have insight: the Hebrew has "I *am* (*ᵃnî*) insight"; but *ᵃnî* is probably a textual error for *lî*, "to me (is)", that is, "I have", as in the accompanying phrases.

16. govern the earth: the Hebrew text in *BHS* has *kolšōpᵉṭê ṣedeq*, that is "all righteous rulers" or – following Dahood, Gemser, Ringgren and Plöger – "all legitimate rulers". *RSV* has followed a variant Hebrew text equally supported in the MSS and Versions and found in some printed Hebrew bibles which has *'ereṣ*, "the earth", instead of *ṣedeq*. The textual alternatives are fairly well balanced. Either *ṣedeq* or *'ereṣ* could be a scribal error, the former influenced by the similar phrase **decree what is just** (*yᵉḥōqᵉqû ṣedeq*) at the end of v. 15, or the latter by the more familiar phrase *šōpᵉṭê 'ereṣ*, "rulers of the earth" in other texts (Ps. 2:10; 148:11; Isa. 40:23).

17. I love those who love me: see on 4:6 and compare 4:6–9 in general. Kethib has "those who love *her* (*'ōhᵃbéhā*)"; *RSV* and most commentators follow Qere (*'ōhᵃbay*). Kayatz's argument (1966, p. 102) that the use of the third person (as in Kethib) is correct, having been influenced by Egyptian usage in similar phrases but subsequently and incorrectly altered by the Massoretes is not convincing as she does not cite any Egyptian examples which mix the persons in this way. On the form *'ēhāb* see *GK* 68f.

18. enduring: this word (*'āṯēq*) has been variously rendered. *REB* has "boundless"; other translations include "venerable" (German *altehrwürdig*, Gemser), "surpassing" (Oesterley), "splendid", "solid" (McKane), "increased" (Plöger). The word occurs nowhere else in the Old Testament, and the cognates *'āṯîq* and *'attîq* are also extremely rare and variously understood. The verb *'āṯaq* means "to advance, move forward"; but this notion can be understood figuratively in a variety of ways: with regard to space, time (compare *'attîq yômîn*, "ancient of days" in the Aramaic Daniel [7:9, 13, 22]), value, quality etc. *RSV* is probably correct in view of the context. As in 3:13–16, the wealth offered by Wisdom is not to be understood in a figurative sense but is quite literally material wealth which, because it is gained through Wisdom rather than directly as an end in itself, is more worthwhile than gold and silver obtained in the usual way without regard to her (v. 19) because it will be **enduring**. See on 3:14 above.

prosperity (*ṣᵉdāqāh*) (literally, "righteousness":) some commentators (Toy Scott, Ringgren, Barucq) together with *RSV* find it incongruous that righteousness should be paired with **wealth** as an attribute or gift of Wisdom, and have taken *ṣᵉdāqāh* to mean "prosperity", "approbation", "success" – that is, the tangible *results* or fruits of righteousness. However, the few passages which they cite in support of this view (1 Sam. 26:23; Ps. 112:3; Isa. 54:17; Ezek. 18:20; Jl 2:23) are not convincing. Moreover, the only other occurrence of *ṣ^e^dāqāh* in chapters 1–9 is in 8:20, where it is paralleled with *mišpāṭ*. In the rest of the book it occurs frequently, always in a moral sense. In fact the association in this verse of **enduring wealth** (*hôn ʿātēq*) with *ṣ^e^dāqāh* here is in line with the moral tone of the chapter as a whole (especially vv. 7, 20), and the phrase **Riches and honour** (*ʿošer w^e^kābôd*) is probably to be understood in the same way. Wealth is presented here as both desirable and attainable through Wisdom, but, as is constantly stressed in the sentence literature of Proverbs, prosperity and moral righteousness are inseparable. A similar view is taken by McKane and Plöger.

19. This verse is similar to 3:14, but also to 16:16, which may suggest that it is modelled on proverbial wisdom. **fruit** and **yield** are often used figuratively in the sense of the result or consequence of an action. Here they refer to the material advantages to be obtained from a devotion to Wisdom. They appear together again in parallelism in a different connection in 18:20. See on vv. 10–11 above.

20–21. Here again the close relationship between Wisdom and morality is stressed.

21. wealth (*yēš*): this is the only place in the Old Testament where this word occurs as a noun (though see below on 13:23), but it is found in Sir. 42:3 in the sense of "property". It is also used as a noun in post-biblical Hebrew.

The LXX translators – or their Hebrew sources – were evidently struck by the abruptness of the transition from v. 21 to v. 22 (see above on 8:1–36), since they added at the end of v. 21 a verse clearly intended to make this transition less harsh: "If I declare to you the things that happen daily, I will remember also to recount the things of old".

22–31. This passage has been widely discussed in recent literature. It has been seen as an elaboration of the statement in 3:19–20 (on which see the remarks in this commentary) that Yahweh founded the earth and established the heavens *by wisdom*: that is, that he used his wisdom as an instrument in his acts of creation of the world. But this passage is not concerned with instrumentality; it is concerned rather to set forth the nature, status and relationship to Yahweh of this wisdom, and to do so in a way which, while stressing Wisdom's subordinate status, also asserts her authority over human lives. In doing so, it calls upon various motifs drawn from a number of traditional sources.

The style and language of this poem are quite different from those employed in the rest of chapter 8, and many scholars have pointed out features resembling texts from the ancient Near East, Egyptian, Mesopotamian and possibly Canaanite (see, for example, Gemser, Ringgren, Kayatz, Albright [1955, pp. 7–8]). The question at issue, however (see Plöger), as with the other passages concerning Wisdom which have already been considered above, is whether these features are to be understood as indicating a real affinity with the polytheistic religious and theological beliefs of the surrounding peoples or whether they are no more than literary allusions intended to reinforce the appeal of Wisdom by presenting her as beloved of Yahweh and so eminently worthy of acceptance as the guide to the "life" which she offers elsewhere in this chapter (vv. 35, 36).

It is important to notice that although the poem is not primarily intended as an account of the creation of the world, it differs markedly from the rest of the chapter in that it is Yahweh, not Wisdom, who is the central figure. The tone is already set by the change of subject at the beginning: the name of Yahweh stands there as the very first word and in an emphatic position (that is, preceding the verb which it governs: see *GK* 142a, f). This emphasis is continued by means of further verbs of which he is the subject in vv. 26, 27, 28, 29, Wisdom's status or presence being defined in relation to these creative acts (vv. 25, 27, 30–31). Wisdom, in other words, is not engaged here in any independent activity (on the correctness of *RSV*'s **like a master workman** in v. 30 see below) or indeed as having any independent existence before, during or even after the acts of creation are performed: it is in *Yahweh's* **inhabited world** (v. 31) that she rejoices. This kind of relationship has no real parallels in the ancient Near Eastern literature, nor does Wisdom's direct appeal to humanity: even the Egyptian Maat does not do this (see G. von Rad, *Wisdom in Israel*, 1972, pp. 150–57). Wisdom stands within the confines of the Israelite monotheistic tradition.

The catalogue of Yahweh's creative acts in vv. 23–9 has frequently been compared with other ancient Near Eastern, especially Eyptian and Babylonian, accounts of the creation of the world by various gods. There are undoubtedly points of similarity here, some of which will be referred to in the detailed comments below. There are also many details which call to mind creation accounts and references to the creation of the world in other Old Testament texts such as Gen. 1; 2; Pss. 93; 104; Job 28; 38; Isa. 40:12; 45:18. There are, however, also substantial differences from all these, just as they all differ among themselves. The body of literature which survives both in the Old Testament and from the surrounding peoples makes it evident that there was a great diversity of traditions about the creation of the world, and it is probable that these traditions intermingled to some extent. Some of their features, however, are also found in creation traditions from parts of the world culturally and religiously quite alien from the ancient Near East – the result of quite independent reflection by different peoples on similar cosmic phenomena (see below). Prov. 8:23–9 is clearly following a particular type of creation tradition which has features in common with other Old Testament as well as Near Eastern traditions, but is not, as far as is known, actually dependent on any given text.

22. created me (*qānānî*): the meaning of this word has been disputed since very early times. LXX, Targ., Pesh. have "created"; Vulg. "possessed". The verb *qānāh*, which occurs frequently, together with its cognates, in the Old Testament, almost always means "acquire" or, more specifically, "purchase" (and so also "possess"). In Proverbs, apart from this verse, it occurs thirteen times. Of these occurrences twelve (including five in chapters 1–9) speak of (the desirability of) acquiring wisdom, skill, knowledge, etc.; in one (20:14) the meaning is "purchase, buy" in a commercial sense. The analyses of Humbert (1950, pp. 259–66) and W. A. Irwin (1961, pp. 133–42) have shown that only in a handful of passages at most (Gen. 4:1; 14:19, 22; Exod. 15:16; Dt. 32:6; Ps. 74:2; 78:54; 139:13; Prov. 8:22) is the meaning "create" a possibility. (Humbert's view that there are two verbs *qānāh* in biblical Hebrew, one meaning "acquire" and the other "create" has not been generally accepted.) In all these passages except Gen. 4:1 God is the subject of the verb. But in none or almost none of them is "create" the only possible meaning.

Some modern scholars have proposed a third meaning for the verb here: "procreate, beget" (Oesterley, Cazelles [1957, pp. 422, 429], W. A. Irwin [1961], Gilbert [pp. 209–10], Plöger, Lang [1986, p. 77]). This view is based partly on a particular interpretation of a few Old Testament passages mentioned above (Gen. 4:1; Dt. 32:6), partly on the interpretation of certain words in Prov. 8:23, 24, 25 as referring to Wisdom's "birth" (see below), partly on analogies from extra-biblical material, especially on the birth of the Egyptian Maat (Kayatz, pp. 93–8), and partly on the – disputed – claim that *qny* in Ugaritic can mean "procreate".

The interpretation of *qānānî* as "begot, procreated me", if taken other than figuratively, clearly has mythological and even polytheistic implications. But some other considerations must be borne in mind. First, the meanings of *qānāh* which have been attested or proposed ("acquire, possess", "make, create" and "beget, procreate") overlap to such an extent that in the crucial passages precision of interpretation is virtually impossible: in particular, acquisition is common to all of them (see Ringgren). Thus in Gen. 4:1 all these senses are acceptable: Eve's words in Gen. 4:1 could mean "I have acquired", "I have made" or "I have given birth to (a man)". Similarly the phrase in Gen. 14:19, 22 could mean either "creator of heaven and earth" or "possessor (master) of heaven and earth".

Secondly, as in Dt. 32:18, where it is stated that the nation Israel has been "begotten" and even "born" *(mᵉḥōlᵉlekā)* by God, a literal meaning of *qanāh* in Prov. 8:22 would obviously be out of the question. The idea of Yahweh's acquiring a child as a consequence of sexual activity is inconceivable in the Old Testament. Thirdly, it should be remembered that Prov. 8:22–31 is a poem, in which figurative images are to be expected. If "begot" were in fact the meaning of *qānānî* here, the word, together with comparable terms in the succeeding verses, would surely be intended figuratively, even if there are mythological overtones (so Irwin, Gilbert).

To conclude: the meaning of *qānānî* here remains uncertain. Of the three possibilities, "begot, procreated" has less evidence to support it than the other two. "Acquired, possessed" is perhaps more likely than "created" in view of the overwhelming number of passages in which this verb has that meaning. But scholars who argue that *qānāh* in the sense of "acquired" must imply that Wisdom is here seen as having pre-existed before Yahweh acquired her (Vawter, 1980, pp. 205–16; de Boer, 1961) are reading too much into the text. This conclusion, however, is subject to the interpretation of 8:22–31 as a whole.

at the beginning of his work (*rē'šît darkô*): *rē'šît* has been interpreted in many ways: "beginning", "first", "best", "first principle", "firstfruits", "origin", "attribute", "essence". Some of these translations reflect the presuppositions of the exegetes more than the original meaning of the text. Such exegesis, which has also distorted the meaning of other parts of the poem, began early with the ancient versions. In view of the context ("before . . .", vv. 25, 26); "when . . . I was there", vv. 27–9) and the parallel (**the first**) in the second line of this verse, a temporal sense is the most probable. But since **at** is not represented in *MT* – though Jerome and possibly some ancient Versions had *bᵉrē'šît*, "at the beginning" in their Hebrew texts – "*as* the beginning" would be more accurate. *rē'šît* stands in apposition to **me** (see *GK* 131c). *darkô* (**his work**) is, literally, "his way". This also has been variously interpreted. Albright's proposal (1955, p. 7) that *derek* here is cognate with Ugaritic *drkt*, "sovereignty" has not been widely accepted. The word is used in Job 26:14; 40:19 of the divine creative activity, and, in view of the parallel in the second line there is no reason to doubt that *RSV*'s rendering is correct.

the first (*qedem*): this word is parallel to *rē'šît*, and, like it, is in apposition to **me**. In v. 23 it means "beginning". The point of the whole verse, which is further elaborated in the verses which follow, is to establish that Wisdom was with Yahweh from before he began to create the world.

23. I was set up (*nissaktî*): this translation assumes that this is the niphal of *nāsak*, and that this verb has here the same sense as in Ps. 2:6 "I have set (*nāsaktî*, qal) my king on Zion, my holy hill" (so Ringgren, Plöger). *LXX* has "He founded me", which is similar in meaning, but may have been based on a form of *yāsad* "to found". Many commentators, however, render *nissaktî* as the niphal of *sākak* which means "to weave", but which in two passages appears to be used figuratively of the formation of a foetus in the womb: Ps. 139:13, "You wove me together in my mother's womb"; Job 10:11, "You wove me together with bones and sinews". (*nissaktî*, however, would be an anomalous form and, if this view is correct, should perhaps be repointed as *nᵉsakkōtî*.) However this may be, a figurative sense must be intended (see on *qānānî* in v. 22).

It should be noted how the writer (in this verse and the preceding one) was so insistent on pressing home the fact of Wisdom's unimaginable antiquity that he piled up every available synonym in a deluge of tautologies: *rē'šît*, **beginning**, *qedem*, **the first**, *mē'āz*, **of old**, *mē'ôlām*, **ages ago**, *mērō'š*, **at the first** or "from the beginning" (compare Isa. 40:21; 41:4, 26), *miqqadᵉmê 'āreṣ*, **before the beginning of the earth**: the emphasis is not so much on the *mode* of Wisdom's coming into existence, whose expression in verbal form (*qānānî*, *nissaktî* and, in vv. 24, 25, *ḥôlāltī*) has constituted such problems for the exegete, but on the *fact* of her antiquity.

24–26. It has been argued by Gemser and Ringgren that the form of these verses, in which the various acts of creation are referred to in a series of negative clauses each beginning with **before**, points to a common ancient Near Eastern tradition and has prototypes in Egyptian and Babylonian accounts of creation such as the Egyptian *Book of the Apophis* (*ANET*, p. 5) and the Babylonian *Enuma Elish* (*ANET*, pp. 60–61) and *The Creation of the World by Marduk* (A. Heidel, *The Babylonian Genesis*, Chicago, 1951, p. 62). However, there are considerable differences between these texts and Prov. 8:24–6; and these, together with the existence of comparable texts from other parts of the world, suggest that the theory of a common Near Eastern tradition explicitly followed in Proverbs is not proven. See Whybray, *VT* 15 [1965], pp. 504–14 for discussion and translations of some of the relevant texts.

24. depths (*tᵉhōmôt*): this is probably not an allusion to the primeval ocean (*tᵉhôm*) of Gen. 1:2 and other passages which God divided into the upper and lower waters (Gen. 1:7) but to the existing terrestrial ocean. Compare 3:20. **I was brought forth**: literally, "I was born". But this is to be understood figuratively, as in Ps. 90:2, where the same verb (the polal of *ḥîl*) is used of the "birth" of the world. Compare also Job 38:8, where the sea is said to have "burst forth from the womb". **abounding with water** (*nikbaddê-māyim*): literally, "made heavy (niphal of *kbd*) with water". LXX has "the fountains of water", which may represent Hebrew *nibᵉkê-māyim*; Job 38:16 has a similar expression: *nibᵉkê-yām*, "the springs of (or, "in") the sea". But MT makes good sense and may be correct.

25. shaped: the usual meaning of this verb (*ṭāba'*) is "to sink". It is used in Job 38:6 of God's sinking or settling the earth on its base or pedestal ("pillars", according to Job 9:6; Ps. 75:3 [Heb. 4]). These and other passages in different words reflect Near Eastern ideas of cosmology which were shared by Israel. "Settled" (that is, on their foundations) would therefore be a more appropriate rendering than that of *RSV*, though McKane, following Albright, also renders the word by "shaped" on the basis of an Arabic word with that meaning and also of post-biblical Hebrew usage. **I was brought forth**: this is the same word as in v. 24 and has the same figurative meaning.

26. with its fields (*w*^{e}*ḥûṣôt*): this word (*ḥûṣ*) mea
outside". In 1:20; 7:12 it clearly denotes, as is other Olc
contexts, that part of the town which is outside its bui...ngs: that is, its streets, squares etc. But it is also used, as here, of what is outside the walls of a town – that is, the open country (for example, in Ps. 144:13). *'ereṣ* (**earth**) and *ḥûṣôt* occur as a parallel pair also in Job 5:10. On the construction with *w*^{e} here see *GK* 154a, note 1. **the first** (*rō'š*): probably better, "the mass". **dust**: *'āpār*, here in the plural, probably denotes the particles of which the soil is composed.

27–29. After claiming that she came into existence *before* Yahweh created the world, Wisdom goes on to assert that she was a witness (**I was there**) to the acts of creation themselves (**When he . . .**). This account of the creation, despite some ambiguities, conforms in general to the current understanding of the matter which is reflected in other Old Testament passages, especially Gen. 1 and the Book of Job. It also covers ground already traversed in vv. 24–6 and may have originally been derived from another source. It is not a complete account: compared, for example, with Gen. 1 there are important omissions. The author was solely concerned with the creation and ordering of the universe itself, and there are no references to the heavenly bodies, vegetation or the animal world, though the poem concludes in v. 31 with a reference to the human race.

27. circle (*ḥûg*): this word occurs in only two other passages in the Old Testament together with a possible reference in Sir. 43:12. The context is cosmological in every case; but its meaning is not always the same. In Job 22:14, where God "walks on the *ḥûg* of heaven", it refers to the solid hemispherical vault of heaven (*rāqîa'* in Gen. 1:7, 8) which separates the upper from the lower waters between which the earth is situated; but in Isa. 40:22, where Yahweh "sits above the *ḥûg* of the earth", it appears to refer to the earth itself, conceived as a flat circular disc. Here in Prov. 8:27, as the object of the verb *ḥāqaq* and in connection with the **deep** or sea (*t*^{e}*hôm*) it could either denote the earth – as surrounded by water – as in Isa. 40:22 or the horizon which appears to constitute its limit.

28. made firm the skies (literally, "the clouds"): whether or not this refers to the creation of the firmament (see on v. 27 above) or vault of heaven, the clouds were believed to be a solid mass by which God controlled the weather (compare Job 37:18). **when he established**: there is no certainty about the meaning of this word. It has the form of the qal infinitive of *'āzaz* "to be strong" (*ba*$^{'a}$*zôz*), which does not make good sense. Some commentators emend it to *bᵉʿazzô*, the piel infinitive with suffix: "when he made strong", which may be the basis of *RSV*'s translation. Other proposals include the retention of MT but in a different sense based on an Arabic usage: "to restrain, control" (see Dahood, p. 16). LXX has "made secure".

29. This verse and v. 30 have three lines each. *BHS* has, perhaps correctly, arranged them as three couplets, with vv. 29c and 30a forming the middle couplet. LXX, however, omits v. 29ab.

The first two lines refer to the belief that the "inhabitable world" (v. 31) was created when God by his almighty word exercised his power over the waters of chaos (Gen. 1:2, 6–10; Ps. 104:6–9; Job 38:8–11; see also on v. 27 above).

so that the waters might not: the Hebrew has "and the waters do not". **transgress his command**: literally, "exceed his mouth" (that is, his words of command). This expression is not specifically poetical but is also found in prose narrative – in Saul's confession of disobedience to Yahweh's and Samuel's orders (1 Sam. 15:24), Moses's warning to the Israelites (Num. 14:41) and Balaam's refusal to disobey Yahweh (Num. 22:18; 24:13) – and was probably a standard expression.

when he marked out (*bᵉḥûqô*): a slight emendation to *bᵉḥazzᵉqô*, "when he made firm", would give a better sense: compare LXX. **the foundations of the earth**: see on v. 25 above.

30. like a master workman: this renders the single word *ʾāmôn* (*RSV*'s **like** is not represented in the Hebrew text). Despite its importance for the understanding of the nature and function of Wisdom as depicted in the poem, there is, as in the case of *qānānî* in v. 22, no agreement about the meaning of this word; and the uncertainty goes back to early times. The Versions translated it in quite different ways and were clearly puzzled by it.

RSV accepts the commonly held view that the word, which occurs nowhere else in the Old Testament except in quite unrelated proper and place-names, is borrowed from Akkadian *ummiānu, ummānu* (W. von Soden, *Akkadisches Handwörterbuch* III, 1981, pp. 1415–16), meaning a skilled craftsman (although it can also mean a court expert or counsellor) rather than being a cognate of the Hebrew *ʾmn*. In favour of this interpretation, apart from the creation context, is the isolated occurrence of a word *ʾommān*, apparently meaning a skilled craftsman, in Ca.7:1 (Heb. 2). It has also been supposed that some of the Versions were aware of this; and the fact that the late

Wisdom of Solomon 7:21 (22) and 8:5 (6) refers to Wisdom as the (female) "artificer (*technitis*) of all things" in a passage which is clearly based on Prov. 8:30 has also influenced this view.

Other interpreters, taking their cue from Aquila and some subsequent Jewish exegetes, relate the word to one of the meanings of the Hebrew verb *'āman*, to care for children as nurse, foster-parent etc. (Num. 11:12; Ru. 4:16; 2 Kg. 10:1, 5; Est. 2:7; Isa. 49:23; Lam. 4:5), suggesting that the word means "nursling", that is, a cherished infant (this would require the repointing of *'āmôn* to *'āmûn*, the passive participle qal of *'āman*, or the postulation of a cognate noun such as **mûn*). Other proposals by modern scholars include "court expert", again *ummānu* (Gaster, 1954, pp. 77–8), "living link" between Creator and creation (Scott, 1960, pp. 213–23, reading *'ōmen*) and "little mother", that is, the mother (*'ēm*) as counsellor (de Boer, 1955, p. 70).

It is admitted that all these proposals are to a greater or lesser extent speculative. For the purposes of the interpretation of the poem as a whole the crucial question is obviously whether Wisdom is here seen as actively participating in the creation of the world or simply as a spectator whose mere presence there gives her eminent status. It is significant that nowhere else in the poem is there any suggestion of such constructive activity on her part (unless her "building a house" 9:1; 14:1 is interpreted in cosmic terms – see on 9:1 below). However the verbs in vv. 22–6 are interpreted, she is not credited there with any form of activity; and in relation to the acts of creation described in vv. 27–30a Wisdom only says of herself "I was there" (v. 27) and "I was beside him" (v. 30). In vv. 30–31 she merely delights in the world that God has made. **master workman**, then, as referring to Wisdom, seems out of place. The interpretations of later Jewish exegetes, and the explicit statement in the Wisdom of Solomon that Wisdom made all things – a view which is *not* held by Ben Sira (Sir. 1; 24) – do not constitute evidence for the original intention of this author: they merely show that Prov. 8:22–31 was the starting-point for later theological speculation. This may have been influenced by the ambiguous statement in Prov. 3:19 that Yahweh created the world *by wisdom* (see above).

The evidence for the view that *'āmôn* here means "nursling" or "cherished infant" is also, however, very precarious. It rests on the single phrase *hā*mūnîm ʿalê tôlāʿ*, "nurtured in purple", in Lam. 4:5. But *'āmûn* there is a participle, and does not function as a noun.

There is no evidence for a *noun* meaning "nursling", whether it is spelled *'āmôn*, *'mûn* or *'āmûn*. (The other interpretations by Scott and de Boer, also linking the word with Hebrew *'mn*, are too speculative to be persuasive.)

There is, however, another possible interpretation of the word which has been pointed out by Keel, 1974, pp. 21–5. This is that *'āmôn* does not refer to Wisdom at all: it refers to Yahweh as Creator. If *'āmôn*, which is a masculine and not a feminine form – or, more probably, in a repointed form, *'ommān*, as in Ca. 7:1 – can mean an artificer or one who is skilled in making things, the phrase may be rendered "then I was beside him, (that is), the Creator". (On this construction, in which a noun stands in apposition to a pronominal suffix, see *GK* 131n and compare *qānānî rē'šît* in v. 22 above.) The problem of the context, which stood in the way of this interpretation, is now removed. (The references to Wisdom's "rejoicing" and "delighting" in vv. 30b-31 need not mean that Wisdom is a small child: see below.) It may be strange that none of the Versions or later exegetes interpreted the word as referring to God as Creator; but they, like modern exegetes, were faced with an unfamiliar and difficult word which they naturally saw as connected in some way with the Hebrew *'mn*, and attempted to find ways to relate to Wisdom's **I was** rather than to **him**.

delight (*ša'ašū'îm*), **rejoicing** (*m^eśaḥ^eqet*): these words, which recur in v. 31, have been interpreted as referring to Wisdom as a child at play. But this interpretation is entirely dependent on the view that *'āmôn* in this verse means "little child" or the like, and finds no support in the meaning of these words themselves. *ša'ašū'îm* simply means something in which one takes pleasure: in Isa. 5:7, for example, Yahweh takes pleasure in the vineyard which he has planted; and the author of Psalm 119 repeatedly declares his delight in Yahweh's laws (Ps. 119:24, 77, 92, 143, 174). In Jer. 31:20 Ephraim is said to be Yahweh's "child of delight" (*yeled ša'ašū'îm*), but this does not imply that the word was especially applied to children; and there are no other passages in which it is associated with them. *m^eśaḥeqet*, "playing, dancing, making merry" also has no such implication. Although in one passage (Zech. 8:5) the verb in this form (piel) refers to children playing or dancing in the streets, it also is not elsewhere used of children. It is used, for example, of the women who greeted David on his return from defeating the Philistines (1 Sam. 18:7), of joyful behaviour in general (Jer. 15:17; 30:19;

31:4), and of making jokes (Prov. 26:19). But dancing could have a more specifically religious or liturgical purpose: David danced "before Yahweh" (2 Sam. 6:5, 21 – compare v. 16), a phrase which is reminiscent of Wisdom's "*dancing* (RSV **rejoicing**) before him" here. The purpose was clearly to give pleasure to Yahweh. Keel (pp. 25–9 and *passim*) has drawn attention to similar references in Egyptian literature, in which dances are performed both before kings and before gods to entertain them (as Samson was forced to "entertain" his captors (*wîśaḥeq-lānû*) at their victory celebrations [Jg. 16:25]). So here, on the supremely auspicious occasion of the creation of the world, Wisdom as spectator acts in an appropriate way, celebrating the daily progress with ritual dance. (Compare Job 38:7, which states that at the creation of the world "the morning stars sang together and all the sons of God shouted for joy".)

I was . . . his delight: the Hebrew has simply "I was delight" (*wā'ehyeh ša*[ʿa]*šū'îm*). But it is unnecessary to follow LXX and emend to *ša* [ʿa]*šū'âw*, "*his* delight". See *GK* 141c and note 2.

31. rejoicing, delighting: these are the same words as in v. 30, but the latter now has a first person suffix: literally, "my delight (was)" (*ša* [ʿa]*šū'ay*). Their order is now reversed, forming a chiasmus which elegently completes the poem. Wisdom now, in the final line of the poem, reveals her purpose in speaking of her primordial ancestry: within the created world in which she plays or dances before God, her special delight is in mankind. Here "delight" is used, in a kind of wordplay, in a slightly different sense from its meaning in v. 30 and elsewhere: whereas in v. 30 Wisdom is the object of *Yahweh's* delight, here *she* delights in mankind: that is, mankind is the object of *her* delight. So Wisdom reveals herself as one who comes from God and at the same time singles out the human race as the object of her special and loving care.

in his inhabited world: this phrase, *b*[e]*tēbel 'arṣô* literally "in the world of his earth", simply means "in his world".

32–36. These verses resume the speech of Wisdom which was interrupted by the interpolation of vv. 22–31. Having set out her virtues and usefulness for mankind and then (v. 21) promised good fortune to those who love her, Wisdom now solemnly pronounces **happy** those who devote themselves to her, and concludes by promising "life" to those who "find" her. But, as is generally recognized, the order of the lines has been seriously disturbed; and other material has been added to the original text. LXX has a substantially different arrangement of the lines as well as a somewhat different text, and various attempts have been made to restore the original order (note especially that of Gemser). It is suggested here that the original text consisted of vv. 34a + 32b, 34bc, 35a + 36a, making three couplets:

Happy is the man who listens to me,
and happy are those who keep my ways,
watching daily at my gates,
waiting beside my doors.
For he who finds me finds life,
but he who misses me injures himself.

Vv. 32a, 33 (missing in LXX), 35b and 36b are later additions. V. 32a is identical with 7:24a and serves a similar purpose: it has been inserted in order to make a smooth transition between vv. 22–31 and the interrupted conclusion of the speech. This is helped by the fact that its address to **my sons** picks up the reference to the "sons of men" in v. 31. But it is out of place in a speech by Wisdom: nowhere else does Wisdom address her audience as "my sons". This form of address, usually in the singular (though 4:1 has the plural form) is characteristic of the language of the human teacher in the preceding Instructions, and this is also true of the admonition **listen to me** (compare, for example, 1:8; 4:1, 10). V. 33 is also strongly reminiscent of the Instructions (compare 1:8; 4:1); it also interrupts the couplet vv. 34a + 32b. V. 35b is identical with 18:22b. It is an interpolation similar to others in the preceding chapters including v. 13a and vv. 22–31, asserting the close association between Wisdom and Yahweh. It interrupts the antithetical parallelism, formed by vv. 35a and 36a. V. 36b is a redundant comment which in terms of style weakens the climax formed by vv. 35a + 36a in an attempt, paradoxically, to strengthen it. It glosses "ruins his life" (*RSV* **injures himself** (v. 36a – see below) with a more explicit threat of death for those who hate Wisdom (perhaps derived from 2:18; 5:5; 7:27, though the notion of *loving* death does not occur elsewhere in these chapters).

With these rearrangements and omissions, these verses form an impressive conclusion to Wisdom's speech. They begin in vv. 34a + 32b with a pronouncement of happiness for Wisdom's adherents (it should be noticed that their placing in this reversed order settles the problem of the word "and" with which v. 32b begins – not translated in *RSV*). V. 34bc extends this thought, depicting the need for assiduity in the pursuit of Wisdom in terms of a lover waiting and hoping for admission to his beloved's house; and vv. 35a + 36a, continuing the imagery of the anxious lover, conclude by emphasizing that he must "find" or obtain the loved one at all costs, for to fail or "miss" her would be a disaster for him. (See R. N. Whybray, *VT* 16 [1966], pp. 492–6 for a fuller account.)

32. happy are: see on 3:13. The repetition of this word (*'ašrê*) here and in v. 34a is not unusual. In Ps. 144:15 it introduces both lines of a couplet as here. **who keep my ways**: this is a reference to v. 20.

33. and be wise: see on 6:6. **do not neglect it**: the object (**it**) is not expressed in the Hebrew. Some commentators hold that a word (*'ōtô*) has accidentally dropped out. This is not necessarily the case, although the line is unusually short (see *GK* 117f).

34. watching . . . at my gates; waiting beside my doors: that Wisdom has a house to which she invites the "simple" is the theme of 9:1–6. In chapter 9 Wisdom's house and what occurs there is contrasted with the house of the "woman Folly" (vv. 13–18), a passage which is clearly reminiscent of the house of the "strange woman" in 2:18–19 and the parallel passages in other preceding Instructions. Here in 8:34–6 as in chapter 9 the imagery of the house is a feature of the offer to young men of a stark choice which is crucial for their future. It has been interpreted (Frankenberg, Plöger) as suggesting a royal palace: according to this theory, Wisdom has presented herself in vv. 22–31 in elevated terms which show her to be a queen or princess who keeps her would-be courtiers waiting outside the palace. Lang, on the other hand, sees her as a schoolmistress whose pupils must rise early to wait beside her house (1986, p. 80). But this is to miss the fact that there are erotic (or marital) overtones here. Wisdom is the beloved, before whose house her suitors wait for admission. The Song of Songs, much of which is built round the theme of "seeking" and "finding", uses the word "door" figuratively in an erotic sense (8:8–10). But the motif of the lover seeking entrance into the loved one's house is much older. It is used – apparently in a literal sense – in Egyptian love songs of the Ramesside period, for example: "I passed by her house in a daze. I knocked, but it was not opened for me"; "She left me standing at the door of her house when she went inside" (M. V. Fox, *The Song of Songs and the Ancient Egyptian Love Songs*, Madison, Wisconsin, 1985,

p. 75; see also p. 14 and the discussion of the theme on pp. 282–3).

35. finds life: read Qere (*māṣā'*) rather than Kethib (*mṣ'y*). On the meaning of **life** in these chapters see on 3:2; 3:18 and compare 4:22.

36. he who misses me: this word (*ḥōṭ^e'î*) is clearly intended to denote the opposite of "he who loves me" (*mōṣ^e'î*) in v. 35. Other examples of this meaning of the verb *ḥāṭā'*, which in the great majority of occurrences in the Old Testament means "to sin", occur in Jg. 20:16; Job 5:24; Isa. 65:20. **injures himself** (*ḥōmēs napšô*): better, "ruins his life", the opposite of "finds life" in v. 35. This is the meaning of *napšô* when it is the object of a verb in comparable phrases in Proverbs such as "preserves his life" (13:3; 16:17; 19:16); "saves his life" (23:14); "hates his life" (29:24).

WISDOM AND FOLLY
9:1–18

This chapter – apart from vv. 7–12 – makes an impressive conclusion to chapters 1–9. The choice between wisdom and folly frequently set out in both the preceding Instructions and the two speeches by Wisdom in chapters 1 and 8 is now presented in two contrasting vignettes (vv. 1–6, 13–18) whose effectiveness is created by the close similarity between the scenes portrayed up to the final devastating conclusion: those who accept Wisdom's invitation will receive the gift of life (v. 6); those who accept that of the woman Folly will join her other guests in death (v. 18).

The similarities between the two scenes are obvious: both Wisdom and Folly invite the **simple** or naive (vv. 4, 16 – the two verses are virtually identical) to their respective houses (vv. 1–4, 14–16) to partake of a meal (vv. 5, 17) which will in each case offer particular attractions (vv. 6, 17). Apart from the stark contrast of the consequences of accepting the invitation, the main differences are the additional statement that Wisdom **has built her house** (v. 1), the different modes of invitation (vv. 3, 14), the description of the character of Folly (v. 13), the contrast between the conversion of Wisdom's guests to **the way of insight** (v. 6) while Folly's guests remain stupid (**he does not know**, v. 18), the immoral inducement offered by Folly (v. 17) and the vivid description of the fate of Folly's guests (v. 18).

Vv. 7–12 do not obviously fit into this scheme. From the aesthetic or literary point of view they are intrusive and seriously weaken the effect of the contrast formed by the two vignettes. Although in v. 11 Wisdom appears to be still speaking (**by me**), and it is possible that this verse was originally the continuation of her words in vv. 5–6, the other verses in the section show no sign of this; they are miscellaneous in character and quite inappropriate as part of her invitation. It is not clear, however, why they should have been added at this point. Unlike the additions which were made to some of the preceding Instructions, they have no theme in common with vv. 1–6, nor – except possibly for v. 11 – can they be easily seen as offering a correction or reinterpretation of those verses. It has been supposed that they may have been inserted to express disillusion with the confident optimism of v. 6 (Goldingay, 1977, pp. 87–93; Gemser, Ringgren), introducing a more sober note based on bitter experience; but if so, this has been done clumsily; nor is the suggestion that they are intended to offer examples of the "food and drink" – that is, the instruction, that Wisdom offers – convincing. The facts that one Hebrew manuscript lacks vv. 9–10 and another vv. 10–12 (see *BHS*) and that LXX has a long addition after v. 12 suggest that there is a complicated textual history behind this section.

Doubt has also been thrown on the unity of vv. 1–6, 13–18 taken together. It is argued by Scott that a later author modelled vv. 13–18 on vv. 1–6 out of earlier material taken from chapters 1–8, especially from chapter 7; Goldingay draws similar conclusions on formal grounds and as part of an elaborate theory about the composition of the chapter as a whole. Vv. 13–18 do in fact have unusual features. Only here is Folly personified, and the figure has evidently been largely modelled on the more concrete figure of the "loose woman" of chapters 2, 5, 6 and 7. Further, the word for "folly" in v. 13, *kᵉsîlût*, is not used anywhere else in these chapters (in fact, this is its only occurrence in the Old Testament). These facts may well suggest that vv. 13–18 are not by the same hand as the earlier chapters; but it does not prove that their author is other than the author of vv. 1–6. As has been pointed out above, there is no reason to suppose a common authorship for the whole of chapters 1–9; on the contrary, it is probable that they are the work of many authors who, however, shared a common purpose and worked within the same general conventions though they differed in various ways. Prov. 9:1–6, 13–18 with their double imagery of a personified Wisdom and a personified Folly come from a slightly variant tradition which was probably aware of some of the material in chapters 1–8 but which carried the imagery further. The aesthetic quality and balance of their form are not to be explained in terms of literary pastiche. (The purely homiletic addition by *LXX* after v. 18, similar in character to other additions by *LXX* in these chapters, does not affect the issue.)

1. Wisdom's possession of a **house** is also mentioned in her speech in chapter 8 (v. 34). Here in 9:1 she is represented as having just built it and as sending out invitations, apparently to a house-warming party. Many theories have been put forward about the significance of this house, in particular with regard to its **seven pillars**. These theories can be divided into three main categories: the cultic, the cosmological and the literal.

i. According to Boström, Albright (1955, pp. 8–9) and Ringgren, the house is to be regarded as a temple: Wisdom is a substitute for a goddess – a foreign goddess of love, or the "Queen of Heaven" – from an alien religious tradition; she prepares a sacrificial feast, but one which consists of intellectual food. This view is based on the evidence of seven-pillared temple structures attested from the third millennium to the Hellenistic period in various parts of the ancient Near East.

ii. Others have postulated a cosmological significance for Wisdom's house. This interpretation is an ancient one. Rashi interpreted the seven pillars as the pillars which uphold the world; and the Midrash connected them with the seven heavens. In modern times Boström (1935, pp. 3–14), citing Iranian and other texts, combined his theory of the house as a temple with one which saw it as representing the world, the pillars standing for the seven planets. Scott saw it as the "inhabitable world" of 8:31, with Wisdom, its builder and resident, as "the constructive power of reason in Yahweh's creation" (compare his interpretation of *'āmôn* in 8:30).

iii. None of the interpretations of Wisdom's house by modern scholars sketched above is derived from information provided by this verse alone: each is a constituent part of, and interdependent with, a wider hypothesis about the figure of Wisdom, whether mythological, cultic or cosmological, based on an interpretation of other texts. It should therefore be asked whether there is any reason why the reference to the house with its pillars should not be an example of poetical imagery comparable with the representation of

Wisdom in 1:20–33 and chapter 8 as a public speaker or preacher and elsewhere in chapters 1–7 as a bride or as an exceedingly precious commodity: that is, why she should not here be pictured somewhat similarly – no doubt with the opposite picture of the "strange woman" in mind – simply as a hostess inviting guests to a meal.

This interpretation depends, however, on a satisfactory explanation of the house's **seven pillars**: that is, it must be demonstrated that such dwelling-houses did, or at least could have, existed in Palestine during the Israelite period. This question has been endlessly debated, with successive archaeological discoveries making their contribution to the debate. Dunand (1940, pp. 69–84) showed that similar houses existed in Phoenicia and Canaan before the Israelite period, but that evidence for later periods was less secure. It now appears that multiple-pillared houses, including some seven-pillared examples, of the Israelite period have been identified (see Lang, 1983, pp. 488–91; 1986, pp. 90–93). These pillars did not support the main structure of the house but the portico which covered half of the inner courtyard. The norm was the four-pillared house; but larger and more luxurious houses had more. The number of pillars was evidently an indication of wealth and social status: the number of guests who could be accommodated obviously depended on the space available. Wisdom's house, then, was a patrician house or mansion. The number seven, however, was not chosen at random here: seven, as is well known, was widely considered in the ancient Near East including Israel as an ideal number signifying completeness or perfection.

If, however, Wisdom's house has neither a cultic nor a cosmological significance, it becomes necessary to enquire what was the purpose of the emphatic statement that she was not only its resident but its builder. There is no parallel to this in what is said about Folly here. Some light may, however, be thrown on this problem by the isolated proverb 14:1, which uses the same imagery. There the line "Wisdom has built her house" (on the text see below on that verse) is followed by the line "but Folly with her own hands tears it down". That is, Wisdom is a builder but Folly a destroyer. Something of the kind is in fact indirectly implied in chapter 9, since here Folly's house (**there**, v. 18), like that of the "loose woman" in 2:18–19, is the anteroom to death: that is, it is not a solid, real house at all but simply a pit (see on 2:18a). The imagery of Wisdom's having built her house is thus probably intended as an assurance that, in contrast to the unstable Folly (v. 13), Wisdom offers a stable and lasting abode for her adherents. The phrase "to build a house" (*bānāh bayit*) has strong positive overtones of stability and permanence (compare 2 Sam. 7:13, 16, 27) and prosperity (Prov. 24:3–4).

Wisdom (*ḥokmôt*): see on 1:20. **has set up**: *RSV* has followed the emendation of the Hebrew *ḥāṣ*ᵉ*bāh*, "has hewn", to *hiṣṣîbāh*, which seems to have been read by LXX, Pesh. and Targ.

2. She has slaughtered her beasts (*ṭāb*ᵉ*ḥāh ṭibḥāh*): literally, "has slaughtered her slaughtering". This is evidently a lavish banquet. Meat was a luxury, and the slaughtering of an animal would be an occasion for keeping open house. Plöger points out that these terms – in contrast to the *z*ᵉ*bāḥîm* or "sacrifices" held out as an inducement by the "loose woman" in 7:14 – were reserved for purely secular butchery: this meal, accordingly, is not a cultic meal. **mixed her wine**: probably with spices to vary the taste or to make it more intoxicating (compare 23:30; Isa. 5:22) rather than with water (note Isa. 1:22!), though the latter practice was normal from Hellenistic times (see 2 Mac. 15:39).

3. sent out . . . to call: it is not clear whether it is Wisdom herself or her maids who call. The Hebrew has not the infinitive but the feminine singular *tiqrā'*, "*she* calls"; and the singular verb "she says" in v. 4 seems to confirm this. Dahood and Scott (compare also Plöger) take *šāl*ᵉ*ḥāh* (**sent out**) as meaning "sent away" (compare Gen. 28:5; Jg. 11:38) and render the words by "she dismissed her maids and called". An alternative solution might be to take the speech in vv. 5–6 as constituting Wisdom's instructions to the maids, which they were to communicate verbatim to the prospective guests. *qārā'* here (**call**) means "to invite".

from (*'al-gappê*): that is, "from a position on". The meaning of *gap*, the presumed singular of *gappîm*, is uncertain. It may be cognate with *gûpāh* (1 Chr. 10:12), "body, corpse" and so something curved like a vault or ridge; if so, the phrase may simply be equivalent to *'al*, "on the top of" (so Toy, Gemser, *KB*³), or, on the basis of Ugaritic *gpt*, "edge" (Albright, 1955, p. 9). Dahood and Ringgren, however, dispute Albright's interpretation of *gpt*. **the highest places in the town** (*m*ᵉ*rōmê qāret*): this phrase is the same as that used of Folly's standpoint in v. 14; the two words also occur separately in the description of Wisdom's location in 8:2–3. *qeret*, "town", is a rare word: see on 8:1–3. Albright, remarking that all the words in this line are "characteristic of Ugaritic", renders it by "on the edge of the acropolis of the town".

4–6. Compare Folly's speech in vv. 16–17. V. 4 is virtually identical with v. 16.

4. simple: see on 1:4. **let him turn in here**: better, "let him turn aside hither", that is, "to me". **here** obviously does not refer to Wisdom's house, as she is not at home when she speaks. She calls to those who are passing by to approach her so that she may issue her invitation. **without sense**: see on 6:32–5. On the construction of the second line (literally, "[as for] him without sense, she says to him") see *GK* 143b.

5. eat: there are only six occurrences of this verb (*lāḥam*) in the Old Testament, of which four are in Proverbs. In Ugaritic literature it occurs several times in parallelism with **drink** (*šātāh*) as here. **bread**: that is, "meal".

6. simpleness: the Hebrew has *p^eṯā'yîm*, "simple ones", that is, their simple companions. There is no need either to emend or to suppose the existence of an abstract noun meaning "simplicity" (so Delitzsch and McKane, and compare *REB*, "the company of simpletons"). **walk**: this verb (*'āšar*) means "go forward" (*REB* "advance").

7. a scoffer (*lēṣ*): this word (on which see also on 1:22) recurs in v. 8, and the cognate verb *lîṣ* in v. 12. (The additional lines in LXX at the end of v. 12 refer to "lying" [*pseudesis*], which probably reflects the cognate abstract noun *lāṣôn*.) There is no agreement on the meaning of *lēṣ* and its cognates; but there is probably a connection with the preceding verses: it is intended here to denote a person who, unlike the "simple" ones of those verses, is by nature malicious and impervious to correction or instruction. This meaning is in line with its use in other contexts in chapters 1–9: in vv. 8 and 12 it is contrasted with the wise, in 1:22 it is contrasted with the simple and associated with the fool, and in 3:34 it is contrasted with the humble. In Ps. 1:1 it is parallel with *rāšā'*, "wicked", as here.

abuse (*qālôn*): better, "contempt". Compare the hiphil of the verb *qālāh* in Dt. 27:16, "to treat with contempt". **injury**: this is not a satisfactory translation of *mûmô*, literally "his blemish". But the sense is not clear. The word has been thought to refer to the moral defect of the wicked man which is somehow transferred to the person who **reproves** him (McKane; Richardson, 1955, p. 173, "he will be charged with the sin of the wicked man"). This hardly seems probable. Equally improbable is the view that the "blemish" or "defect" is that of the reprover himself. It has been proposed that the word should be emended to *k^e^limmāh* or *ḥerpāh* (compare 18:3), both of which can mean "insult" or "humiliation". Either would make a good parallel with *qālôn*. LXX has *mōmēsetai*, "will be blamed", probably because of its similarity to *mûmô*.

8. This verse and v. 9 continue the theme introduced in v. 7. The three verses are, however, best seen as a short collection of proverbs juxtaposed and linked by catchwords to form a chain: v. 7, *lēṣ*, *hôkîaḥ* (**reprove**), *rāšā'* (**wicked**); v. 8 *lēṣ*, *hôkîaḥ*, *ḥākām* (**wise**); v. 9 *ḥākām*, *ṣaddîq* (**righteous**). This device is frequently used in the sentence literature to join a series of proverbs together (see below, *passim*).

9. Give instruction: the Hebrew has simply "Give" (*tēn*). That what is to be given is instruction is clear from the context. This is a straightforward case of ellipsis, and no emendation is required. *REB* has "Lecture", based on the repointing of *tēn* as *tan*, supposedly the imperative piel of a rare verb *tānāh* II; but it is doubtful whether this verb, which can mean "to teach" in post-biblical Hebrew and Aramaic (compare Tannaim, the sages of early post-biblical times) can have this meaning in biblical Hebrew (see *KB*[3]).

10. On the first line see above on 1:7. This is the only reference to God in this chapter. As with other such additions to chapters 1–9 the purpose of the verse is to assert that Wisdom is not an independent entity but only attainable by those who serve Yahweh. It thus qualifies v. 11. **the Holy One**: the plural *q^e^dōšîm* usually refers to holy or saintly persons or to heavenly beings or angels. This verse, with 30:3 and Hos. 11:12 (Heb. 12:1) are the only places in the Old Testament where it may refer to God. However, almost all commentators (Ringgren and Barucq are undecided) take it to be an epithet of Yahweh, who of course is frequently referred to (in the singular, *qādôš*) as "holy". The plural form here may be an example of the so-called "plural of majesty" like *'^e^lōhîm* (*GK* 124g).

11. The phraseology of this verse is very similar to that employed by the human teacher about his own words in 3:2; 4:10; compare also Wisdom's offer of long life in 3:16.

by me (*bî*): Pesh. and Targ. read *bāh*, "by her" (compare LXX). This may be an accommodation to the present context rather than evidence of an original reading. It is the context which is probably not original. If the verse did not originally follow v. 6 it is probably a fragment of a lost speech by Wisdom. **and . . . will be added**:

the form of the verb (*wᵉyôsîpû*, hiphil) is active (literally, "and they will add"); but this is probably an example of an indefinite third person active form with a passive meaning (*GK* 144g). *BHS* suggests emendation to the niphal (*wᵉyiwwāsᵉpû*).

12. Although this verse presents no textual or philological problems, its purport is not easy to understand. Its concern with the same human types as vv. 7–9 suggests that it was at one time juxtaposed to those verses, but there is no development of thought, and it must be seen as an originally isolated proverb which, like many of those in the sentence literature, is too brief to convey a clear meaning. It may, however, be said that its point must lie in the words **for yourself** and **you alone**: that is, that the effects of both wisdom and its opposite are confined to their possessors – others are not affected. The verse has therefore generally been interpreted as an assertion of individual responsibility: neither the benefits conferred by the possession of wisdom nor the punishment meted out to the "scoffer" can be transferred to others. These commentators, however, have failed to note the fact that, in the case of wisdom, such an assertion is contrary not only to human experience but to the constant teaching of chapters 1–9, and indeed of the whole book, that wisdom *can* be taught to others and that those who heed that teaching will themselves become wise and so receive the benefits of the possession of wisdom together with their teachers. The LXX translators were aware of the problem, and completely reversed the sense of the line: "If you are wise for yourself, you will be wise also for your neighbours": thus wisdom *can* and should be communicated to others, but the wicked must suffer alone. McKane attempts to interpret the verse along psychological lines: both wisdom and the wickedness of the "scoffer" are inalienable characteristics and cannot be altered. Wisdom "is part of the man who has it; it makes him what he is and no man can take it from him"; and similarly the attitude of the "man who has intellectual pride" is "constitutive of him in the most inward parts of his selfhood" so that "in his loneliness . . . he must endure the consequences on his personality as they work themselves out inexorably". This is perhaps to read too much into the verse, whose true meaning remains obscure.

13. A foolish woman (*'ēšet kᵉsîlût*): rather, "The woman Folly". This is an explicative genitive (see *GK* 128k and Driver, Gemser and *REB*). **noisy** (*hōmiyyāh*): see on 7:11. **wanton** (*pᵉtayyût*): this word and *kᵉsîlût* occur only here. It is agreed that *pᵉtayyût*, whose form may have been influences by Aramaic (see Toy), is derived from *pātāh* (like *petî*, "simple"); but in the piel this verb means "to persuade". This fact has given rise to two different types of translation: "simple, ignorant" (from the qal – so Driver, *JTS* 41 [1940], p. 173 –) and "persuasive, seductive" – hence *RSV*'s **wanton** – so Toy, Plöger, Lang (1986, p. 170).

and knows no shame (*ûbal-yādᵉʿāh māh*); the Hebrew text has no word here meaning "shame", but reads "and does not know *māh*." The older translations took *māh* here to mean "anything": that is, Folly is completely ignorant. *RSV*, however, has followed many commentators who, on the basis of LXX, emend *māh* to *kᵉlimmāh* "shame" or *hikkālēm*, "to be ashamed". The reason for these proposals is that *māh* (most frequently "what") supposedly never has the meaning "something" or "anything". But this is not so. Sometimes it has this meaning when, as here, it stands as the object of a verb. This is so in Gen. 39:8 and 2 Sam. 18:29; in both instances the governing verb is, as here, *yādaʿ* in the negative (*lōʾ-yādaʿ*). "and knows nothing" is therefore a possible translation here. But there is another possible rendering of the phrase: *yādaʿ* can also mean "to care about, be concerned about" (Gen. 39:6; Job 9:21); the best translation may therefore be "and she cares about nothing" (so *REB*). (On Thomas's view that *yādaʿ* here means "to be quiet, be at rest" see on 5:6 above.)

14. the high places of the town: this is the same phrase as in v. 3. Folly's double location here is puzzling. The view of Boström and Ringgren that there is a cultic implication here, Folly's house, like that of Wisdom, being a temple and not an ordinary dwelling-house may be ruled out (see on v. 1). Folly's **house** and the **high places** cannot, then, be identical. Perhaps the best explanation is that the author wanted to make the similarity of these verses with vv. 1–6 as complete as possible despite the discrepancy.

16. This verse is almost identical with v. 4. **she says** (*wᵉʾāmᵉrāh*): on the construction see *GK* 143d; S. R. Driver, *Tenses*, section 123.

17. This verse corresponds with v. 5 in that "food" and "drink" are offered as inducements; but the point is the complete contrast between the true nature of what is offered in the respective cases. Wisdom offers instruction for the mind; Folly offers sexual pleasure. **water** (not the "wine" offered by Wisdom) is a metaphor for sexual intercourse as in 5:15; its being **Stolen** means that it is forbidden and clandestine. **bread eaten in secret**: eating is a frequent metaphor for sexual intercourse: compare 30:20. **sweet**; **pleasant**: the clandestine nature of the action proposed makes it all the more desirable.

18. The similarity of this verse to 2:18 and 7:27 raises the question whether the author was familiar with those passages. **the dead**: literally, "the shades"; see on 2:18.

The verse makes a fitting climax to the poem. The long passage in LXX which follows is not original and weakens the effect.

"PROVERBS OF SOLOMON"
A COLLECTION OF SHORT PROVERBS
10:1–22:16

(The following remarks apply also to chapters 25–9.) See also the Introduction.

From the points of view both of contents and of form these chapters are quite different from chapters 1–9. Although the latter contain a few individual proverbs which have been incorporated into or appended to larger compositions, chapters 10:1–22:16 consist almost entirely of short individual proverbs each having the form of a single couplet. Apart from this formal distinction there are two other important differences: (1) the proverbs in question did not for the most part originate in a specifically educational setting like the Instructions; and (2) there is virtually no personification of Wisdom in these chapters.

The fact that these proverbs have been collected, committed to writing and handed down presupposes the work of scribes, some of whom were probably connected with the royal court (note the headings in 10:1 and 25:1). But the original background, setting and purpose of the material can be assessed only on the basis of the internal evidence of the proverbs themselves. This shows that the main preoccupation of the authors was the prudent conduct of the life of the individual, as regarded both his personal interests and those of the society of which he was a member. The frequent alternation of the contrasts between wise and foolish on the one hand and righteous and wicked on the other shows that the two spheres – of wisdom and religion – were closely related if not identical. With certain reservations – notably the recognition that Yahweh was sovereign and sometimes acted to overrule human plans, and that the existence of an underprivileged class was believed to be inevitable – it was constantly asserted that human beings are free to choose their own destinies.

To this extent the *message* of these proverbs closely resembles that of the Instructions of chapters 1–9, except that it is not ostensibly addressed to a specific class or age-group. However, a study of the allusions to practical details of life and the use of socio-economic terms used in the proverbs show that this section of the book, too, has a specific social background. The setting is predominantly agricultural, and the proverbs represent a class of small farmers who are relatively prosperous but aware of the precariousness of their economic situation. They aspire to greater prosperity and yet detest those who have enriched themselves by immoral means and who oppress the less fortunate; they fear a fall into poverty, yet believe that the poor have usually brought their misfortunes on themselves by fecklessness or irresponsibility, while recognizing a duty to be charitable towards them. They strongly advocate the virtues of hard work and frugality. (References to the king – and to kings in general – do not, as has been widely believed, prove that any of the proverbs originated in the setting of the royal court: see below on the various so-called "royal proverbs"; and see Whybray, 1990 on the social background and especially pp. 45–59 on the "royal proverbs".)

The *purpose and function* of these proverbs are disputed. (The terminology used of them ("proverb") is also contentious; some commentators, therefore, avoid the term "proverb" altogether as too specific, preferring "neutral" terms such as "saying" and "sentence". For recent discussions of this question see Fontaine, 1982; Thompson, 1974; J. G. Williams, 1981.) They must have been culled from various sources, and it would be unwise to assume that they were all originally intended to serve the same kind of basic purpose, or to attempt to classify them rigidly in this respect. Each one makes a distinct observation about how things are, and was evidently considered to be of practical utility and so memorable. The view that they represent an attempt to discover an overarching "order" in the world is inaccurate; rather, they testify to the existence of order in the world (see Murphy, 1967, 1981), but on the whole they do this piecemeal and do not attempt a systematic approach. Many of them, however, do attempt to enunciate principles for the ordering of society, and to that extent they may be regarded as contributing to its cohesion.

Scholars have classified these proverbs in various ways. Some of these distinctions pertain to their *form*. Most of the proverbs consist of parallel couplets; and these may be antithetical, for example, 10:5,

A son who gathers in summer is prudent,
but a son who sleeps in harvest brings shame,

or synonymous, for example 16:18,

Pride goes before destruction,
and a haughty spirit before a fall,

though in some there is no parallelism: the second line simply continues the thought of the first, as in 16:4:

The Lord has made everything for its purpose,
even the wicked for the day of trouble.

Another form which occurs frequently is the so-called "Better-saying" such as 15:16:

Better is a little with the fear of the Lord
than great treasure and trouble with it.

These are all speech-forms used for emphasis and effective communication which are also found in other literature, both oral and written, of the ancient Near Eastern and other cultures.

Another formal distinction is that between the "statement" – for example, 14:5:

A faithful witness does not lie,
but a false witness breathes out lies

and the "admonition" for example, 16:3:

Commit your work to the Lord,
and your plans will be established

The latter form, which is predominant – though usually at greater length – in chapters 1–9, is, however, rare in these chapters. It has been argued (especially by Audet and Gerstenberger) that these two forms have quite separate origins; but in these chapters at least it is difficult to distinguish between their functions: a statement like 10:5 (see above), for example, is clearly no less a piece of advice, and is no less effective, than the imperative form of 20:13:

Love not sleep, lest you come to poverty;
open your eyes, and you will have plenty of bread;

nor is the point of 13:24

He who spares the rod hates his son,
but he who loves him is diligent to discipline him

in any way different from that of 19:18:

Discipline your son while there is hope;
do not set your heart on his destruction.

In the Introduction to chapters 1–9 above and in the comments on subsequent sections it was maintained that some at least of the *references* there *to Yahweh* in both the Instructions and in the speeches by Wisdom had been added to older material in order to make it clear that the "wisdom" taught by the human teachers and embodied in the personified figure of Wisdom was in fact Yahweh's wisdom: the pursuit of wisdom advocated by the teachers was, in other words, inseparable from the "fear of Yahweh". A comparable process seems to have taken place also in the case of 10:1–22:16 and chapters 25–9. This does not, however, mean that those proverbs which do not mention Yahweh should be characterized as "secular". The idea of a non-religious "old wisdom" later "baptized", as it were, into the Yahwistic faith is no longer tenable (see the Introduction above). Rather it was a question of making these collections of proverbs more explicitly theological and specifically "Yahweh-oriented". (This opinion entails some modification of my earlier views [1979, pp. 153–165].)

A final distinction which has been made between types of proverb in these chapters is that of McKane, who divided them into three types: (A) proverbs concerned with the education of the individual; (B) proverbs concerned with the wellbeing of the community; and (C) proverbs concerned with "a moralism which derives from Yahwistic piety" (p. 415). Apart from the question of type C, already considered in the preceding paragraph, the distinction between McKane's types A and B is also questionable. Although it is certainly possible to pick out many proverbs in these chapters which are superficially concerned exclusively either with the interests of the individual or with the wellbeing of the community, this is in fact a false distinction, since the life of the individual in a society like that of ancient Israel was inextricably bound up with that of the society in which he or she lived – in the case of these chapters, primarily the family and the village or small town. Without the good will of his fellows the individual could not prosper: the community knew what sort of person he was, and judged him accordingly (compare 5:9–14 and 6:32–5). The two kinds of proverb, in as far as they can be distinguished at all, belong together, and nothing is to be gained by separating them.

The *process by which these chapters were compiled* remains obscure. It is unlikely that it was a single one, or that it was completed in a short space of time. There are many features which point to the formation of smaller collections prior to the final redaction. It has been pointed out, for example, that there is a stylistic difference between chapters 10–15 and 16:1–22:16 in that the former consists overwhelmingly of antithetical proverbs while the latter consists mainly of other types, especially the synonymous proverb. However, identical or almost identical lines or proverbs appear in both sections (for example, 10:15a and 18:11a; 15:33b and 18:12b). But such repetition is also found within a single section (for example, 14:12 and 16:25); this suggests that these sections were themselves formed from even smaller collections, since it is difficult to account for such repetitions in any other way.

There are also groups of proverbs dealing with the same general theme (for example, 16:10–15, all of which except v. 11 are concerned with kings); but this is a rare phenomenon. The task of compositional analysis is made the harder in that nowhere within the entire section 10:1–22:16 – or within chapters 25–9 – is there a distinct heading or any other overt indication of the existence of smaller groups of proverbs. Any evidence there may be of this must be sought in the text of the proverbs themselves. Even between chapters 15 and 16 there is no indication of a break: chapter 16 runs on from chapter 15 as if the composition were entirely seamless. Nor is there any substantial difference in subject-matter between 10–15 and 16:1–22:16, despite Skladny's attempt to establish this statistically. Thus the whole collection gives the impression of deriving from the same social background.

The individual proverb, then, remains the basic unit. Each is complete in itself; and whatever may be the rationale of their present arrangement, there is every reason to suppose that the great majority of them once existed separately. There has been much discussion of their style. It was often supposed that the proverbs are too skilfully composed to be of popular origin; but it has now been demonstrated that this is not so: numerous examples of proverbs current among modern pre-literate, especially African, peoples have been collected which are closely comparable with those in the book of Proverbs not only in content and moral tone, but also in stylistic characteristics, even including the phenomenon of parallelism, formerly believed to be a special characteristic of ancient Near Eastern poetry (see Barucq, 1972, cols 1415–19; Westermann, *Gesammelte Studien* II, 1974, pp. 149–61; Naré, 1986 for examples and discussion). Further, the idea that the proverbs in Prov. 10:1–22:16 and 25–9 are too numerous to have been current simultaneously in ancient Israel has been rendered otiose by the listing of about 1900 proverbs of the Mossi people by Naré in the book referred to above.

Incidentally, these discoveries also make less probable the theory that the typical two-line proverb or couplet in Proverbs was a development from the simpler one-line proverb, although this may have been the case in some instances. In general parallelism was used not for the purpose of literary decoration or adornment but in order to persuade by repetition – made more effective by the variation of detail in the second line – or by the dramatic presentation of stark contrasts.

One of the essential characteristics of the proverb in any language is its *brevity*, which gives it a peculiarly pithy effect. The most typical examples in these chapters of Proverbs contain no more than three words in each line. Since in most cases each single line contains a complete statement, meaning is conveyed solely by sentences of no more than three, or at the most four, words, and an entire topic is dealt with in six or eight. Many of these topics are extremely wide-ranging, and would require an entire treatise for adequate discussion. But the proverb is the *result* rather than the starting-point of such discussion: it is a distillation of reflection on experience. But, for the modern reader at least, this brevity often causes obscurity. It is possible that some of the proverbs are actually intended to be ambiguous or "open-ended". Certainly they are intended to be applicable in various different circumstances in quite different ways; and the modern interpreter is at a disadvantage owing to his limited knowledge of the daily life of those for whom they were composed.

One of the most difficult problems encountered in studying these chapters is, however, their *present arrangement*. For some commentators this is completely haphazard. Thus McKane asserts that, apart from some minor editorial groupings, "there is, for the most part, no context in the sentence literature"; and he speaks of "the random way in which wisdom sentences follow one upon the other in any chapter" (commentary, p. 10). On the level of subject matter at least, a superficial reading of these chapters tends to confirm this view; and in fact no investigation of the question so far undertaken has produced a plausible hypothesis which accounts for the arrangement of the collection as a whole.

Nevertheless, the unquestionable fact of the existence of *a few* obvious groupings of proverbs indicates that some persons acting in an "editorial" capacity at some time before the final redaction were aware of the desirability of some kind of systematization and had some notion how to go about it. This is an encouragement to further exploration of the question, since it suggests that there may be other groups of proverbs hitherto unsuspected by modern scholars, based on other principles of arrangement. Boström (1928) was the first to take up this challenge, studying the *sounds* of the language used (alliteration, assonance, wordplay and the like – see Watson, pp. 222–50) to see how these were used to link juxtaposed units together. Various attempts have since been made to find other principles of arrangement; but so far little progress has been made in the search for a basis for more than the formation of quite small groups of proverbs (see, however, Van Leeuwen [1988] and Krispenz). Some possible evidence for the existence of such groups is set out in the commentary below. (See also my forthcoming study on this question to be published in the *JSOT* Supplement Series.) One value of the discovery of such groups for the interpreter is that it provides a miniature context which may assist the interpretation of the individual proverbs within the group.

CHAPTER 10

Although the present division of the books of the Old Testament into chapters is no older than the fourteenth century AD, it presumably reflects a perception at that time, not necessarily of the individual chapters as distinct literary entities or as authorial or editorial divisions of the text, but at least of appropriate places to make a pause without marring the continuity of a work. In the case of Prov. 10:1–22:16, although this perception was not sufficiently acute to detect the major break at 22:17, the unequal numbers of verses in these chapters, ranging from twenty-four to thirty-five, suggests that each chapter was seen as having some kind of formal or thematic cohesion, or at least a beginning and an ending: otherwise there appears to be no reason for these unequal lengths. Recently some scholars have attempted to demonstrate the unity of certain chapters (see especially on ch. 25, below). It is therefore not entirely inappropriate to follow some other commentators in naming some dominant forms and themes to be found in individual chapters.

Chapter ten, as has already been observed, consists almost entirely of proverbs in antithetical parallelism. Its two main themes are the contrasts between the righteous and the wicked and between the wise and foolish. (It should be observed, however, that the "positive" and "negative" lines in a single proverb are not always placed in the same order.) At least half of the verses fall into the first category; specific examples of the second are somewhat less numerous (vv. 1, 8, 13, 17, 23). However, several sub-categories belong to this latter category in a wider sense: clearly diligence and laziness (vv. 4, 5, 26) are in fact examples of wisdom and folly respectively; and this is also true of the prudent and imprudent use of speech (v. 19). Contrasts are also made between rich and poor (v. 15) and between love and hatred (v. 12). The point which is common to the great majority of these proverbs is that the material destiny in life of each of the contrasted human types will be appropriately determined by its behaviour; but the behaviour itself is clearly not predetermined: if a choice were not available, the proverb would have no point. Both the various kinds of behaviour referred to and the expected consequences are mainly expressed in very general terms; but it is clear that no distinction is made between wisdom and righteousness on the one hand and folly and wickedness on the other as far as the consequences are concerned. The chapter contains four Yahweh-proverbs (vv. 3, 22, 27, 29) which appear to be not unrelated to the contexts in which they stand.

1–5. Plöger has pointed out that these verses form a thematic group, though a loose one. This is not a single literary entity but an editorial arrangement of originally unconnected proverbs, and there is no progression of thought but rather an interior linkage of a different kind. Vv. 1 and 5 form a framework for the verses in between. The general statement about wise and foolish sons in v. 1 receives greater precision in v. 5, where their respective wisdom and folly are expressed in concrete terms respectively of diligence and neglect in the matter, vital to the farmer, of bringing in the harvest. Within this framework, v. 4 states even more unequivocally than v. 5 what are the ultimate respective consequences of the two modes of behaviour: that is, wealth and poverty. Verse 3, the central verse of the group, makes a similar assertion but expresses it in terms of righteousness and wickedness rather than of wisdom and folly, and also introduces Yahweh as the one who presides over the process; and v. 2 picks up the theme of wealth treated in vv. 3 and 4 with a warning note: wealth profits its recipient only if it is earned by righteousness and diligence; if it is obtained by immoral means it will in the end ruin him. To this thematic argument Plöger adds a formal one: in vv. 1, 3 and 5 the "positive" line (wisdom, righteousness, diligence) precedes the "negative" one, whereas in vv. 2 and 4 the order is reversed: wickedness and laziness precede their opposites. He also maintains that there is no such clear evidence of a deliberate arrangement of proverbs elsewhere in the chapter. If this is correct, this initial group may have been intended to "set the tone" for what follows. (But see below.)

1. The proverbs of Solomon: see the Introduction. The theme of this verse is a frequent one in Proverbs. Not only are very similar proverbs found in the sentence literature (see especially 13:1; 17:21, 25, and 15:20, whose first line is identical with 10:1a), but this is also the leading theme of the Instructions in chapters 1–9, where in very different social circumstances it is the aim of the teacher to persuade his pupils to be "wise sons". We may also compare the royal instruction in 31:1–9 and the teaching of the "good wife" (31:26–8). The same theme is also found frequently in the other literatures of the ancient Near East. The purpose of the editor in placing this verse and those which immediately follow it at the head of the collection was probably to give the whole collection the appearance of an educational instruction, whereas the bulk of the individual proverbs do not suggest this at all. The theme was, however, an important one because the maintenance of the family and its social standing depended on the character of the son and heir who would inherit the property, whether this was great or small, quite apart from the importance to the small farmer of a son who would be not only able but willing to assist with the work of the farm. **his mother**: on the role of the Israelite mother see on 1:8.

2. death: see on 2:18; 5:5 and compare vv. 16, 21, 27 and 30 in this chapter. The second line is identical with 11:4b.

3. the righteous: the Hebrew has *nepeš ṣaddîq*, probably "the *appetite* of the righteous". **the wicked**: some MSS have "the treacherous"; but this is probably an assimilation to 11:6.

4. A slack hand causes poverty: the order of the words in the Hebrew text – object, verb, subject – is unusual; but the alternative translation "poverty causes a slack hand", meaning that the unemployed become idle, is improbable in view of the parallelism. The arrangement of the words in this line is no doubt made in order to create a chiasm with the second line which puts the verb before the subject. **poverty**: the Hebrew has "a poor man" (*rā'š*). *RSV* follows the proposal found in *BHS*, to repoint the word as *rē'š*, "poverty"; this would then entail the repointing of the masculine participle *'ōśeh* (**causes**) to the feminine *'ośāh* since **hand** (*kap*) in this line is a feminine noun.

rā'š (also spelled *rāš*), "poor", is the word most frequently used in Proverbs with that meaning (the others are *'ebyôn* and *'ānî*). All these words have exactly the same connotation of actual destitution. *rā'š* occurs fourteen times in Proverbs and only seven times in the remainder of the Old Testament. *rēš*, **poverty**, is peculiar to Proverbs. The frequency of the references in these chapters to poverty and, more generally, to other potential disasters, is an indication of the precariousness of life for the small farmer, who for various reasons was particularly vulnerable and could easily find himself ruined. One the other hand, he also believed that by hard work or by being **diligent**, there was a possibility of improving his situation. **makes rich** (*he"šîr*): probably better, "makes his fortune". The word in this context does not necessarily mean the acquisition of great wealth, but rather of sufficient prosperity to confer an economic security which at present the farmer does not have: compare v. 15a, where wealth is described as "a strong city" – that is, it protects its possessor from the vicissitudes of the ordinary life of the small farmer.

5. The first line could equally well be translated "A prudent son gathers in summer"; similarly the second line. **prudent** (*maśkîl*), **brings shame** (*mēbîš*): the first of these words can also mean "intelligent" or "successful". The second may mean either "brings disgrace" – that is, on the son's family – or "acts shamefully", that is, "is worthless". It is difficult to decide between these meanings; but if the preceding verse may be regarded as a kind of commentary, the point of the verse is that neglect of proper attention to the harvest will lead to destitution, a state which if due to one's own fault is one which the community regarded as a disgrace. **summer**, **harvest**: see on 6:8.

McKane regards this and other "agricultural" proverbs in these chapters as having a much wider application: he speaks of their language as "figurative". While it may be characteristic of the proverb to be open to a variety of applications, it is improbable that these chapters would teem, as they do, with allusions to farming if they were not intended in the first place to reflect a specific socio-economic situation.

6–11. These verses do not have the same thematic coherence as vv. 1–5, but there are a number of verbal repetitions. In the Hebrew text (but not in *RSV*, which in v. 10b follows the quite different text of LXX), vv. 8b and 10b are identical; and this is also true of vv. 6b and 11b. There are also verbal links between vv. 6 and 7, both of which speak of a **blessing** (*b^erākāh*) and both of which contrast the **righteous** and the **wicked**, as also does v. 11. The question is whether these repetitions indicate an editorial attempt to form a coherent group.

It should be noted that all of these verses except v. 8, where the contrast is between the wise and the fool, are concerned with ethically right and wrong conduct. Recent commentators have, however, regarded the identity of vv. 6b and 11b and of vv. 8b and 10b as indications that the Hebrew text is in disorder. They argue that whereas vv. 8 and 11 form acceptable parallelisms, the second lines of vv. 6 and 10 do not match the first lines. This is not entirely true, however, as in v. 6 there is a contrast between **head** and **mouth** and in v. 10 between **eye** and (in the Hebrew text) "lips". The use of parts of the body seems to dominate this group of verses: in v. 6 **head** and **mouth** are set against one another; in v. 8 **heart** and "lips" (*RSV* **prating fool**, literally "fool of lips") occur as a pair; and in v. 11 **mouth** occurs (twice).

It could thus be argued that the similarity of wording between vv. 6 and 11 is intended to mark out the beginning and conclusion of a self-contained group of proverbs. Internally, from the thematic point of view, it could be said that v. 7 follows logically from v. 6 in that v. 7 extends the thought of the **blessings . . . on the head of the righteous** to include his posthumous reputation (**memory**, **name**). There is no obvious connection between the themes of vv. 7 and 8, but v. 9 may have been placed immediately after v. 8 in order to interpret wisdom and folly in terms of moral conduct (**integrity**, **perverts his ways**). There is also probably a verbal connection between vv. 10 and 11 in that the "lips" (in the Hebrew) of v. 10b are echoed by the **mouth** of v. 11. So while no progression of thought can be traced in this group of verses, there are enough verbal associations, together with some limited thematic connections, to suggest that an editorial attempt has been made to group them into some kind of meaningful order. If, as is widely held, there is some disorder in the text, this may be the result of editorial manipulation rather than an accident of scribal transmission.

6. Blessings . . . on the head: Israel's (Jacob's) blessing of his family exemplifies the custom of placing the hands on the head of a recipient of a blessing (Gen. 48:14–22). Here the expression is used figuratively. *LXX* and Vulg. add "of the Lord" after **Blessings**, and this may be a correct interpretation. Compare v. 22.

It is usually supposed that the text of this verse is in disorder, since there appears to be no parallelism: instead of a statement in the second line about the *fate* of the **wicked** corresponding to the positive statement about the good fortune of the **righteous** in the first line, the second line appears to refer only to the *activities* of the wicked. Consequently it has been supposed that the second line is an intrusion into the text from v. 11b, perhaps to fill in a gap left by a lost line. But a better solution may lie in the proposal of Gemser that the piel of the verb *ksh* here, usually taken to mean "cover" (*RSV* **conceals**) in fact means "fill (to the brim)". He points out that in Isa. 11:9; Hab. 2:14; 3:3 *ksh* is equivalent to *ml'*, "to be full": thus in Isa. 11:9 the waters *fill* (*m^ekassîm*) the sea (rather than "covering" it, which makes no sense), the sea being regarded as a vessel whose interior is hidden from view when filled to the brim. If this interpretation is accepted, the line may be rendered "but violence fills the mouth of the wicked" – that is, the wicked will *suffer* violence or harm, like the man who by his foolish actions "drinks violence" in 26:6. This rendering would provide the parallelism with the first line which is otherwise lacking.

7. memory (*zēker*); **name** (*šēm*): these words, which occur as a parallel pair also in Exod. 3:15; Job 18:17; Ps. 135:13, are here, as often in the Old Testament, virtually synonymous. They denote the reputation or esteem in which a person was held not only in his lifetime but also after his death. This applied, however, only to the **righteous**, the memory of whose exemplary life was a source of

blessing to others who modelled their lives on theirs: an extension of the blessing which they had themselves received during their lives (v. 6). The **wicked**, on the other hand, were not so remembered, and so their name would **rot** – that is, it would be forgotten after their death and so be as useless as a piece of rotting wood.

8. The wise of heart (*ḥ^akam-lēb*): this emphatic expression denotes the opposite of *ḥ^asar-lēb*, the person without sense (6:32; 7:7; 9:4, 16). On the meaning of **heart** see on 2:2; 4:21. **commandments**: this word (*miṣwāh*) is used in some of the Instructions (2:1; 3:1; 4:4; 7:1, 2), where either in the plural or the singular it denotes the contents of the teaching; but here it does not necessarily denote formal teaching but may refer to parental or other authority in general (compare 6:20). **a prating fool**: literally, "a fool of lips" (*'ᵉwîl śᵉpātayim*). On *'ᵉwîl*, "fool", see on 1:7. The phrase presumably means "a foolish talker", that is, a person who speaks foolishly or without thinking. The parallelism between the two lines of this verse is not obvious, but the thought may be that whereas to conform to the recognized norms of society is a prudent course of action, "talking out of turn" implies a refusal to do so. **will come to ruin**: this verb (*lbṭ*, niphal) occurs in the Old Testament only here and in v. 10 and in Hos. 4:14. Its precise meaning is uncertain. In mishnaic Hebrew it can mean "to be troubled"; but the passive participle qal denotes an outcast, while the noun *lebeṭ* means "misery".

9. He who walks in integrity (*hôlēk battōm*) **walks securely** (*yēlēk beṭaḥ*): here, as in the Instructions of chapters 1–9 and elsewhere in the Old Testament, human life is envisaged in terms of making a journey on foot. Almost identical phrases occur in the Instructions: in 3:23 it is those who make "sound wisdom" their guide who "walk securely", that is, who enjoy the assurance that no danger can overtake them; in 2:7 those who "walk in integrity" receive the protection of Yahweh. In this verse, in which the two phrases are brought together, it is probably implied that, as in 2:7, it is Yahweh who gives this assurance. The line is a good example of the confident optimism of Proverbs which was challenged in the presentation of Job as a man whose integrity was unparalleled (Job 1:1) but gave him no such protection.

he who perverts his ways: literally, "makes his ways crooked", that is, "behaves deceitfully or dishonestly".

will be found out (*yiwwādēa'*): literally, "will be known" – possibly by his fellows or associates, but more probably by God (see above on the first line). This reading has been questioned on the grounds that the parallelism requires a stronger verb conveying the idea of punishment, or at least of some kind of misfortune. It has therefore been suggested that the original reading was *yērōa'* (the niphal of *r''*), "will suffer harm", which occurs in similar contexts in 11:15; 13:20. An alternative solution proposed is that of Gemser and Ringgren, following Thomas, that the word is an example of a verb *yāda'* distinct from that which means "to know", which would here yield the meaning "will be humiliated" (see on 5:6 above for this theory). But in fact no such proposals are required: the rendering "will be known" (or, "is known") is quite satisfactory. If it means that the deviousness of the person in question will become known to his fellows, his fate at their hands does not need to be specifically mentioned: whether actual punishment or ostracism is implied, it can be taken for granted. Such pregnant use of words is not infrequent in these brief and compact proverbs. This is even more true if the reference is to *God*'s knowledge. That Yahweh sees (*rā'āh*) and knows (*yāda'*) the human heart is a commonplace in the Old Testament; and in Proverbs also it is three times asserted that he weighs, or weighs up human spirits or hearts (16:2; 21:2; 24:12). In these, as in other passages, this knowledge is clearly not purely academic, but forms the basis of Yahweh's judgement and of his consequent actions towards the persons concerned. An example of the use of the verb *yāda'*, "know", in a similarly pregnant sense is Ps. 1:6: "Yahweh *knows* the way of the righteous, but the way of the wicked *will perish*".

10. He who winks the eye: as in 6:13 and Ps. 35:19 the exact significance of this evidently malicious action is not clear. It may be magical (compare the "evil eye") or deceitful (a secret sign) or contemptuous. **trouble** (*'aṣṣebet*): this noun, cognate with *'āṣab*, "to hurt, pain", occurs only five times in the Old Testament. In Prov. 15:13 and Ps. 147:3 the "pain" is not physical but mental – grief or sorrow. Here it is probably something which is inflicted (*nātan*, *RSV* **causes**) by the winker on other people, although in 13:15 ("Good sense wins favour") *nātan* is used in a similar way of obtaining something for oneself.

The second line in Hebrew is identical with v. 8b (see above on vv. 6–11). There seems to be no connection between it and the first line. Most commentators, followed by *RSV*, supply a line based on LXX which is entirely different. If winking in the first line refers to insincerity, this would provide a reasonable antithesis to the first line; but LXX is not supported by Vulg., and the line may have been supplied by LXX to fill a gap or to replace a mutilated Hebrew text which has dropped out of *MT*.

11. The second line of this verse is identical with v. 6b, on which see the comments above. The order is chiastic: the Hebrew of the first line has "A fountain of life is the mouth of the righteous". If *RSV*'s translation is correct, it may be possible to see a certain thematic parallelism here. McKane comments: "The speech of a righteous man fructifies and enriches the common life, whereas when wicked men speak, there is a deep-seated malevolence behind what they say". However, to interpret "conceals violence" as an expression for "deep-seated malevolence" is a rather forced interpretation. The alternative rendering of the line ("violence fills the mouth of the wicked" – see above on v. 6) does not provide a thematic parallelism, since the first line speaks about speech and its effect on others while the second is not about speech at all but rather a comment on the fate of the wicked. But there is a formal link between the two lines in the similarity, yet contrast, between the phrases "the mouth of the righteous" and "the mouth of the wicked" which have been chiastically juxtaposed – perhaps the work of an editor rather than of an author (see on vv. 6–11 above).

a fountain of life: this phrase occurs again in three other passages: in Prov. 14:27 it is associated with the fear of Yahweh, and in Ps. 36:9 (Heb. 10) it is an attribute of Yahweh himself. In Prov. 16:22 it is Wisdom, who in chapters 1–9 offers "life" to those who follow her, who is said to be a fountain of life to her possessors. (Cf. also Jer. 17:13.) Thus what is elsewhere an attribute either of Yahweh or of Wisdom is here attributed to the speech of **the righteous**, who are thus by implication identified with the pious or with the wise. The metaphor of water which gives life ("living water", that is, water from a spring or "fountain", Jer. 17:13) is an obvious one, especially in a country like Palestine, and is frequently found in the Old Testament (see P. Reymond, *VT* Suppl. 6, 1958).

12. There is a verbal link between this verse and v. 11 (*tᵉkasseh*, **covers**; v. 11 *yᵉkasseh*, *RSV* **conceals**); but if *yᵉkasseh* in v. 11 means "fills" (see on v. 6b, which is identical with v. 11b) it is one of homophony rather than of sense.

This proverb is concerned with personal relationships which, however, affect the wellbeing of the community (this is implied by *mᵉdānîm*, **strife**). **offences**: this word (*peša'*), which elsewhere in the Old Testament often denotes sin against God, is used here – and often in Proverbs – of (undefined) personal offences committed by one individual against another (compare 19:11). **love** (*'ahᵃbāh*) here means a harmonious and affectionate relationship between individuals or within a family (compare 15:17; 17:9). Here this takes the form of forgiveness (this is the meaning of *ksh* piel here – *RSV* **covers**). The proverb is thus an indirect exhortation to love one's enemies.

13. The accumulated experience of the person **who has understanding** (*nābôn*, compare 1:5) finds expression in his speech. Many of these proverbs – and much of Egyptian wisdom literature – are concerned with this question of speech. The wise man knows when to keep silent and when to speak; and when he speaks he chooses his words carefully and appropriately to the occasion, whereas the fool speaks without thinking (v. 8b). The use of the faculty of speech is thus an indication of character.

The second line, however, does not provide an obvious parallel to the first. It is almost identical with 26:3b (the only difference is that 26:3 has *kᵉsîlîm*, "fools", instead of **him who lacks sense**), and there it is entirely appropriate to its context. LXX here links the two lines: "He that brings forth wisdom from his lips smites the fool with a rod"; but this is not supported by the other Versions, and there is no reason to suppose that LXX was following an alternative Hebrew text. The suggestions for emendation in *BHS* are also unsupported. The line may mean that the fool inevitably gets into trouble and is punished by being beaten up or flogged. If it is implied that the cause of his trouble is something which he has said, there may be a kind of connection with the first line; but a more explicit indication of this would be expected, and this is probably to read too much into the text.

14. This verse continues the theme of appropriate speech. The first line may be understood in slightly different ways according to the interpretation of the verb *ṣāpan* (**lay up**), which can mean either "to hide" or "to treasure up" (*REB* "store up"). According to Wildeboer and Toy the line means that wise men are reticent: they avert misfortune either to themselves or others by concealing potentially dangerous information. This interpretation may be supported by comparison with 12:23, where it is said that a shrewd man (*'ārûm* – see the comment on the cognate noun *'ormāh*, 1:4) *conceals* (*kōseh*) knowledge; compare also v. 19 and other proverbs in the book. Plöger, however, following Bühlmann, p. 194, takes the line to mean that the wise "store up" their knowledge in the sense of having it ready to be brought out at an appropriate moment, citing this use of *ṣāpan* in 13:22 and Ca. 7:13 (Heb. 14). Both interpretations make excellent parallels with the second line, and both have parallels elsewhere in these proverbs. The thought is similar to that of v. 13. Compare also 10:19; 12:23; 13:16; 15:2 and similar sentiments in Egyptian wisdom books.

The second line of the verse in Hebrew is aphoristic: literally, "but the mouth of a fool (*'ewîl*) – ruin near" (*ûpî 'ewîl mᵉḥittāh qᵉrōbāh*).

15. This verse is linked verbally but not thematically with v. 14 by the occurrence in both of *mᵉḥittāh*, **ruin**. Its form is chiastic. The first line is identical with 18:11a.

The point made by the verse is that **wealth** protects the **rich** from the vicissitudes of life, while the **poor**, having no resources to fall back on, are easily vulnerable to total disaster. It is clear from this and other verses which contrast rich and poor that their authors regarded their own economic status as belonging to neither class. Although they entertained hopes of increasing their own wealth by the legitimate means of constant toil (see on v. 4 above), they were well aware of those who had become rich by illegitimate means (v. 2 above); and it may be that these were the men whom they designated by the term **rich man** (*'āšîr*). At any rate, their references to the *'āšîr* are always hostile (see especially 18:23; 22:7; 28:6, 11 and Whybray, 1990, pp. 22–3), as though the *'āšîr*, the "truly rich", belonged to a particular class seen as arrogant and oppressive. But the "truly poor" (here *dal*, elsewhere *'ānī*, *rāš*, or *'ebyôn* – these terms are synonymous: see Whybray, 1990, pp. 15–22) are also always seen in these proverbs as a separate group not to be identified with the authors themselves. They are the totally destitute; and although their **poverty** is often due to their own fecklessness (see for example vv. 4, 5 above) it is an acknowledged duty to be generous towards them (14:21, 31; 19:17; 22:9; 28:27).

his strong city: the metaphor is of a fortified, and supposedly invulnerable, town.

16–17. These verses are linked by the occurrence in each of the expression **to life** (*lᵉḥayyîm*); there may also be a thematic connection (see below on v. 17). But there is also possibly a superficial connection between v. 16 and v. 15 in that **wage** and **gain** in v. 16, though there used in a figurative sense, are terms which in their literal meaning are associated with wealth.

16. wage (*pᵉʿullāh*): so in a literal sense in Lev. 19:13, but here in a more general sense of "reward, recompense" as in Isa. 49:4; 61:8. **leads to life** (simply *lᵉḥayyîm* in the Hebrew): rather, "*is* life". On the emphatic *lamedh* see Brockelmann, section 31a; F. Nötscher, *VT* 3 (1953), pp. 372–80; Dahood, p. 19; *KB*[3]; and Ec. 9:4. **gain** (*tᵉbû'āh*): literally, "income, profit": the word is parallel with *saḥar*, "gain" in 3:14; compare also Prov. 11:18. **(leads) to sin** (*lᵉḥaṭṭāt*): this may be another example of the emphatic *lamedh*; but to say that **the gain of the wicked** *is* sin is as inappropriate to the context as to say that it *leads* to sin: sin would naturally be the *cause*, not the result, of the fate of the wicked. Some kind of contrast is required here to the **life** which is the reward of the righteous. Some commentators propose to emend *ḥaṭṭāt* to *mᵉḥittāh*, **ruin**. If this were allowable, it would link the verse with vv. 14 and 15; but textual corruption would be more likely to have occurred in the contrary direction. It may be that *hāṭṭāt* here has a sense similar to that of the cognate verb *hāṭā'* in 8:36, "to miss": the wicked gains nothing, or loses everything, because he misses, or fails to attain, "life". This also seems to be the meaning of the verb in 20:2, where the person who angers the king "misses", or forfeits, his life.

17. instruction (*mûsār*); **reproof** (*tôkaḥat*): these terms are used regularly in the Instructions of chapters 1–9 to refer to the words of the father or teacher. In this verse also the reference may be to parental teaching (compare 13:1, 24; 15:5; 22:15; 29:15), though in some other proverbs the reference may be general.

is on the path to life: MT has or *'ōraḥ lᵉḥayyîm*, "*is* a path to life": in other words, the person who has himself profited by instruction is able to give "life" to others by instructing them (cf. v. 11a). But many commentators, followed by *RSV*, repoint *'ōraḥ* to *'ōrēaḥ*, the qal participle of *'āraḥ*: "is travelling (towards)", "is on the way to". This question is interrelated with that of the interpretation of *mat'eh* (**goes astray**) in the second line. This is the hiphil participle of *tā'āh*, "to go astray". Since the most common meaning of the hiphil of an intransitive verb is causative, some commentators (for example, McKane) take the word to mean "leads others astray". This would make a suitable contrast with "is a path to life" in the first line. But Gemser, followed by *RSV*, takes the form as an "internal hiphil", that is, as intransitive (**goes astray**), comparing its use in Isa. 63:17 (KB^3 also cites Jer. 42:20 in this connection).

Whichever of these interpretations of the verse is correct, the verse may have been placed here as a comment on v. 16, associating wisdom and folly respectively with righteousness and wickedness (Plöger).

18–21. A group of proverbs about true and false speech (compare vv. 11, 13, 14).

18. This verse is unusual in this section of the book in that it does not exhibit an antithetical parallelism. It presents a number of problems. 1. It is not certain whether the two lines are synonymous or whether the whole verse is a single sentence with a double subject: "Both he who conceals hatred with lying lips (see *GK* 118 m, q on the 'adverbial accusative') and he who utters slander is a fool" (so Gemser, Scott, Ringgren, Plöger). The other problems concern the first line: 2. If this line is an independent statement it is a nominal (that is, non-verbal) sentence; but as with many other such sentences in these chapters and elsewhere it is not clear which is the subject and which the predicate: hence *REB*'s "Lying lips conceal hatred". 3. **conceals** (*m^ekasseh*) is a masculine singular participle, and neither **hatred** (*śin'āh*, feminine singular) nor **lying lips** (*śip^etê-šāqer*, feminine dual) can be its subject. 4. According to Dahood (p. 19) and Scott, *m^ekasseh* here does not mean "conceal" but its opposite, "reveal", "uncover". 5. LXX has "*Righteous* lips cover up hatred" – that is, a righteous man is able to assuage enmity. This might presuppose a Hebrew text which read *ṣedeq* rather than *šāqer*, **lying**.

Of the above interpretations the most plausible is that which sees the whole verse as a single sentence (see 1. above). The point would then be that it is equally stupid – and so presumably self-destructive – to nurture hatred and let it fester, and to express it in slanderous accusations. Of the other interpretations, those of *RSV* and *REB* fail to account for the grammatical difficulties; Dahood's interpretation of *m^ekasseh* does not carry conviction; and LXX's rendering may be no more than an attempt to make sense of a difficult verse.

19. See on v. 13 above and compare 13:3; 15:28; 17:27. **transgression** (*peša'*) is here used not of sin against God but of giving offence to others (compare *REB*). **is not lacking**: so most commentators. But this verb (*ḥādal*) normally means "to cease, come to an end", and Bühlmann (pp. 176–7), followed by Plöger, takes it in this sense here: when one has committed an offence, no amount of excuses or explanations will put things right. The second line would then be a continuation of the theme: the prudent course in such a situation is to say nothing in one's defence, since "Qui s'excuse s'accuse". This would then be another example of the importance of knowing when to speak and when to keep silence.

20. The form of this verse is chiastic. **choice** (*nibḥār*): this expression occurs also in 8:19. Here, however – though not in 8:19 – LXX has "melted in the fire", that is, "purified, refined", which has been thought to presuppose Hebrew *nibḥān*. But Gemser argues on the basis of Akkadian and Syriac that *nibḥār* itself may have that meaning. In any case the sense of the line is that the speech of the righteous is of great value – either to himself or to others.

mind: literally, "heart" (*lēb*). The parallelism with **tongue** is inexact; but, as is stressed elsewhere in the book, it is the mind or intelligence that determines what a person says, and speech is an indication of character. The verse may be intended as a comment on v. 19.

of little worth (*kimᵉʿāṭ*): this word, which usually means "almost", is here probably an emphatic form of *mᵉʿaṭ*, "little" (see *GK* 118x). The proposal (see Bühlmann, pp. 40–41) to emend it to *kᵉmāʿāh*, "like a grain of corn", is unnecessary and improbable.

21. feed: this verb (*rāʿāh*) means to tend a flock. No emendation is necessary. The metaphor is to be explained in terms of the common Near Eastern concept of kings and leaders generally as shepherds, a concept frequently to be found in the Old Testament, both of human rulers and of God as shepherd of his people. Since one of the main functions of a shepherd is to find good pasture for his flock, the verb is often used in that restricted sense; but shepherds – and so rulers – have other important functions, especially that of protecting their "flock" from danger. Hence Bühlmann (pp. 284–8) interprets the word here as meaning "care for" rather than "feed". Either interpretation makes good sense: the point of the verse (compare v. 11a) is that the well-chosen and well-intentioned words of the **righteous** are beneficial not only to themselves but also to others, whereas **fools** not only fail to preserve their own lives but are also of no use to others. The contrast between righteous and fools in this verse indicates how closely intellectual and moral qualities were associated.

die: on the concept of "death" in Proverbs see on 2:18. Here, however, a literal sense is not necessarily excluded. **lack**: we should probably repoint the adjective *ḥᵃsar* ("lacking") as *ḥeser* or *ḥōser*. **of sense**: Hebrew *lēb*, "heart"; but *RSV*'s translation is correct. There is a verbal link here with v. 20b, where it is the mind (*lēb*) of the *wicked* to which reference is made.

22. This verse interrupts a series of antithetical proverbs. Since it is also one of the rare references in the chapter to Yahweh, it has been suggested that it may be an addition to the series, making the point that the good things attributed to the influence of the prudent or the righteous in the preceding verses are ultimately provided by him. Certainly the first line in the Hebrew text makes a more emphatic statement than appears in *RSV*. *REB* renders the meaning accurately: "The blessing of the Lord *is what brings* riches" (*hī' taᶜᵃšîr*) – in other words, there can be no material success unless Yahweh sees fit to confer it. This is a correction, or at least adds a theological dimension, to the thought expressed in v. 4b.

There are two ways of reading the second line. Almost all the commentators (Toy is an exception, and also *REB*) take the view expressed in *RSV*mg., according to which *ᶜeṣeb* (*RSV* **sorrow**) is the subject but has the meaning "toil", as in 5:10; 14:23; Ps. 127:1–2: Yahweh's blessing is amply sufficient as a cause of success, and hard work cannot **add** to this. This makes a more effective conclusion to the proverb than *RSV*'s translation in its main text. The line thus completes the theological reinterpretation of the assertion of v. 4b begun in the first line; though it would hardly be correct to draw the conclusion from it that hard work is being dismissed as unnecessary. The meaning is probably the same as that of Ps. 127:1–2: no human effort can succeed without Yahweh. This may be the reason for the choice of the phrase **with it** (*ᶜimmāẖ*) rather than the usual "to it" (*ᶜālehāh*), suggesting that *both* Yahweh's **blessing** *and* hard work are necessary.

23–26. The antithetical form is resumed in v. 23 and is continued in vv. 24 and 25. In all of these, however, the "negative" side of the antithesis (**fool**, **wicked**) precedes the "positive". V. 26 is not antithetical, but is wholly concerned with the "negative" character of the **sluggard**. Vv. 24 and 25 are closely connected in thought.

23. The first line of this verse might be better rendered by "Doing wrong is to the fool just a joke". *zimmāh* (**wrong**) also has the meaning "plan"; but the context here demands a word meaning some kind of wrongdoing. *zimmāh* in this sense is reserved for particularly heinous crimes such as incest, adultery and idolatry; the phrase *ʿāśāh zimmāh* (**to do wrong**), in the only other passage in the Old Testament where it occurs, refers to mass rape and is designated "an abomination in Israel". *śᵉḥôq* (**sport**) properly means "laughter"; the particle *ke* which is prefixed to it (*RSV* **like**) is probably for emphasis: see on *kimᵉʿāṭ* in v. 20 above. The line thus means that fools are incapable of understanding the seriousness of their actions; the implication is that their ignorance will not save them if they commit crimes.

The second line is more difficult. The form is antithetical, making some kind of contrast between wisdom and folly. A literal translation of the Hebrew would be: "and (or "but") wisdom to a man of understanding": **is pleasure** is unrepresented in the Hebrew text. *RSV* has here followed those commentators who take the reference to **sport** – that is, pleasure – in the first line to apply also to the second: sensible persons take pleasure in wisdom as fools take pleasure in crime (so *REB*). Others (for example, Plöger) take the line to mean "but wisdom *belongs* to the man of understanding". Either of these interpretations makes a rather poor parallel to the first line. The text may be corrupt. Several commentators have proposed the emendation of the word *ḥokmāh* (**wise conduct**) to a word of "negative" meaning such as *kᵉlimmāh* ("humiliation"), *ḥēmāh* ("wrath") or *tôʿēbāh* ("abomination"), for example, Toy: "but it (that is, wrongdoing) is an abomination to a man of sense".

24. The contrast in this verse is between two kinds of anticipation. Both will be fulfilled; but a complete contrast is drawn between the respective *states* of the two types of person *before* that fulfilment takes place. The **wicked** person, aware of the current belief, attested frequently in these proverbs, that although they may seem to enjoy impunity, he and his like will eventually come to a bad end, already lives in a state of terror (*mᵉgôrāh RSV* **dreads**), while the **righteous** person lives in a state of happy anticipation (**desire**, *taʾᵃwāh*, almost means "hope" here).

will be granted: the verb is active (*yittēn*). This has been explained in three different ways: it may be an "impersonal qal" with a passive meaning, literally "one gives" (Delitzsch, Wildeboer); the subject may be Yahweh (unexpressed): "*he* will give" (Frankenberg, Gemser); or the verb should be repointed as passive (*yuttān*, Toy, Ringgren, Plöger). Others (for example, McKane) are undecided. LXX and other versions have passive forms, but this cannot be taken as a proof of a passive verb in Hebrew: the consonantal text can be read either way.

25. The theme of this verse is similar to that of v. 24. In its present position it serves the purpose of stating more explicitly – though in poetic imagery – the nature of "what the wicked dreads" and what is "the desire of the righteous" referred to in that verse. The image is the common one of the effects of a violent storm on differently constructed houses (compare Mt. 7:24–7). *sûpāh*, **tempest** – perhaps better, "whirlwind" – is a poetical word used mainly figuratively to denote the destructive wrath of God. The theme is most impressively elaborated in Job 27:13–23, where the "house" of the wicked man, despite his material wealth, proves to be the flimsiest of structures (v. 18) and so he himself is carried away by the storm (v. 20). That the imagery of a house is present in this verse also is shown by the use of the word *yᵉsôd*, "foundation", in the second line. A literal translation of this line would be "but the righteous is a foundation for ever". This should be taken with the temporal clause in the first line: the righteous, or his "house", is likewise struck by the storm, but he is unaffected by it because his righteousness gives him strength and stability.

On the syntax of the first line see *GK* 164g.

26. the sluggard: that is, the lazy person (*'āṣēl*). Sloth or laziness was evidently a major concern for the authors of these proverbs: the word *'āṣēl* occurs fourteen times in the book, but only once in the rest of the Old Testament, also in a proverb (Ec. 10:18). In Proverbs the theme occurs even when the word itself is not used: for example, in vv. 4, 5 above).

Several of the proverbs about the *'āṣēl* are specifically concerned with the life of the farmer, pointing out that his slackness will inevitably lead to poverty. This verse, however, is about lazy *servants*, whose irritating behaviour is vividly potrayed through striking similes. **those who send him** (*šōlᵉḥâw*): this does not necessarily refer to the sending of a message by a servant. This verb (*šālaḥ*) may also refer to the setting of a task, with no spatial implication other than removal from the immediate presence of the person issuing the order (e.g., Isa. 6:8; Jer. 14:14, 15). *REB* renders the word by "his master". The apparently plural suffix (**those**) is in fact probably an anomalous singular form (*GK* 124k).

27–32. These six proverbs have several features in common which suggest a deliberate grouping. 1. They all have antithetical form, and in each case the "positive" side precedes the "negative". 2. In every case the contrast made is a moral one rather than one between wisdom and folly. 3. The words *ṣaddîq*, **righteous** and *rāšā'*, **wicked** occur no fewer than four times, including three verses in which they form a contrasting pair. 4. The series is unmistakably oriented towards Yahwistic piety. The series begins with the phrase **The fear of the Lord**, an all-embracing formula which sets the tone for the whole group (see on 1:7). Yahweh also appears in v. 29, as protector of the **upright**.

27. prolongs life: in chapters 1–9 the same claim is made for the father's teaching (3:2) and for Wisdom (3:16; 9:11). The phrase **The fear of the Lord** occurs frequently in these proverbs. Its moral quality is indicated in 14:26; 15:16; 16:6, and its rewards – life, riches, honour – in 14:27; 15:33; 19:23; 22:4. That the years of the wicked will be short – that is, that they will die a premature death – is implied, though less explicitly, in v. 25 above ("is no more"); in 11:10; 19:9; 21:28 ("perish"); 13:9; 20:20 (their "lamp will be put out"); and also in 19:16, where "die" clearly refers to a death which is premature. There is no reason to doubt that these proverbs are to be understood literally.

28. ends in gladness: the Hebrew has simply "The hope of the righteous (is) gladness". An alternative interpretation of this extremely terse line is to take the joy or gladness to be the content rather than the outcome of the righteous man's expectation: in other words, the righteous man is essentially an optimistic person, it being implied that he is justified in his optimism (so McKane, Plöger). The difference between the two interpretations is very small. **gladness** (*śimḥah*) is so obviously to be expected for the righteous according to the thought-world of these proverbs that there is no need to emend the word to *ṣām^{e}ḥāh* (*REB* "blossoms" – see *BHS*) in order to make a supposedly better contrast with *tō'bēd*, "perish" (*RSV* **comes to naught**) in the second line.

29. This verse uses two expressions which link it with the piety of the Psalms. *mā'ôz* (**stronghold**, better "[(place of] refuge") occurs nowhere else in Proverbs; but it is found a number of times in the Psalms where the same metaphor is employed: that Yahweh *is* a place of refuge for those who appeal to him in times of trouble or persecution. Here in Prov. 10:29 the thought is similar to that of v. 25, where the righteous is depicted as safe in his house, unaffected by the storm which sweeps away the wicked. The second expression reminiscent of the Psalms is evildoers (*pō*ᵃ*lê 'āwen*). This phrase occurs in Proverbs only once more, and in a line which is identical with this. The precise meaning of *pō*ᵃ*lê 'āwen* when it occurs in the Psalms has been the subject of discussion ever since the publication of Mowinckel's *Psalmenstudien I* (Oslo, 1921); but here, where it signifies the opposite of the **upright**, it clearly has the general sense of "wicked".

to him whose way is upright: *RSV* has here followed most commentators in repointing *lattōm*, "to uprightness", as *l*ᵉ*tām*, which makes better sense. This line could also be rendered as "The way of the Lord is a stronghold to the upright"; but there is general agreement that **way** (*derek*) here makes better sense as denoting the behaviour of the righteous than in connection with Yahweh (compare also 11:20; 13:6). The "way" of Yahweh, whatever it may mean here, can hardly be termed a place of refuge.

It has already been noted that the second line of this verse and 21:15b are identical. There, where **destruction** (*RSV* translates *m*ᵉ*ḥittāh* there by "dismay") to the evildoers is contrasted with "a joy to the righteous", it makes better parallelism than it does here, a fact which may suggest that here it was not originally intended for its present position, though if *m*ᵉ*ḥittāh* is given its alternative meaning of "terror" the parallelism, though not complete, is not entirely absent.

30. The thought of this verse is similar to that of v. 29 but is expressed in different imagery (compare the somewhat similar pair vv. 24 and 25). The first line (**will never be removed**) reinforces the general notion of the security which is enjoyed by **the righteous** in times of insecurity; the second line with its reference to the exclusion of **the wicked** from **the land** is more concrete. The notion of the promise of the land (see on 2:21–2), being here applied to individuals rather than to the whole nation, is clearly a figure of speech, but one which reveals the importance of the theme for the ancient Israelites.

31–32. These two verses, both of which are concerned, like several others in this chapter, with the words spoken by the **righteous** and the **wicked**, are also linked together verbally by the word *tahpūkôt* (**perverse**). Since **mouth** (*peh*) and **righteous** (*ṣaddîq*) also occur in each, almost half of their total contents (six words out of fourteen) is common to both. They are in a sense complementary: neither verse by itself offers an entirely satisfactory parallelism. This fact has given rise to a number of textual and philological proposals intended to remedy this defect.

31. This verse can only be understood if it is realized that the phrases **The mouth of the righteous** and **the perverse tongue** are examples of the device, frequent in biblical poetry, by which relevant parts of the body stand for whole persons in particular activities (for example, when Yahweh is addressed in Isa. 51:9 with the words "Awake, awake, put on strength, O arm of Yahweh"). Thus these phrases here stand for the *persons* whose speech is "righteous" or "perverse".

The first line of the verse, and probably also the second, employs the metaphor of the life of plants or trees. The verb *nûb* (*RSV* **brings forth**) means "to flourish", primarily of plants; but it is intransitive; and it is doubtful – despite Dahood's arguments – whether it can have the transitive meaning assigned to it here by *RSV*. Bühlmann's suggestion (pp. 303–6) that *ḥokmāh* (**wisdom**) here is an instrumental or adverbial accusative (see Brockelmann, *Syntax*, § 93n; compare *GK* 117z, 118q, 144m, note 4) is probably correct: the righteous speaker flourishes *with respect to* wisdom.

The plant metaphor is probably continued in the second line, since the niphal of *kārat* "to cut" (*RSV* **will be cut off**), often used of annihilation, is particularly appropriate to the cutting down of a tree or plant – though it may have a double meaning here, as the word can also mean "cut out", appropriate to a **perverse tongue**.

Seen, then, as an instance of plant metaphor, this verse exhibits a reasonable parallelism, and the various suggestions for alternative meanings of *nûb* (Dahood; J. Hoftijzer [*VT* 11 (1961), pp. 344–5]) are not needed (so also Plöger).

32. In some degree this verse may be said to clarify the meaning of v. 31. The **righteous** flourish because they **know** how to choose their words (*REB* "suit words to the occasion"), while the only skill of the **wicked** is to cause trouble (*tahpūkôt*, **perverse**). We may compare Amos 3:10: "they do not know how to do right". **what is acceptable** (*rāṣôn*): the notion of acceptability as regards speech is found also in Ps. 19:14 (Heb. 15). Such words may be acceptable either to God or to human beings. (See also on 11:1.) Proposals to emend *yēdᵉʿûn* (**know**) or to assign it a different meaning based on an Arabic root (see Thomas, *VT* 3 Suppl [1955], pp. 284–5) are rightly discarded as unnecessary by McKane, Bühlmann (pp. 289–92), Plöger and *REB*.

CHAPTER 11

In this chapter each proverb takes the form of antithetical parallelism with the exception of v. 7, whose parallelism is synonymous, v. 22, which is a simile or comparison, and v. 31, which exhibits progressive parallelism ("If ... how much more ...!"). As in chapter 10, some of the antithetical couplets begin with a "positive" statement and others with a "negative", but there is no regular alternation between these two types. With regard to contents, proverbs contrasting the **righteous** with the **wicked** predominate, with a number of other proverbs making a similar point using different terms. Very few of these proverbs are concerned with contrasts between the **wise** and the **fool**. Other contrasts include those between the proud and the humble (v. 2) and between the generous and the mean person (vv. 24–6). Wealth is explicitly treated in vv. 4, 16 and 28, and by implication in vv. 24–6. Yahweh is mentioned only in vv. 1 and 20, and in both instances in the phrase **an abomination to the Lord**; however, his agency in determining the fate of both righteous and wicked is probably implied elsewhere, for example in v. 4 (**the day of wrath**). There is some reason to believe that both vv. 1 and 20 have been placed in their present positions in order to comment on adjacent verses (see below). Three verses stand out in the particularity of their topics: v. 1 on honest trading, v. 14 on the importance of acting on advice, and v. 15 on the danger of standing surety for others.

1. Cheating customers by using false weights or tampering with the scales by which goods were weighed was evidently as common a practice in the ancient Near East as it has been in other places and at other times. In Proverbs it is condemned as **an abomination to the Lord** not only here and in 20:10, 23 (compare also 16:11), but also in the Old Testament laws (Dt. 25:14–15; Lev. 19:35–6) and in the prophetical literature (Ezek. 45:10; Hos. 12:7 [Heb. 8]; Am. 8:5; Mic. 6:10–11). It is also condemned in Egyptian and Mesopotamian literature (*Amenope* ch. 16, *ANET*, p. 423; Babylonian Hymn to the Sun God, *ANET*, p. 388). In most of the Old Testament passages concerned, the same or similar language is used; in particular, the identical expression **A false balance** (*mō'zᵉnê mirmāh*, literally, "scales of deceit", occurs in Prov. 20:23; Am. 8:5; Hos. 12:7 and **a just weight** (*'eben šᵉlēmāh*, literally, "a complete [or 'perfect'] stone") in Dt. 25:15. The expression "dual weights" (*'eben wā'eben*, literally, "a stone and a stone") is also used in this connection (see also on 20:10). In view of the wide spread of these passages and the similarity of terms employed, it is hardly possible to determine whether it was in the legal, wisdom (or prophetic) tradition that the topic first appeared in Israel.

an abomination to the Lord: see on 6:16. **his delight** (*r^e ṣônô*): this word is clearly intended to express the antithesis of *tô'ēbāh*, **abomination**; but **delight** is too strong. *rāṣôn* means what is acceptable and so pleasing to a person or to God (see on 10:32). LXX correctly has *dekton*, "acceptable"; *REB* similarly, "accurate weights win his favour".

rāṣôn occurs fairly frequently in Proverbs. Nevertheless, its occurrence in the two consecutive verses 10:32 and 11:1 is likely to be deliberate. Although the particular topics dealt with in the two verses are not the same, both verses set out criteria of acceptable behaviour as distingushing the righteous from the wicked. 11:1 may then be regarded as a comment on 10:32 in that it makes it clear that moral and immoral conduct are matters not only for the approval of society but also for the judgment of Yahweh himself.

2. The first line of this verse has an unmistakable assonance and rhyme: *bā'-zādôn wayyābō' qālôn*, literally, "pride has come and then comes disgrace". This feature, together with the compactness and unusual form of the syntax, which has the effect of a conditional sentence (see *GK* 159h; Driver, *Tenses*, section 153) suggests that the line may be a quotation of a popular aphorism which has been subsequently turned into a more sententious proverb by the addition of the second line. Another example is Prov. 18:22a, *māṣā' 'iššāh māṣā' ṭôb*, "He who finds a wife finds a good thing".

qālôn, **disgrace** or dishonour, is the opposite of *kābôd*, "honour", with which it is contrasted in 3:35. *ṣ^e nûa'* (**humble**) occurs only here in the Old Testament. In Sir. and Mishnaic Hebrew it has the sense of discretion or prudence rather than of humility. Hence McKane and Plöger, probably correctly, take it here to mean "modest": that is, one who is "humble" not in the sense of meekness, but rather of self-restraint or not putting oneself forward. This makes a suitable contrast to "arrogant" or proud. It is such a person who has **wisdom**, which is the road to success rather than to dishonour.

3. guides them: the same verb is used of the parents' teaching in 6:22. Here it is the innate quality of the **upright** (*y^e šārîm*) which governs their behaviour. The implication is the same as in the more explicit statement of 6:22–23 that this "guidance" will see a person safely through his daily life, ensuring that he takes the road to "life" and not to death. *tummāh* (**integrity**) occurs elsewhere in the Old Testament only in Job (2:3, 9; 27:5; 31:6), where it is applied to Job himself, the man who was "blameless and upright" (*tām wᵉyāšār*) *par excellence*. The kind of confident assertion made in this and many other proverbs in the book is precisely what is challenged by Job, who, though his integrity has signally *not* protected him but has allowed him to suffer the fate here said to be reserved for the wicked, yet refuses to abandon his claim to it.

destroys them: better, "ruins them". Qere's *yšdm* = *yᵉšaddēm* is clearly the correct reading as against Kethib's *wšdm*.

4–6. These somewhat similar proverbs are grouped together under the keyword *ṣᵉdāqāh*, "righteousness".

4. The second line of this verse is identical with 10:2b. The first lines of the two verses differ in that here the **riches** which **do not profit** are not specifically stated to have been obtained through wickedness as they are in 10:2. However, the phrase **in the day of wrath** shows that this is implied. This phrase is reminiscent of prophetical denunciation: the prophets frequently speak of Yahweh's "day" in threatening terms, and in fact both Ezekiel (7:19) and Zephaniah (1:18; compare also Isa. 10:3) employ precisely the same phrase as here, specifying that the "wrath" is that of Yahweh (*yôm ʿebrat yhwh*). This is certainly implied here. This is not a condemnation of wealth as such; rather, it is a warning that if a person has brought Yahweh's wrath on himself – that is, through wickedness – the fact that he is wealthy will not protect him from its dire consequences.

5. keeps . . . straight: this is the same verb as in 3:6. The metaphor of the **way** is the same as in 4:11–19 and other passages in chapters 1–9. **falls** (*yippōl*): this verb (*nāpal*), frequently employed in these proverbs as a metaphor for disaster, is particularly appropriate here in view of the metaphor of the "way". This proverb is a straightforward expression of the belief that human behaviour reaps its own reward.

6. The thought in this verse is very similar to that of v. 5. In the first line the subject is identical with that of v. 5a, and the rest of the line differs only in the choice of words. **delivers** (the verb is *hiṣṣîl*) also recalls v. 4a. The second line reads, according to the Hebrew text, literally "but in the *hawwāh* of the treacherous (they) are caught". *hawwāh* can mean either "desire, avidity" as probably in 10:3, or, more frequently, "ruin, destruction"; but whichever is its meaning here there is a difficulty: the verb has no subject (the persons who are **taken captive** can hardly be **the upright** of the first line). *RSV* has accepted the proposal of many commentators to emend *b^{e}hawwat* ("in the *hawwāh* of . . .") to *b^{e}hawwātām*, that is, "in (or 'by') *their hawwāh*". This emendation, which is supported by LXX and Vulg., makes **the treacherous** the subject of the verb. If this is correct it would suggest, on the analogy of v. 5b ("falls by his own wickedness") that *hawwāh* here means not **lust** as in *RSV* but "ruin" or "destruction". The **treacherous**, like the wicked of v. 5b, will be caught by their *own* destruction of others: they will themselves suffer the same fate as those whom they have ruined.

7. Toy, Gemser and *BHS* regard the text of this verse as seriously corrupt and so of uncertain meaning. *RSV* understands it as in synonymous parallelism; but even this is not certain. The first line has been seen by some commentators as metrically too long; but those who hold this view are not agreed on which word should be dropped as redundant. The two words in question are *'ādām rāšā'*, literally, "a wicked man" (*RSV* has simply **the wicked**). If it is *'ādām* which is redundant (so Toy, Gemser, Ringgren), the sense remains unchanged; but if it is *rāšā'*, "wicked" (Scott, Plöger) it is completely altered, since the line must then read "When *any* man dies . . .".

The meaning of the second line is equally uncertain. *'ônîm* (*RSV* **the godless**) has been understood in several quite different ways: "strength" (Oesterley), "deceitfulness" (Gemser, Ringgren), "wickedness", that is, wicked persons (Plöger), "riches" (as in Hos. 12:8 [Heb. 9]; Job 20:10 – so van der Weiden, McKane, *REB*). Others have proposed its emendation, on the one hand to *'^{e}wîlîm*, "foolish persons" (following LXX – see *BHS*), or, on the other, to *'^{e}mûnîm*, "faithful ones" (Reider [1952], p. 124).

With all these uncertainties the possible interpretations of the verse as a whole are almost endless. If it is antithetical, the tenses of the verbs (imperfect followed by perfect of *'ābad* – *RSV* has concealed that this is the same verb by rendering its two occurrences differently as **perishes** and **comes to naught** –) may be significant: whereas the hope of *everyone* will come to an end at death, the fate of the godless has *already* come upon them by retribution *before* their death. Perhaps the best solution, however, is to take the parallelism as synonymous and to understand *'ônîm* as meaning "riches", and so to render the whole verse with *REB*:

> *When someone wicked dies, all his hopes perish,*
> *and any expectation of affluence ends.*

It then becomes a statement about expectations of wealth – that the wicked will not be allowed to succeed in their attempt to amass a fortune (compare 10:3b, 28b).

8. The point of this proverb is the same as that of Ps. 7:15 (Heb. 16); Prov. 26:27; 28:10, where it is affirmed that the wicked will fall into the pit which they have dug to trap others. The situation is presented more vividly than in the generalities of such proverbs as v. 3: the first line emphasizes that the **wicked** comes close to success with his plot, since the **righteous** is in real danger of disaster (*ṣārāh*, trouble) and has to be "snatched away" (*ḥālaṣ*, niphal [*RSV* **is delivered**], a stronger verb than the *hiṣṣîl* of 10:2; 11:4, 6) at the last moment, while a corresponding disaster falls on the criminal. The proverb has been compared to 21:18 (see below), in which the wicked becomes a "ransom" or substitute for the righteous; but this is probably to read too much into it.

9–14. Plöger comments that these verses form a group which is concerned with the relationship of the individual to the community as a whole rather than simply with individuals and their dealings with other individuals (**neighbour**, vv. 9, 12; **city**, vv. 10–11; **tale-bearer**, v. 13; **people**, v. 14). However, the fact that two words for city (*qiryāh*, *qeret*) are used in two successive verses is a further indication that these proverbs were composed separately and then linked together, if at all, by various formal or thematic features. The verb *ḥlṣ* (**are delivered**) both in v. 9 and v. 8, a word which occurs nowhere else in Proverbs, similarly forms a link between this group of verses and what precedes.

9. the godless man: this word (*ḥānēp*) has the meaning "hypocrite" in later Hebrew: see Bühlmann, p. 296. **would destroy**: perhaps better, "can destroy". The proposed emendations referred to in *BHS* are unnecessary. The second line may mean either that the **righteous** can save themselves from such "destruction" (presumably of their reputation) by their wisdom (**knowledge**), or that those who possess such wisdom are able to rescue others from it (see on 10:14). A small community can be wrecked by unwise or malicious speech, but peace can be preserved equally by judicious words (or by self-restraint).

10–11. These two proverbs have clearly been grouped as a pair. (LXX omits v. 10b, 11a, putting vv. 10a, 11b together as a single proverb; but although this makes an adequate parallelism the omission is probably accidental.) Both proverbs are concerned with the well-being of urban life; the only other references to cities in the sentence literature are 10:15; 16:32; 18:11, 19; 21:22; 29:8, and of these only 29:8 has a literal sense. V. 11 may be regarded as a comment on v. 10 in that it gives a reason for the reactions of the inhabitants stated there. There is also a connection between v. 11b and v. 9a, both of which refer to the evil effects of the *speech* (**mouth**) of the **wicked**.

11. blessing: that is, prosperity. **is exalted** (*tārûm*): this verb (*rûm*), literally "to be high", can refer to enhanced status (Ps. 89:16 [Heb. 17]; Isa. 52:13), and here may refer to that or to prosperity in general. However, Gemser, followed by van der Weiden, in view of **is overthrown** in the second line, proposes to repoint the word as *tĕrôm*, which he takes to be a form of a verb *rmm*, "to build, build up" on the basis of Ugaritic and Arabic analogies. However this may be, the line means that a city shares in the good fortune of one of its inhabitants.

12–14. There is an obvious affinity between vv. 12 and 13: both are concerned with the importance of self-restraint in speech and the destructive effects on the community of derogatory comments by individuals. Plöger also finds a connection between these two verses and v. 14, seeing the latter as stating in general terms the principle of the importance of communal consensus of which the former are illustrations. But there is also a connection with v. 11: vv. 11 and 14 are both concerned with the causes of the wellbeing and collapse of a community.

12. belittles: this verb (*bûz*), generally rendered by "despise" (see 6:30), can also signify the verbal expression of contempt (compare 30:17; 2 Kg. 19:21 and Isa. 37:22, where it is associated with *lāʿag*, "to mock"). In 14:21a in a similar line this behaviour is castigated not as foolish but as sinful. That it refers to speech and not to unexpressed contempt here is confirmed by the **remains silent**, referring to the **man of understanding**, in the second line. This silence, commended elsewhere in the sentence literature as the mark of a wise man, may here be due either to self-regarding caution or, more probably in view of the other proverbs in this group, to a sense of responsibility towards the community.

13. He who goes about as a talebearer (*hôlēk rākîl*): in all of the six occurrences of *rākîl* in the Old Testament with one exception (Ezek. 22:9) it is associated with the verb *hālak*, "go, walk" in the sense of going around. It appears to be an abstract noun used adverbially (see *GK* 118q), and in each case denotes *slander* except possibly in Prov. 20:19a, which is almost identical with 11:13a and which may refer to non-malicious gossip or chatter. Here, where the phrase is contrasted with *ne'man-rûaḥ* (**trustworthy in spirit**) it could refer either to malicious or merely injudicious speech; but the general import of the verse is the same as that of v. 12: the responsible person **keeps a thing hidden** – that is, he keeps to himself any **secrets** or private information about other people which has come to his knowledge, in the interests of harmony within the community.

14. The occurrence of the words *'am* (**a people**), *t^ešû'āh* **safety**, sometimes used in the sense of military victory) and *yô'ēṣ* (**counsellors**) in this verse, together with the fact that in 24:6, whose second line is identical with the second line of this verse, there is a reference to waging war, has led some commentators to suppose that the verse presupposes an intimate knowledge of royal circles. But this is not so: indeed, its point would be so self-evident to members of those circles as to be entirely superfluous. It is rather an observation of persons remote from national affairs who have noted its truth and now apply it to their own, or indeed to any, situations. While the particular choice of words may be intended to advert to national policies, the keywords all have double or multiple meanings. *'am* is a word of many meanings including "the common people" (Jer. 21:7; Neh. 5:1), people in general (Gen. 50:20) and the inhabitants of a city (Gen. 19:4; 1 Sam. 9:13; Jer. 29:16) as well as "nation". *t^ešû'āh*, often "victory", is here correctly rendered by *RSV* by **safety**. *yô'ēṣ*, although it can mean "royal counsellor", also has the general sense of one who gives private advice (Prov. 12:20). On *taḥbūlôt* (**guidance**) see on 1:5. The verse is thus of quite general application and appropriately rounds off this group of verses.

15. See on 6:1–5 and especially 6:1. This theme is peculiar to Proverbs (see also 17:18; 20:16; 22:26–7; 27:13). If, as is probable, **stranger** (*zār*) refers not to foreigners but to fellow-Israelites outside the family or the circle of intimates, the frequency of its occurrence in the sentence literature illustrates the economic insecurity of the circles from which these proverbs come. Once in the hands of his creditors the debtor evidently had little chance of freeing himself from his debt, and was likely to drag down his kindly guarantor into a similar predicament. This and other similar proverbs in no way contradict the expressions of approval of generosity found in such proverbs as vv. 24–5 below: generosity when one has the means to help those poorer than oneself is not the same thing as signing a blank cheque.

will smart for it (*raʿ-yērôaʿ*): that is, will suffer (from his generous impulse). *raʿ* here should probably be repointed as the infinitive absolute *rōaʿ*. **he who hates**: the verb *śānēʾ* here has a milder sense: to keep away from, to have nothing to do with.

16. The point of this proverb is not immediately obvious, and some commentators (Wildeboer, Oesterley, Gemser, Ringgren) have concluded that there is a lacuna in the text here, and have preferred – at least in general terms – the longer LXX text:

A gracious wife brings glory to her husband,
but a woman who hates righteousness is a throne (!) of dishonour.
The slothful come to want,
but the diligent support themselves with wealth.

LXX thus has two proverbs here rather than one, each antithetical. However, other commentators, probably rightly, regard its additional lines as an attempt to make sense out of a difficult Hebrew text.

If *MT* represents the original Hebrew text, the main problem is to know where the essential antithesis is to be found. Is it between **honour** and **riches** (so *REB*, "a bold man gets *only* a fortune"), between men and women, or between gentle and violent ways of achieving one's ends? The problem is complicated by the fact that doubt has been thrown on the correctness of the translation **violent men** (Heb., plural, *ʿārîṣîm*) in the second line. Driver (*Bibl* 32 [1951], p. 180) argued that the word here means "vigorous" (so *REB* "bold"), while others propose, on the basis of LXX, to emend it to *ḥārûṣîm*, "diligent".

Of the various solutions proposed, two are perhaps the most plausible. One is that the proverb is concerned to state that gentle methods (such as those employed by a charming woman, *ʾēšet ḥēn*) can achieve more than ruthlessness (or boldness, or diligence) because it is more important to acquire **honour** (*kābôd*) than *riches*. Alternatively, the verse may be a simile, of the type in which the two elements are not connected by the usual *k*ᵉ ("as" or "like") but are simply juxtaposed, being joined only by the simple *w*ᵉ (*RSV* **and**). This construction, the so-called *waw adequaetionis* (*GK* 161a), is especially characteristic of Job and Proverbs: compare Job 5:7; 14:11–12; Prov. 17:3; 25:3; 26:3, 9, 14. The order in which the two elements, the thing compared and the thing with which it is compared, appear is variable. In this case the most probable rendering would be "As energetic men acquire riches, so a charming woman gains honour". If this is correct, the verse falls into the category of those proverbs (11:22; 12:4; 18:22; 19:13, 14; 21:9; 25:24; 27:15 – and compare the longer poem 31:10–31) which give advice of various kinds about the choice of a wife. It advocates the quality of charm, since a charming woman will be able to obtain an honourable status for her family simply by being what she is, and so enhance what her husband can only obtain – that is, wealth – by hard work (so Plöger). This assessment of feminine charm was not, however, universally accepted: the author of 31:10–31 preferred an intelligent and hardworking wife, and held that "charm (*ḥēn*) is deceitful, and beauty is vain".

17. himself: the Hebrew uses two different words: *nepeš* and *š*ᵉ*'ēr*. The first of these regularly has the meaning of "self"; the latter, elsewhere "body, flesh", appears here to be synonymous with it. The point of the proverb is that one's behaviour towards others, whether good or bad, has unintended or unexpected consequences for oneself. It may be interpreted simply as an assertion of the certainty of eventual divine retribution; but it probably also expresses a belief that the effects of good and evil, once they are unleashed, cannot be confined or controlled.

18–21. In a variety of ways each of these verses expresses an identical belief. In their present position they may all be regarded as expounding further the statements of v. 17. Vv. 18, 19 & 21 define the "benefits himself" and the "hurts himself" of that verse in terms of a secure future, "life" and safety as opposed to disappointment, death and punishment respectively. V. 20 further interprets these as the consequence of pleasing or offending Yahweh.

18. The thought closely resembles that of v. 4. **deceptive wages** (pᵉ*'ullat-šāqer*): on the first of these words see on 10:16. The second word elsewhere, and almost always in Proverbs, denotes the telling of a deliberate lie (e.g. 12:22). In 25:14 it refers to the making of a false promise, and its meaning here is similar: the reward received by the wicked man is **deceptive** in that it is not what he had expected. 11:4a puts the thought more precisely.

There is a play on words here between *šeqer* and *śeker* in the second line: in contrast to the deceptiveness of the reward of the wicked, the righteous receives a *śeker* (**reward**, literally "wages") which is "true" (*'emet*, *RSV* **sure**), that is, genuine, or reliable.

one who sows righteousness: a similar expression occurs in Hos. 10:12, where it refers to actions which will "*reap* the fruit" (of steadfast love). So here also the thought is of "reaping the harvest" of a virtuous life.

19. He who is steadfast (*kēn*): *RSV*, probably rightly, takes this word as an adjective. Elsewhere it frequently means "in the right" or "honest" (so frequently in Gen. 42). But "honest in righteousness" hardly makes sense; and *RSV* follows those commentators who take the word as derived – as an adjective or a participle – from *kûn*, "to be firm". Other suggestions are less probable, and emendation, following LXX, to *ben* (so, literally, "a son of righteousness") is unnecessary and problematical.

20. The form of this verse is chiasmic. On **abomination** see on 3:32; 6:16; on **delight** (*rāṣôn*) see on 11:1. **Men of perverse mind** (*'iqqešê-lēb*): other proverbs speak of perverse speech (e.g. 8:8) or way of life (2:15); but all actions, whether good or bad, are the outward manifestations of the inner self, the heart (*lēb*) or mind: compare *ḥakam-lēb*, "wise of heart" (10:8); "lacking in mind" (6:32; 10:13, 21 etc.). The consequences of Yahweh's approval or disfavour are made explicit in v. 21.

21. Again the form is chiasmic. **Be assured**: literally, "hand to hand" (*yād leyād*). The same expression, also followed by **will not go unpunished**, occurs in 16:5b. Plöger has pointed out that there as here the phrase *yād leyād* is closely associated with "abomination to Yahweh" (there in the previous line, here in the preceding verse), a verbal association which may partly account for the association of the two verses here. Although it is generally agreed that the phrase *yād leyād* expresses a strong asseveration perhaps derived from popular speech, its original significance is unknown. It may have been derived from a custom of sealing an agreement by striking hands together, also reflected in the expression *tāqa' kap* (see on 6:1–5).

will not go unpunished (*lō'-yinnāqeh*): this verb is a forensic term denoting acquittal, in this case presumably by Yahweh as judge, since being **an evil man** is hardly in itself an indictable offence in law. **will be delivered**: literally, "will escape", here from the punishment inflicted on the wicked.

those who are righteous: the Hebrew has "the seed of the righteous" (*zeraʿ ṣaddîqîm*). The commentators are divided on the meaning of "seed" (*zeraʿ*) here. It is not clear that this word can mean a particular kind of person as *RSV* takes it. *REB*'s "the righteous and all their descendants" almost certainly interprets the phrase correctly. If so, the verse may be making a further distinction between the fates of the wicked and the righteous: the family of the former will become extinct while the progeny of the latter will prosper – compare Job 18:19; 21:19.

22. This is a simple comparison, similar to v. 16 except that here the two elements are juxtaposed with no connecting particle at all (see again *GK* 161a – *RSV*'s **Like . . . is** is not expressed in the Hebrew). This rather crude proverb belongs to the category of those which purport to give advice about the choice of a wife – see on v. 16. That beauty is not a reliable guide in this matter agrees with 31:30 – except that the latter verse also dismisses charm; and indeed the whole of that poem (31:10–31) might be seen as an extended commendation of a wife who has **discretion**.

a gold ring: nose rings were items of feminine jewellery (Gen. 24:47; Isa. 3:21; Ezek. 16:12). **without** (*sārat*): literally, "turned away (from)" – a unique use of this verb. **discretion** (*ṭaʿam*): literally, "taste", that is, good taste; but the word is also used of good sense or judgement (Prov. 26:16; 1 Sam. 25:33; Job 12:20).

23–27. Plöger, perhaps not entirely convincingly, sees a connection between these verses: vv. 24–6 extend the thought of vv. 23 and 27 by illustrations showing that the righteous and the wicked receive their due rewards despite what might be expected from their actions. However this may be, there is no doubt that vv. 24–6 belong together: they all express the paradox that liberality will ultimately increase the wealth of the donor rather than decrease it, while meanness will lead to impoverishment.

23. Compare 10:24, 28; 11:7. As there is no verb in the Hebrew, the first line could be rendered "The righteous desire only what is good" (so *REB*); but the parallelism demands a translation like that of *RSV*. **good** refers to the wellbeing of the righteous, not of others. **wrath** (*ʿebrāh*): compare v. 4. No emendation is required.

24. This proverb points no explicit moral, but merely states observable facts, though it does not claim that the instances which it gives are necessarily typical. In the Hebrew text **One man** and **another** are represented merely by "There is (one who) . . . and (one who) . . .": in other words, such things do sometimes happen. McKane points out that the proverb could be interpreted in strictly economic terms: "you have to speculate in order to accumulate"; but with other commentators he thinks it more likely that it is commending enlightened self-interest: "philanthropy is the best policy". The latter interpretation is made probable by the use of the verb *pizzēr* (**gives freely**), which elsewhere generally means "scatter" in a general sense, but in Ps. 112:9, the only other passage in which it refers to the spending of money, is associated with giving to the poor – compare Lk. 6:38. **what he should give**: literally, "what is due" or "proper" (*yōšer*).

25. This proverb in synonymous parallelism expresses the same thought as v. 24a. **A liberal man** (*nepeš-b^erākāh*): literally, "a 'soul' of blessing". *b^erākāh* is here used in the sense of "gift" (compare Gen. 33:11; Jos. 15:19; 1 Sam. 25:27 etc.), and *nepeš* in the sense of "a person" (compare 19:15), that is, "anyone". **will be enriched**: literally, "will be made fat". The same meaning as here is found also in 13:4; 28:25.

waters: this verb (the hiphil of *rāwāh*) occurs in a similar metaphorical sense in Jer. 31:25. **will . . . be watered** (*yôre'*): this is probably to be understood as an anomalous form of the hophal of the same verb (see *GK* 69w).

26. This verse has been placed here partly because of the word *b^erākāh* (**blessing**), which occurs also in v. 25; but, more significantly, because it provides a concrete example of the liberality and meanness of which vv. 24 and 25 speak. The situation presupposed is that of a scarcity of food due to poor harvests, a not uncommon state of affairs which bore heavily on ordinary people. Of those well-to-do persons who have providently kept back and stored up part of their harvested grain in anticipation of future shortages (compare the action of Joseph, on a national scale, in Gen. 41:48, 49), the profiteers refuse to sell to those in need knowing that the price will rise, and are cursed by the populace, while those who relieve distress by selling their goods without regard for personal gain will receive the people's blessing (compare Gen. 41:55–7). If the two verses (25 and 26) are taken together, the meaning of *b^erākāh* in v. 25

("gift") is complemented in v. 26: "blessing" here is not just "good will" (as opposed to "curse" as an expression of hostility) but also includes the sense of *material* gain. The benefactor will receive a material "blessing" in the form of an even greater prosperity than before, as in v. 25.

27. The first line of this verse can be interpreted in three ways: 1. The person who **diligently seeks good** is thereby seeking God's **favour** (*rāṣôn*): 2. he is seeking the good will of the community for himself; 3. he is seeking God's favour (*rāṣôn*) – that is, prosperity – *for* the community. The first two of these interpretations imply *self*-seeking, and this hardly agrees with the general attitude of these proverbs. The third interpretation is tautologous, since **good** (*ṭôb*) must mean "what is good for others", and this has the same meaning as **favour**. It would be more in keeping with the attitude of this literature if it was said that the man who seeks good *wins* favour; and several commentators translate the verb in this way. But *biqqēš* = "seek" cannot mean "win" or "obtain". Driver (*JSS* 12 [1967], p. 108), however, maintains that *biqqēš* here is cognate with Akkadian *baqāšu* which could permit the meaning "win". If this proposal is not accepted the line remains obscure. **evil** (*rā'āh*): i.e., misfortune; but there is a double meaning here: **it** clearly refers back to *rā'āh*, now having the other sense of *moral* evil, which such a person commits (Heb. *dōrēš*, "pursues" [*RSV* **searches for**].

28. This verse is not concerned with dishonestly acquired wealth like 10:2 and 11:4, nor with the ephemeral nature of wealth as in 27:24; equally, it expresses no disapproval of wealth in itself. It is rather a general warning to those who possess it that it is sinful to rely on it as a protection against future disaster. The proverb should be understood in the light of those (16:20; 28:25; 29:25) which stress that it is in God that one should put one's trust. Those who forget this and so put God in second place are here seen as having placed themselves outside the category of **the righteous**, and will suffer the consequences of their apostasy.

will wither: *RSV* appears to have followed those commentators who emend *yippōl*, "will fall" (found in 11:5, 14 and elsewhere in Proverbs) to *yibbōl*. Although this would match the language of Ps. 1:3, where the righteous is compared to a tree whose "leaf does not wither", making a good parallel between the two lines, this emendation, which is not supported by the Versions, is hardly necessary. The simile in the second line (**will flourish like a green leaf**) is found not only in Ps. 1:3 but also in Ps. 92:12–14 (Heb. 13–15) and elsewhere.

29. This proverb in synonymous parallelism is probably to be classed among those which speak of the fate of those who fail, in various ways, to manage their affairs competently, for example, 10:4; 12:11, 24; 17:2; 18:9; 21:17. **He who troubles his household** (literally, "his house", meaning his personal property – compare Gen. 39:4, 5): the same phrase occurs in 15:27 of dishonest persons; but the verb (*'ākar*) does not necessarily have such an implication here, where the second line shows that the reference is to a **fool** rather than a rogue. Such a person **will inherit wind**, that is, will find that he is insolvent, and so will be reduced to becoming the slave (*'ebed*, *RSV* **servant**) of his more prudent (*ḥakam-lēb*, *RSV* **wise**) creditor when he is unable to pay his debts. Such a situation is widely attested in the Old Testament; (in Proverbs, compare 22:7). The verse illustrates the precarious situation of the social class from which these proverbs come. It does not specify any of the possible ways in which a person might "trouble" or injure his economic situation through his own fault. There is an interesting reversal of the situation in 17:2, where a clever slave can contrive to get part of a property into his own hands.

30. This verse is difficult to interpret. Most commentators, followed by *RSV*, emend the Hebrew *ḥākām*, "a wise man", in the second line to *ḥāmās*, "violence" (**lawlessness**) which may have been the reading of LXX. If the Hebrew text is correct, the line makes sense only if *lōqēaḥ nᵉpāšôt* (**takes away lives**) means "wins lives" (so Delitzsch). But it is doubtful whether the verb *lāqaḥ* can have this meaning, whereas *lāqaḥ nepeš* occurs in Ps. 31:13 (Heb. 14) in the sense of "take away life", that is, "murder". But in any case the parallelism is weak (it should be noted that **life** and **lives** are different words in the Hebrew).

The first line has its own difficulties: to call a **fruit** a **tree** makes no sense, and a proposed emendation of *ṣaddîq* (**righteous**) to *ṣedeq* ("righteousness") does not solve the problem. Possibly **tree of life** (if that is the meaning of the phrase – see on 3:18 and compare 13:12; 15:4) had become a stereotyped expression whose original meaning was no longer remembered.

31. The *a fortiori* argument (**If . . . how much more . . . !**) is used several times in these proverbs (compare 15:11; 17:7; 19:7, 10; 21:27). But if *RSV*'s translation is correct, there is no such argument here, since the belief that people get what they deserve in the world applies equally to the righteous and the wicked: the fate of the latter is not more certain than that of the former. The **how much more** (*'ap kî*) is then no more than a rhetorical device to add emphasis to the statement of the second line. There is, however, another way of understanding the proverb. The verb *šillēm* (here in the passive, **is requited**) may be intended in a negative sense with regard to both lines: if even the **righteous** must pay for their moral lapses, the **wicked** will have even less chance of escaping due retribution. That the righteous have imperfections is admittedly contrary to the general belief expressed in these proverbs, but it corresponds to the assertion in Ec. 7:20 that "Surely there is not a righteous man on earth who does good and never sins", and may receive some support in Proverbs from 25:26. If this is the correct interpretation of the verse, it may be regarded as a theological correction of v. 30 and perhaps of the attitude of these proverbs in general. It has been suggested that 1 Pet. 4:18 is a deliberate interpretation of the verse in this sense (see Toy and Plöger).

on earth: this phrase can also be rendered "in the land" (compare 2:21, 22; 10:30). It does not imply a doctrine of eternal punishment for the wicked as suggested by Dahood. Some commentators regard the phrase here as otiose, and propose various emendations, partly on the basis of LXX and 1 Pet. 4:18 (see Barr, 1975, pp. 149–64). But more probably it should be taken with **righteous**: it is "the righteous in the land" who is the subject of the verb; compare "the afflicted in the land", Ps. 76:9 (Heb. 10) and elsewhere.

CHAPTER 12

In this chapter almost every verse is in antithetical parallelism, the exceptions being v. 9 (**Better is**. . .) and v. 14 (synonymous parallelism). Once again proverbs contrasting the righteous with the wicked – expressed in a variety of terms – predominate over those concerning the wise and foolish; among the latter are three about diligence and laziness (vv. 11, 24, 27). There are two references to Yahweh as granting favour (*rāṣôn*, **favour**, v. 2; **delight**, v. 22) to the good or faithful and correspondingly condemning their opposites; the latter of these employs the phrase **an abomination to the Lord** already noted in 11:1, 20. There is one reference to women (v. 4) which belongs to the category of proverbs which proffer advice to men about the choice of a wife.

The chapter contains only one clearly defined extended thematic group: vv. 14–25 are almost all concerned in various ways with the use of speech.

1. Like chapters 10 and 13 this chapter begins with a general statement about the importance of acquiring and living by the accepted norms of society as laid down especially by parents though also obtainable from other "wise" persons. This ordering of initial verses is unlikely to be unintentional: it is one of the many indications of an editorial shaping of the material. **discipline** (*mûsār*): this is the same word as that rendered in *RSV* in 1:2, 8; 10:17 and elserwhere by "instruction". The first line, with its repetition of **loves** (*'ōhēb*), gives the impression of having once been a popular or pedagogical saying. It would be possible to translate the first line by "He who loves knowledge loves discipline" (or "instruction"), and this would give a slightly better sense: if one wishes to acquire knowledge one must recognize the desirability of undergoing instruction. The second line could also be reversed; but it gives a better sense if left as in *RSV* (where it gives the verse a chiastic form). If one must undergo instruction in order to acquire knowledge, then to refuse **reproof** (= instruction) is the mark of an excessively stupid person. **knowledge** (*da'at*) here, as in 1:7; 11:9, is equivalent to wisdom; and it may be presumed that the editor who placed the verse here intended the reader to see the verses which follow as constituting the contents of such knowledge.

stupid: this word (*ba 'ar*) occurs only five times in the Old Testament: here, in 30:2 and in the "wisdom psalms", Ps. 49:10 (Heb. 11); 73:22; 92:6 (Heb. 7). It is thus peculiar to the wisdom literature. It is cognate with *b^e'îr*, "cattle". and in Ps. 73:22 it is parallel to *b^{e}hēmôt*, "cattle". It thus signifies a person of extremely dull intelligence.

2. obtains favour from the Lord: this line is virtually identical with 8:35b, which is an interpolation made in order to identify the gifts of Wisdom with those conferred by Yahweh. Somewhat similarly this verse seems to be intended as an interpretation of the verse which follows, making it clear that it is the approval or condemnation of Yahweh which lies behind the process of retribution. On **favour** (*rāṣôn*) see on 11:1; on **evil devices** (*m^{e}zimmôt*) see on 1:4.

condemns: this verb (*hiršîa'*) is properly a juristic term, but is here used in a general sense.

3. The sentiment expressed in this verse is repeated many times in these proverbs, and the language used is conventional. The phrase *bal-yimmôṭ* (**will never be moved** – but the Hebrew has "not" rather than "never") occurs also in the similar 10:30, and **the root of the righteous** again in 12:12. **established**: literally, "made firm", in contrast with the verb in the second line. These are "conventionalized metaphors" (see Watson, p. 264) or clichés. There is no real intention to see the fates of righteous and wicked respectively in terms of a vigorous tree or plant or of one which has been weakened by transplanting or uprooting. Thus in v. 12 the same word **root** is used probably to denote stability without any corresponding plant metaphor in the parallel line.

4. This proverb, like others in the book (see on 11:16) is concerned with the importance of choosing a suitable wife. The phrase *'ēšet-ḥayil* (**A good wife**) is the same as that applied to the wife whose virtues are extolled in detail in 31:10–31. The meaning of *ḥayil* as applied to a wife has been variously understood. *ḥayil*, perhaps primarily "strength", has a wide range of meanings in the Old Testament. In 31:10–31 the main activities of the *'ēšet-ḥayil* suggest the meaning "capability" or "efficiency"; but as here the emphasis is on her value as a wife: she loyally brings her husband both wealth and public esteem. This is strongly emphasized here both by the word **crown** and by the contrast with a wife **who brings shame**. The **crown** (*ᵃṭārāh*), properly the symbol of royalty, is used here, as often, figuratively of that which confers honour or esteem on a person: compare 14:24; 16:31; 17:6. **rottenness in his bones**: a modern equivalent expression might be "a cancer" – some disease which progressively saps a person's vitality.

5–7. These verses in their present arrangement form a logical progression. They are all concerned with the **righteous** (*ṣaddîqîm*) or upright (*yᵉšārîm*) and the wicked (*rᵉšā'îm*), first with their thoughts or intentions (v. 5), then with the expression of those thoughts in action (v. 6) and finally with the consequences of those actions (v. 7).

5. No distinction is intended here between *maḥšᵉbôt*, **thoughts** and *taḥbūlôt*, **counsels**. Both denote the forming of concrete plans. *taḥbūlôt*, which in 11:14; 20:18; 24:6 refers to corporate planning carried out by a group in order to ensure success, here probably denotes the forming of plans by individuals for their own ends (compare

1:5; Job 37:12). It is therefore not correct, as many commentators maintain, to speak of its being used, only here in Proverbs, in a "bad" sense. It is an ethically neutral term. The point of the verse is similar to that of Mt. 7:16–20: "By their fruits you shall know them" (Toy).

6. It is not specified in what way the **wicked** can kill, or how the **righteous** can save by the use of words, but it is not difficult to envisage such situations, for example in a criminal trial. **lie in wait**: literally, "are a lying in wait". Almost the same expression is used in 1:11, though the reference there is to physical violence. As in 1:11 there is no justification for emending *dām*, **blood** to *tām*, "the innocent". *dām* is a term closely associated with violent death (see, for example, 1 Kg. 2:9) and also with the death penalty (Ezek. 18:13; 33:4).

delivers men: the Hebrew has "them" (verbal suffix). This can hardly refer back either to the wicked or the righteous, and there is no other antecedent. *RSV* takes the suffix as having an impersonal sense; others omit it as a scribal error.

Bühlmann (p. 299) draws attention to the effective use of alliteration in this verse: *rš'ym/yšrm* (**wicked/upright**) and *dbry/'rb-dm* (**words/lie in wait**).

7. are overthrown: on this use of the infinitive absolute see *GK* 113ff. **the house of the righteous**: see on 10:25. The two verses make the same point. Whether **house** here refers to the physical home (compare Job 8:15) of the righteous or to his family and descendants, this proverb, like many in these chapters, probably reflects the harsh economic conditions of agricultural life in which total disaster – loss of house and land and a fall into destitution and possibly slavery – was a daily possibility. **will stand** (*ya'amōd*): that is, stand firm when disaster threatens.

8–9. Plöger finds here a loose arrangement of proverbs extending from v. 8 to v. 11, seeing vv. 9–11 as illustrations of a general principle enunciated in v. 8. However this may be, there is certainly such a link between vv. 8 and 9.

8. good sense: on the meanings of this word (*śēkel/sekel*) see on 3:4. Its meaning here is the same as in the similar proverb 13:15. **is commended, is despised**: that is, by the other members of the community. To stand well with one's fellows was of particular importance in Israelite society (compare 31:23).

one of perverse mind (*na'awēh lēb*): some commentators emend the first of these words, on the basis of LXX, to *na'abēh* which, they claim, means "stupid" or "thick-witted", on the grounds that it makes a better contrast with **good sense**. But there are several objections to this. *naʿᵃbêh* itself is suspect, being a dubious form of a verb occurring only twice in the Old Testament, where it means "to be fat" rather than "to be stupid". It is best to retain MT, especially since this verb (*ʿāwāh*, niphal) elsewhere (Ps. 38:6 [Heb. 7]; Isa. 21:3) appears to denote a state of confusion rather than of perversity.

9. Better is: that is, "It is better to be . . .". **who works for himself** (*wᵉʿebed lô*): the most obvious meaning of this phrase is "who has a slave". Most commentators have accepted this, seeing the significance of the phrase to lie in the use of the singular *ʿebed* rather than the plural: in other words, the possession of *only one* servant is a mark of a modest standard of living, contrasted with that of the person who **plays the great man**. This view is probably correct. *RSV* and some other modern translations, however, have accepted the proposal to repoint the noun *ʿebed* to some form of the verb *ʿābad* "to work": "Better is one who . . . works for himself" (*REB* "earns one's living"). Ringgren retains MT, but nevertheless interprets the phrase in the same way: "one who is his own slave"; this interpretation, however, is linguistically dubious (see Delitzsch). The general meaning of the proverb is not affected. It reflects the prudent attitude of persons of small means, and suggests that one should be content with one's lot (compare 15:16, 17; 16:8; 17:1; 19:1; 28:6). The portrait in the second line of the man who tries to impress others with his social prestige while actually starving at home is a deliberate caricature but an effective one.

10. This proverb appears to be concerned with a fundamental psychological contrast between two human types: the **righteous man**'s nature is spontaneous and outgoing, knowing no bounds and overflowing even into the consideration with which he treats his livestock, while that of the **wicked** man is grudging; even when, uncharacteristically, he attempts to do a kindness (*raḥᵃmîm*, *RSV* **mercy**), his **cruel** instincts hold him back. *nepeš*, **life**, should perhaps be rendered "feelings". Consideration for the needs and well-being of animals is prescribed in the laws of the Old Testament (e.g. in Exod. 23:12) and elsewhere, but most notably in Dt. 25:4.

11. This verse is identical with 28:19 except that the latter ends with "will have plenty of poverty" rather than **has no sense**. The inclusion of virtually identical proverbs in two quite separate collections supports the view that there was a common stock of proverbs on which the editors of the different collections were able to draw; it also shows that these could exist in variant forms. The proverb is one of many which warn the small farmer about the absolute necessity of constant hard work. The phrase **will have plenty of bread** links the verse with v. 9, and the agricultural theme links it with v. 10 and also perhaps with vv. 8 and 9 (see above on 12:8–9).

12. It is generally agreed that the text of this verse is seriously corrupt, especially the first line. *RSV*'s translation is based on a heavily emended text. The best clue to its original sense is the phrase **the root of the righteous** in the second line. This phrase occurs also in v. 3, where the accompanying verb is "will not be moved". This has suggested the emendation of the meaningless *yittēn*, "will give", to *(bᵉ)'ētām*, "(is) enduring" (*RSV* **stands firm**), an emendation suggested by LXX. If this is accepted, parallelism would suggest that the first line, which in MT is unintelligible, originally made a statement about the discomfiture of the wicked. On some of the numerous proposals for emendation to give the line such a meaning see *BHS* and McKane.

13–23. The importance attached by ordinary people in Israel – and in the ancient Near East generally – to the spoken word both in its consequences and in its revelation of character is well illustrated in this group of proverbs, which cover a wide range of circumstances. Speech is seen here as capable of producing important consequences both desirable and undesirable both for the speaker and for those to whom he speaks; and it also provides a means by which one can discern the underlying goodness, wickedness, common sense or folly of the speaker. (See Bühlmann, especially pp. 326–30.)

13. The first line of this verse, *bᵉpešaʿ śᵉpātayim môqēš rāʿ*, has been interpreted in three quite different ways. 1. *RSV*, following several commentators, assumes that *môqēš rāʿ* means "(there is) a snare for the wicked" (or, more probably, repoints or emends the noun *môqēš* as a passive verb). The proverb then states the principle of retribution: the slanderer or deceiver gets what he deserves, but the **righteous** (presumably because his words are honest and true) can talk himself out of trouble. 2. On the other hand, McKane, on the analogy of 11:9, takes *môqēš rāʿ* as a subjective genitive: the snare is *set by* the wicked for others and takes the form of malicious speech, by which, however, the righteous are not affected. 3. A third interpretation of *môqēš rā'* is to take it as meaning "an evil snare" (Scott, Barucq, Bühlmann [p. 302], Plöger). The "evil man" (*rā'*) of the other translations thus disappears from the verse altogether. *peša' śᵉpātayim* (*RSV* **the transgression of his lips**) then becomes no more than "a slip of the tongue", and the meaning of the proverb is that although a slip of the tongue (which may be committed by anyone) can lead to disaster, the righteous person will be able to talk himself out of its unfortunate consequences. But it is doubtful whether *peša'* can have such a weak meaning. Of the other two interpretations, either provides a satisfactory parallelism, and *RSV* may be right.

14. The first line of this verse in its present position carries the thought of v. 13b a further stage: by choosing one's words one can not only extricate oneself from trouble, but can achieve material prosperity. The second line appears to add the somewhat trite comment that this is also true of one's actions; but it may be that the whole verse is a comparative sentence (see on 11:16, 22) intended to make the point that words can be *as* effective as deeds. (LXX in the second line has "lips" instead of **hand**, but although this reading creates a neat parallelism its very smoothness invites suspicion.) The first line may originally have been an independent saying complete in itself: it recurs with variants in 13:2 and 18:20, but with quite different second lines. See further on 18:20.

From the fruit of his words: literally, "of his mouth". The Hebrew is alliterative: *mippᵉrî pî*). **fruit**: see on 1:31; 8:19. **is satisfied with good**: "good" here (*ṭôb*) denotes material sufficiency or even wealth: compare 13:2, "*eats* good". The second line (*gᵉmûl yᵉdê-'ādām yāšûb lô*, literally, "the *reward* of a man's hands . . .") means that a man will receive a reward – whether good or bad – corresponding to his actions. The meaning of *gᵉmûl . . . yāšûb* (literally, "the reward will return") is well illustrated in Ob. 15, where it is paralleled by "As you have done, it shall be done to you". **comes back**: Kethib *yāšûb* is to be preferred to Qere's *yāšîb*, "brings back", with Yahweh assumed to be the subject.

15–16. These two proverbs are linked not only by the recurrence of *'ᵉwîl*, **fool**, but also by their theme. The general characterization of the fool as being so sure that he is right that he refuses to take advice like a sensible person (v. 15) is followed (v. 16) by a concrete example: the fool is not only quick to take offence, but also quick to show it in public, while a sensible person if he is insulted refuses to be provoked and plays the situation down. The meaning of the second line is perhaps brought out more clearly if *ḥākām* (**a wise man**) and *ʿārûm* (**the prudent man**) are taken as the predicates rather than the subjects: "but he who listens to advice is wise"; "but he who ignores an insult is prudent".

15. listens to advice: Proverbs as a whole and also the Egyptian wisdom literature regard "hearing" (that is, paying attention) and "speaking" as equally important for the properly conducted person. Only by such listening can one become wise (cf. 1:2–5) and so be saved from precipitate and foolish behaviour.

16. vexation: that is, anger when provoked: compare Ec. 7:9. **at once**: literally, "on the (same) day". **is known**: MT has, literally, "(As for) the fool, his vexation is known". LXX and some other Versions have "A fool declares his anger". This may presuppose a different vocalization, and may be correct, but MT is not impossible. The general sense is not affected. **ignores**: the Hebrew has "conceals": compare v. 23. **prudent** (*ʿārûm*): rather, "clever" or "shrewd". The word is used in a bad sense in Gen. 3:1 (*RSV* "subtle"), but in Proverbs it always has a morally neutral sense, being contrasted with "simple" or "fool". **insult**: properly "humiliation".

17. The meaning of this verse may not be as trite as first appears. The situation envisaged is that of legal testimony, as is shown not only by the word *ʿēd*, **witness**, in the second line, but also by the verb *yāpîaḥ* (**speaks**) in the first. In Proverbs this verb is used several times (6:19; 14:5, 25; 19:5, 9) of giving legal testimony. *RSV*'s **honest evidence**, however, may misrepresent what is intended by the Hebrew, which has the single word *ṣedeq*, here probably "justice". Thus the truthful witness proclaims (*yaggîd*, *RSV* **gives**) the principle of justice, which is the very basis of Israel's claim "to inherit the land which Yahweh your God gives you" (Dt. 16:20), whereas **deceit** (*mirmāh*) is elsewhere (11:1) singled out as "an abomination to Yahweh". On the frequent use of the theme see on 19:5.

18. There is: see on 11:24. This proverb is concerned with thoughtless words which may cause trouble in the community which only the tactful intervention of the **wise** can put right. Its placing between two verses about lying may be intended to emphasize the fact that inconsidered remarks can be as destructive of social harmony as malicious lies.

19. Truthful lips: the Hebrew has the singular, literally "lip of truth" (*śᵉpat ᵓᵉmet*). The line becomes less strange when it is realized not only that "lip", like "mouth" and "tongue", simply means "speech" or "language", but also that *ᵓᵉmet* has a far deeper meaning than simply "truth" as opposed to "lies" (compare *ṣedeq* in v. 17). It implies such qualities as durability, permanence and reliability. Speech which has this quality will **endure** (literally, "will be established") **for ever** because it will be found to be reliable, in contrast with the **lying tongue** (compare v. 22) which may deceive **for a moment** but cannot prevail when put to the test.

There is a play on words here: *lāʿad* (**for ever**) is immediately followed in the second line by *wᵉʿad* (**but for**).

20. There is no clear antithesis between the lines of this verse unless **Deceit** here means "self-deceit", a solution which is accepted by Gemser, Scott and McKane. If this is correct, the verse means that those who hatch schemes to harm others find that they have harmed only themselves (**in the heart**), while those who plan for the common good (*yōᵃṣê šālôm*, *RSV* **plan good**) find due satisfaction.

22. Compare v. 19, on which this may be a comment. As in 11:1,20, *tôʿēbāh* (**abomination**) and *rāṣôn* (**delight**) express the opposite poles of Yahweh's assessment. **act faithfully** (*ʿōśê ᵓᵉmūnāh*): this noun (*ᵓᵉmūnāh*) is the same as that rendered by "the truth" in v. 17; and, in view of the contrast with the first line, probably refers primarily to speech.

23. prudent (*ʿārûm*): see on v. 16. **conceals his knowledge**: this proverb, like 10:14, 19, belongs to the category of proverbs which deal with the art of knowing when to keep silent.

24. The respective consequences of industry and idleness (compare 10:4, 5; 12:11 and other proverbs in these chapters) are here set out forcefully in hyperbolic language. **forced labour** (*mas*) always denotes a particularly oppressive form of slavery reminiscent of the oppression of the Israelites in Egypt (Gen. 49:15; Exod. 1:11) and of the oppressive policies of Solomon (1 Kg. 5:13 [Heb. 28]). It is never used of private or domestic slavery. Here it stands for the ultimate in human wretchedness, but is clearly not intended to be taken literally. The same is true of the verb *māšal* (**rule**), which denotes the wielding of absolute power, equally unrealistic in the present context.

25. In view of the uncertainty of life for the Israelite farmer, it is not surprising to find references to **Anxiety** or fear for the future (also in 15:13; 17:22), despite the many assurances of other proverbs that the righteous, the wise and the diligent need have no such fears. The proverb is also interesting for its concern with the psychological state of the individual; but its main point is to be found in the second line, which is a further testimony to the power of speech and the way in which it can change a situation. **good** (*ṭôb*) in this context may simply mean "kindly", but more probably means "reassuring" or "encouraging" (compare 15:23, 30; 25:25). **weighs him down**: that is, depresses him.

The verse contains two grammatical anomalies: *deʾāgāh* (**Anxiety**), a feminine noun, has a masculine verb; and both verbs have feminine instead of masculine suffixes ("her" instead of **him**). For possible explanations see Plöger.

26. The first line of this verse is seriously corrupt and no satisfactory solution has been found despite many attempts to emend it or to make sense of it as it stands. None of these has succeeded in finding a tolerable parallelism with the second line, and all are unsatisfactory in one way or another. A literal translation of the first line (*yātēr mērēʿēhû ṣaddîq*) could be "A righteous man seeks out (or, 'spies out') his neighbour". *RSV* probably reads *yāsûr mērāʿāh ṣaddîq*. Among other proposals, Barucq and McKane retain MT, taking *yātēr* to mean "shows the way to"; Plöger has "the righteous looks for his pasture" (*yātūr mirʿēhû*); Emerton (*ZAW* 76 [1964], pp. 191–192) "the righteous is freed from evil" (*yuttar mērāʿāh ṣaddîq*).

27. The general sense of this proverb is clear, although there are difficulties in the Hebrew text. The first line may have originally been a popular saying like "The early bird catches the worm". But the verb rendered **catch** in *RSV* – *ḥārak* – occurs nowhere else in the Old Testament, and its meaning is not clear. In modern Hebrew it can mean "to roast", and mediaeval Jewish commentators took it in this sense; but earlier post-biblical Hebrew and Aramaic attest for it only the meaning of "singe" or "char", not in a culinary sense. LXX, however, has "catch", which Gemser and others have taken to be a translation of *yadrîk* (hiphil of *drk*), which seems to have this meaning ("obtain") in the Hebrew text of Sir. 15:1, 7. One of several other suggestions is that the verb is cognate with an Arabic verb meaning "to set in motion": so *REB* "put up (game)", a term used in hunting.

28. This proverb employs the imagery of the two ways found elsewhere in Proverbs: see on 2:12. On **life** and **death** see on 2:18–

19; 5:5 and compare 11:19; 13:14; 14:27; 18:21. As with verse 27 the general sense is clear, but there is a textual problem in the second line, where the Hebrew has "but the way *of the path* (*n^e tîbāh*) (leads) to death". Most commentators agree that *n^e tîbāh* is a textual error. The antithetical parallelism requires a word which makes a contrast with *ṣ^e dāqāh*, **righteousness**; but it is not clear what this may have been. *nit'āb*, "abominable", is a common suggestion; Gemser and others propose *m^e šûbāh*, "apostasy", literally "turning away" – that is, from righteousness. Tournay, (*RB* 69 [1962,], pp. 495–7) suggested *p^e tî bā'*, which would produce the line "and the path *of folly leads* to death"; but this produces a weakened parallelism.

One other proposal requires mention. Dahood, who against the view of most scholars found a number of allusions to life after death in Proverbs, noted that the word generally rendered **to** in the second line is not the usual *'el* but the negative particle *'al*, and rendered the final phrase *'al-māwet* by "immortality" (literally, "not-death"). The proverb would then be an example of synonymous parallelism: "And the treading of her path is immortality". This, however, involves both lexicographical and grammatical difficulties. In fact many MSS (but not MT) read *'el*. (It has been suggested that the reading *'al* was a theological interpretation of the verse by a later scribe.)

Like 10:1, which it resembles, 13:1 has the marks of a new beginning, and the present verse (12:28) may be regarded as a general conclusion to the chapter or at least to the preceding group of verses. (So Delitzsch, who regarded it as the conclusion to the whole preceding section 10:1–12:28.)

CHAPTER 13

Like 10:1, the very similar 13:1 may mark the beginning of an originally distinct collection intended to function as instruction. Delitzsch regarded it as the beginning of a section ending with 15:19. But 14:1 also clearly marks a new beginning. Throughout the present chapter there are warnings about the need to follow the advice or instruction of the teacher or of persons known for their wisdom. V. 1 sets the tone with a proverb about the wise and obedient child, and this is complemented in the penultimate verse (24) which explains how such wisdom and obedience can be achieved. Vv. 10, 13–14, 18 and

20 all build on this theme, leaving it to be understood that the need for instruction and advice is not confined to children. This basic theme is then developed in various ways in many of the other verses. Vv. 2–3 take up from v. 1 the topic of wise speech, and vv. 12–19 form a group of proverbs related in various ways to the main theme (see below).

Some smaller groups are linked together in other ways: vv. 2–4 and 21–2 have common elements of vocabulary; v. 6 looks like a comment on v. 5; vv. 7–8 both have a paradoxical character. Other topics – indolence, wisdom and folly, individual psychology – are familiar from earlier chapters. There are no references to Yahweh (though see on v. 21) and none to women.

The lack of a comprehensive structure and the presence of unrelated verses show that as in the chapters already considered the present arrangement is editorial and not authorial.

1. In the Hebrew text the first line of this verse has no verb. It reads "A wise son (is) a father's instruction (*mûsar 'āb*)". (The variant reading of a single MS cited in *BHS* does not necessarily point to the original reading, nor do the readings of the Versions referred to there.) Almost all commentators have recognized that the text is corrupt. *RSV* has adopted the view that the verb **hears** (*yišma'*) has dropped out, although its inclusion would make an exceptionally long line. Others have suggested that *mûsar* has been *substituted* for *yišma'*, perhaps because a copyist had the phrase *mûsar 'āb* in mind from 4:1 (compare also 1:8). The line would then have read "A wise son listens to (his) father". An alternative proposal is *'āhēb* or *'ōhēb*, "loves" (the phrase *'ōhēb dā'at*, "loves knowledge", occurs in 12:1). Driver (*JTS* 41 [1940], p. 174) suggested a slight emendation of *mûsar* to *myussar*, "is disciplined (by)". Whatever may be the true solution, the general sense of the verse is clear, and there is a reasonable parallelism, although a phrase like "a foolish son" such as occurs in the comparable 10:1 might have been expected in the second line. On **scoffer** (*lēṣ*) see on 1:22.

2–4. If vv. 1–3 are linked by a common topic, vv. 2–4 are linked by the common word *nepeš*; but this word does not have the same meaning in each case (see below), and the link is purely formal or external. There is no thematic connection between verses 3 and 4.

2. a good man: the Hebrew speaks only of "a man" (*'îš*), and the line is a variant of 12:14a (which has "is satisfied with" rather than **eats**) and also, somewhat more remotely, of 18:20a. See on

12:14. *RSV*'s addition of the adjective **good** qualifying **man** constitutes an interpretation of the Hebrew rather than a translation; and although this interpretation has a long ancestry, Emerton (*JTS* NS 35, 1984, pp. 91–5) rightly takes *RSV* to task for introducing it. Emerton sees no need for emendation, and renders the line by "From the fruit of a man's lips he *may* eat good" – that is, "every man has a chance of eating good as a result of his words". This provides a contrasting parallel with the second line, which then refers to a certain kind of person (**the treacherous**) who is set on the opposite course. LXX's "A good man shall eat of the fruits of righteousness" probably took the word *ṭôb* (**good**) at the *end* of the line as the subject of the sentence and probably read *mišpāṭ*, "righteousness" instead of *pî-'îš* (*RSV* **mouth** and **man**); but there is no reason to prefer LXX to MT. See further on 18:20.

The second line may mean that **the desire** (*nepeš*) **of the treacherous** – that is, their evil intentions – is turned to **violence** against themselves (the Hebrew has simply "(is) violence") (compare 12:14b). This would give an even better parallel to the verse.

3. Compare 10:14, 19, 21; 18:7; 21:23. *nepeš* here (**life**) is used in a quite different sense from its meaning in v. 2.

4. This is yet another proverb contrasting the fate of the indolent (*'āṣēl*) with that of the diligent (*ḥārûṣ*). *nepeš* (**soul**) here means "appetite" in a literal sense (the lazy starve, the diligent have plenty to eat). Both types of person have appetites, but in the case of the lazy one indolence wins. **and gets nothing**: the Hebrew has simply "and – nothing". The small farmer has literally nothing to fall back on if he fails to produce his own food. **is richly supplied** (*t^edušš ān*); see on 11:25.

In the first line the Hebrew has *napšô*, ostensibly "his *nepeš*," where the construct form *nepeš* (with no suffix) would be expected. The form has been explained as an anticipatory suffix as found in Aramaic, or as the survival of an archaic nominative (see *GK* 90k, o); but it may be simply due to scribal error.

5. Further characteristics of the **righteous** and the **wicked** are stated here. *d^ebar-šeqer* (**falsehood**): literally, "a word of deceit", in other words, a lie. The other main meaning of *dābār*, that is, "thing, matter", is less probable here than "word". (Compare a similar expression in Ps. 101:7). **acts shamefully and disgracefully** (*yab'îš w^eyaḥpîr*): this juxtaposition of two virtually synonymous words (compare 19:26) is presumably intended for emphasis, but may be a colloquialism like the French "*une honte et un scandale*". *yab'îš* (hiphil of *bā'aš*, literally, "to stink") may be an internally intransitive hiphil (see *GK* 53f). It is used metaphorically: "behaves offensively". Some commentators, however, regard the word as an error for *yābîš*, the hiphil of *bôš*, "to be ashamed", which occurs several times in Proverbs and is combined with the same word as here in 19:26. The meaning is hardly affected.

6. This verse may be intended to constitute a comment on v. 5: both the righteous and the wicked respectively reap the fruits of their own conduct. **Righteousness** (*ṣᵉdāqāh*) and **sin** (*ḥaṭṭā't*) appear to be personified (compare Gen. 4:7, "sin is crouching at the door") and are represented as able to protect or to overthrow a person. In the second line the Hebrew has an abstract noun, *riš'āh*, rather than the concrete **the wicked**, so it would be possible to take this as the subject of the sentence: *REB* has "but wickedness brings sinners down". **him whose way is upright** (*tām-dārek*): literally, "the blameless of way"; compare the similar phrase in 11:20. *tām* ("blameless", in the absolute state), should be repointed as construct (*tam*).

7–8. These two proverbs are ostensibly simply detached observations of different aspects of wealth and poverty. Plöger sees them as having an ironical tone in common.

7. If this is more than a simple observation of actual oddities of human behaviour (compare the first line with 12:9b), several interpretations are possible: that one should not judge by appearances; that one should not, or cannot, conceal one's true circumstances from neighbours; that one should avoid extremes of behaviour; etc. It may be that these possibilities – and perhaps others – have been deliberately left open. There is, however, a danger of overinterpretation here. This is illustrated by Oesterley's "one man, though poor, is really rich because he is content with a little . . . while another, who has plenty, is never satisfied . . . and therefore from his own point of view . . . is a poor man". This thought may be in accordance with wisdom teaching, but is not what the text says.

8. The point of this verse, like that of v. 7, is by no means clear. The first line appears to state that the rich have the particular characteristic that they have the means to save their lives by paying a **ransom**. Nothing is said about the circumstances in which such a need might arise, and no metaphorical meaning springs to mind.

The second line is also obscure. *RSV* is based on an emendation, the literal translation of the Hebrew text being placed in the margin. This is for two reasons: 1. The statement about the **poor** in the Hebrew seems simply not to be true. 2. This line has been seen as suspect because it is almost identical with v. 1b except for the first word, where v. 1b has "scoffer", not "poor", making good sense in its context. It has therefore been supposed that v. 8b except for the first word has been borrowed from v. 1b to fill a gap left when the original line dropped out in the course of transmission. *RSV* represents one attempt (made by Steuernagel and Gemser) to restore the original line.

These emendations, however, are purely speculative and may be unnecessary. Most modern commentators and translations (for example, McKane, Plöger, *NEB*, *JB*, *REB*) retain the text of MT but render *g*ᵉ*'ārāh* (*RSV* mg, "rebuke") by "threats" – thus *REB* has "but one who is poor is immune from threats". If this is correct, it is possible to find a parallelism in the verse by rendering the first line by "one who is rich *has to pay* a ransom" (so again *REB*) – that is, the poor have an *advantage* over the rich in that they cannot be subjected to demands for money! (It is not entirely clear, however, that *g*ᵉ*'ārāh* can mean "threat".) It is in such an interpretation that Plöger sees irony and "gallows humour" (*Galgenhumor*) in the proverb: certainly to tell the poor that they are more fortunate than the rich one would have to have one's tongue in one's cheek. (This is not the point of 15:16; 16:8; 15:17; 17:1, on which see below.)

9. On this metaphorical use of **light** (*'ôr*) and **lamp** (*nēr*) see on 6:23. The phrase **the lamp of the wicked will be put out** was evidently a stock phrase in wisdom poetry: it occurs again in 20:20; 24:20, and also in Job 18:6; 21:17, and with *'ôr* as a variant in Job 18:5. The lighted lamp in the house at night was a sign of family life and activity (compare Jer. 25:10; Prov. 31:18), and its (permanent) extinguishing signified the extermination of a household (compare 2 Sam. 21:17; 1 Kg. 11:36).

rejoices (*yiśmāḥ*): if this is correct it is a somewhat extreme example of personification (for other examples see L. Alonso Schökel, *A Manual of Hebrew Poetics*, Rome, 1988, pp. 123ff). It may be better to repoint the verb as a causative (piel): "causes joy". Alternatively, it has been suggested that this may be another *śmḥ*, cognate either with an Ugaritic (Driver, *Bib* 23 [1951], p. 180) or an Arabic (Kopf, 1959, p. 276) word meaning "to shine brightly". Various suggestions for emendation have been made, but are not compelling.

10. This proverb is somewhat similar to 12:15 and several others, and is concerned with the need to think carefully and take advice before endangering good relations between members of the community by intemperate speech. It is particularly appropriate to a collection which begins with v. 1. **the heedless**: this is not represented in MT, which has *raq*, which usually means "only". This has been thought to be inappropriate and to create a syntactical difficulty in the line as a whole. *RSV*, together with Gemser, Scott and McKane, has plausibly repointed it as *rēq*, literally "an empty (=lightweight) person". Others less plausibly, on the basis of LXX, have emended it to *raʿ*, "a wicked person", while Toy and Oesterley wished to omit *raq* and the following letter (*bᵉ*) as a dittography of the somewhat similar final words of v. 9. The line would then read simply "Insolence makes strife". Plöger retains *raq* but renders it by "truly"; but it is doubtful whether it can have that meaning (see Jongeling, 1973, pp. 97–107, especially p. 106).

those who take advice (*nôʿāṣîm*): this is probably the true text, although some commentators emend the word to *ṣᵉnûʿîm*, "humble", in conformity with 11:2b, which is otherwise identical with this line.

11. hastily gotten: *RSV* has here accepted an emendation of MT's *mēhebel* ("from worthlessness, nothingness, impermanence") to *mᵉbōhāl*. But Driver (*ZAW* 50 [1932], p. 144) repoints the Hebrew consonantal text as *mᵉhubbāl* (from the verb *hābal* rather than the noun *hebel*) which, he argues, means "got by scheming". Only Plöger retains MT, supposing the line to refer to persons who made a fortune though they began with nothing. However, it is questionable whether *hebel* can simply mean "nothing".

Any one of these readings would fit the general point of view of the proverbs in these chapters, and there is little to choose between them. Wealth obtained by fraud or other illegitimate means is of course condemned (for example, in 10:2; 11:4, 18; 21:6), but a sudden access of wealth was also suspect (20:21; 28:20), probably because in the social and economic circumstances in which these proverbs were formed there were no innocent ways in which it could be so acquired.

little by little: if this is the meaning of the Hebrew *'al-yād* (literally, "on/by the hand"), it perhaps makes the best parallelism with the **hastily gotten** of *RSV* in the first line. Wealth in itself is never regarded as evil in Proverbs, or indeed in the Old Testament generally; it is rather regarded as a sign of divine blessing and, especially in these proverbs, as a well deserved reward for slow and laborious manual work (e.g. 10:4b).

12–19. With the exception of v. 17, these verses form a distinct group which is arranged concentrically. Vv. 13–14 and 18 stress the need to pay attention to the teaching of the wise, which is the keynote sounded at the beginning of the chapter (v. 1). Between these come two proverbs (vv. 15, 16) which advocate the qualities of good sense taught by the wise. These speak of material rewards, life, favour, honour; and in the same vein vv. 12b and 19a, which closely resemble one another and are concerned with the fulfilment of ambitions, provide the envelope which encloses the whole. The fact that vv. 12a and 19b are not relevant to the theme does not detract from this view; it merely gives some indication of the way in which proverbs could be forced into a mould which was not wholly appropriate to them.

12. This is a psychological observation rather than a piece of practical advice (compare 12:25). Plöger suggests that it has been placed after v. 11 because the two verses both speak of the time taken to achieve an ambition; but this would be a rather remote connection. On **tree of life** see on 3:18 and 11:30.

13–14. These verses are virtually identical in meaning. **word** (*dābār*), **commandment** (*miṣwāh*) and **teaching** (*tôrāh*) are all used interchangeably in the Instructions of chapters 1–9 to denote that instruction which is also specifically the subject of the initial verse of this chapter.

13. brings destruction upon himself: this translation is probably correct (so *KB*[3], *REB*), although many commentators derive the verb (*yēḥābel*) from another *ḥbl* meaning "to be under a pledge", that is, under an obligation. **respects**: literally, "fears".

14. a fountain of life: see on 10:11. **the snares of death**: behind this metaphor lies a concept of a personal figure, Death, who ensnares his victims. On **life** and **death** see on 2:18–19.

Plöger, noting that the theme of this verse is the same as that of v. 1, sees it as marking the conclusion of a group; but he also notes that vv. 15 and 16 may be intended to exemplify the consequences of acting or not acting on the teaching to which it refers, so that it could also be seen as marking a new beginning.

15. Good sense: here this phrase (*śēkel-ṭôb*) clearly denotes intelligence rather than success (see on 3:4). An example of the use of intelligence to secure **favour** (*ḥēn*) is that of Abigail (1 Sam. 25), who is described as *ṭôbat-śekel* (v. 3).

The second line of the verse makes no sense: the Hebrew text declares that the way of the treacherous is *eternal* or enduring. *RSV* has adopted a frequently proposed emendation, substituting *'êdām*, (**is**) **their ruin** for *'êtān*, on the basis of LXX. Other alternative emendations include that of Driver (*ZAW* 50 [1932], p. 144), who suggested that the rare particle *'î*, "not", had dropped out before *'êtān*. The line is clearly in disorder. Even if emended as mentioned above, it still makes no parallel with the first line. It may be that some lines have dropped out between the two extant lines. LXX has an additional line there, but almost certainly does not represent the original text.

16. prudent (*'ārûm*): see on 12:16. **knowledge** (*da'at*) here as frequently in Proverbs (e.g. 1:4, 7; 12:1) is a synonym for wisdom. It is sometimes expressed by silence or caution in speech (10:14; 12:23). The verse is an interesting variant of 12:23. The statements, here that the wise man **acts with** (rather, "by") knowledge and in 12:23 that he *conceals knowledge* are not opposed to one another, but rather complementary: in contrast to the **fool** who reveals his true nature by his speech and actions, the wise man does not draw attention to himself, his self-restraint being itself a proof of his wisdom.

17. The **messenger** (*mal'āk*) or **envoy** (*ṣîr*) was a necessary means of communication in private life as well as in the public service (ambassador) even when the distance between sender and destination was short (compare 2 Kg. 6:32). Messengers could be used simply to make a report (Job 1:14) or as intermediaries (Gen. 32:3, 6 [Heb. 4, 7]), when as representatives of the sender they might be responsible for carrying on negotiations. In the context of these proverbs such negotiations might be about the buying or selling of livestock, farm products or land and the fixing of a price. The point of this proverb is not the content of the message but the character of the messenger. *rāšā'* (**bad**) is a strong word: it can hardly mean "incompetent", but implies the messenger's deliberate misuse of his commission for his own ends (compare the behaviour of

Gehazi, 2 Kg. 5:19–24), as opposed to the messenger who is **faithful** (*ṣîr ᵉmûnîm*).

plunges men into trouble: the Hebrew has *yippōl*, "*falls* (into trouble)". This would mean that the unfaithful messenger will be found out and punished (MT is retained by Barucq and Bühlmann; compare LXX and Vulg.). The second line would then presumably mean that the faithful messenger has nothing to fear, and the proverb would be a warning to potential messengers. But in 25:13, which is similar to the second line, it is the sender who stands to benefit from sending a reliable messenger. If this is also the meaning of the second line here, *RSV*'s rendering of the first line following the majority of commentators, which is based on the repointing of *yippōl* to the causative (hiphil) *yappīl* may be justified. In that case the proverb is a warning to exercise prudence in the choice of messengers – a further example of the "teaching of the wise" in v. 14.

healing: this word (*marpē'*) is almost always used in a figurative sense. Here it probably has the same meaning as *lēb marpē'*, "peace of mind", in 14:30.

18. The use, in parallelism, of the words *mûsār* (**instruction**) and *tôkaḥat* (**reproof**) recalls 12:1 (where *mûsār* is rendered in *RSV* by "discipline"). These two verses – and also 13:1 – are very close in meaning, though 13:18 goes further in making specific reference to the *consequences* of the two types of behaviour mentioned. As in many other proverbs in these chapters, the point at issue is social approval of (or rejection by) the local community, which had decisive economic consequences for the individual concerned and his family. **Poverty** (*rēš*) and **disgrace** (*qālôn*) are significantly mentioned together, while the root *kbd* – here in the pual, **is honoured** – denotes both social esteem and wealth.

There is no verb in the first line which, rendered literally, asserts that the person **who ignores instruction** *is* **poverty and disgrace**. Some commentators emend the text in order to "improve" the syntax (see *BHS*); but the Hebrew text as it stands is probably correct: it is to be interpreted as a strong metaphor (compare GK 127g, 131c and Watson, 1984, pp. 263–71).

19. The thought of the first line of this verse is very similar to that of v. 12b; but whereas the latter line is complemented by an appropriate parallel in the accompanying line, there is no such parallelism apparent here. Many commentators, probably rightly, consider the two lines to have originally been quite independent of one another, their present juxtaposition being fortuitous. Delitzsch pointed out the similarity of sound between the initial words of the respective lines, *ta'ᵃwāh* (**desire**) and *tô'ᵃbat* (**abomination** [**to**]), which may have led to their association in oral transmission. Plöger attempted to find an association of sense, seeing the second line as a warning that to have one's **desire fulfilled** was conditional on having the sense **to turn away from evil**; but this is hardly convincing. Nor has any emendation which has been proposed carried conviction.

to the soul: *nepeš* here probably means "person", but, as often, with a particularly emotional overtone: compare, for example, the phrase "hated by David's *nepeš*" in 2 Sam. 5:8.

20. This verse shows that in the circles in which these proverbs had their origin the acquisition of wisdom was not thought to be exclusively a matter of the education of youth. It was communicated by constant association with persons recognized by the community as possessing it, presumably by following their example as well as by listening to their advice. The thought is similar to that of v. 18, and is in line not only with v. 1 but also with several other verses in this chapter. The antithesis between **walks with wise men** and **companion of fools** indicates that **wise** (*ḥākām*) here is descriptive and not a technical term.

In the first line Kethib has imperatives: "Walk with wise men and become wise". Qere, on which *RSV*'s translation is based, is preferable in that the imperfect **becomes wise** corresponds to the imperfect in the second line.

There is alliteration in the verse, seen not only in the double occurrence of the root *ḥkm* in the first line, but more strikingly in the similarity of *rō'eh* (**companion**) and *yērôa'* (**will suffer harm**) in the second. Scott suggested that this line may have originally been a "popular epigram".

21–22. These two verses are linked by a common vocabulary (*ḥaṭṭā'/ḥôṭē'*, **sinner**; *ṭôb* (**prosperity**, **good man**); *ṣaddîq*, **righteous**) and also in theme. In fact v. 22 provides a concrete example of the statement in v. 21, which is expressed in very general terms (**Misfortune**; **prosperity**).

21. *RSV*'s rendering of the second line is probably correct. *ṭôb* (**prosperity**): perhaps rather "happiness" or "good fortune". Some commentators have doubted whether this can be so personified as to be envisaged as dispensing rewards, and have either taken the subject to be God, who is otherwise not mentioned in the chapter (so "*He* rewards the righteous *with* good"), or have emended the verb (LXX has "overtakes").

22. In the Hebrew text the first word of this verse (*ṭôb*, **A good man**) is identical with the last word of v. 21 (**prosperity**). No doubt this partly accounts for the juxtaposition of the two verses. It is tempting to suppose that the word should be omitted from v. 21 as an instance of dittography (see *BHS*); but this would involve considerable emendation of the rest of the line which is not justified.

This verse has to be understood in the light of the great importance attached in ancient Israel to lineage and inheritance. The possibility of being childless and/or losing one's family possessions through misfortune and having nothing to hand on to the next generation was regarded as the greatest possible calamity (Ec. 2:18–21; 4:7–8; 6:1–2), and was a fate which the pious Israelite hoped would befall the wicked (Ps. 109:6ff.; Job 27: 13ff.). In this verse, which in its present position emphasizes the truth of the bare statement about retribution made in v. 21, it is the element of inheritance which is stressed: that a **sinner** may acquire **wealth** is not in doubt; but the assertion that in some unspecified way it will end up in the hands of the **righteous**, thus giving him a double portion of wealth, is to give a double incentive to righteous behaviour in society.

23. *RSV*'s translation of this verse (compare also *REB*) makes it into a condemnation of those who by flouting or corrupting the legal process snatch away from the poor even their hard-won livelihood. But various objections have been made to this interpretation, and several commentators have regarded the verse as irremediably corrupt. They have pointed out that the **poor** in Proverbs are always totally destitute persons who have *no* land, not even rough, previously uncultivated ground (*nîr*, **fallow ground**); and also that it is unlikely that such land could produce a rich harvest (**much food**). It has also been noted that the Hebrew of the second line does not read **it is swept away**, but states only that this *sometimes* occurs (*yēš*), an impossibly feeble statement.

These difficulties have not been solved by different interpretations of particular words. McKane, for example, pointed out that *rā'šîm* (*RSV* **poor**) may in fact be the plural of *rō'š*, literally "heads", and renders it by "grandees"; Gemser derives it from an Arabic word meaning "arrogant"; others emend it to *rᵉšā'îm*, "wicked". Frankenberg took *yēš* (not translated in *RSV*) as a noun meaning "property" or "wealth", as in 8:21. But the adoption of none of these proposals would produce a satisfactory meaning for the verse as a whole.

24. The view that corporal punishment was an essential element in the education of children, repeated several times in Proverbs (22:15; 23:13–14; 29:15; compare 3:12; 19:18; 29:17) was firmly held not only in Israel but elsewhere in the ancient Near East, and is very frequently expressed in Egyptian literature. **is diligent**: the precise meaning of this verb (*šḥr*, Piel) is uncertain, although the general sense is clear. Elsewhere it means "to seek out", perhaps with the added nuance of "diligently", but possibly rather "early" (see Driver, *JTS* 41 [1940], p. 174). If the latter is the case, the verse means that such treatment ought to begin at an early age before the child's character is formed. On the double accusative see *GK* 117ff.

Plöger points out that this penultimate verse of the chapter is closely connected with v. 1, and suggests that it may once have followed v. 25, so that the chapter would have constituted an independent collection enclosed within an "instructional" framework.

25. Compare 10:3.

CHAPTER 14

There are no clear signs of a fully integrated structure in this chapter, although the reference to Wisdom's "house" in v. 1 suggests that what follows was regarded at some point by an editor as a compendium of wisdom sayings. How far this section originally extended is not clear; but it is just possible that v. 11, which states that the "house" of the *wicked* will be destroyed may at some time have marked its conclusion. V. 12, which is a very general observation, could then have introduced a new section.

Within the chapter a number of small, mainly thematic, groups may be tentatively postulated: vv. 1–3, 6–8 (9), 12–13, 15–18, 19–21, 25–8, 29–30; and, extending into the next chapter, 34–15:3.

References to God are comparatively frequent. Three verses (2, 26, 27) mention Yahweh by name, and all employ the formula "the fear of Yahweh", a phrase closely associated with wisdom in the preface to the book (1:7) and elsewhere in chapters 1–9. There is also a reference to God as Creator in v. 31 (on v. 9 see below). There is reason to believe that the three Yahweh-proverbs have been placed in positions where they comment on adjacent proverbs. Other topics include caution and prudence, relations between rich and poor, and psychological aspects of human character.

1–3. This placing of a verse which speaks of the fear of Yahweh (2) in the immediate context of a proverb (v. 1) or passage on the virtues of wisdom follows the same pattern as in chapters 1–9 (1:7, 29; 2:5; 3:7; 8:13; 9:10). The effect in each case, whether Wisdom is personified there or not, is to assert that the way of wisdom is inseparable from, or is to be defined in terms of, the faithful service of Yahweh. But this little group of verses probably also includes v. 3, which may be regarded as a further but distinct comment on verse 1, providing a concrete illustration of the general statement made in that verse.

1. The first line of this verse in *RSV* is based on an emendation which has been accepted by the majority of modern commentators. The Hebrew text as pointed in MT reads, literally, "The wisest (plural) of women *has* built *her* house" (*ḥakmôt nāšîm bānᵉtā bêtāh̲*). The emendation represented by *RSV* involves the omission of *nāšîm* ("women") and the repointing of *ḥakmôt* to *ḥokmôt*, "wisdom" (the unusual form found in 9:1). The chief attraction of this reading, apart from the avoidance of the problem of a singular verb governed by a plural subject, is that it is then exactly identical with 9:1a. It also has the advantage that **Wisdom** as an abstract noun corresponds to **folly** in the second line, making a good parallelism between the two lines. The whole verse would then make a statement corresponding closely to the fuller picture of 9:1–6, 13–18 in which a personified Wisdom is contrasted with a personified Folly, differing only in that whereas in chapter 9 Folly has her own rival establishment to that of Wisdom, here she is represented as demolishing the house built by Wisdom.

Not all commentators accept this emendation. Plöger accepts the emendation to *ḥokmôt*, but retains "women": "The wisdom of women builds her house" (compare also *REB*). He points out that the weakness of the generally accepted emendation is that it is difficult to account for the subsequent addition of this word, which was already present in the text translated by LXX. He also refers to 24:3, which states that "By wisdom a house is built" in a context in which the reference is clearly to housebuilding in the literal sense: that is, as in other enterprises, wisdom – that is, skill – is required in building a house. The interpretation of 14:1 in a similar sense is plausible, but still does not account for the reference to women, since house-building was not a normal activity of flesh-and-blood women. An alternative suggestion is that building a house in 14:1 may be a figurative way of referring to founding a family; but this interpretation makes no sense of the second line.

On balance the emendation represented by *RSV* remains the most probable solution to the problem. With regard to the presence of the word "women" in the traditional Hebrew text, it may have been added as a gloss by a scribe who misunderstood *ḥkmwt* as a feminine adjective meaning "wise" rather than as a noun meaning "wisdom", though in view of the LXX reading this would have to have been a very early gloss.

If **Wisdom builds her house** represents the original text, the point of the verse appears to be that the achievements of a life based on wisdom can be brought to nothing by subsequent acts of folly: continuous vigilance is essential (compare Ec. 10:1).

3. The general sense of this verse is similar to that of some already considered: foolish talk gets one into trouble, but intelligent discourse can keep one out of it. (Compare 10:13, 21; 12:16). But the precise meaning of the first line is uncertain. *RSV* has followed a number of commentators is emending the Hebrew text, which reads "In the mouth of a fool is a *ḥōter* of pride". *ḥōter* is usually taken to mean "rod", although in its only other occurrence in the Old Testament (Isa. 11:1) it is a shoot springing from the stem or stock of a tree. "A rod of pride", however, hardly makes sense in the context, and *RSV* here represents the emendation of *gaʾ*ᵃ*wāh* "pride", to *gēwô*, **his back**. The phrase "a rod for the back" denoting the fate suffered by fools occurs in 10:13 and 26:3, though it should be noted that in those two passages a different word, *šēbeṭ*, is used for "rod".

will preserve them: better, "will protect them" – that is, **the wise** (plural). On the unusual verbal form see *GK* 47g.

4. This is a straightforward piece of advice to the small farmer. Only if he farms his land properly and keeps oxen to plough his fields will he grow sufficient crops to make an adequate living (compare similar agricultural advice in 12:11 = 28:19; 27:23–7). However, the meaning of the first line has been disputed. *RSV*'s **there is no grain** represents a common emendation of the Hebrew text, replacing *'ēbûs*, "crib, manger" by the negative particle *'epes*. This gives a satisfactory meaning, but is speculative and probably unnecessary. The principal difficulty of the line is the meaning of the word *bar* (*RSV* **grain**). There is another *bar* which elsewhere means "pure", but which several commentators (Gemser, Scott, Dahood, Barucq, Plöger; also *KB*[3], and compare *REB*) take here to mean "clean", that is, here, bare or empty (LXX also has "clean"). The line could then be rendered "Where there are no oxen, the manger is empty"; and this has been interpreted as meaning that although the farmer can save himself work or expense by not keeping oxen, that is a false economy.

crops: literally, "what comes in", that is, "produce": compare this meaning of the word in 3:9.

5. The second line of this verse is identical with 6:19a, where it appears (as a relative clause: "a false witness *who* . . .") in a list of things which Yahweh hates. The verse as a whole is similar to 12:17. It appears to be a statement of the obvious; but although expressed in a form typical of the wisdom literature it probably corresponds in intention to a legal prescription (see on 6:16–19). The phrase **false witness** (*'ēd šeqer*) occurs in the Decalogue (Exod. 20:16) and also in Dt. 19:18. The heinousness of perjury is frequently stressed both in the laws and the wisdom instructions of the Old Testament and in the literature of the ancient Near East. **faithful**: better, "truthful". See also on 19:5.

6–8. These three verses are all concerned in various ways with wisdom and folly, and are also linked verbally: *ḥokmāh* (**wisdom**) occurs in vv. 6 and 8; *da'at* (**knowledge**) in vv. 6 and 7; *kᵉsîl* (**fool**) in vv. 7 and 8. If the Hebrew text of v. 9 is correct there is also a verbal link between vv. 8 and 9: *'iwwelet* (**folly**), v. 8; **wīlîm* ("fools" – but not in *RSV*: see below), v. 9.

6. The point of this verse is that wisdom is not a commodity which anyone may acquire whenever he feels the need for it: it only comes to those who by their way of life have disposed themselves to receive it, and then it comes easily and increasingly (compare 1:5). This proverb thus strikes the same note as the exhortations to the pupil in the instructions of chapters 1–9 in which he is urged to lose no time in choosing the right path. **wisdom** (*ḥokmāh*) and **knowledge** (*da'at*) here denote primarily the ability to cope with the practical problems of life; this explains why it can be said of the scoffer (*lēṣ*, perhaps better, "arrogant person"; see on 1:22), who is elsewhere contrasted with the wise, that he **seeks wisdom**.

in vain: literally, "but there is none" – that is, for him.

7. The second line of this verse has been held by a number of commentators to be obscure and to require emendation (see *BHS*, Gemser, Scott, Dahood); but the Hebrew text makes good sense: literally, "for you do not learn (*yāda'tā*) lips of knowledge" – that is, "you will not hear a word of sense from him" (*REB*). In its present position the verse elucidates what is meant by "a man of understanding" in v. 6b: such a man does not consort with, or pay attention to, known fools, who have no knowledge to impart.

8. This proverb, which may be seen as a further elucidation of v. 6, employs the metaphor of the **way** (here *derek*) familiar from its repeated use in the instructions of chapters 1–9 (compare "you will understand . . . every good path", 2:9). As in v. 6 the choice between the right and wrong "way" (of living) is a crucial one. The intelligent person (*'ārûm*, *RSV* **prudent** – see on 12:16 and compare 12:23; 13:16) will make the right choice, while **fools**, making the wrong one, will meet with disappointment and frustration. **deceiving** (*mirmāh*): better, "disappointment" (self-deceit). The proposal to repoint this noun as a participle *m^e^rammāh*, "misleads" (Thomas, *VT* Suppl. 3, 1955, pp. 285–6; Gemser; compare also *REB*) is unnecessary despite the reading of LXX, as are also more radical emendations.

9. The first line of this verse is seriously corrupt, and it is doubtful whether it can be restored. The Hebrew has "Guilt (or, A guilt-offering – *'āšām*) scorns fools". A slight emendation (of the verb from singular to plural) would give "Fools scorn an *'āšām*". This word, which denotes a particular type of propitiatory sacrifice in the great majority of cases, mainly in the priestly legislation of the Pentateuch, and "guilt" only in a few cases elsewhere in the Old Testament, never occurs elsewhere in Proverbs or in the other wisdom books; and its choice here would be extremely surprising even if the line could be made to mean that fools are contemptuous either of the penalties consequent upon sin or of the sacrificial means provided for its expiation. *RSV* represents an unsupported radical emendation which changes "fools" (*'ewīlîm*) into **God** (*'elōhîm*) and *'āšām* into *r^e^šā'îm* (**the wicked**), leaving only the verb of the Hebrew untouched. Other emendations which have been proposed are equally unsupported.

The second line also presents difficulties. The Hebrew has "and (or, 'but') between the upright is *rāṣôn*". *bên*, "between", has been rendered by "among" by some commentators, and *rāṣôn* (see on 10:32) by "good will" or something similar, so that the line is made to speak of harmonious human relationships (*RSV*'s **his**, referring to God, is not represented in the Hebrew). But *bên* means "between" and not "among". Driver (*Bib.* 32 [1951], p. 181) proposed the emendation of *ûbên*, "and among", to *ûbān* or *ûbanû* (from the verb *bîn*): "but upright men *discern* what is acceptable" – that is, to God (so also McKane). But it is questionable whether *rāṣôn* by itself without further specification can refer to *divine* favour.

10. For similar psychological statements about the private thoughts and feelings of the individual see 12:25a; 13:12a, 19a; 14:13. The proverb does not mean that joys and sorrows cannot at all be shared with others, but expresses an awareness that there is in every person an inviolate private area which no-one can fully penetrate. In other proverbs (17:3; 21:2; 24:12) and elsewhere in the Old Testament (for example, Ps. 44:21 [Heb. 22]) it is stated or implied that only God has access to what goes on in a person's **heart** – that is, in this private realm. *zār* (**stranger**) here means "anyone, another person" (compare 27:2; Job 19:27).

11. This verse has affinities with 11:28 and 12:7. It has a strong alliterative character: *r*[e]*šā'îm* (**the wicked**), *yiššāmēd* (**will be destroyed**); *y*[e]*šārîm* (**the upright**). **tent** (*'ōhel*): as in some other instances in poetry this word means simply "home" or "dwelling-place", and has been chosen to make a parallel pair with **house** (*bêt*).

12–13. These two verses are linked by the occurrence in each of *'aḥ*[a]*rît*, **end**, and also perhaps thematically by the common thought that appearances may be misleading.

12. This verse is identical with 16:25. This repetition, surprising in a single collection, points to the combination of two (or more) originally independent earlier collections.

The thought of a **way** which when embarked upon leads inevitably to death is reminiscent of warnings against being seduced by the "strange woman" (5:5; 7:25–7); but there is no suggestion here of the making of a choice between good and evil or between wisdom and folly. The proverb simply states that life contains hidden snares: the road ahead may seem to lead straight (*yāšār*, "straight" or "straightforward" rather than *RSV*'s **right** with its moral overtones) to the desired goal, but there may be (**There is**, Hebrew *yēš*) hidden and fatal dangers further on. This thought is in conflict with the general confidence of Proverbs that the guiltless will be free from trouble (compare v. 11), but represents a realistic strain more characteristic of Job and Ecclesiastes, but not entirely unrepresented in Proverbs; it reappears in the next verse (13).

13. As translated by *RSV* this verse expresses a depressing view of human nature which is entirely contrary to the prevailing attitude of Proverbs and indeed of the Old Testament as a whole. But this is a misunderstanding of its meaning. In the first line the verb *yik'ab* (*RSV* **is sad**; literally, "aches" or "is in pain") is an example of the potential use of the imperfect (*GK* 107r; S. R. Driver, *Tenses*, Section 37) and should be rendered "may be . . .". Similarly in the second line, where there is no verb in Hebrew, "may" or "can be" renders the sense better than **is**. This is a further example of a "psychological" proverb which, like v. 12, recognizes that the view which polarizes joy and sorrow as the respective and inevitable rewards of conduct does not do justice to the complexities of human experience, in which the two can exist side by side, or in which the one may give place to the other. (Ec. 7:3 has been compared with this verse, but the point made there is somewhat different.) An alternative interpretation of the first line taken by itself is that one should not judge by appearances: an external show of happiness may conceal a secret sorrow.

the end: the Hebrew has "*its* end". This is probably a slip by a scribe who was thinking of the word "its end" in the previous verse.

14. The occurrence of *lēb*, "heart" in the Hebrew both here and in v. 13 (see below on **perverse man**) may be the cause of the juxtaposition of the two verses; otherwise they have nothing in common. This proverb reiterates the notion of reward such as appears in v. 11 and elsewhere in these proverbs. The verb in the first line (*śāba'* + *min-*, RSV **will be filled with the fruit of**) applies to both lines, but there is an ironical play on its two senses. As referring to the fate of the **good man** it means to be satisfied or to receive in abundance (compare 12:11, 14), whereas in the case of the **perverse man** it means to have too much – with unfortunate results (compare 1:31; 25:16).

perverse man (*sûg lēb*): literally, one who has turned away in his heart (here, from the right way). **his deeds**: *RSV* has here followed the majority of commentators in emending *mē'ālâw* (literally, "from upon him") to *ma'alālâw*.

15–18. There are both thematic and formal links between these verses. Although different terms are used, all are concerned with the wise and the foolish. In vv. 15–17 the same or similar characteristics are attributed respectively to the two types of person: caution and prudence on the one side; credulousness, recklessness and impatience on the other. V. 18 concludes the group with a general statement. Formally the use of the same terms (*petî*, **simple**; *'ārûm*, **prudent**, or rather, "clever") in the opening and closing verses (15 and 18) knits the group together, while the repetition of *'iwwelet*, **foolishly**, **folly** in vv. 17 and 18 forms an additional link.

15. simple (*petî*): see on 1:4. **everything** (*kol-dābār*): probably better, "every word" – that is, everything that he hears. **looks where he is going**: literally, "gives heed to his step".

16. cautious: literally, "fearful", that is, aware of hidden dangers. **evil** (*rā'*): this word also means "misfortune", and this is almost certainly the meaning here. In other words, there is no moral implication: the wise man simply avoids trouble by taking care. **throws off all restraint**: the meaning of this verb (*hit'abbēr*) is uncertain. It may mean to become angry or excited and so to lose self-control. Gemser suggested that it is cognate with a Syriac verb meaning "to be careless" (cf. Driver, *JTS* 41 [1940], p. 174). This, however, would make it synonymous with the following word *bôṭēaḥ* (**careless**), perhaps better, "overconfident".

17. Both text and meaning of the second line of this verse are disputed. One problem is the meaning of *'îš m^ezimmôt*, rendered in *RSV* by **a man of discretion**. The word *m^ezimmāh*, however, has two quite distinct senses (see on 1:4). In the majority of instances in Proverbs it denotes cleverness (so *RSV* **discretion**) – a neutral term with no moral connotations. However, in 12:2, where the same phrase *'îš m^ezimmôt* is used, and in some other passages in the Old Testament, it has the pejorative sense of wicked scheming – in 12:2 the *'îš m^ezimmôt* is the opposite of the "good man" (*ṭôb*), and is condemned by Yahweh.

Most commentators, followed by *RSV*, have understood the word in its neutral or favourable sense, on the ground that only this interpretation affords a suitable contrast to the **man of quick temper**. But this creates a further problem: the Hebrew verb which governs the phrase is distinctly *un*favourable: "is hated" (*yiśśānē'*). Since this is totally unsuitable as a description of a "man of discretion", it has been assumed that the text is corrupt: hence *RSV*'s **is patient**, which represents an emendation (perhaps supported by the LXX's "endures") to *yiśśē'* – an intransitive use of the verb *nāśā'* which is attested also in 30:21 and Isa. 11:14; Jer. 44:22. Other proposals include that of Thomas (*VT* Suppl. 3, 1955, p. 286) to emend the word to *yiśneh*, "become exalted" (on *śānāh* [III] in this sense see *KB*³). So also McKane, "holds office": the clever man is bound to rise in the world. But it must be said (with Plöger) that provided that *m*ᵉ*zimmāh* is taken in its *un*favourable sense MT is by no means impossible ("the evil schemer is hated").

18. This is a generalizing statement about the characteristics of the simple and the clever (*RSV* **prudent**): compare v. 15. **acquire**: literally, "inherit" or "take possession of" (*nāḥ*ᵃ*lû*). Driver (*Bib.* 32 [1951], p. 181) suggested that a better parallelism would be obtained if this verb were repointed as *neḥ*ᵉ*lû*, the verb *ḥālāh* being supposedly a denominative verb from *ḥ*ᵃ*lî*, "ornament" – so *REB* "wear the trappings of". Thus the simple person adorns himself with folly as the clever person crowns himself with knowledge (= wisdom): both wear the outward marks of their respective characters. **are crowned with** (*yaktīrû*): this appears to be an impersonal hiphil (*GK* 53d, g) of a verb derived from the late Hebrew noun *keter*, "crown", attested elsewhere only in Est. 1:11; 2:17. Elsewhere Proverbs uses "crown" as a metaphor, but employs a different noun, *ᵃṭārāh*.

19–21. These verses have a certain thematic unity. Vv. 20–21 give the impression of being intended to qualify the absoluteness of v. 19's uncompromising division of mankind into two classes, the wicked and the righteous. V. 20 describes a social evil which is to be deplored, but is evidently widespread and hardly deserves a simple condemnation as "wicked". V. 21 then comments on v. 20, but again in relatively mild terms (see below).

19. This uncompromising statement is, unusually, in synonymous parallelism. It is implied that the wicked – the nature of their wickedness is not defined – will initially have some success, but that this will not last. Their punishment will be that they will end by being reduced to the humiliation of begging at the good man's door.

20. The social evils described here were evidently not rare in the society in which these proverbs arose: they are condemned again in 19:4 and 19:7. The standpoint of the proverb is that of an observer who considered himself to be neither **rich** (*ʿāšîr*) nor **poor** (*rāš*, that is, destitute). The *ʿāšîr* is always regarded unfavourably in these proverbs. **is disliked**: literally, "is hated". This was probably because the poor begged from their neighbours, who themselves had little to spare. Nevertheless it is implied that they have a duty towards those in less fortunate circumstances than themselves. The second line refers to hangers-on of the rich. **friends**: literally, "lovers". The statement is ironical: their "love" is insincere: they are out for what they can get.

21. The first words of this verse (*bāz-lᵉrēʿēhû*), **He who despises his neighbour**, echoes the first words of v. 20 (*gam-lᵉrēʿēhû*), "even by his neighbour", and this no doubt partly accounts for the juxtaposition of the two verses. But there is also a thematic connection: **despises** and **is kind to** undoubtedly refer to the provision or otherwise of material assistance to the needy who come to beg from their neighbours. LXX confirms this interpretation in that it reads *penētas*, "needy", in place of MT's **neighbour**. This does not necessarily mean, however, that Gemser's suggestion that the Hebrew originally read *rāʿēb*, "the hungry", rather than *rēʿēhû*, the corruption being due to an unconscious scribal repetition of *rēʿēhû* from v. 20.

a sinner (*ḥôṭēʾ*): in view of the contrast between this word and **happy is he who**. . . (*ʾašrâw*) in the second line, this word may mean no more than "one who misses (that is, fails to obtain) happiness". The same contrast between the two words is found in 8:32–6. If this is correct, the parallelism is improved: both lines speak, respectively, of the *consequences* of meanness or generosity respectively. The attitude of the neighbour in v. 20a is thus rebuked, but in relatively mild terms. **the poor**: read Kethib (*ʿaniyyîm*) rather than Qere (*ʿanāwîm*).

22. This proverb is a plain statement about the respective fates of good and evil persons. **err** (*tāʿāh*) means to go astray, here in the sense of taking the wrong road, the road that leads to death (compare 7:25–7; 21:16). The use of the word **devise** (*ḥāraš*) implies a deliberate decision. **meet**: there is no verb in the Hebrew. This omission is probably a mark of the concise style in which some of these proverbs are couched, and no emendation is required. The meaning of this line appears to be that the good man's conduct is equivalent to **loyalty and faithfulness** (*ḥesed weʾemet*), which in 16:6 are equated with the fear of Yahweh, which puts a person right with God and protects him from harm (see also on 3:3).

23. The effectiveness of this proverb lies in the irony of the strong assonance of the final, and therefore most emphatic, words of the two lines: *môtār*, **profit** and *maḥsôr*, **want**, which are similar in sound and form but opposite in meaning. This emphasis on the need for and rewards of hard work and the harsh fate of those who waste their time in other activities is characteristic of these proverbs (compare 12:11; 21:17; 28:19; also 27:23–7) and reflects the harsh life of the small farmer. (*'eṣeb*, **toil**, here has a harsh connotation – compare 10:22.) What is surprising in view of the high value placed elsewhere in these proverbs on speech is the deprecation of **talk** (literally, "the word of the lips", *RSV* **mere talk**); but other proverbs speak of the talk of fools, and what is meant here is presumably endless foolish chatter or idle boasting unaccompanied by actual physical labour.

24. This verse has been held by many commentators to be incomprehensible and in need of radical emendation. In the first line *RSV* has adopted one of the proposed emendations in substituting **their wisdom** (*'ormātām*) for the Hebrew *'ošrām*, "their wealth", following LXX. But the Hebrew makes good sense (so McKane, Plöger). *'ōšer*, "wealth", is a neutral term with no intrinsic moral connotations; but in 3:16; 8:18 it is used in a positive context, being one of the rewards conferred by personified Wisdom on those who follow her, and in 22:4 it is a reward for fearing Yahweh. **crown** (*[a]ṭārāh*) in Proverbs, where it is a favourite metaphor, stands for the conferring of esteem or honour on a person (12:4; 16:31; 17:6), and in 4:9 is itself something which is conferred by Wisdom. The line therefore means that riches are the "crown" or reward properly conferred on the **wise**.

The second line is more difficult. The Hebrew reads, "the folly (*'iwwelet*) of fools (*k[e]sîlîm*) is folly (*'iwwelet*)". Although this might perhaps mean that fools are incorrigible and always remain fools, almost all commentators propose the emendation of *'iwwelet* on its first occurrence (before **of fools**) to *liwyat*, "wreath" or (*RSV*) **garland**. (Some also emend *'iwwelet* on its second occurrence to *'iwwaltām*, ("*their* folly".) This proposal, which creates an excellent parallelism, gains further plausibility from the fact that both *liwyāh* and *[a]ṭarāh* occur in parallelism in 4:9. If this emendation is accepted, the line is ironical: elsewhere *liwyāh* (it only occurs in 1:9 and 4:9) is reserved exclusively for those who have heeded instruction or followed wisdom. As an adornment for **fools** it is ludicrous.

25. This verse has strong affinities with v. 5, where also the faithful or **truthful witness** (*'ēd [x]mûnîm*, here *'ēd [x]met*) is contrasted with the person who **utters lies**. The frequent occurrence of the theme in these proverbs (compare 6:19a; 19:5, 9; 21:28 among others) as well as in the laws of the Old Testament points to the existence of a serious social evil. This verse points out most clearly the consequences for others of true and false witness. The witness who tells the truth at the trial of a falsely accused person may be able to save him from conviction and execution, while a perjured witness by deceiving the judges may bring about his conviction (see on v. 5 above). **is a betrayer**: literally, "is deceit". This may be a case of the use of the abstract for the concrete (*GK* 83a); many commentators however, propose the repointing of the word (*mirmāh*) as the piel participle of the verb "to deceive" (*m^erammeh*). See also on 19:5.

26–28. Plöger suggests that there are not only internal links between vv. 26 and 27 but also with those which precede and follow them. Vvv. 26 and 27 are obviously related in that they both speak of the practice of the **fear of the Lord** as a guarantee of safety and good fortune (compare also v. 2). It is certainly possible that they have been inserted here as comment on v. 25, to suggest that truthfulness is closely linked with Yahweh's ethical demands and that it saves the lives not only of the falsely accused but of those who practise it. But there may also be a connection between vv. 27 and 28, which is a proverb about kings. Although there is no obvious thematic connection, it is significant that this is only one of several instances in these proverbs where originally distinct "royal proverbs" have been placed in close proximity with Yahweh-proverbs: 14:34–15:3; 20:26–21:3; 21:1–4; 22:11–12; 25:2–7; 29:12–14; and above all 15:33–16:15, where a long string of Yahweh-proverbs is immediately followed by a long string of royal proverbs. (See below on these passages.) The main purpose of such juxtaposition seems to be to stress that obedience to Yahweh is particularly important for kings, in whose hands are the lives of all his people. Plöger also finds links between v. 28 and the remainder of the chapter, noting that the "royal proverbs" vv. 28 and 35 enclose a group of sayings which can mainly be interpreted as especially relevant for kings. While some of the arguments put forward along such lines are fragile and liable to undue subjectivism, they often give at least a limited insight into what appear to be compositional methods and patterns of thought.

26. one has: these words are not represented in the Hebrew text which is a nominal (non-verbal) sentence. Since this means that **his children** has no antecedent, it has been proposed that *'ōz*, literally "(of) strength (*RSV* **strong**)" should be repointed to *'āz*, "a strong person". So *REB*, "One who is strong and trusts in the fear of the Lord . . .". However, this rendering has its own difficulties, and MT may be right despite its apparent syntactical lapse.

27. This verse is identical with 13:14 except that the subject here is not "The teaching of the wise" but **The fear of the Lord**. This is a further example of the reinterpretation of wisdom in specifically Yahwistic terms which characterizes some of the instructions in chapters 1–9 – for example, chapter 2.

28. This is the first example in these chapters of a so-called "royal proverb". These proverbs in fact have nothing in common except that they refer to kings and rulers. They reflect several quite different attitudes towards the king (or to kings in general), and do not presuppose a court origin, a school for courtiers, or a personal acquaintance with kings. (See Whybray, 1990, pp. 45–59.) This proverb states the obvious fact that the importance and power of kings depend on the size and importance of the kingdom over which they rule. It is more difficult, however, to understand the reason for this statement. The second line, conjuring up a picture of a king with no people to govern, seems to present an "upside down" world. The usual view was that kings were indispensable: without a *king* it was the *people* that was ruined (compare 2 Sam. 21:17; Lam. 4:20; and the paradox of the locusts, which form a well organized fighting force despite their lack of a king, Prov. 30:27). It is possible that this proverb reflects some event in the turbulent history of Judah in which a king had been deserted by his subjects.

29–30. There is an obvious affinity between these two verses, but also between v. 29 and v. 33 (**great understanding**, *rab-tᵉbûnāh*; **a man of understanding**, (*lēb nābôn*). Both verses could be applicable to kings, though not exclusively so.

29. exalts: this verb (*mērîm*, hiphil participle of *rûm*, "to be high") does not give a very satisfactory sense. Some commentators therefore propose its emendation to *marbeh*, "increases", which gives better sense and also makes a satisfactory parallelism. But see on 3:35.

30. A tranquil mind (*lēb marpē'*): perhaps better, "A healthy mind" (see on 4:22). But some scholars regard *marpē'* here as derived not from *rāpā'* "to heal" but from *rāpāh* "to be relaxed" (so KB^3; and compare *GK*75nn on a similar interchange of letters in the case of verbal forms). **makes the bones rot**: see on 12:4. Such a contrast between the calm (or "cool") and the passionate (or "heated") person was a commonplace of Egyptian wisdom books: see especially *Amenope* IV 6:1–12 (*ANET*, p. 422).

31. This verse goes beyond v. 21 in giving a reason for the judgement there made that only those who treat the poor with generosity can receive blessing. Here it is affirmed that the poor person no less than others has been created by God, and not just as part of the created universe but individually (note **his Maker**), and is thus under his personal protection. To maltreat him is therefore to insult God himself, while to recognize his full status as a fellow human being is to honour God (compare also 20:12). The theological implications of this thought are immense. Similar thoughts are, however, found elsewhere in ancient Near Eastern wisdom books – compare, for example, *Amenope* XXV (ANET, p. 424).

oppresses: this verb (*'āšaq*) is often used in the Old Testament of the actions of the rich and powerful, but there are also passages (Lev. 6:2 [Heb. 5:21]; 19:13; Hos. 12:7 [Heb. 8]) where it refers to common robbery or cheating of "neighbours", that is, of fellow-members of the same intimate community.

32. through his integrity: this translation is based on an emendation accepted by the great majority of commentators. The Hebrew has *b^emôtô*, "in his death"; this makes sense only if it is taken as an expression of a belief in personal immortality, which, despite the arguments of Dahood and others, is extremely improbable in Proverbs. The proposed emendation to *b^etummô* represented in *RSV* (with metathesis of consonants) may be supported by LXX ("in his holiness"). It makes a good parallelism with **through his evildoing** in the first line.

33. In the second line of this verse *RSV* follows the majority of commentators; the Hebrew text, however, lacks the word **not**! It is generally assumed that LXX's *ou diaginōsketai*, "it is not discerned", reflects the original text, and that "not" has fallen out of the Hebrew text accidentally. The accidental loss of a whole word, and that one which is vital to the meaning of the text, has, however, been regarded by some commentators as unlikely, and various suggestions have been made to emend the *verb* (*tiwwādēa'*, *RSV* **is . . . known**) or to interpret it differently. Some early commentators emend it to *'iwwelet*, "folly" (so, "but folly [abides] in the heart of fools"). Thomas (*JTS* 35 [1934], pp. 302–3) in connection with his special theory about the meanings of the verb *yāda'* (see pp. 86 above) took the verb to mean "it is suppressed". Emerton, however (*VT* 41 [1991], pp. 161–2) rejects Thomas's theory and suggests emendation to *tērōa'*, "suffers harm". But if that were the original reading it is difficult to explain the reading of LXX, which may after all be right. If this is so, the point of the verse may lie in the verb *tānûaḥ*,

abides: in the heart of the **man of understanding** wisdom is not a temporary but a permanent "guest" (*REB* "is at home"), but it is a stranger (**is not known**) to the heart of fools.

34–15:3: Although these proverbs may not at first appear to have a common theme, there are indications that they have been arranged in order to assert that human conduct is rewarded and punished by Yahweh or by the king as his representative. The opening verse (34) speaks of the consequences for a nation of righteousness and sin, while the closing verse (15:3) affirms that nothing escapes the universal scrutiny of Yahweh. Vv. 34 and 35 taken together imply that the king's function is to observe the behaviour of his subjects and to mete out favour or wrath to them as they deserve. 15:1 may then be seen as a comment on v. 35, and 15:2 as a comment on v. 1. The king may thus be said to possess God-given ability to discern and to reward or punish. As with some other proverbs in these chapters, there is perhaps a reminiscence here of the tradition about Solomon recorded in 1 Kg. 3 (especially vv. 8–9, 28). V. 3 makes it clear that this ability is dependent on Yahweh's universal omniscience and power.

34. exalts: that is, makes great or prosperous. **reproach** (*ḥesed*): better, "degradation" (compare *REB*). No emendation (such as that suggested in *BHS*) is needed: this word *ḥesed*, also found in Lev. 20:17 (and compare the corresponding verb in Prov. 25:10) is unconnected with that meaning "love" or "loyalty". The thought, which may be compared with the teaching of the prophets, is unusual among these proverbs in its concern with matters beyond the local community; but compare also v. 28. It may refer to the behaviour of the king or the ruling class rather than to the common people at large.

35. Although this proverb is concerned with skill and incompetence rather than moral qualities (on the two verbs see on 10:5), it has some relevance to the theme of this group of proverbs in that it speaks of the king's ability to perceive and judge others. **servant** (*'ebed*) here probably means a member of the royal administration, though its wider meaning lies in the background. Like other "royal proverbs", this one does not presuppose personal acquaintance with the court.

falls on: the Hebrew has *tihyeh*, literally "is" or "will be". No emendation is necessary, although *l*^{e} (literally "to") would normally be expected before *mēbîš*, **one who acts shamefully** (compare *l*^{e}*'ebed* in the first line). But these brief proverbs do not always strictly obey the "normal" rules of grammar.

CHAPTER 15

This chapter is chiefly remarkable for the high proportion (nine in thirty-three verses) of its references to Yahweh (vv. 3, 8, 9, 11, 16, 25, 26, 29, 33). Much of the chapter appears to have been built round these: vv. 8–11, 12–17, 25–33. V. 33 is also a pivotal verse which introduces a further group consisting almost entirely of Yahweh-proverbs (see on 16:1–9 below).

The other most notable feature of the chapter is that almost half of its constituent proverbs are concerned with the teaching and acquiring of knowledge and instruction and the importance of these for daily living. The two themes are brought together in the final verse (33) in which instruction in wisdom is identified with the fear of Yahweh. It is not clear, however, that the chapter as a whole originally formed a single collection. V. 20 may have once marked the beginning of a separate collection.

1. Like others in these chapters this proverb lays great emphasis on the power of the spoken word, in this case on its power to promote harmony or to cause disharmony in a community (compare 12:18). It is clearly intended to be universally applicable, though in its present position it can be seen as an extension of the thought of 14:35, applying the "royal" saying to everyday life. **wrath** and **anger** pick up the "wrath" of that verse, though there quite different words are used. **a harsh word**: literally, "a word of pain" (*d*ᵉ*bar-ʿẹseb*), that is, a word which *causes* pain.

2. This verse is a further general statement about wise and foolish talk, probably meaning that a person's talk is a key to his character.

dispenses: this represents a common emendation of the Hebrew *têṭîb* to *taṭṭîp*, literally, "drops" or "drips". Other emendations have also been proposed; but the Hebrew makes acceptable sense (so also Bühlmann and Plöger). *hêṭîb*, the hiphil imperfect of *yṭb*, here has the not infrequent meaning of making something – here one's **knowledge** – acceptable or pleasant to others. This fits well with v. 1 and with 14:35 and probably accounts for the verse's present position. The purpose of the proposed emendations is to create a good parallelism with **pour out** in the second line; but good parallelism is not an essential feature of these proverbs; and to emend a reasonably satisfactory Hebrew text without supporting evidence and solely for the sake of style is a questionable procedure.

3. The notion that the gods (or a particular god, who might be identified with a heavenly body passing through the sky) were all-seeing and scrutinized human behaviour is a commonplace of Egyptian literature and other literature of the ancient Near East. In the Old Testament we find it for example in Am. 9:2–4; Ps. 33:13–15, 18–19; 139:1–12. This proverb, which concludes the group that began with 14:34, is a reminder that the whole range of national as well as private behaviour comes under Yahweh's inexorable scrutiny.

4. This proverb has affinities with vv. 1 and 2, especially with the former: it concerns the *effects* of the spoken word on others. It is not entirely clear, however, what kinds of speech are here contrasted. *marpē'* (*RSV* **gentle**) has more than one possible meaning (see on 14:30); *selep* (**perverseness**) occurs in the Old Testament only here and in 11:3, where it appears to denote what is twisted or false, though the corresponding verb (*slp*, piel) can mean "to ruin". Probably the contrast is between speech which heals or soothes (compare its use in 12:18) and so enhances the life of the hearer (on **tree of life** see on 3:18) and malicious or hurtful speech which can ruin the lives of others by driving them to despair (*šeber bᵉrûaḥ*, *RSV* **breaks the spirit** – compare *šeber rûaḥ* in Isa. 65:14 and the "broken spirit" of the Psalmist in Ps. 51:17 [Heb. 19]).

5. Compare v. 20. The language of this verse (**his father's instruction**, *mûsar 'āḇîw*; **heeds**, literally, "keeps", *šāmar*; **despises**, *nā'aṣ*; compare 5:12 and see also 1:30) is that of the Instructions of chapters 1–9. **is prudent**: perhaps better, "will *acquire* shrewdness", that is, as a *result* of heeding the admonition.

6. Compare 10:2; 11:4. The grammar of the second line is anomalous: see *BHS*. On *tᵉbû'āh* (**income**) see on 10:16; 14:4.

7. spread: this verb (*zrh*) is elsewhere always used in an unfavourable sense of "scatter". Of the emendations and repointings that have been proposed, that noted in *BHS* (*yiṣṣᵉrû*, "keep, guard", is probably the most plausible. The expression "guard knowledge" (*nāṣar da'at*) occurs also in 5:2 in connection with **lips** or speech, and Symmachus's translation probably supports this emendation.

not so (*lō'-kēn*); here *kēn* is almost certainly an adjective as in 11:19, and the phrase should be rendered "not right", that is, probably, not reliable or untrustworthy. So the meaning of the verse seems to be that whereas the speech of the **wise** is disciplined in accordance with the knowledge – that is, the wisdom – that they have acquired, **fools** cannot be relied on because their **minds** (literally, "heart") have not acquired, or have rejected, that self-discipline.

8–11. These verses are linked both formally and thematically. Formally, vv. 8 and 9 are closely parallel. They both speak of **the wicked** (*rāšā'*, plural in v. 8; singular in v. 9), whose behaviour is **an abomination to the Lord**, and also, on the other hand, of Yahweh's affection (*rāṣôn*, **delight**, in v. 8; *yeʾhāb*, **loves**, in v. 9) for the righteous (*yᵉšārîm*, **the upright**, in v. 8; *mᵉraddēp ṣᵉdāqāh*, **him who pursues righteousness**, in v. 9). Vv. 9 and 10 are associated not only by the motif of the **way** (*derek*, v. 9; *'ōraḥ*, v. 10), but also by the contrast between **loves** (*yeʾhāb*, v. 9) and **hates** (*śōnē'*, v. 10). Vv. 10 and 11 are linked by references to death (**will die**, v. 10; **Sheol**, v. 11); and the reference there to Yahweh looks back to vv. 8 and 9.

A thematic thread also runs through these verses: the reference to specific religious acts (**sacrifice**, **prayer**) in v. 8 leads to a wider appraisal of moral conduct in v. 9, while v. 10 extends the general references in vv. 8 and 9 to God's disapproval of the wicked (**abomination to the Lord**) in specific terms – such people **will die**. V. 11 concludes the series with a reminder (cf. v. 3) that there is no escape from this fate because nothing – not even the inner thoughts (**hearts**) of men from which their actions proceed – is hidden from Yahweh, who is the master of death as well as of life.

More than one explanation is possible of the way in which this group of verses has been built up. It may be that the three Yahweh-proverbs (vv. 8, 9, 11) have been assembled round v. 10, the only verse in the group which does not mention Yahweh, in order to make it clear that the otherwise undefined **way** of v. 10 is to be seen as a matter of obedience to the demands of Yahweh (compare the additions to the Instructions of chapters 1–9). Alternatively, vv. 9–11 may be seen as an expansion of v. 8, underlining the point that worship of Yahweh unaccompanied by obedience to Yahweh's moral demands is not only unacceptable to him but a heinous sin which will lead to the destruction of its practitioners. However this may be, there is reason to suppose that this group of verses in its present form, together with the other references to Yahweh in the chapter, is intended to put a particular stamp on the chapter as a whole. These verses have many points of contact with other verses in the chapter: in particular, v. 8 has contacts with vv. 3, 6 and 29; v. 9 with vv. 16 and 17; v. 10 with vv. 5, 20, 31 and 32; and v. 11 with vv. 24–6.

8. Although some passages in the Old Testament (for example, Ps. 51:15–17 [Heb. 17–19]; Mic. 6:6–8; Prov. 21:3) express the view that the only sacrifice acceptable to God is a righteous and humble life, and in Ps. 141:2 prayer appears to be regarded as a substitute for sacrifice, the view of some early commentators that *in this verse* a contrast is intended between sacrifice and prayer is mistaken. Prayer (*tᵉpillāh*) and the offering of animal or vegetable sacrifice were never regarded as mutually exclusive forms of worship in ancient Israel. Although prayer obviously could, and often was, offered without the accompaniment of sacrifice, it was a regular accompaniment of ritual sacrifice: in Isa. 56:7, for example, Yahweh, in speaking of his acceptance of animal sacrifice, refers to the Temple where that sacrifice is offered as "my house of prayer"; and the two forms of worship are associated in other passages: see for example Isa. 1:12–17; Jon. 2:7–9 [Heb. 8–10]. Both were acceptable forms of worship; and prayer, which was primarily petition, or an appeal to God for favourable treatment or help, was no more acceptable to him if offered by the unrighteous than was animal sacrifice (so Prov. 15:29; 28:9). The contrast drawn in this verse is not between alternative forms of worship but between God's response to those who approach him: whether they are **wicked** or **upright**. It should be noted that although it has often been alleged that these proverbs are only marginally interested in worship, whether sacrificial or not, this proverb – as also 15:29; 21:27 and 28:9 – appears to take it for granted as a normal activity (see Perdue, 1977, pp. 155–62).

On *tôʿᵃbat yhwh* (**abomination to the Lord**) see on 6:16. On *rāṣôn* (**delight**) see on 11:1.

9. pursues righteousness: that is, tries to lead a righteous life. The verb is in the intensive (piel) form, indicating a serious and fixed intention.

10. severe discipline (*mûsār rāʿ*): better, "severe hardship" or "severe punishment". On this meaning of *mûsār* see on 1:2. The synonymous parallelism of this verse equates this with "death". On what is meant by "death", however, see on 2:18–19. **forsakes the way**: this must refer to the way or path of life or of wisdom (compare

2:19; 4:11) frequently contrasted in the Instructions of chapters 1–9 with the path or way of life chosen by the wicked or the foolish. "The way" (*derek*) is used similarly in an absolute sense in Ps. 119:1.

11. Abaddon, literally "destruction", associated with Sheol also in 27:20; Job 26:6, and with death in Job 28:22, is another name for the underworld, the place of the dead. The first line of this verse presupposes a common belief that even the underworld is subject to the scrutiny of Yahweh; the second line proceeds by means of an *a fortiori* argument (*'ap kî*, **how much more . . . !**) to point out the absurdity of supposing that he is incapable of performing the presumably simpler action of seeing into the **hearts** of the living (compare Am. 9:2) – in other words, that not only human actions but human nature itself, that is, the good or evil propensities of individual human beings, is an open book to him.

Krispenz (pp. 71–4) observes that the word "heart" (*lēb*) which occurs in this verse recurs also in vv. 13, 14 and 15 as a "catchword", and concludes that this verse (11) is the beginning rather than the end of a series. There is, however, no contradiction here: if, as seems probable, v. 11 is a pivotal verse pointing both backwards and forwards, this should be regarded as a valuable pointer to the compositional methods employed by the editors of this proverb material. (See below.)

12–17. These verses (and v. 11) are linked by a vocabulary chain, but only partly by theme. As has already been noted, *lēb* (**heart**, **mind**) occurs in vv. 11, 13, 14 and 15; it has also been pointed out that even v. 12, which does not contain that word, begins with the same letter as vv. 13 and 14. Vv. 15–17 are, further, linked by the occurrence in each of the word *ṭôb* (**cheerful**, **Better**); vv. 16 and 17 are particularly closely linked by their syntactical form (*ṭôb . . . min* –, **Better is** . . . **than** . . .). These formal editorial links are unlikely to be coincidental. But only between (13 and) 15–17 is there a thematic link (see below). Krispenz's argument for a thematic link between the whole of (11 and) 12–15 is not convincing. The word *lēb* in these verses has quite different meanings. In v. 11 it refers to Yahweh's ability to see into the **hearts** – that is, the inner *thoughts* or plans of men and women, but in vv. 13 and 15 it denotes not their mental processes but their *emotions*: these are psychological observations and have nothing to do with Yahweh's powers of observation; indeed, v. 13a speaks rather of the way in which a person's inner *feelings* can be detected by his *human* acquaintances. V. 12 is also quite unconnected with its context.

12. On the **scoffer** (*lēṣ*) see on 1:22. His arrogance and obstinacy are a constant theme of these proverbs: compare 9:7, 8; 13:1; 14:6. The statement that **he will not go to the wise** probably does not specifically refer to consultation but to *associating* with wise persons. LXX has "consort *with*", which may presuppose *'et*, "with", rather than *'el*, **to**, in the Hebrew; compare "walks with" in 13:20. *ḥᵃkāmîm*, *RSV* "*the* wise", is used in a general sense, as elsewhere in these proverbs, of ordinary members of the community who have a reputation for common sense.

13. The two lines of this verse are not strictly parallel: the first observes the fact that happiness shows itself externally in the face, while the second is purely psychological: mental suffering can end by wrecking one's entire life – compare 15:4, where the "breaking of the spirit" is the opposite of possession of the "tree of life".

14. At first sight there seems to be no correspondence between the two lines of this verse: **seek** (*biqqēš*) and **feed on** (*rā'āh*) seem to offer no parallel. Various emendations of the second of these verbs have therefore been proposed. However, Bühlmann (pp. 190–93) has plausibly argued that the metaphor of shepherding which is used in the second line is the key to the whole verse. As in 10:21, *rā'āh* is used not in its intransitive but in its transitive sense of leading sheep to pasture and protecting them from harm, while *biqqēš* here has a similar sense: the good shepherd seeks good pasture for the sheep, and also seeks out and cares for the lost sheep (so Ezek. 34:1–10). So here the person **who has understanding** (*nābôn*, compare 1:5; 10:13) is seen as a shepherd who takes thought (*lēb*, "understanding") for the welfare of the community, while **fools** have only their own folly to offer.

15–17. V. 15 picks up v. 13, expressing a similar thought but reversing the order of the lines. The metaphor in the second line, which represents **a cheerful heart** (*ṭôb-lēb*) as **a continual feast**, suggested to the collector another proverb (v. 17) which also connects a meal (*'ᵃrūḥāh*), **dinner**) with a happy state of mind (again *ṭôb*, *RSV* **Better**). V. 17 can thus be seen as a possible – though not the only possible – interpretation of v. 15, giving its own definition of the nature of a "feast", which, in contrast with what is generally assumed and taken for granted, is to be found not in its lavishness or abundance (**a fatted ox**), but in its being eaten in the context of a loving, harmonious family. V. 16, which substitutes **the fear of the Lord** for the simple *love*, and the rather vague **great treasure** for the concrete **fatted ox**, is clearly based on v. 17 and must be reckoned as one of those additions, found in these collections as well as in the Instructions of chapters 1–9, whose pious purpose is to bring all acceptable human activities under the aegis of religion.

15. The second line of this verse reads like a popular proverb complete in itself: literally, "merry of heart – perpetual feast". As with some other such short proverbs, the syntax is minimal, and the text needs no correction: it speaks for itself. But the first line appears to contradict it: it states that it is impossible for the truly poor or indigent (*'ānî* means "poor" rather than **afflicted** here) ever to enjoy happiness, since their whole life is wretched (*ra'*, *RSV* **evil**). McKane's interpretation of the whole verse, that "There is an inner resilience which is invulnerable to the whims of fortune", does not take into account the absoluteness of the statement in the first line of this apparently contradictory proverb.

16–17. Although these two verses are probably intended to be extensions of the thought of v. 15b, their standpoint is quite different from that of v. 15a. Neither **a little** nor even **a dinner of herbs** reflects the situation of the "poor" of that verse. Those who are envisaged in these two verses are not "poor" in any absolute sense: the contrast made here is with the truly rich, who have **great treasure** and can afford to dine on **a fatted ox**. They are in fact the small farmers, whose circumstances may well be, at least at times, straitened, but who are by no means entirely without resources; here they are warned not to envy the rich, whose wealth does not necessarily bring them happiness.

16. On **the fear of the Lord** see on 1:7; 10:27. This verse is almost identical with 16:8 except that whereas 16:8 has "righteousness" (*s^e dāqāh*) in the first line and "injustice" (*lōṣ 'mišpāṭ*) in the second, this verse has **the fear of the Lord** and **trouble**. The two verses are really different versions of the same proverb, but in 15:16 Yahwistic piety has taken over the role of morality. Compare the similar process exemplified in the pair 13:14 and 14:27, in which the fear of Yahweh has taken the place of "the teaching of the wise". The kind of **trouble** envisaged here as a possible accompaniment of great wealth is not specified; Ec. 5:10–20 [Heb. 9–19] may provide a clue to this.

17. A dish of vegetables (*RSV*'s **dinner of herbs**) would not be an unusually meagre meal for an Israelite farmer (contrast, however, the "dry morsel" of 17:1), nor would a **fatted ox** be out of the way for him on a special occasion such as that alluded to in 7:14. The point of the proverb is that there are more important things in life than comfortable living. **love** and **hatred** may refer either to family relationships or to relations between neighbours who gather for a communal meal.

18. stirs up strife: in 29:22a the same phrase is used of the "man of wrath"; in 28:25 it is used of the greedy man. Here the contrast is between the **hot-tempered** and the person who is **slow to anger**, a theme which was also a favourite of Egyptian wisdom literature. Like so many other of these proverbs, this verse expresses a concern for harmonious relations between members of the local community – for the building up of society and against whatever threatened to disrupt or destroy it. There is a certain link with v. 17: both verses speak of good and bad personal relations.

19. overgrown with thorns: the Hebrew has "like a thorn-hedge". The metaphor is probably intended to represent the excuse which the *sluggard* makes for his failure to achieve anything: that whatever he tries to do, unsurmountable obstacles stand in his way. Many commentators, on the grounds that **upright** (*y^e^šārîm*) is not a true parallel with **sluggard** (*ʿāṣēl*), propose to emend it to *ḥ^a^rūṣîm*, "diligent", following LXX (cf. also 13:4). However, Plöger points out that there is a tendency in some of these proverbs to equate good with wise and bad with foolish.

a level highway: all that is meant by the Hebrew here is "a highway", that is, a properly constructed road from which obstacles have been removed.

20–23 (24): If v. 20 once stood as the opening verse of a collection (see the introduction to chapter 15 above), there is no clear indication where this ended, though vv. 31 and 32 could be seen as rounding off its message by returning to the theme of v. 20. (Delitzsch held that it ended only in 17:20.) On a smaller scale, however, there are clear signs of a deliberate arrangement of vv. 20–23 (possibly also v. 24). Formally, the root *śmḥ* (the verb **make . . . glad** and the noun *śimḥāh*, **joy**) is common to vv. 20, 21 and 23. Thematically, vv. 21–3 are all concerned with aspects of human behaviour which have their roots in the attitudes of children towards their parents alluded to in v. 20: responsible and irresponsible behaviour in general (v. 21); taking or refusing to take advice from others (v. 22); knowing how and when to speak (v. 23). V. 24, with its promise of "life" to the wise, may have been intended to close this short series.

20. This verse is a variant of 10:1 (compare also 12:1 and 13:1). The first line is identical with 10:1a; the second is slightly different – 10:1b has "is a sorrow to" rather than **despises**. Proverbs, like other books of the OT including the Decalogue, puts great emphasis on the duty of obeying and honouring parents, and is extremely severe towards those who do not do so (19:26; 20:20; 28:24; 30:11, 17). This verse probably alludes to acceptance or rejection by children of parental instruction (compare 1:8), which according to the Instructions of chapters 1–9 was essential for forming character and instilling right attitudes to life.

a foolish man: literally, "a fool of a man" (*kᵉsîl 'ādām*). On this expression, which occurs again in 21:20, see *GK* 128 l. There is no need to emend to "a foolish son" with LXX to conform with 10:1b.

21. This verse is thematically somewhat similar to v. 19. It contrasts the irresponsible person who wastes his life on amusing trivialities (compare 10:23) with the person who takes life seriously, moving steadily through it (once again the metaphor of the "way", found also in vv. 19 and 24 and constantly in the book, is used).

22. This is a variant of 11:14, differing in that it does not draw on a political analogy. **counsel** (*sôd*): that is, consultation. The emphasis placed in this and many others of these proverbs on the importance of acting only with the co-operation of other members of the community is a mark of a conservative society which mistrusts individual initiative.

23. There is a certain appropriateness in the placing of this proverb in that it may be taken to constitute advice to the advisers whose assistance is recommended in v. 22! The theme is similar to that of v. 1; but *RSV* has here gone beyond the Hebrew text in introducing the word **apt**. A literal translation of this first line might be "There is joy (or, "satisfaction") to a man in the answer of his mouth". The verse as a whole is probably an instance of the use of the *a fortiori* argument (*mah-ṭṭôb* can mean "how much better . . . !" as well as **how good** . . .!). A man may be pleased with the answer he has given; but it will be fully effective only if it is made at an appropriate moment. This is an example of the emphasis laid by these proverbs on the importance of mastering the difficult art of persuasive speech. The time is not always ripe: when to speak is as important as what to say and how to say it. This idea of the "right time" pervades the wisdom books: compare, for example, Ec. 3:1–8.

24. This verse may have been placed here to form the conclusion of the group which begins in v. 20: it is a general statement which picks up the thought of that verse and elaborates its implications.

As it stands in the Hebrew text, this verse, which presents the choice to be made between two ways of life and their consequences, the one leading **upward** (*l^ema'lāh*) and the other downward (*māṭṭāh*, *RSV* **beneath**), may appear to suggest a doctrine of personal immortality – of eternal life in heaven and of eternal punishment in the underworld (compare Dan. 12:2–3 and an alleged allusion to such a belief in Ec. 3:21). Most commentators, however, agree that such a belief is extremely improbable here in view of its absence otherwise from Proverbs and of the comparatively early date attributed to these proverbs: the reference is to the future of the wise during their existence in this world and to the "paths of life" and "death" in the same sense as in, for example, 4:18–22 and 12:28. Others, while agreeing with this view, hold that "upward" and "downward" (especially the former, with its implication of a heavenly afterlife) can only be interpreted in an eschatological sense, but see these words as later glosses inserted into a text in which no such sense was originally implied. It is significant that they are not represented in LXX.

25–33. There is agreement among those scholars who are interested in tracing the composition of these chapters (Hermisson, Plöger, Krispenz) that these verses form a distinct group. Their most notable characteristic is the predominance in them of Yahweh-proverbs – four out of nine verses (25, 26, 29, 33), including the first two and the last. On the verbal level there is a chain of links which cannot be coincidental: vv. 25 and 27 have the word *bêt* (**house**, **household**) in common; vv. 28 and 29 both speak of the **righteous** (*ṣaddîq*) and the **wicked** (*rāšā'*); the root *šm'* (the verb "hear", *šāma'*, three times; news, *š^emû'ā* [literally, "what is heard"]) occurs in each of the four consecutive verses 29–32, and vv. 31 and 32 are also linked by *tôkaḥat*, **admonition**; *mûsār*, **instruction**, is common to vv. 32 and 33.

On the thematic level it is not possible to trace a single continuous thread; but at least vv. 25–9 are all concerned with righteousness and wickedness, and vv. 31–3 with the theme of **instruction** and

admonition. It is, however, the Yahweh-proverbs as commenting on their contexts which give this group of proverbs their distinct character. Vv. 25–6 may in fact be pivotal: they can be seen as commenting on v. 24, interpreting the "life" and "death" set before the *wise* man in that verse as the consequence of pleasing or displeasing Yahweh, but also, together with v. 29, as attributing the fate of the *wicked* and *righteous* of vv. 27 and 28 as equally due to his favour or disfavour. Similarly v. 33 defines the **instruction in wisdom** commended in vv. 31 and 32 as equivalent to **The fear of the Lord**. The non-Yahweh proverbs in this group are thus brought specifically into the sphere of Yahweh's moral demands. It is also significant that this group of proverbs is immediately followed by another group (16:1–9) of which every verse but one (v. 8) is a Yahweh-proverb (see below).

25. One of the greatest misfortunes which could befall a family in ancient Israel was the loss of its ancestral portion of land, on which its livelihood, and often the status of free citizens, depended. Those who were responsible for driving such people off their land for their own profit are frequently condemned in the Old Testament. The powerful had many ways of doing this, one of which was the use of either force or deceit to enlarge their own property by changing the position of the boundary stones (*g^{e}bûl*, *RSV* **boundaries**) which marked the limits of fields; this is prohibited in Dt. 19:14; 27:17, and also in the wisdom books (e.g. Prov. 22:28; 23:10–11; Job 24:2). To act in this way against those who were particularly vulnerable to exploitation, that is, the **widow**, mentioned here, and the orphan or fatherless (Prov. 23:10–11) was regarded as a particularly heinous crime. Neither the practice nor its denunciation was, however, peculiar to Israel. For example, the Egyptian *Amenope* (VI 7:10–15, *ANET*, p. 422) strongly condemns the practice, and in the ancient Near East in general it was acknowledged to be a special duty of rulers to put widows, orphans and other disadvantaged persons under their protection. To this extent, therefore, the Old Testament attitude to this problem is by no means unique. What is striking, however, in this verse is the assertion – characteristic, indeed, of much Old Testament teaching – that Yahweh himself will act directly to defend widows from exploitation and to root out the offenders. This may suggest that the practice was a common one (cf. Job 24:2 ff.) which the king, despite his acknowledged duty in this matter, might be unable or unwilling to suppress. **tears down**

the house of the proud: compare 10:25; 12:7. The **proud** (*gē'îm*) are the powerful or wealthy, who recognize no moral law.

26. The meaning of the second line of this verse is uncertain. The Hebrew has "pleasant words are pure". LXX ("the words of the pure are held in honour") appears to presuppose a reversal of the order of the words. However, the Hebrew text may be correct, although **pure** (*ṭāhôr*) is an unusual word to be used as the opposite of **abomination to the Lord**. It is primarily a technical term for *ritual* purity, but is also used in an ethical sense (Ps. 51:10 [Heb. 12]; Job 17:9, where it is equivalent to "righteous"). Since human purity whether ritual or ethical is always purity in the eyes of Yahweh, it may have this sense here. "Pleasing words" (*'imrê-nō'am*) may mean speech which makes for communal harmony (compare Prov. 16:24; 3:17, where *nō'am* is parallel with *šālôm*) and so is contrasted with the **thoughts** or plans **of the wicked**, which cause dissension.

27. He who is greedy for unjust gain: this phrase (*bôṣēa' bāṣa'*) is rendered by *RSV* in 1:19 by "who get gain by violence"; but here the emphasis appears to be on the heinousness of the crime rather than on the means by which it is committed. Its precise nature is not stated here; but the parallel in the second line suggests that it is some kind of extortion. **makes trouble for his household**: see on 11:29. Clearly the verb (*'ākar*) here signifies a major calamity.

bribes: this word (*mattānāh*) means "gift". It is used in a neutral sense in 19:6. Another word for "bribe" used in Proverbs is *šōḥad* (17:23; 21:14). Bribery – of witnesses or judges – was evidently a common practice and is severely condemned in the laws (Exod. 23:8; Dt. 16:19; 27:25) and elsewhere in the Old Testament. In Proverbs it is condemned here and in 17:23; but a different attitude towards it seems to be implied in 21:14, which simply notes – without comment – that it is sometimes expedient (contrast 6:35). **will live**: on the meaning of "life" in Proverbs see the note on 3:2.

28. The second line of this verse is a variant of v. 2b; but there the contrast is between wise and fools, here between **righteous** and **wicked**. Such ambivalence occurs frequently in these proverbs. There is a contrast here between considered speech (**ponders**) and rash speech (**pours out**); but more important is an implied contrast between responsible and anti-social speech. The righteous man takes time to consider how he can ease a difficult situation, while the wicked man is ready and eager to stir up trouble.

29. The point of this proverb is not that divine help can only be obtained through prayer. Rather, like 28:9, it assumes that prayer is offered to God by **wicked** and **righteous** alike, but that God will only respond to the petitions of the latter. The complaint frequently made in the psalms of lamentation that Yahweh **is far from** the petitioner is always a complaint that he has failed to respond to his prayers.

30. This is the only verse in the group which appears to be thematically isolated. It is a psychological observation comparable to 10:26; 12:25; 13:12, 17; 14:30; 15:13, 15. **The light of the eyes**: this phrase (*mᵉ'ôr-'ênayim*) is strange. Elsewhere *mā'ôr* means a lamp or source of light. Here the phrase may refer to a radiant look seen in the face of a happy person (so Scott; compare *REB*'s "a bright look"). Emendation is probably unnecessary.

31. He whose ear: literally, "The ear that . . .". It may be the reference to the *eyes* in v. 30 that has led to the placing immediately after it of this proverb which begins with the word *ear*. It may also be that the same preoccupation with the parts of the body accounts for the position of v. 32, which refers to the *heart* (*lēb*, *RSV* "understanding"). Compare the use of the same device in another form in 6:16–19.

wholesome admonition: literally, "admonition of life" (*tôkaḥat ḥayyîm*), that is, admonition which leads to or confers "life" in the sense in which that word is understood in Proverbs (compare *'ōraḥ ḥayyîm*, "the path which leads to life", in 5:6).

It is not clear whether the second line of this verse states the contents of the admonition – that is, to seek the company of wise men – or whether its meaning is that heeding such admonition will give the entrée to their company or will be considered to do so by others. However this may be, the proverb reiterates the standard teaching that only by willingness to listen to good advice can one achieve wisdom.

32. This verse echoes in antithetical parallelism what v. 31 states in a single positive sentence. The first line would be better rendered as "He who *neglects* instruction *rejects* himself" (contrast "loves himself" in 19:8). There is a play on two different meanings of *lēb* (**understanding**) here: in its meaning of "heart" this word is close to *nepeš* (*RSV* **self**) which occurs in the first line. One line of conduct *rejects* the *nepeš* while the other *acquires* the "heart".

33. The first line of this verse, which equates the **fear of the Lord** with readiness to accept **instruction in wisdom**, echoes 1:7

and 9:10, suggesting that it belongs to a later editorial stratum than the preceding verses. Its function here is to interpret the vocabulary of vv. 31 and 32 (admonition, wise, instruction, understanding) in terms of obedience to the demands of Yahweh, and so to round off this group of proverbs. The second line is identical with 18:12b, and may have originally been a popular saying. Here, however, as in 22:4, it acquires a specifically religious connotation. It does not contradict 22:4, which states that "the reward for humility and the fear of the Lord is riches and honour and life", but is in agreement with it: it means, not that **honour** is of little worth compared with humility, but that honour, that is, an honourable and prosperous position in society, can only be obtained by those who have *already* (**goes before**) shown themselves to be humble towards God.

CHAPTER 16

Even more than chapter 15, this chapter is dominated by Yahweh-proverbs. In vv. 1–9 every verse except one (v. 8) is a Yahweh-proverb, and the final verse (33) is also a Yahweh-proverb, and one which echoes verse 1, so forming a framework for the chapter. There are also Yahweh-proverbs in vv. 11 and 20. Vv. 1–9 are immediately followed by a second series (vv. 10–15) of which every verse but one (v. 11) is a royal proverb.

These two series, which occupy almost half the chapter, have clearly been placed in their present sequence deliberately (see below on 16:10–15). It is to be noted that their respective topics have been intertwined in vv. 9–12, where the sequence is Yahweh-proverb, royal proverb, Yahweh-proverb, royal proverb.

It is almost certainly significant that this double series of proverbs has been placed precisely in a central position in the book: the Masora points out that the central verse in the whole of the Book of Proverbs is 16:17. This arrangement clearly reflects an editorial view about the central importance for the reader of these statements about Yahweh, about the king, and, implicitly, about the relationship between the two. A link between chapters 15 and 16 is provided by 15:33.

It has frequently been noted that chapters 16:1–22:16 differ formally from chapters 10–15 in that in the former synonymous parallelism prevails, while in the latter antithetical parallelism is dominant. But whatever may have been the origin of this difference in the history of the composition of the book, there is no sign of a break in the text as it stands.

In the remainder of the chapter there is particular emphasis on positive virtues associated with wisdom – humility, the proper use of speech, patience – rather than on the enemies of society; the latter theme is almost entirely confined to the short section vv. 27–30.

1–9. The only verse in this group which stands in isolation from the rest is v. 8, which contains no reference to Yahweh and has no close connection, either thematical or formal, with its context (though see below). Its presence here may be due to a subsequent dislocation of the text. Otherwise the verses have been arranged in a logical order. Vv. 1 and 9, both of which stress Yahweh's sovereignty over the lives of men, the success of whose plans is entirely dependent on him, constitute the framework of the group and determine its tone. Vv. 2–4 further elaborate the thought of v. 1: Yahweh has complete knowledge of human motives (v. 2); he will give success to those who commit their plans to him (v. 3); all created things answer to his purpose, including the punishment of the wicked (v. 4). Vv. 5–7 speak in more detail of his dealings with mankind: he will punish the arrogant (v. 5, which is closely linked with v. 4) and protect and give peace to those whose lives meet with his approval (vv. 6, 7). The verse which precedes this section (15:33) identifies the fear of Yahweh (v. 6) with the "instruction in wisdom" of which Proverbs speaks elsewhere. Together, these verses make up a theological compendium and have deliberately been given the central place in the book.

1. This proverb is often taken to mean that all human attempts to control events are pointless: it is God who is in control, and what he decides may be quite different from what men and women want to happen: "Man proposes, but God disposes". Similar notions are found in non-Israelite Near Eastern wisdom literature, for example, "One thing are the words which men say, another is what the god does" (*Amenope* XVIII 19:6–7; *ANET*, p. 423). There can be no doubt that Yahweh's sovereignty is stressed here, but it is not so clear that the intention is to belittle human enterprise. The interpretation of the verse depends on the meaning of **the answer of the tongue** in the second line. Some commentators (Barucq, McKane) understand this to refer to Yahweh's decision; but this is an unnatural interpretation of **answer**. There is, moreover, a close connection between **answer** and **tongue** in this line and **plans** and **mind** in the first. In other words, it is man who both plans and answers: man decides what he wants to say (compare 15:23 on the "apt answer" and the "word in season"), but he is dependent on God for the ability to choose the right words. If this is the correct interpretation of the verse, its intention is not to denigrate all human plans as useless but to stress human dependence on God for their successful execution.

2. This verse, probably placed here because of the logical sequence from *thoughts* ("plans of the mind", v. 1) to *actions* (literally, **ways**), is concerned with a rather different attribute of Yahweh: his ability to discern human motives. A man *may* (the Hebrew does not require the translation **are**) believe that the motives for his actions are entirely disinterested, but Yahweh assesses them at their true value. (See further on 20:9.) **weighs the spirit**: the Hebrew has "spirits" (*rûḥôt*). The meaning of the phrase is the same as "weighs hearts (*libbôt*)" in 21:2, which is otherwise almost identical with this verse except that it has *yāšār* "right" – that is, righteous – instead of **pure** (*zak*).

There is a slight difference of opinion among commentators about the meaning of *tōkēn*, **weighs**. Driver (*VT* 1 [1951], pp. 242–3) held that the verb *tākan* means "to fix a standard (for)"; Gemser and others that it means "tests". In Prov. 24:12, which like 21:2 has *tōkēn libbôt*, the verb is paralleled by "keeps watch, watches over". The meaning of the line is, however, hardly affected by these different interpretations. It should be noted that the meaning of the verse is not that *impure* motives cannot be hidden from Yahweh, but the more subtle one that he is a more accurate judge of the purity of a person's motives than that person himself. This point is taken up by the next verse, which is a warning that plans will only succeed if they are first subjected to Yahweh's scrutiny.

3. Despite the difference of terminology ("ways" in v. 2 and *ma'a-śîm*, **work**, here both refer to human actions) which indicates that the two verses were originally unconnected, this verse, which is in the form of an admonition, neatly fits its context (see on v. 2 above). The second line is virtually the same as 4:26b, where, however, it is the human "father" who guarantees success. In another passage (Prov. 20:18) where the same phrase "plans will be established" occurs, it is again human advice which will ensure this.

Commit: literally, "roll" (*gālal*). This curious metaphor occurs also in Ps. 22:8 (Heb. 9) and Ps. 37:5. The meaning may be similar to that of 1 Pet. 5:7, "casting all your care upon him". Pesh., Targ. and Vulg. appear to have regarded this verb as derived from *gālāh*, "to reveal" (reading *gal* instead of *gōl*).

4. for its purpose (*lamma'ᵃnēhû*: the usual meaning of *ma'ᵃneh* (for example, in v. 1) is "answer". This is hardly an adequate meaning here; and the majority of commentators render it by "purpose", citing Arabic usage and the Hebrew expression *(lᵉ)ma'an*, which can mean "for the purpose of", as evidence. McKane, however, takes the word here as meaning "in relation to its (not Yahweh's) counterpart" – that is, Yahweh has made everything correspond to ("answer") the proper order of things: **the day of trouble** is an *appropriate* fate for the wicked. The same ambiguity appears in the use of the verb *'ānāh*, normally "answer", in Ec. 10:19.

A more important problem on which the commentaries do not agree is whether this verse implies that the wicked are *predestined* by their creator to their punishment and so have no choice in the matter. Ben Sira (Sir. 39:16–25) perceived this moral problem, and, after a discussion, took refuge in the thought that it is wrong for man to question what God does. Probably the author of this verse, holding the view expressed elsewhere in the Old Testament (for example, Am. 3:6; Isa. 45:7) that everything that happens is directly due to Yahweh because nothing exists outside what he has created, was unaware of the moral problem.

lamma'ᵃnēhû: this form – the use of the article with a noun which has a pronominal suffix – is anomalous. It may be due to an erroneous pointing by the Massoretes; if not, the reason for it is not fully understood (see *GK* 127 i; Brockelmann, *Syntax*, 73d).

5–6. These two verses are probably intended to act as different kinds of comment on the second line of v. 4. V. 5 offers a definition of the kind of wicked person whose punishment is certain; v. 6, however, offers reassurance that it *is* possible for atonement to be made for sin.

5. To be **arrogant** (literally, "lifted up in heart") is an unforgivable sin because it is an offence directly against Yahweh (compare Isa. 2:11–17). On **abomination to the Lord** see on 6:16; on **be assured** see on 11:21. **will not go unpunished**: literally, "will not be acquitted". Yahweh is here clearly seen in his capacity of judge.

6. The two lines of this formally synonymous proverb are synonymous also in meaning. On **loyalty and faithfulness** (*ḥesed weᵓmet*) see on 3:3. **is atoned for**: this verb (*kippēr*) is primarily, though not exclusively, a technical term of the sacrificial cult. McKane, who takes **loyalty and faithfulness** as referring solely to moral qualities, holds that its use in this context betrays an anti-cultic attitude; but the verb is probably used here in the same sense as "covers (all offences)" in 10:12. The idea that obedience is more highly regarded by Yahweh than sacrifice is not an anti-cultic one: it was also the view of the Deuteronomists (1 Sam. 15:22). **avoids evil**: that is, escapes misfortune (compare **is atoned for**).

7. This proverb has affinities with v. 2 (the same phrase **a man's ways** occurs in both verses) and with vv. 3 and 6. The background is local community life with its unpleasantnesses so often referred to in these chapters: the man whose **ways please the Lord**, that is, whose behaviour meets with Yahweh's approval, will enjoy harmonious relations with all his neighbours: even his former **enemies** will wish to become his friends.

8. See on the similar proverbs 15:16 and 17 and compare also 17:1. This verse may have been inserted here to provide an illustration of what is meant in v. 7 by "pleasing the Lord". If this is so, it is particularly close to 15:16, which speaks of "the fear of the Lord" – this may be implied here by the words **righteousness** (*ṣᵉdāqāh*) and **justice** (*mišpāṭ*) – compare 21:3.

9. This group of verses ends with a proverb similar in meaning to v. 1: it also states that the plans formed by **A man** (*'ādām*) in his **mind** (*lēb*) can only be brought to fruition with the help and approval of Yahweh; but the thought is here extended to all of a person's activities in life (**way**, *derek*): each of his **steps** along the way (*ṣa'ad*) need Yahweh's guidance.

10–15. On the relationship between this group of proverbs and the preceding one see on 16:1–33. These "royal proverbs" have been brought together to stimulate thought about the role of the king just as vv. 1–9 are a compendium of thoughts about God. They do not all reflect the same standpoint: for example, v. 14 may envisage the possibility of arbitrary destruction, while vv. 10 and 13, taken by themselves, are quite uncritical of kings.

But the two passages (vv. 1–9 and 10–15) seen consecutively and as a whole echo one another in many ways and are clearly intended to react upon one another. As vv. 1–9 are concerned with the dependence of men and women in general on Yahweh, so vv. 10–15 are concerned by implication not only with the king as ruler but also with the king as a man, and not only in his relationship to his subjects but also in his relationship to his God. This double topic closely conforms to Israelite beliefs about the king's position as Yahweh's representative: he has been endowed with both power and responsibility, and is answerable to him. (This may be one of the reasons for the inclusion in this series of one Yahweh-proverb, which speaks of the supervision of weights and measures, which was one of the king's duties [see 2 Sam. 14:26], as ultimately under Yahweh's care.)

The relationship between the two passages can be seen in some of the specific statements about the king, which echo statements in vv. 1–9. For example, the king fulfils the role of a judge over his people, including power over life and death (vv. 10, 14, 15) which Yahweh himself exercises (vv. 4, 5,), but at the same time he is responsible for his actions, and will retain his throne only if he maintains righteousness and punishes evil (v. 12). He, like others, will be judged by his actions (v. 12, compare vv. 5, 6, 7). Kings make plans, but like others can only carry them out with Yahweh's help (v. 10, **inspired decisions**; compare vv. 1, 3, 9). The king's words are dictated by Yahweh like those of other persons (v. 1). It should also be noted that the same word **abomination** is used in v. 12 in connection with the king's duty to right wrong as is used in v. 5 of Yahweh's own punishment of wrong. So by the careful choice and assembly of diverse proverbs, kingship is seen in its proper light in accordance with Israelite notions. Like the other Yahweh-proverbs in these chapters, none of the proverbs in this group necessarily reflects a personal acquaintance with kings or royal courts (see Whybray, 1990, pp. 45–59).

10. Inspired decisions (*qesem*): elsewhere in the Old Testament this word always denotes divination or the like, and is strictly condemned as both an illegitimate and a fraudulent practice of persons who claimed by this means to discover and so to make known the divine will. Here alone it is used in a clearly positive sense, and is paralleled by the pronouncing by the king of judgment (*mišpāṭ*) – that is, of a judicial decision made with respect to cases brought to him as judge. No satisfactory explanation has been found of the use of the word here; but it probably reflects a naive view of royal judicial pronouncements comparable to that of the woman of Tekoa (2 Sam. 14:17) who in asking for a legal decision claimed to believe that David was "like the angel of God to discern good and evil".

This does not mean that the king was believed to be God's mouthpiece, but that God had endowed him with his own ability to make right judgments (compare 1 Kg. 3:28).

11. See on 11:1. The **weights** (literally, "stones") were kept in a **bag** or purse (Dt. 25:13; Mic. 6:11). (On the connection of this verse with the topic of kings see on 16:10–15 above.) It has been suggested, partly on grammatical grounds and partly on the grounds that it would be more logical to say that *every* weighing device, whether accurate or not, belongs to Yahweh, that the word *mišpāṭ* (**just**) is a later addition to the text; but this is hypercriticism. The LXX text suggests that it is original, and also the fact that in the text as it stands *mišpāṭ* ("judgment" in v. 10) acts as a key-word linking these two verses. (On the grammatical point see *GK* 128a, n. 1.)

This proverb, more clearly than others which speak of Yahweh's detestation of dishonest trading, implies a very close relationship between Yahweh and the ordinary details of human life: it asserts that commerce, here represented by the weighing of goods, is not merely subject to his scrutiny and judgment, as stated in the Old Testament laws and in Israelite and Near Eastern wisdom literature generally, but is **his work** – that is, it is not a man-made enterprise but actually a part of the created order.

12. *RSV*'s rendering of the first line of this verse gives the impression that it is the **kings** who do evil. But it is more probable that the line should be rendered "Doing evil is an abomination (that is, is abhorrent) to kings": that is, kings cannot tolerate wicked persons because the upholding of **righteousness** is the basis of their rule. This interpretation is supported by the similarity of the phrase **an abomination to kings** to the frequently occurring "an abomination to the Lord".

The statement here that the royal throne is founded on righteousness clearly implies that the king is regarded as the representative of Yahweh on earth, since precisely the same language is used elsewhere (Ps. 89:14 [Heb. 15]; 97:2) in passages which refer to Yahweh's own sovereignty. The imagery may have originated in Egypt (see Brunner, 1958, pp. 426–8), though McKane regards it as "so commonplace and obvious that it might occur to anyone at any time".

13. Righteous (*ṣedeq*) here echoes "righteousness" (*ṣ*ᵉ*dāqāh*) in v. 12. The general sense of the two verses is also similar. Plöger points out that, as in v. 12, what is said of the king here is elsewhere said of Yahweh himself (e.g. in 12:22). The verse expresses a general belief: there is no specific reference to advice given to a king by his courtiers, which might suggest a court background for the proverb.

a king: the Hebrew has the plural, although the verb is singular. LXX and other Versions and some MSS have "king" (see *BHS*). **him who speaks what is right**: the Hebrew phrase is somewhat strange. Some commentators (and see *BHS*) propose emendation to "words of righteousness" or the like.

14–15. These two verses speak simply of the king's sovereign power, without making any adverse judgement.

14. Just as punishment is in store for those who anger Yahweh (v. 5 above), yet forgiveness is possible for those whose conduct pleases him (vv. 6–7), so with the king, whose power is here regarded as absolute, but whose anger can be deflected by wise conduct. (The analogy is particularly suggested by the use of the same verb *kippēr*, **appease**, in both this verse and in v. 6, where it appears in the passive form "is atoned for".) **a messenger of death**: the Hebrew has "messengers". For the meaning of the phrase compare Ps. 78:49–50, where Yahweh's "messengers" (also in the plural) do not simply convey information but act as the agents of his anger, actually inflicting disease and death on his people. For an example of a royal "messenger of death" see 2 Kg. 6:32–3. The picture here of a king who as a matter of course sends his agents to despatch those who have angered him – although such things could happen in very exceptional circumstances (1 Kg. 2:25, 34) – belongs to the realm of the imagination rather than of real life, and reflects a naive awe of kings such as might be expected of people who had no direct knowledge of the way in which kings ordinarily behaved.

15. This proverb, placed here because it depicts the opposite aspect of the exercise of royal power to that depicted on v. 14 (the king can confer **life** as well as death!), could equally refer in its entirety to God. The phrase *'ôr pānîm* (**the light of**. . . [the] **face**) is used in one other passage in the Old Testament (Job 29:24) of the favourable disposition of one human person to another; but it is pre-eminently used of *Yahweh's* favour (Ps. 4:6 [Heb. 7]; 44:3 [Heb. 4]; 89:15 [Heb. 16]), and elsewhere Yahweh is entreated similarly to "make his face shine" on his worshippers, e.g. in the blessing of Aaron: "May Yahweh cause his face to shine on you and be gracious to you" (Num. 6:25).

the clouds that bring the spring rain: this simile reflects the fact that the spring rain, which was eagerly awaited because without it there would be a poor fruit crop, was preceded by the appearance of clouds. This appearance was therefore a moment for joy and relief.

16–23. There are many links both verbal and thematic between these verses. Thus "wise" and "wisdom" occur in vv. 16, 21 and 23; vv. 20, 22 and 23 have the root *śkl* in common (*maśkîl*, **He who gives heed**; *sēkel*, wisdom; *yaśkîl*, **makes . . . judicious**); *rûaḥ*, **spirit**, occurs in vv. 18 and 19; *lēb*, **heart**, **mind**, in vv. 21 and 23; *ṭôb* in vv. 16, 19 and 20 (**better**; *māṣā' ṭôb*, **will prosper**); *yōsîp leqaḥ*, **increases persuasiveness**, in vv. 21 and 23. The themes, apart from the desirability of acquiring or possessing wisdom in vv. 16, 21, 22, 23, are also appropriate: general uprightness (v. 17); humility as opposed to pride (vv. 18, 19); heeding the "word" (that is, of wisdom or instruction, v. 20); wise speech (vv. 21, 23).

It is possible that v. 16 (compare 10:1; 12:1; 13:1; 15:5, 20) marks the beginning of a small group of proverbs fashioned to function as a miniature "instruction" in the manner of those in chapters 1–9. The language of "getting", that is, acquiring, **wisdom** (*qānāh ḥokmāh*) and **understanding** (*qānāh bînāh*) clearly associates this verse with 4:5, 7, where the importance of this is a main feature of an instruction, and more generally with the introductory sections of other instructions (3:14; compare 2:4); and in the speech of personified Wisdom in chapter 8 (vv. 10, 19) there is the same comparison, in Wisdom's favour, between its value and that of silver and/or gold. If this hypothesis of a miniature instruction is correct, v. 23 probably marks its conclusion: it then begins with a general statement about the importance of wisdom (v. 16) and concludes with an emphatic three-verse repetition of the same theme (vv. 21–23). It is noteworthy that at the centre of the group – perhaps properly to be regarded as its kernel – is a Yahweh-proverb (v. 20). There is also a possible link with the preceding sections (vv. 1–9 and 10–15) in that wisdom is seen as necessary to all, both kings and men and women in general.

16. The grammar of the first line of this verse is somewhat strange in the Hebrew, which has "To acquire wisdom, how much better than gold!". *RSV*, following the Versions and many commentaries, omits **how much** (*mah*), which may be a dittography, its consonants being identical with the final consonants of the previous word *ḥokmāh*. In the first line also the form *qᵉnōh* (**To get**) is anomalous; the second line has the normal form of the infinitive, *qᵉnôt*. But emendation is probably unnecessary: see *GK* 75n.

17. turns aside from evil: that is, "avoids evil". "Evil" here means "harm" rather than "wickedness"; the righteous will come to no harm. **highway** (*mᵉsillāh*): this is the theme of choosing the right way so prominent in the book, especially in chapters 1–9. The word *mᵉsillāh*, which occurs only here in Proverbs, means a raised **highway**, which would be free of obstacles and difficulties. The second line, in synonymous parallelism, puts the thought in a slightly different way. **guards his way**: that is, "watches his step" (so *REB*).

18. The condemnation of **Pride** is a commonplace of Proverbs, although a variety of different terms is used. The word employed here (*gā'ôn*) is cognate with *gē'îm* ("the proud") in v. 19. The first line of the verse, probably the origin of the English proverb "Pride goes before a fall", may here also have originally been an independent popular saying.

19. the poor: Kethib has *ʿᵃniyyîm*, "poor"; Qere *ʿᵃnāwîm*, "humble". *RSV* is probably correct, although some commentators take the opposite view. **of a lowly spirit** is paralleled by **proud**; **poor** by **divide the spoil**.

divide the spoil was probably originally a military term, but here means to be wealthy – to be among those who between them share this world's goods (compare 31:11; Isa. 53:12). On **the proud** (*gē'îm*) as both wealthy and rapacious see on 15:25.

20. He who gives heed to the word (*maśkîl ʿal-dābār*): it is not clear whether this refers to the teaching of the wise (as in, e.g., 1:23; 4:4) or of God. The former may have originally been the meaning of this line; but it was clearly open to a theological interpretation, and the second line may have been added to provide that interpretation.

21. The difficulty with the first line of this verse is that **wise** (*ḥākām*) and **man of discernment** (*nābôn*) are synonymous (cf., e.g., 10:13; 14:6; 18:15). Some commentators attempt to obtain some significant meaning for the line by stressing the importance of the verb **is called** (*yiqqārē'*): the wise man's wisdom will *come to be recognized* in the community. But this interpretation is hardly convincing. There is probably textual confusion here, but no convincing solution has been found. *REB*'s "The sensible person (*nābôn*) seeks advice from the wise (*ḥᵃkam-lēb*)", repointing *yiqqārē'* to *yiqrā'*, literally, "calls upon", does not improve the sense. The fact that there seems to be no connection between this line and the second one (except, perhaps, in the progression from "heart") (*lēb*) or "mind", to speech) tends to lend support to the view that it is corrupt.

pleasant speech: literally, "sweetness of the lips" (*meteq śᵉpātayim*). The expression occurs in the Old Testament only here; but Dahood pointed out a similar expression (though not a metaphorical one) in Ugaritic (see Gibson, 1978, p. 125). **increases persuasiveness** (*yōsîp leqaḥ*): this phrase seems to have been a commonplace of Israelite wisdom literature, occurring again not only in v. 23 but also in 1:5 and 9:9. It is not certain, however, that *leqaḥ* here means "persuasiveness". It appears to have something of that meaning in 7:21; but elsewhere it means either learning or acquiring knowledge (1:5; 9:9) or teaching, instruction (4:2; Dt. 32:2; Isa. 29:24). Here, then, the line may mean either that an agreeable or attractive way of speaking by a wise man or teacher will enable him to persuade his hearers, or that it will encourage learning – the difference is not great.

22. a fountain of life: see on 10:11. **to him who has it**: the Hebrew lacks "to"; almost all commentators propose emending *bᵉʿālâw* to *libᵉʿālâw*, the *lᵉ* having dropped out by haplography (compare LXX).

The second line probably means that fools bring punishment on themselves by their folly (*mûsār*, **chastisement**, being used here in the same sense as in 13:24 and 22:15, not in the more usual sense of "instruction"). But Scott takes the line as meaning that fools are *educated* only in folly, and McKane that to try to educate fools is folly.

23. The point of this verse is similar to that of v. 21. **makes . . . judicious**: the verb *hiśkîl* has a different meaning here from that which it has in v. 20 (compare also 21:11). "Guides" or "instructs" would be a better rendering than that of *RSV*.

As perhaps in v. 21 there is a progression from **mind** (*lēb*) to speech, that is, from the inner character to the outward expression. On **adds persuasiveness** (*yōsîp leqaḥ*) see on v. 21b. But if *leqaḥ* does not mean "persuasiveness" but "learning, instruction" (see above), the meaning of the line is not clear; and in that case the proposal of several commentators to emend *wᵉʿal* (**and . . . to**) to *ûbaʿal*, "master" (so McKane, "and an expert speaker promotes learning") may be justified.

24. This verse has connections with vv. 21–23 in various ways. Both it and v. 21 speak of **Pleasant words**, though not in the same terms: here *'imrê-nō'am*, there *meteq śᵉpātayim*, literally, "sweetness of the lips". The occurrence of *mātôq*, **sweetness**, here in the second line and *meteq* in v. 21, however, is unlikely to be accidental, in view of the rarity of these two words: *meteq* occurs only twice in the whole of the Old Testament, and *mātôq* only in one other verse in Proverbs. There is also a certain thematic connection with v. 23. However, this verse reads like an anti-climax after v. 23, and was probably added to vv. 16–23 after those verses were formed into a group, rather than having originally been part of the group itself.

The phrase *'imrê-nō'am* occurs also in 15:26. On *marpē'* as meaning **health** see on 14:30. *nepeš* here means "palate" (literally, "throat") rather than **soul**; there is no idea here of a dichotomy between soul and body. The verse, like 15:26, probably refers to speech which makes for communal harmony. The first line may originally have been a popular proverb. **honeycomb**. (*ṣûp-dᵉbaš*): the idea is of honey which *drips* from the honeycomb. The metaphor of the dripping of words upon the hearers – although other words are used – is relatively frequent in the Old Testament: compare, e.g. Prov. 5:3; Job 29:22; Am. 7:16.

25. This verse is identical with 14:12.

26. *nepeš* (**appetite**, perhaps here "hunger"), which picks up the same word in v. 24, has a similar meaning, but is used literally rather than metaphorically. **mouth** in the second line is equivalent in sense. There is a play on words in the phrase *'āmēl 'āmᵉlāh*, **worker . . . works**, perhaps suggesting that this line was originally a popular proverb. **worker** (*'āmēl*): that is, a manual labourer (compare Judg. 5:26).

This proverb makes a "neutral" observation in the first line and then makes this more explicit in the second: the labouring man must work in order to live. But it is also open to other and wider interpretations, and was probably intended to be so. Two other interpretations are, for example, suggested by Qoheleth, who (Ec. 4:7–8) speaks of the *rich* man who toils (*'āmēl*) not out of necessity but because he is greedy for even greater wealth, and also (3:9) of toil (*'āmāl*) as futile because it brings no real gain. It would be possible to interpret this verse in either of these two ways, or in other ways.

27–30. These four verses clearly form a group. They have no thematic connection with what precedes, though their present position may be due to the fact that the previous verse contains the word "mouth" – though it is there not used in connection with speech – and v. 27 speaks of **speech** (literally, "lips"). These four verses are all implicit warnings – though couched in the form of statements – against types of persons who, mainly by the things they say, deliberately set out to cause trouble and to endanger the wellbeing of the community. The series has close links with 6:12–15 and 6:16–19; but here each item in the list has been expanded by the addition of a second line. The first three are bound together by the form of their first lines, each of which begins with the word *'îš*, "A man of . . .", followed by a noun which characterizes the type of person in question. The form of the last item (v. 30) is different from that of the other three, but it rounds off the series by pointing out what are the outward signs by which such persons can be recognized (compare the way in which 6:12–15 is juxtaposed to 6:16–19).

These verses contain a remarkable number of words and phrases which are identical or very similar to terms employed in 6:12–19. *'îš bᵉliyya'al* (**A worthless man**) in v. 27 is equivalent to *'ādām bᵉliyya'al* in 6:12; **perverse** (*tahpūkôt*, vv. 28, 30) occurs also in 6:14; **spreads strife** (*šillaḥ mādôn*, v. 28) is found also in 6:14 ("sowing discord"); **plots evil** (*kōreh rā'āh*, v. 27) is similar to "devise wicked plans" (*ḥōrēš maḥšᵉbôt 'āwen*) in 6:18; the rare verb *qāraṣ*, here used (v. 30) of the man who **compresses his lips**, occurs also in 6:13, where it refers to winking with the eyes, an action which is itself referred to in the first line of this verse, using a different verb.

27. On **A worthless man** see on 6:12. **plots**: this verb (*kārāh*) means literally "to dig". This is a variant on the common metaphor of "digging a pit" (e.g. 26:27) for others, meaning to attempt to destroy them: *rā'āh*, **evil**, here means trouble or disaster. Gemser and Scott propose the emendation of *kōreh*, "digging", to *kûr*, "furnace" (". . . is like a furnace of wickedness") on the grounds that this makes a better parallelism with the second line; but MT makes adequate sense and is supported by LXX. The mischief-maker forms his plans and then puts them into action with words which are calculated to be destructive of social harmony: **fire** is frequently used in the Old Testmament as a symbol of total destruction.

28. A perverse man (*'îš tahpūkôt*): see on 2:12. **a whisperer** (*nirgān*): this word is peculiar to Proverbs (here and 18:8; 26:20, 22) and its meaning is uncertain. The context suggests the meaning "slanderer". The verb (*rāgan*) is used of Israel's "murmuring" in the wilderness: hence *RSV*'s translation.

29. 1:10–19 – where the same word *pātāh* (piel) is used as here (**entices**) – gives a fuller description of the kind of action here attributed to the man of violence. **not good** is probably an euphemism for either "criminal" or "disastrous".

30. Compare 6:13–14; but whatever may be the significance there of the bodily actions listed, here the meaning seems to be that wicked persons may be detected by observing these signs. The verb *'āṣāh* (**winks**) occurs only here in the Old Testament, and its meaning is uncertain. It may be connected with an Arabic verb meaning "to shut".

plans: the Hebrew has what appears to be the infinitive form. This may be an unusual form of the third mascular singular of the imperfect (Dahood), or it may be a case of the infinitive construct used in the sense of "to be about to" or "to be likely to (do something)". See GK 114i, k and notes, and Driver, *Bib* 32 (1951), p. 196. Some commentators draw attention to the fact that in the second line of the verse the verb (*RSV* **brings . . . to pass**) is in the perfect tense (*killāh*). This might suggest that whereas a wink indicated an *intention* to do evil, the pursing of the lips was taken to be a sign that evil had already been done (so, e.g., McKane, "has completed mischief").

31. a crown of glory: the same phrase is used in 4:9, where it is a gift of Wisdom (compare also 14:24). **A hoary head**: that is, grey hair as a sign of old age. This line may have originally been a popular saying expressing the deference given to the aged as being repositories of wisdom. The second line seeks to draw a moral from this saying, connecting old age not only to the possession of wisdom but, more specifically, to virtuous conduct. Since, as is constantly reiterated in Proverbs, the wicked die before their time, longevity must be a reward for **a righteous life** (Heb. *derek ṣᵉdāqāh*, literally "the way of righteousness").

32. Self-control and patience under provocation are marks of the wise man not only in Proverbs (compare, e.g., 15:1; 17:27; 25:15; 25:28) but also in the wisdom literature of Egypt. **is better than**: *RSV*'s rendering of this line lacks liveliness. The Hebrew ("It is better to be . . . than") is more accurate. **slow to anger**: see on 15:18, where the same expression is contrasted with "hot-tempered".

The references to **the mighty** (Heb. *gibbôr*, "warrior") and **he who takes a city** do not necessarily imply familiarity with military operations, nor should the proverb be seen as speaking of top-level diplomacy as preferable to war. Rather, it simply uses a comparison with warfare to make the point that wisdom can achieve more than brute force (compare 24:5–6 and Ec. 9:13–16).

33. The general purport of this proverb is the same as in vv. 1, 9. The casting of the **lot** (*gôrāl*) as a means of reaching a decision was evidently a common practice, not necessarily a religious one (compare 1:14; 18:18); but it was also practised as a means of discerning the will of Yahweh – notably in the form of the Urim and Thummim (e.g. Exod. 28: 30–31; Lev. 16:8–10 etc.; but compare also 1 Sam. 14:41–3; Jon. 1:7). In this verse it is not clear for what purpose the lot was cast; the point is that whatever human **decision** may be taken by this means, the ultimate decision (*mišpāt*) is in Yahweh's hands. McKane sees the verse as in some sense a defence of the practice, but there is no reason to suppose that its rightness was questioned. **into the lap**: this has been thought to refer to the pocket in the High Priest's breastplace where the Urim and Thummim were kept; but this interpretation is hardly compatible with the local and social background of these chapters. The practice was evidently widespread and not at all confined to the priests, who are never mentioned in Proverbs. The **lap** (*ḥêq*) was the fold of a garment, which formed a lap when the wearer was seated. But too little is known about the practice for any specific assertions to be made about its mechanics. On the use of *'et-* here before *haggôrāl* see *GK* 121a, b.

On the possible connection between this verse and the first verses of chapter 17 see immediately below.

CHAPTER 17

Most commentators are in agreement that there are few indications of deliberate arrangement of the proverbs in this chapter, although Delitzsch connected the first six verses with 16:31–3 on the grounds of the occurrence of the word **crown** in 16:31 and 17:6, and Krispenz saw a connection between the final verses (26–8) and 18:1–8. On vv. 1–3 see below.

The most frequently occurring theme is that of fools and their folly (vv. 2, 7, 10, 12, 16, 18, 21, 24, 25, 28), a theme which is treated in a variety of ways. There are four references to sons (vv. 2, 6, 21, 25), of which three are warnings, presumably to parents, about the misfortune attendant upon their stupidity or folly, and are therefore presumably indicative of an educational concern. There are three references to God (Yahweh, vv. 3, 15; **his Maker**, v. 5). Formally the chapter contains few antithetical proverbs but a variety of other types.

16:33–17:3. 16:33, as has already been stated, belongs to chapter 16 in that together with 16:1, which it closely resembles, it forms a framework for the whole chapter. But it is also a *pivotal* verse: that is, it is also the first of a group of four proverbs. 17:1 and 2 are related in that they both refer to the ruin of a family (**a house**, **the inheritance**), either through **strife** among its members or through the worthlessness of the heir. These two proverbs are flanked by two Yahweh-proverbs (16:33; 17:3) which set these situations in a new context and so re-interpret them. The **strife** between members of the family (v. 1), it is implied by 16:33, will not be settled by human means (like the casting of lots), because it will be Yahweh who makes the decisions; and the question of the **inheritance** (v. 2) will also be settled by Yahweh, who **tries hearts** – that is, he will decide between the claims of the **slave** and the **brothers** on the basis of his assessment of them. This arrangement of these verses also unobtrusively introduces a different meaning into the word *maśkîl* (**who deals wisely**) from that which it originally had: it now denotes not simply a person who possesses shrewdness or cunning (as in 10:5; 14:35) but the person whose "path leads upward to life" (15:24, where *maśkîl* is rendered in *RSV* by "The wise man"). Similarly *mebîš* (**acts shamefully** – compare 10:5; 12:4; 14:35) acquires a moral connotation (compare its use in Hos. 2:5 [Heb. 7]).

1. Compare 15:16, 17; 16:8, especially 15:17. **morsel** (*pat*), that is, a scrap, almost always refers to bread (compare 28:21). **quiet** (*šalwāh*), which can also mean "ease" or "security", here takes its meaning from the context: freedom from quarrels between members of a family. Such quarrels would probably be, as in v. 2, between brothers about their share of the inheritance. **feasting** (*zeʿbāḥîm*): literally, "(communion-)sacrifices"; but the reference is to the eating of the meat at a family feast after the sacrifice had been carried out (see on 7:14–15). Presumably only the well-to-do could afford to have their **house full of feasting**, that is, to hold such feasts frequently.

2. The situation envisaged here appears to be that an unsatisfactory **son** may be disinherited by his father, and a domestic **slave** freed and promoted in his place, even being given his share of the inheritance. *maśkîl* (**who deals wisely**) is always used in Proverbs in an approving sense: there is no suggestion that the author of this proverb was appalled by such a social overturn as was the author of 30:22. It is not stated in what way the son **acts shamefully**, but the reference is probably to laziness – to a refusal to take an active part in the work of the farm, so bringing poverty upon the family (compare the same phrase in 10:5). The principle involved is enunciated in general terms in 12:24. It is not known whether such a practice was common (though see Ec. 10:7). This proverb is not primarily concerned with the status of slaves but is a warning to sons to pull their weight, and about the need for hard work if poverty is to be avoided.

3. tries hearts (*bōḥēn libbôt*): compare *tōkēn libbôt*, "weighs – or tests – hearts" in the apparently similar 21:2; 24:12 and *tōkēn rûḥôt*, "weighs spirits" in 16:2 (see also 15:11). However, the meaning of this verse may be somewhat different. The verb *bāḥan* means "to test, to prove" (compare Ps. 11:4–5), which may imply judgement; but the simile in the first line of the verse – the melting of metals in a crucible or furnace – refers not (only) to the testing of their purity but to a process of purification. This verse may therefore mean that Yahweh is capable of purifying the hearts of men rather than simply that he judges them.

The first line of this verse occurs again in 27:21 but in an entirely different context: it may have been a current phrase, evidently usable in different ways.

4. This verse makes better sense if the first line is rendered "He who listens to wicked talk is (the same as) an evildoer"; and similarly in the second line. The reference appears to be to the person who deliberately keeps his ears open to catch any scrap of malicious gossip that he can pass on in order to make trouble. Such a person can also be called **a liar**, since he passes on as true what he knows to be false. **a liar**: MT has the abstract "lies" (*šeqer*) probably a mispointing for *šaqqār*, "liar" or "deceitful person", a word which does not otherwise occur in the Old Testament but was current in later Hebrew (compare LXX here).

5. the poor (*rāš*): on words for "poor" in Proverbs see on 10:15. **glad at calamity**: this also characterizes the type of person described in v. 4. Probably this verse is intended as a comment on v. 4, in two ways: it states that the evildoer will not escape punishment – this is not made clear in v. 4 – , and that this is because a sin committed against fellow human beings is also an attack on the honour of God, who will not tolerate it.

insults his Maker: compare 14:31; 22:2; 29:13. **will not go unpunished**: see on 16:5.

The expression **is glad at calamity** (*śāmēaḥ lᵉ'êd*) does not make a very close parallel with the first line: reference to a person rather than to a situation might be expected here. Several commentators have proposed an emendation to *śāmēaḥ lᵉ'ōbēd*, "rejoices (arrogantly) over those who are ruined" (compare LXX, "rejoices at the destruction of another"). Plöger suggests *'êdō*, "*his* distress" – viz. of the **poor** man; Driver (*Bib.* 32 [1951], p. 82) connects *'êd* with an Arabic verb meaning "to be bent, weighed down" – hence a person in distress. The Hebrew text with its conventional translation (as in *RSV*) may, however, be correct.

6. Elsewhere (4:9; 16:31) the two words **crown** (*ᵃṭārāh*) and **glory** (*tip'eret* – also "beauty") form a single phrase ("beautiful crown", "crown of glory"). Here in parallelism they are virtually synonymous. By putting these two statements together the proverb describes the mutual respect and pride which ought to exist among three generations of a family. The basis of the first line is the importance which was attached to the preservation of the family line by the birth of male children: grandchildren are the crown of the aged grandparents when they have survived to see them, because they are assured of this. The other side of family pride is expressed in the second line: **sons** can take pride in the esteem with which their fathers are held in the community. This is a picture of an *ideal* family: other proverbs are well aware of the existence of worthless sons (and also, at least by implication, worthless fathers) who bring shame rather than **glory** upon their families.

7. The word *nābāl*, here rendered by **fool**, is not one of those regularly employed in Proverbs (its only occurrences in the book are here and in 17:21; 30:22); and it has a somewhat different connotation from the others. It denotes a person who, in the words of *KB*³, "takes a negative stance in every area of life, contributes nothing (i.e. to society), gives no help, respects nothing, *is* a nothing", and who ought therefore to be excluded from normal society (see Roth, *VT* 10 [1960], pp. 394–409). He thus exists at the opposite social extreme to the *nādîb*, **prince**, that is, the person of high rank. (For another possible meaning of *nādîb*, however, see on v. 26 below.) The first line of this verse, then, states that if a *nābāl* were to be heard making an outstanding verbal contribution to the welfare of society (*śᵉpat yeter*, literally, "a lip of excellence"), this would be completely out of character (**not becoming**); see also on 19:10; 30:21–3. (The proposed emendation of *yeter* to *yōšer*, "righteousness", is not necessary: compare Gen. 49:3, where *yeter* is correctly rendered in *RSV* by "pre-eminence").

But the main point of the verse is expressed in the second line: **false speech** – that is, deceitful or lying speech – uttered by a person of power and influence is, or ought to be, even more unthinkable than what is envisaged in the first line.

8. him who gives it (*bᵉʿālâw*): this use of *baʿal* is ambiguous (see on 3:27); and some commentators take the word here to mean "him who *receives* it", while others are undecided. The context suggests that *RSV* is correct: bribes, although obviously useful to the dishonest person who accepts them, are more likely to bring permanent success in life (*yaśkîl*, **he prospers**) to the one who offers them. (*hiśkîl* can also mean to be wise or prudent, but this interpretation does not make good sense here.) **a magic stone** (*'eben-ḥēn*): this probably means an amulet, thought to bring good luck.

Like 21:14, this proverb merely states a fact of life without expressing either approval or disapproval. 17:23, which refers specifically to bribery in legal cases, where its purpose would be either to secure the acquittal of the guilty or the conviction of the innocent, expresses the consensus of the laws and wisdom books both of Israel and the ancient Near East in condemning such practices.

9. The first line of this proverb is the counterpart of 10:12b, "love covers all offences". Whereas in 10:12 **love** – that is, good will or friendship (compare 15:17) – disposes a person to forgive an offence, here the motive for forgiveness is a desire for *future* friendship. Both proverbs are concerned, like many of these proverbs, for social harmony. The second line interprets the verb *kissāh* (*RSV* **forgives**) in a slightly different way from 10:12, as meaning "conceals": the person who seeks to be friends conceals the offence: in other words, he does not repeat the matter to others, while the person who does so makes future good relations impossible.

10. goes deeper: this rather unusual use of the verb *nāḥat* may be compared with Ps. 38:2 [Heb. 3], where it is used of divine punishment. The point of the proverb, which is echoed in other literatures, is obvious.

11. A few commentators have taken the first word of this verse (*mᵉrî*, **rebellion**) to be the subject rather than the object of the verb: it is rebels (the abstract noun is taken to stand for the concrete) who seek evil. But *RSV*'s rendering is the more natural one.

It has not been generally noted by the commentators that – apart from one or two textually doubtful occurrences – *mᵉrî* is used exclusively in the Old Testament of rebellion *against God* (and the corresponding verb, *mārāh*, also almost without exception). In 1 Sam. 15:23 as here it is used in that sense without qualification. This verse does not, then, as most commentators hold, refer to particular or imaginary cases of attempted *political* or military insurrection, but to deliberate sins against God. The identity of the **cruel messenger** who will be sent to punish the rebel is, perhaps deliberately, not stated but left vague; he may be a "messenger of death" like the one mentioned in 16:14, but here sent by God rather than by a human king – compare Ps. 78:49. This interpretation makes better sense of the verse and is more appropriate than that which gives it a reference to *political* rebellion, a topic which is altogether outside the sphere of interest of the authors of these proverbs, even though a few do refer, somewhat naively, to the king or the "rulers".

cruel (*'azkārî*): probably better, "merciless"; the word has a somewhat sinister feel. Note the wordplay between *'azkārî* and *'ak-mᵉrî*. This rules out emendation of the text as proposed by some commentators to read *'îš mᵉrî*, "a *man* of rebellion" (a point made by Gemser, following G. Boström, 1928, pp. 168–9).

12. Although there is no obvious thematic connection between the two verses, it is hardly coincidental that immediately after the reference to the "cruel messenger" sent by God in v. 11 we meet **a she-bear robbed of her cubs**. Bears, whether bereaved or not, are rightly regarded throughout the Old Testament as particularly dangerous animals, and are in several passages compared in this respect with lions. Meeting a bear is sometimes seen as a punishment inflicted by God. In 2 Kg 2:23–4 bears attack and kill children as the result of Elisha's cursing them in the name of Yahweh; and in several passages (Hos. 13:8; Lam. 3:10; compare Am. 5:19) Yahweh himself is compared to a ferocious bear. The phrase used here about the bereaved she-bear was evidently a common one: it occurs also in 2 Sam. 17:8; Hos. 13:8. The propensity of bears to appear without warning is well known to those who have had this experience (compare also the stage direction in *The Winter's Tale*, Act III, scene 3 ["Exit, pursued by a bear"].

This is the most emphatic statement in Proverbs that involvement with a **fool** (here *kᵉsîl*, but the reference to **his folly** [*'iwwelet*] shows that no distinction is made between *kᵉsīl* and *'ĕwīl*) is a calamitous experience, though many other proverbs (e.g. 13:20; 19:13; 26:24–5; 29:11) regard fools as in various ways a menace to society. The exaggeration of the comparison with a dangerous animal here suggests that the proverb is intended to be humorous, though this is a humour born of bitter experience.

13. This is a straightforward statement of the principle of exact retribution. The case is that of a person who is not only ungrateful for benefits or kindnesses which he has received but even turns against his benefactor to do him harm (there is an example of this in Joseph's accusation of his brothers in Gen. 44:4). The **evil** that he does to him will rebound on him in turn, and its effects will be permanent, even extending to his family (**house**).

14. There is no comparative particle in the first line of this verse, which simply reads "One who releases water – start of quarrelling". The laconic style together with a degree of alliteration suggests that this may originally have been a popular saying. The meaning is that as a flow of water – for example, one caused by the opening of a sluice – is difficult to stop once it has started, so too quarrels get out of hand and are difficult to stop. This plea against quarrelling is characteristic of ancient Near Eastern wisdom literature. The second line is a comment on the first, taking the form of a warning: a dispute should be settled or abandoned (*nāṭaš*, *RSV* **quit**) at the outset, before it becomes too serious (*hitgalla'*, perhaps literally, "show one's teeth"; *REB* "come to blows").

15. By translating the Hebrew *maṣdîq* by **justifies** and *maršîa'* by the general term **condemns**, *RSV* fails to make it clear that these are forensic terms ("acquits" and "convicts" respectively), and that this verse is about the misconduct of judges. The verse turns the normal phrases "acquit the innocent" and "convict the guilty" (see Dt. 25:1, where they define the proper functions of judges) upside down. Here, however, it is Yahweh himself who is judge: he judges the human judges (on **abomination to the Lord** see on 6:16).

There is probably a connection between this verse and the preceding verses 11, 12 and 13, all of which speak of mysterious fates which will befall the enemies of society. This verse may be seen as a comment on those verses, making it clear that such calamities are not due to chance or to human contriving but come directly from Yahweh himself. Thus apart from v. 14, which may be a later intrusion, vv. 11–15 may be regarded as a deliberate editorial grouping.

The point made by this verse is, of course, not new. Corrupt judges are universally condemned in ancient Near Eastern literature as well as in the Old Testament, especially in the laws, wisdom literature and prophetical books. In the laws – Exod. 23:6–8 and Dt. 16:18–20, both of which claim divine authority – it is presumed that these offences will be punished by human means; but they were evidently often committed with impunity: hence the reminder here that the offenders will have to reckon directly with *divine* justice.

16. The commentators are divided on the meaning of this verse. Some see it as proof that there was a class of professional "wise men" who taught "wisdom" for a fee; others take it simply as an assertion – in the form of a rhetorical question – that wisdom, unlike other commodities, cannot be bought for money: it can never be acquired by a **fool** (*kᵉsîl*) because he lacks the mental capacity (**mind**, literally, "heart") to comprehend it. Although there were those in Israel – parents or others; see chapters 1–9 – who claimed to teach wisdom, there is no evidence (in contrast to the Greek practice) that there were *paid* teachers, at least before Hellenistic times. The second of the above interpretations is therefore the more probable.

17. It is not clear whether the parallelism in this verse is synonymous or antithetical: in other words, whether a distinction is intended between the behaviour of a **friend** (*rēaʿ*) and a brother (*'āḥ*). 18:24b, which also speaks of the two relationships, suggests that while brothers might normally be expected to help one another, sometimes a friend may show even more loyalty (compare also 27:10). The present verse perhaps expresses a somewhat similar view: there is no intention to contrast brotherly love unfavourably with that of friendship, but a distinction may be intended in that while a **brother**, who is bound to his brother from birth by natural ties, can normally be expected to assist him in a real crisis (**adversity**) and may even be said to have been **born for** this, the **friend** (*hārēa'* – the unusual use of the article is perhaps intended to suggest that true friends are always like this: see *GK* 126m – has bound himself to his friend by a spontaneous and enduring affection which manifests itself not only in crises but **at all times**.

18. Compare 6:1; 11:15; 20:16; 27:13. **gives a pledge** (*tôqēa' kāp*); **becomes surety** (*'ōrēb ʿᵃrubbāh*): see on 6:1–5. This verse seems to regard the offering of any kind of financial guarantee as completely foolish. **in the presence of his neighbour** (*lipᵉnê rē'ēhû*): this can hardly mean "on behalf of his neighbour", though that is perhaps what is implied. **neighbour**, *rēa'*, which occurs in v. 17 in the sense of "friend", here means no more than an acquaintance; but it is probably because the word occurs in both verses that they have been juxtaposed.

19. The meaning of each line of this verse is uncertain, as also is their relationship to one another. The first line perhaps makes the best sense if it is rendered "He who loves strife loves transgression", branding as wicked the "perverse" person who enjoys stirring up trouble for its own sake (compare v. 20 and 10:12a; 11:9a; 12:6a; 16:27). The interpretation of the second line is obscured by the difficulty of the unusual phrase **he who makes his door** (*pitḥô*, literally, "gateway") **high**. This would be an odd way of referring to ostentatious building, and a literal interpretation seems hardly possible. But the cognate adjective *gābōah̠*, "high" often has the sense of "proud" (compare 16:5); and it is probable that the reference here also is to pride or arrogance, which will lead to **destruction** (*šeber*) as in 16:18, where the same word is used of the fate of the proud (*gōbah̠-rûaḥ*, "haughty spirit"). This does not, however, explain the reference to **his door**. Some commentators have proposed the emendation of *pitḥô* to *peh*, "mouth", referring to arrogant speech; but this is purely conjectural.

20: On **crooked mind** see on 11:20, where the same phrase is used, and where the reason why such a person **does not prosper** is given: he is "an abomination to Yahweh". **prosper**: literally, "find good" (*māṣā' ṭôb*); compare 16:20. **perverse** (*nehpāk*): this form of niphal participle (*hāpak*) occurs only here; it is clearly connected, however, with *tahpūkôt*, "perversity", which occurs in 2:14 and elsewhere in Proverbs.

21–25. The frequency in these chapters of similar proverbs about the sorrow or joy to parents caused by a **stupid** (10:1; 15:20; 17:25; 19:13) and/or wise (10:1; 13:1; 15:20) **son** may be due to editorial adaptation of these proverbs for educational purposes (see on 10:1–5; 12:1; 13:1–25). In this chapter the similarity of v. 21 to v. 25 may suggest that, like 10:1–5, vv. 21–5 was once a distinct group. V. 24 has a suitably educational flavour, though this is less obviously so in the case of vv. 22 and 23. Delitzsch regarded v. 21 as the beginning of a much longer section (17:21–22:16).

21. fool (*nābāl*): see on v. 7. Here it stands in parallelism with *kᵉsîl*, **stupid**; this does not necessarily mean, however, that the two words were regarded as exactly synonymous.

22. This is one of a number of proverbs (compare 14:10, 13, 30; 15:13, 15, 30; 16:24; 18:14) which reflect on the states of mind of individuals to a large extent in the same or equivalent terms. Thus **A cheerful heart** (*lēb śāmēaḥ*) occurs also in 15:13 (compare also 15:30) and **a downcast spirit** (*rûaḥ nᵉkē'āh*) in 15:13 and 18:14, while there are phrases comparable to or contrasting with **dries up the bones** in 14:30 and 15:13. The thought of this verse is especially close to 14:30 and 15:13. This is a psychosomatic observation.

is a good medicine (*yêṭīb gēhāh*, literally "does good to the *gēhāh*"): The meaning of the latter word, which occurs only here in the Old Testament, is uncertain. Driver (1950, p. 344) took it as related to an Arabic word meaning "face" (compare 15:13); but more probably it is related to the rare verb *gāhāh* (Hos. 5:13) which appears to mean "to heal".

23. See on v. 8 above and on 15:27. In these verses, and also in 21:14, opposite views are expressed about the morality of giving and taking bribes (here *šōḥad*, elsewhere also *mattānāh*, "gift"; but the two words stand in parallelism together in 17:8). The offering of a gift when asking a favour is still in many countries and in the present writer's own experience not only customary but socially mandatory, and is not normally regarded as "bribery": it simply helps to get things done and is also a form of politeness. It is only immoral if the purpose for which the "gift" is offered is itself immoral. This is true of 15:27, and also here: corruption of judges or witnesses was universally condemned in the ancient Near East as elsewhere, particularly if its purpose was to secure the condemnation of an innocent person (compare v. 26 below).

accepts: the verb is *lāqaḥ*, "to take". Grammatically the subject could be either the corrupt judge or witness who *accepts* a bribe, or the briber, who secretly *takes* the bribe **from the bosom** to give it to the person whom he is bribing. The commentators and translators are divided on this point; but as both taking and giving bribes for such purposes were regarded as equally reprehensible, the point is an academic one. **bosom**: see on 16:33. The bribe has been carried hidden in the folds of the briber's garment.

24. In Hebrew the first line of this verse has simply "In the presence of (*'et-pᵉnê-*) the man of understanding is Wisdom" – that is, Wisdom is "never out of sight" of such a person (so *REB*). The thought of the verse is similar to that of 14:6. While the wise person "keeps his sights" on Wisdom, the **fool** is incapable of concentration: to say that his **eyes** are **on the ends of the earth** can only mean that his attention is always wandering. The verse is reminiscent, with its personification – or, at least, partial personification – of Wisdom, of those verses in chapters 1–9 (e.g. 2:2–4; 4:5; 7:4) which have been inserted into the father's admonitions in order to associate Wisdom with his teaching. It serves a similar purpose with regard to the "mundane" teaching of vv. 25 and 21.

25. This proverb, which is similar to v. 21 except for the introduction of the mother (compare 10:1) probably marks the end of a short section (see on vv. 21–5 above). Some older commentators (Ewald, Delitzsch), however, regard it as the *beginning* of a more extended section, though without giving sufficient reasons.

26. This verse, like v. 23, refers to corruption in the lawcourts. **righteous**: this word (*ṣaddîq*) here has its proper legal sense of "innocent". **to impose a fine** (*ᵃnôš*): this verb may have a rather broader sense of "punish" here; but to impose fines was a recognized punishment in certain cases: compare Exod. 21:22. **to flog**: literally, "to beat": compare Dt. 25:2–3. **noble men** (*nᵉdîbîm*): this word usually denotes men of noble rank (see on v. 7 above, where *RSV* has "prince"); but here it probably means persons of exceptional nobility of character (compare Isa. 32:5–8 and also the double meaning of "noble" in English). **not good**: see on 16:29.

wrong (*'al-yōšer*): this may mean "contrary to what is right"; but the expression is unusual, and some commentators propose emendation to *'al-yeter*, "beyond (reasonable) measure", "excessive" (compare Ps. 31:23 [Heb. 24], *RSV* "abundantly"). If this is correct, it suggests an *a fortiori* progression: if fining the innocent is (always) wrong, subjecting persons of exceptional nobility of character to the humiliation of public corporal punishment is even more so. This in interpretation may be supported by the word *gam*, "also, even" (not translated in *RSV*) with which the verse begins.

27–28. The common theme of silence accounts for the juxtaposition of these two verses, though the fact that quite different verbs are employed shows that they were originally independent proverbs. Krispenz (pp. 91–2), noting that 18:2 has a similar theme, regards 17:(26) 27–18:2 as a distinct unit; but 18:1 hardly fits into this scheme.

27. The second line of this verse broadens the scope of the first: keeping control over one's words is only one aspect or manifestation of the possession of **a cool spirit**: that is, of self-control or moderation. Compare 10:19; 11:12; 13:3 with the first line and 14:29; 15:18; 16:32 with the second. The theme is also a commonplace of Egyptian wisdom. **and he who has a cool spirit** (*wᵉqar-rûaḥ*): this reading (Kethib) is to be preferred to Qere's *yᵉqar-rûaḥ*, "precious (= "worthy, esteemed"?) of spirit".

28. There is a certain irony in this proverb: it is characteristic of the **fool** that he is *incapable* of keeping quiet (compare, e.g., 12:23). The theme is, however, also represented in ancient Near Eastern wisdom literature: compare *Ankhsheshonqy* 23:4, "Silence conceals folly" (see Lichtheim, 1983, pp. 47, 88). In its present context this proverb is perhaps intended to reinforce v. 27a: it is *always* best to say as little as possible for fear of making a fool of oneself.

CHAPTER 18

As in chapter 17 there are very few antithetical proverbs in this chapter. There is also no indication of the incorporation of substantial sub-groups unless v. 15 can be regarded as having originally functioned as the introduction to such a group (see below). However, some topics have been grouped together on a smaller scale: vv. 6–8, 10–11 (12), 16–18 (19), 20–21, 22–4.

Only two proverbs are specifically concerned with the wicked (vv. 3, 5) and three with fools (vv. 2, 6, 7). Several deal with aspects of the proper use of speech (vv. 4, 6–8, 13, 20, 21). Some have a legal background (vv. 16–18) and two refer to the behaviour of the rich (vv. 11, 23). One verse has a psychological theme (v. 14). Yahweh is mentioned twice (vv. 10, 22). Other topics include arrogance (v. 12), bribery (v. 16) and friendship (v. 24).

1. The meaning of this verse is not entirely clear. *niprād*, **estranged**, means, literally, "separated". It is used absolutely only here, but probably refers to exclusion from the local community, either voluntarily or by expulsion: it is not clear which. **pretexts**: this translation is based on the widely accepted emendation, possibly attested in LXX, of *ta'ᵃwāh*, "desire, object of desire", to *tō'ᵃnāh*, a word which elsewhere occurs only in Judg. 14:4, where Samson seeks an occasion, or pretext, to attack the Philistines. MT is, however, retained by Scott, McKane, Plöger and *REB*, who take the line to mean that such a person disregards all conventions and acts according to his own whims. This interpretation fits reasonably well with the second line.

to break out: *RSV* here suggests a continuity between the two lines which is not present in the Hebrew text, which has "*he* breaks out". Moreover, "quarrels" would be a better translation – see on 17:14 and also 20:3, where *RSV* itself understands this verb as meaning "quarrel". The line thus probably means that the estranged person "quarrels" with all sensible practical conventions or decisions (*tûšiyyāh*; see on 2:7). Thus the purpose of the proverb is probably to point out the dangers either of anti-social behaviour or of ostracism of undesirable individuals.

2. The reason for the present position of this verse is undoubtedly the superficial similarity between *hitgallôt* (**expressing his opinion**) here and *yitgalla'* (**break out**) in v. 1. Otherwise any affinity with this verse would be with v. 4 or with 17:28. The two verbs are totally unconnected.

in expressing his opinion: literally, "in revealing his heart (that is, mind)". It is characteristic of the fool that he loves to air his views but does not reflect before he speaks.

3. The commentators have been able to make little of this verse. The three words *bûz* (**contempt**), *qālôn* (**dishonour**) and *ḥerpāh* (**reproach**) overlap to a large extent in meaning. In Ps. 119:22 *bûz* and *ḥerpāh* stand in parallelism. It is possible that the succession of the three words is intended to mark progressive stages in the social disgrace which befalls, or *ought* to befall, the wicked; but our understanding of the distinctions between them is insufficiently precise to be sure of this.

When wickedness comes: the Hebrew reads "When the wicked person (*rāšā'*) comes". Most commentators, probably rightly, repoint the word as *reša'*, "wickedness".

4. The first line of this verse is to be understood in the light of 20:5a, where it is what a man *thinks* with his mind (*lēb*) that is compared to **deep waters**. That the words which one speaks are the result of, and an indication of, one's mind or character is a commonplace of Proverbs (see especially 16:23): consequently there is little difference in saying that the mind or the speech is like deep water. What is being said here is that the nature of a person's character is almost impenetrable to an observer – according to 20:5, it takes a particularly perceptive person to understand it. This line is therefore a general statement, based on experience, about human nature; and in spite of the reference to **wisdom** in the second line, there is no justification for emending **a man's mouth** (*pî-'îš*) to "wise men" (*ḥ^akāmîm*) or something similar as proposed by Toy and Oesterley.

The second line constitutes a problem. Many commentators take it, as does *RSV*, as a nominal sentence (like the first line) with **the fountain of wisdom** as the subject. Others, however (Toy, Oesterley, McKane), take it as the continuation of the first line: **The words of a man's mouth** are then characterized in terms of *three* images connected with water (that is, in English translation the two phrases in this line should be seen as in apposition, with no **is**). The former interpretation is the more probable. If the first line is concerned with mankind in general (see above), the reference to **wisdom** in the second line marks this out as an independent proverb, probably placed here because of the related imagery and perhaps especially because of a supposed contrast between the static **deep waters** and the **gushing stream**.

Toy maintained that it makes no sense to define a **fountain** (*māqôr*, properly "spring" or "source") as a **gushing stream**. But this is hypercriticism. In 5:15–18 no fewer than six words and phrases, including *māqôr* and *nōzᵉlîm*, "flowing water", are used, apparently without significant difference of meaning, of sexual activity; and in 5:16, *ma'yōnôt*, "springs", is clearly used as the equivalent of "streams of water" (*palᵉgê māyim*). This imagery is evidently used imprecisely. The point of the present line appears to be that **wisdom** (*mᵉqôr ḥokmāh*, "the fountain of wisdom – compare *mᵉqôr ḥayyîm*, "a fountain of life", 10:11; 13:14; 14:27; 16:22 – MT is to be preferred to the alternative reading of LXX and some MSS; see *BHS*) is a constant source of strength and refreshment.

5. This verse is a condemnation of corrupt judges (compare

17:23). *rāšā‘* (**a wicked man**) and *ṣaddîq* (**a righteous man**) are technical terms for "guilty" and "innocent" respectively. The phrase *nāśā' pānîm* (**to be partial**, literally, "to lift the face [of someone]") is used of judicial bias in Lev. 19:15 and Ps. 82:2, and also in Dt. 10:17, where it is specifically associated with the taking of bribes. The hiphil of *nāṭāh* (**deprive . . . of justice**, *mišpāṭ*), literally "thrust aside", is regularly used in the OT in this sense (e.g. Exod. 23:6; 1 Sam. 8:3 [in connection with bribery]; and compare Prov. 17:23). **not good**: see on 16:29.

In the second line the Hebrew begins with the infinitive "*to* deprive . . .", linking the rejection of the case of the innocent with bias towards the guilty. This makes excellent sense, and the addition in *RSV* of **or**, following LXX and some commentaries and turning a continuous sentence into a synonymous parallelism, is not necessary.

6–8. The juxtaposition of vv. 6 and 7 which are similar in form and also have a common theme – the harmful effects of the talk of fools – is obviously intentional. This is probably also true of v. 8. But v. 8 is identical with 26:22, where it forms part of a much larger group (vv. 17–26) and where it fits more satisfactorily as those proverbs are mainly concerned with malicious rather than foolish talk. This verse was evidently a "floating" proverb which was incorporated quite independently into two different contexts.

6. This proverb is concerned, like many others, with harmonious relations within the community (compare, e.g., 15:18; 17:14; 20:3). Irresponsible talk can obviously cause trouble; but it is not clear whether the second line refers to the punishment of the **fool**, or whether it simply repeats the thought of the first line. *RSV*'s **flogging** interprets it, probably correctly, in the former way; but this word (*mah*^{a}*lūmôt*) appears simply to mean "blows", and could, especially in view of the corresponding **strife** in the first line, refer to the physical outcome of a quarrel caused by the fool's malice. *REB*'s "his words provoke blows" leaves the question open.

bring strife: MT has *yābō'û b*^{e}*rîb*, which would normally mean "enters strife". Driver (*VT* 1 [1951], p. 249) defended MT on the grounds that "come with" can mean "bring"; but the supporting texts which he cited are not comparable. The suggestion of many commentators that the verb should be repointed as the causative (hiphil) *yābî'û*, "bring", is probably correct.

7. The theme of this proverb – the disastrous effects of irresponsible talk – is the same as that of v. 6; but in this case it is clearly the **fool** who suffers the consequences. The verse may be intended as a clarification of v. 6b. There is no reference here to the effect of the fool's behaviour on others, though this may be taken for granted: it is regarded by others as intolerable. **ruin** (*m^eḥiṯṯāh*), rendered variously by *RSV* elsewhere in these proverbs by "ruin", "destruction", "dismay", is an imprecise but uncompromising word. **are a snare to himself** (*môqēš napšô*): *nepeš* can mean either "self" or "life"; and McKane's "a lethal snare" may be right.

8. This verse is identical with 26:22. **whisperer**: probably better, "slanderer" or "gossip" (see on 16:28). The verse is a warning to resist the natural human propensity to listen eagerly to gossip. **the inner parts** (*ḥ^adārîm*): literally "the inner rooms"). The same expression is found in 20:27, 30. This noun (*ḥeḏer*) is also used of a storeroom; and McKane may be right in supposing that it is here implied that gossip is not only greedily absorbed by the hearer but is also prone to be remembered – and so repeated at a later time. **they**: the Hebrew resumes the subject of the first line with *w^ehēm*, literally, "and they", probably for emphasis: "it is *these* words which . . ."

9. Although the word rendered by **slack** here in *RSV* (*mitrappeh*) is unusual (McKane translates it by "half-hearted"), this verse, though expressed in strong, dramatic terms, is yet another example of the warnings about the disastrous consequences of laziness so frequent in these collections of proverbs. The slack worker is compared with, or put in the same category as (for another example of this use of **brother** see Job 30:29, and also compare Prov. 28:24, "*companion* of a man who destroys") **him who destroys** (*ba'al mašḥît*), that is, a deliberate wrecker or enemy of society.

RSV has left untranslated the first word of this verse: *gam*, most frequently rendered by "also" or "even". Here it is probably used as a strong asseverative: see C. J. Labuschagne, 1966, p. 199.

10–12. It is generally acknowledged that the juxtaposition of vv. 10 and 11 is no coincidence; but there is also a case for the inclusion of v. 12 in this small group.

The verbal agreements between vv. 10 and 11 are obvious. The noun *'ōz*, "strength", is common to both, and occurs in virtually synonymous phrases: *migdal-'ōz*, **a strong tower** (v. 10), *qiryat 'uzzô*, **his strong city** (v. 11). The niphal participle *niśgāb* (**safe**) appears in v. 10, and its feminine form *niśgābāh* (**high**) in v. 11. The two verses also have a common theme: each is in effect an answer to the question "How can a man ensure his safety?" (that is, from the chances and misfortunes of life). Both the answers to this question are given in terms of reliance on reliable defences; but what is meant by these is expressed in contrasting images: the **rich man** (*'āšîr*) relies on his **wealth** to protect him, while the defences of the **righteous man** (*ṣaddîq*) are defined as **The name of the Lord**.

V. 10 is clearly an example of a Yahweh-proverb commenting on an adjacent one. Its purpose seems to be to modify, or possibly to deny (see on v. 11 below) the truth of the assertion made in v. 11: it asserts in effect that wealth does *not* protect a man from misfortune; only Yahweh can be relied on to do this, and he will do it not for the **rich** but only for the **righteous**. It is possible, but by no means certain, that v. 10 was composed for this specific purpose: the terminology is not identical, and v. 10 can well have originally stood on its own. V. 12, which speaks of the **destruction** (*šeber*, "collapse") of the **haughty** (literally, "high", but the word used is not the same as that used in v. 11) may also have been placed here as a disapproving comment on that verse.

10. The phrase **The name of the Lord** occurs only here in Proverbs (though we may compare "the name of my God" in 30:9). The concept of Yahweh's **name** in the Old Testament does not always have precisely the same connotation. But in 10:29 he himself is said to be a stronghold (*mā'ôz*) to the upright, and this kind of imagery is found in a manner of the Psalms. Here, whatever may be the precise significance of speaking of the name rather than directly of Yahweh himself, the general meaning is clear from the context. In Ps. 61:3 [Heb. 4] Yahweh is addressed as a strong tower (*migdal 'ōz* – the same phrase as is used here) against enemies. **runs into it**: the reference is to the inhabitants of a town taking refuge in the town's fortified tower at the approach of an enemy, as in Jg. 9:51. **is safe**: this verb (*śgb*) means "to be high", but with the implication of being out of reach of danger below.

11. The first line of this verse is identical with 10:15a; but whereas in that verse it forms part of an antithetical proverb contrasting the situation of the **rich man** with that of the poor, here the parallelism is synonymous. The sense of the second line, however, is not clear because of uncertainty about the meaning of the final word, *b^emaśkîtô* (*RSV* **protecting him**). *RSV* is based on an emendation favoured by some commentators on the supposed basis of LXX and other Versions (see *BHS*); the Hebrew word is somewhat obscure, but

McKane, Plöger, *REB* and *JB*, who retain the text of MT, take it to mean something like "in his imagination" or "as he believes". This may mean that his wealth does *not* in fact protect the rich man; if so, this gives a quite different meaning to the verse from that of 10:15. It also means that the function of the previous verse (10) is not to deny the truth of v. 11 (see above on vv. 10–12) but rather to confirm it in Yahwistic terms: the rich man *thinks* that his wealth will protect him, but in fact only reliance on Yahweh can do this. This interpretation is probably to be preferred: the quite different reading of the Versions may be due to a misunderstanding of the rare *maśkît*.

12. The first line of this verse resembles, but is not identical with, 16:18a; the second is completely identical with 15:33b. Both of those verses are examples of synonymous parallelism. Here, where the second line is a short, crisp non-verbal sentence which may once have been an independent popular saying (see also on 15:33), the first is stylistically more laboured, and has probably been added to it to make a more impressive antithetical statement. **destruction** (*šeber*, that is, ruin) is the antithesis of **honour** (*kābôd*, that is, prosperity and esteem).

13. This is probably a general comment on the person who cannot wait to express his opinion and does so without waiting for his interlocutor to finish speaking. His behaviour is a particular example of the lack of control so frequently castigated in these proverbs. The view that the verse refers to the specific case of the pronouncement of premature decisions in legal hearings (see M. A. Klopfenstein, *Scham und Schande nach dem Alten Testament*, ATANT, 1972, pp. 119–36) is not proven. (See Bühlmann, pp. 196–8; Plöger.)

shame (*kᵉlimmāh*): that is, disgrace or humiliation incurred by such conduct. Some commentators, however, render the word by "insulting" – that is, such behaviour is insulting to the other speaker (so *REB*).

14. This proverb is clearly related to 15:13 and 17:22, the only other two passages in the Old Testament where the phrase *rûaḥ nᵉkē'āh* occurs; but it presents a special problem of interpretation. In the other two proverbs a contrast is made between the "broken spirit" and a glad or cheerful heart (*lēb śāmēaḥ*), and all three proverbs make the point that the former is a sad case, with the implication that it is incurable. But whereas in the other two cases the sadness of this condition is emphasized by a contrast with the opposite state of happiness, here the point appears to be made by contrasting two cases of adversity of different degrees of intensity, the lesser one endurable, the greater one unendurable. So much is clear; but the use of the same word **spirit** in both lines is confusing, at least to the modern interpreter, and raises more acutely than in the other two cases the question of what is meant by **a broken spirit**. If a man's spirit is strong enough (or *may* be strong enough) to overcome the misfortune of **sickness** (it is not clear whether this word is intended literally or metaphorically), what is this *broken* spirit that is apparently *un*endurable or incurable? The commentators have been unable to find a satisfactory answer to this question. It has been suggested that it refers to a state of irrational acute depression; but speculations of this kind about ancient texts, particularly such brief ones, are unwise. The question remains unanswered.

15. The first line of this proverb is identical with 15:14a except for the verb; but the second line also resembles 15:14a, which also contains the phrase *seeks knowledge*. Thus all three lines (15:14a; 18:15a; 18:15b) are variants of the same didactic statement that a desire for further education is the mark of the wise man (compare 1:5). This verse reflects the attitude of the introduction to the book (1:2–6), and may mark the beginning of a sub-collection of proverbs collected with an educational purpose. The **ear** as the organ by which the father's (oral) instruction is to be received is characteristic of the Instructions in chapters 1–9 (2:2; 4:20; 5:1, 13; compare also 15:31), and stands in parallelism, as here, with the heart (**mind**) in a similar context in 2:2.

16–19. Vv. 17 and 18 are specifically concerned with legal processes; and this is probably also true of v. 16. The meaning of v. 19 is uncertain; but the occurrence of the word *midyānîm/mᵉdônîm* (**disputes, quarrelling**) both here and in v. 18 suggests that this verse too may have belonged to a small group of proverbs to which v. 15 may have been the introduction (see above).

16. The word *mattān* (**gift**), though it may be used in a general sense, also has the more restricted meaning of "bribe" (compare 21:14, and the use of the cognate *mattānāh* in 15:27). Here the immediate context shows that it means a bribe, but the commentators are divided on the question whether it refers to the particular practice of bribing judges or witnesses, a practice attested elsewhere in these proverbs (especially clearly in 17:23), or more generally to the bribing of officials or servants in order to secure privileges, whether social, political or commercial. The fact that the two following verses are concerned with forensic matters suggests the former, as perhaps does also the term *g^edōlîm*, **great men**: this term is used generally of influential persons, persons who might be presumed to be able to influence the course of justice; and it may be significant that in mic. 7:3 they are associated with corrupt judges.

On the anomalous *mattān* where the construct *mattan* would normally be expected see *GK* 92g.

17. seems right: *ṣaddîq* here as elsewhere means "innocent". Driver (*Bib.* 32 [1951], p. 183) has argued convincingly that the setting is that of a legal trial: **He who states his case first** (in the Hebrew, simply *hārī'šōn*, "the first one") is the defendant, and **the other** (*rē'ēhû*, literally, "his neighbour") the plaintiff or accuser. The verse is addressed to judges, warning them against making premature judgements before all the evidence and arguments have been heard. A more general setting (note that **states his case** is an interpretation by *RSV* and has nothing corresponding to it in the Hebrew), that is, of an ordinary discussion among neighbours, is not impossible, but a legal setting is more probable in the light of the wider context.

comes: read Kethib *yābō'* rather than Qere *ûbā'*.

18. On the casting of the **lot** see on 16:33. This is the only reference in the Old Testament to its use in ordinary disputes, presumably in cases where other methods had proved impossible. **puts an end to**: according to Albright (1955, p. 10) this verb (*hišbît*) may have been a technical term for reaching a legal decision.

The meaning of the second line is not entirely clear. The verb rendered in *RSV* by **decides** (**between**), *hiprîd*, normally means to separate, or even (16:28; 17:9) to alienate. Further, the reason why "*powerful* contenders" (*ᵃṣûmîm*) are singled out as a special case is also not clear, unless to imply that disputes between such persons are likely to be more socially disruptive than disputes between others. Driver (*Bib.* 32 [1951]; p. 183) thought the word to be inappropriate here, and proposed its emendation to *'ōṣ^emîm*, which he rendered by "litigants" on the basis of a Syriac cognate and the Hebrew word *ᵃṣûmôt*, "pleas", which occurs in Isa. 41:21. So *REB* "keep(s) litigants apart".

19. This verse is particularly difficult, and several commentators have regarded the Hebrew text as corrupt beyond the possibility of correction. The second line may mean that disputes can lead to complete alienation between the disputants; but the first line has not been satisfactorily elucidated by any commentator. *RSV*'s **helped** follows an emendation derived from the Versions; but this offers no more satisfactory sense than the Hebrew, which has *nipšā'*, the niphal participle of *pāša'*, "to rebel", or, in religious terms, "to sin". Some commentators take this to mean "sinned against" (so Ringgren and Gemser, "deceived": McKane, "aggrieved"); but this is a dubious translation.

20–21. These two proverbs are both about the power of speech. There is one verbal connection between them: the occurrence in both of the word **fruit** as meaning the consequences which flow from a person's words. V. 20 speaks of the beneficial effects of speech on the speaker; v. 21, in stronger terms, emphasizes its power both for good and evil.

20. The first line of this verse has strong verbal affinities with 12:14a and 13:2a, and it is probable that all three are variants of some common saying, which has been used in different ways with the addition of different second lines. This variant has one signifcant difference from the other two: whereas 12:14 has (literally) "is satisfied with good (*ṭôb*)" and 13:2 has "*eats* good", here the word *ṭôb* is replaced by *biṭnô* "his belly": "his belly is satisfied" (this word is not represented in *RSV*). This opens the line up to different interpretations. Whatever "eats good" may mean in 13:2, the word "belly" here in conjunction with **fruit** suggests the idea of literally satisfying one's hunger. But to say that one satisfies one's hunger by what *comes out* of one's mouth rather than by what goes into it appears at first to be an absurdity. Clearly the author of this variant, like Jesus in Mt. 15:11, is using a rhetorical device (a verbal contradiction known as oxymoron) to make a point. But this is not the only verbal device used in the line. The verb *śāba'* (**is satisfied**) has more than one meaning: whereas in 12:11; 20:13; 28:19 it has the positive sense of satisfying hunger (either literally or metaphorically), in 25:16 it means to have *too much* for one's good; in 1:31 it means to suffer the consequences of one's evil deeds; and in 25:17 it means to become weary – to have too much – of someone's company. In 14:14 it has both a good and a bad sense in the same proverb. The word "belly" (*beṭen*) too can be used in two distinct ways: whereas in 13:25 it denotes the belly as the seat of physical hunger, in 18:8 and 20:27 it has a more psychological sense of the inner or essential man. (Together with *śāba'*, therefore, it could have the same meaning as the English expression "to have a bellyful").

There is thus scope for different interpretations of this line. Of those which have been proposed, the most natural is, taking both the oxymoron and the puns seriously, to see it as meaning that just as eating fruit may either leave one pleasantly satisfied or – if it is taken in excess – unpleasantly surfeited (with unfortunate results – compare 25:16, on eating honey –), so also what *comes out* of the mouth – that is, words – has consequences which may be either good or bad: so it is important to use them with discretion. The meaning of this first line, therefore, is not very different from that of 12:14a or 13:2a taken by themselves, but the point is made with greater verbal subtlety. The second line, unlike the second lines of 12:14 and 13:2, simply echoes the first.

21. This verse expresses the same thought as v. 20 but both more simply and more strongly. **those who love it**: that is, those who like to chatter or to express their opinions. **eat its fruits**: as in v. 20, such people will be faced by the consequences of their loquacity. It is not stated whether these will be good or bad; the latter is probably implied. On the use of the distributive singular (*yō'kal*, **eat**) with a plural subject see *GK* 145 l.

22–24. Toy and Plöger point out that these three verses deal with different but important aspects of ordinary life: marriage, wealth, friendship. They are in fact more closely related than at first appears, in that they are all concerned, in various ways, with the importance of having reliable human relationships: a happy marriage means to have a lifelong companion (v. 22); the poor man, elsewhere described as one who has no friends (14:20) or as deserted by his friends (19:4), is isolated and vulnerable in his poverty (v. 23); there are true friends, but also false ones (v. 24). Some of these themes recur in chapter 19; but there is no reason to suppose the existence of a longer subsection beginning here.

22. The first line of this verse was probably originally a popular saying, as its style suggests. Although several of these proverbs (11:22; 19:13; 21:19; 25:24; 27:15) reflect the fact that marriages are not always blissful, this is clearly one of those (compare 11:16; 12:4; 19:14, and especially 31:10–31) which extol the joys of marriage. (In Proverbs, of course, marriages are always assessed from the point of view of the husband.) The reference is obviously to marriage with a "good" wife, although this is not explicitly stated (LXX adds the word "good", but this clearly does not represent an original Hebrew text). **finds a good thing**: this expression (*māṣā' ṭôb*) elsewhere (16:20; 17:20) means "to prosper" (on the construction see *GK*159b, h).

The second line is identical with 8:35b, which refers to the "finding" of personified Wisdom but is an addition to an earlier poem, asserting Wisdom's connection with Yahweh (see on 8:32–6). Somewhat similarly, it has been added here to the older proverb in order to assert that the ordinary circumstances of life such as happy marriages are the work of Yahweh. Whether the assurance that the happy husband receives **favour from the Lord** refers to the *choice* of a wife or to the *consequences* of such a choice, a point on which the commentators differ, is hardly significant. But see on 19:14.

23. This is one of several proverbs in these chapters (also 10:15; 14:20; 22:2, 7, 16; 28:6, 11) which specifically contrast the characteristics or behaviour of **rich** and **poor**. On these terms, and on the hostile attitude of these authors towards the rich, see on 10:15 and 14:20. This verse does not necessarily favour the poor as against the rich, but is a "neutral" comment on a fact of social life and relationships.

24. There are: in this first line MT has *'îš*, "A man (of)". *RSV*, following the majority but not all of the commentators, has taken this to be a mispointing of *yēš*, "There is", bringing the line into formal conformity with the second line. The line clearly draws a contrast between "friends" whose friendship is in some way faulty, and the true **friend** who can be relied on in trouble. But the precise way in which the "false" friend proves unsatisfactory is unclear because the meaning of the word rendered in *RSV* by **who pretend** to be friends (*hitrō'ēa'*) is uncertain; and some commentators offer alternative explanations of it. Delitzsch derived it from *r''* "to be harmful" and rendered the line by "A man with many friends comes to grief". Wildeboer, Ringgren and Plöger produce a similar meaning by deriving it from another *r''* (an Aramaizing form equivalent to *rṣṣ*), "to break". Toy, followed by Oesterley, with a slight emendation (to *hitrā'ôt*) (from *rā'āh*, "to be a companion"), offered the translation "seeks society" – in other words, there are friends who are no more than social companions. Finally Driver (*Bib.* 32 [1951], pp. 183–4), followed by McKane, derived the form from *rw'*, "to shout", but saw it as used in a weakened form attested in Syriac meaning "to chatter".

sticks closer than a brother: the value of true friends in time of trouble as (even) greater than that of brothers is also the theme of 27:10 and possibly also of 17:17. On the other hand, 19:7 puts no trust in either.

CHAPTER 19

As in the immediately preceding chapters there are only a few examples of antithetical parallelism in this chapter, and a prominence of synonymous ones. Very few of these proverbs contrast the righteous and the wicked, although various kinds of reprehensible conduct are mentioned. Wisdom and prudence are frequently advocated (vv. 8, 11, 14, 20, 25, 27), but there are few verses extolling goodness for its own sake. The importance of education and instruction is frequently stressed, and of these proverbs four (vv. 8, 16, 20, 27) use language strongly reminiscent of the Instructions in chapters 1–9. The rich and the poor are frequently mentioned (vv. 1, 4, 6, 7, 17, 22). Three proverbs are concerned with false witnesses (vv. 5, 9, 28) and two with sloth (vv. 15, 24).

As in chapter 18 there are few clear signs of extensive groupings, though v. 27, an admonition to "my son", has the appearance of the introduction to an Instruction, and vv. 16 and 20 may mark out a small such group. There are several examples of pairing of proverbs: vv. 2–3, 6–7, 11–12, 13–14, 20–21. Yahweh is mentioned five times (vv. 3, 14, 17, 21, 23), and in three of these cases the Yahweh-proverb appears to be a comment on the previous verse (v. 3 on v. 2, v. 14 on v. 13, v. 21 on v. 20). Plöger finds a connected group in vv. 18–23.

1. This verse is identical with 28:6 except that in the second lines the latter has "a rich man" (*'āšîr*) rather than **a fool** and "ways" rather than **speech**. Some MSS and Versions have "ways" in both verses; but the notion of "perverted speech" – that is, telling lies in order to deceive – is no less appropriate to the context (compare 8:8; 17:20).

MT's **fool** (*k^esîl*), however, has been thought to be inappropriate here, and most commentators, following Pesh. as well as 28:6, emend the word to "rich", which admittedly provides a good parallelism with **poor**. However, it is not clear how MT's reading could have arisen. If **fool** is in fact the correct reading a reasonably good sense for the verse can be obtained. The implication may be that liars are in fact fools because – as is axiomatic in these proverbs – wickedness does not pay in the long run. Thus, somewhat analogously to those proverbs (15:16, 17; 16:8, 19; 17:1) which declare that the rich are not necessarily to be envied for their luxurious style of living, this proverb may be saying that the state of the poor man whose conduct is irreproachable is preferable to that of the persuasive liar because the former will in the end be blessed with prosperity while the latter is a fool who will not escape divine punishment. See also on 28:6.

2. The parallelism of this verse is improved if the word *nepeš* (*RSV* **a man**) is rendered by "desire" (compare 10:3; 13:4, 25; 16:26), that is, ambition: to desire to do something without giving proper thought to ways and means will lead to disaster (on this meaning of *lōʾ ṭob*, literally, **not good**, see on 16:29); similarly the person who is in too great a hurry (literally, **makes haste with his feet**) will fail to reach his objective (*ḥôṭēʾ*, **misses his way** – on this meaning of *ḥāṭāʾ* see on 8:36). The expression is of course metaphorical.

On the word with which the verse begins (*gam*, untranslated in *RSV*) see on 18:9.

3. This verse is probably intended as a comment on v. 2 (and perhaps also on v. 1). Its point is somewhat weakened in *RSV*'s translation: a better translation would be "It is a man's own folly which ruins his life, yet it is *against Yahweh*" (emphatic) "that he rages". Folly and blasphemy are closely linked here. Von Rad (*Wisdom in Israel*, p. 65), who refers specifically to this verse among others, characterized folly as "practical atheism" similar to that expressed in Ps. 14:1, "The fool (*nābāl*) says in his heart, 'There is no God' ". But, as Plöger points out, this is not quite what is meant here. The fool does not deny or discount God's power; rather, he accuses him of misapplying it, manifesting an arrogance and self-conceit which is a form of blasphemy rather than any kind of atheism. It is a denial of the principle expressed frequently in these proverbs and elsewhere in the Old Testament that God is righteous. This is a question urgently raised in the Book of Job.

4. Compare v. 7 and see the comments on 14:20. **is deserted by his friend** (*mērēʿēhû yippārēd*), the word for "friend" being *rēaʿ*. Some MSS read *mᵉrēʿēhû*, *mērēaʿ* being another word meaning "friend": "As for the poor man, his friend deserts (literally, "separates himself from") him". Either pointing is possible; the sense is unaffected.

5. This proverb is one of a group of verses (6:19; 12:17; 14:5, 25;

19:9; 21:28) which contain partial variants, or in some cases identical phrases. Every one of its words and phrases occurs also in one or more of the other verses in the group; and, in this chapter, v. 9 is its almost exact doublet. The problem of lying witnesses was evidently a major problem for the community which produced these proverbs; the use of a common vocabulary points to a common, probably oral, source. **will not go unpunished** (*lō' yinnāqeh*): that is, will not be acquitted.

6–7b. These two verses form an excellent antithesis, although they were almost certainly originally separate proverbs. Compare 14:20 with its equally strong implicit condemnation of those who fawn on the rich and despise the poor, and 18:24 on true and false friends in general. On the third line of v. 7 see below.

6. a generous man: this word (*nādîb*) has several distinct though related meanings (see on 17:7 and 17:26). *RSV*'s translation (compare Exod. 35:5, 22) makes a good parallel with **a man who gives gifts** in the second line, although "noble" – that is, in rank; compare Prov. 8:16; 17:7; 25:7 – is also a possible meaning here. Such a person might be expected to reward those who gained his favour by flattery. **gifts** (*mattān*): here the reference is to generosity rather than to bribes (see on 18:16).

every one is a friend: the Hebrew (which has the article before "friend") is somewhat strange, but emendation is probably not necessary.

7. This verse, unusually, consists of three lines. The first two form a typical parallel couplet of the *a fortiori* kind (*'ap kî*, **how much more . . .!**). A few commentators have attempted to find some way of relating the final line to the previous two; but others have regarded it as unintelligible, perhaps a fragment of which the rest has been lost, and almost certainly the result of textual corruption. A literal translation of it would be "pursuing words not these". LXX's variant of the verse is of no assistance. It has a garbled version of the first two lines and then a long addition of its own (two couplets) which is unrelated to what precedes and throws no light on the Hebrew line.

hate him: this verb (*śānē'*) has a wide range of meanings (see E. Jenni, *THAT* II, 1976, cols. 835–6). Here it means no more than "dislike" or even "avoid" (compare its use in 11:15; 25:17). **his friends**: the form is singular in the Hebrew; this may be intended in a collective sense, or it may be simply due to a minor scribal slip.

8. wisdom: literally, "heart". See on 15:32. **loves himself**: that is, does himself a good turn. **keeps understanding**: see on 5:2; 7:1–3. This is the technical language of education (see on 19:1–29). **will prosper**: on this meaning of *māṣā' ṭôb* see 16:20; 17:20; 18:22. Some commentators emend the infinitive here to the imperfect; but the text may be correct: see *GK* 114h, i and Dahood, p. 40.

9. This verse is almost identical with v. 5.

10. The first line of this verse is a variant of 17:7a. The significance of **not fitting** here is perhaps illuminated by 30:21–3, which lists virtually the same examples as here with others under the heading of "things under which the earth trembles"; in other words, they are not merely incongruous but actually destructive of the divinely established order of things. **a slave** (*'ebed*) **to rule over princes**: this means to become king, as is clearly stated in 30:22. The acquisition of wealth and power by fools or by slaves was not unknown in the ancient world, and it is of interest to note that Zimri, probably a person of low birth, who ascended the throne after assassinating his "master", King Elah of North Israel (1 Kg. 16:9; 2 Kg. 9:31), is called an *'ebed*. However, the example used here probably does not refer specifically to any historical event. If it did, it would probably be unique in the Book of Proverbs.

luxury (*ta'anûg*, literally, "delight"): Thomas (*JTS* 38 [1937], p. 400) and Driver (*VT* Suppl. 3, 1955, p. 84) render this word by "leadership" or "control", on the basis of an Arabic root. This would give an excellent parallel with the second line, but the word does not have this meaning elsewhere in the Old Testament, and an exact parallelism is not necessarily required here (compare again 30:21–3). The reason why the second example of unfittedness is regarded as more deplorable than the first does not appear, and must probably remain obscure in the absence – as, of course, with the other proverbs in these collections – of any information about the precise circumstances in which the proverb originated.

11–12. The common topic of **anger** (*'ap* in v. 11; *za'ap* in v. 12) is sufficient to account for the juxtaposition of these two verses. On the question whether there is a further thematic connection between them see on v. 12.

11. makes . . . slow to anger (*he'rīk 'appō*): the repointing of the perfect form *he'rîk* as the infinitive *ha'rîk* proposed by a number of commentators provides a better parallel to the second line: "it is (a sign of) a man's good sense *to* be slow to anger". Patience or forbearance was a particular characteristic of the wise men (compare especially 14:17, 29). Here this takes the form of the avoidance of a quarrel even under provocation; the wisdom literature both biblical and extrabiblical constantly stresses the importance of avoiding acrimonious disputes for the sake of the wellbeing of the community. **it is his glory**: that is, it contributes to his reputation as a wise man. This word (*tip'eret*) is regularly used of the greatness or splendour of kings – perhaps another link with v. 12.

12. On this picture of absolute monarchy in the perception of ordinary people see on 16:14. The first line, probably a popular saying, has a variant in 20:2a, where, however, it is used in a different way. Here the wording of the second line shows that the point is not the necessity to placate kings who can destroy or advance those who are in his service, but that the king is the protector and benefactor of his people. The **dew**, which in the climatic conditions of Palestine was essential to the survival of vegetation in the hot, dry, summer, was regarded as a gift from God which he could either confer on his people or withhold from them (see, e.g., Dt. 33:28; 1 Kg. 17:1; Hos. 14:5 [Heb. 6]; Hag. 1:10; Zech. 8:12). In Gen. 27:28 it is one of the items specified in the blessing of Jacob by Isaac, but is withheld from Esau (v. 39). Thus the **king** is here compared with God, or, more probably, regarded as his representative or agent in his power to confer this blessing, and in the dependence of the gift on his **favour** (*rāṣôn*). Correspondingly the king's **wrath** in the first line presumably refers to his power to destroy those wicked persons who threaten the wellbeing of his people.

If this interpretation is correct, no criticism is intended in this proverb of the king's actions or of his motives. However, it is possible that v. 11, with its implied criticism of those who too hastily give vent to their anger and are unforgiving, has been placed in its present position to create a paradox, or even perhaps to suggest that between the two extremes of **wrath** and **favour** those in authority ought to find room for the exercise of a third option: tolerance or forgiveness.

like the growling of a lion (*naham kakk*ᵉ*pîr*, literally, "a growling like a lion"): Seeligman (1953, p. 164) refers to a suggestion of Ehrlich that originally this line – and also 20:2a – referred not to a lion (*k*ᵉ*pîr*) but to hoar frost (*k*ᵉ*pôr*). This would provide a very neat contrast with dew, but is speculative and unnecessary. The image of the king as a lion, like that of the gift of dew, seems to be a reflection of that of *Yahweh* as a lion which may fall upon Israel and destroy it (e.g. Hos. 5:14; 13:7–8) or, on the other hand, may act to protect Israel (Isa. 31:4–5) or to attack her enemies (Jer. 49:19).

13–14. It is the references to wives in v. 13b and in v. 14b which accounts for the juxtaposition of these two proverbs; but there is a further relationship between the two verses: while in v. 13 the quarrelling wife is only one of a pair of examples of what can go wrong in family life, v. 14 is wholly concerned with the choice of a suitable wife, and is to be understood as a comment on v. 13b.

13. Each line of this verse has variants elsewhere in these chapters: compare the first line with 10:1b; 17:21a, 25a and the second with 21:9b, 19b; 25:24. In 27:15–16 what was originally probably an independent popular saying has been further expanded in a more literary style. **a continual dripping of rain**: perhaps better, "an endlessly leaking roof" (compare Ec. 10:18).

14. prudent: this word (*maśkelet*) is the feminine of *maśkîl*, "intelligent, wise", a term frequently used in these proverbs and one which occurs as the antonym of *mēbîš*, "(one who) brings shame" in 10:5. The *'iššāh maśkelet* here is thus the opposite of the *m*ᵉ*bîšāh* of 12:4, and also of the quarrelling wife of v. 13.

The second line is reminiscent of 18:22, especially if that verse means that the *choice* of a good wife is due to the guidance of Yahweh. There is, however, some difficulty about its logical relationship to the first line. A contrast seems to be intended between the regularity of the process by which a man can confidently expect to inherit family property and the unpredictability inherent in the selection of a wife. We might expect the second line to say that "a prudent wife comes by chance". But the affirmation that a prudent wife is from the Lord raises questions about the author's view of the part played by Yahweh in human affairs. While several of these proverbs (e.g. v. 21 and 16:1, 9, 33) maintain that human choices are *wholly* subject to Yahweh's control, this verse may seem to imply that – in contrast with the general view – the acquisition of wealth – and perhaps also of an *unsuitable* wife – is outside his control.

In attempting to account for this anomaly it should first be noted that the second line – which could well have originally been a popular saying – presents no problem in itself, especially if **the Lord** (*yhwh*) has here a weakened sense analogous to that proposed for its occasional use in an adjectival sense by Thomas (*VT* 18 [1968], pp. 120–24) and de Boer (1974, pp. 233–5). If this is the case the phrase **is from the Lord** may mean no more than "(is) an unexpected piece of good fortune" (compare perhaps also Eve's comment on the birth of a son in Gen. 4:1). At a later stage the first line may have been added, without serious theological reflection, in order to make the point that if a man who has already been blessed by good fortune through the normal law of inheritance has his happiness completed by a happy marriage, this is a mark of exceptional divine favour. At an even later stage the whole verse may have been brought into connection with v. 13b in order to remind the reader further that, since in fact wives often prove to be unsatisfactory, thanks are especially due to Yahweh when a marriage turns out well.

15. casts into a deep sleep: literally, "causes a deep sleep (*tardēmāh*) to fall". The verb cognate to this noun (*rdm*) is used of the sleep of the worthless son in 10:5. The verse makes good sense (compare the self-destructiveness of the half-awake sluggard in 19:24), and Dahood's and Gemser's proposals, on the basis respectively of Ugaritic and Arabic roots, to find new meanings for *tardēmāh* are unnecessary and improbable.

16. The language of this verse is that of the teacher in chapters 1–9. **keeps the commandment**: that is, of the teacher (so 4:4 and 7:2; compare similar phrases *passim* in those chapters). Similar language occurs also, as has been seen, in a number of the proverbs in this section of the book (10:1–22:16), for example 10:17; 13:18; 15:5; 19:8 – an indication of an educational motive in the collection of these proverbs. **keeps his life**: the same expression occurs in 16:17 and 22:5.

he who despises the word: the Hebrew has "despises his ways" (*bôzēh d^e rākâw*); *RSV*, following several commentators, has emended *d^e rākâw* to *dābār*, on the analogy of 13:13. This would make a more complete parallelism, but is hardly necessary: to "despise one's ways" may be understood as paying little attention to, or being careless of, one's behaviour. Dahood's suggestion that *derek* here may mean "authority" (on the basis of Ugaritic *drkt*) is too speculative. The view that "*his* ways" may refer either to the ways of the teacher or to those of Yahweh (see McKane and Plöger) is not plausible as there is no antecedent.

will die: *RSV* here correctly reads the Qere in preference to Kethib's "will be put to death".

17. The five proverbs in these chapters which speak of generosity to the poor all explicitly or implicitly promise a reward to the giver: he will be "happy" (14:21b); he will be blessed (22:9); he will not want (28:27a). In 14:31b a reward is implied: such generosity honours Yahweh; and the giver will surely be rewarded. Here in 19:17 the relationship between the giver and Yahweh is expressed in the language of usury (**lends to the Lord, and he will repay him**). The same phraseology is used negatively in Isa. 59:18, where Yahweh will "repay" his enemies "according to their deeds". In the present verse as in 14:31 Yahweh is seen as involving himself so closely with the poor that what is *given* to them (who are unable to repay) is regarded as *lent* to him so that repayment – presumably in the form of blessing and material prosperity – will surely be made. But there is no idea here of a *quid pro quo*: no intention to encourage generosity simply for the reward which it will bring. The underlying thought is that generosity is a characteristic of a person who is righteous; and the proverb reflects the basic belief that righteousness is, and ought to be, materially rewarded. The **poor** here, as elsewhere in these proverbs, are those who are totally destitute; the generous giver is himself not rich but merely a person who has enough for himself and perhaps a little to spare.

The relationship of this Yahweh-proverb to its context is not clear. It may have been placed here to make the point that obedience to the human "commandment" of v. 16 has the backing of Yahweh, who will duly reward it. There may also be a remote connection with vv. 18–23 in that those verses taken as a whole (see below) also see Yahweh as a source of "life" to those who accept his guidance.

18–23. Plöger sees vv. 18, 20, 21, 23 as a connected sequence, with vv. 19 and 22 as interpolations. V. 18 is addressed to a father, with a recommendation to firm, though not excessive, discipline of his son; v. 20 is addressed to the child, who is beginning his education, admonishing him to attend to his studies and informing him of their purpose, that he should eventually attain to wisdom; v. 21 states that this purpose cannot be attained by human means alone but only under Yahweh's direction; finally v. 23 expatiates on the meaning of the "wisdom" referred to in v. 20, pointing out the great rewards which will eventually accrue from this programme. V. 19 is intended to reinforce the warning of v. 18b; v. 22 presents serious problems of interpretation, and its relationship to the context in which it now stands cannot be clearly determined. Plöger is probably correct in seeing a connection between the verses in question; but the fact that the father is first addressed and then the child shows that this is not an "Instruction" in the proper sense, but a collection of proverbs on a single theme.

18. Discipline (*yassēr*): on the corporal punishment of children see on 13:24 and compare 23:13–14. **hope**: that is, of amendment. The meaning of the second line is disputed. It is unlikely to be a warning against beating the child to death (so *REB*), since although the execution of a rebellious child was permitted, it could only be carried out by the decision of the elders of the city (Dt. 21:18–21). Two main interpretations have been proposed: 1) that his destruction (literally, "to kill him") is not to be taken literally but in a weakened sense, "do not chastise him excessively" (Thomas, *VT* Supplement 3, 1955, pp. 288–9); 2) that the reference is not to death as a result of the beating but to the fate of "death" which will be the son's if he does not amend his ways (compare 23:14; so Toy, Scott, McKane).

do not set your heart on: this expression (*nāśā' nepeš ['el]*) has also been variously interpreted: as *RSV* (Toy, McKane; compare Ringgren); "either lose one's temper" or "be carried away by passion" (Barucq, Plöger; compare LXX).

19. If v. 18b refers to excessive punishment, this verse may have been placed here as a further warning against such violence. **A man of great wrath**: Kethib's *gōral-ḥēmāh* makes no sense. One should read, with Qere, *g*ᵉ*dol-ḥēmāh*, "one whose wrath is great", or possibly, following LXX and other Versions, emend to *g*ᵉ*bar-ḥēmāh*, "a man of wrath". *'ōneš*, penalty: literally, "fine"; but see on 17:26. **pay**: literally, "bear": compare *REB*, "must bear the consequences" – presumably of whatever violent act has been committed.

The meaning of the second line is uncertain, and the text may be corrupt. **deliver him** could mean "pay his fine" or, more generally, "extricate him from his predicament"; but the Hebrew lacks the suffix **him**. **you will only have to do it again** (*w*ᵉ*'ôd tôsīp*): literally, "and again you will add". This verb can mean "to add", "to increase" or "to repeat". An alternative translation might be "you will make matters worse" – because the man will not have learned his lesson.

20–21. V. 21 is clearly a comment on v. 20 after the manner of the additions to the Instructions of chapters 1–9 (for example, in 2:1–9). V. 20 is typical of the introductory sections of the father's instructions except that it is expressed in impersonal terms. V. 21

picked up the word *'ēṣāh* (**advice**) in v. 20 and speaks of *Yahweh*'s *'ēṣāh* (**purpose**), asserting that while sound human advice should be heeded, it will be efficacious only in so far as it is in accordance with the will of Yahweh.

20. Listen to advice: see on 12:15, where the same expression (*šāma' 'ēṣāh*) is used. As in the Instructions of chapters 1–9, this is the singular imperative of the verb: that is, it is addressed to an individual pupil. On the meaning of **instruction** (*mûsār*) see on 1:2. **for the future**: literally, "in your *'aḥ^arît*". Although in 5:11 the same expression probably simply means "afterwards", here it probably refers to the goal or final stage of the process of acquiring wisdom (compare 14:12; 16:25, where *'aḥ^arît* is used of a *bad* end).

21. The thought of this verse is similar to that of 16:1, 9. There is a play on the two meanings of *'ēṣāh* here (**purpose**) and in v. 20 ("advice"). Yahweh's *'ēṣāh* overrules that of human teachers.

22. The Hebrew of the first line of this verse reads, "The desire of a man is his *ḥesed*" – a word which normally means kindness, love, loyalty, or possibly charm. *RSV* treats the first phrase as an example of an objective genitive (see *GK* 128h): so, "The desire (of others) *for* a man", that is, his desirability or **What is desired** in him (so also Barucq). This is not impossible, but it offers no parallelism to the second line. *JB* and *REB*, on the other hand, take *ḥesed* here to be a quite different word having the same form which occurs also in 14:34, meaning "disgrace" or "humiliation": so *REB*, "Greed is a disgrace to a man". (This interpretation was already put forward by Rabbi Levi ben Gershom [Ralbag], and in modern times by Greenstone; compare also van der Ploeg.) This has the advantage of providing a reasonable parallelism: both lines then affirm that poverty is no disgrace. If it is correct, the various emendations which have been proposed are unnecessary. **a liar**: elsewhere in Proverbs (6:19; 14:5, 25; 19:9; 21:28) this word (*kāzāb*) is used exclusively to designate a perjured witness. If this is implied here the point of this line is that it is better to remain poor than to seek to gain an advantage by perjury.

23. The first line of this verse has parallels elsewhere in these chapters: 10:27; 14:27; 22:4. 16:6 to some extent parallels the second line in asserting that "by the fear of Yahweh a man avoids evil" (*rā'*, here **harm**). But the Hebrew of this line (from **he who has it** to **by harm** – there are only the usual two lines in the Hebrew) is difficult. A literal translation might be "and a satisfied (one) spends the night (and is) not visited by harm". *RSV*'s **he who has it** is lacking in the Hebrew and is interpretation rather than translation. Nevertheless with some reservations most recent commentators (Scott, Barucq, McKane, Plöger; also *REB*) also suppose an impersonal subject to be implied – thus, for example, Ringgren, "a man sleeps satisfied . . ."; McKane, "and one passes the night replete. . . ." This is probably better than unsupported emendations such as that of Toy.

24. This verse is almost identical with 26:15, which forms one of a group of four (26:13–16) about the **sluggard**. The lazy person was evidently regarded as a warning to others, several of the proverbs in these chapters affirming that he is destined for poverty and actual want; but also, as here (and also in 22:13; 26:13–15) he was a figure of fun. This proverb is obviously an exaggeration: a vivid caricature of the sluggard's lack of energy – or perhaps more precisely of his tendency to fall suddenly asleep; compare the "deep sleep" of v. 15 and the reference to his exhaustion in 26:15.

25. On the **scoffer** (*lēṣ*) see on 1:22; on the **simple** (*petî*) see on 1:4. The difference between the two is that the first is incorrigible, while the latter is teachable, open to the influence of others whether good or bad. The first line states that when the *petî* sees that the way of life of the *lēṣ* gets him into trouble (**Strike** may refer to punishment for a crime [see, for example, Dt. 25:1–3] or simply to an "unofficial" thrashing), he will learn his lesson.

The point of the verse taken as a whole is not, however, entirely clear. A parallelism is clearly intended between the two lines: **Strike/reprove**; **scoffer/man of understanding** (*nābôn*); **learn prudence/gain knowledge**. For a perfect parallelism, however, one would expect the first line to end with something like ". . . and he will not profit by it": in other words, the *lēṣ* does not learn even if he suffers physical chastisement, but the *nābôn*, if he errs, needs only a verbal reproof to learn his lesson. The introduction of the *petî* into the equation is thus difficult to account for on this interpretation, and a different reading of the verse may be required. Gemser pointed out that **he** in the second line could refer not to the *nābôn* but to the *petî* of the first line, and this suggestion has been adopted by Plöger: so the *petî*, who can learn from the fate of the *lēṣ*, can also learn (perhaps even more?) from seeing even a "man of understanding" admonished for a fault.

26. To honour or show respect to one's parents was for an

Israelite a fundamental duty enshrined in the Decalogue (Exod. 20:12; Dt. 5:16). Yet several proverbs (20:20; 28:24; 30:11 in addition to the present one) attest the fact that this duty was by no means always observed. Some scholars have, however, contested the usually accepted meanings of the verbs in the first line. The verb *šdd* (piel; *RSV* **does violence to**) was understood here by Thomas (*VT* Suppl. 3, 1955, p. 289) to be derived from a root otherwise unattested in Hebrew but found in the Arabic *sadada* meaning "to expel" or "to reject". This suggestion would make the parallelism between the two lines exact, and has been accepted by *JB* and *REB*, though none of the modern commentators accepts it without reservation. On the other hand, Driver (*ThZ* 11 [1955], pp. 372–3) connected the two verbs in a different parallelism: he associated the first with Arabic *ṣadda*, "to silence (by striking on the mouth)", and the second (*yabrîaḥ*, *RSV* **chases away**) with Arabic *barraḥa*, meaning "to afflict". If Thomas is right, the verse probably refers to an adult son who takes over the family property which his aged parents are unable any longer to manage and, with no sense of shame or respect (on the combination of the two verbs **causes shame** and **brings reproach** see on 13:5), evicts them. If Driver is right, both lines refer more generally to violence committed by the son against his parents. But it is doubtful whether either of these interpretations is necessary, since there seems to be no absolute need for an exact parallelism, and *RSV*'s translation makes perfectly good sense.

27. The form of this verse, which begins with an imperative and an address by a father to a son (**my son**, *b^enî*, occurs nowhere else in 10:1–22:16), is unmistakably that of the formal Instruction (compare, for example, 1:8), but it has an unique feature: in order to suggest the disastrous consequences of failure to take the father's instruction to heart, it ironically tells him to go ahead and *be* inattentive. This kind of irony occurs nowhere else in chapters 1–9 or indeed anywhere in the Book of Proverbs. **only to stray** (*lišgōt*): better, "straying" (see *GK* 114 o).

Some commentators, unable to accept the verse as ironical and alleging a grammatical awkwardness in the use of the infinitive *lišgôt*, have regarded the text with suspicion; and several proposals have been made for its correction. The most plausible of these are those based on the LXX's "A son who ceases . . . will stray . . .". The emendations needed to produce a Hebrew text on this basis would be the repointing of the imperative *ḥ^adal* (**Cease**) as the qal participle, the emendation of *lišgôt* to the imperfect *yišgeh*, "will stray", and the change of *b^enî* to *bēn*, "a son", together with the removal of the last of these to stand at the beginning of the verse. Many commentators, however, probably rightly, retain MT.

This verse may be understood as a comment on the awful example of the wicked and impious son of v. 26, made by an editor who collected these proverbs to form a body of educational, that is, instructional, material.

28. devours: more precisely, "swallows". This is the usual meaning of this verb (*bāla'*), and, if this meaning is retained, **devours iniquity** presumably means something like "gets pleasure from iniquity". But there are no other clear examples of this metaphor, and several commentators have suggested the emendation of *y^eballa'* to *yabbîa'*, "pours out" (compare 1:23; 15:2, and especially 15:28, "the mouth of the wicked pours out evil things"). Others postulate the existence of another verb *bāla'* cognate with an Arabic verb, which would mean "communicate" or "spread", or possibly "afflict" (see McKane for details). This is accepted by *KB*[3]. Such a meaning would be more appropriate than "devour", as in these proverbs the **mouth** is frequently – and almost always – the organ of speech rather than of ingestion.

29. Condemnation: this word (*š^epāṭîm*), literally "judgements", occurs almost exclusively in Exodus and Ezekiel, and always refers to actions – mainly, but not always, punitive – of God himself (occasionally of human beings at God's direction). Its counterpart here, however – *mah^alūmôt*, *RSV* **flogging**, literally "blows" (compare 18:6) – clearly refers to punishment inflicted by human beings. The verse may thus be saying that the punishment for **scoffers** and **fools** respectively are of different orders: God punishes scoffers, man (perhaps less drastically?) punishes fools. But LXX (*mastiges*, "whips") seems to have read not *š^epāṭîm* but *š^ebāṭîm*, the plural of *šēbeṭ*, "rod, stick", a word which occurs frequently in these proverbs and is stated in 26:3 to be appropriate "for the back of fools", a phrase identical with that used in the first line of this verse. This reading would make a good parallelism between the two lines, though it is curious that nowhere else in Proverbs is it used in the plural. There is thus a balance of probability between MT and the proposed emendation. The majority of commentators accept the emendation and also *REB* and *JB*, but Barucq and McKane retain MT. That the *k^esîl* (**fool**) is not merely a harmless idiot but constitutes a menace to society and so deserves punishment is stated several times in these proverbs (see on 17:12).

CHAPTER 20

This chapter is characterized by a variety of both forms and themes. Proverbs with antithetical parallelism are outnumbered by other literary forms which include the interrogatory sentence (vv. 6, 9, 24), indirect speech (vv. 9, 14, 22, 25), the admonitory imperative (vv. 13, 16, 19, 22) and the *'ašrê*-form (see on 3:13). The topics include observations on the human mind or heart (vv. 5, 9, 27), quarrelling (v. 3), the evils of drink (v. 1), laziness (vv. 4, 13), honesty and dishonesty in commerce (vv. 10, 14, 23) and others which occur elsewhere in these chapters. There are six Yahweh-proverbs (vv. 10, 12, 22, 23, 24, 27) and four proverbs about the king (vv. 2, 8, 26, 28). The next chapter also begins with three Yahweh-proverbs of which the first (v. 1) is also a royal proverb; and there is reason to suppose that 20:20 marks the beginning of a sub-group somewhat similar to 16:1–15 which was intended to show and expound the relationship between Yahweh and the king and which extended as far as 21:4 (see below). There are also signs of composition in vv. 7–9 and 8–12.

1. More detailed warnings against drunkenness are found in 23:19–21; 23:29–35; 31:4–5. In this verse **Wine** and **strong drink** (perhaps "beer") are vividly personified as drinking companions whose company is best avoided. **a mocker**: Hebrew *lēṣ*, usually rendered in *RSV* by "scoffer". Plöger suggests that there may be a link here with 19:29, where the same word occurs. **a brawler** (*hōmeh*): this word is used of the seductress in 7:11 (*RSV* "loud") and of the woman Folly in 9:13 (*RSV* "noisy"). **is led astray**: perhaps better, "staggers": in Isa. 28:7 this verb (*šāgāh*) is used of drunkards reeling under the influence of drink. **is not wise**: the Hebrew may mean either that a wise person does not get drunk or that a drunken person behaves stupidly.

2. The first line of this verse is a variant of 19:12a, which uses a different word of the king's anger. Here *'êmāh*, **dread wrath**, is, literally, "terror": that is, the terror which the king inspires in others. On the question whether Israelite kings had arbitrary power over their subjects, and on the social background of these "royal proverbs", see on 16:14. Compare also 14:35; 16:15. **provokes him to anger**: for another possible meaning of this difficult verb (*hit-'abbēr*) see on 14:16. *REB* has "one who ignores it puts his life in jeopardy". **forfeits his life**: on this meaning of the verb *ḥāṭā'* see on 8:36.

3. This is one of a number of proverbs (compare 15:18; 17:14; 18:6) which speak of the need for harmonious relations within the community and the folly of stirring up **strife** (this word, *rîb*, may mean either simply "quarrelling" or "lawsuits"). **keep aloof**: this word (*šebet*) may be either the infinitive construct of *yāšab*, "to sit, dwell" (but also "remain", and so here, with **from** (*min-*) "avoid"), or a verbal noun from *šābat*, "to cease" or "to desist". The view that here it has the meaning of "to settle (a lawsuit – see on 18:18) is improbable. **an honour**: that is, such conduct will enhance a man's reputation. **will be quarrelling**: on this verb (*hitgalla'*) see on 17:14; 18:1.

4. Like 10:5 which refers to the "son who sleeps in harvest", this proverb is a warning not to follow the example of the agricultural worker who fails through indolence to provide for his livelihood. The **autumn** (*ḥorep*) in Palestine, the season following the early rains in October to November, is the time to **plough** and sow the seed for the next crop. Since no reference is made here to sowing, the meaning may be that the sluggard *does* sow – otherwise he would hardly expect a crop – but does not take the trouble to prepare the ground properly first. At any rate, when he does **seek at harvest** – that is, expect a crop the following year at harvest-time – he will **have nothing** (literally, "and nothing" – compare 13:4).

5. Compare 18:4. This proverb may be no more than a statement that a clever person can discover the plans or plots of others; but the word here rendered by **purpose** (*'ēṣāh*) may also denote something like "wisdom" (compare 8:14; 21:30). If this is what is meant, **deep water** may, as McKane suggests, refer to the profundity rather than the secrecy of a person's thoughts. Plöger suggests that two distinct kinds of wisdom may be referred to here: one which is profound but not easily made accessible to others, and one which can communicate itself without difficulty. This might be interpreted as an assertion that practical wisdom is superior to theoretical thinking; but Plöger is perhaps reading too much into the proverb. However, it is quite possible that it has been intended from the first to be tantalizingly obscure and so to provoke thought.

6. The first line of this disillusioned proverb is susceptible of several interpretations. Most modern commentators correctly understand the line more or less in the same way as *RSV*, though they vary slightly in their understanding of *ḥesed* (**loyalty**), some preferring such renderings as "kindness", "goodness", "friendship". However this may be, the second line makes it clear what is the point of the proverb: that although many men may make protestations of friendship (or loyalty), very few are in fact trustworthy (*'îš 'ᵉmûnîm*, **a faithful man**; cf. 18:24). The question **who can find?** demands a negative reply: the meaning is that such people are rarely – if at all – to be found (compare 31:10).

Other interpretations of the first line – "Many a man is *called* a man of kindness" (Oesterley, following Targ., Pesh. and Vulg., which apparently read the consonants of the verb *yiqrā'* [**proclaims**] as the passive (niphal) *yiqqārē'*); "Many a man *meets* a man of kindness" (*qārā'* also has this meaning – not only make a less effective parallelism but also fail to account for the Hebrew *ḥasdô*, "*his* kindness".

7–9. It is possible that these three verses have been placed here as commenting in various ways on the pessimism about human nature expressed in v. 6. V. 7 with its enthusiastic praise of the **righteous man** may be taken as an affirmation that such people do exist – though it could also be taken to imply that they are exceptional. V. 8, on the other hand, confidently affirms that under a righteous king **evil** will always be discovered and dealt with. V. 9 is a sober reflection on the fact that no one can claim to be untainted by sin. This interpretation of these verses is not necessarily incompatible with the view expressed below about the composition of vv. 8–12; on the contrary, this "overlapping" may be a pointer to different stages of composition in these chapters.

7. There has been much discussion of the syntactical relationship between the two lines of this verse; but this is probably simply a case of the phenomenon known as *casus pendens*: "As for him who walks . . ." (see *GK* 143a).

According to the order of the words of the first line a literal translation of it would be "One who walks in his integrity *as* a righteous man", the final word (*ṣaddîq*) defining "integrity" more precisely. **blessed are**: see on 3:13. **after him**: this probably reflects the notion of family solidarity, in which future generations share in the fortunes or the character of the father or ancestor (compare 13:22; 14:11, 26).

8–12. These five proverbs appear to have been arranged in a group centred on the two Yahweh-proverbs, vv. 10 and 12. Their mutual relationship can be understood in a variety of ways. They speak both of the impossibility of concealing sins from God, and of the close relationship which exists between the king and Yahweh: the king's ability to see and judge human beings is, as it were, a reflection of Yahweh's own ability, as their creator, to do so. Vv. 8 and 12 both refer to the "seeing eye" – first as a peculiar gift conferred by Yahweh on the king, and secondly in more general terms as an organ created by Yahweh and given to *all* human beings. (It may also be noted that vv. 10 and 12 are also linked by the phrase *gam-šᵉnêhem*, "both of them", which occurs in both verses.)

Vv. 9–11 enlarge on the theme: v. 9 in its present position can be taken to mean that in view of the king's special gift it is dangerous to be complacent about one's own freedom from guilt; and v. 11 further remarks that it is dangerous to attempt to conceal one's own true character. V. 10 may at first seem to be unrelated to its context; but its relevance lies in the implication that God sees and punishes dishonesty even if man does not.

These verses, then, are among other things concerned with the power of *discernment*, both human and divine. The king with his special gift *sees* into the hearts of his subjects (v. 8); but he is dependent on God, who himself does not fail to *discern* dishonesty (v. 10). Between these verses comes v. 9, which points out the inability of *all* human beings (including the king?) to *discern* their own motives and character. V. 11 is also about *discernment*: human character is revealed – whether to God or to other human beings is not stated – by a person's actions. V. 12, which is clearly linked with v. 8 – the two verses form a framework to this whole group of proverbs – refers to the *ear* and the *eye*, the *organs* of *discernment*, which God has given to his creatures. It is not entirely clear why the editor who collected and arranged these verses chose to place them in precisely their present order, but it is clear that there is an interplay here between statements about the all-discerning nature of Yahweh and the *relative* and partial powers of discernment which he has given to his creatures.

8. This proverb belongs to the category of those which express a simple faith in both the impartiality and the effectiveness of the royal administration of justice (compare 16:10, 13; 20:28). **winnows all evil**: v. 26a uses the same expression about the punitive actions of the king, who is there specified as "wise" (LXX has "wise" here also, but this is almost certainly an addition, though the king's wisdom is *implied* here). In v. 26 also the object of the verb is not **evil** (*ra'*) but "evil persons" (*rešā'îm*). **winnows**: that is, "sifts". This is an agricultural term meaning to sift the grain from the chaff. It has, however, been observed that the primary meaning of this verb (*zārāh*, piel) is "scatter" – the king could thus be said to "scatter" or drive away evil (or, "a wicked person", since *ra'* also has this meaning). But the addition of **with his eyes**, which refers to the belief that kings had a special God-given ability to discern the truth (compare 1 Kg. 3:9–12, 16–28), makes this interpretation less probable.

9. It is a commonplace of ancient Near Eastern thought, and especially of its wisdom literature, that all men and women are morally imperfect – compare, for example, 1 Kg. 8:46; Ps. 51:5 (Heb. 7); 143:2; Job 4:17; the Sumerian poem known as "Man and His God" (Kramer, 1955, pp. 170–82 and lines 101–3 of that poem; *ANET*, p. 590 [Supplement, p. 154]; the Egyptian *Amenemope* XVIII, 19:18 (*ANET*, p. 423). The thought was not a purely abstract one but was prompted by reflection on the problem of theodicy: if all human beings are sinful, all deserve divine punishment. All this is taken for granted in this proverb. But it was difficult to reconcile with – and perhaps was a reaction to, and in a sense a criticism of – the neat polarization of human beings into two categories which is so frequent in Proverbs and in the other literatures: the righteous, who will be divinely blessed and rewarded, and the wicked, who are doomed to destruction. It is with those who *claim*, or even genuinely believe, that they belong to the first category that this proverb, like 16:2, is concerned.

10. Compare v. 23 and see on 11:1. **diverse measures**: the Hebrew has "ephah and ephah". Both this expression and *'eben wā'eben* (**Diverse weights**, literally "A stone and a stone") occur in the law of Dt. 25:13–16, where it is explained that they refer to the possession and use of "a large and a small" weight or measure, enabling the dishonest merchant to cheat both when buying and selling goods. The ephah was a standard quantity of dry goods and also, as here, the receptacle or "measure" employed.

11. This verse presents some difficulties with regard to the

Hebrew. First, the word **Even** (*gam*) is placed in such a position that a literal translation of the first line would be "Even by his acts a child makes himself known". Some commentators consider *gam* to have been misplaced; others (most recently Plöger) follow Ewald in taking the word *ma'ᵃlālâw*, **his acts**, to be cognate here with a root *'ll* which may denote a child's play: so, "Even in his play . . .". Secondly, with regard to the second line, it has been suggested that **what he does** (*po'ᵒlô*) should be rendered "his character" (see *KB*³). Thirdly, the literal meaning of this line is "whether (*'im*) **what he does** is pure *or* (*wᵉ'im*) is right (*yāšār*)". Some commentators propose the emendation of *yāšār* to *rāšā'*, "wicked" in order to obviate this apparent contrast between two synonymous adjectives.

Whatever may be the correctness of these proposals, the *general* sense of the verse is clear enough. Its purpose – that is, the point which it is intended to make – is, however, more difficult to discern. It appears on the surface simply to make an observation about children: how a child may turn out can already be recognized (*yitnakker*, **makes himself known**) from his early behaviour. This notion, according to Plöger, runs contrary to the more usual belief expressed in Proverbs (especially chapters 1–9) that education can *form* a person's character (*na'ar*, **child**, can mean either a child or a young man). On the other hand, the proverb may be pointing to the *necessity* of the proper education of the young: a character formed early will determine the whole of a person's life.

However, it is probable that this verse is not primarily about children or young men. The use of the word **Even**, wherever it should be placed in the verse, points to an implied *a fortiori* argument: if even a child's character can be discerned from his behaviour, this is even more true of grown men and women.

12. The difficulty presented by this verse is not dissimilar to that of v. 11: ostensibly it simply states an incontrovertible fact; it is the underlying purpose of the statement that is difficult to discern. Some commentators (e.g. Wildeboer and Toy) supposed that the point implied is the same as that which is made explicitly in Ps. 94:9, where the psalmist, in reply to the boast of the wicked that God does not observe – and so, by implication, punish – their crimes (vv. 6–7), points out the absurdity of this claim by asking, "He who planted the ear, does he not hear? He who formed the eye, does he not see?". A similar interpretation of this verse would certainly fit the general tenor of this group of proverbs in its present form; but if the verse is viewed as an originally independent proverb it must be said that it gives no hint of such a meaning. It is more natural to assume that it means that **ear** and **eye** – the organs of human perception – ought to be put to the use for which their creator intended them. This interpretation still leaves the proverb open to more than one application, since eyes and ears can be used for more than one purpose. Of these interpretations the most probable, and one which is accepted by the majority of commentators, connects the verse with the many passages in Proverbs, not only in the Instructions of chapters 1–9 but also in the sentence literature (15:31; 18:15; 25:12), where it is through the use of eye and/or ear that a person, by paying attention to the teaching of the wise and to the path on which he walks, himself attains wisdom and prosperity. The purpose of this verse would then be to assert that it is Yahweh, who created both eye and ear, through whom true wisdom can be attained.

13. See on v. 4. Although this verse clearly belongs to the class of proverb which depicts the lazy worker and his fate, it has probably been placed here because, with its admonition to **open your eyes**, it has some affinities with both the theme and the language of vv. 8–12. The obvious verbal link is with vv. 8 and 12, and there is a closer link with the latter verse, if, as proposed above, that verse is concerned with the *proper use* of the eyes: since Yahweh made the eye to be used properly, the person who spends most of the daylight hours ignoring this divine gift is courting disaster. The sleeping sluggard may also be seen as one who, on the one hand, lacks the capacity for self-examination (compare v. 9) and, on the other hand, plainly reveals his character to others (compare v. 11). But the verse hardly has a structural place in the more tightly knit group of vv. 8–12, and is probably to be seen as making an additional comment on those verses.

come to poverty: more precisely, "lose your property" (or, "your inheritance") (niphal of *yāraš*). **and you will have plenty**: the verb is in the imperative, which gives the line a pithiness and directness characteristic of the popular proverb: "open your eyes, have plenty of bread". The addition of "and" to the Hebrew text as proposed by some commentators is unnecessary and somewhat pedantic.

14. The situation envisaged here is the bargaining over goods offered for sale, for which there was traditionally no fixed price. The astute purchaser pretends that the goods in question are worthless or of inferior quality, and so forces the price down; but once out of the hearing of the vendor he congratulates himself on bringing off a good bargain. This may be just a humorous observation on one aspect of life, or may be intended as a warning to the simple farmer not to be taken in by crafty merchants who travel about looking to buy the farmers' surplus crops. It evokes a vivid picture while employing as few words as possible. **but when he goes away** (*wᵉʾōzēl lô*): on the construction see *GK* 119s.

15. Apart from the first word *yēš* (**There is**), which, though not strictly a verb, often functions in this way, this verse contains no verb (**are** in the second line is not represented in the Hebrew). This leaves the verse open to a variety of interpretations; but that of *RSV* is the most probable. The imagery employed to commend wisdom (the equivalent of **knowledge**) by presenting it as of greater value than gold, silver and jewels is a commonplace of the book (compare 3:13–15; 8:10–11; 16:16). **lips of knowledge** (the same phrase occurs in 14:7): that is, "informed speech" (*REB*). There is here, as in the comparable passages mentioned above, no intention to disparage wealth, but rather to put forward the ability to speak effectively as the first priority – the rest, as is stated clearly in those passages and elsewhere, will then follow.

There is: the view of Frankenberg, Toy and others that this word (*yēš*) is here treated as a noun meaning "property, possessions" is improbable: see also on 8:21 (compare also 13:23). **costly stones**: this word (*pᵉnînîm*), which occurs also in 8:11 (compare also 3:15), probably means "red coral", which was highly prized. **jewel**: this word (*kᵉlî*) can denote any kind of material object, for example tool, weapon, cup, musical instrument. There is no particular reason to suppose that it means "jewel" here; but since it is **precious**, "ornament" may be an appropriate translation. The intention is, however, to denote something superlative: compared with the other things mentioned in the verse, effective speech is the most valuable possession of all. Plöger, probably correctly, considers that the verse has been placed here as a comment on verse 14: that which is truly most valuable cannot be obtained "over the counter" or through sordid deals.

16. See on 6:1; 11:15; 17:18, where a comparable situation is envisaged; compare also 22:26–7; 27:13. Three persons were involved in this kind of transaction: the **stranger** or **foreigner** (on the meaning of these terms see on 6:1) whose credit is being guaranteed; the guarantor; and the guarantee or creditor. This proverb, in the form of an admonition, is a warning addressed not to the guarantor but to the guarantee, who in the case of default by the "stranger" may find that the guarantor does not have the means to fulfil his self-imposed obligation (compare 22:27). The advice given is that the guarantee should obtain some security at the time of the transaction (**hold him in pledge**) by impounding the guarantor's **garment** (compare Dt. 24:10–14, 17 on the practice of using garments as security for loans).

Take: this form (*l^eqaḥ*) of the imperative of *lāqaḥ* is unusual but not unique (see *GK* 66g). The almost identical 27:13 has the more usual form *qaḥ*. **a man's garment**: Hebrew has simply "*his* garment". **foreigners**: Qere has *nokriyyāh*, "a foreign woman", perhaps influenced by the frequent reference to such women in chapters 1–9. Kethib's masculine plural *nokrîm* is to be preferred (see also on 27:13).

17. This verse is linked with v. 16 by wordplay. Its first word in the Hebrew, *'ārēb*, **sweet** (a rare word of which there is only one other occurrence in the Old Testament: Ca. 2:14, where it describes the voice of the beloved as "pleasant") echoes the *'ārab* ("has given surety") – a quite different verb – of v. 16. Two verses later (v. 19) yet another verb *'ārab* occurs in the hithpael form *hit'ārēb* ("associate with"). This triple occurrence of *'rb* suggests a deliberate grouping, even though there is no thematic connection between the three verses and there is no occurrence in v. 18.

The thought of this verse is expressed more fully in Job 20:12–16. **Bread gained by deceit** (*leḥem šāqer*): *RSV* here follows many commentators in the interpretation of this phrase. On this view, **bread** (which frequently has the wider meaning of food or material sustenance or even livelihood – compare, for example, 9:5; 12:9, 11; 20:13) here presumably stands for the material profit which can be obtained by devious means. However, in 4:17 (and compare Job 20:12) it is their wicked deeds themselves which give pleasure to the wicked; and this is probably the meaning of the phrase (literally, "bread of deceit") here. In any case this is a figurative way of expressing the axiom so characteristic of this book that the satisfaction gained by the wicked is shortlived.

18. This theme – the importance of taking advice if plans are to succeed – is also found in 11:14; 15:22 and 24:6, all of which are to a large extent variants of one another, sometimes using identical vocabulary (for example, *maḥašābôt*, **Plans**, occurs also in 15:22 and *taḥbūlôt*, **wise guidance**, also in 11:14 and 24:6; *tešû'āh*, "safety", "victory", occurs in 11:14 and 24:6) and sometimes using equivalents (for example, the abstract *be'ēṣāh*, **by counsel**, is synonymous with *berob- [berōb] yô'ēṣ*, "in an abundance of counsellors", 11:14 and 24:6 and *berob yô'aṣîm*, "with many advisers", in 15:22; *tikkôn*, **are established**, is equivalent to *tāqûm*, "succeed", in 15:22; *yippol*, "falls" in 11:14 corresponds to *hāpēr*, "go wrong", in 15:22). All these proverbs are of general import and refer to the circumstances of ordinary life rather than to political policies or military strategy, of which the authors of these proverbs would have had no knowledge or experience. This is true even of the reference to "making war", which occurs here and in 24:6, which is to be taken metaphorically of the struggle to succeed or survive in daily life (so Wildeboer, Oesterley, Gemser and Plöger; for a similar metaphor see, for example, Ps. 35:1; 56:1–2 [Heb. 2–3]; 120:7 etc.).

are established (*tikkôn*): on the use of a singular verb with a plural subject see *GK* 145k. **wise guidance** (*taḥbūlôt*): see on 1:5. **wage** (*'aśēh*, literally, "make", the imperative of *'āśāh*): it is not certain that the text is correct. The verse, together with several others, is lacking in LXX. The virtually equivalent line in 24:6 has *ta'aśeh*, "you can make". Some commentators follow Pesh. which has the passive: "war is made".

19. Although the two lines of this verse appear to have a common theme, the connection between them is not clear (*RSV*'s **therefore** is represented in the Hebrew only by *ū* ("and"). Another unusual feature of the verse is the use in the second line of the "prohibitive" form *lō'*, **Do not** (the same form as the "Thou shalt not" of the Decalogue and other "apodictic" laws) rather than the milder *'al* which introduces an admonition rather than a command – the usual form employed in these proverbs (the *lō'*-form occurs only in one other verse in Proverbs, in 22:24). This may suggest that this line is a quotation from a more authoritarian or legislative tradition, quoted to reinforce the statement made in the first line.

The first line is a variant of 11:13a (see the note there on *rākîl*, **gossiping**). Its point may be that the gossiper or chatterer, however innocent his intention may be, is dangerous – and therefore to be avoided – because he or she inevitably ends by blurting out information which has been made in confidence.

The meaning of the word rendered in *RSV* by **one who speaks**

foolishly (*pōtēh śᵉpātayim*) is uncertain. The verb may be the participle of the common verb *pātāh* "to be simple or foolish": the literal meaning would be "one who is foolish with his lips". But Gemser, followed by *KB*[3], postulates the existence of another verb *pātāh*, attested in Mishnaic Hebrew and meaning "to open". The meaning might then be "chatterer", possibly with the same implication as with *rākîl* in the first line (*REB* has "talebearer").

20–21:4: Of these fifteen verses, no fewer than seven (vv. 22, 23, 24, 27; 21:1, 2, 3) are Yahweh-proverbs, all of which with one exception are arranged in clusters of three. There are also three royal proverbs (vv. 26, 28; 21:1) in the group, of which one (21:1) is also a Yahweh-proverb. There is some reason to suppose that this grouping is not accidental. The intention of this arrangement seems to be to explore three relationships: between Yahweh and man; between Yahweh and the king; and between the king and other men.

The first subsection (vv. 20–25) is concerned with the first of these relationships. After an assurance given respectively in vv. 20 and 21 that crimes will not go unpunished (**lamp will be put out**; **will . . . not be blessed**), v. 22 points out that it is Yahweh whose function it is to avenge crime, and that he can be relied on eventually to assist its victims. A further statement in v. 23 that he hates dishonest practices is followed in v. 24 by a proverb which if taken by itself might seem to be a denial of human free will and so as relieving men and women of moral responsibility for their crimes, but which in this context is probably intended to have the force of a second admonition (compare v. 22) to leave the punishment of crime in the hands of Yahweh, who alone understands human motives and controls human destiny. In the light of this, v. 25 acts as a warning not to make rash and thoughtless vows which may prove impossible to fulfil to this all-seeing and all-powerful God.

The second sub-section (vv. 26–21:4) turns to the position of the king, both with regard to Yahweh and to his fellow-men (compare this sequence with the juxtaposition of 16:1–9 and 16:10–15). V. 26 speaks of the king as given wisdom to see and punish the wicked; but v. 27 points out that it is Yahweh who sees into men's hearts – thus by implication relativizing the superiority of the king, since he is presumably also subject to this scrutiny. V. 28 insists that the king's position depends on his loyalty and faithfulness. Vv. 29 and 30 seem at first sight to lie outside this sequence of ideas, but v. 29

could be seen as commending the wise king (compare v. 26) who gains additional wisdom (compare 1:5) through a lifetime of experience, while v. 30 (possibly: see below) draws attention to an aspect of punishment – either at the hands of Yahweh or of the king – as purgative, in contrast to the destructive aspect in which it is the king's duty to eliminate the irretrievably wicked (but see below).

21:1 reverts to the theme of the subordination of the king to the direction of Yahweh, and 21:2, like 20:27, stresses Yahweh's scrutiny of the human heart (again including, by implication, that of the king). 21:3, on Yahweh's insistence on righteousness and justice, is also applicable to the king as well as to other men, as is also 21:4, against human pride. Finally, it should be noted that a further indication of the unity of the passage as a coherent collection of once independent proverbs into which Yahweh-proverbs have been inserted, is the repetition of the word **lamp** in the first and last verses of this group and also in the middle: the lamp (*nēr*) of the wicked in 20:20, the lamp (*nēr*) of Yahweh in 20:27 and the lamp or light (*nīr*, if the text is correct) of the wicked again in 21:4. This group of verses is less closely knit than 16:1–15, but the intertwining of the three themes mentioned above, involving Yahweh, the king and men in general, is unmistakable.

20. See on 19:26. To curse another person in the world of Israel and of other ancient Near Eastern peoples was not merely to wish that person harm but to invoke or set in motion forces which would injure or destroy him (compare, for example, Josh. 24:9–10; Ps. 62:4 [Heb. 5]; Neh. 13:2; Job 24:18). In the Covenant Code (Exod. 21:17) and in Leviticus (20:9) the penalty for cursing one's own father and/or mother was death. Here, however, it is to be understood that the source of the punishment is not human but divine: it is Yahweh who will himself impose the "death sentence". No reason is given why a man should curse his parents; but see on v. 21 below.

his lamp will be put out: see on 13:9. **utter**: *RSV* follows some Versions and the majority of commentators in reading the Kethib *ʾĕšôn*, literally "pupil (of the eye)", which is generally taken here – though without really adequate explanation – to mean "centre, middle": that is, the middle or darkest part of the night (so Vulg., *in mediis tenebris*). Qere, however, has *ʾĕšûn*, "time": so "in a time of darkness". A similar problem arises in 7:9.

21. This proverb, although no doubt originally independent, may have been placed here to illuminate v. 20 by describing the kind of person who might curse his parents. **inheritance** (*naḥᵃlāh*) here means "inheritable property" as in 19:14 (*naḥᵃlat 'ābôt*, literally "property inherited from ancestors"). It is not certain what is implied here by **gotten hastily** (*mᵉbōhelet*, Qere; the meaning of Kethib's *mᵉbōḥelet* is obscure), but the verse may refer to the premature acquisition by a son of the family farm from his parents, perhaps by some fraudulent means. Such a man would be one who cursed his parents. 13:11 and 28:20 also refer to wealth quickly amassed, but without specific reference to a *naḥᵃlāh*.

22. This verse makes an appropriate comment on vv. 20 and 21, both of which give assurances that sin and crime will in the end receive due punishment. It affirms that such punishment will be inflicted by Yahweh, who will also right the wrongs (*yš'*, hiphil; *RSV* **help**) from which the victims have suffered, and on this account gives a warning against their taking the law into their own hands, no doubt with the general good of the community in mind. The same thought appears also to lie behind 24:29 (compare also Dt. 32:35–6). The point is, however, quite different from that of 24:17–18 and 25:21–2 (compare also Lev. 19:18; Job 31:29–30), where there is no thought that aggressors should be punished but, on the contrary, a divine requirement that one should desire the wellbeing of one's enemies.

In general there is agreement in the Old Testament about the necessity and desirability of punishing sin and crime; but it may seem at first sight that there are two views about the direct agent of such punishment. The Old Testament laws prescribe the trial and conviction of offenders and their due punishment at the hands of society (Exod. 21:23–5; Lev. 24:19–20 and Dt. 19:21 preserve the principle of exact retribution, but regulate it by bringing it under the rule of law). The view that punishment should be left to the direct action of God is characteristic of Proverbs but was also found outside Israel (for example, in *Amenope* XXI 22:1–8 – *ANET*, p. 424). Whether it was due to the influence of the wider wisdom tradition or to a refinement of native Israelite theology is disputed.

It should not be supposed, however, that the authors of these proverbs regarded direct divine punishment as an *alternative* to the due processes of law: these proverbs contain many references to legal processes, e.g. 12:17; 14:5, 25; 16:10; 17:15, 23; 18:17; 19:5, 9, 28; 20:8; 21:15, 28; 29:4, 14. This verse must be presumed to refer to offences which could not for some reason be dealt with by the judges, or to cases where the offender had been wrongfully acquitted. This could not, however, be tolerated if the harmony of the community was to be maintained; and although immediate redress was not to be expected, it was believed that it would eventually come, for those who were able with patience to **wait for the Lord**.

23. This verse is a variant of v. 10 above; see also 11:1a. On **Diverse weights** see v. 10. **false scales**: this phrase is rendered in 11:1 (*RSV*) by "A false balance". **abomination to the Lord**: see on 6:16. **not good**: see on 16:29.

24. This verse employs the metaphor of human life as a journey which is prevalent in the book. The first line expresses the belief that human destiny is controlled by God (compare 16:1–9); but it is also important to note that it is precisely identical with Ps. 37:23. In the context of the psalm, Yahweh's control is seen as entirely beneficial: he provides his creatures with protection and guidance, enabling them to "walk" in the way which will be for their ultimate benefit. Nothing is said there about their ignorance of what is going on. This verse, however (taken by itself; see on 20:20–21:4 for its function in its present context) appears to understand the matter differently. The first line is probably a quotation of a familiar aphorism (which also appears in Ps. 37:23) on which the second line is a negative comment (the interrogative form beginning with **how** (*mah*) . . . ? frequently has the force of a statement that something is impossible – compare, for example, Num. 23:8; 1 Sam. 10:27; Job 9:2; 25:4; 31:1). Yahweh is seen as concealing from men the direction in which he is leading them, so that the significance and consequences of their actions (**steps**) are hidden from them: their lives do not make sense, and they have a sense of totally lacking control of them. McKane sees the verse as an expression of faith, countering what he sees as the general view of Proverbs that **man** is his own master (compare Prov. 14:8, which also uses the phrase **understand his way**, but asserts that the clever person is quite capable of doing this). However, it is perhaps more likely to be a despairing protest against the contrary dogma which reduces man's role to nothing and so oppresses and bewilders the author.

are ordered by the Lord: the Hebrew has simply "are (from) Yahweh". **how then can man . . .?**: the Hebrew is emphatic: "but (as for) man, how can he . . . ?". **understand** (*yābîn*): some MSS have *yākîn*, "establish", "order". If this is correct, it may slightly strengthen the sense; but there is no reason to reject MT.

25. The syntax of this verse is difficult, perhaps the sign of a corrupt text; but the sense is reasonably clear. This is a warning against hastily or rashly making **vows** to Yahweh which when the time comes it may prove impossible to carry out. Such a vow was a promise to consecrate to Yahweh part of one's own possessions in return for receiving some favour from him, pronouncing them to be **holy**. The thing promised might be a sacrificial animal or some other kind of sacrifical offering (so Lev. 7:16–17; 22:18–23); but it could also be money, a house or a piece of land (Lev. 27:11–25). The vow might be made hastily or **rashly**, for example by a person in danger or distress who was not calculating the cost but would promise anything in order to be restored to safety. To make such a vow was a purely voluntary act (Dt. 23:22; Ec. 5:5 [Heb. 4]), but once it was made the vow could not be recalled and must be fulfilled (Num. 30:2 [Heb. 3]; Dt. 23:21; Ec. 5:4 [Heb. 3]): it could thus be a **snare** or danger to the person who had made it.

say rashly: the meaning of this word (*yāla'*) is uncertain, as also is its form. LXX has no verb of speech here: "It is a snare to a man to consecrate part of his property hastily (*tachu*)". The word may be an imperfect form of a verb cognate with Arabic *laġā*, "to babble or talk wildly". The only – probable – other occurrence in the Old Testament is in Job 6:3.

to reflect: this verb (*biqqēr*) elsewhere means to seek, to examine or to enquire. *REB* has "have second thoughts".

26. This verse is a variant of v. 8. The reference to the **wheel** in the second line, however, has been the subject of much debate. The phrase *wayyāšeb ᶜᵃlêhem 'ôpān*, literally, "and causes the wheel to return on them" (*RSV* **and drives the wheel over them**) has been interpreted variously as referring to some form of torture (not clearly specified – see Snell, 1959, pp. 503–507) or to the turning of the "wheel of fortune" (so Driver, *Bib.* 32 [1951], p. 184; so also *REB*). But several older commentaries (Delitzsch, Wildeboer, Frankenberg, Toy; more recently only Thomas, *JJS* 15 [1964], pp. 155–6, Franzmann, 1991, pp. 121–3 and Plöger) rightly saw that the line simply continues the imagery of the first line: as is clear from Isa. 28:27–8, winnowing – that is, the use of wind to blow away the useless chaff, leaving the kernel of the grain – was carried out after the ears of grain had been pressed down or crushed by the wheels of a threshing sledge which separated the one from the other.

The verb *hēšîb* (*RSV* **drives**, literally "causes to return") may refer to a repetition of the process. On the use of the waw consecutive imperfect here see *GK* 111 r, u. The proposal to emend *'ôpān*, **wheel** to *'ônām*, "their sin", and so to render the line by "and brings their sin upon them" is feeble and unnecessary.

27. The thought of this verse bears a close resemblance to 15:3, 11; 16:2; 21:2: that is, it is impossible for man to conceal his private thoughts and motives from God. But the terms employed are variable: according to 21:2 (compare also 15:11) Yahweh "weighs the hearts (*libbôt*)"; in 16:2 he "weighs spirits (*rûḥôt*)"; here he searches a person's **innermost parts**. There is, however, room for somewhat different interpretations of the verse. In the first line it is clear that **the lamp of the Lord** is identified with the **spirit** (literally, *nᵉšāmāh*, "breath") **of man** which he breathed into man's nostrils to make him a living being (Gen. 2:7 – but *nᵉšāmāh* is probably the equivalent here of *rûaḥ*, "spirit"). But it is not clear whether the purpose of the searching lamp is to reveal man's secret thoughts to God or to man himself. According to the more probable interpretation, man's breath or **spirit** functions as a **lamp** inside men's body which enables *God* to penetrate its innermost recesses; but several commentators see the lamp as standing for the human conscience by which man sees his own true self. Support for this view has been sought, not very convincingly, in passages like Job 29:3; Ps. 18:28 [Heb. 29]; 119:105, where God shines a lamp on human beings to guide their steps; in any case this concept of "conscience" may be too modern. Plöger, however, suggests that the two interpretations are compatible and that both may be correct: God sees a man's true nature, but also reveals this knowledge to the man himself.

The proposal to emend *nēr*, **lamp** to *nōṣēr*, "watching over" (so "Yahweh watches over the spirit of man") on the analogy of 24:12 and Job 7:20 is unnecessary, as *MT* makes good sense. **innermost parts**: see on 18:8.

28. This proverb should probably be seen as one of those which express confidence in the conduct of kings rather than as merely expressing a pious hope. On **Loyalty and faithfulness** (*ḥesed weᵓᵉmet*) see on 3:3. As in that verse, these are partly personified and are regarded as divinely appointed powers which guard the king (compare Ps. 89:24 [Heb. 25]). *BHS* accepts a proposed emendation of the plural verb *yiṣṣᵉrû*, **preserve**, to the singular *yiṣṣôr*, making the king the subject of this line as well as of the second (see below): "The king guards loyalty and faithfulness". But this is hardly necessary.

A literal translation of the second line would be "and he establishes his throne by faithfulness" (*ḥesed* again). Here LXX has "righteousness", perhaps implying Hebrew *ṣedeq* or *ṣᵉdāqāh* (compare 16:12).

29. At first sight this verse may seem to do no more than to make the trite observation that youth and old age have each its own advantages or characteristics. More probably, however, it is intended to assert the superiority of the latter over the former. (No distinction is intended between the terms **glory** [*tip'eret*] and **beauty** [*hādār*]: these terms are virtually identical in meaning [compare, for example, their use interchangeably in Ezek. 16:12 and 16:14], as also is *ᵃṭārāh*, "crown" (17:6).

The real meaning of the verse is to be understood in the light of two other proverbs which have been considered above. On the one hand, in 17:6, as here, both youth and old age are said each to have their own honourable status: fathers are the "glory" (*tip'eret*) of their children as grandchildren are the "crown" of the aged. On the other hand, in 16:31, whose first line is almost identical in sense with the second line of the present verse, "A hoary head" (*śēbāh*, the same word as that rendered here by **grey hair**) is said to be in itself a "crown of glory" (*ᵃṭeret tip'eret*) because a happy longevity can only be obtained by a righteous life. So here it is implied that while physical **strength** (*kōaḥ*) is a splendid thing in youth, it does not last, whereas **grey hair** is the symbol of a more rewarding gift, which can only be obtained by a righteous life (or, perhaps, by experience in wisdom). In its present context, however, the verse may perhaps be intended as a comment on the preceding royal proverb (v. 28), implying that the wise ruler is the experienced one, possibly with the further implication that the young should learn from the old.

In the first line LXX has "wisdom" in place of MT's **strength**. But this is probably a reinterpretation of the text, commending the "wise young man", of whom Joseph is the pre-eminent example (see G. Bertram, 1957, p. 228).

30. The meaning of this verse is obscure, and some commentators regard the text as corrupt. The principal difficulty is the otherwise unattested word *tamrîq* (so Kethib; Qere *tamrûq*). This has frequently been taken to be the feminine singular (qal or hiphil) of the verb *māraq*, "to rub, polish" – so *RSV* **cleanse away**. However, apart from the anomaly of a singular verb with a plural subject, this would be the only use of the verb in a figurative sense, and the word is now generally regarded as a noun – thus, for example, "Blows that wound are a cleansing from evil". It has been associated with Akkadian *marāqu*, supposedly a medical term (so McKane; compare also Plöger). W. von Soden, however (1990, pp. 120–21), takes it and the whole verse in a quite different sense. According to him, *tamrîq* is a Hebraized form of an Old Aramaic word meaning an insult or a deliberate injury. He also takes *makkôt*, which normally means "blows" (*RSV* **strokes**) to mean "scars", repointing it as *mikwôt*, the plural of a term found in Lev. 13:24, 25, 28. He thus interprets the verse as a whole as meaning that a malicious injury leaves a permanent scar on the victim's innermost character (it should be noted that the verb in the second line in *RSV* is not represented in the Hebrew). It must be said, however, that von Soden does not deal satisfactorily with some of the other difficulties of the verse, and it must be concluded that no satisfactory solution to the difficulties has been found. If *RSV*, which represents the views of a number of scholars and also of *REB*, is correct, the verse presumably means that a severe beating has a salutary effect on the character of the victim. This would agree with the general view expressed in the wisdom literature of the ancient Near East and of a number of the proverbs in these chapters in particular, but the obscurity of the language in comparison with that of the comparable proverbs makes the interpretation very uncertain.

CHAPTER 21

This chapter contains a larger proportion of antithetical proverbs than the immediately preceding ones. The contrasts include those between wicked and righteous, rich and poor, and diligent and lazy. There are also three examples of comparative sentences (vv. 3, 9, 19). Two verses refer to women (vv. 9, 19).

On the connection of vv. 1–4 with the previous chapter see above on 20:20–21:4. Krispenz finds no such connection but, on the other hand, sees vv. 1–8 as a distinct group. She notes that the three words *'îš*, **man** (not apparent in *RSV* in the case of v. 8), *yāšār*, **right** and *derek*, **way** occur in both v. 2 and v. 8, and also that *mišpāṭ*, **justice/just** is found in both vv. 3 and 7 and *rᵉšā'îm*, **wicked**, in vv. 4 and 7. Vv. 1–3 are of course linked as Yahweh-proverbs, while *lēb*, **heart** is found in vv. 1, 2 and 4. A weak point in this supposed verbal network or "system" binding vv. 1–8 together is the fact that vv. 5 and 6 stand completely outside it, having no such verbal repetitions at all. Thematically, Krispenz sees the group as intended to show that the "ways" and the "heart" of man, that is, his deeds and his disposition, whether good or evil, are known and judged by Yahweh. This thesis would be more convincing if the supposed group ended with a Yahweh-proverb. In fact, after v. 3 Yahweh is not mentioned again until the final verses 30 and 31 (though see on v. 27). The fact that the chapter begins (vv. 1–3) and ends (vv. 30–31) with Yahweh-proverbs is probably to be accounted for as belonging to a somewhat different compositional scheme imposed on the material at some point in the development of the book (see further on v. 27 below).

1. In contrast with those proverbs (14:35; 16:14, 15; 19:12; 20:2) which taken by themselves appear to attribute unrestricted power to the king, this verse, further reinforced by v. 2, asserts that, like other human beings, kings are subject to Yahweh's control. A similar message is conveyed by the juxtaposition of 16:10–15 with 16:1–9 and of 20:27 with 20:26 (see above). (Scott suggested that the words **in the hand of the Lord** are not original to the proverb, which originally stated that "The king's heart is a stream of water which he (that is, the king) directs wherever he will". This suggestion, however, although it would also produce a more regular poetical line, is purely speculative.) The metaphor is derived from the practice of irrigation: the **stream of water** (*palᵉgê-mayim*) refers to water-channels which can be diverted into any desired direction (compare Isa. 32:2, where the same phrase is used of the beneficial rule of the king and his ministers). The choice of this phrase with its connotation of fertility (compare also its use in Ps. 1:3; Prov. 5:16) indicates that the rule of the king under Yahweh's direction and as subject to his will is seen, as elsewhere in these proverbs, as essentially beneficent: the point is not, as in v. 2, that the king will be held responsible for any evil actions that he may do, but rather that since he is guided by Yahweh one may be confident of his good will and his justice.

2. This verse is a variant of 16:2. The observation that Yahweh sees and assesses the human heart or spirit is a constant theme of these Yahweh-proverbs (compare 15:3, 11; 17:3; 20:9, 27; 24:12). **the heart**: the Hebrew has the plural, "hearts" (*libbôt*); compare also "spirits", *rûḥôt*, in 16:2. This shows clearly that the verse did not originally specify the king but referred to human beings in general; but placed as it now is immediately after v. 1 it makes the point that the king, however exalted he may be and although he may enjoy a special relationship with God, is after all only a man, who cannot escape this divine scrutiny and assessment.

3. See on 15:8. This verse has been compared with a number of prophetical sayings (Isa. 1:11–17; Hos. 6:6; Mic. 6:6–8), all of which state that Yahweh regards a virtuous life, especially as regards the just treatment of others, as of more importance to him than the offering of sacrifice; compare also 1 Sam. 15:22. That this understanding was not confined to Israel is exemplified in the Egyptian *Instruction for King Merikare* (129; *ANET*, p. 417), in the context of advice concerning the administration of justice: "More acceptable (to the gods) is the character of the upright of heart than the (sacrificial) ox of the evildoer". In none of these passages is there an intention to reject sacrificial worship; rather what is implied here is the same as what is clearly stated in v. 27, that it is the sacrifice of the *wicked* that is unacceptable to God.

The fact that **To do righteousness and justice** (*'āśāh ṣᵉdāqāh ûmišpāṭ* – the order in which these terms are placed is variable) is a requirement of Yahweh which was especially – though not exclusively – regarded as a function of kingly rule (1 Kg. 10:9; Jer. 22:3, 15; Ezek. 45:9) probably accounts for the present position of this verse.

4. The first line of this verbless verse consists of two phrases both of which refer to arrogance. (**haughty eyes** refers not to the appearance of a person's eyes as seen by others but to his particular way of perceiving, and treating, the world around him: compare the "bountiful eye" of 22:9 and the "wicked eye" of 23:6 (*RSV* "stingy") and 28:22 (*RSV* "miserly".) In Ps. 101:5b there is a similar double reference to arrogance, which is there regarded with abhorrence; and in Prov. 6:17 "haughty eyes" are listed as one of the things which are an abomination to Yahweh; compare also 30:13.

But the connection of the first line with the second is not clear. The problem is made more difficult by the fact that **the lamp of the wicked** is obscure. But whatever this phrase may mean (see below), it hardly seems to be comparable with the straightforward references to arrogance in the first line. The two lines are therefore taken by some commentators to be fragments of quite different proverbs. Gemser suggested that two additional lines, now lost, may have originally stood between them. The first line, if it was in fact originally unconnected with the second, may have been part of a list of "abominable things" similar to that in 6:16–19. Its reference to the **heart** (*lēb*), a key word in vv. 1 and 2, is probably at least partly responsible for its present position, while it may also have served as a contrast to the statement in v. 3, this group of verses together setting out what God requires of kings and other persons and what he abominates.

lamp: MT has *nīr*, which can mean either "lamp" or "fallow, uncultivated land" (compare 13:23). The spelling, however, suggests *nēr*, "lamp", a more common variant of *nīr* and one which, as has already been pointed out, occurs in two of the other proverbs in this group (20:20, 27). LXX and other Versions have "lamp". But whichever of the two above senses is accepted, and whether or not the line is syntactically connected with the first line, no satisfactory meaning seems obtainable. The phrase **the lamp of the wicked** (*nēr rᵉšāʿîm*) occurs also in 13:9 and 24:20, where "lamp" seems to denote life or prosperity (the phrase is parallel with "the light of the righteous" in 13:9), but this meaning makes no sense here: what is required is a pejorative sense denoting or alluding to some kind of sin. But "fallow ground" also makes no sense. Driver (*Bib.* 32 [1951], p. 185) suggested, on the basis of an Arabic word, that *nēr* or *nīr* here may mean "mark": "a high look and proud heart (which are) the mark of sin" (compare *REB*); but he put forward this suggestion only tentatively, and it is very speculative. The line remains obscure, and the text may be corrupt.

5. Unlike 10:2; 11:4, 18 this proverb does not, at least overtly, make the assumption that hastily acquired wealth is necessarily due to dishonest practice. Rather it seems to be intended to qualify the axiom (see, for example, 10:4) that the way to enduring prosperity is honest toil by adding a further axiom somewhat along the lines of our "More haste, less speed". **diligence** is not enough: **plans** must be made, and their execution must be steady, not unduly **hasty**. On the choice of the terms *môtār*, **abundance** and *maḥsôr*, **want** see on 14:23.

6. This verse has probably been placed here as a comment on v. 5: wealth may also be acquired by mendacity or perjury (see on 6:17 and compare 12:19, 22), but this also will lead to disaster. In terms of composition it is perhaps significant that **lying tongue**

occurs also in 6:17 in the same list of "abominations" as, and in proximity to, "haughty eyes" which are condemned as sin in v. 4. (There may also be significance in the fact that v. 7, on violence, corresponds to the next item in that list.)

The first line is straightforward except that the noun translated in *RSV* by **getting** (*pō'al*) should probably be pointed, following LXX, as the participle *pō'ēl*, "he who gets", since *pō'al* elsewhere (compare its other occurrences in Proverbs – v. 8; 20:11; 24:12, 29) never means the process of acquisition but its result, something made or done. But the second line is almost certainly corrupt. A literal translation would be "(is) a breath which is driven, seekers of death". *RSV*'s **snare of death** is based on an emendation suggested by LXX. LXX has "He that gathers treasures with a lying tongue pursues vanity on (to) the snares of death". This may in some respects represent a better Hebrew text; but the only words in this line which appear certain are *hebel*, "breath, vanity" and *māwet*, "death". These at least give some impression of the general import of the line.

7. Compare 1:18–19. **will sweep them away**: this rare verb probably means "to drag away" – presumably to death; compare its use in Hab. 1:15 with reference to catching fish in a net.

8. This proverb may have been placed here as an elaboration of v. 7, defining the distinguishing marks of the wicked (*RSV* **guilty**) as contrasted with the righteous: the former are underhand or devious (**crooked**) in their dealings, while the righteous (*pure*) are open and straightforward (**right**, literally, "upright").

The phrase translated in *RSV* by **guilty** (*'îš wāzār*) presents a problem, however, although its general sense is determined by its opposition to *zak*, **pure**. Its form is strange (words beginning with *w* are very rare indeed in Hebrew), and it occurs nowhere else. Despite a variety of attempts to explain *wāzār* by comparative philology (e.g. by Driver, *Bib.* 32 [1951], p. 185; L. A. Snijders, 1954, p. 96, note 69), its precise meaning remains obscure. The text is probably irrecoverably corrupt. *BHS* suggests emendation to *kāzāb* – the phrase *'îš kāzāb*, "liar", occurs in 19:22.

9. This verse is virtually identical with 25:24, and there is also a variant in this chapter (21:19). The nagging wife is also mentioned as an irritating hazard of married life in 19:13 and 27:15. **in a corner of the housetop**: the precise location and mode of living envisaged in this expression have been solemnly discussed by the commentators. But a comparison with v. 19, where the corresponding expression is "in a desert land", shows that such literalism is misplaced: these are examples of humorous fantasy such as is frequently found in popular proverbs – compare the English "I'd rather be hanged!" This proverb does not go quite as far as that; but corners of roofs, like deserts, while being extremely uncomfortable places for permanent residence, are at least, the proverb implies, out of earshot of a wife's continual nagging.

a house shared: the Hebrew *bêt ḥāber* may possibly bear this meaning, but there are no other examples of this use of a rather rare word *ḥeber*. However, LXX seems to have interpreted it in this way. Albright (1955, pp. 10–12) took the phrase, on the basis of a similar root in Akkadian and Ugaritic, to mean a brewery or alehouse; but this hardly seems an appropriate allusion; nor does the proposal referred to in *BHS* to emend *ḥāber* by metathesis to *rāḥāb*, "broad, spacious" greatly improve the sense.

10. The point of this verse seems to be that the criminal mind desires evil for its own sake, sparing no-one. **soul** (*nepeš*): that is, the person in his rapacious or predatory character – compare the use of the word in 10:3; 13:2, 4.

11. See on the somewhat similar verse 19:25, with regard to which there is a similar divergence of interpretation. Here most commentators, probably rightly, understand the proverb as concerned to contrast the **simple** (*petî* – see on 1:4) with the **wise man**. Whereas the latter gains knowledge – that is, increases in understanding – simply by following the teaching of those even wiser than himself (compare 1:5), the former will only turn to wisdom when he sees the fate of those who reject it; so, apparently, *RSV*. Plöger, however, takes **the simple** to be the subject of both clauses: he can gain wisdom in either of two ways: by seeing and learning from the punishment suffered by the scoffer, or by heeding the teaching given by the wise man. The interpretation of the verse thus turns on a matter of syntax: the second line may mean either "a wise man when he is instructed gains knowledge" or, "by the instruction of the wise man he . . . (that is, the simple) gains knowledge".

Neither of the above interpretations solves the problem of the fact that *ḥākām* (**wise man**) is preceded by the preposition *l*[e], "to, for". It has been suggested that this has crept into the text by dittography of the last letter of the preceding word *ûb*[e]*haśkîl*.

12. There is a verbal link between this verse and v. 11 in that both contain the verb *hiśkîl* (here **observes**). On its meaning see below.

By using a passive verb in the second line where the Hebrew has an active one, *RSV* has concealed a problem. The Hebrew has "*he* casts the wicked down to ruin"; and this "he" can only refer to **The righteous** (*ṣaddîq*) of the first line. But nowhere else is it stated that the righteous man causes the ruin of the wicked: that is God's privilege and function. The majority of commentators therefore assume that here *ṣaddîq* refers to God ("the Just One"), although this epithet is never used of him in any of the many verses in Proverbs in which the word occurs. Indeed, although elsewhere in the Old Testament Yahweh is frequently said to be "just" or "righteous" (*ṣaddîq*), there is no other passage in which "the Righteous One" is used as a divine title (Job 34:17, sometimes cited in this connection, is no exception). If the text is correct, then (this is doubted by Toy), it would appear that the two lines of the verse are fragments of two originally separate proverbs wrongly assembled by a scribe (so Oesterley).

observes (*maśkîl*): this verb has several meanings (for example, in v. 11 it means "to instruct"); but there is no justification for the view of Plöger and of the *REB* that it can mean "deal effectively with", which, if allowed, would support the view that *ṣaddîq* here refers to God. **the house of** (*l^ebêt*): LXX has "the hearts of", which suggests the reading *libbôt*.

13. This is a strongly persuasive variant on the theme of the duty to help the poor (compare 14:21, 31; 22:9; 28:27). It is expressed in terms of exact retribution. The **cry of the poor** person is presumably a desperate appeal either for food or for justice. It is assumed that the person whose help is now sought could himself at some time in the future be in need of such help – a further indication that those addressed in these proverbs are not the wealthy who live in total security (see, for example, 10:15) but persons of limited means who have no such security.

14. See the comments on 15:27; 17:8, 23; 18:16. This verse, like 17:8, makes no comment on the morality of bribery, but merely points out its effectiveness in getting the briber out of trouble. It is not stated whose **anger** and **strong wrath** are to be appeased; but the situation envisaged may be similar to that of 6:32–5: an offender offers secret compensation to the offended party to persuade him not to prosecute.

averts (*yikpeh*): this verb (*kāpāh*) occurs only here in the Old

Testament; it may mean "satisfy" (Gemser) or "appease" (see *KB*³). Some of the Versions (Targ., Symm., Vulg. [extinguit]) seem to have read *yᵉkabbeh*, "quenches"; Oesterley proposed *yᵉkappēr*, "propitiates, pacifies".

15. *RSV* and some commentaries take the phrase *ᵃśôt mišpāṭ* (**When justice is done**) in a passive sense: the **righteous** and the **evildoers** are witnesses to the making of just decisions by others. But it is more natural to take it in an active sense: "There is joy for the righteous in doing what is right, but for those who do evil there is disaster" (so Delitzsch, Barucq, McKane, Plöger). This assertion about the working of the retributory process has probably been placed here as a comment on v. 14, asserting that those who obstruct the proper course of justice – for example, by offering bribes – will *ultimately* not escape the consequences.

16. This proverb in its present position suggests that the character of the evildoer (v. 15) is the consequence of failing to heed the instruction of the wise (**the way of understanding**) – one of the main themes of the Instructions of chapters 1–9, where the foolish young man who **wanders** (*tāʿāh*) into evil paths finds himself in the **assembly** or company **of the dead** (e.g. 9:18). Once there he will settle or remain (**rest**): that is, he will die an early death. This is a dramatic way of expressing a warning found elsewhere in these proverbs (for example, 10:21; 21:6).

The recurrence of the verb *hiśkîl*, also found in vv. 11 and 12 (here serving as a verbal noun, *haśkēl*, **understanding**), suggests that vv. 10–16, all of which are concerned in one way or another with the wicked and his fate, may once have formed a separate group.

17. This warning against an extravagant lifestyle reflects the economic status of those addressed in these proverbs. By hard work (10:4) and with Yahweh's blessing (10:22) they might aspire to wealth; but they could not afford to squander their capital on luxurious living: poverty was always a threatening possibility. *śimḥāh* (**pleasure**), elsewhere "joy, happiness" (10:28; 12:20; 14:10; 15:23; 21:15) here denotes festivity, as in Ec. 2:1, 2; 8:15; 9:7 (compare "house of mirth in Ec. 7:4). **wine and oil** (the latter for anointing the head) were frequently associated as concomitants of festivity (compare Jg. 9:9, 13; Ec. 9:7–8).

18. This enigmatic verse seems to be saying that the punishment of the **wicked** will be accepted – presumably by God – as a kind of compensation for letting the **righteous** – that is, the innocent –

go free from punishment. *kōper* (*RSV* **ransom**) is used in the Old Testament in various ways, but always with the notion of substitution or compensation (so, for example, in Prov. 6:35 and 13:8); but it is not clear why the righteous, who elsewhere in these proverbs deserve and will receive a positive reward rather than punishment, should need to be ransomed. There is a somewhat similar problem in 13:8 (see the comment on that verse).

19. This verse is a variant of v. 9. **fretful**: better, "ill-tempered" (so *REB*).

20. This verse as rendered in *RSV* appears to mean that if a wise man possesses a fortune he will keep it intact, whereas a foolish man will squander it. This contrast may be intended simply as a warning against extravagance or to inculcate the importance of acquiring wisdom. Alternatively, it could be a sombre comment on the ephemeral nature of wealth in the same vein as Ec. 2:18–19, pointing out that it is futile to nurse a fortune if it may be inherited by a fool who will simply spend it all.

But there are problems in the Hebrew text which *RSV*'s rendering conceals. **remains** is not represented in MT but is derived from the LXX: the Hebrew has "Precious treasure *and oil* (are) in the wise man's dwelling". This text has its own difficulties (see below); but LXX ("A desirable treasure rests on the mouth of the wise") is even less probable. There is a further difficulty in the second line: the Hebrew word **devours** (*bālaʿ*, piel) is not elsewhere found in the sense implied, that is, "to squander". The meaning of the verse thus remains obscure.

I. Eitan 1937, pp. 55–8), followed by Gemser and *REB*, proposed the repointing of *šemen*, "oil" to *šāmīn* or *šāmēn*, which he took on the analogy of an Arabic word to mean "costly". But however this may be it does not solve the problem of the meaning of the verse as a whole.

21. Compare 8:18; 11:19; 12:28. In the second line the Hebrew has "life, *righteousness* and honour". *RSV* correctly omits this repetition of "righteousness", which is lacking in LXX, as a scribal error.

22. Compare 16:32; 24:5, and also Ec. 9:14–18, where a similar image is employed. The point is that brains can achieve more than mere brute force, an axiom of no great originality applicable to any human situation including that of personal relations within a small community. No allusion to actual military operations is intended; but there may be overtones of a modest farmer's antagonism towards the "strong city" of the arrogant wealthy (compare 10:15; 12:12). **the city of the mighty** (*'îr gibbōrîm*): that is, a strongly defended town (*gibbôr* here means an armed soldier as in Isa. 21:17; Jer. 48:41; Ezek. 39:20; Joel 2:7; 3:9 [Heb. 4:9]). **stronghold**: this word (*'ōz*), usually "strength", is used in this sense also in Am 3:11.

23. This verse is an expanded variant of 13:3a, on which see the comments. On the importance attached to reticence see also 10:13, 19; 12:23; 17:27–8. **keeps**: this word (*šōmēr*) is used twice here but with subtly different nuances: "guards" and "preserves". **himself** (*napšô*): perhaps better, "his life".

24. The syntax of this verse is not clear. Most commentators and modern translations take it in the same way as *RSV*, as a kind of definition of the *lēṣ* ("**Scoffer**") as an arrogant person. However, such a definition does not correspond very well to what is said about the *lēṣ* elsewhere in the book, where other characteristics are to the fore: see on 9:7 and compare 13:1; 14:6; 19:29; 21:11. It is difficult to grasp the purpose of the verse, which is overloaded with virtually synonymous terms – **proud** (*zēd*), **haughty** (*yāhîr*), **pride** (*zādôn*) – and is also tautologous: to say that the **proud** (*zēd*) acts with **pride** (*zādôn*) is meaningless.

with arrogant pride (*b*e*'ebrat zādôn*): this phrase, however, is probably not tautologous and would probably be better rendered by "with excessive pride": see Driver (*Biḇ* 32 [1951], pp. 185–6), followed by Gemser and Ringgren; see also *KB*³.

25. This is a dramatic way of expressing the warning about the fate of the **sluggard** which occurs frequently in these chapters. **desire** (*ta*ₐ*wāh*) means "appetite" in a literal sense (compare 13:4): it will eventually "kill" the indolent person in that he will starve to death because he lacks the energy to satisfy it by working (compare 19:24).

26. In the first line of this verse *RSV*, following Gemser, Scott and Ringgren, has adopted the reading of LXX. This provides a suitable contrast between the behaviour of the "wicked" and the "righteous", but probably represents an attempt to "improve" a difficult verse (so also McKane). In the Hebrew of MT there is no mention of the wicked, and in fact no indication of a subject at all: it reads, literally, "All day long he desires a desire (*hit'awwāh tā*a*wah*)"; the natural interpretation of this is that it is the sluggard of v. 25 who is the implied subject. But although there is a verbal link between the two verses ("desire"), there is no obvious continuation of sense from one verse to the next; nor, on this view, is there a convincing relationship between the two lines of this verse (26). Plöger's solution is perhaps the most probable: he proposes the slight emendation of *hit'awwāh*, "(he) desires" to the participle *(ha)mit'awweh*, "the person who desires", that is, who is greedy: so, "the greedy covets all day long". The noun which follows, *ta*^{a}*wāh*, "desire", is then seen as an "internal object" intensifying the meaning (compare Lk. 22:13 and see *GK* 117q). The greedy miser and the generous righteous man then make a reasonable contrast.

27. This verse is a variant of 15:8 in that the two verses have a common first line which has subsequently been expanded in different ways. See on 15:8 and also on 21:3. LXX adds "to the Lord" after **abomination**, thus making the line precisely the same as 15:8a; whether this is the original reading here or not, it correctly interprets the proverb's meaning.

It is not clear how an **evil intent** (*zimmāh* – see on 10:23) can have increased the heinousness of the **sacrifice of the wicked**, already "abominable" in God's eyes. It must be presumed that such a sacrifice would *always* be offered insincerely, since *rāšāʿ* (**wicked**), one of the most frequently used words in Proverbs – it occurs more than fifty times in these chapters alone – never refers to a repentant sinner seeking to atone for his sin, but always denotes an incorrigibly evil person already doomed to destruction. The solution to the problem may lie with LXX, which has "*for* they offer them wickedly". This suggests that in this instance *'ap kî* does not have the meaning **how much more when** but, literally translated, "indeed, because". If this is so the line may be rendered "because undoubtedly his intention in bringing it is evil". That a wicked person should offer the conventional sacrifice to hide his true intentions is readily understandable. (On the singular verb see *GK* 145 l.)

This verse – virtually a Yahweh-proverb – is perhaps to be seen as the beginning of an arrangement of proverbs at the close of the chapter designed at some editorial stage to correspond to those with which the chapter begins, asserting Yahweh's control over all human activities.

28. The first line of this verse is a variant of 19:5a and 19:9a, but has been expanded to form an antithetical proverb. There appears to be a subtle play on two meanings of the verb *'ābad* (**perish**). At first sight this seems to have the same meaning as elsewhere in the book, referring to the total destruction of a wicked person (so, for example, in 19:5b and 19:9b, where it is used of liars); but the addition of the second line suggests that it is also used here in the sense of being shortlived or ineffective, and applied by implication not to the **false witness**'s person, but to his words: whereas the speech of the "hearer" will have a lasting effect, it will "perish" in the sense of failing in its purpose. (So *REB*, "A lying witness will be cut short, but a truthful witness will speak on".) This interpretation provides a good parallel between the lines.

But the identity of the **man who hears** (*'îš šômēa'*) is disputed. In view of the context, the verb *šāma'*, "to hear", is most probably used here in the judicial sense of "hearing" a legal case (compare, for example, Dt. 1:16, 17; 2 Sam. 14:17; 15:3; 1 Kg. 3:11), or of acting as an arbiter who hears both sides of an argument and then makes a decision (so in Jg. 11:10). It is this decision, based on an attentive hearing of all the witnesses, that **will endure** – that is, which has binding force for the future. The thought is similar to that of 18:17. (For a somewhat different interpretation of *'îš šômēa'* as a perspicacious witness who refutes the testimony of his opponent see Emerton, *ZAW* 100 [Suppl], 1988, pp. 161–70.)

29–31. There is a clear sequence in the arrangement of these verses. V. 30 is concerned to prevent a misunderstanding of v. 29b, which taken by itself might seem to assert – contrary to, for example, 16:9 – that it is possible for a righteous person to order his life wholly without divine help; v. 30 makes it clear that such human "wisdom" is useless, or even irreligious (**against the Lord**); see McKane on this verse. V. 31 then provides a concrete example of the fact that nothing can be achieved without the approval and help of Yahweh.

29. considers his ways (literally, "his way" *-yābîn darkô*): *RSV* has here followed Qere, which is supported by a few Hebrew manuscripts and by LXX. Virtually the same expression occurs in 14:8 and 20:24, where it means to be in control of one's life and so to be able to make the right choices. Kethib, followed by Targ., Pesh. and Vulg., has *yakîn d^erākâw*, literally, "establishes his ways". Despite some views expressed in the commentaries, the difference between the two is not great. A similar expression in 16:9 (*RSV* "directs his steps") is used of Yahweh's control of human life.

This proverb, then, contrasts the upright man, who openly orders his conduct in accordance with consistent principles, with the wicked man, who deviously hides his true character behind a mask (**puts**

on a bold face – see Garrett, 1990, pp. 681–2); compare the use of this expression in 7:13.

30. This triple negative assertion is intended to cover the whole range of human claims to self-determination. **wisdom** (*ḥokmāh*), **understanding** (*t^ebûnāh*) and **counsel** (*'eṣāh*) are technical terms of wisdom vocabulary (see McKane). This verse belongs to that strand in Proverbs, particularly evident in chapters 1–9 but not exclusively so (compare 19:21 on Yahweh's *'ēṣāh* ["purpose"]) which asserts that these qualities are all derived from and dependent on Yahweh. **can avail**: these words are not represented in the Hebrew, which has simply "There is no wisdom, no understanding and no counsel face to face with (*l^eneged*, perhaps but not certainly **against**) Yahweh".

31. As with other proverbs in these chapters which employ similar imagery (for example, 16:32; 20:18; 21:22), this verse does not imply familiarity with military matters. The thought is similar to that of 16:9, 33; 21:1.

CHAPTER 22, VERSES 1–16

These verses conclude the section which began at 10:1. V. 17 clearly marks the beginning of a new section. A wide range of subjects is covered here, of which the most prominent is that of the relationship between rich and poor (vv. 2, 7, 9, 16); two other proverbs (vv. 1, 4) also refer to material wealth. There are two proverbs on the education of children (vv. 6, 15). There are four Yahweh-proverbs (vv. 2, 4, 12, 14), of which at least two (vv. 2 and 12) appear to comment on the verses which immediately precede. (On v. 11 as a possible Yahweh proverb see below.) Formally antithetical proverbs are few (vv. 3, 5, 12, 15) in comparison with examples of synonymous or synthetic parallelism. There is no indication of the formation of major groups. (on vv. 1–9 see R. E. Murphy, *Interpretation* 41 [1987], pp. 398–402.)

1. For other indications of the importance attached to a person's **name** or social reputation see 3:4; Ec. 7:1. It is not without significance that the kind of comparison with **riches**, **silver** and **gold** that is made here is elsewhere made with respect to wisdom or instruction in wisdom (2:4; 3:14; 8:10–11, 19; 16:16) as the means for achieving success in life. Here, as in the other passages in question, there is no intention to despise wealth; rather, the implication is that a blameless reputation (**A good name**) and public approval (*ḥēn*, **favour**) are a more certain basis for a successful life than the mere acquisition of wealth. Here again the social background of these proverbs can be seen: wealth is – in theory, at least – attainable and is not despised, but does not by itself command respect.

A good name: the Hebrew has simply "A name"; but *RSV* has correctly understood the meaning. LXX's "A good name" is to be seen as a similar interpretation and not as evidence of an original Hebrew text.

2. Compare 14:31; 17:5; 29:13, which are also concerned with the implications of Yahweh's creation of all human beings for a proper attitude towards the poor. In all of those proverbs the point is made, directly or indirectly, that Yahweh, because he has created the poor, will not tolerate their ill-treatment. Here, however, no explicit moral is drawn, and the proverb can be interpreted in various ways. Interpretation depends partly on the meaning of **meet together** (*nipgāšû*). This line may mean simply that in every society there are rich and poor mixed together and coming into contact with one another, and that that is how Yahweh made them: in effect, a defence of the *status quo*. But the word should more probably be understood figuratively as meaning that rich and poor have something in common: their status as Yahweh's creatures (see Ps. 85:10 [Heb. 11] for a somewhat similar use of this verb). The verse may then be interpreted in the light of 14:31 and 17:5: since Yahweh deliberately gave to the poor the same human status as he gave to the rich, to treat them as less than human or as intrinsically inferior is to commit the sin of insulting God himself. At the same time it should be noted that this is not a statement about the need for *social* or economic equality: as elsewhere in Proverbs, the existence of the poor is not considered to be disgraceful but is taken for granted as intended by God (compare the statement in 16:4 that he "made the wicked for the day of trouble" and the comment on that verse).

The fact that both this verse and v. 1 are concerned with wealth has no doubt led to their juxtaposition. There is no obvious thematic connection between them, but the Yahweh-proverb sets the previous verse is a wider framework: wealth, like poverty, is bestowed by Yahweh alone and cannot be acquired unless he permits it.

3–6. These verses have been arranged to form a coherent group. The Yahweh-proverb (v. 4) may be seen as a comment on vv. 3

and 5, which speak of the dangers which threaten the **simple** or untutored and the **perverse** persons respectively and of the ways in which these can be avoided by the **prudent**. V. 4 identifies the latter in terms of the **fear of the Lord**. V. 6 then adds a piece of advice to parents: only a rigorous training from an early age can ensure that a child will follow the right path in adult life.

3. This verse is virtually identical with 27:12. The thought is similar to that of 14:15 and 14:18, where also the conduct of the **prudent man** (*'ārûm*) is contrasted with that of the **simple** (*petî*). **sees danger**: literally, "sees trouble" – that is, sees it coming towards him. The wordplay (*rā'āh rā'āh*) is obviously intentional. **go on**: that is, they ignore it – once more a metaphor taken from walking along a road. **hides himself**: Kethib and Qere have different forms of the same verb; the meaning is not affected. **suffer for it**: the Hebrew has "are punished"; the same verb (*'nš*) occurs in 17:26 and 21:11 as well as in 27:12.

4. The syntax of this verse is difficult. Some commentators render it differently: "The reward for humility is the fear of the Lord [the word "and" is not represented in the Hebrew], together with riches . . ." etc. But this would be a strange doctrine. In the LXX there is no mention of humility; and the best solution to the problem is perhaps that of Toy, who suggested that **humility** may be a scribal gloss intended to define that is meant by the **fear of the Lord** (compare 15:33, where the two stand in parallelism). The first line would then originally have read "The reward (better, "the consequence") for fearing Yahweh is riches . . ." etc.

5. Thorns and snares (*ṣinnîm paḥîm*): note the absence of "and" in the Hebrew. The meaning of the first of these words is uncertain (see *KB*^{3}). Driver (*Bib.* 32 [1951], p. 186) somewhat tentatively postulated the existence of a word *ṣēn* (singular) cognate with Arabic and Aramaic terms meaning "basket", which he thought might have developed the further meaning "cage"; but this is very speculative. The second word, **snares** (*paḥîm*), may be a gloss attempting to define the meaning of an already obscure word, though LXX also has two words here, which it joins by "and".

guards himself (*šōmēr napšô*): elsewhere in Proverbs this phrase means "preserves his life".

6. The admonition in the imperative addressed to a father is an indication of the instructional character of this section – compare 19:18; 29:17. **Train up**: elsewhere in the Old Testament this verb (*ḥānak*) always means to dedicate or inaugurate a temple or house (Dt. 20:5; 1 Kg. 8:63; 2 Chr. 7:5); but it is attested in some other Semitic languages in the sense of instruction or direction. (This verse is lacking in the *LXX*.) **in the way he should go** (*'al-pî darkô*): the translation "at the beginning of his way", favoured by some commentators, is less probable. The principle expressed in this verse conforms exactly to that of the Instructions in chapters 1–9 (for example, 2:1–5; 4:10, 20–22).

7. This proverb is ostensibly simply a statement about the harsh facts of life, though a warning not to fall into debt may be implied. On debt slavery see on 11:29, and on the economic standpoint of these proverbs – that of a class of persons who identify themselves neither with the rich nor with the poor – see on 14:20; 18:23.

8. The first line of this proverb is a straightforward expression of the principle of retribution. The second line, however, makes little sense if translated literally as in *RSV*. The sense is hardly improved by taking the noun *'ebrāh* (*RSV* **fury**) in its other meaning of "excess" or "pride" (so Gemser, Ringgren, McKane), or by following *LXX*, which has "his deeds", possibly a rendering of Hebrew *'ᵃbōdātô*. The connotation of **rod** (*šēbeṭ*) here is clear: in Proverbs it always denotes an instrument of punishment; but it can hardly be said of it that it **will fail** or come to an end (*yikleh*). Several commentators have proposed either to repoint this verb as *yᵉkallēhū*, "will destroy him", or to emend it to *yakkēhû*, "will smite him". Either of these would give a somewhat better sense; but "the rod of his anger/pride" remains obscure, and it is probable that the original text of this line is irrecoverable.

9. To have **a bountiful eye** (*ṭôb-'ayin*) means simply to be generous: compare *ra' 'ayin* (literally, "bad of eye"), meaning "miserly" (23:6; 28:22). The eye was believed in general to reveal a person's character and disposition. **shares his bread**: literally, "gives (some) of his bread", that is, of his food. Of the several proverbs in these chapters which advocate generosity towards the poor, this one most clearly reflects the economic situation of the giver, who is able to spare something for the truly destitute, but from a limited budget rather than from great wealth.

10. The situation envisaged in this verse is of a community whose harmony is endangered by the activities of a **scoffer** (*lēṣ*). Such a man must be expelled from society. *dîn* (**qarrelling**) here means (the bringing of) a lawsuit, as in Job 35:14; *qālôn* (**abuse**) elsewhere means "disgrace" or "humiliation"; but here, as in Isa. 22:18, it denotes the bringing of disgrace on others – presumably by abusing them or bringing them into court. LXX has a different text which has been used as the basis for emendations of MT; but no emendation appears to be necessary.

11. This verse hardly makes sense in the Hebrew: "One who loves the pure in heart – grace of his lips – the king is his friend". LXX has a quite different text: "The Lord loves holy hearts, and all blameless persons are acceptable to him; a king rules with his lips"; this is hardly more satisfactory. Various emendations, partly influenced by LXX, have been proposed. The presence of "The Lord" – absent from MT – in the LXX as the subject of the first line raises the question whether this is a Yahweh-proverb as well as (or possibly rather than) a royal proverb. Of the emendations which have been proposed, that of Driver (*Bib.* 32 [1951], pp. 186–7; compare *REB*) involves the least change in the text: "Yahweh loves a person who is pure in heart, and his lips make a friend of the king". But there is no agreement among the commentators on this verse. The fact that the following verse is a Yahweh-proverb may help to support the view that this also is one.

12. The eyes of the Lord: compare 15:3. **knowledge**: that is, those who possess or aim for God-given wisdom (compare 30:3). **faithless**: this word (*bōgēd*) is frequently used in these chapters in the general sense of "wicked" (in contrast with such terms as "righteous", "upright", "good"). The verse thus states that Yahweh, who sees into the hearts of men (compare 15:3, 11 etc.), will act to protect those who seek to live and to speak by wisdom while punishing their slanderers. It may have been placed here to expound the reference to Yahweh's love for the pure in heart of v. 11a (if that is the meaning of that line – see above) more concretely in terms of divine action; it may also be intended to refer back to v. 10.

13. Like 19:24 and 26:13–15 (this verse is a variant of 26:13), this is a humorous but contemptuous saying about the lazy person who will make any excuse, however improbable, for not going out to do his work.

14–15. Only here in these chapters is there a reference to the danger of associating with a **loose woman** (*zārāh*, here in the plural in the Hebrew) which is a major theme of chapters 1–9 (2:16–19; 5:3–6; 6:24–25; 7:5–27). In their present juxtaposition these two verses may be said to epitomize the teaching of the final edition of the Instructions of chapters 1–9 in that they stress the vital importance of a strict training as the only way to guard the young from **folly** (compare chapter 2, *passim*), while making it clear that it is Yahweh who is the ultimate source of the "wisdom" so communicated (compare 2:5–8). The appearance of such a theme here and the way in which teaching corresponding to that of the "father" of the Instructions has been glossed by a Yahweh-proverb confirm the conclusion that both sections of the book (chapters 1–9 and 10:1–22:16) have been finally edited in the same spirit. The fact that these verses occur at the end of the section supports this view.

14. mouth: that is, her seductive speech: compare 2:16; 5:3; 6:24; 7:5, 13–21. In the variant 23:27 a prostitute is said to be *herself* a deep pit. In 2:18–19; 5:5–6; 7:27 the imagery employed is death, the "shades" or Sheol.

15. Compare 13:24; 22:6; 23:13; 29:15, 21. The idea that children are naturally foolish and that corporal punishment is an essential part of the inculcation of wisdom was common to ancient Near Eastern, classical and also much later educational theory.

16. This is a very difficult verse concerning which there is no agreement among the commentators. *RSV*'s translation, which takes it to be a single continuous sentence, is improbable; the connecting particle **or** which is essential to it is entirely unrepresented in the Hebrew. Rather, the form is that of a parallel couplet: the subject of the first line, *'ōšēq dāl* (**He who oppresses the poor**), is exactly paralleled in the second line by *nōtēn lᵉ'āšîr* ("he who gives to the rich" [*RSV* **or gives to the rich**]), and *lᵉharbôt lô*, "increases his own wealth" (*RSV* **to increase his own wealth** – but see on 19:8 on this use of the infinitive) corresponds exactly to *'ak-lᵉmaḥsôr*, **will only come to want**.

However, the existence of this formal parallelism does not solve the problems of the meaning and purpose of this verse as a whole. Each line contains ambiguities. The Hebrew of the first line could bear the meaning that it is the recipient of the oppression – the poor – and not the oppressor whose wealth is increased; and similarly it could be the recipient of gifts – the rich – and not the giver who will come to want. These somewhat paradoxical interpretations have been defended by some commentators, who have argued that the poor may be said to gain from oppression because God will come to their aid and bless them, and that giving to the rich will serve to make the rich extravagant and so bring them to poverty. These interpretations, though ingenious, are extremely improbable. The contrary interpretation of *RSV* is in both cases a more natural one.

Difficulties, however, remain. The first line appears to run entirely counter to the spirit of these proverbs and seems even to encourage the oppression of the poor rather than, as would be expected, to promise the ruin of the wicked. Further, despite the parallelism of form, the two lines show no parallelism of sense. It may be best to see them as originally unconnected fragments which have been erroneously set side by side because of their formal parallelism. Although it is not possible to supply the missing lines with certainty, it may be that the first line was originally followed by one which qualified it or negated it by stating that wealth so gained will not last (compare 10:2a; 11:4a, 28; 21:6). The second line appears to state that, contrary to what is asserted in such proverbs as 18:16; 17:8, giving presents to the rich to curry favour will fail in its purpose and only impoverish the giver; it may originally have been part of an appropriate two-line proverb, whether in antithetical or synonymous parallelism.

"SAYINGS OF WISE MEN"
A SERIES OF INSTRUCTIONS
22:17–24:22

For the last seventy years, since the publication of the Egyptian work known as *The Wisdom of Amenope*, it has been generally believed that there is a direct literary relationship between this section of Proverbs and the Egyptian work. Scholarly opinions have differed, however, on the question whether the Hebrew work was influenced by the Egyptian or *vice versa*. A third possibility has also been discussed: that both works might be dependent on some no longer extant earlier work, whether Hebrew or Egyptian (see Bryce, 1979, for a full account of the discussion).

The arguments which have been employed are partly linguistic (the supposed existence of "Egyptianisms" in the Hebrew text or of "Semitisms" in the Egyptian one, and in particular of close verbal equivalences in certain passages), partly thematic and partly structural: it has been supposed that the Hebrew word in Prov. 22:20 which *RSV* has rendered by **thirty sayings** refers to the structure of the ensuing section as a whole and corresponds in some way to

Amenope's "thirty chapters". With regard to this point, it should be remarked that 1) it is not certain that this is a correct translation of the word (see below); 2) it is a matter of considerable doubt whether the Hebrew text does in fact consist of thirty sayings; and 3) even if this is the case, the themes of *Amnenope* only partly correspond to those in these chapters of Proverbs, and in any case their sequence is quite different from that in *Amenope* – a fact which has never been satisfactorily accounted for.

The question has been exhaustively discussed by Egyptologists as well as by Old Testament scholars. Some have recently re-examined all the supposedly parallel passages and have qualified or altogether rejected the idea of a direct connection between the two works (Ruffle, 1977, Bryce, 1979, Kitchen, 1988, Krispenz, 1989). The question of direct dependence of one literary work on another is always a difficult matter. The difficulties in this case are compounded by the fact that extant Egyptian – and perhaps also Hebrew – texts of this kind are undoubtedly only a small sample of what once existed in this genre. Both the themes and the phraseology of *Amenope* may well have been found in other examples of a genre which was in many respects traditional, and to which in general the wisdom books of the Old Testament belonged. A general acquaintance of the author(s) of these chapters of Proverbs with the Egyptian instruction genre is accepted by some of those scholars who reject the theory of a direct connection between Proverbs and *Amenope* (for example, Bryce and Kitchen).

A further consideration which may throw doubt on the theory of such a direct connection between the two works is that there is reason to believe that Prov. 22:17–24:22 is not an unitary composition but is composed of a number of originally separate and independent instructions rather than being a single work comprising thirty "chapters" (Niccacci).

The question of the relationship, if any, of these chapters to *Amenope* must therefore be left open. The chapters are thoroughly Israelite in character and have many links with other parts of Proverbs. The commentary which follows here will be concerned with the meaning of the Hebrew text rather than with extra-biblical parallels, although the affinities between these instructions and the Egyptian instruction genre in general are fully recognised.

The material in these chapters is quite different in character from the collection of short proverbs which precedes them, and belongs to the same instructional or educational genre as the instructions in chapters 1–9, which in many ways it resembles. The units are almost all longer than the single couplet, and are addressed to young men of the upper class. The admonition (imperative) form, which rarely occurs in the proverb collections, is here the dominant one.

Niccacci (1979) has made a plausible case for 22:17–23:11 as a single extended Instruction consisting of an introduction (22:17–21) followed by a series of ten admonitions arranged in a coherent structure. The first four of these (22:22–8) and the last four (23:4–11) are all negative admonitions counselling the avoidance of certain actions, while the two central items (22:29–23:3) constitute advice to a would-be courtier. The first and the last (22:22–3, against robbing or oppressing the poor, and 23:10–11, against the removal of landmarks) are thematically related, indicating the completion of a single composition.

On the basis of what appear to be new introductory verses in 23:12 and 23:26, Niccacci has concluded that the remainder of the section (23:12–24:22) comprises two originally independent works. However, there are clear signs that these verses are made up of not two but several independent, though brief, Instructions. They include several passages (23:15–19, 22–6; 24:3–7, 13–14) which have the characteristics of introductory material rather than of concrete admonitions: these contain no instruction on particular matters, but are general exhortations by the father to the son praising wisdom in general terms and advocating its acquisition through paying attention to the father's teaching, entirely in the manner of the general *introductions* to the Instructions of chapters 1–9. These passages have generally been counted by many commentators as constituting distinct Instructions in themselves, making up the number of thirty for the whole section 22:17–24:22. But if this is not the case, the number of items falls considerably short of the twenty required by the theory of "thirty sayings" supposedly corresponding to *Amenope* (for details, see below).

The new general heading in 24:23 clearly indicates the beginning of a new section of the book.

22:17–21. This is the longest and most elaborate introduction in this section of the book, and is clearly intended to be the general introduction to the admonitions which follow. Its similarities to the Prologue to *Amenope* have often been pointed out; but its affinities – especially as regards vv. 17–18 – with the introductions to the

Instructions in chapters 1–9 are also quite obvious. Although the phrase "my son" does not occur here, it is clear that the speaker is a teacher instructing a pupil. He refers to himself in the first person (**my knowledge**, v. 17; **I have made** . . . **known to you**, v. 19; **Have I not written for you** . . . ?, v. 20), and addresses his pupil in the singular imperative (**Incline your ear, and hear**, v. 17). In vv. 17 and 18 much of the vocabulary and phraseology is the same as that of the earlier introductions: **Incline your ear** (v. 17) occurs also in 4:20; 5:1, and **hear** (imperative) in 4:1, 10; **apply your mind** (literally, "heart") to **my knowledge** is closely paralleled in 2:2; **keep them within you** (literally, "in your belly") is reminiscent of similar expressions in 4:21; 6:21; 7:3. The verb *šāmar*, **keep**, together with its virtual synonym *nāṣar*, is used in similar contexts in 4:21; 5:2; 7:1 (*šāmar*); 3:1; 5:2; 6:20 (*nāṣar*). The adjective **pleasant** (*nāʿîm*), referring to the teacher's words, corresponds to the references in the earlier Instructions to their beauty (for example, in 1:9); the corresponding verb *nāʿam* is used in 2:10 of **knowledge**, a word which also occurs here in vv. 17, 20. Such coincidences of expression point to a common tradition of educational literature which was shared by Hebrew and Egyptian writers alike.

There is reason to suppose, however, that these verses are not a single composition but that additions have been made to an originally shorter introduction which closely resembles its counterparts in chapters 1–9, or that more than one introduction has been combined. The reference to **trust** . . . **in the Lord** in v. 19a may be such an addition. Syntactically it is somewhat loosely attached, probably to v. 18 (rather than, as in *RSV*, to v. 19b), by an infinitive clause (see Richter, 1966, p. 179). It has been noted above that similar references to Yahweh have been added to some of the Instructions in chapters 1–9 to introduce a specifically Yahwistic note to their teaching which is absent from others, and also that Yahweh-proverbs have similarly been inserted into the sentence literature of 10:1–22:16. Some of those additions, like v. 19a here, specifically refer to trust in Yahweh (14:26; 16:20b; compare also 28:25).

V. 19b, then, is probably to be taken with what follows (*RSV*'s **them** is not represented in the Hebrew). Vv. 19b–21, although to some extent they repeat what has already been said in the earlier verses about the nature of the teaching which is to follow, are somewhat different in character. Whereas v. 17 ostensibly refers, like the earlier instructions, to teaching originally given orally – even though the admonition to **hear** is not necessarily exclusive of a written text which could be read aloud – here in v. 20 we have the only reference in the whole of the Book of Proverbs to writing (except in a metaphorical sense, 3:3; 7:3) and to a book which the pupil is to study. Another unique feature of these verses is the strictly personal note – **even to you** – in v. 19b.

17. the words of the wise (*dibᵉrê ḥᵃkāmîm*): in the other Instructions in Proverbs the teacher always recommends his own teaching, not that of the wise men in general. Most modern commentators believe that this phrase was not originally an integral part of this verse, but is an editorial heading to the whole section (compare 24:23, which heads the section which follows), which has been inserted by error into it. It is supposed, partly on the evidence of the LXX, that the original text had "my words" (*dᵉbāray*) here. On the other hand, since elsewhere the teacher never speaks of **my knowledge**, but simply of "knowledge", the text may have originally read "knowledge".

18. within you: literally, "in your belly" – that is "in your innermost self". Compare 18:8; 20:27, 30. **all of them**: the Hebrew has *yaḥdāw*, literally, "together". It is probably unnecessary to emend this word on the analogy of a phrase in *Amenope* (see Plöger). The thought is that the teaching as a whole should be present to the pupil's mind and so available to guide him when he speaks. Compare 5:2.

19. I have made them known to you: the Hebrew (*hôdaʿtîkā*) lacks **them**. In view of the time-indicator **today** this should be rendered "I am instructing you" (compare 9:9 for the use of this verb in an absolute sense, and see *GK* 106i on this use of the perfect tense). **even to you** (*'ap-'āttā*): some commentators regard this expression as meaningless or inappropriate and follow LXX, seeing it as a corruption of "your ways" (*'orḥōtekā*) and so as the object of *hôdaʿtîkā*. But this is unnecessary: *RSV* makes good sense (so also McKane, Plöger). *'ap* is an emphatic particle; the phrase means "to you personally" (on the construction see *GK* 135d–h and compare 23:15).

20. thirty sayings: the Hebrew has only one word here: *šilšôm* (Kethib) or *šālîšîm* (Qere); of these variants the latter, a term denoting a military rank or function, is clearly inappropriate here; and there is no warrant for the "excellent things" of some older translations. Commentators writing since the publication of *Amenope* have emended the word to *šelōšîm*, "thirty" (see above on vv. 17–21). There is, however, no equivalent to **sayings** in the text. *šilšôm*, literally "(on) the third day", meaning "the day before yesterday", elsewhere occurs only together with *temôl*, literally "yesterday", in the idiomatic phrase *temôl šilšôm*, "yesterday (and) the previous day", always in the more general sense of "in the past", "formerly". Its occurrence by itself is thus unique; but it is reasonable to suppose that it may here have a similar meaning to the full phrase. That it does so receives support from the fact that the previous verse (v. 19) also contains a temporal expression, *hayyôm*, "today" or "now". The line may therefore be rendered "Did I not write to you earlier . . . ?". The question form here as frequently elsewhere, has the sense of a strong positive asseveration: "I have (certainly) written . . .". This may be taken to refer to some previous Instruction composed (or perhaps transcribed) by the same writer to the same pupil. The text as it stands in the Kethib thus presents fewer difficulties than is supposed by the advocates of a reference to the "thirty chapters" of *Amenope*.

of admonition and knowledge: this is probably a hendiadys meaning "some pieces of sage advice" (on this use of *be* see *GK* 119i).

21. what is right (*qōšṭ*): this is an Aramaic word which occurs nowhere else in the Hebrew of the Old Testament but is found in the Aramaic chapters of Daniel (2:47; 4:37 [Heb. 34]). It has been suggested that the following words *'imrê *met*, literally "words of truth", are an explanatory Hebrew gloss. **give a true answer** (literally, "return words, truth". The two nouns are probably to be regarded as in apposition (*GK* 131c – but see Dahood, van der Weiden). **true** (**met*): in both lines this word probably means "reliable" rather than "truthful". **to those who sent you** (better, "(may) send you"): the use of messengers was clearly a common practice, and is referred to several times in Proverbs. In several cases (10:26; 13:17; 26:6) a concern is shown with their abilities or sense of responsibility either in conveying the original message correctly or in reporting the answer reliably (see on 13:17). But there was probably more to the messenger's function than accurate reporting: he acted as a representative of the sender, carrying out negotiations on his behalf. He would therefore need the education which the teacher is offering his pupil here.

22–23. This admonition, like many others in this section of the book, is provided with a motive-clause: the poor must not be exploited because Yahweh is their protector and will severely punish those who do so. That he is the protector of the poor is affirmed in the laws (Exod. 22:21–3; 23:6; Dt. 24:14–15) and elsewhere in the Old Testament (e.g. Ps. 68:5 [Heb. 6]; 146:9), and also in the wisdom literature of the ancient Near East. **the afflicted** (*'ānî*): this word is generally synonymous with *dal*, **poor**, but probably has here an added nuance of weakness or helplessness. **at the gate**: that is, in court. The gate of the city was the place where justice was administered. The reference is probably to the ruthless seizure by legal process – immoral if not illegal – of the property or even the person of debtors unable to repay their debts. **the Lord will plead their cause**: this is also a forensic term, but is here used metaphor ically of Yahweh's protection of the poor. When Yahweh "pleads someone's cause" the phrase is equivalent to his vindicating that person and executing judgement against his opponents or attackers (compare, for example, Mic. 7:9). The second line makes this clear: the judgement is a sentence of death. Those who have robbed the poor will themselves be robbed (*RSV* **despoil**, but see Driver, *ZAW* 50 [1932], p. 145) of their lives (on the construction see *GK* 117cc-ff).

24–25. A further example of an admonition with motive-clause. **a wrathful man**: see on 15:18 (and compare 29:22), where an almost identical phrase is rendered in *RSV* by "a hot-tempered man", and where it is stated that his characteristic is that he "stirs up strife". Such warnings are also characteristic of various Egyptian instructions including *Amenope*, and are also found in Babylonian literature. **go with**: that is, associate with. **learn**: or possibly "become accustomed to". This verb (*'ālap*) occurs in the Old Testament elsewhere only in Job. It appears to be a late borrowing from Aramaic.

26–27. Compare 6:1–5; 11:15; 17:18; 20:16; 27:13 and see especially on 6:1–5. The frequency of the topic in Proverbs speaks for the seriousness of the problem in ancient Israel. **for debts**: that is, for debts owed by a third person. **why . . . ?**: this word (*lāmmāh*) is not represented in the Versions: LXX has simply "they will take your bed . . .". Several commentators have supposed a dittograph in MT (that is, an inadvertent repetition of letters from the previous word *lšlm*, **to pay**; Gemser defended MT but proposed the meaning "beware" for *lāmmāh* supposedly found in the corresponding word in Syriac. However, it makes good sense in its usual meaning **why . . . ?** The line belongs to a well-known class of what Barr (1985, pp. 19–22) has called "hypothetical deprecations" in which the speaker "asks the question 'Why should such a thing happen (when it might well be avoided)'?". The point is that to become surety for debts, like going bail in modern times, carries with it the risk of the loss of all one's possessions if the guarantor has insufficient funds to meet his commitment. Here the warning, presumably addressed to persons in comfortable circumstances, is perhaps not intended to be taken literally, but may be a general quasi-humorous warning against making financial commitments without due thought.

28. On this crime of seizing the property of others, presumably of those who are powerless to prevent it (compare v. 22 on robbing the poor) see on 15:25. It is surprising that this admonition, which does not include a motive-clause, should be repeated a few verses later in 23:10–11; its first line is in fact identical with 23:10a. It is also a close variant of part of Dt. 19:14, where it appears as a law of Moses. In Dt. 27:17 those guilty of this offence are pronounced accursed. Prov. 23:10–11 has a fuller form, complete with motive-clause. **fathers**: that is, ancestors. Dt. 19:14 has "men of former times" (*rī'šōnîm*). In 1 Kg. 21:4 Naboth refers to "the inheritance of my fathers", inalienable property which must not be tampered with, even by its present holder.

29. The form of this verse is not that of an admonition; nevertheless it teaches a lesson by means of an example: only by diligently acquiring special and superior qualifications can one hope to rise to the top. **Do you see . . . ?**: there is no indication that this is a question, and such may not be intended. But there is no justification for following some commentators and omitting the word. A similar rhetorical device is employed in 26:12; 29:20.

The first two lines of this verse have been compared with the final lines of *Amenope* (XXX 27:16, 17 [*ANET*, p. 424]) which speak of the experienced scribe who is worthy to serve in the royal court. There is, however, no reference to professional scribes either here or anywhere else in these admonitions. The adjectives *māhîr*, **skilful** (or "ready, well-prepared") occurs only three other times in the Old Testament. In two of those passages (Ezr. 7:6; Ps. 45:1 [Heb. 2]) it is used to describe the characteristic of a good scribe in the phrase *sōpēr māhîr*, an expression which seems to have been the Hebrew equivalent of a standard expression in Aramaic and Canaanite; but *māhîr* is not used exclusively in this connection. In Isa. 16:5 *māhîr* is used in a slightly different sense of a future Davidic ruler who will be ready (or eager) to do justice. In the verse under consideration here (v. 29) the person who is held up as a model for the pupil is said to be **skilful in his work**. The latter word, *m^elā'kāh*, is a very general word for work, business or workmanship. The phrase a **man . . . skilful in his work** (*'îš māhîr bim^ela'ktô*) may, for example, refer to a skilful artisan (compare the craftsmanship -*m^elā'kāh*- of the skilled artisans who made the furnishings for the tabernacle in Exod. 31), the quality of whose workmanship might bring him to the notice of **kings** (there is no allusion to any particular king). There is then no reason to suppose that the phrase refers to the work of a scribe.

The third line hardly adds anything to the sense of the previous lines and itself makes little sense: no-one would be said to **stand before**, that is, serve, **obscure men**. The line is probably corrupt and may originally have been, in its original form, part of a separate statement. But no convincing emendation has been proposed.

23:1–3. Although formally these verses comprise three admonitions they constitute a single whole on a single topic. This topic occurs frequently in Egyptian instructions beginning with the earliest, *Ptahhotep* and *Kagemni* and including *Amenope*. In Jewish wisdom literature it reappears in Sir. 31:12ff. This passage presupposes an upper-class readership – a society in which dinner parties were a part of social life. The advice given here is addressed to a young man as yet inexperienced in the fine points of social etiquette; there is no indication, however, of the nature of any profession which he might be hoping to enter. The host is a **ruler** – that is, a person possessing political power, able to influence the young man's career for good or ill. It is important that the young man should make a favourable impression on him.

1. what is before you: that is, the food being served. But an alternative translation could be "*who* is before you" – that is, your host. If *RSV* is correct, the line means "be careful about how you eat your food", an interpretation which fits well with v. 2. If the reference is to the host, it may mean "give consideration to your host's rank" – that is, behave towards him with due deference (compare 14:15 for a similar use of this verb [*bîn*]).

2. put a knife to your throat: these two nouns occur nowhere else in biblical Hebrew, and are probably borrowed from Aramaic. This is an otherwise unknown idiomatic expression; the context indicates that it means "restrain your appetite". **given to appetite**: that is, greedy.

3. do not desire: better, "do not hanker after" – a warning against gluttony. Compare Sir. 31:14: "Do not reach out for everything you see". **deceptive**: it is not made clear in what sense this word is to be understood. It may refer to the unfortunate consequences of eating too much rich food (compare Sir. 31:20), hardly, in the context, to some sinister intention on the part of the host.

4–5. This admonition is somewhat surprising in that ostensibly it holds the acquisition of wealth to be of no importance – an attitude quite different from that of the sentence literature, which by no means despised wealth and condemned only those who had acquired it dishonestly or unscrupulously, affirming that such wealth would be ephemeral (e.g. 10:2; 11:4, 18; 20:17). Possibly the emphasis here is to be placed on **toil**: to devote all one's time and energy to making a fortune is futile, because wealth does not last (compare Ec 5:13–17 [Heb [12–16]). Yet even if that is what is meant here, it is contrary to the teaching of the sentence literature of Proverbs, which is that wealth gained honestly and laboriously *does* last (e.g. 12:27; 14:23; 28:20). Elsewhere, too, in these admonitions (24:4) wealth appears to be a desirable goal obtainable by wisdom. In general, attitudes towards wealth in Proverbs are complex and may to some extent appear contradictory. This admonition remains something of an enigma; but this is also true of attitudes towards wealth elsewhere in the wisdom literature of the ancient Near East – compare, in one of the earliest of the Egyptian instructions (*Ptahhotep*) the enigmatic "If a man says 'I shall be rich', he will have to say, 'My cleverness has ensnared me' ". It may be that in the circles in which the author of these admonitions moved the really unforgivable offence was the vulgarity of the self-made man (compare those proverbs which condemn those who become rich *quickly*: 13:11; 20:21; 28:20, 22).

4. be wise enough to desist: literally, "cease, in consequence of your understanding" (*mibbînāt^{e}kā* – on this use of *min-* see *GK* 119z).

5. When your eyes light upon it: literally, "Do you cause your eyes to fly" (reading Qere) "on it?" The interrogative form is here equivalent to a conditional sentence. But the syntax of the line is anomalous (**upon it**, *bô*, has no antecedent, since in the Hebrew of v. 4 there is no noun: "acquire wealth" is represented in the Hebrew text by a verb). The use of the word "to fly" (*'ûp*) in this sense is unique. The line may be a gloss.

suddenly: this appears to be *RSV*'s rendering of the infinitive absolute (*'āśōh*) which, when it immediately precedes a finite form of the same verb as here (*ya'aśeh*) has the effect of strengthening its force. But, as in v. 4, there is no antecedent, and it may be that *'āśōh* should be emended to *'ōšer*, "wealth", which would then be the subject of the sentence.

The image of wealth growing wings and flying off into the sky occurs also in *Amenope* (VII 10:4–5 [*ANET*, p. 422]), where it is expressed similarly (though it refers not to an **eagle** but to geese). However, the figure is older than *Amenope*: it occurs in a Sumerian proverb of the early second millennium B.C.: "Possessions are spar rows in flight which can find no place to alight" (E. I. Gordon, *Sumerian Proverbs*, New York, 1968, p. 50). The relevant passage in *Amenope*, which is considerably longer than the present admonition, also differs from it in that its concern is specifically with wealth obtained by robbery.

flying: the Hebrew has "it will fly" (reading *yā'ûp* with Qere).

6–8. This admonition returns to the topic of the dinner party, but its point is quite different from that of vv. 1–3. The pupil is here warned against accepting an invitation from a certain kind of man. *RSV* is probably correct in rendering *ra' 'ayin* in v. 6, literally, "evil of eye", by **stingy**. The only other place where this phrase occurs is 28:22, where its meaning cannot be precisely determined from the context; but in 22:9 *ṭôb-'ayin*, literally, "good of eye", which is presumably its opposite, clearly means "generous". However, some commentators take *ra' 'ayin* here to mean not "miserly" but "malicious" or "malevolent". Unfortunately these verses present so many detailed problems of interpretation that the precise situation envisaged is not clear.

6. The second line of this verse is identical with v. 3a.

7. The first line of this verse is difficult, and has been pronounced unintelligible and hopelessly corrupt by some commentators. The main problem is the meaning of *kᵉmô-šā'ar bᵉnapšô* (*RSV* **like one who is inwardly reckoning**). This verb *šā'ar* is not found elsewhere in the Old Testament, though it occurs in Mishnaic Hebrew in the sense of "to measure, calculate". If the consonantal text here is correct, it should probably be repointed as the participle *šō'ēr*. J. Gray (*The Legacy of Canaan*, 2nd edition, 1965, p. 266) suggests that the verb may be cognate with an Ugaritic verb meaning "to prepare, arrange": the miser (or the malevolent person) is like one who prepares or arranges his thoughts – an interpretation not far from that of *RSV*. Other suggestions, however, have been made. One of these was suggested by LXX's "as if anyone should swallow a hair". This may suggest that the word should be *śē'ār*, "a hair", and that *nepeš* here denotes not the man's inward self but, as is the case in other passages, "throat": so *REB*, "(they) will stick in your throat like a hair" – a possible cause of vomiting (compare v. 8).

Whatever may be the meaning of the first line, the remainder of the verse clearly means that the host's ostensibly hospitable words are a sham. **his heart is not with you** may mean either that he grudges his expenditure in giving the party, or that he harbours some hidden animosity towards his guest (for the expression compare 2 Kg. 10:15).

8. waste: literally, "spoil". The **pleasant words** in question may be the compliments which the guest has made to his host on arrival or during dinner. **vomit up**, like the (possible) reference to the hair in the throat in v. 7, is presumably not to be taken literally. The meaning is that the guest will afterwards regret and be revolted by the whole incident.

9. in the hearing of: literally, "in the ears of". The meaning of this brief admonition is not that one should not let the fool overhear what one says to a third person, but that one should not attempt to give him advice. To "speak in the ears" of someone frequently means to speak seriously or urgently (Bühlmann, p. 220; also Plöger). A similar idea is expressed in 9:7, 8; 17:10; 26:4; 27:22.

10–11. See on 22:28. **an ancient landmark** (*gᵉbûl 'ôlām*): it has been suggested that this should read "a widow's landmark" (*gᵉbûl 'almānāh*), since widows and orphans are frequently paired as being persons especially vulnerable to exploitation; it is supposed that *'ôlām* has been subsequently introduced into the text to make it conform to 22:28. However, the Versions support MT.

11. their Redeemer: in law the "redeemer" (*gô'ēl*) was the kinsman whose duty it was to buy back ("redeem") property which poverty had compelled the owner to sell (Lev. 25:25; Ru. 4:1–4). Here Yahweh himself will act as "redeemer" since the **fatherless** presumably have no relative to perform that office, and will also **plead their cause** (on the meaning of this phrase see on 22:23), punishing the offender.

12–28. V. 12 has all the marks of the beginning of a new section. It is general in character; it has strong affinities both verbally and in contents with 22:17; and every word in it is identical with terminology found in the introductions to the Instructions of chapters 1–9, or in the general preface (1:1–7). But how far this new section extends is not at all clear. The admonitions in vv. 12–28 are interspersed with further introduction-like verses (15–19, 22, 26) which give the impression of beginning yet more brief, but distinct, sections.

13–14. Although v. 12 gives the impression of being the beginning of a new section, Plöger has noted that there is an apparent incongruity between it and the verses which follow it. That is, while v. 12 is addressed, like other similar passages, by a parent or teacher to his pupil, vv. 13–14 are clearly addressed *to* a parent or teacher of a child. Plöger therefore suggests that v. 12 is not the beginning of a new section but is to be seen as the conclusion of the foregoing Instruction, while vv. 13–14 are an appendix addressed to parents or teachers quite outside the body of the Instruction. He considers, accordingly, that the next section begins only with v. 15. There are, however, two difficulties about this hypothesis: firstly, this kind of change of standpoint here is not unique, but is found also in a comparable passage in *Ahikar* (part of which is quoted below); and secondly, there are no other examples of such a conclusion to an Instruction such as Plöger proposes.

With regard to this topic see on 13:24; 19:18; and compare also 22:15; 29:15.

13. discipline: as in 13:24; 22:15 this word (*mûsār*) is here virtually equivalent to corporal punishment. **he will not die**: this may be interpreted in two ways: 1) simply, corporal punishment is not (normally) fatal; 2) if the child is not given salutary beatings to make him learn wisdom, he will come to a bad end. The latter interpretation is supported by 13:24 and by 19:18, where *RSV*'s "on his destruction" is, literally, "to kill him" (*'el-hamîtô*).

This verse has a very close parallel in *Ahikar*, lines 81–82: "Do not withhold your son from the rod . . . If I beat you, my son, you will not die, and if I leave you to your own heart . . ." (the following words are missing, but it has been conjectured that the line originally ended with "you will not live"). This is much closer to the present verse than anything in comparable passages in Egyptian literature. It would seem that the sources of this section of Proverbs are not confined to Egyptian models but include Semitic ones. There may well be a direct connection between these two passages, though it has been suggested that here the passage of *Ahikar* is modelled on Proverbs and not *vice versa*.

14. If you beat him: better, "You must beat him" (and so save his life). Great stress is placed here on the first word *'attā*, "you", perhaps to draw the reader's attention to the extreme importance of the matter. **from Sheol**: that is, from the fate which attends those who refuse to learn and practise wisdom (compare 1:12; 7:27; 9:18; 15:24).

15–18. These verses mark a resumption of the usual address to a son or pupil. They form a distinct short Instruction of which vv. 15–16 are the introduction and vv. 17–18 the main body containing a single admonition.

15. My son: this phrase, occurring as the initial formula of the introduction to an Instruction, is that which is found most frequently in the Instructions of chapters 1–9 (2:1; 3:1; 5:1, 20; 6:1; 7:1). In two of those passages it is immediately followed, as here, by a conditional clause (**if** . . .). The appeal to the pupil to acquire a **heart** that is **wise** expresses the whole intention of such Instructions (compare especially 2:10). The tone is more personal than that of the other introductions, but these verses clearly belong to the same genre.

16. My soul: literally, "My kidneys", the seat of the emotions and affections in Hebrew thought. **what is right**: in 8:6 Wisdom herself claims this quality (*mêšārîm*) for the words which she speaks.

17–18. The advice not to **envy** the wicked is found also in 3:31; 24:1, 19. It must be presumed that **sinners** aroused envy because they were so successful: they were committing crimes with apparent impunity and living prosperously on their illicit gains. The background to these passages is evidently a growing scepticism about the principle of just retribution which the teacher here attempts to counter simply by emphatically reiterating that principle (compare also 1:10–19).

17. but continue in: there is no verb in MT, which has simply "but (in) the fear of Yahweh." Some commentators take "the fear of Yahweh" to be a second object of the verb in the first line, since this verb (*qn'*, piel) has what are now often regarded as two meanings, though they are actually related: to envy, and to be zealous. If this view is correct, the pupil is here being advised to apply his "zeal" to "fearing Yahweh" rather than to the emulation of sinners.

Driver (*Bib.* 32 [1951], p. 196) has plausibly suggested that "fear" here is a collective noun standing for "those who fear": it is those whom the pupil should envy rather than sinners. Other commentators suppose that a verb has dropped out from the second line: but the line is already long in MT. Toy more plausibly, followed by Oesterley, proposed the emendation of *bᵉyir'at-yhwh*, "(in) the fear of Yahweh" to *yᵉrā'-'et-yhwh*, "fear Yahweh" (imperative). (See 24:21). **all the day**: that is, "always".

18. Surely: the words so rendered here by *RSV* (*kî 'im*) can hardly have that meaning. In v. 17, where also they occur, they have been rendered by "but"; but this meaning would be inappropriate in the context of the present verse. An alternative meaning is "For if . . ."; but one would then expect a verb to follow. In MT there is no such verb; but LXX may provide a clue to the original text: "For if you keep these things". Several commentators (Oesterley, Gemser, McKane) have accepted such an emendation.

future (*'aḥᵃrît*); **hope** (*tiqwāh*): *'aḥᵃrît* means literally "what comes after", "end", and it has this meaning in most of the other passages in which it occurs in Proverbs. But here and in 22:14, 20a, where also it occurs in parallelism with **hope**, it denotes a happy and successful life in store for the young pupil. Both words occur together in a similar sense also in Jer. 29:11, where Yahweh promises a happy existence for the exiles in Babylon, whom he will restore to their homes. Despite Dahood, *'aḥᵃrît* does not here refer to life after death.

19–21. This is another brief Instruction, consisting of introduction (v. 19), admonition (v. 20) and motive-clause (v. 21).

19. Although brief, this verse is typical of such introductions: **Hear, my son** occurs also in 1:8 and 4:10, though here there is the addition of the emphatic *'attā*, "you!". **be wise** (imperative): compare 6:6. **direct your mind** (literally, "heart") **in the way** (*'aššēr badderek libbekā*); compare the use of the same verb but with an intransitive sense in 4:14: "do not walk in the way of evil men" (*'al-tᵉaššēr bᵉderek rā'îm*). **the way** here is equivalent to the way of wisdom (4:11) or the way of life (6:23).

20–21. This topic – or more precisely that part of it which is concerned with drunkenness – occurs again in vv. 29–35, where it is treated very differently. The latter passage lacks both an introduction and the form of an admonition, and is probably an isolated piece. Plöger suggests that it may have been placed at the conclusion of this series of admonitions in order to develop the topic in a humorous vein.

20. winebibbers (*sōbᵉʾê yāyin*); **gluttonous eaters of meat** (*zōlᵉlê bāśār*): these terms (drunkard, *sōbē'* and glutton, *zōlēl*) occur together in the law concerning the rebellious son in Dt. 21:20. They may have formed a pair of stock epithets. It may be significant that both passages are concerned with the behaviour of youth. The verb *zālal* properly means "to be reckless, extravagant" – here in overeating. In Hebrew the verse ends with the word *lāmô*, literally, "for themselves", presumably indicating the self-centredness of this kind of person, whose company the pupil is advised to avoid (**Be not among** . . .).

21. will come to poverty: presumably as a result of extravagance or inattention to work. On the meaning of this verb see on 20:13. **drowsiness**: that is, the torpor which comes from overindulgence. Compare the various proverbs in the sentence literature which speak of the lazy person's propensity to fall asleep.

22–28. These verses all contain material reminiscent of the earlier Instructions in the book and particularly of their introductions; but they hardly constitute a stylistic unity. V. 26 is the only verse in which the "father" specifically addresses his "son", but he is probably also the speaker in v. 22 (for another example of his referring to himself in the third person see 4:1; 6:20): the appeal to hear (*RSV* **Hearken**) and the reference to both parents (compare 1:8; 6:20) make this likely. But vv. 24 and 25 do not appear to be part of his speech. V. 24 seems to be an independent proverb, which is then "personalized" by v. 25. In their present form vv. 22–25 are linked together by their especial emphasis on the desirability of a son's giving his parents pleasure by obeying his parents' teaching and so setting out on the proper course in life. However, it is improbable that these verses originally formed a literary unity. Vv. 24 and 25, as has already been suggested, do not appear to belong to the "father"'s speech.

But it is also doubtful whether even vv. 22–3 alone constitute an original instruction. If they do, v. 23 is clearly the admonitory part of it. But although this verse, with its advice to **Buy truth** etc., verbally resembles 4:5, 7 (the same verb, *qānāh*, is employed there as here, but is there rendered in *RSV* by "Get"), the long list of things to be acquired (**truth, wisdom, instruction, and understanding**) is general in character and entirely lacks the intimacy of the appeal to "love" and "embrace" Wisdom in 4:1ff.; it is more reminiscent of the abstract list of accomplishments to be acquired which is set out in the general introduction of 1:2–5.

Thus v. 23 is probably to be understood as an expanded form of the introduction to this Instruction rather than as a specific admonition in itself. If this is so, vv. 22–8 contain only one instruction: this is to be found in vv. 26–8, or perhaps in vv. 22, 26–8, the body of the Instruction consisting of vv. 27–8. The other verses (23–5) are elaborations, probably added at a late stage in the editorial process.

22. who: on this construction (*zeh* introducing a relative clause) see *GK* 138g.

24. Compare 17:21; 23:15. Note the parallelism between **righteous** and **wise**.

25. and mother (*wᵉʾimmekā*): the mention of the mother twice in the same verse is strange. It has been suggested that this word should be emended to *ʿimmᵉkā*: so, "Let your father be glad *at you*".

26. give me your heart: the heart (*lēb*) was the seat of the will and the intelligence, not of the affections. Several commentators take this phrase to mean "pay attention"; but it probably means more than that. The father is demanding that his son should submit his will to his. **observe**: *RSV* here, together with the Versions, follows Qere (*tiṣṣōrnāh*). This verb *nāṣar* occurs frequently in Proverbs in the sense of "watch, keep, guard". Here the pupil is to watch the behaviour or way of life (**ways**) of the father with a view to imitation. Kethib, however, reads *tirṣénāh* from *rāṣāh*, "delight in, approve". The meaning is not very different.

27. Compare the similar 22:14a, which uses the same expression **deep pit** (*šûḥāh ᵃmuqqāh*) of the words (literally, "mouth") of "loose women" (*zārôt*). Here the word *zônāh*, "prostitute" (*RSV* **harlot**) is used, though the LXX (which otherwise has a different text) may suggest an original reading *zārāh*. The latter word appears in parallelism with *nokriyyāh* (**adventuress**) in the warnings on the same subject in the Instructions of chapters 1–9 (2:16; 5:20; 7:5). Those Instructions, although they do not employ the words **pit** and **well**, speak of the woman's house as "sinking down to death" (2:18) or of her paths as leading to Sheol (5;5; compare also 7:27). They may be elaborations of more succinct admonitions such as the present one.

28. The second line of this verse hardly makes sense. Two solutions have been proposed: 1) to read the passive participle *b^e gûdîm*, "deceived", "betrayed", instead of the active participle *bôg^e dîm*, "treacherous" (*RSV* **faithless**) – so Gemser; 2) to take *bôg^e dîm* as a collective noun meaning "deceit", or "treachery": the line would then mean "she repeatedly acts treacherously (literally, 'repeats acts of treachery') towards men" (so Driver, *Bib.* 32 [1951], p. 196.).

29–35. This passage is quite different from anything else in Proverbs (though compare 27:23–27) and is somewhat reminiscent of the "miniature essays" of Ecclesiasticus. It is built round the admonition in v. 31, with regard to which the verses which follow function in the same way as a motive-clause. Although it is written in a jocular, not to say burlesque, style, it has a serious purpose and is an excellent example of effective teaching method. The six questions with which it begins in v. 29 constitute a single riddle which requires the pupil to identify the kind of person whom the teacher has in mind (compare the use of the same question-and-answer technique in Ecclesiasticus, for example Sir. 10:19); the last of these gives an unmistakable hint of the correct answer which is supplied in v. 30, while vv. 32–5 paint the deplorable condition of the drunkard in vivid colours.

29. The first line of this verse is perhaps better rendered by "Who cries 'Woe!'? who cries 'Alas!'?" **strife**: that is, drunken quarrels. **complaining**: perhaps better, "trouble". **wounds without cause**: viz., acquired in a drunken quarrel. **redness**: the meaning of this word is not certain. It may mean "clouding" or "dimness" – that is, inability to see clearly.

30. tarry long: the same word is used in Isa. 5:11 of late drinkers. **to try mixed wine** (*laḥqōr mimsāk*): this noun, which occurs in the Old Testament only here and in Isa. 65:11, may mean "mixing bowl" (so Dahood and *KB*^{3}, on the basis of an Ugaritic word). The phrase may then mean "to inspect (the bottom of) the bowl", that is, to drain it. If on the other hand **mixed wine** is correct, it refers to wine to which spices had been added to increase its potency, especially appropriate to a banquet (compare 9:2). In later times (see 2 Mac. 15:39) the custom of mixing wine with water was adopted by the Jews from the Greeks; but in Old Testament times this was regarded as an undesirable adulteration (Isa. 1:22).

31. Do not look at: although the mere contemplation of a cup of wine might give an irresistible thirst to an alcoholic, it is unlikely that the writer would express his warning so indirectly as this.

Driver's suggestion that this line should be rendered by "Do not drink deeply of . . ." (taking the verb to be not the more common *rā'āh* meaning "see, look at" but an alternative form of *rāwāh*, "to be saturated, to drink one's fill" – a form attested elsewhere (*Bib.* 32 [1951], p. 187) makes better sense. **when it sparkles**: literally, "when it gives (out) its eye". *'ayin* in the sense of "gleam, sparkle" occurs also in Ezek. 1:7; 10:9; Dan. 10:6: see P. Auvray, 1954, pp. 4–5.

and goes down smoothly: this odd third line in a poem otherwise consisting entirely of parallel couplets has aroused the suspicion of some commentators. There is a similar line, also referring to wine, in Ca. 7:9 (Heb. 10). Toy and Oesterley suggested that the line here is a gloss, perhaps for some reason borrowed from the passage in the Song of Songs; but Gemser suggested that a line has dropped out of what was originally a second couplet in the verse, such as that which follows in the other passage: "gliding over lips and teeth". Plöger, however, defended the line, as possibly being a common expression which the author thought to be appropriate to his theme.

32. At the last: that is, "in the end, afterwards". **stings** (*yapriš*): the meaning of this word is not precisely known (so *KB*[3]). If it is identical with the common verb *pāraš* it could mean "spray, squirt" in this context, with "venom" (probably Hebrew *rôš*) either to be understood as an unexpressed object or possibly omitted by haplography (LXX speaks of "poison" here). But it has been suggested that it is cognate with an Arabic verb meaning "to wound" (Gemser). This would then be its only occurrence in the Old Testament. **adder**: this is clearly some kind of poisonous snake, but as it has not been precisely identified its method of injecting its venom – whether by biting, stinging or spraying – is unfortunately not known.

33. strange things: such as pink elephants! **your mind** (*lēb*) **will utter perverse things** (*tahpūkôt*): the heart (or **mind**) can be said to "speak" in the sense that it produces the thoughts which are then expressed in speech (compare 15:28; 16:23). *tahpūkôt* elsewhere refers to malicious speech; but here it appears to mean muddled or confused speech (see on 2:12 on the cognate verb *hāpak*, "to overturn, change").

34. in the midst of the sea: that is, "out to sea" or "on the high seas" (compare the use of the expression in Ezek. 27:25, 26; 28:2, Jon. 2:3 [Heb. 4]). The verse describes the sensation of the drunken man, whose surroundings seem to be bewilderingly in constant motion as if he were lying in his bunk in a ship out to sea. **on the top of a mast**: *ḥibbēl* (*RSV* **mast**) occurs only here in the Old Testament. It may be presumed that it is a nautical term cognate with *ḥebel*, "a cord, rope" and *ḥôbél*, "a sailor" (as one whose business is with ropes). But there is no certainty that it means "mast". LXX appears to have read *ḥôbēl*; but it has a substantially different text: "and as a pilot in a great storm"; there is no reason to accept such a major emendation. McKane, Plöger and *REB* take the word to mean "rigging" or "tackle": to be lying at the topmost point of the ship's rigging may be required of sailors, but they are even more subject to a violent rocking motion than the passenger below in his bunk. On this interpretation the second line of the verse would heighten the effect beyond that of the first.

35. "They struck me . . .": the drunkard now recognizes that he has been involved in a fight, but that his condition at the time was such that he did not feel his injuries. **you will say**: this is not in the Hebrew text (it is supplied by LXX), but correctly interprets these last two verses as being the words of the hypothetical drunkard. **I did not feel it**: this verb (*ḥālāh*) generally means "to be ill" or "to suffer an injury"; most commentators, however, take it here to mean "to *feel* pain", as apparently in Jer. 5:3. However, Driver (*JTS* 29 [1928], p. 392), followed by Gemser, interprets it quite differently. He links the verb with an Ethiopic word and takes the phrase to mean "but I did not care". Driver also interprets *bal-yādā'tī* (*RSV* **I did not feel it**) similarly, arguing for this interpretation on the grounds that *yāda'*, which most frequently means "to know", also frequently means "to be concerned (for)" (especially with respect to individuals).

When shall I awake?: presumably the man is still suffering from a hangover and cannot be said to have recovered complete consciousness. The sense of the phrase – though hardly its strict grammatical sense – may be "When I wake up . . .". **I will seek another drink**: literally, "I shall yet again look for it, once more". This is the teacher's final warning: habitual drunkenness can lead to alcoholism.

24:1–2. V. 1 reverts to the admonition form and appears to be the beginning of a new and isolated admonition (LXX introduces it with "My son"). That its theme has already been dealt with in 23:17 and will appear again in v. 19 is the more readily accounted for if all these verses occur in what were originally separate pieces.

The same theme occurs also in 3:31–2; compare also 1:10ff. This verse differs, however, from all these passages in that, while they reinforce their admonitions either by depicting the downfall of the wicked or by a reference to an alternative way of life which has the blessing of Yahweh, here the motive clause seems inadequate, as it does no more than describe the activities of the **evil men** in question, of which those who emulate them must already be aware. Presumably it must be the apparent success and prosperity of such men rather than their wickedness as such which the pupil may be tempted to emulate, though this is not specifically stated (compare 1:11–14, where a successful prize is promised). **be with them**: that is, join them in their activities (compare again 1:11, 14).

3–9. Here the style changes once more, this time to that of the sentence literature. These verses contain no admonitions at all: they all have the form of statements. Vv. 3–4 describe the gifts of wisdom in terms of a well-founded and luxurious house; vv. 5–6 speak of the power conferred by wisdom (v. 5), with a particular illustration (v. 6); vv. 7–9 are distinct short proverbial statements in couplet form. All these verses, however, have an educational purpose, and have probably been editorially assembled and placed here to follow vv. 1 and 2 in order to present the attractions of wisdom to the young men who are envisaged in vv. 1–2 as tempted to follow the example of the wicked. It is probably significant that vv. 8 and 9 revert to the theme of vv. 1 and 2, so creating a well-rounded whole.

3–4. The statements made in these verses are in the first place to be understood literally. It is a general principle of the teaching of the book that **wisdom** will confer material prosperity on those who follow her (see, for example, 8:18, 21; 21:21), or that such prosperity will be given to the righteous (see especially 15:6) or to those who fear and honour Yahweh (so 3:9–10; 22:4). Such promises are sometimes associated with the **house** of such persons, for example in 15:6: "In the house of the righteous there is much treasure". So what is stated here is that the followers of wisdom will so prosper materially that they will be able to build their house and furnish it with every luxury.

The above is the simple meaning of these verses. But more is probably intended here: there are various allusions to other aspects of the teaching of the book, in which the word **house** is used in a variety of ways. Apart from its literal meaning and the extended meanings of "household" and "family", common in biblical

Hebrew, there is the house that Wisdom builds for herself (9:1; 14:1) and where she plays the part of hostess, offering wholesome "food" to her guests (9:1–6), which is contrasted with the house of the "strange woman" (2:18; 5:8; 7:8, 27) or of the "woman Folly" (9:14–18) which leads to death. In fact, it is possible to interpret the statement that **By wisdom a house is built** here as referring to a house built for herself by Wisdom (see *GK* 121f), who then offers both stability and prosperity to those who possess her. (We may also compare Ps. 127:1, where it is Yahweh who is the builder.)

It is also possible that there is an echo here of Wisdom's connection with the creation of the world by Yahweh (cf. 8:22–31). In 3:19–20 it is stated that Yahweh created the universe by **wisdom** (*ḥokmāh*), by **understanding** (*tᵉbûnāh*) and by his **knowledge** (*da'at*). It is perhaps not a coincidence that the same three words in the same order are employed here of the building of a *house* by Wisdom, especially since the same verb *kûn* (**established**) is used in both passages, though in different modes.

Finally, there is a curious reminiscence here of a verse in the first Instruction of chapters 1–9 (1:8ff.). Both these passages speak of gaining possession of treasure. In 1:13 the thieves who seek to persuade the young man to join them claim, "We shall find all precious goods (*kol-hôn-yāqār*), we shall fill our houses with spoil (*nᵉmallē'* bāttênū šālāl)". Here in 24:3–4 the same material goods (*kol-hôn yāqār*, *RSV* **all precious . . . riches**), with which the **rooms** of the house (*bayit*) will be **filled** (*yimmālᵉ'u*) are promised, not as the illegal "spoil" of the criminals who are doomed to destruction (1:16–19) but to those who, on the contrary, follow the teaching of Wisdom.

These two verses, then, although they are expressed in the form of an apparently simple statement about the material benefits conferred on those who set themselves to acquire wisdom, may be among the latest additions to the book. They show knowledge of various passages in the earlier chapters and subtly build on them.

5–6. See on 21:22 for the theme, and compare Ec. 9:16.

5. In the first line of this verse MT has, literally, "A wise man (is) in strength" (*geber-ḥakām ba'ôz*). Most commentators, however, together with RSV (and see BHS) follow LXX, which has "A wise man is superior to a strong one", perhaps a rendering of the Hebrew *gābar ḥākām mē'āz*. In the second line, MT has "and a man of knowledge consolidates strength" (*wᵉ'îš-da'at mᵉ'ammeṣ-kōaḥ*), but most commentators again find a comparison here by emending the last two words to *mē'ammîṣ-kōaḥ*, (["is superior] to one mighty in strength"). Plöger, however, finds MT satisfactory in both lines, and McKane suggests emendation only in the case of the first. The general sense of the verse is unaffected: real strength resides in intellectual superiority, not in brute force.

6. The particle *kî* (**for**) normally introduces an explanation of, or motivation for, what precedes. In this case it seems that the explanation is intended to give support to v. 5 by citing particular circumstances in which the wise man is shown to be superior to the physically powerful. However, this intention is not really fulfilled by this verse. A slightly different theme is introduced: the need for a person to receive good advice from persons wiser than himself, which is not at all the point of verse 5. What seems to have happened is that an originally not very appropriate proverbial saying has been tacked on. It expresses a theme which was evidently a commonplace of current proverbial wisdom, having parallels and variants elsewhere in the book. The first line is almost identical with 20:18b, and the second exactly identical with 11:14b; compare also 15:22. *taḥbūlôt*, **wise guidance** (see on 1:5) also occurs in 11:14 and 20:18. **you can wage**: this direct address, though not strictly an admonition (compare 20:18), is somewhat at variance with the style of the context.

As in the case of 20:18, this reference to military activity is not to be taken literally, as if addressed to a king or general, but is a figurative expression referring to the "battle of life".

7. Wisdom: on this form (*ḥokmôt*) see on 1:20. **is too high for**: this translation is based on the supposition that *rā'môt* (elsewhere some kind of precious substance, probably "black coral" and used as jewellery) is here an unusual spelling of *rāmôt* "high" (feminine plural). Some comentators, however, take the word in its more usual sense (it occurs in Job 28:18 and Ezek. 27:16). The line would then mean that wisdom is as unattainable by a **fool** as coral would be. There is thus little difference in meaning between the two interpretations. The reason why the feminine plural form is used is not clear; it may be in order to conform to the (apparent) feminine ending of *ḥokmôt*.

in the gate: this does not necessarily mean "in court" as in 22:22. The city gate was also the place where general discussion of affairs took place. The line presumably means that the **fool** is incapable of making a sensible contribution to this and so keeps silent. This may seem to contradict those proverbs which speak of the fool as very ready to **open his mouth** (for example, 10:14; 12:23; 14:3; 15:2; 18:6, 7), but the meaning may be that in a serious and formal debate he will be overawed.

8–9. These two proverbs are linked verbally (*mezimmôt*, mischief, v. 8; *zimmāh*, devising, v. 9) and to some extent in theme. V. 9 also picks up the thought about the fool in v. 7.

8. The point of this verse is not clear. It may be that **mischief-maker** (*ba'al-mezimmôt*) was a technical term for a person whose exclusion from the community was axiomatic (compare *'îš mezimmôt* in 12:2, a person who was subject to Yahweh's condemnation).

9. In its present position this proverb carries the thought of v. 8 further. **folly** (*'iwwelet*) should perhaps be rendered by "a fool" (abstract for concrete: see Driver, *Bib.* 32 [1951], p. 196). In Proverbs the fool (*'ewîl*) is not a simple-minded and harmless person: he is an obstinate and incorrigible person (see on 1:7) who equally with the "mischief-maker" of v. 8 is a schemer (*zimmāh*, **devising**) who sins against society in such ways as gossiping, picking quarrels, stirring up dissension etc. (see, for example, 10:14; 11:29; 12:15, 16; 20:3) and is consequently equated with the **scoffer** (*lēṣ*) as one whose presence in society is intolerable.

10–12. There is a return to the admonitory style in v. 11 with the singular imperative **Rescue . . .**! This admonition is followed in v. 12 by a question which has the force of a motive clause. V. 10, also an address in the second person singular, could be an isolated saying but is more probably related to the verses which follow.

There are serious problems of detail in these verses, but the literal meaning of the admonition in v. 11 is sufficiently clear. However, it is not immediately clear who are the persons **being taken away to death** and who are **stumbling to the slaughter**, who must be rescued by the person addressed on pain of Yahweh's displeasure. It has been widely supposed that they are persons who have been sentenced to death either justly or unjustly by the court or by the authorities, and who are now being **taken away** to a place of execution. But this is quite impossible. Firstly, if this is the case, it is taken for granted that the person addressed is in a position to intervene and prevent the executions. Such a person would presumably have to be a revolutionary leader able to defy the authority of the established government; and for this there is no warrant in the text. Secondly, if these persons had been justly convicted, to interfere with the course of justice in this way would be both illegal and immoral – but v. 12 shows that this is not the case. Thirdly, the reference cannot be to persons *unjustly* convicted, since this is clearly not envisaged in the text, which makes no such distinction but is a general admonition to rescue people threatened with death.

It is important to observe that in fact the text says nothing at all about a legal trial or about a legal or arbitrary sentence of death. It refers simply to persons who are about to be killed. Only one situation is possible: it is that these are persons who have been set upon by robbers who are intent on murdering their victims and whose activities are observed by the person addressed. Such criminal activities are attested elsewhere in the book of Proverbs (1:11; compare 24:1, 15). The victims have been waylaid, seized (*lᵉqūḥîm*, literally, "taken"; *RSV* **being taken away**) and are about to be killed (*lammāwet*, **to death**; *hereg*, **slaughter**). To intervene and come to their assistance (*haṣṣēl*, **Rescue**) is presented to the – presumably – active young man as a positive duty (v. 12); and faintheartedness or cowardice cannot be regarded as an excuse for avoiding this duty (v. 10).

10. If you faint: literally, "Have you been slack . . . ?" **your strength is small**: this line is unusually short, and some commentators suppose that some words have fallen out. Gemser proposed the addition of "when you need it" at the end; but such suggestions have not been universally accepted. There is a play on words between *ṣārāh*, **adversity** and *ṣar*, **small**, literally, "narrow, limited".

11. hold back: the verb, in the second person masculine imperfect (*taḥśôk*), is preceded by the particle *'im*, whose normal connotation is "if", which clearly makes no sense here. Opinions are divided about its meaning here, since it has two other connotations, one positive and the other negative. On the one hand, it may express a wish: "O that . . . !, Would that . . . !" (*GK* 151e – compare Ps. 81:8 [Heb. 9]). This is apparently how *RSV* understands it: the verb *ḥāśak* can mean "to hold back" and so "to prevent". Driver, however (*Bib.* 32 [1951], pp. 188–9) suggested the meaning "keep safe, save", on the basis of a cognate Syriac verb; this, if correct, would give a somewhat better sense. (Vulg. also has "save".) On the other hand, it has been pointed out that *'im* can have a negative sense which in this case would have almost the force of a prohibition: "Thou shalt not . . ." (compare LXX). In that case *ḥāsak* may have its intransitive meaning of "to hold *oneself* back". Thus despite these syntactical differences there is little difference ultimately in the interpretation of the line: the pupil is admonished not to hesitate in going to the help of those in imminent danger of death.

those who are stumbling (*māṭîm*): several commentators prefer to point this word as *muṭṭîm*, the hophal participle of *nāṭāh*, literally "stretched out", that is, "made ready"; Driver accepts this reading, but (*ZAW* 50 [1932], p. 146) derives it from a postulated verb cognate with an Aramaic word, literally "to arrive at", giving a similar meaning, "ready for", "on the point of".

slaughter: this noun (*hereg*), it should be noted, is never used of judicial execution, and the cognate verb *hārag* very rarely so.

12. we did not know: the plural is unexpected, since **you say** is singular. LXX has the singular, which is probably the correct reading. **this**: on *zeh* in a neutral sense, less common than *zō't*, see *GK* 136b and the lexica. **who weighs the heart**; **who keeps watch over your soul**: see on 16:2 and 21:2. **soul** (*nepeš*): better, "your life" or simply "you". The final line is a succinct expression of the notion of retribution.

13–14. The combination of **my son** with a general statement about the importance of acquiring wisdom – compare 23:15, 19 as well as the introductions to the Instructions in chapters 1–9 – suggests that these verses are yet another introduction to a series of more precise admonitions constituting a distinct Instruction (vv. 15–16, 17–18, 19–20, 21–2). The form is unique, however, in that it begins with what is ostensibly a very precise admonition – to **eat honey**. It has been supposed by some commentators that this should be taken literally: that the instructor here concerns himself with a small and ephemeral matter of pleasing the palate. This is improbable. Neither is this true of the other three references to honey in Proverbs (16:24; 25:16; 25:27). Nowhere else in the Instructions in this book is advice given about purely physical enjoyment. Here the topic of the sweetness and goodness of honey is introduced simply as analogy: if honey is **good** and **sweet** and so desirable, so also is **wisdom** (compare the other qualities attributed to it in the other Instructions, for example pleasantness [*nō'am*,], 3:17; beautification, 3:22; companionship, 7:4).

13. the drippings of the honeycomb: this phrase in *RSV* corresponds to a single word in the Hebrew, *nōpet*, which may simply be another word for "honey", or perhaps "honeycomb". Honey eaten straight from the honeycomb is of course particularly sweet and delicious. The same word occurs in 5:3; 27:7. **your taste**: literally, "your palate".

14. The first line of this verse is difficult. It is probably all that remains of a couplet from which several words have been lost. As it stands it reads "So know (on the unusual form of this imperative *–dᵉʿeh–* see GK 48l) for yourself (*lᵉnapšekā*)". Various suggestions have been made for the restoration of the original couplet and/or for the emendation of the text. Thus Gemser suggested "So is knowledge (*daʿat*) sweet for your heart, and wisdom is good for your soul"; later, however, in the second edition of his commentary Gemser accepted the suggestion of Thomas (*JTS* 38 [1937], p. 401) which associated *dᵉʿeh* with an Arabic verb meaning "to seek". All the suggestions of this kind which have been made are speculative, and the original text is no doubt irrecoverable.

The last two lines, except for the addition of **If you find it**, are identical with 23:18 (see on that verse). Here they are hardly appropriate to what precedes, and may be a later addition. They may have been a current cliché.

15–16. This warning against criminal activity can hardly be addressed to the same young man as in vv. 10–12, where the teacher's requirement of acts of altruism by the pupil necessarily presupposes a basic decency of character. The verb *ʾārab* (**Lie . . . in wait**) is reminiscent of 1:10–18, although the crime mentioned here appears to be an attack on property alone rather than robbery with violence. Its precise nature is not specified: it may be an attempt to bring about the ruin of another person by damaging his property in his absence.

15. dwelling, *nāweh*, properly a shepherd's hut, and **home**, *rēbeṣ*, literally "lair" or "place for lying down" – of animals, are "high-flown and poetic language" indicating a "picturesqueness of expression" (McKane) rather than an indication of a rural setting (as Oesterley, Gemser). **as a wicked man**: grammatically this word (simply *rāšāʿ* in Hebrew) could have a vocative sense: "O wicked man!", and has so been taken by some commentators, who, however, recognize that it is inappropriate since this is an admonition addressed by a teacher to a pupil, and who therefore omit it as a gloss (so Toy, Gemser, McKane; the last of these explains it as mistakenly introduced to make a contrast with **righteous** [(*ṣaddîq*]). But *RSV* is correct: the noun defines the category into which those who commit such acts fall (see *GK* 118q).

16. This motive clause is a straightforward statement of the principle of retribution. The **righteous man** may appear to be crushed, but will ultimately, even after many (literally, **seven**) attacks on him have seemed at the time to succeed in their aim, win through (presumably by divine help), and the **wicked** will come to a bad end.

17–18. This admonition is closely connected with the previous one. The same verbs are used in vv. 16 and 17: v. 16 speaks of the temporary fall (*nāpal*) of the righteous, and of the overthrow (*kšl*, niphal) of the wicked; v. 17 of the fall (*nāpal*) of the enemy and of his stumbling (*kšl*, niphal). Vv. 17 and 18 pick up the topic of the fall of the wicked and pursue it further with a warning not to gloat over the fall of a personal enemy. It is interesting that it is taken for granted here and elsewhere in the Old Testament that hatred and malice are regular features of Israelite society, but a number of passages show a concern to set limits to them, or at least to their overt expression.

17. This verse, if taken by itself, would seem to express an attitude calculated to limit the social damage caused by such feuds. It does not, however, go as far as 25:21–2, which enjoins positive assistance to an enemy fallen into indigence as an action worthy of divine reward, or as Exod. 23:4–5, which makes assistance to an enemy in difficulties a divine command. Job 31:29 regards rejoicing over the ruin of an enemy as a serious sin deserving divine punishment, and in Ps. 35:13–15 the psalmist claims credit for grieving over his enemy's troubles. Prov. 20:22 warns against taking revenge for losses or injuries inflicted by an enemy, but counsels trust that Yahweh himself will do this.

18. This verse, which functions as a motive clause, has been seen by a number of commentators as falling seriously behind the ethical standard which v. 17, taken by itself, might naturally be taken to reflect: that is, it appears to assume that it is quite acceptable for a person to *hope* that his enemy will meet with a bad end, and indeed expresses the hope that Yahweh will not be deflected from destroying him. Refraining from gloating over his discomfiture, therefore, is not inspired by sympathy for him, but, on the contrary, is intended to ensure that Yahweh does so. In other words, the spirit of revenge appears to be approved rather than disapproved. This does indeed seem to be the meaning of the verse. It is not clear why looking for revenge is acceptable to Yahweh provided that one does not openly express pleasure in it. It may be that such rejoicing is held to be premature and usurps the function of Yahweh as avenger (compare 20:22). The verse may be a later addition to the admonition, asserting the prerogative of Yahweh.

Lest (*pen-*): better, "or". It is not implied that Yahweh might *not* see: the meaning is that *if* one gloats over one's enemy's discomfiture, he will certainly refrain from punishing that enemy. No explanation is given why Yahweh should **turn away his anger from him** (that is, from the enemy); but it may be implied that there is now nothing to choose between the two persons: *Schadenfreude* (deriving pleasure from the misfortune of others) is evidently, as in Job 31:29, regarded as being as serious a sin as that committed by the enemy (this is not defined), and as being one which causes Yahweh's displeasure (*ra' b^e'ênâw*, literally, "it is evil in his eyes"), and he might justifiably not only turn his anger away from the enemy but also turn it *towards* the other person.

Whether the above interpretation is correct or not, McKane is probably justified in his observation that in their present form these verses show a lack of human feeling and sympathy.

19–20. This topic is the same as that of vv. 1–2, on which see the comment. It is appropriate to its context here, as pursuing further the theme of the proper reaction to the activities of the wicked. The second line of v. 19 and v. 1a are close variants. The motive clause (v. 20) here, however, is a plain statement of the principle of retribution.

19. Fret not yourself: that is, "Do not become overheated or indignant".

20. On this meaning of *'aḥ^a rît* (**future**) see on 23:18; on the image of the putting out of the lamp see on 13:9.

21–22. This admonition may have originally been an isolated short Instruction (it has the formal introduction, **My son**). There is nothing to suggest that it was placed here as being a suitable conclusion to the section, as has been suggested by some commentators, who took it as a concluding appeal to the pupil to observe religious and patriotic obligations. Apart from the first line the text presents serious difficulties of interpretation.

21. the Lord and the king: the king in Israel was closely associated with Yahweh, as is attested by a number of proverbs in this book, both in that he derived his power from him and in that he acted as his earthly representative. It was natural, therefore, that the two should be associated together as the source of supreme power whom all must **fear**.

However, both text and meaning of the second line are disputed. The ostensible meaning of MT is "do not associate (*'al-tit'ārāb*) with persons who change" (or "differ" – *šônîm*, the participle of *šānāh*). This meaning was accepted by Toy, Barucq and Plöger, who explained *šônîm* as referring to persons who were disposed to rebel against, or who wished to change, traditional ideas or systems. This, however, is dubious. The quite different rendering of *RSV* is taken from the LXX. In this rendering, **either of them** presupposes reading *šᵉnêhem* for *šônîm*; but **disobey** is more difficult to account for. LXX may have read *tit'abbār* for *tit'ārāb* (so Gemser), but *tit'abbār* seems to mean to become angry or excited rather than to be disobedient (see on 14:16; 20:2).

A different proposal has been made which does not necessitate any emendation of MT. Thomas (*ZAW* 52 [1934], p. 237 and Driver (*Bib.* 32 [1951], p. 189), followed by Emerton (*VT* 24 [1974], pp. 25–30) and by KB^3, proposed the view that *šônîm* here means "noblemen". They postulated the existence, previously unrecognized, of a Hebrew verb meaning "to be exalted", cognate with an Arabic word of similar meaning and attested in a number of places in the Old Testament. If this view is correct, the pupil here addressed is advised on the one hand to fear God and the king but, on the other hand, to avoid having anything to do with noblemen or persons of high but lesser rank. The reason for this advice is then given in the following verse.

22. disaster from them; ruin . . . from both: Hebrew has "their disaster"; "the ruin of both". *RSV*, on the assumption that the persons referred to here are Yahweh and the king (see on v. 21 above), translates in a way which makes these the *agents* of the ruin of those who are disobedient (subjective genitive). But if in fact "they" are the noblemen (*šônîm*) of v. 21b, an objective genitive is more probable: the pupil is advised to have nothing to do with noblemen, as they are prone to intrigues, which may be discovered at any time, and it will be *their* ruin that will follow, together with that of their associates. This interpretation requires the emendation of *šᵉnêhem*, *RSV* **them both**, to *šônîm* (or *haššônîm*, Driver): "the ruin of noblemen, who knows (when it will come)?".

It would be foolish to pretend that any of the attempted interpretations of these two verses is other than uncertain.

MORE "SAYINGS OF WISE MEN" PROVERBS, ADMONITIONS AND AN EXAMPLE STORY 24:23–34

V. 23a is one of the headings provided by the final editor of the book, marking the beginning of a major section. The section continues only to the end of the chapter: 25:1 is another main heading introducing a new section, consisting, like 10:1–22:16, of collected proverbs. The word **also** in v. 23a suggests, however, that this section, as a second collection attributed to "wise men", was at one time placed here as an appendix to 22:17–24:22 (compare, and see the comment on, 22:17). It is interesting to note that in the LXX this section is placed after 30:14, a fact which may suggest that its status as an appendix is not original. All this shows that the book has had a complex history of composition of which we know little.

This section has a more miscellaneous character than the preceding one. Vv. 23b and 26 are one-line proverbs – a rarity in the book. Vv. 24–5 is an extended, four-line proverb of a type of which there are a few other examples in the book. Vv. 27–9 are instructions. Vv. 30–34 are a short moral tale comparable with 4:3ff.; 7:6–23; Ps. 37:35–6, in which a teacher refers to his own experiences – whether real or imagined – as a way of teaching by example.

The choice of material to form this section is not entirely haphazard. Two main topics are dealt with: honesty and impartiality in the administration of justice (vv. 23b–26, 28–9) and advice to the farmer (vv. 30–34).

23. The Hebrew of the first line has simply "These also are of wise men" (*laḥªkāmîm*). The second line is almost identical with 28:21a and is also a variant of 18:5a; but in those verses it is part of a two-line proverb. **Partiality in judging**: the same phraseology occurs in Dt. 1:17 in an address to judges, and also in Dt. 16:19, which is addressed to the whole people. In fact the administration of justice in Israel was not confined to "professional" judges: ordinary Israelites had responsibility for it, not only as witnesses but also as judges. The similarity of this line to the laws of Deuteronomy suggests that it was generally familiar as a legal maxim. It may, however, have originally been part of a more extended proverb as in 28:21 and 18:5. **not good**: see on 16:29.

24–25. The legal principle stated in v. 23b is now elaborated, and the consequences of obeying or disobeying it are set out.

24. "You are innocent" (*ṣaddîq 'āttāh*) was probably the legal phrase used as a declaration of acquittal by a judge: compare, for example, Ezek. 18:9, where this legal formula, "he is innocent, he shall live", together with, in the same chapter, its opposite, "he shall die", is put into the mouth of Yahweh as judge. **wicked** (*rāšā'*) here means "guilty". **peoples**; **nations**: many commentators take this to refer only to Israelites, the plural forms signifying "all kinds of people"; but this would be a unique example of this use of the plural, and there is no reason to take these words otherwise than literally as a recognition that corruption of justice was an *universal* crime.

25. those who rebuke the wicked: the Hebrew has simply "those who convict" ("them", that is, the guilty, being understood). **will have delight**: that is, it will go well with them. **a good blessing**: this is a mistranslation of *birkat-ṭôb*, which means "the blessing of prosperity".

26. This verse is too short and too allusive for its meaning to be clear. **He who gives a right answer** (*mēšîb dᵉbārîm nᵉkōḥîm*): literally, "he who returns honest words". This is taken by some commentators to mean no more than "he who speaks plainly" or "he who gives an honest answer"; but the meaning may be "he who makes an honest legal judgement" (so Oesterley; see on 18:13). If that is so, the verse has a common theme with vv. 24–5, although it was probably originally a separate short proverb. **kisses the lips**: kissing was a sign of love or affection. Its employment here as a metaphor is unique. Perhaps the most probable interpretation of the verse is that the honest judge or witness is as welcome to the innocent as the kisses of a lover. It has, however, been argued by Cohen (1982, pp. 420–22) that this verb (*nāšaq*) here means "to seal the lips": giving a right judgement seals (hostile) lips.

27. This admonition, if understood literally, is addressed to the young farmer, not to a young man of the upper class. But it may also be taken in a figurative sense: don't undertake anything hastily without due preparation. **for you** (*lāk*): Gemser proposed that this word should be repointed as *lēk*, "go!", and attached to the following line: "after that go and build". In the Hebrew text **and** *follows* **after that**; this has led to the suggestion that a preceding verb or phrase has been omitted – either "go" (see above) or something like "take a wife", which would complete an otherwise incomplete couplet (Toy). The latter suggestion, however, is quite speculative. In fact the construction as it stands (the perfect consecutive) is not impossible here: see *GK* 112 oo. **build your house**: this may refer to the literal construction of a house or to the founding of a family (compare Ru. 4:11).

28. This is probably a further example of the many warnings against perjury in the book. LXX, which renders **a witness without a cause** by "a false witness", has probably correctly understood the verse. Accusations made in court which one knows to be groundless (*ḥinnām*, **without a cause**) are perjury. If v. 29 is a continuation of this verse, the perjury in question may be the action of an aggrieved person to get his own back by accusing his enemy of a crime which he has in fact not committed; but such a connection between the two verses is doubtful (see below).

and do not deceive: MT has "and have you deceived . . . ?", which does not make a satisfactory parallelism with the first line; moreover, this verb would be expected to govern an object, and this is not the case. LXX has a second prohibition here, and it has been proposed that MT should simply be emended to conform to it. However, another reading is possible: two manuscripts have here a different verb *ptt*, "to break up", and this corresponds to Pesh: "do not break him in pieces" – that is, slander him. Driver (*Bib.* 32 [1951], p. 189) suggested a transposition of the letters of the word which, if the *'al* (**not**) of the first line is understood as governing both verbs, would correspond exactly to the reading of Pesh.

29. The first part of this verse is similar to 20:22a. For a discussion of the issue see the comment on that verse. It is doubtful whether this admonition was originally connected with v. 28, which refers simply to "your neighbour". The verse has no poetical form and is probably to be defined as prose. The final words ("I will pay . . .") merely repeat the gist of the earlier part of the verse. They are similar to v. 12b, where however it is Yahweh who will avenge human shortcomings. They may be a gloss.

30–34. This passage, together with 6:6–11, provides an insight into the teaching methods of the ancient Israelite father or teacher. The subject is the familiar one of the sluggard or lazy person; and both passages show how the single two-line proverb could be expanded and presented in a vivid way. In both cases the moral is the same and is the same as in several other proverbs (10:4; 13:4; 15:19; 20:4, 13). Vv. 33–4 are virtually identical with 6:10–11. In

6:6–11 the pupil is urged to consider an example of industry from the animal world; here, as in 7:6–23, the teacher recounts his own experience and observations.

30–32. The various examples of this kind of teaching story, in which the teacher recounts what he has observed and then draws a moral from it, have common features – though with some variation of detail – and, to a large extent, a common vocabulary. Here the teacher **passed by** (*'ābartî*), **and lo** (*wᵉhinnēh*) . . . ; he **looked and received instruction** (*rā'îtî lāqaḥtî mûsār*). In Ps. 37:25 the moral lies not in what the teacher has seen but in what he has *not* seen (*lō' rā'îtî*): that is, "the righteous forsaken". Ps. 37:35–6 a similar experience is recounted in two stages: the psalmist compares his first sight (*rā'îtî*) of the wicked man in his then flourishing state with his subsequent sight of him obtained when he "passed by" again (reading *'ābartî* with the Versions), "and lo (*wᵉhinnēh*) he (the wicked man) was no more". In Prov. 7:6–8 the verb *'ābar* is again used, but there it was not the teacher who "passed along" but the young man, seen (*wā'ēre'*) by the teacher on his way (*'ōbēr*) to his destruction.

31. nettles: or, possibly, "chickweed". This verse, unusually, contains three lines. LXX, which has a somewhat different text, has four. Gemser suggested that a line may have dropped out from *MT*; other commentators, on the contrary, suggest that the third line may be a later addition.

32. instruction (*mûsār*): the teacher hands on to his pupil the lesson which he himself has received (compare 4:3–5).

33–34. See on the almost identical 6:10–11. **like a robber** (*mithallēk*): a number of manuscripts have *kimᵉhallēk* as in 6:11. **poverty**: *MT* has an unaccountable plural form; but here also some manuscripts agree with the singular form found in 6:11.

MORE "PROVERBS OF SOLOMON" TRANSCRIBED BY THE MEN OF HEZEKIAH
25–29

On the general character of these chapters see on 10:1–22:16. They form a major section of the book, delimited by the heading in 25:1 and the heading to the next section, 30:1. But it is generally recognized that there are differences both of form and content between the first three and the last two of these chapters which suggest that they originally formed not one but two major collections. Chapters 25–7 are characterized by the virtual absence of references to Yahweh, by the large number of similes and metaphors, and by the relative absence of antithetical parallelism, while they have a relatively high number of admonitions. Chapters 28 and 29 on the whole possess the contrary characteristics. It has also been argued that there are more clear signs of deliberate arrangement of individual proverbs into sub-groups in chapter 25–7, or at least in chapters 25 and 26, than in the remaining chapters.

On the ascription to Solomon see the Introduction. The fact that in the heading (25:1) the words **proverbs of Solomon**, which constitute the heading in 10:1, are repeated here, prefaced by **These also are** is a clear indication that these chapters were intended to be an appendix to the first "Solomonic" collection; why they are now separated from it is not known.

The further information provided in 25:1 – **which the men of Hezekiah copied** – is of a different kind from the attributions to Solomon here and in 1:1; 10:1. It refers to a particular stage in the literary history of the book, naming the group of men who were responsible for it and specifying the period and the milieu in which the work was carried out (see Weinfeld, *Deuteronomy and the Deuteronomic School*, Oxford, 1972, pp. 161–2; M. Fishbane, *Biblical Interpretation in Ancient Israel*, Oxford, 1985, pp. 32–3). The **men of Hezekiah** may be presumed to have been scribes employed at the Judaean court. The reign of Hezekiah may well have been a period of exceptional literary activity (see Scott, 1955, pp. 273–9). This does not, however, imply that these scribes were the authors of these proverbs; it is perhaps significant that there are fewer references to the king (six) in these chapters than in 10:1–22:16.

The precise meaning of the verb (*he'tîqû*) rendered by *RSV* as **copied** is not certain: it may mean "transcribed", "transmitted" or "published", but hardly "composed". This note or colophon, if it is to be taken at face value, which there is no reason not to do, is evidence for a concern at Hezekiah's court to preserve or to collect already existing proverbial material. The individual proverbs themselves, however, derive from the same milieu as 10:1–22:16.

CHAPTER 25

This chapter shows clear signs of editorial work in the formation of groups of proverbs linked both thematically and by the use of such devices as keywords, assonance etc. Two recent writers, however, Bryce, 1972, pp. 145–57 and Van Leeuwen (1988) have pursued the question of the composition of the chapter much further and have argued – the latter mainly by means of structuralist analysis – that the whole chapter (more precisely, vv. 2–27) constitutes a single integrated "wisdom-book" or "proverb-poem" conceived as a literary unity on the model of two Egyptian texts, the *Instruction of Sehetepibre* and the *Kemit*.

According to Bryce, the chapter falls into two main sections with an introduction (vv. 1–5), each containing six units. The theme of the first part (vv. 6–15) is concerned with the king or ruler and is subdivided into vv. 6–7, 8–9a, 9b-10, 11–12, 13–14, 15. The second (vv. 16–17, 18, 19–20, 21–2, 23–4, 25–6) is a series of units dealing with various types of wicked person. The final verse (27) forms a conclusion which picks up the theme of v. 2 and also that of v. 16. V. 28 is unconnected with the rest of the chapter. The aim of the "book" is to provide the young courtier with advice which will guide him in his career at the royal court. Van Leeuwen's view of the aim and setting of the chapter is similar to that of Bryce, but he divides the second half into two subsections, vv. 16–20 and 21–7.

Much of Bryce's and Van Leeuwen's detailed analysis is correct and will be taken into account in the commentary which follows. But their thesis as a whole is unconvincing. The hypothesis of a court setting depends on their assumption that the references to kings or rulers in vv. 2–7, 15 indicate such a situation (compare the interpretation of other "royal proverbs" given in this commentary on the earlier parts of Proverbs). Further, the admonitions and proverbs in vv. 8–15 are of a general kind and not particularly relevant to the concerns of a courtier. It is also hardly the case that vv. 16–27 can be described as depicting different types of wicked men, or that they are closely connected with the earlier part of the chapter.

Formally the chapter differs from the earlier sentence literature in the large number of admonitions (vv. 6–7b, 7c–10, 16, 17, 21–2), in the greater length of many of the units (vv. 2–3, 4–5, 6–7, 8–10, 21–2) and in the frequency of similes and comparisons (vv. 3,

11, 12, 13, 14, 18, 19, 20, 24, 25, 26, 28). These marked differences, together with the total absence of antithetical parallelism, bear out the indication in v. 1 that the chapter belongs to an *appendix* to the earlier collection of "proverbs of Solomon", having been collected from partly different sources by a different set of editors. However, the original milieu of the individual proverbs was similar to that of 10:1–22:16. Most of the topics dealt with are the same as those which occur there: for example, the nature of kingship (vv. 2–7, 15), behaviour in the law court (vv. 8–10), the importance of the spoken word (vv. 8–10, 11, 12, 15, 23), relations with neighbours and with the community in general (vv. 17, 18, 19, 21–2) and the nagging wife (v. 24). This identity of social background is confirmed by the number of proverbs which are variants of, or are closely similar to, proverbs found in the earlier collection: compare v. 5 with 16:12; v. 11 with 15:23; v. 13 with 13:17; v. 15 with 15:1; v. 24 with 21:9; v. 25 with 15:30; v. 28 with 16:32.

2–7b. These verses consist of four short units, of which the first two (vv. 2 and 3) are statements about **kings** (*m^e lākîm*), the third (vv. 4–5) is essentially a statement about the (or a) king (singular, *melek*) and the fourth (vv. 6–7b) an admonition which also refers to a king but also to **the great** and **the prince**. The occurrence of this key word is obviously the reason why these verses have been grouped together; otherwise they have no more thematic unity than the other group of "royal" proverbs in 16:10–15.

There are some affinities here with some of the other royal proverbs: verse 2 associates kings with God, though not in the same way as 16:10 and 21:1; both vv. 2 and 3 credit kings with superior powers of judgement as do 16:10 and 20:8. Vv. 4–5, however, like 16:12 (compare also 29:4, 12) are far from adopting an uncritical view of kings, and specify what is required of them if their rule is to continue. The second line of v. 5 occurs also, with variants, in three other verses (16:12b; 20:28b; 29:14b). The theme of vv. 6–7b is not, however, the nature of kingship: it is about social pretensions, and the reference to a king is merely illustrative (see below).

There is, then, nothing in any of these verses to justify the view that either singly or in their present grouping these verses constitute advice to a courtier; they do not present a single consistent viewpoint. Vv. 2–3 reflect the awe in which monarchs were held by ordinary persons who had never seen one; vv. 4–5 apparently reflect an awareness by such people of injustices done by persons standing near the throne, coupled with an attempt to reconcile this with a respect for monarchy by blaming the king's advisers, but would be quite fatal if offered as advice to an experienced courtier. Vv. 6–7b are a warning against social climbing in general.

2. Although there is no difficulty in understanding the plain meaning of this verse, its implications are by no means clear, and the commentators vary considerably in its interpretation. It is possible that it was intended to be a riddle (*ḥîdā*) or "hard saying", open to more than one interpretation.

The second line presents fewer difficulties than the first. It is reasonable to suppose that the verse is primarily a statement about **kings**. **glory** (*kābôd*) in both lines means that which brings due honour to a person; in the case of a king, it therefore means that he fulfils his proper function in a worthy manner. That function, it is here stated, is **to search things out**: to know what is going on in his kingdom and to take appropriate action. This is tantamount to saying that he possesses exceptional wisdom (compare 2 Sam. 14:17; 1 Kg. 3:9). The statement may refer to his ability to distinguish between the good and the bad among his subjects (compare 16:10), or to his general competence to rule his kingdom justly and successfully in both war and peace.

That God's thoughts and plans are inscrutable – that he does not wholly reveal **things** (*dābār*) to his human creatures (including kings!) – is a commonplace of Old Testament belief (compare, for example, Dt. 29:29 (Heb. 28); Isa. 45:15; Job 11:8; 15:8; 26:14; Ec. 8:17). What is not clear is the relationship of the first line to the second. Ostensibly the verse is concerned to point out a contrast between God and the king. Whereas God's function is to **conceal things**, that of kings is to **search them out** – that is, to bring them to light. Each has his own proper **glory**, but the natures of these are diametrically opposed. It is not clear, however, whether the **things** in question are the same. If they are, the meaning of the verse may be that information (God's plans), which is generally inaccessible to men and women, may become (at least partly?) accessible to kings if they use their God-given wisdom rightly. If there is no identity between the two **things**, we appear here to have two statements which have been placed together simply for the sake of the paradox which they present.

God: this use of the word *ᵉlōhîm* rather than Yhwh is unique in the sentence literature of Proverbs and extremely rare in the rest of the book. Its use here may be due to a concern to stress the difference between the divine and human natures in general, although there is no doubt that for the authors of this book there is no question of other gods (compare 2:5, where "the fear of Yahweh" and "the knowledge of God" are clearly synonymous).

3. unsearchable (*'ên ḥēqer*): the word *ḥēqer*, literally "a searching out", picks up the verb *ḥāqar* ("to search out") from v. 2, but makes a quite different point. The **mind** (literally, "heart") of kings, that is, their inner disposition and consequently their intention, is *not* to be discovered or "searched out" by others: it is as mysterious as the **height** of the **heavens** or the **depth** of the **earth** (*'ereṣ* here may mean "underworld"). This statement, originally an independent proverb, points to a characteristic of kings which they have *in common* with God: like him, they *conceal* their intentions from others; their behaviour is unpredictable.

4–5. This double couplet is not an admonition. *hāgô* (**Take away**) in both verses is not an imperative but an infinite absolute functioning as a finite verb (see *GK* 113aa, ff). The sense in each case is that of a conditional sentence: "If one takes away . . .". The two verses together draw an analogy. The criticism is not directed against the **king** *per se*, for he is compared with a precious metal; it is directed against **wicked** persons who give him bad advice which may endanger his throne (compare 1 Kg. 12:6–15).

4. dross (*sîgîm*): **silver** is smelted in order to remove lead and copper impurities. The same analogy is used elsewhere in the Old Testament (Ps. 119:119; Isa. 1:22, 25; Ezek. 22:18, 19). **and the smith has material for a vessel**: literally, "and a vessel comes out for the smith". It has been pointed out that the smelting process cannot of itself produce a vessel but only the material for one; and the suggestion that *k*ᵉ*lî* (vessel, tool, ornament, equipment etc.) can mean "material" is not entirely convincing. LXX has "and it will be made entirely pure", a rendering which suggests a different text (*kullô*, "all of it", for *k*ᵉ*lî*; a passive participle meaning "purified" for *ṣōrēp*, **smith**); this would require a considerable emendation. The proposal of Dahood and of Driver (*Bib.* 32 [1951], p. 190) to render "will shine" for "come out" on the basis of supposed Arabic and Akkadian cognates ("and the vase will shine for the smith") does not solve the problem. The most recent commentators (McKane and Plöger) regard MT as satisfactory, regarding the two lines of the verse as referring to consecutive, not identical, operations: "and the smith will produce a work of art" (McKane). This is probably correct.

6–7b. These four lines constitute a single admonition; v. 7c ("What your eyes have seen"), as is generally agreed by the commentators, belongs to v. 8. The admonition, against claiming a social standing which one does not in fact possess, is strikingly similar to Lk. 14:7–11. Both passages are intended to be of general application (so also Plöger), the point being illustrated by a particular example. Here the imagined setting is some kind of assembly of notables; in Luke it is a wedding feast. In the case of the passage in Luke its illustrative character is obvious, since the saying out of which it has been developed, and which is found elsewhere in quite different contexts (Lk. 18:14; Mt. 23:12), has been retained in the final verse (11). Here no such saying has been included; but the variety of settings (**the king's presence**; **the place of the great**; **the presence of the prince**) rules out the possibility that these verses are addressed specifically to a courtier.

the great: see on 18:16. **the place of the great** may mean a place where leading citizens gather (so *REB*). **the prince** (*nādîb*): this term appears in a variety of contexts in the Old Testament. It is a non-specific term denoting persons of high rank and often of power and influence, and does not necessarily, or even probably, refer to a king.

7c-8. do not . . . bring: MT has "do not go" (*'al-tēṣē'*); but *RSV*, in common with the majority of commentators, repoints the verb as causative (hiphil), *tōṣē'*. If MT is correct in other respects, this appears to be an admonition against being in a hurry to go to law or to act as witness against someone observed committing a criminal act. However, if this is so it is not clear why the observer should end by being humiliated. It may be best, following a clue from Symmachus, to repoint *lārīb*, **into court**, as *lārōb* "to the crowd" (on this meaning of *lārōb* see *KB*[3]): "Do not broadcast to the crowd . . ." (Toy, Gemser, McKane). If this is correct, the admonition is concerned not with criminal proceedings but with scandal-mongering. Scandalous revelations to all and sundry may not find a welcome, and the **neighbour** who is their recipient may respond with contempt or abuse (*RSV* **puts you to shame**, but probably better, "abuses you"), so that in the end the tale-bearer rather than the object of his vilification is the one who suffers public disgrace. **for**: the Hebrew has *pen-*, usually rendered by "lest, that not". Some commentators emend the word to *kî*, "for"; but this is an unsupported reading and probably unnecessary. *pen-* here and in some other passages means "else", introducing an alternative to the action warned against. (See Bühlmann, pp. 245–6, cited by Plöger).

9–10. If the above interpretation of vv. 7c-8 is correct, this admonition has been juxtaposed to it because the two have similar themes. Both stress the importance, in a small community, of reticence about the affairs of others. The situation envisaged here is a private dispute (*rîb*, **case**, can have a legal connotation but probably does not here). **and do not**: rather, "*but* do not . . .". That two people should engage in a private dispute is acceptable, but it would be totally undesirable for one of the parties to reveal to outsiders any private information which he may have acquired in the course of the dispute. As in v. 8c, the person who does so will be denounced by the person to whom he reveals it (*šōmēaʿ*, **he who hears you**). This was evidently regarded as a very serious offence entailing public disgrace which the offender would never be able to live down.

11–14. These four metaphorical proverbs are in the form of statements, and are all concerned with the spoken word: the *mot juste*, the wise advice, the message safely delivered, the boastful word. They have a loose connection with the immediately preceding admonitions (vv. 7c-10) in that they also are concerned with words: the indiscreet or malicious word.

These verses are arranged in pairs. In both vv. 11 and 12 the word of wisdom is compared with precious items of jewellery, both of gold. Vv. 13–14 both use imagery taken from the weather; they also make a contrast between the reliable (*neʾmān*) person and the unreliable braggart.

Formally, three of these four verses (11, 12 and 14) are metaphors in the strict sense (*RSV* has turned them into similes). In these the thing compared is juxtaposed to the thing with which it is compared, with no connecting particle ("like", "and"). But v. 13 is a true simile. The variation in form points to an editorial assembly of originally independent proverbs, though in all three verses the same order is followed: the comparison precedes the thing with which it is compared (*RSV* has reversed the order in v. 11).

11. The general import of this verse is clear: it asserts, in hyperbolic terms, the beneficial effect which an appropriate word or piece of advice can have. The precise meaning of several words, however, is doubtful. What is said to be of equal value with appropriate speech is clearly some kind of elaborate ornament made of **gold** and **silver**. The word rendered by **apples of** (*tappûḥê*) denotes some kind of fruit (compare Ca. 2:3, 5; 7:8 [Heb. 9]; 8:5; Joel 1:12), but not the apple, which had not been introduced into Palestine in Old Testament times. An ornament such as is described here is otherwise unknown. It has been suggested that the order of the letters has been accidentally reversed, and that the word should be *pittûḥê*, "engravings" or "decoration" (Toy, Scott, McKane); but MT may be correct (so Plöger, *REB*). *maśkiyyôt* (**setting**) also probably refers to some kind of carved work (*KB*³). Toy thought that two kinds of ornament are referred to: "graved work of gold and carved work of silver".

fitly (*'al-'opnâw*): the meaning of this word *'ōpen*, which occurs only here, is obscure. As pointed in MT it can hardly be a form of *'ôpān*, "wheel", which in any case, despite some ingenious attempts to find such a meaning here, makes no sense (for example, that of McKane, on the basis of the occurrence of what appears to be the same word in the Hebrew of Sir. 50:27). The word may be cognate with Arabic *'iffān*, "time" (*KB*³). If this is so, a literal translation of the phrase would be "at the (right) time" (so Symmachus, Vulg., Köhler; compare 15:23, *bᵉ'ittô*).

12. The metaphor is similar to that in v. 11. The notion of wisdom as more precious than jewels is a commonplace of the wisdom literature: compare, for example, 8:11. McKane remarks that this verse expresses an "ideal teacher-student relationship". **ornament**: perhaps better, "necklace". **a listening ear**: that is, a receptive pupil. **gold** (second occurrence): this word (*ketem*) is found only in poetry. It may denote a particular kind or quality of gold – "Nubian gold" (so *REB*).

13. The third line of this verse is probably an explanatory gloss. Although a fall of snow in Palestine at harvest-time – that is, in the heat of the summer – is not entirely unknown, some commentators (McKane, Bühlmann [pp. 137–41], Plöger) think it more probable that the reference is to ice-cold water (from a spring) either as a drink or to refresh the brows of the workers in the hot sun. (See also B. Lang, 1981, pp. 219–232. LXX has "heat" (*ḥōm*) for *yôm*, "day" (*RSV* **time**); this may be the true reading. **faithful messenger**: see on 13:17. The word used here for messenger (*ṣîr*) is a play on *qāṣîr* (**harvest**) in the first line. **refreshes the spirit**: literally, "brings back the life".

14. The common feature of the comparison and the thing compared here is failure to produce what is expected. The **clouds** in question (*n^eśî'îm*) are mists which, accompanied by wind, normally precede the onset of the **rain** (compare Jer. 10:13; 51:16; Ps. 135:7). **a gift he does not give**: literally, "a gift of deception (*šeqer*)", that is, a non-existent gift. The person in question is one who "poses as a great benefactor" (McKane) but whose resources are insufficient to enable him to carry out his promises.

15. The second line of this verse is a general statement about the persuasive power of speech (compare 15:1). **will break a bone**: a hyperbolic expression meaning "is irresistible" (compare a similar expression in Ahiqar, lines 105–6 [ANET, p. 429]). The first line gives a particular example of the same principle; it may be an older proverb of which the second line is a secondary generalization. Even a high functionary (*qāṣîn*, *RSV* **ruler**; compare 6:7) may be open to persuasion.

Frankenberg and Toy considered the reference to **patience** (they prefer "forbearance") on the part of a lesser person towards a ruler to be unlikely, and proposed emendations; but these are unnecessary. The view that a high official may be open to persuasion is expressed elsewhere in the book. 11:14 and 15:22 stress the importance of the offering of advice, and the possibility that even a king may be governed by his ministers is envisaged in 25:5.

persuaded: this verb (*pth*) in the piel (here its passive, pual, is used) frequently has a pejorative sense of "entice", "deceive"; but here it is probably used in the neutral sense of "persuade" as in Hos. 2:14 (Heb. 16), although *RSV* there renders it by "allure".

16–17. These two verses, both admonitions, are obviously connected, although like the two lines of v. 15 one may have been modelled on the other. V. 16, ostensibly a warning against over-indulgence in honey, is – and was intended to be – a warning against excess of any kind. V. 17 gives a particular illustration of the danger in a particular case. The second lines are closely similar in wording and structure; the syntactical form (**lest . . . and**) is identical, the initial verb (*śāba'*, *RSV* respectively **be sated**, **become weary**) is the same, and the final verbs **vomit** and **hate** are alike in signifying violent rejection.

16. Like 16:24 and 24:13, this verse regards **honey** – that is, wild honey found unexpectedly – entirely positively; the point is that even pleasures may do harm if indulged in to excess.

17. This verse, which is a commonplace of international wisdom literature, illustrates the meaning of v. 16 with a warning about a particular point of social etiquette. Dropping in on a neighbour and his family is a pleasant habit which may be welcomed and makes for good relations, but not if indulged in too frequently. **Let your foot be seldom**: literally, "make your foot precious", that is, make your visits rare. **hate**: this is probably too strong a rendering; "dislike" would be better. A state of active enmity is hardly envisaged.

18–20. Each of these verses is a metaphorical proverb like vv. 11, 12 and 14. In vv. 18 and 19 *RSV* has reversed the order of the lines: the Hebrew puts the object of the comparison first. But the text of v. 20 is uncertain (see below).

18. The first line of this verse (in *RSV*) is expressed in the language of the Ninth Commandment of the Decalogue (Exod. 20:16; Dt. 5:20). Perjury, frequently condemned in this book and whose potential role in the conviction of the innocent is the theme of 14:25, is here likened to a lethal weapon. In 6:19 it is listed as one of the things which are especially hated by Yahweh. **a war club**: *RSV* has accepted the universal emendation of *mēpîṣ*, "one who scatters", to *mappēṣ* (see Jer. 51:20), following LXX.

19. Trust in: Gemser proposed the omission of this word, making the **faithless man** himself the object of the comparison; but MT makes adequate sense: reliance on such a person is as useless as a **bad tooth** or a sprained ankle. (On the form, *mibṭāḥ*, **Trust**, see *GK* 92g). **bad**: the Hebrew, *rō'āh*, makes no sense unless it is a contraction of *rō^{a}'āh*, "broken" (see *GK* 67s); alternatively it could be repointed as *rā'āh*, "bad" as by *RSV*. **that slips** (*mû'ādet*): this could be an anomalous form of the pual (passive) participle (*GK* 52s); but it should probably be repointed as the qal (active) participle *mô'ādet*.

20. The Hebrew text of this verse is seriously corrupt, and no convincing restoration has been proposed. *RSV* prints it as consisting of three lines; but one of these (**and like vinegar on a wound** – the Hebrew has simply "vinegar on soda" and has neither a verb nor a comparative particle; *RSV* has followed LXX) is extremely short, and another (**one who takes off a garment on a cold day**) is probably a corrupt dittograph of a line in v. 19.

Thus **He who sings songs to a heavy heart** appears simply to be compared with "vinegar on soda"; but almost every commentator assumes that something has been omitted. Various reconstructions have been proposed, some of which propose the addition of one or more lines supposedly omitted accidentally. But even in the Hebrew text as it stands there are ambiguities.

To Oesterley, the point of vinegar poured on soda is the resulting effervescence, which symbolizes cheerfulness, while for Scott the opposite is the case: it is adding one bitter thing to another. Again, the final line (the first in *RSV*) could mean "One who sings in chorus" (reading *b^{e}šārîm*, "among singers", for *baššīrîm*) *with* a sad heart rather than "to a heavy heart" (so Driver, *VT* 4 [1954], pp. 241–2). LXX has a quite different and much longer text, probably of little use for textual criticism.

21–22. This admonition goes beyond comparable verses in Proverbs (14:29; 19:11; 20:22; 24:17, 29) in advocating kindness towards a personal enemy (*śōna^{a}kā*, literally, "one who hates you"). The situation envisaged is one in which such a person has fallen into a state of desperate penury; the duty to help him here prescribed is in the spirit of Exod. 23:4–5. The promise in the last line of v. 22 that **the Lord will reward you** should be regarded rather as a consequence of the helpful action than as constituting the motive for it. It sets the seal of Yahweh's approval on the action. St Paul, who quotes this passage – except for the final line – verbatim in Rom. 12:20, goes on to interpret it correctly: "Do not be overcome by evil, but overcome evil with good". Like many other passages in Proverbs, these verses are concerned with the harmony and well-being of the local community, which ought to override the selfish interests and feuds of individuals. *Love* of enemies, however, is not prescribed.

heap (literally, "snatch up") **coals of fire on his head**: there is nothing in the Old Testament to compare with this expression. It has been variously interpreted, for example, as meaning that the enemy will be caused to feel shame or contrition; but such interpretations are based on the context rather than on a convincing explanation of the reason for this choice of words. Fire is a purgative element, but not as applied to a person's head! Elsewhere in the Old Testament (Ps. 18:8, 12; 2 Sam. 22:9, 13; Ps. 140: 10 [Heb. 11]) the raining down of live coals signifies punishment or destruction. S. Morenz, 1953, cols. 187–92, suggests a reminiscence of an Egyptian rite in which a penitent endured such a punishment as a mark of his contrition; but there is no evidence of a similar custom in ancient Israel.

The problem is that the expression itself must refer to an

unpleasant experience for the enemy, while on the other hand the result achieved is clearly positive. The reward from Yahweh is presumably for achieving reconciliation between the two persons involved. This could only be due to a change of heart on the part of the enemy. The context does therefore seem to compel some idea of shame or contrition, though the expression itself remains unexplained except perhaps as irony.

23–28. These six verses consist entirely of statements (metaphorical proverbs, except for v. 24 and the obscure v. 27). For Bryce and Van Leeuwen, v. 27 marks the end of a "wisdom-book" or "proverb-poem" which began in v. 1, v. 28 being entirely unrelated to this. For Krispenz, however (pp. 103–6), following Delitzsch, vv. 23–8 form a single group: she points out that the first word of v. 23 and the last word of v. 28 are the same: *rûaḥ*. This, however, may be a coincidence; it has no thematic significance. Clearly the methods of compositional research have not yet been satisfactorily refined.

There is, however, some indication of arrangements in pairs here. Vv. 23 and 24 are both about destructive or anti-social speech; vv. 25 and 26 both use *water* as a point of comparison, contrasting the benefit of clear, pure water with the uselessness of polluted or muddied water. In the case of vv. 27 and 28 no pairing is observable; but the text and meaning of v. 27 are too problematic to make a conclusion possible.

23. The main difficulty with regard to this verse is that in Palestine the **north wind** emphatically does *not* bring rain; rather, the reverse is true. Various explanations have been offered, but no consensus has emerged. 1. This proverb had its origin in Egypt, where the north wind brings rain, but not with acceptable results (Gemser). It is, however, hardly conceivable that it should have been transferred unchanged to Palestine, where it makes no sense. 2. **north** is not to be taken literally: it is used vaguely with no particular significance, or it stands for the north-west wind which sometimes does bring rain (Toy), or the word is used because the north was a mysterious and frightening region. However, the coming of the rain was regarded in Israel as beneficial rather than as menacing. 3. The word *ṣāpôn* does not mean "north" here, but is connected with the verb *ṣāpan* "to hide": if repointed as the passive participle *ṣāpûn* it would mean hidden or mysterious – that is, as coming from some unknown heavenly place where it had been stored (van der

Ploeg, 1953, pp. 189–91; compare Job 38:22). 4. The word rendered in *RSV* by **brings** (*tᵉḥôlēl*, normally "gives birth to") here means "holds back" (so *REB*) or even "repels" (Saadia). This appears dubious. It also raises the question of the meaning of the second line of the verse, as this verb serves both lines. *REB* solves this problem by reversing subject and object in the second line (so, incidentally, avoiding a chiasmus): "so an angry glance holds back slander".

In assessing the above proposals it is important to consider which makes for the most satisfactory comparison. It may be significant that the literal meaning of the phrase rendered in *RSV* by **backbiting** is, in the Hebrew, *lᵉšôn sāter*, literally "a tongue of hiddenness" that is, a person who whispers secrets. This would correspond to the "hidden wind" of proposal number three above: as the mysterious wind darkens the sky with black clouds, so does a "hidden" tongue darken the face of those who suffer from it (so Ringgren, Plöger). However, it must be admitted that the problem remains unsolved.

24. See on 21:9, with which this verse is virtually identical. There is clearly a link intended between the nagging wife of this verse and the backbiting tongue of v. 23. The recurrence of the proverb is an indication that these are separate collections but derived from similar sources.

25. On sending and receiving messages see on 13:17 and compare 15:30; 25:13. *'ereṣ* (**country**) does not necessarily refer to a territory outside Israel, but merely to places beyond the immediate locality, for which a journey (on foot) of more than a day or two may be required and which may therefore be hazardous. *nepeš* (*RSV* **soul**) probably means "throat" here; *nepeš ʿᵃyēpâ*, literally, "a tired (that is, parched) throat."

26. *māṭ*, *RSV* **gives way**, here almost certainly refers neither to a moral lapse gleefully observed by the wicked (Oesterley) nor to a lack of stamina (McKane), but to a disaster which befalls **a righteous man** at the hands of a **wicked** one. Such an event would be a total reversal of the proper order of things: compare 12:3, where the same word is used in making the assertion that "the righteous will never be moved", while the wicked will have no stability, and similar passages in the Psalms, for example, Ps. 55:22 [Heb. 23]: "he (Yahweh) will never permit the righteous to be moved". If such a thing occurs it is as disastrous as the pollution of the supply of water on which life depends – a **spring, muddied** and made useless by trampling feet or made undrinkable (**polluted**) in some other way. There is, then, a recognition here (compare the Book of Job and many of the psalms of lamentation) that the wicked do sometimes triumph over the righteous.

27. The first line of this verse presents no particular problem; its import is the same as that of v. 16. But the second line in MT makes no sense: "and searching out their glory is glory". It also appears to be unrelated to the first line. LXX has a different text, but one which is hardly an improvement: "but it is fitting to esteem notable words". *RSV* has followed an emendation proposed by Frankenberg partly based on LXX and accepted by Gemser, Ringgren and McKane. Of the many proposals made involving emendation, repointing, unusual senses of words, etc., perhaps the most plausible are those which retain the consonantal Hebrew text but repoint and divide it differently from MT, transferring the final letter of *kbdm* (*RV* "their glory") to the next word. This can, however, lead to several contradictory interpretations: thus Driver (*Bib.* 32 [1951], pp. 190–91) has "but the search for honour is honourable (*m^ekubbād*)"; Barucq, "nor seeking after glory upon glory (*mikkābōd*)"; Plöger, "and seeking after glory (remains) without glory (*mikkābōd*)".

28. This proverb appears to be unrelated to the previous verse. It points out that the person who cannot control his temper (literally, "having no restraint over his *rûaḥ*"; compare a similar use of this term in 14:29; 16:32; 17:27) is totally vulnerable – presumably to retaliation from those whom he has offended; but the implication is wider than that. For the authors of these proverbs as well as for their counterparts in Egypt, coolness of spirit (compare 17:27) was the sign of a competent and successful person, while lack of self-control indicated weakness of character.

CHAPTER 26

This chapter is much more closely integrated than most of the chapters in the sentence literature. The individual proverbs are grouped under three main topics: the fool (vv. 1–12), the sluggard (vv. 13–16), and various kinds of person who damage social relations by injudicious or malicious speech (vv. 17–28) are all depicted with disapproval. A number of verses are also linked by catchwords.

Formally the chapter is marked by a large number of comparisons or metaphors; these account for half the total number of verses, and they are arranged in groups: vv. 1–3, 6–11, 17–23. They are of more than one type: vv. 1, 2, 8, 11, 18 are similes; vv. 3, 7, 9, 14, 21 link the two lines simply by "and"; and in vv. 6, 17, 23 there is simple juxtaposition of the two lines with no connecting link. The whole chapter is a series of warnings against various forms of abnormal behaviour which are harmful either to the individual concerned or to society as a whole.

Van Leeuwen (pp. 87–122), using similar methods as with chapter 25, which he saw as a *single* "proverb-poem", divides this chapter into *three distinct* proverb-poems: vv. 1–12, 13–16, 17–28. Krispenz (pp. 107–16) finds *two* "Spruchkompositionen" here: vv. 1–16 and 17–22. The final two verses (27–8) she links with 27:1–2.

There is no reference to Yahweh in this chapter.

1–12. This group of verses is linked together partly by the repetition of certain words and phrases: **fool** (*kᵉsîl*) in every verse except v. 2; **honour** (*kābôd*) in vv. 1 and 8; **wise in his own eyes** in vv. 5 and 12; **is a proverb in the mouth of fools**, vv. 7 and 9. There is also a thematic link, in that several verses are concerned with what is fitting for a fool or for those who deal with fools.

1. Plöger sees this verse as making a significant initial statement about the proper position of fools in society. Toy sees it as a protest against a contemporary practice of giving important responsibilities to persons incapable of carrying them out. **honour** (*kābôd*) here perhaps deliberately picks up the thought of 25:27 and even of 25:2. The word denotes an established position in society. **not fitting**: the other occurrences of this phrase in Proverbs (17:7 and 19:10) also refer to fools; see also 30:21–3. The proverb is saying that to give honour to a fool is to reverse the proper order of things – a catastrophe comparable to the disruption of the normal sequence of the seasons.

2. This is the only verse in vv. 1–12 which makes no reference to the fool. Oesterley thought that it may be a quite unrelated secondary addition. However, Van Leeuwen (1988, p. 102) sees vv. 1–3 as all concerned with the concept of fitness or appropriateness: after the statement in v. 1 that honour does not befit a fool comes a corresponding statement that **a curse that is causeless** – that is, an attempt to *dishonour* an innocent person – is *un*fitting and so ineffective. Finally in v. 3 comes a statement of what *is* fitting for a fool. Plöger also sees the figure of the fool lurking behind this verse (v. 2); Krispenz (pp. 110–11) sees the figure of the fool here as the perpretator of the curse.

The identity of the two birds here is uncertain, but irrelevant. The point is that (to the uninformed observer) their flight is aimless. **causeless** (*ḥinnām*): compare 24:28. The verse, by implication, holds to the traditional view of the effectiveness of the curse, but modifies it: its effectiveness depends on whether the curse is justified by the behaviour of the recipient.

3. What **fools** have in common with the **horse** and the **ass** is lack of understanding: persuasion is ineffective for them, and coercion is the only fitting treatment. Compare 10:13.

4–5. The deliberate paradox created in the juxtaposition of these two verses is an example of a device more frequent in other wisdom books, for example, Ecclesiastes. Whatever may have been the intention of the editor responsible for the paradox, the verses continue the theme of what is fitting or appropriate: it asks, "Should one answer a fool or not? What is the most fitting response – to take him seriously, or to ignore him?" V. 3 has suggested that to answer him would be useless: only physical violence would have any effect on him.

These verses have been much discussed, not only by the commentators but also in general works on the nature of the wisdom literature. For example, Skladny (1962, p. 51) supposed that the reader is being advised to follow a middle way of treating fools between aloofness and acceptance; H. H. Schmid (1966, p. 172) thought that the intention was to leave the decision to the reader; Bühlmann (pp. 134–6) detected a slight nuance of meaning in the double use of the verb **Answer**: it is, he argued, used in a straightforward way in v. 4, but in the sense of "rebuke" in v. 5. McKane's view was that two different ways of dealing with the fool are held to be appropriate in different circumstances.

Another solution is proposed here: that by putting together two proverbs which give completely contrary advice to follow in precisely the same situation, the editor was concerned, like the later Ecclesiastes, to demonstrate that no human wisdom can encompass the whole truth; in particular, that a short proverb can express only one aspect of it. The existence of pairs of popular proverbs which appear to contradict each other such as "Many hands make light work" and "Too many cooks spoil the broth" confirms this view; but only when the two are deliberately juxtaposed as here does this truth become evident.

according to his folly (literally, "like his folly"): this phrase is used in two somewhat different senses in the two verses. V. 4 is a warning against taking a fool at his own estimation and giving him a proper answer, which would be to share in his folly; v. 5 is an admonition to answer a fool's words as they deserve to be answered – that is, by showing up the fact that he is a fool –, because otherwise he will think himself exceptionally shrewd and offer disastrous advice to all and sundry.

6. A further illustration of the uselessness of fools and an illustration of what is unfitting for them: to be used as messengers. (*RSV* has reversed the clauses.) This proverb resembles 10:26, where it is the sluggard – always a kind of fool in Proverbs – who is more than useless in this capacity. Here the **fool**, sent to deliver what is probably a verbal message (*dᵉbārîm*, "words"), either fails altogether to deliver it or gets it wrong. **cuts off his own feet**: this is an appropriate metaphor. The point of using a messenger rather than delivering it oneself is, as it were, to provide oneself with an extra pair of feet; but if the sender chooses a fool as messenger it is as if he has no feet. **and drinks violence**: this is a strange expression. "To drink" might just possibly mean "to suffer" (compare Job 21:20); but **violence** (*ḥāmās*) is much too strong a word for the context: it always denotes deliberate harm or injury, whether physical or not. That is not what is suffered by the sender of the idiot messenger. The text is clearly corrupt. *LXX* has "blame", perhaps a rendering of *ḥerpāh*; other emendations proposed are *ḥōmeṣ*, "vinegar" (compare 10:26); *ḥēmāh*, "anger". None of these is very plausible.

7. V. 9 is a variant of this verse: the second lines are identical, but different metaphors are employed. As in earlier verses the meaning turns on the question of what is or is not fitting: the cripple has **legs**, but they are useless and so not fitting to be so called; **fools** may try to say something wise, but it turns out to be unworthy of the name **proverb**.

which hang useless: the Hebrew has only one word here: *dalyû*. This is an anomalous form which should probably be emended to *dallû*, the third person plural qal of *dālal*, "to hang (down)"; compare the use of this verb in Job 28:4. **Like a lame man's legs**: the Hebrew *šōqayim mippissēaḥ* should probably be emended to *šōqê mᵉpassᵉḥîm*

(Driver, *Bib.* 32 [1951], p. 191). The literal meaning of the line would then be "(As) cripples' legs hang down".

8. The meaning of the simile in this proverb is obscure. The theme is similar to that of v. 1: that honour is not fitting for a fool. But the Hebrew of the first line is ambiguous.

The word *margēmân*, *RSV* **sling**, occurs nowhere else in Hebrew, but it is presumably cognate with *rāgam*, "to stone, to kill by stoning". *margēmân* has been thought to mean either a sling or a heap of stones. The word *ṣ*ᵉ*rôr*, an infinitive meaning "to bind" (*RSV* **one who binds**, probably emending it, following LXX, as the participle *ṣôrēr*) also has two other meanings: a stone or pebble, and a bag or bottle. The line might, then, be rendered in either of two ways: either as in *RSV* or by "Like a bag of pebbles in a heap of stones". But the latter interpretation only makes sense if *'eben*, stone, means a *precious* stone: its presence on a heap of ordinary stones could then be compared to an honour conferred on a fool – it would be incongruous or unfitting. But *'eben* does not in fact mean "precious stone" except, as in Zech. 3:9, where this is clearly indicated by the context.

The interpretation represented by *RSV* is, then, the more plausible: if one ties a stone on to the sling by means of which it is intended to hurl it, the operation will be ineffectual because obviously the stone will not leave the sling; similarly giving honour to a fool is ineffectual because he is incapable of living up to it.

9. that goes up into the hand: probably better, "in the hand": this verb *'ālāh*, literally "to go up", can be used, with an inanimate subject, in a passive sense of being placed in or on something or someone, for example clothes on a person (Lev. 19:19) or grain on a threshingfloor (Job 5:26). The image is of a **drunkard** in a rage who snatches up a stick (*ḥôaḥ* is a thornbush, or part of one, rather than a tiny thorn), or even a dangerous grappling-hook (*ḥôaḥ* also has that meaning in Job 41:2 [Heb. 40:26]) as a weapon but being incapable of inflicting injury with it; equally ineffective (compare v. 7b) is a fool's attempt to impress others with a **proverb**.

10. The Hebrew text of this verse is certainly corrupt. LXX has a quite different but also unsatisfactory version: "All the flesh of fools endures much hardship, for their fury is brought to nought". If *RSV* is correct in following Bickell (1891) and some later commentators in taking the word *rab*, more commonly "much, many" to be a rare word (occurring elsewhere only in Job 16:13 and Jer. 50:29) meaning "archer", it is possible to make some limited sense of the metaphor, although it would make better sense if it were the fool rather than his employer who were said to cause indiscriminate injury.

or a drunkard: MT has "he who hires (*śōkēr*) a fool and hires (*śōkēr*) passers by (*'ōbᵉrîm*)." *RSV* has followed the suggestion of Gemser and others, supported by Targ. and Pesh., that the second *śōkēr* should be pointed *šikkōr*, "drunkard"; but **passing fool** can hardly be correct. Gemser's further suggestion that *'ōbᵉrîm* originally stood at the end of the first line has much to be said for it: the verse would then read: "like an archer who wounds all the passers by is he who hires a fool or a drunkard". The solution proposed by Snell, 1991, pp. 350–56, which involves the emendation of *mᵉḥôlēl*, **wounds** to *mᵉhôlēl*, "makes a fool of", is ingenious but not convincing.

11. The observation that **a dog** . . . **returns to its vomit** is sufficiently clear in its implication and needs no further explanation. It may well have been a popular saying in origin, and has in fact re-acquired that status in modern times. The second line is a rather pedantic explanation. It assumes that the fool in question will already have experienced the unpleasant consequences of his folly, but still goes on committing it. In other words, the **fool** (*kᵉsîl*) is an incorrigible, hopeless case. It is interesting that the first line is quoted in 2 Pet. 2:22 without the second.

12. Do you see . . . ?: see on 22:29. **wise in his own eyes** is a kind of leitmotiv in this chapter, occurring also in vv. 5 and 16. It can be used of the **fool**, but is not restricted to him (compare 3:7; 28:11).

Unlike the preceding verses, this is not a proverb about the fool, who is introduced here only to afford a comparison. It is the self-confident person who believes that he needs no advice from anyone who is the subject of the proverb. For him there is little, or no, **hope** – that is, no hope of future success. The fool (here *kᵉsîl*) is, however, assessed more favourably here than in the preceding verses: he is usually characterized as incorrigible, but here he is less so than the complacent person. The verse can therefore not be considered as a conclusion to the preceding verses, but is more probably a later addition to the group, placed here partly because of the catchword **fool** (*kᵉsîl*), but partly also to make a slight correction to the impression given by those verses. There are worse kinds of folly than those which are obvious: the self-opinionated person may not appear to be a fool at all (compare 28:11, where the rich man is said to be "wise in his own eyes"), but he may in fact be more so than the more obvious cases.

13–16. This group of proverbs has been appropriately placed, since the lazy man or **sluggard** is a particular kind of fool. Two of these verses have almost exact variants elsewhere in the sentence literature of the book: v. 13 is a variant of 22:13 and v. 15 of 19:24.

13. The variant in 22:13 gives a more vivid picture than this verse, where the **sluggard** simply repeats his first remark in different words. But it is not possible to determine which is the older form of the proverb.

14. This is a simile of which the two parts are joined simply by *wᵉ*, literally, "and". Like v. 13 and some other proverbs about the sluggard, it is clearly humorous, although this is a humour which, by pointing the finger of scorn, is intended to make the sluggard ashamed of himself and so stir him to action. The point of comparison is that neither situation advances anything: the **sluggard** remains attached to his **bed** just as the **door** is held in place by its **hinges** and cannot move from one place to another.

15. it wears him out (*nil'āh*, literally, "he is (too) weary") – a slight difference from 19:24.

16. It is not clear why the sluggard is particularly singled out as intellectually arrogant. The **seven men who can answer discreetly**, literally, "who return sound judgement (*ṭāʿam*, compare 11:22)", are probably simply people who possess common sense; **seven** simply stands for "any number of". The proverb perhaps refers to the tendency of the lazy to find excuses for themselves.

17–28. These proverbs are almost all either similes or metaphors; there are no admonitions. They form a coherent group in that they are all concerned with persons who are guilty of actions damaging to the well-being of the community: quarrels, lies, deceit, gossip, slander, malice. They are also linked by the repetition of certain keywords: *rîb* (**quarrel**, **strife**, vv. 17 and 21); *'ēš* (**fire**, vv. 20 and 21; compare also *ziqqîm*, **firebrands**, in v. 18); *mādôn* (**quarrel**, **quarrelsome**, vv. 20 and 21); *nirgān* (**whisperer**, vv. 20 and 22); *śᵉpātayim* (**lips**, vv. 23 and 24); *śānā'/śin'āh* (**hates**, **hatred**, vv. 24, 26, 28).

17–19. These two proverbs (vv. 18 and 19 form a single proverb) are concerned with stupid rather than malicious behaviour.

17. The order of lines in the Hebrew has been reversed in *RSV*. This verse constitutes a metaphor rather than a simile, the two lines being simply placed together with no connecting particle. **meddles**: The Hebrew has *mit'abbēr*, which probably means "is furious" (compare the use of this verb in 14:16 and 20:2). *RSV*, following several commentators, emends it to *mit'ārēb*; compare Targ. and Pesh. **a passing dog**: according to the accents in MT it is the man who is passing, not the dog; but it is probably preferable to translate as *RSV* with many commentators, ignoring the accents. Toy considered that **passing** (*'ōbēr*) should be omitted as a dittograph. It is lacking in LXX. McKane comments that if it is the dog that is passing there is a contrast between the **dog**, which is minding its own business, and the man, who is not.

18–19. This four-line proverb is a simile: **Like** (*kᵉ*) in v. 18 is picked up in v. 19 by "so" (*kēn*).

18. madman (*mitlahlēaḥ*): this word occurs in Hebrew only here and in the Hebrew Ecclesiasticus (32:15). It has Syriac and Arabic cognates and may be a loanword. **firebrands**, **arrows**, **and death**: the meaning is "lethal firebrands and lethal arrows". (See Watson, pp. 324–5.) **firebrands** (*ziqqîm*): that is, flaming arrows. The point is that just as the madman hurls his lethal weapons entirely at random, so this kind of joker cannot foresee the unfortunate effects of his practical joking.

20–22. These three proverbs have a common topic: troublemakers who provoke quarrels.

20–21. These two proverbs are virtually identical in meaning. In both, the heat engendered in **quarrelling** is aptly compared to **fire**, and the **whisperer** (*nirgān* – see on 16:28) and the **quarrelsome man**, though not identical, are equally guilty of perpetuating **strife**. Both verses refer to **wood** (*'ēṣîm*) as fuel.

21. charcoal: this is probably the meaning of *peḥām*. Wildeboer, partly followed by Gemser, Oesterley and Ringgren, proposed that it should be emended to *mappûaḥ*, "bellows" (compare Jer. 6:29); supposedly on the basis of LXX's *esqara*; but in fact *esqara* does not specifically mean "bellows", but either a fireplace, or *any* unspecified means of procuring fire. *RSV*'s translation is perfectly satisfactory.

22. This verse is identical with 18:8, on which see the comments. It refers to the eagerness with which slander is listened to, and is very appropriate in the present context.

23–26. These verses are warnings against malicious persons who hide their hatred under a cloak of friendship.

23. glaze: MT has *kesep sîgîm*, "silver dross", that is, lead monoxide, a silver-like substance left over from the process of purifying of silver and used to cover pottery to make it look like silver. *RSV* has adopted a proposal (see Driver, *Bib.* 32 [1951], p. 191; Albright, 1955, pp. 12–13) to read *k^esapsāg*, **Like . . . glaze**, this otherwise unknown Hebrew word being supposedly found in Ugaritic and Hittite. Dressler, however (1988, pp. 117–25) has rejected this hypothesis.

smooth: here again *RSV* has accepted a probably unnecessary emendation. MT has *dōl^eqîm*, "burning", referring to a kiss of warm friendship or love; Toy and others have proposed emendation to *ḥ^alāqîm*, following LXX.

24–26. These verses may be a somewhat long-winded and repetitious elaboration of v. 23.

24. He who hates (*śônē'*): that is, a personal enemy (compare 27:6). **harbours**: literally, "puts" (*yāšît*).

25. seven abominations: see on 6:16. **seven**: see on v. 16 above.

26. be covered (*tikkasseh*): on this form of the hithpael see *GK* 54c. **the assembly** (*qāhāl*): see on 5:14.

27. The same metaphor, though expressed in different words, recurs in Ps. 7:15 [Heb. 16] and Ec. 10:8 and no doubt had its origin in a popular proverb. The idea that the person who plans the ruin of others will be "hoist with his own petard" is one which appeals to the popular imagination. It is frequently found in fairy stories and other popular tales: compare Dan. 6:24 (Aram. 25); Est. 7:10.

28. hates its victims (*yiśnā' dakkâw*) literally, "its crushed ones": this makes little sense, and the text is evidently corrupt. It has been suggested that *dak* here is an Aramaism, since *dak* is the Aramaic equivalent of the Hebrew *zak*, "pure, righteous" (compare 16:2; 20:11; 21:8). But the occurrence of an Aramaism here needs an explanation, and in any case the form remains difficult to account for: "its pure ones" makes no more sense than "its crushed ones". Driver (*JTS* 41 [1940], pp. 174–5) attempted to overcome part of the difficulty by proposing that *dakkâw* should be repointed as *dikyû*, which means "innocence" in Aramaic.

Whatever may be the meaning of the first line, there is no satisfactory parallel between the two. It is not clear whose **ruin** is envisaged, that of the liar or of his victim. If it is the latter, the verse must be regarded as standing in isolation from the preceding group of verses, which speak of the discomfiture of the malicious speaker.

CHAPTER 27

Malchow, 1985, pp. 238–45 has argued that chapters 27–9 as a whole form a thematic unity; but such a unity is hard to see. In fact, apart from vv. 23–7, which constitute an extended admonition, this chapter consists mainly of short individual statements and admonitions. Even Van Leeuwen, who discerned "proverb-poems" in both chapters 25 and 26, has found no such unity here ("no overarching thematic concern"), and speaks of "the aphoristic, somewhat isolated nature of the Sayings and Admonitions of this chapter" (1988, p. 129).

There are in fact a few cases of paired verses (at least vv. 1–2, 3–4, 5–6, 15–16); and Krispenz argued for vv. 3–9 as a distinct group. On vv. 11–22 or 11–27 as a loose collection of proverbs see below.

As in chapter 25 there are a number of admonitions, although the statement form – including some similes and comparisons – predominates. Antithetical parallelism is again rare. Several verses have variants elsewhere in the sentence literature. Van Leeuwen correctly notes that the most frequent topic treated is friendship (at least vv. 5–6, 10, 17). As in chapter 26 there is no reference to Yahweh.

1–2. There are both thematic and verbal links between these two admonitions: they both deprecate self-praise, and they both employ the verb *hll* (**praise** in v. 2, and, in a reflexive mood, "praise oneself" *RSV* **boast**) in v. 1. But they do not constitute an original unit: each makes a somewhat different point.

1. To **boast about tomorrow** means to make a confident prediction of one's future achievements. But the main purpose of this verse is not so much to recommend modesty as to stress the impotence of human beings. This is a commonplace of ancient Near Eastern thought, attested as early as the third millennium BC in Egypt in *Ptahhotep* ("One does not know what may happen, so that he may understand the morrow", *ANET*, p. 413b) and reiterated in later writings including *Amenope* and *Ahiqar* and later still, most emphatically, in Ecclesiastes. Some of the non-biblical texts in question add that the future is known only to God; this is no doubt implied here also (compare 16:9).

2. another (*zār*); **a stranger** (*nokrî*): these two terms are evidently used here in a weaker sense than in 2:16; 5:20; 7:5, since they must refer to acquaintances belonging to the same community, who are the only persons entitled to express an opinion about the merits of a neighbour. Self-advertisement is apt to have the opposite effect than the one intended.

3–4. These verses are formally similar in their mode of expression ("Z is worse than either X or Y"). In the Hebrew their first lines are more effective than in *RSV*'s translation: "The weight of stones and the heaviness of sand!"; "The cruelty of wrath and the devastation of anger!".

3. a fool's provocation: that is, the irritation or vexation caused by the behaviour of a fool.

4. The second line of this verse means "but jealousy is intolerable".

5–6. These proverbs are both concerned with friendship (*'ahābāh*; **love**, v. 5; *'ôhēb*, **friend**, v. 6) and the importance of frankness in such a relationship.

5. hidden (*m^esuttāret*): literally, "which has been concealed". The meaning is not clear. Frankenberg thought that the word here means "withdrawn": that is, that the alternative presented is either to be frank in criticizing a friend, or to withdraw from a relationship with one whose conduct has been unsatisfactory. It is doubtful whether the word can have such a meaning; but van der Weiden suggested that a similar sense can be retained if it is understood not as a form of *sātar* "to hide" but as an unusual form (the so-called "infixed 't' conjugation") of *sûr*, "to turn away". A more general view is that the **love** in question is "hidden" in the sense of failing to express itself openly.

6. The topic dealt with in this verse is the same as in v. 5: the nature of true friendship. The **wounds of a friend** – that is, his harsh criticism (compare the use of "wound" in English in a metaphorical sense) – are **faithful**, that is, they are reliable or "true" in the sense that they have been called forth with a good intention. They demonstrate the sincerity of the friendship.

The antithesis of this is **the kisses of an enemy**: the sign of a *pretended* friendship. But in this second line, as in v. 5, there is one word which defies attempts at comprehension. *RSV*'s rendering of this word (*na'tārôt*) by **profuse** is based on the view that in addition to the more common verb *'âtar* "to pray, supplicate" there is a second *'âtar*, a loanword from Aramaic meaning "to be rich" (cognate with Hebrew *'āšar*). But the existence of such a word in Hebrew is dubious (it is listed in BDB, but not in *KB*³). A satisfactory parallelism would require a word opposite in meaning to **faithful**; and various emendations have been proposed, including *nᵉʿōtôt*, "treacherous" (Gemser); *nᵉrāʿôt*, "corrupt"; *ʿiqqᵉšôt*, "crooked" (Toy, Oesterley). None of these, however, receives any support from MSS or Versions. Driver's suggestion that the word is cognate with an Arabic word meaning "unruly, disordered" also does not yield good sense.

7. As elsewhere in these proverbs (16:24; 24:13; 25:16, 27) the topic of finding and eating **honey** here suggests an application which goes beyond its literal meaning. This proverb is open to several different interpretations concerning aspects of human nature, such as the indifference or complacency of the rich and the desperation of the poor, or the relativity of human values. *Ahiqar* (line 188; *ANET* p. 430) has a very similar proverb, unfortunately only partly preserved: "Hunger makes sweet what is bitter". **loathes**: the Hebrew has *tābûs*, literally, "tramples". The proposal to emend this to *tābûz*, "despises" perhaps produces a slightly better sense but is hardly necessary.

8. This proverb is not concerned with travellers in general but to people who, for whatever reason, leave their homes and settle elsewhere. They are compared with the **bird that strays** (*nādad*) or flees **from its nest** – a symbol not of wilfulness but of exile or banishment (Isa. 16:2–3). So the man who leaves his **home** (*māqôm*, literally, "place" – that is, the place where he belongs), whether voluntarily or not, suffers loneliness and isolation. The precise circumstances, if any, to which this proverb originally referred are not apparent. It may simply be a plea for community solidarity: everyone has a place in the community in which he ought, and ought to be allowed, to stay.

9. The first line of this verse presents no difficulties: it makes a somewhat trite comment about the soothing effect of physical self-indulgence on the mind. It may be presumed that the real point of the proverb originally lay in the second line; but this is unfortunately completely obscure. The Hebrew text makes no sense and is clearly corrupt: "and/but the sweetness of his friend from the advice of the soul". *RSV* has followed the very different text of LXX, from which some commentators have attempted to reconstruct an original Hebrew. Alternatively, others have seen a positive comparison here, emending *rēʿēhû*, "his friend", to *raʿᵃwāh*, thought to be a loan-word from Aramaic meaning "friendship", and *mēʿaṣat*, "from the advice of", to *mᵉʾammēṣ*, "strengthens": "the sweetness of friendship strengthens the soul". But the corruption of MT is so great that speculations are probably useless.

10. If v. 9 originally contained a reference to friends or friendship, these two verses may have formed a pair. However this may be, this verse, which contains three lines, is concerned with friends (*rēaʿ*), brothers (*ʾāḥ*) and neighbours (*šākēn*). The first two lines are admonitions; the third may be a popular proverb.

The three lines appear to be completely independent of one another; unity of thought cannot be obtained simply by omitting the second line (Scott). The first line is addressed to young men, advising them not to scorn or neglect old family friends (read *rēaʿ* with Qere at the second occurrence of **friend**); it makes no reference to brothers. The second line, which is unusually long and may have been secondarily expanded, is concerned only with brothers. It appears completely to contradict the idea, expressed in 17:17, that brothers may be especially relied on to help one another in trouble, but gives no reason for this view. The third line points out that brothers may live too far apart to be able to offer such help, and stresses the practical importance of cultivating local solidarity in the community. There is no point in trying to relate these points of view. The first and third lines have extremely close parallels in the Syriac version of *Ahikar*.

11–22. V. 11 has probably been placed here because like v. 10 it is addressed to a young man; and these verses, together with vv. 23–7, may have been assembled to make a kind of compendium of educational material. V. 11a, which strongly resembles 23:15, has the form of the introduction to a "parental" Instruction, and v. 12 makes a fitting continuation of this. Of the eleven verses (12–22), no fewer than four are variants of, or reminiscences of, proverbs occurring in earlier chapters of the sentence literature. V. 12 is virtually identical with 22:3; v. 13 with 20:16; v. 15 closely resembles part of 19:13; v. 21a is identical with 17:3a.

11. him who reproaches me: that a stupid or wicked son brought shame on his parents in the form of reproaches by neighbours, and that, conversely, a wise or righteous son was a credit to them is a commonplace of these proverbs. Some commentators have attempted to draw a distinction between this and otherwise comparable verses, alleging that here the father is thinking of himself and of his standing in the community rather than of his son's welfare; but this is mistaken. In fact the two elements are always mixed, and cannot be separated, as every parent knows.

12. This verse is identical with 22:3 except for the absence of a connecting particle (*RSV* has **and**) between the lines with a consequent change of tense (see *GK* 120g, h), and for the spelling of **simple** (*p^etā'îm* – see *GK* 93x).

13. foreigners: MT has *nokriyyāh*, "a strange woman"; but see on the virtually identical 20:16. There is a wordplay between *'ārab*, **goes surety** and *'ārûm*, "prudent" in v. 12.

14. blesses: this probably refers to a greeting as in, for example, 1 Sam. 13:10; 2 Kg. 4:29; 10:15; but the notion of invoking a blessing was no doubt also always present. **rising early in the morning**: this phrase, which is lacking in one manuscript and which overloads the poetical line, is considered by many commentators to be an explanatory gloss; if so, it is probably a mistaken one. The phrase **will be counted as cursing** (literally, "a curse will be reckoned to him") is an extreme one; and this makes it unlikely that the offence in question was nothing more than the boisterous waking up of a sleeping person too early in the morning. It may be relevant that "bless" is sometimes used as an euphemism for "curse" (1 Kg. 21:10, 13; Job 1:5, 11; 2:5, 9; Ps. 10:3). The point of the proverb is, however, uncertain. It has been suggested that such a public greeting (**with a loud voice**) might have been interpreted as insincere or even as having the opposite intention to the ostensible one.

15–16. These two verses now form a single unit; but v. 16, which elaborates the point that there is no way to stop the woman's continual flow of speech, may be an expansion of an originally independent proverb.

15. A continual dripping: see on 19:13, where the identical expression is used. **a contentious woman**: in 21:9, 19; 25:24, where the same expression is used, it is stated that to live with such a woman is so intolerable that the only solution is to move away. This is probably also implied here. **a rainy day** (*yôm sagrîr*): this word (*sagrîr*) occurs only here in the Old Testament, but means "rainstorm" or "downpour" in Mishnaic Hebrew. **are alike** (*ništāwāh*): this may be a niphal form with transposed consonants or simply a scribal error for *nišwātāh* (*GK* 75x).

16. to restrain her: literally, "those who restrain her" (*ṣôp^eneḥā*). This is not a usual meaning of the verb *ṣāpan* "to hide, keep, preserve"; but it has been argued that a somewhat similar meaning is to be found in Hos. 13:12 (see Driver, *JTS* 41 [1940], p. 175). If *RSV*'s translation is thus to be accepted as correct, the meaning would be that to try to control or confine such a woman is as futile as to try to control the wind (some minor adjustments would still need to be made to the text). If not, the line is unintelligible. (LXX has a quite different text which refers to the north wind, Heb. *ṣāpôn*).

The Hebrew of the second line may be rendered by "and oil meets his right hand" (taking the verb *qārā'* here, normally "call", as a variant of *qārāh* "to meet" (so presumably *RSV*, **grasp**). This has generally been understood as meaning that such a woman is as slippery as **oil** and slips out of one's **hand** when one tries to catch her – a thought only loosely related to that of the first line.

17. sharpens: in both cases the pointing of the Hebrew is anomalous. Most commentators repoint the first as passive hophal, "is sharpened by" and the other as hiphil, "sharpens".

another: the Hebrew has "the face of his friend". No entirely convincing explanation has been found of the meaning of the word "face" (*pānîm*) here. It is just possible that it means "person", but this is rather meaningless. "Behaviour" and "manners" have been suggested, but with little plausibility. Toy and Oesterley proposed that the word should be omitted as a gloss. It can, however, mean the "edge" or "cutting edge" of a tool or weapon; and Wildeboer's suggestion that it is used in this way here to continue the metaphor of the first line is perhaps the most convincing: social intercourse or conversation between two people can sharpen the *wits* (compare *REB*).

18. This is a straightforward statement that a servant who has faithfully looked after his master may expect to be suitably rewarded as surely as the person who has faithfully tended a fruit-tree may look forward to a time when he will be able to enjoy its fruit. Like most proverbs, however, it is open to a wider application.

19. answers; **reflects**: these words are interpretation rather than translation. In the Hebrew text there are no verbs at all: it reads simply, "Like water, a face to a face, so the heart of man to man". What this means is far from clear. LXX has no reference to **water**, and this led some commentators to suppose that *kammayim* ("As water") is a corruption of the particle *k^emô*, "like, as" (corresponding to *k^e* in prose texts). So Toy: "As face answers to face, so men's minds one to another": that is, men's minds may be as like or unlike as their faces.

Most commentators, however, accept *MT* as it stands. It is also agreed that the point of the proverb is a statement about human character (*lēb*, *RSV* **mind**), and that a comparison is made with what can only be, in the first line, the reflection of one's face in water. If this line is referring, as seems to be the case, with the *recognition* of one's own reflected face, the second line may be supposed to be saying something about recognizing one's own character. The major difference between the commentators is on the question whether the second **man** in that line is identical with the first: in other words, is it being said that the observation of another person enables one to understand one's own nature (so Gemser, Ringgren – one may perhaps compare v. 17 –) or that one can understand it by looking into one's *own* heart (McKane; compare Scott)?

20. Sheol and Abaddon: see on 15:11. **Abaddon** is curiously spelled *ᵃbaddōh* (Kethib) or *ᵃbaddō* (Qere) here, but a few *MSS* have the more usual *ᵃbaddôn*. Sheol and Abaddon are called insatiable because they continue endlessly to swallow up the dead – a remnant of the mythological notion of Sheol as a monster equipped with a mouth and an appetite. They thus provide an apt comparison with the cupidity (literally, **eyes**) of human beings.

Plöger points out the contrast between this verse and the picture drawn in v. 18 of the faithful servant who *is*, it is implied, satisfied with the reward of his care for his master. Since v. 19 is also concerned with the "mind of man", these three verses may have been intentionally juxtaposed. Vv. 21 and 22 also have somewhat germane themes: the criterion for the assessment of human worth and the irradicability of folly.

21. The first line of this verse is identical with 17:3a; but it is used here to make a different point. The second line has no verb: the Hebrew has simply "and a man according to his praise". "is tested" would probably express its meaning better than *RSV*'s **is judged**, since the first line is about the assaying of metals. As the true nature of **gold** or **silver** is tested and so made known through the means of **crucible** and **furnace**, so a man's true character is assessed and known by the amount of **praise** that he receives from others – that is, by his public reputation. There is a somewhat similar thought in 12:8a, where it is stated that "a man is praised" (the verb used corresponds to the noun in 27:21) "according to his good sense".

22. This is not an admonition but a conditional sentence in Hebrew: "Though you may crush . . . his folly will not . . .". What is said elsewhere of the *kᵉsîl* (17:10; 26:11) as being incorrigible is now said of the *ʾewîl* (the two words for **fool** are hardly distinguishable in meaning). The metaphors employed in this verse and v. 21 are somewhat similar. In both cases the imagery is one of the conversion of raw materials into useful products. The purpose of crushing grain **in a mortar** is not only to reduce it to flour but also to get rid of the inedible and worthless husks. In the case of a **fool**, no amount of pounding will succeed in separating the "husk" of his **folly** from him, rendering him a useful member of society.

The first line of the verse is metrically too long. The view of most commentators that **with a pestle along with crushed grain** is a gloss is probably correct. The meaning of *rîpôt*, *RSV* **crushed grain**, a word which occurs elsewhere only in 2 Sam. 17:19, is not certain.

23–27. These five verses stand apart from the rest of the chapter. They form a single whole. They are, ostensibly at least, addressed to the sheep- and goat-breeder and can be interpreted as an expanded example of the kind of proverb which points out the necessity of unremitting hard work on the farm, one which usually takes the form of a statement but occasionally appears, as here, as an admonition (20:13; 24:27). It shows knowledge of the nature of the work involved, and in that respect has its clearest parallel in Isa. 28:23–8, where the topic is employed metaphorically.

The passage has been interpreted in various ways. Toy called it "a treatise on the culture of animals", and compared it to other ancient agricultural treatises. Ringgren, followed by McKane, saw it as a commendation of pastoral life and perhaps even as polemic against urban luxury. Van Leeuwen (pp. 131–43), while admitting that it "makes sense" as straightforward advice to a farmer, believes it to be a kind of parable or "metaphor for kingship", addressed to a king as shepherd of his people. He takes his cue from the word *nēzer*, "crown" in v. 24, a verse which he understands as a warning that royal dynasties are not secure for ever.

The point of the passage must indeed lie in v. 24, which provides the motive for the initial admonition in v. 23. But there is insufficient ground for Van Leeuwen's interpretation, which would require a specific allegorical explanation of all the details given in these verses. Apart from the word "crown", which is lacking in the LXX and which several commentators propose to emend, there is little to suggest such a royal allegory. The point of v. 24 is that there must be a continuous effort to preserve one's livelihood: to "rest on one's laurels" is a recipe for disaster. Time does not stand still, and a farm does not look after itself. This axiom is certainly applicable to the life of a farmer of similar standing to those addressed elsewhere in these proverbs, but like most proverbs it is also capable of a much wider interpretation.

23. Know well: the form (infinitive absolute followed by a second person singular imperfect) is very emphatic: see *GK* 113bb. **the condition of**: literally, "the face of", that is, their appearance, by which it can be judged whether they are healthy. **flocks, herds**: that is, sheep and goats rather than larger cattle (see v. 26).

24. riches: this word (*ḥōsen*) means what is stored up, normally treasure. This verse has been taken to refer to wealth gained by trade, which can easily be lost, in contrast with the solid wealth represented by farming stock; but this is not certain. It may refer to the wealth or store of the successful farmer, which will nevertheless melt away if the stock is not properly looked after.

a crown: this word, which denotes an item of exclusively royal regalia and symbolizes royal power, is regarded by the commentaries as incomprehensible in this context and is usually emended either to *'ôṣār*, "treasure" or to *'ōšer*, "wealth". However, this may be an example of a "royal" proverb in which ordinary persons are compared and contrasted with kings: the point may be that since even a royal dynasty may not last for ever, a private fortune is even more precarious: nothing is certain in this world. The possibility of a king's (not necessarily any specific king's) losing his throne is envisaged in 14:28.

25–27. These verses envisage the conditions and rewards of good animal husbandry.

25. grass (*ḥāṣîr*); **new growth** (*deše'*); **herbage** (*'iśśᵉbôt*): these terms are roughly synonymous, although *deše'* is sometimes used specifically of fresh, new vegetation. Here they all refer to food for the sheep and goats, who are fed with first and second crops of vegetation and also with hay (**herbage**) gathered from the mountain slopes. **is gone**: for a similar meaning of *gālāh* compare Isa. 24:11; Job 20:28. Here it means "is removed", that is, taken off as hay. **When**: the Hebrew has simply "the grass has been removed"; but

RSV, probably correctly, renders the whole verse as an extended temporal clause.

26–27. The solid advantages of the enterprise are now presented. The **lambs** provide wool for clothing; the **goats** can be sold and the estate extended in size out of the proceeds. The **field** in this context is probably a meadow to provide grazing for a larger flock. **food**: literally, "bread". **for the food of your household**: this phrase, which is lacking in the LXX, makes the line too long and is probably to be omitted as a gloss added because the original text did not refer specifically to the male household. **maintenance** or sustenance: literally, "life" (*ḥayyîm*). This unusual meaning is supported by Toy, Gemser, Dahood, van der Weiden and *KB*[3].

Considered as a whole, this passage depicts a pastoral way of life which is, as McKane remarks, "self-contained" if not idyllic. There is no mention of a need for divine blessing: success depends on technical skill combined with hard work. Why the pastoral rather than other modes of agriculture was selected for depiction is not clear.

CHAPTER 28

The unusually long passage 27:23–7 marks the conclusion of what was evidently originally a separate collection of proverbs. This chapter, which reverts to the two-line proverb, begins another, but without a new heading. Unlike chapters 25–7 it contains a great preponderance of antithetical proverbs and very few examples of simile, metaphor or imagery in general.

There are only two explicitly Yahweh-proverbs in the chapter (vv. 5 and 25); but, as Plöger pointed out, the operation of divine norms of justice seems to be implied throughout – another difference from the immediately preceding chapters. The great majority of verses in one way or another contrast the righteous with the wicked, and state that the latter will suffer an unpleasant fate. In view of the general character of the chapter, the three verses which refer to *tôrāh* (*RSV* **law**) are of particular interest. Elsewhere in the book – except perhaps in 6:23 – this word denotes the teaching given by parents or teachers to their children or pupils; here, however, it is used without qualification, and the reference appears to be to *divine* teaching (though not necessarily to the "Law" in the Deuteronomic sense). In v. 7 it is associtated, as elsewhere in the book, with wisdom; but in v. 4 to keep it is to stand against the wicked, and in v. 9 it is only those who hear – that is, who obey – it whose prayers are acceptable to God. It may also be significant that these three verses are grouped together in close proximity to one of the Yahweh-proverbs (v. 5), though in general internal groupings in the chapter are fairly rare.

1. bold: better, "confident". This verb, *bāṭaḥ*, means "to trust", and is used elsewhere in Proverbs, together with the cognate noun *mibṭaḥ*, of putting one's trust in Yahweh (3:5; 14:26; 16:20; 22:19). Here also it is probably implied that the confidence of the **righteous** is not *self*-confidence but is given them by Yahweh's assurances. It is usually the **wicked** who are depicted in Proverbs as on the attack; but here they are the fearful ones, pursued not by real enemies but by a bad conscience, whereas the righteous have a good conscience and so cannot be frightened.

wicked (singular, *rāšā'*) is here construed with a plural verb and **righteous** (plural, *ṣaddîqîm*) with a singular one. This remains a minor puzzle despite various attempts to explain it, but the sense is not affected.

2. The meaning of this verse is uncertain. *RSV*'s translation of the first line, which closely follows MT, makes a kind of sense but not a very satisfactory one: when a country sins against God, it is punished with political and military unrest, with **many** would-be **rulers** pitted one against another. But *RSV*'s translation of the second line is hardly possible. Several commentators prefer the version of the LXX, which is quite different, for the whole verse: "By reason of the sins of ungodly men quarrels arise, but a wise man will quell them". To correct MT along these lines would, however, require a massive series of emendations.

3. It has been supposed by many commentators that the situation envisaged in this verse is an impossible one: the **poor** (here *rāš*) do not oppress the **poor** (*dallîm* -*dal* and *rāš* are synonymous). It has therefore been proposed to emend *rāš* to some more appropriate word such as *rāšā'*, "wicked person", *'ārîṣ*, "violent person" or *rō'š*, "chief". But this is to misunderstand the range of meanings of the verb *'āšaq* (*RSV* **oppresses**). Although this verb is frequently used of the tyranny of the rich and powerful over the poor and defenceless, it can also denote robbery of one's (presumably equal) neighbour (Lev. 6:2–4 [Heb. 5:21–3]; 19:13) or the cheating of customers by a tradesman (Hos. 12:7). Here for a poor man to steal food from his equally poor neighbour is singled out as particularly disastrous: it is compared to torrential rain which devastates the standing crops and thus causes famine (Heb. *wᵉʾên leḥem*, literally, "and there is no bread").

4–6. Paronomasia makes an aural (or oral) link between these verses and v. 3: *rāš* (**a poor man**) in v. 6 picks up the earlier occurrence of that word in v. 3, closing the group; and between those two verses v. 4 has *rāšāʿ* (**the wicked**) and v. 5 *ʾanᵉšê-rāʿ* (**Evil men**).

4. Whether or not *tôrāh* (**the law**) here refers specifically to divine law (see on 28:1–28 above), there is certainly a thematic connection between this verse and v. 5 in that to **keep the law**, even if "law" means the teaching of the wise, is to fight against the wicked, and it is precisely such "Evil men" who set themselves against those who "seek Yahweh" in v. 5. These proverbs belong to the same strand as verses like 9:10, where wisdom is only attainable by those who "seek the Lord" (Plöger).

5. Evil men: this phrase (*ʾanᵉšê-rāʿ*) is emphatic. It means men who have completely devoted themselves to evil. In this verse (see on v. 4 above) devotion to Yahweh is expressed in terms of wisdom or understanding (the verb is *bîn*), and wickedness is defined as a lack of this. **understand it completely**: the Hebrew has "understand all" (*yabînû kôl*), meaning everything concerning **justice** – perhaps an echo of the "knowledge of good and evil" in Gen. 2:9, 17; 3:5).

6. The first line of this verse is identical with 19:1a; the second is a variant of 19:1b in that it has precisely the same structure; but here it is the **rich man**, not the fool, who is **perverse in his ways** and is contrasted with the righteous poor man.

Better (*ṭôb*): the question precisely what is meant by "better" in these proverbs is not always easy to answer, and the answers are not always the same. There may be a clue in the Hebrew of the second line, where the emphasis is different from what would be supposed from *RSV*: it reads, "than one who is perverse in his ways, although (*wᵉhûʾ*) he may be rich". This probably means that wealth will not enable a rich man to escape the consequences of his evil deeds: it is better to be honest, though poor, because then there will be no fear of divine punishment. See also on 19:1.

his ways: MT has the dual form, "two ways". This is either a scribal error or a later interpretation of the consonantal text as referring to the doctrine of the "two ways" – that is, to the moral choice which has to be made in life.

7. The first line of this verse should perhaps be rendered by "It is a wise son who keeps the law". On **the law** see on 28:1–28 above. **gluttons**: or, perhaps better, "frivolous persons" or "wastrels". **shames his father**: compare, for example, 10:1; 27:11.

8. Lending at interest to fellow-Israelites was forbidden in the laws of the Old Testament (Exod. 22:25 [Heb. 24]; Lev. 25:36; Dt. 23:19 [Heb. 20]; compare Ps. 15:5; Ezek. 18:8, 13, 18 [Heb. 17]; 22:12); but was evidently practised. The words *nešek* (**interest**) and *tarbît* (**increase**) occur as a pair in most of those passages. The difference between the two is never explained in the Old Testament; but later Jewish usage and the etymology of the two words suggest that *nešek* (related to *nāšak*, "to bite") was interest which was levied by deduction from the original loan but which had to be repaid in full, while *tarbît* (related to *hirbāh*, "to increase") was an additional charge levied on repayment. The point of the verse is that while one man may extort money from the poor by usury, his heir may be a generous person who "pays it back" through gifts to the poor.

9. See on 15:8 and 15:29. It was evidently taken for granted that **prayer** to Yahweh was generally practised in the communities to whom these proverbs were addressed, even by those who are censured by them. In 15:8b the prayer of the upright is acceptable to Yahweh (*reṣônô*, *RSV* "his delight", the opposite of *tô'ēbāh*, "abomination" – see on 11:1) while the sacrifice of the wicked is his "abomination". Here, where it is the person who refuses to "hear", that is, obey, **the law** whose prayer is **an abomination** (presumably to Yahweh), it would seem that this law must be Yahweh's own moral law or instruction by which he seeks to provide guidance through life (compare 6:23a).

10. This is a straightforward statement of the principle of exact retribution. The second line is a variant of 26:27a. **misleads**: better, "entices" (properly, "causes to go astray"). **pit**: this word (*šeḥût*) occurs only here. It is a byform of *šaḥat*, which is the word used in 26:27. Since **pit** is the most appropriate meaning, suggestions of a different derivation and meaning (Thomas, *JTS* 38 [1937], pp. 402–3; L. Kopf, 1959, pp. 256–7; van der Weiden) are beside the point.

The third line (**but the blameless** . . .), an anomaly in a series of two-line proverbs, is regarded by most commentators as either a gloss or as a fragment of an otherwise lost proverb. **will have a**

goodly inheritance: literally, "will inherit good". This means no more than that they will prosper (compare 3:35). The line is present in the LXX, and is not inappropriate in the context, as it completes an antithesis.

11. To be "wise in one's own eyes" is, in these proverbs, not a fault confined to any one kind of person. In the case of the **rich man**, who may fancy himself in an impregnable position (compare 10:15; 18:11), such arrogance is not particularly surprising. But these proverbs consistently compare the rich unfavourably with the poor in various ways, and it is quite in character that this proverb should point out that a poor man may be more intelligent than a rich one. However, there may be a hidden irony here: the **poor man** may be able to "find out" (literally, "search" – compare 1 Sam. 20:12) and expose the pretensions of the rich, but he nevertheless remains poor and at a disadvantage.

12. This verse is a partial variant of v. 28. Its first line is identical with v. 28b except for the main verb, and both verses are concerned with the reactions of the populace (*'ādām*, **men**) to the respective rise and fall from power of **righteous** (*ṣaddîqîm*) and **wicked** (*rᵉšā'îm*) claimants to political dominance. There is also a strong resemblance to 29:2.

In the first line there is a difficulty which *RSV* has concealed by its use of the word **triumph**. Although in English this word can mean to win a victory or to gain a success, the Hebrew word (*'ālaṣ*) does not have this meaning: it means to rejoice or to be jubilant. The cause of this rejoicing is not disclosed. What is required here is a verb with a meaning similar to **rise** (*qûm*) in the second line. Some commentators (Toy and Scott, less certainly Gemser and Plöger) have proposed an emendation to the infinitive of *'ālāh*, literally "to ascend". In the same line it is the word **glory** (*tip'eret*) which signifies the expression of triumph or something to boast about. (Compare 17:6; 20:29.)

In the second line also the verb (*yᵉḥuppaś*, **hide themselves**) has been questioned. This may mean "is sought for", that is, "is in hiding"; a slight emendation to *yitḥuppaś* would yield the meaning "hide themselves" (so *KB*³). That this is correct is strongly confirmed by the parallel in v. 28, where the meaning of *yissātēr*, "hide themselves", is not in doubt. Driver's proposal (*Bib.* 32 [1951], pp. 192–3) of "are trampled down", based on an Arabic word, is unnecessary.

13. Several commentators have pointed out that this is the only verse in Proverbs which refers to God's forgiveness of the penitent sinner. **confesses**: this verb, the hiphil of *yādāh*, normally means "to thank" or "to praise" (compare the noun *tôdāh*, "thanksgiving"). But in Ps. 32:5 also it appears to mean "to confess", and this is a regular meaning of the hithpael. **will obtain mercy**: in practical terms this presumably means that Yahweh will remove the obstacles to his prosperity.

14. fears the Lord: the Hebrew has simply "fears", or, better, "is in dread". The commentators are divided on the question whether Yahweh is in fact the implied object of the verb. LXX does not mention God, but on the other hand it interprets the verb along those lines by adding "with reverence". The verb used is *pḥd* (piel), which is not the verb used elsewhere for fearing God. But if this is not the meaning it is difficult to see why continual dread should make a person **Blessed** (*'ašrê*).

The relationship between the first and second lines is not clear. **hardens his heart**: this phrase in Hebrew denotes not a lack of compassion for others but rather stubbornness (Exod. 7:3) and, in Ps. 95:8, a refusal to listen to Yahweh's words or to acknowledge his actions. It is thus just possible to see in this a convincing antithesis to the "fear" of the first line, though nothing in the verse is expressed clearly.

15–16. As comments on the disastrous results of the rule of the wicked, these verses take up and illustrate the general assertion of v. 12b. Compare 17:7; 29:4, 26 for other examples of proverbs critical of oppressive rulers.

15. This verse is a metaphor rather than a simile in the Hebrew. **roaring** (*nōhēm*): perhaps better, "growling". See on 5:11. **people** (*'ām*): that is, the common people: see on 11:14.

16. There appears to be no logical connection between the lines of this verse. The text of the first line is also probably corrupt. The Hebrew has "*and* a cruel oppressor" (literally, "and great in oppressions"). Some commentators (possibly followed by *RSV*) have suggested the emendation of *w^erab* to a verb such as *yereb*, literally, "makes many (oppressions)"; but there is still no parallelism. Something like "will perish" or "will not live long" would correspond to the **will prolong his days** of the second line; but this would require a major and improbable emendation. The second line, however, makes sense by itself. In the first line LXX has "A king in need of revenues", apparently reading *tᵉbû'ôt*, "income" for *tᵉbûnôt*, **understanding**. Another suggestion is to omit the first word *nāgîd* (**A ruler**), so that the first line would read simply "One who lacks . . .", making the whole verse generally applicable. None of these proposals is satisfactory.

17. This verse also is beset with difficulties. The first line appears to refer to a murderer. But **burdened** (*'āšūq*), whether it refers to a criminal charge (so *REB*) or to the burden of a guilty conscience, would be a unique use of the verb *'āšaq*, which ordinarily means "to oppress" or "to wrong". The Hebrew of the second line (*RSV* **let him be a fugitive until death**) is, literally, "as far as a pit (*bôr*) he will (or, "let him") flee". "Pit" has been taken by *RSV* and others to mean the grave, that is, **death**, though *REB* renders the line by "will jump into a well to escape arrest" (compare also Ringgren). Finally in the last line (which may be a gloss) *yitmᵉkû* (*RSV* **help**) is ambiguous and is capable of opposite meanings – either "seize" or "support, help". If *RSV's* translation is the correct one, this may be a warning not to help murderers to escape; and some commentators (Toy, Oesterley) have supposed that this verse is not a proverb at all, but that a law has been mistakenly included among these proverbs.

18–20. These three proverbs have a certain thematic unity in that they all deal antithetically with the consequences of acceptable and unacceptable behaviour: of honesty, diligence and trustworthiness respectively and their opposites.

18. will be delivered: that is, will be safe from any kind of adversity. **perverse in his ways**: that is, devious or dishonest. On the dual form of *dᵉrākayim*, literally, "two ways", see on v. 6. **into a pit**: the Hebrew has *bᵉ'eḥāt*, literally "into one". This was taken by some early commentators to mean "into one of the two ways"; but most modern commentators and *RSV* and *REB*, regarding "two ways" as an error, emend the word, following Pesh., to *bᵉšāḥat* "into a pit", as *RSV*. Oesterley and Toy, however, suggested that the word is unnecessary and should be omitted; it is not represented in LXX.

19. This verse is a variant of 12:11, the only difference between the two being that 12:11 ends with "has no sense". The warning that the farmer who neglects his work will end in poverty is a commonplace of these proverbs.

20. It appears to be assumed in this proverb that the sudden acquisition of wealth implies the use of unscrupulous or dishonest devices: compare 13:11; 20:21. This reflects the circumstances of small farming communities where there were few honest opportunities to make a fortune and where everyone knew his neighbour's business. **go unpunished**: that is, escape a condemnation and punishment imposed by God.

21. This proverb, on the venality of witnesses – or perhaps judges – at a trial or lawsuit, is appropriately placed between two proverbs condemning those who use unscrupulous means to acquire wealth, and may be seen as an example of how this can be done, together with a warning against it. The first line is a variant of the single-line proverb 24:23b, the main difference between the two being that the latter's "in judging" (*b^e mišpāṭ*) is lacking here. But the expression *hikkîr pānîm*, literally "pay regard to faces", is used only in this connection (Dt. 1:17; 16:19, where the practice is formally condemned). **is not good**: on the strong force of this – or an analogous – expression see on 16:29; compare also 18:5.

The second line comments, probably with some exagerration, on the ease with which witnesses can often be bribed.

22. miserly: on the difficulty of determining the precise meaning of this expression (*ra' 'āyin*) see on 23:6, the only other place where it occurs in the Old Testament. Here the context suggests that it may mean "greedy" or "grasping". **hastens after wealth**: this phrase has the same meaning as "hastens to be rich" in v. 20, although the terminology is not the same. As in v. 20 it is assumed that wealth can only be suddenly acquired by wrongful means: hence, according to the principle of exact retribution, such a person will be reduced to complete destitution (*ḥeser*, **want**) by Yahweh's punitive action.

23. This proverb expresses approval of plain speaking to a friend or neighbour and disapproval of sycophantic or weak-minded flattery. 9:8; 19:25; 25:12 and 27:5 similarly point out that a sensible person will receive reproof in good part and will be all the better for it. **favour** (*ḥēn*): this probably means that the candid friend will rise in the estimation of the recipient of the rebuke.

afterwards: the Hebrew has *'aḥ^a ray*, literally, "after me", which makes no sense. The majority of commentators (e.g. Scott, Ringgren, Barucq, Plöger and *RSV* and *REB*), probably correctly, propose emendation to *'aḥar*, **afterward**, meaning that the person rebuked may not appreciate the rebuke at the time but will eventually do so. Other solutions have been offered: McKane, on the basis of LXX, emends to *'orḥōt*: "(reproves . . .) about his conduct". Driver (*ZAW* 49 [1932], p. 147) rather implausibly postulates a word with an Aramaizing ending meaning "(as) a common man". **flatters with his tongue**: literally, "makes his tongue smooth". This verb is used in 2:16 and 7:5 of the seductive speech of the "loose woman".

24–26. These verses are thematically related, v. 25 (a Yahweh-proverb) being perhaps intended as a comment on both vv. 24 and 26. The theme is the sin of selfishness or self-centredness. The criminal in v. 24 is so self-centred that he does not admit that what he is doing is wrong; v. 26 depicts a man who stupidly relies on his intelligence to protect him. V. 25 sets out trust in Yahweh as the true road to prosperity.

24. This proverb is expressed in very strong terms. *gāzal* (**robs**) implies violence; *mašḥît*, **destroyer**, evidently denotes the worst kind of criminal – some commentators take it to mean "murderer" – though in 18:9 it seems to have a milder sense. **companion**: this word is used here, as in Isa. 1:23; Ps. 119:63, to indicate similarity of character. The reference is probably to a son and heir who, instead of caring for his parents, anticipates his inheritance and deprives them of their own property and livelihood by main force (compare 19:26; 20:21). This kind of theft is not specifically dealt with in the Old Testament laws; it is here regarded as a violation of an obligation towards parents which was basic to Israelite ethics. The crime is made the more heinous by the fact that the offender apparently regards his conduct as blameless.

or his mother: several commentators omit this word as overloading the metrical line and also as superfluous, since inheritance was from the father alone.

25. In this verse, clichés found elsewhere in Proverbs are applied to the **greedy** (literally, "wide of appetite") and the truly pious. **stirs up strife** – that is, causes trouble in the community – is used of the "hot-tempered" in 15:18 and the "man of wrath" in 29:22; the second line is a variant of 16:20 and 29:25; **will be enriched** (*yᵉduššān*) is applied to the "liberal man" in 11:25 and to the "diligent" in 13:4. The constant recurrence of the theme of greed in this part of the chapter – not only in v. 24 but also in vv. 20 and 22 – is unlikely to be accidental.

26. Here again the contrast is between relying entirely on oneself (**mind**, *lēb* here means "intelligence" or "cleverness") and living one's life according to the sound principles (**wisdom**) which have been inculcated by one's teachers. This wisdom is interpreted in the previous verse as "trusting in Yahweh". **will be delivered**, or "will escape" (*yimmālēṭ*) has the same meaning here as "will be delivered" in v. 18, though the verb employed (which is used in the same sense in 11:21) is different.

27. The affirmation that giving away part of one's wealth to the poor will paradoxically lead to an *increase* in one's wealth or prosperity is made in various ways also in 11:24, 25; 19:17; 22:9. **many a curse**: it is not clear whether the curses will come directly from Yahweh as in 3:33 or from the poor themselves; in the latter case they should be seen as an indirect punishment imposed by Yahweh: all well-deserved curses had the power to blight the lives of the recipients. It should be noted that the generosity envisaged does not imply great wealth on the part of the giver.

28. See on v. 12 above, of which this verse is a variant. **increase**: this verb (*rābāh*) can mean either "to become many" or "to become great". In view of the parallel with *qûm*, **rise** in the first line and the general sense requirement of the context, the latter meaning is the more probable: so *REB*, "come into power". It is curious that in the similar verses 29:2 and 29:16, where the same verb is used, *RSV* has "are in authority" – though *RSV* may there be following the unnecessary emendations referred to in *BHS*.

CHAPTER 29

In this chapter as in chapter 28 antithetical proverbs predominate, although there are a number of verses consisting each of a single continuous sentence, and one admonition. There is little vivid imagery and a dearth of similes or metaphors. The themes treated are very diverse, and many verses are variants of, or similar to, proverbs which appear in the earlier chapters of the book. There are three proverbs about the education of children (vv. 3, 15, 17); the contrast is frequently drawn between wicked and righteous (vv. 2, 6, 7, 16, 27); there are three references to the poor (vv. 7, 13, 14). It is striking that the references to kings or rulers (vv. 4, 12, 14, 26; compare also vv. 2, 16) are all critical or partially so; this is also true of the references in chapter 28, but contrasts strongly with the situation in 10:1–22:16 and in chapters 25–7, where the great majority are either adulatory or at least neutral (speaking of royal power or wisdom). But it is significant that as elsewhere the three references to Yahweh (vv. 13, 25, 26) occur in close proximity to the references to the king or to rulers, forming two small groups (vv. 12–14, 25–6). Otherwise there is little sign of the formation of such groups.

1. The theme of the incorrigibility of the fool who will not listen to reproof is a commonplace of these proverbs (compare, for example, 13:18; 15:10). **He who is often reproved**: literally, "a man of reproofs"; the Hebrew plural is represented in *RSV* by **often. stiffens his neck**: this is a standard expression in biblical Hebrew for stubbornness in the sense of refusing to accept teaching or rebuke.

The second line of the verse is identical with 6:15b, where it is applied to various kinds of wicked person. Evidently the type of person referred to here was equally regarded as a menace to society. Plöger rather implausibly takes the first line as a complete non-verbal sentence: "He who has suffered rebuke becomes obstinate" – a warning against unduly harsh educational methods.

2. This is a further variant of a proverb which occurs several times in this and the previous chapter – v. 16; 28:12, 28. The reason for its frequency is not apparent. **are in authority**: this verb (*rābāh*) has the same meaning as in 28:28, on which see the comment above. Here it is paralleled with *māšal*, **rule**.

3. He who loves wisdom: the Hebrew has "*The man* who loves wisdom". Some commentators propose the omission of "The man (*'îš*)" partly on metrical grounds but also as being inappropriate when applied to a young pupil.

This is the language of the Instructions and poems of chapters 1–9 (4:6; 8:17, 36). The second line also reflects the teaching of those chapters (for example, 5:9–10).

4. This verse is related to v. 2 in that it provides a concrete illustration of the effects of the rule of good and evil rulers. The equitable administration of **justice** (*mišpāṭ*) was one of the most important duties of kings both in Israel and in the ancient Near East generally (compare 16:10; 29:26; see also 21:3, 15). That the king's throne was established by righteousness is reiterated several times in these proverbs (16:12; 20:28; 25:5; 29:14); if this was lacking there could be no **stability** for the nation.

The second line of the verse presumably refers to a particular kind or cause of injustice; but the meaning of the phrase *'îš t^erûmôt*, *RSV* **one who exacts gifts**, is uncertain. Some commentators take it to refer to the taking by the king of bribes; but this word *t^e^rûmāh* elsewhere always denotes a sacrificial offering. The phrase more probably means "one who levies extortionate taxation". It has been suggested that this transference of *t^e^rûmāh* from the cultic to the administrative sphere may be in some way connected with the prescription in Ezek. 45:13–16 that taxes for the purpose of providing for sacrificial offerings were to be collected by the secular "prince".

5. flatters: this is the same word as in 28:23, but used absolutely (28:23 adds "with his tongue"). **his feet**: this is ambiguous: it could refer either to the flatterer or to the recipient of the flattery; the commentators are divided on this point. If the latter interpretation is correct, the flattery in question must be seen as carried out with a malicious intent to deceive, and the proverb is an assertion of exact retribution: the flatterer has intended to ruin his victim by giving him an exaggerated opinion of his capabilities, but will in fact suffer ruin himself. But on the former interpretation this is a warning of the danger of being taken in by flattery. 28:23 may suggest that this is the right view (but see below on v. 6).

6. is ensnared: the Hebrew has "In the sin of an evil man (there is) a snare (*môqēš*)". The suggestion that this word should be repointed as the participle *mûqāš*, **ensnared** is supported by Targ. and Pesh. Otherwise, despite various suggestions for emendation, MT is probably correct. **sings** (*yārûn*): this is the qal imperfect third person singular of *rānan* (see *GK*. 67q), "to be jubilant". This verse may be intended as an interpretation of v. 5, regarding it as a statement of retribution.

7. rights (*dîn*): that is, legal rights. **knows**: this verb (*yāda'*) is here used in the sense of "to be concerned for" as in 12:10. The line thus expresses a concern which is characteristic of these proverbs.

The meaning of the second line, however, is not clear. The Hebrew, literally, ". . . does not understand knowledge", hardly makes sense: the view of some commentators that **understand** (*yābîn*) also means "concerned with" lacks support. *bîn* can, however, mean "to pay attention to"; and that may be its meaning here. *da'at*, however, means "knowledge"; and cannot mean "*such* knowledge" as in *RSV*. The best solution may be that of Thomas (*JTS* 38 [1937], pp. 401–2; *VT* Suppl. 3, 1955, p. 285), followed by Plöger and *KB*^{3}, who postulated another *da'at* cognate with an Arabic word meaning "legal claim", at the same time emending the word to *da'tô* (adding a personal suffix). The line would then read "a wicked man does not recognize his (that is, the poor man's) claim" (*dallîm*, **the poor**, in the first line is plural, but such alternation is not unknown in these proverbs). This would give a satisfactory parallelism.

8. scoffers: this phrase (*'anᵉšê lāṣôn*) occurs also in Isa. 28:14, where it refers to unscrupulous politicians. Here also in this verse, which is one of the rare references in the sentence literature to the life of the **city** (*qiryāh* – but compare 11:10) there appears to be a reference to political unrest; the proverb states that it takes **wise men** to calm things down and restore order.

9. Several of these proverbs (for example, 13:20; 14:7; 26:4) advise having as little to do with fools as possible. Here it is pointed out that to quarrel with a **fool** (or perhaps to go to law against him – the verb *nišpāṭ* may have either meaning) is profitless.

The proverb sets two sentences side by side with no conditional particle (**If**) in the Hebrew; but the meaning is as in *RSV*. The second line is ambiguous (the words **the fool** in this line are an addition by *RSV*). The subject may be the fool, who makes a mockery of the dispute by refusing to argue rationally, or it may be the **wise man** of the first line, who tries every possible means to deal with his adversary but to no avail. The verbs employed (*rāgaz*, *RSV* **rages**, better, "becomes excited") and *śāḥaq*, to laugh derisively, suggest the former. If this is correct, **and there is no quiet** presumably means that the fool's ranting and abuse make a rational solution to the dispute impossible.

10. the wicked: this is based on an emendation. MT has the exact contrary: "the upright". The emendation of *yᵉšārîm* to *rᵉšā'îm* made by *RSV* following Frankenberg and others is based simply on the grounds that the idea of the "upright" seeking to kill is unthinkable. This emendation turns the verse into an example of a synonymous rather than an antithetical parallelism, a form which occurs only very rarely in this chapter. An alternative type of solution to the problem is to see whether *yᵉbaqᵉšû napšô* (*RSV* **seek his life**) can be interpreted in a positive sense or should be emended. The former suggestion is improbable: this is a standard expression which always denotes an intention to kill. Toy's proposal of a slight emendation (*yᵉbaqᵉrû* for *yᵉbaqᵉšû*), which has been accepted by several other commentaries, supposedly giving the meaning "are concerned for", is also somewhat precarious as this verb normally means "to seek", and it is not certain that it means "be concerned for" in the one text (Ezek. 34:11) which has been cited in this connection. A further suggestion is that of Driver (*JSS* 12 [1967], p. 108), who postulated a second verb *bqš*, cognate with Akkadian *baqāšū* (to be large), which he thought could in the causative (piel) form mean "esteem" here. No satisfactory solution has been found.

11. It is not clear whether the second line of this verse refers to the self-restraint of the **wise man** with regard to his own anger (compare, for example, 14:29; 16:32) or to his action in restraining the anger, or the effects of the anger, of the **fool** (compare 15:18). **quietly holds it back** (*bᵉʾāḥôr yᵉšabbᵉḥennāh*): the verb means "to soothe" or "to quieten". The form *bᵉʾāḥôr* is unique and its meaning problematic. *ʾāḥôr* by itself has both a spatial meaning ("behind, back") and a temporal one ("after"). *RSV* (**quietly**) presumably takes it to mean "remaining in the background"; *REB* understands it – or probably a repointed version of it – in a temporal sense: "wise men wait for it to cool". Despite the difficulties, *MT* is probably correct and no emendation necessary.

12–14. These three verses are thematically related. V. 12 is concerned with the evil effects on the people of a weak king and evil officials; v. 13 considers the oppressors of the poor; v. 14 returns to the responsibility of the king for seeing that the poor get justice.

12. The theme of this proverb is the same as that of 25:5, which envisages the collapse of the state when such conditions prevail. It does not imply personal acquaintance with the court, but it probably reflects experience of injustices committed by officials who rule in the name of a weak or gullible king. The Hebrew text is not formulated as a conditional sentence, but sets cause and effect side by side without specifically linking them: literally, "A king paying attention to lies – all his officials wicked".

13. This proverb is a variant of 22:2. The first line of both verses is identical except that here the two classes mentioned are **poor man** and **oppressor**, whereas in 22:2 they are rich and poor. The change to **oppressor** was no doubt made in order to adapt the proverb more closely to its immediate context – though the rich (*ʿāšîr*) are elsewhere seen as oppressors in these proverbs. On **meet together** (*nipgāšû*) see on 22:2. The second line is identical in meaning with 22:2b though expressed in different words. **gives light to the eyes**: that is, gives life: to "see light" means to live (compare, for example, Job 3:16; Ps. 49:19 [Heb. 20]). **oppressor**: *LXX* and Vulg. have "creditor"; this meaning is certainly included, though the Hebrew term has a wider connotation.

14. This verse expresses the same thought as v. 4a, but more particularly refers to the king's duty towards the **poor**, who as stated in other proverbs are vulnerable and need special protection if their rights are to be safeguarded. **with equity**: that is, impartially. Although the king cannot act personally as judge in all cases, he is responsible for the probity of all legal judgements. The second line is a variant of 16:12b and 20:28b. As in v. 12 the two lines are set side by side with no connecting conditional particle.

15. As appears also in 13:24; 22:15; 23:13–14 corporal punishment was regarded as an essential ingredient of the education of children. **left to himself**: this word *m^e^šullāḥ*, which more frequently means "sent away, dismissed", here probably means "let loose" in the sense of undisciplined, freed from proper discipline. **brings shame**: compare 10:5; 12:4. The **mother** may be specifically mentioned here because she was responsible for a child's early education. The subject of education is resumed in v. 17.

16. This verse and its variants 28:12, 28; 29:2 are similarly constructed and to a large extent employ the same vocabulary. They all contrast the **wicked** and the **righteous** and their respective rise and fall; they all use the temporal construction *b^e^* followed by an infinitive (**When**), and in every case but this one use it twice, once in each line. The clause "When the wicked rise" occurs both in 28:12 and 28:28; otherwise synonyms are employed. **When . . . are** in authority, (*bir^e^bôt*, see on 29:2) is used in 29:2 of the righteous and here of the wicked.

In this verse the verb *rābāh* is used twice, with different meanings: **When . . . are in authority** (*bir^e^bôt*) and **increases** (*yirbeh*). This is clearly a deliberate play on the meaning of words. The second line states that the rule of the wicked will collapse – following the retributive principle – and that the righteous **will look upon their downfall**. The verb *rā'āh*, "to see, look" when followed by *b^e^* (**upon**) rather than by the direct object often has an emotive connotation. Here as in other passages (for example, Mic. 7:10; Ob. 12, 13; Ps. 22:17 [Heb. 18]; 54:7 [Heb. 9]; 118:7) it means "to look with triumph at" or "to gloat over".

17. Discipline your son: see on 19:18 and compare v. 15 and 23:13. **give you rest**: that is, relief from the kind of worry referred to in such proverbs as v. 15. **delight to your heart** (*ma^ca^dannîm l^e^napšekā*): this may mean "the delights you desire" (*REB*). *ma^ca^dannîm*, used here metaphorically, elsewhere means rich or luxurious food, and *nepeš* frequently means "desire, appetite". This is the only admonition in this chapter.

18. This verse has been variously interpreted. Ostensibly it states that when no prophetic message (*ḥāzôn*, *RSV* **prophecy**, can only mean "prophetic vision") is available to guide the people, chaos ensues, but that the individual person who observes the teaching (*tôrāh*, *RSV* **law**, which may refer either to the "Law" in the Deuteronomic or priestly sense or to the teaching of the wise men) will nevertheless be **Blessed** (*'ašrēhû* –see on 3:13). This may be a correct understanding of the verse. Some commentators, holding this view, have supposed that it must be a late addition to the book, reflecting a situation in the post-exilic period when prophecy had ceased and when the Law (that is, the Pentateuch) had become the sole source of divine guidance; but this is not necessarily so. Amos in the eighth century BC spoke of a famine of the word of Yahweh when no prophetic message would be available though it was urgently required and sought for (8:11–12); and this proverb may be giving an assurance that even in such times the individual who is obedient to traditional teaching will escape the disaster which will fall on the people as a whole.

Some commentators (Gemser and Driver, who pointed to an Akkadian cognate), finding it difficult to accept the presence of this unique reference to prophecy in the book, have proposed the repointing of *ḥāzôn* to *ḥazzān*, a word which does not otherwise occur in the Old Testament but which in Mishnaic Hebrew denotes an overseer or magistrate, and which might mean a magistrate or political leader here. It may be significant that the LXX also understood the word to refer to a person ("interpreter").

19–21. Vv. 19 and 21 are closely related, and there is also a thematic connection with vv. 15 and 17: if strict discipline is required for the upbringing of children, it is no less necessary for securing proper service from slaves. V. 20 appears to have been inserted between vv. 19 and 21 because of the occurrence of **words** (*d^ebārîm*) in both vv. 19 and 20.

19. The implication of the first line of this verse is that only a beating will obtain results. **give heed**: literally, "answer". This does not mean a refusal to reply but a general unwillingness to obey orders. Compare *Papyrus Insinger* 14:11: "If the rod is far from his master, the servant will not obey him".

20. This verse is virtually identical with 26:12 except that in the latter it is the person who is "wise in his own eyes" who is said to be a less hopeful case than the **fool**. See on 26:12. According to other proverbs (for example, 10:13; 12:16, 23; 14:3) speaking without reflection is precisely a characteristic of the fool.

21. pampers (*mᵉpannēq*): this word occurs only here in the Old Testament, but is found, with this meaning in Mishnaic Hebrew. **his heir**: this word (*mānôn*) has completely baffled the interpreters. It is probably corrupt. It is most unlikely to mean "heir", even if – which is most improbable – it is related to *nîn*, a rare word meaning "offspring, progeny". Emendations which have been proposed are mainly based simply on guessing what kind of meaning seems most appropriate, for example *mādôn*, "(source of) strife" (Wildeboer, Plöger), *yāgôn*, "grief, sorrow" (Frankenberg); "ungrateful" (*REB*). Several commentators (Gemser, Scott, Ringgren, McKane) simply follow Vulg. (*contumax*, "refractory") without being able to suggest what the original Hebrew word might have been. Reider (1954, pp. 285–6) retained MT and rendered it by "weakling", citing a cognate Arabic word. LXX, has "ultimately he will be with sorrow concerning himself"; but LXX also has a quite different first line: "He that lives wantonly from a child will be a slave".

22. The first line of this verse is a close variant of 15:18a, but unlike the latter is in synonymous parallelism. The short-tempered man not only creates quarrels with his neighbours but also **causes much transgression** – that is, he frequently commits some social or legal offence.

23. The consequences of pride and humility respectively are similarly contrasted in other proverbs in these chapters (11:2; 16:18, 19). Here there is a play on words between *tašpîlennû*, **bring him low** (in the sense of humiliation or material poverty) and *šᵉpal-rûaḥ*, **lowly in spirit**. 25:6–7 provides a concrete example of the humiliation of the proud.

24. The partner of a thief: literally, "One who shares out with a thief". In 16:19 it is the proud who are said to "divide the spoil", and they are contrasted with those who are "of a lowly spirit" (the same phrase as is used in v. 23). Here, however, the reference to partners in theft is probably to be taken literally, though a distinction is made between the thief himself and the person who receives part of the proceeds of the theft, presumably as a reward for assisting the thief in some unspecified way. It is said of this **partner** that he

hates his own life: that is, he will suffer a severe penalty, probably a divine rather than a legal punishment.

The meaning of the second line has been disputed, but it probably refers to a legal oath or curse requiring witnesses to a crime or those involved in it to come forward and reveal their knowledge of it. This requirement is set out in the law of Lev. 5:1–6, where also the expression *šāmaʿ ʾālāh* (*RSV* **hears the curse**) is used (compare also Jg. 17:2). For those who refused to speak after the "curse" or oath had been pronounced, it had the effect of a divine curse, which could only be averted by subsequent confession and the offering of a propitiatory sacrifice.

25–27. It is probably no coincidence that these final verses, like the opening verses, of this section of the book (chapters 25–9), refer to Yahweh and to kings, and that the last verse of all may be said to sum up the whole message of the collection with a reminder that there are only two ways in which a person may walk: no middle way, no compromise, is available between that of the **righteous** and that of the **wicked**.

25. The fear of man: this could mean either "a man's fear" or "being afraid of men". In either case the meaning of the proverb is virtually the same. **lays a snare**: this is a misleading translation. *REB*'s "may prove a snare" is better. The point of the verse is the contrast between the person who has no effective religious faith and the one who knows that Yahweh will guide and support him. The former is in a perpetual state of anxiety (**fear**, *ḥ^a^rādāh*, is a strong word – "trembling", "terror") because human relations are unpredictable, and in this state he may be led into a **snare**, that is, he may find himself forced into some kind of foolish or dishonest behaviour, whereas with Yahweh as his guide and support he has nothing to fear but is **safe** (for the meaning of this verb *śgb* see on 18:10).

26. There is a close connection between this verse and v. 25 in their present positions. In both, a contrast is made between what is to be expected from human beings and from God respectively. The verse may not originally have been intended to condemn the practice of trying to obtain favour – or, more probably, justice – from an influential person. The point of the proverb is in the second line: whatever human beings may be able to do for one, one can be sure that Yahweh will be impartial in giving a person what he deserves – a confident statement of the principle of divine retribution.

27. Although Yahweh is not specifically mentioned in this verse, the thought is similar to that of 11:20. See on vv. 25–7 above.

"WORDS OF AGUR"
CHAPTER 30

Chapters 30 and 31 are often seen as a series of appendices to the book. 30:1 and 31:1 are headings – the last in a series beginning in 1:1 which marks all the main sections of the book up to this point. (The final twenty-two verses of chapter 31 form a third "appendix" which, although it has no heading, is marked out as a separate section not only by its distinctive theme but also because it is an alphabetic acrostic poem: each verse begins with a consecutive letter of the alphabet.)

But it is not clear how much of chapter 30 belongs to the "words of Agur" announced in v. 1. The *LXX* is instructive at this point. It represents a quite different recension of the Hebrew text from *MT*, placing whole sections in a different order. After the long section 22:17–24:22 the remainder of the book is distributed by *LXX* as follows (giving the equivalents in *MT*): 30:1–14; 24:23–34; 30:15–33; 31:1–9; chapters 25–9; 31:10–31. This recension presumably reflects a situation when 30:1–14 and 30:15–31 were recognized as independent units but whose order had not yet been fixed.

The unity of vv. 1–14, however, is itself disputed. Taking this group of verses from the end, vv. 11–14 consists of a list of types of unpleasant persons which has little in common with what precedes and more affinities with the "numerical proverbs" which follow. Some of the earlier verses may have been strung together simply on the basis of the occurrence of identical or similar words. Thus v. 10 appears to be an isolated admonition, but may owe its present position to the occurrence of the word **curse** (*qll*) common to it and to v. 11. There is also some similarity between **curse** (v. 10) and **profane** (v. 9); and **lying** (*d^ebar-kāzāb*), together with **falsehood** in v. 8 echoes **be found a liar** (*kāzab*, niphal) in v. 6 (Gemser). McKane even restricts the "words of Agur" to vv. lb-3, while on the other hand some scholars (Scott; Franklyn, 1983, pp. 238–52) find a genuine sequence of thought throughout vv. 1–9.

The remainder of the chapter consists mainly of "numerical proverbs" (using the term broadly), vv. 7–9, 11–14, 15–16, 18–19,

21–3, 24–8, 29–31, 32–3, together with two isolated proverbs (vv. 17 and 20).

1–4. Although v. 1b (from **The man**) is totally obscure in *MT* and some commentators have entirely given up any attempt to make sense of it, it seems clear that these verses form a unity. There are two speakers: in vv. lb-3 a speaker either out of scepticism or despair declares his lack of wisdom and his inability to attain to any knowledge of God; in v. 4 God himself, or possibly a human "orthodox" interlocuter, speaks, answering him in the manner of the divine speeches out of the whirlwind in Job 38–41, by asking him questions by which he implicitly reveals the identity of the sovereign creator and master of the universe, whose name ought to be familiar to his self-styled ignoramus. This is a form of "wisdom" otherwise not represented in Proverbs.

1. *LXX* has a quite different text in which there are no proper names. **Agur son of Jakeh**: these are not Hebrew names; they are probably of non-Israelite origin. There is a proper name *ugr* in Ugaritic, but Jakeh is unknown. **of Massa**: *MT* has "the oracle" (*hammaśśâ'*). The word occurs also in 31:1, but without the article: Massa. Here *RSV* has adopted an emendation to *mimmaśśā'*, "from Massa"; others emend to *hammaśśā'ī*, "the Massaite". The commentators are divided between taking the word as meaning "oracle" and seeing it as a proper name: Massa, a North Arabian tribe mentioned in Gen. 25:14 and 1 Chr. 1:30 as a "son" of Ishmael. The latter is the more probable interpretation in view of 31:1, where the phrase *l^{e}mû'ēl melek maśśā'* is more likely to mean "King Lemuel of Massa" than "Lemuel, a king. An oracle".

The man says: this phrase (*n^e'ūm haggeber*) occurs elsewhere in the Old Testament only in Num. 24:3, 15, where it introduces an oracle spoken by the seer Balaam, and in 2 Sam. 23:1, where it introduces an inspired poem or "oracle" composed by David. *n^e'ūm* by itself occurs frequently in the prophetical books meaning a prophetical oracle. Its use here introducing a speech by an ordinary person is thus unique; the reason for this is unexplained.

to Ithiel, to Ithiel and Ucal: it is widely agreed that these are not real names and that this is not a possible translation. While some scholars reject the whole phrase as incomprehensible and impossible to restore to its original state, a wide variety of reconstructions has been offered by others based on repointing, emendation and different word division (see *BHS* for some of these). "I am weary, O God, . . . and am consumed (that is, exhausted)" is favoured by several commentaries and translations; "O that God would be with me . . . that I might understand" is another suggestion; Scott has "There is no God . . . and I cannot (know anything)"; C. C. Torrey (1954, pp. 93–6), taking the sentence as Aramaic, proposed "I am not a god . . . that I should have power". The above list of proposals is not exhaustive. The final word in the sentence (*w*ᵉ*'ūkāl*) has variously been taken as a form of *yākōl*, "to be able, have power, prevail", *'ākal*, "to consume" or *kālāh*, "to be finished, spent, exhausted". There is no certainty about any of these proposals. Perhaps that which best fits the context (that is, vv. 2–3) is the first one given above. The only matter on which there is wide agreement is that this sentence contains the beginning of the speech which continues in vv. 2–3.

2–3. Agur continues his speech, confessing his stupidity and ignorance of God. His words are similar to the confession of Job in Job 42:1–3, and even more so to Ps. 73:22, which uses the same language as v. 2. It seems clear, therefore, that although the heading in v. 1 proclaims a foreign origin for these verses, their present form is Yahwistic.

2. Surely: or, if the interpretation of v. 1b suggested above is correct, "For". **too stupid to be a man**: or, "more stupid than (other) men". On **stupid** (*ba'ar*) see on 12:1.

3. nor have I . . . : there is no negative particle in this line. Either the **not** of the first line governs the second, or the line should be rendered by "that I should have knowledge of the Holy One" (see *GK* 166a). **the Holy One** (*q*ᵉ*dōšîm*): see on 9:10, where the parallelism shows that the word is an epithet of Yahweh. LXX has positive statements: "God has taught me wisdom, and I have knowledge of the Holy". It has also been suggested (see *BHS* and Franklyn, p. 245) that *lō'* (**not**) should be emended to *lû* or *lû'*, expressing a wish: "O that . . . !". But MT is perfectly satisfactory in the context.

4. There is no agreement among the commentators whether the speaker in this verse is the same as in vv. 2–3 or whether it is God or another human speaker. These questions strongly resemble questions put to Job by God in Job 38–9, though their form and purpose are those of Isa. 40:12–14. There is no reason to suppose that, apart from the last two, they are ironical or sceptical.

The speaker – whether God himself or one speaking on his behalf – replies to Agur by enquiring who is the creator and master of the universe. To these questions the only possible answer is "God" or "Yahweh": no human being can make such a claim (compare Job's confession in Job 42:1). The effect of the questions is to show that God is not in fact unknown to Agur as he supposes: he has revealed himself in creation.

The dwelling-place of God is in **heaven**; but the first question points to the fact that he is able to move at will between heaven and earth (Gen. 11:7; 35:13; Ps. 68:18 [Heb. 19]; Ezek. 1 etc.). Gen. 28:12 speaks of a ladder or staircase linking heaven and earth which only God and his angels are able to use. In this question the ascent to heaven is placed before the descent, probably in order to stress human inability to make that ascent – a point made by God to Job in Job 38, when he taunts Job for his ignorance of what takes place in the heavens.

The remaining questions are expressed in a language found elsewhere in the Old Testament, especially in Job and the Psalms, which is of mythological origin. Thus God's control of the **wind**, also mentioned in Am. 4:13, is referred to in Job 38:24, where he scatters it on the earth; in Job 28:25, where he regulates its force; and in Ps. 135:7, where he brings it out of his storehouses. Here he has **gathered the wind in his fists** (compare Isa. 40:12 for a similar anthropomorphism). The statement that he has **wrapped up** or confined (*ṣārar*) **the waters in a garment** is verbally very similar to Job 26:8; compare also, again, Isa. 40:12); the **garment** is the clouds. Finally, **established all the ends of the earth** may be compared with Job 38:4, 6 and Isa. 40:12.

What is his name?: this and the following question are ironical. This is not an enquiry after the identity of the creator-god; rather, Agur is asked ironically to name a human being able to do these things. Some scholars (for example Scott, Franklyn), on the analogy of similar passages in the Old Testament which put questions or make statements about creative activity and conclude with a positive identification of the creator with Yahweh (for example, Am. 4:13, "Yahweh, the God of hosts is his name!"; compare also Am. 5:8; 9:6; Isa. 51:15; Jer. 31:35) have concluded that it is this identification that is called for here; but this interpretation is ruled out by the following question: **and what is his son's name**? Even if LXX's reading "sons" (plural) is accepted, the idea that the "sons" in question are to be identified with the "sons of God" who form Yahweh's heavenly court (Gen. 6:2, 4; Job 1:6; 2:1) is impossible, since it is a notable fact that these, in contrast with the named "families" of gods in the surrounding polytheistic religions, are never identified by name in the Old Testament.

The reason for enquiring about the name of a person's son as well as that of the person himself is not clear: there are no other examples of such a request for identification in the Old Testament with which these questions can be compared. It is more usual to enquire about a person's *father*. This may be a way of enquiring – here ironically, of course – about a family which such a remarkable person might have founded and whose descendants might still be living. **Surely you know!**: these words occur also in Job 38:5 after God has ironically asked Job if he was present at the creation of the world and so knows who laid its foundations and fixed its dimensions. Here, however, they have a somewhat different purpose: they answer Agur's claim that he knows nothing of God: he is, after all, familiar with the identity of the Creator.

5–6. These verses may have been placed here with the idea of giving a further, "orthodox" answer to Agur's complaint that he does not know God by pointing to his "word" (in the Law? in prophecy?) as a completely reliable and sufficient guide and source of revelation, and warning him against profitless and heretical thoughts of his own. But it is unlikely that they were originally part of the same composition. Not only are they not directly relevant to the matter of the preceding verses; they are also composed almost entirely of quotations from and reminiscences of other texts. V. 5 – apart from the use of *ʾlôah̲* for God instead of *yhwh* – is a simple quotation from Ps. 18:30 (Heb. 31) = 2 Sam. 22:31. The command not to add to God's words in the first line of v. 6 is taken from Dt. 4:2 and 12:32 (Heb. 13:1), though without the further command in the Deuteronomy text not to take away from them; and the second line is strongly reminiscent of Job 13:10 and shows familiarity with the whole of Job 13:7–12 and with Job 24:25. There are also similarities with various passages in the Psalms (for example, Ps. 12:6 [Heb. 7] and 119:140).

5. God: this word (*ʾlôah̲*) does not occur elsewhere in Proverbs, a fact which marks these verses out as somewhat apart from the rest of the book. It is used here as a substitute for *yhwh*, which is the word used in the otherwise identical verse Ps. 18:30. Its use in Hebrew may be archaic in origin, but in the Old Testament it occurs mainly in late poetical texts. The great majority of its occurrences are in the poem of the Book of Job. **proves true**: literally, "is tested" (*ṣᵉrûpāh*) – a metaphor from the smelting or refining of metals. It is used of Joseph as tested by God in Ps. 105: 19.

7–9. These verses, despite the lack of address and the references to Yahweh and "my God" in the third person, are a prayer addressed to Yahweh (Plöger suggested that such an address might have been contained in a line which has fallen out from v. 8, but this is an unsupported proposal.) But the verses are also the first of a series of "numerical proverbs" which form almost the whole of the remainder of the chapter. (On this type of proverb see on 6:16–19 above.) They differ, however, from the remainder in their religious tone. Sauer pointed out that from the formal point of view there are strictly three requests, not two as stated, and suggested that "three" has dropped out, but this also is improbable: numerical proverbs with only two items and lacking the "x, x+1" formula are found elsewhere in the Old Testament: compare Job 13:20–21.

The inclusion of this prayer, a genre unique in Proverbs, suggests that, like the Lord's Prayer, which may have been partly based on it, it has a didactic purpose: that it is intended as a model prayer, composed by a pious wise man for imitation and reflection. It has a high theological character. Its request to be given neither wealth nor poverty but simply a sufficiency, although it has partial echoes elsewhere in the book, is also unique.

The first person form has suggested to some commentators that the verses are a continuation of Agur's speech in vv. 1–3; but there is really nothing in their contents to suggest this. There is a link with v. 6 (see above on 30:1–33), but this is a purely verbal one.

Toy, Gemser and Oesterley proposed the deletion of some parts of the prayer, especially the last line of v. 8, as later glosses; but there is no justification for this. The prayer as it stands has an unusual beauty and carries conviction. The structure is clear: an introduction (v. 7); the petitions (v. 8); the motives, which, contrary to the opinion of some commentators, relate not merely to the second petition but to both (v. 9).

8. falsehood and lying: the first of these (*šāwʾ*) stands at the head of the list of crimes of which Job claims to be innocent when he makes his protestation of innocence to God (Job 31:5). But this word also occurs in the Decalogue (Exod. 20:7; Dt. 5:11) in a prohibition against taking the name of Yahweh *lāšāwʾ* – a phrase usually rendered by "in vain", but which may mean the use of his name for magical purposes, in making false oaths, or blasphemously. Here the author may have been thinking not just of common dishonesty but of offences against Yahweh such as are alluded to in v. 9.

neither poverty nor riches: 15:16–17; 16:8; 17:1 all express the view that there are worse things than living in straitened circumstances; but **poverty** (*rē'š*) is something quite different from that: it is absolute destitution and desperate hunger (compare 6:30). On the other hand, although the achievement of **riches** is generally regarded in the sentence literature as desirable, its danger is recognized there, and the "rich man" (*'āšîr*) is not regarded as an admirable person. The author of this prayer asks to be given a modest sufficiency – an attitude not far removed from that of the proverbs referred to above; but only here is there a total renunciation of any desire for wealth.

that is needful for me: literally, "of my portion". This word (*ḥuqqî*) could also mean "which is due to me" or, more probably, "which is sufficient for me".

9. be full: that is, "have too much". **Who is the Lord?**: LXX has "Who sees me?". **deny**: literally, "deceive". The reference may be to deceitfully swearing oaths to other gods, not recognizing the true source of wealth. **profane**: this verb (*tāpaś*) normally means "to lay hold of, grasp", but may here mean "misuse" (see on v. 8). Driver proposed "besmirch" on the basis of a supposed Arabic cognate.

10. This verse was clearly originally an independent admonition. Its position here is usually accounted for by the occurrence of the word "curse" both here and in v. 11. But the connection, in an editorial sense, is probably closer than that. The verse refers to an unpleasant kind of behaviour, and might well have been included with the four others listed in vv. 11–14 except for its different form. Its intention – to give a warning against unacceptable behaviour – is similar.

he in the second line could in principle refer either to the **servant** or the **master**. The latter is the more probable, since the servant would probably be unable to prove his innocence. The proverb may rather be a warning against interference in the domestic affairs of a neighbour than against **slander** – compare 25:17, where this can lead to hatred. The use of the word rendered **slander** (literally, "to use one's tongue") does not necessarily imply that the accusation is a false one. **be held guilty** (*'āšam*): that is, by God, as a consequence of the curse.

11–14. Unlike the other "numerical proverbs" in this chapter, this passage lacks the usual specific reference to the number of items (four) in the list. Several commentators have supposed that an introductory line similar to 6:16 has fallen out; but this is not necessarily so. The fact that each item begins with the same word (*dôr*, *RSV* **those who**) may have been regarded as a sufficient link between them (so Plöger).

Each verse describes a kind of behaviour which is condemned elsewhere in Proverbs. Roth found a thematic link between the items in that they all refer to "offenders in the social sphere"; but it is not clear why these particular items were chosen. The reprehensible nature of the behaviour described has to be inferred simply from the description of the behaviour itself: there is no formal condemnation. The words **There are** have been supplied by *RSV*: each verse begins simply with the noun *dôr*, elsewhere generally rendered by "generation", but here meaning a class of person (see Ackroyd, 1968, pp. 3–10). These are respectively the unfilial (compare 19:26; 20:20; 28:24), the self-righteous (compare 16:2; 20:9), the arrogant (compare 6:17a; 21:4) and the rapacious (compare 1:10–19; 6:17b; 12:6).

12. filth: this is a very strong word. The self-righteousness of these people conceals an unsuspected depth of iniquity.

13. eyelids: see on 4:25, where *RSV* renders the same word by "gaze".

14. teeth: the Hebrew has two synonymous words here. The expressions in the first two lines are metaphorical, but they express the ruthlessness of these enemies of society who prey on others. The last two lines are widely regarded as a gloss explaining the metaphors of the first two. (The same activity is condemned in 22:22.) Plöger, however, regards them as the climax of the whole passage: it is those who are guilty of *all* the above crimes who are responsible for the destruction of the poor. **from among men** (*mē'ādām*): Gemser and Dahood, for the sake of parallelism, wish to read "the earth" here (Gemser emends to *ᵃdāmāh*; Dahood adopts this translation without emendation). But this is not necessary: **among men** gives a sufficient parallelism.

15–16. The much longer text of LXX takes these verses together as forming a single proverb; but there can be no doubt that there are two separate units here. The first lines of v. 15 (to **they cry**) stand on their own, while the remainder of the verse together with

v. 16 constitutes a typical numerical proverb consisting of introduction and list of items (compare vv. 18–19, 21–3, 24–8, 29–31). As with v. 10, v. 15a has been juxtaposed to the numerical proverb which follows because of a common theme: insatiability.

V. 15a, which is syntactically incomplete (*RSV*'s **they say** is not represented in the Hebrew text), is probably a fragment of a longer proverb. The Hebrew has simply: "The leech has two daughters, Give! give!". The sense is less problematical than has often been supposed (see North, 1965, pp. 281–2). **The leech**: there have been various interpretations of this word (*ᵃlûqāh*): it has been understood as a proper name Aluqah, supposedly the author of the remainder of the chapter; it has been divided into two, making two verbs (Gemser); and it has been thought to be the name of a demon or an epithet of the underworld. But there is no reason to doubt that it means "leech". Although this is its only occurrence in the Old Testament, it is attested in Arabic and Syriac and also in Mishnaic Hebrew (see BL^3). **two daughters**: these are the two suckers of the leech, situated at the two ends of its body, with which it sucks the blood of the human being or animal to which it has attached itself. "**Give, give**": this is the reiterated imperative of a conjectural verb *yāhab*, which occurs only in the imperative. The meaning is probably something like "More! more!". The leech continues to suck blood until it is completely bloated and incapable of absorbing more. As it stands, the text merely states a fact, based on observation, about the nature of leeches; but as in some other numerical proverbs about the animal world (for example, 6:6–11) the intention may be to draw an analogy with the character of some human beings.

V. 16 has three lines. Of the four examples given, the last two are provided with explanations while the first two are not. The reason for this may be to fill out the poetical lines (Plöger suggests that the first two items are self-explanatory; but this is hardly convincing). That **Sheol** is insatiable is a commonplace of Hebrew belief (compare 27:20 and see on 1:12). **the barren womb**: this is generally interpreted as referring to the urgent desire of barren women for children – compare Rachel's appeal to Jacob in Gen. 30:1: "Give me (*hābāh*) sons, or I die!". (Thomas's rendering of this phrase by "the voraciousness of the carrion-eagle" [*VT* Suppl. 3, 1955, p. 290] is an unnecessary rejection of the obvious meaning.) The recurrent drought in Palestine explains the reference to the thirst of the **earth** for **water**, and the capacity of **fire** to consume everything within reach is a further obvious example of insatiability. Whether this proverb is an implied warning against human greed (McKane) or is simply an example of the classification of phenomena as part of an attempt to understand the world (Roth; see on 6:16–19) is not clear.

"**Enough**": this word (*hôn*), which occurs frequently in Proverbs, always elsewhere means "wealth, possessions". The universal view that here (both in v. 15 and v. 16) it has the meaning of "sufficiency" is based mainly on the context.

17. This is an isolated proverb, probably placed here because of the occurrence of the word *nešer*, "vulture, eagle", here and in v. 19. Of the proverbs which condemn unfilial behaviour (see on v. 11 above) this is the most severe, though 20:20 states that such a person's "lamp will be put out". Here the corpse of the offender will – or should be – exposed in the open country to be attacked by scavenging birds; appropriately, it is his **eye** with which he has disdained his parents which is specifically mentioned. As may be seen from other proverbs in the book, the eye is the organ which reveals or expresses a person's true character. **to obey** (*lîqqᵃhat*): this word has generally been taken, as by *RSV*, as a somewhat anomalous form (see *GK* 20b) of a word in Gen. 49:10, similarly unique in the Old Testament, usually rendered by "obedience"; but the view of Driver (*JTS* 29 [1928], p. 394) and Thomas (*JTS* 42 [1941], pp. 151–5) who connect it with an Ethiopic word meaning "old age" has been accepted by *KB*³. Pesh., Targ. and LXX also have "old age", previously thought to be based on an original *ziqnat*; but the newer suggestion is more probable. The line should therefore be rendered "and scorns his aged mother".

18–19. This numerical proverb combines the formula "x, x + 1" (see on 6:16–19) with the device employed in vv. 11–14: each item begins with the same word, *derek* (**the way**). The introduction (v. 18) defines the common characteristic of the items in the list: they are all **wonderful** – things which are beyond human (or at least, the author's) comprehension. A different view, that their common feature is that they are all phenomena which leave no trace, though it may apply to the first three examples, fails to explain in what way this can be said of the final one.

The word *derek*, literally "road" or "journey", also means "mode" or "manner", and this is its meaning here: all these phenomena are mysterious in the *manner* of their occurrence: it is impossible to answer the question, "How is it done?". The eagle appears to float and move in the sky with no physical support; the snake is capable of movement, yet has no legs; there is no visible cause of the movement of a sailing ship at sea. The final item may be intended to constitute a climax: the proverb moves from the animal world to the human one. But it is not clear what is wonderful or mysterious about the action referred to here. Probably the reference is not to the act of copulation itself but to what follows: human gestation and birth – the formation of a child in the womb, which is equally seen as a great mystery in Job 10:10–11. It is no doubt to be inferred that all these things are part of the mysterious action of God.

A notable feature of this proverb – though we might compare the speeches of God in the Book of Job – is that, although based on observation, it is a list of things which the author, although he is familiar with them, does *not* understand – which are beyond his comprehension. It is thus an attestation not of what human beings can achieve for themselves through wisdom but of the *limitations* of human wisdom, a fact acknowledged in general terms elsewhere in the book, for example in 16:1,9.

maiden: this word (*'almāh*) does not mean a virgin but simply a young woman, who may be married.

20. This verse is linked to v. 19 by the occurrence of the word *derek*, **way**. But it is not clear whether it was originally an independent proverb placed here solely for that reason, or whether it is a gloss on the last line of v. 19 added by someone who misunderstood that line as referring to an immoral relationship. The answer to this question turns on the meaning here of *kēn* (*RSV* **This is**), a word which usually refers to what precedes, but which may sometimes have the forward-looking meaning attributed to it by *RSV* and also by Scott, McKane and *REB* (see Mulder, 1981, pp. 222–3). **eats**: here a metaphor for sexual intercourse: compare 9:17. The metaphor is continued with **and wipes her mouth**. The **adulteress** has no sense of guilt: her sin, once perpetrated, is soon forgotten like a completed meal.

21–23. In this numerical proverb all the four items refer to situations in human society. V. 21 speaks in metaphorical language of an universal cataclysm which would result from certain surprising social reversals – what Van Leeuwen (1986, pp. 599–610) has appropriately called "a world upside down". But it may be questioned how seriously this cataclysmic language is to be taken. Both Roth and Van Leeuwen regard the proverb very seriously as a warning against a social revolution caused by a general abandonment of the pillars on which society rests. Others, however, especially McKane, see it in a humorous light. In fact the four items listed – a rather arbitrary selection from a large number of possible examples – hardly support the former view. In fact the only example which would justify it is the first – that of the **slave** who becomes **king**. The other three are trivial matters, no doubt not entirely unusual occurrences, and far from earthshaking. Although they all refer to reversals of the normal order of things, it is difficult to believe that they are intended to be taken with great seriousness.

Formally the introductory verse (v. 21) and all the items which follow are linked in the Hebrew text by the fact that they all begin with the same word, *taḥat*, **Under** – a feature suppressed in *RSV*. But the four items have yet another common feature: each depicts the unexpected rise to influence or position of a kind of person normally despised or dismissed by society as of no importance. Two of these are men, two women. But it is not the change of fortune in itself which is felt to be intolerable. The use of the temporal clause (*kî*, **when** . . .) in each case shows that the point of the proverb lies in the behaviour of such persons after their elevation or promotion. The proverb in its brevity only hints at this; but the kind of behaviour which best fits all these cases is probably an intolerable conceit or arrogance (so Ringgren): that of the slave who finds himself in a position to lord it over those who have previously lorded it over him (compare 19:10); of the social outcast (*nābāl*, *RSV* **fool**; see on 17:7) who finds himself living in unaccustomed luxury and boasts of it as if it had been achieved by his own cleverness; of the unpopular woman who has found a husband against all expectations and thinks highly of herself as a consequence; and of the servant girl who, having supplanted her mistress in the affections of the master of the house, gives herself airs.

21. In the second line of this verse the Hebrew has the anomalous sentence "under four it cannot bear". This second *under* should probably be omitted.

22. is filled with food: this verb (*śāba'*) can mean to be sated or to have too much – for example, eating too much honey leads to vomiting, 25:16. But with *leḥem* (**food**) as its object it always in Proverbs (12:11; 20:13; 28:19) denotes an ample sufficiency of food – that is, relative prosperity – attained by hard work and diligence. So although some interpreters have taken the phrase here to refer to gluttony (for example, *REB* "a fool gorging himself"), prosperity is the more probable meaning. This is also the meaning of this verb in 30:9, where it is stated that a consequence of wealth may be arrogance (in the form of contempt of God).

23. an unloved woman: literally, "a hated woman". The brevity of the reference makes this line difficult to interpret, and the commentators are divided. Several commentators (Delitzsch, Wildeboer, Toy, Oesterley, Plöger) think that it refers to an unattractive old maid who unexpectedly finds a husband, and this is probably correct. But others think that the woman in question is a divorcee; according to Roth, Sauer and Driver, the term "unloved" may be a technical term having this meaning. While several passages in the Old Testament deal with divorce (Dt. 21:15–17 and Gen. 29:31–3) they cannot, as has been suggested, be relevant here because although they refer to situations in which a man has two wives and loves one but "hates" (that is, does not love, or is repelled by) the other, there is there no question of divorce and so none of remarriage. Only Dt. 24:1–4 connects the word "hate" with divorce; this is a case where the husband has found some "indecency" in his wife, and his hatred is followed by divorce. It is possible that the present text refers to such a woman, who remarries despite her past reputation; but this is by no means certain. The view that "hated" is actually a technical term for a divorcee cannot be sustained. The "old maid" theory fits the text adequately. Van der Ploeg proposes a repointing of the Hebrew word rendered **gets a husband** by *RSV*, which would produce a translation such as "an unloved wife when she takes control (of the household)"; but this hardly seems necessary.

succeeds: better, "supplants".

24–28. This numerical proverb lacks the "x, x + 1" formula (see on 6:16–19). It has been suggested that this is an indication of a late date; the formula also occurs in Sir. (23:16; 25:7; 50:25). Although no moral is explicitly drawn (contrast 6:6–11), the fact that all the animals listed have been selected for their exceptional *wisdom* is a clear pointer to such a moral. This moral must lie in the relationship between this wisdom and the other characteristic common to all four examples, that is, their apparent insignificance or weakness (the word *qāṭān/qāṭôn*, *RSV* **small**, has this meaning rather than that of physical smallness – compare, for example, Exod. 18:22; 1 Sam. 15:17; Isa. 60:22; Am. 7: 2, 5 for this meaning).

The point of the proverb is that these apparently feeble creatures achieve success in various ways through their wisdom; so, it is implied, human beings who acquire wisdom can overcome their natural disadvantages.

At the same time the proverb is the result of unusually acute observation of the natural world, and as such marks a stage in progress towards a scientific understanding of it.

25. Compare 6:6–8. Another characteristic of **ants** is referred to in a proverb incorporated into Amarna Letter no. 252 (*ANET*, p. 486). The ants are here called a **people** (*ʿam*), implying a high level of organization.

26. badgers: probably the so-called rock-badger, not the European kind, thought to be capable of building its home in particularly difficult terrain. They also are called a **people**.

27. locusts: one of a number of different kinds of locust mentioned in the Old Testament. The fact that they have **no king** (compare what is said about ants in 6:7) to organize and lead them was regarded as a testimony to their unusual wisdom shown in their ability to organize themselves (see Jg. 21:25 for a pronouncement on this subject). The second line apparently refers to the appearance of military organization in the relentless march of a swarm of locusts. **march in rank**: literally, "go out, dividing". *yāṣā*, "to go out", is a regular term used of an army on the march; *ḥāṣaṣ*, "to divide", may refer to a formation into divisions or ranks. The effectiveness of a swarm of locusts in achieving its purpose was too well known to require specific mention.

28. lizard (*śᵉmāmît*): the gecko or house-lizard, remarkable for its ability to climb walls. **you can take**: this verb should perhaps be re-pointed as passive: "can be taken" – a reference to its harmlessness. While the other three creatures are represented as taking positive action, the lizard is simply unobtrusively "there". But this example also differs from the other three in that the lizard's finding its way into **kings' palaces** is hardly an achievement beneficial to itself. This is, rather, a humorous comment on its cheekiness: in a Pickwickian sense, it does better than all the others; and "kings' palaces" makes a climax for the whole group.

29–31. This numerical proverb is difficult to interpret, mainly owing to the obscurity of the last line of v. 31, which as it stands in MT is almost certainly corrupt. In MT the first three examples cited are animal but the fourth is human (**a king**). However, Thomas

(*VTS* Suppl. 3, 1955, p. 291), Roth and Scott proposed reconstructions of the final line which would make that line also refer to an animal, so making the whole proverb an animal proverb similar to vv. 24–8.

29. are stately: the verb employed here means "to do (something) well". The examples which follow make it clear that the stateliness of carriage is seen as an indication of superiority or leadership.

30. The **lion** has a magnificent appearance which matches its courage. Of the four examples given, only this one has a detailed description extending over a whole verse. For a possible reason see on v. 31 below.

31. the strutting cock: this is the interpretation of the ancient versions, but is not necessarily the correct one. MT has a phrase, "girt of loins", perhaps an epithet which would be familiar to the original readers but not to us, designating a particular animal, rather than an actual name, though attempts have been made by some modern scholars to find a name concealed behind it. Suggestions about its identity include cockerel, war-horse, greyhound and a kind of raven. Gemser suggested the emendation of *motnayim*, "loins", to *mitnaśśē'*: "(a cockerel) raising itself up (above the hens)".

the he-goat: this animal was presumably included because of an obvious dominance over the herd. The word is preceded by a redundant *'ô*, "or", which has led some commentators to suppose that the corruption which follows begins here.

and a king standing before his people: MT has *ûmelek 'alqûm 'immō*, "and a king *'alqûm* with him". The word *'alqûm*, which is unique, is unintelligible – the suggestion that it is an Arabic word meaning "troop of soldiers" is quite impossible, and some commentators have regarded the whole line as impossible to understand or even to restore. *RSV*'s translation, accepted with reservations by McKane (compare Driver, *Bib.* 32 [1951], p. 194) is based on an emendation to *ûmelek qām 'el-'ammô*. Among other proposals for emendation, Ringgren suggested *ûmelek kᵉ'ēl qām bᵉ'ammô*, "and the king who appears like a god to his people". A major alternative to this type of interpretation is *ûmelek lō' qāmû 'immô*, "and a king against whom no-one rises up" (Barucq; compare again Driver). T. C. Vriezen (1965, pp. 345–52) improbably suggested that *qûm* is an error for *qôs*, the name of the Edomite war-god.

There is no certainty about these or any other suggestions which have been made. It may, however, be said that the picture of a king leading his people best fits the rest of the proverb. This line would then form its climax: it would be an encomium on kingship in which kings are compared with the "kings" of the animal world as being the greatest of them, in particular with the lion, to which attention is especially drawn (compare 2 Sam. 1:23, where Saul and Jonathan are said to have been swifter than eagles and stronger than lions).

32–33. The form of this proverb resembles that of an admonition (v. 32) followed by the reason for it (v. 33). There are obscurities in v. 32, but v. 33 suggests that the point of the proverb is a warning that actions always entail consequences.

32. have been foolish: elsewhere this verb (*nbl*), like the noun *nābāl* (see on 17:7), has a stronger connotation than that of mere folly, and here may imply contempt for others. **have been devising evil**: this verb (*zāmam*) does not always have a pejorative sense: in 31:16 it is used positively or neutrally of making plans. Plöger thinks that it has such a sense here, and renders the line by "and when you reflect on it afterwards".

put your hand on your mouth: the Hebrew has no verb, but simply "hand on mouth". Elsewhere (Job 21:5; 29:9; 40:4) putting the hand over the mouth or lips is a sign that one is amazed or overwhelmed; here it presumably means to be appalled by a realization of the probable consequences of one's actions. McKane, however, renders the line by "if you dabble in intrigue with your hand on your mouth" – that is, secretly – leaving some expression such as "watch your step!" to be inferred.

33. The point of the proverb lies in the last, or possibly the second, line of this verse. The second line probably refers to a punch on the **nose** and its consequences. The third line, which plays on two meanings of *'ap* – singular, "nose", dual *'appayim*, **anger** – is somewhat similar in meaning to the second; some commentators hold it to be a later gloss. The point of the verse is that just as when sour milk is shaken and then squeezed it **produces curds**, so resentment caused by behaviour such as is described in v. 32 will, when provoked beyond a certain point, break out in violent retaliation (**strife**).

Although the triple form of this verse probably accounts for its placement here, this is not a numerical proverb in the usual sense.

"WORDS OF KING LEMUEL"
AN INSTRUCTION
CHAPTER 31, VERSES 1–9

That these verses constitute a distinct section of the book was already known to the LXX translators: in that version they are separated from vv. 10–31 by chapters 25–9. (See above on 30:1–33.) This is a brief example of the genre of the "royal Instruction" of which there are examples extant from both Egypt and Mesopotamia, notably the Egyptian *Instruction for King Merikare* (*ANET*, pp. 414–18) and the *Instruction of King Amenemhet* (*ANET*, pp. 418–19) and the Babylonian *Advice to a Prince* (W. G. Lambert, *Babylonian Wisdom Literature*, Oxford, 1960, pp. 110–15). This is, however, the only extant example of a royal Instruction given by a mother rather than a father. But it must be remembered that the queen mother occupied a position of power in the kingdom of Judah, and apparently also in some other kingdoms of the ancient Semitic world.

The Instruction appears to be of non-Israelite origin like the "Words of Agur". The name Lemuel is a Semitic but not a Hebrew name, and Massa may be a territory in North Arabia (see above on 30:1). As with 30:1, LXX has no proper names in 31:1: it appears to have divided the word Lemuel into two words, *lᵉmô ʾēl*, "(spoken by God"); and it rendered Massa by "divine oracle", so disguising the foreign origin of the Instruction. The latter is, however, confirmed by the language, which includes some non-Hebraic forms.

The Instruction, probably placed here at the end of the book as summing up the teaching of earlier chapters, presents a picture of a model ruler. It consists of a series of admonitions to a young king about his duties, primarily of a judicial nature. He is to avoid involvement with women who may exercise a pernicious influence on him, to keep sober so that his judgement may not be impaired, and, as judge of his people, to maintain the legal rights of the poor and helpless – a principal duty of ancient Near Eastern kings.

2. What?: since there is no verb, the implication of the use of this thrice repeated word, and indeed the reason why it is repeated, are unclear. Toy and Ringgren suggested "What shall I say to you?", with some support from LXX; Dahood, "What ails you?"; Scott, "Now then!". Alternatively, it has been suggested that the word (*mah*) is Arabic and means "Take heed!" (so McKane and Plöger). But *bar* (**son**) is neither Hebrew nor Arabic, but Aramaic! **son of**

my vows: compare Hannah's vow in 1 Sam. 1:11.

3. *ḥayil*, **strength**, here denotes virility or sexual power. **your ways** (*derākekā*) is hardly an adequate parallel. Scott and others proposed emendation to *yerākekā*, literally, "your loins", a word which also has a sexual connotation. On the other hand, Bauer (1958, p. 91) interpreted MT in a political sense as referring to "power" and "dominion" (the latter on the basis of Ugaritic *drkt*). **who destroy**: MT has an infinitive here (*meḥôt*); but some commentators, probably correctly, repoint the word as a feminine plural participle, *mōḥôt*. **kings**: the form of this word is not Hebrew but Aramaic. A biblical example of a man "destroyed" in this way by a woman is Samson (Jg. 16).

4. It is not . . . to drink: perhaps better, "Let there be . . . no drinking" (Driver, *Bib.* 32 [1951], pp. 194–5). The repetition of **It is not for kings** is difficult to account for, and may be a scribal error, together with this second occurrence of *Lemuel* (here pointed as *lemō'ēl*). With these omissions, the verse becomes a normal parallel couplet. **to drink** (*šetô*): on this unusual form of the infinitive see again Driver. The context (v. 5) suggests that this is not an absolute prohibition but a warning not to drink too much. **to desire**: this word, whether read as Kethib (*'ô*, "or") or as Qere *'ê* ("where?"), is difficult. It is probably a corruption of *'awwāh*, "desire". **strong drink** (*šēkār*): this word, frequently paralleled, as here with *yayin*, **wine**, may denote a kind of strong beer (compare 20:1).

5. All the verbs in this verse are unaccountably singular forms. LXX, however, has plurals. The verse is characteristic of the tone of the whole instruction, which is concerned entirely with the *duties* of a king, not with his undoubted rights and privileges. As judges, kings are not above the law but must observe law and custom (**what has been decreed**) and are to ensure in particular that the legal rights of those citizens who, being poor or otherwise defenceless (*benê-'ōnî*, **afflicted**; compare the note on *'ānî* at 22:22) are not disregarded (**pervert**, literally, "alter").

6–7. There is a deliberate antithesis between these two verses and vv. 4–5 which is strongly emphasized by the repetition of the same words. Indulgence in **strong drink** and **wine** – now chiastically placed in reverse order – is again the theme. But whereas these are bad for kings, they are now commanded (**Give**, imperative) to be made available to certain other classes of person: the **perishing** and those **in . . . distress**. To **drink and forget**, which has a bad connotation for kings, is now said to be right for such people.

This rather strange couplet, which seems out of keeping in a list of royal duties, has been very differently regarded by the commentators. Oesterley regarded it as "a cynical piece of advice wholly out of harmony with the ideals of the wisdom writers in general". Some commentators, taking a similar view, considered it to be a later addition to the instruction. Others saw it as showing genuine concern for unfortunates who, as they no longer had anything to live for, ought to be allowed to get drunk in order to make them oblivious of their sufferings. Dahood saw here a possible allusion to a common practice of offering a "cup of consolation" referred to in Jer. 16:7. The view that the couplet is an addition to the original text is supported by the fact that it is not addressed (or not solely addressed) to King Lemuel, since the imperative **Give** is plural.

6. perishing; **in bitter distress**: these are both somewhat vague terms. The first, *'ōbēd*, is rendered "going to die" by McKane, "pining away" by Plöger and "despairing" by *REB*. In view of the context (**poverty**, v. 7) and passages such as Job 31:19, where it is used of those who lack clothing and is paralleled with "the poor", it almost certainly denotes the destitute and starving. If this is so, Oesterley's comment may be justified: to offer drink to such persons without offering material help may be described as "cynical". **in bitter distress** would of course include such persons, but has a wider connotation.

8–9. These verses revert to, or continue, the theme of vv. 4–5. The general considerations of those verses are now followed by imperatives addressed in the singular to Lemuel. **Open your mouth**: that is, deliver legal judgements. The king was evidently ultimately responsible for the administration of justice. **the dumb**; **all who are left desolate**: as in v. 6, the identity of these classes of person is not clear. **dumb**: most commentators have understood this word figuratively, as referring to persons who are incapable of conducting their own defence or prevented from doing so through intimidation exercised by powerful opponents. In either case, a parallel with the second phrase is required; but the meaning of *bᵉnê ḥᵃlôp* (*RSV* **left desolate**, literally, "sons of *ḥᵃlôp*") is completely obscure. The Hebrew verb *ḥālap* can mean to pass away or vanish, but is not elsewhere used of human beings. The phrase can hardly mean "orphaned", an interpretation favoured by a number of commentators. Others have interpreted it by invoking the cognate languages.

Thomas (*VT* 15 [1965], p. 277) conjectured "imbeciles" on the basis of an Arabic word, and McKane "victims of circumstance" by comparison with a Nabatean one; Driver, (*Bib.* 32 [1951], pp. 195–6), referring to Aramaic and Arabic roots, suggested that the phrase may mean "opponents", and rendered the line by "Open your mouth against the suit of all his adversaries". But no consensus has been reached, and the meaning of the phrase remains obscure.

A POEM IN PRAISE OF THE "GOOD WIFE" AN ACROSTIC POEM

31:10–31

Discussion – from a man's point of view – of good and bad women runs through the wisdom literature. In particular, most Egyptian instructions from *Ptahhotep* onwards (third millennium BC) include the topic, and often in connection with marriage: the choice of a suitable wife was a matter of great importance to a man with regard both to his domestic happiness and his career. The Book of Proverbs is no exception. 31:10–31 is a poem which stands fully within the wisdom tradition. Yet it has its own particular character.

E. Jacob (1971, pp. 287–95) pointed out that much of what is said here about this woman goes far beyond what any real woman could aspire to, and suggested that the whole poem is an allegory in which the woman is personified Wisdom herself. McCreesh (1985, pp. 25–46) also saw the poem as a description of omnicompetent Wisdom, and pointed out a further significant characteristic: that, in contrast to the treatment of the theme in the earlier non-Israelite instructions, it is here the woman who completely dominates the scene, while the husband, although he "sits with the elders of the land" (v. 23), is a very minor character, whose only other function is to praise her (v. 28), so giving her what is due to Wisdom from an ordinary mortal. M. B. Crook (1954, pp. 137–40) also observed that the description is an ideal one, but accounted for this by arguing that the poem was originally an instruction for young girls leaving school, intended as a model of wifely virtues to which they ought to aspire. E. L. Lyons (1987, pp. 237–45), less plausibly, saw it as a pre-monarchical portrait of a matriarch.

However this may be, there can be no doubt that in its present position in the book the poem – which in form is not an Instruction but a hymn of praise (Wolters 1988, pp. 446–57) – is intended to recall not only what is said about wives in general in the sentence literature, but also the figure of Wisdom in chapters 1–9. Together with 31:1–9, which sums up the earlier teaching about kings, the poem forms the climax of the book, rounding it off by recalling a principal theme of the first section. It is significant that its setting is the *house*; and the final editor of the book has clearly intended that the reader should remember that Wisdom is the builder of her own house (9:1; 14:1). This house which she has built and to which she invites her guests (9:3–6) is a house of peace, well-being, industry and successful living in which, in contrast to that of the woman Folly or of the "strange woman", those who love her enjoy perfect contentment and an honourable position in life (v. 23).

The poem is, like a number of the psalms in the Psalter and Lam. 1–4, an alphabetic acrostic, in which the successive verses begin with the successive letters (twenty-two) of the Hebrew alphabet. It presupposes a literate readership (it must have been a written composition from the start), and is probably a relatively late composition. As with other examples of the form, the necessity of observing this *formal* sequence has resulted in a lack of *thematic* sequence. Within the constraints of the general theme, the topics dealt with, although they all contribute to the picture, are arranged in no thematic order, and there are repetitions. Only the first and concluding verses give the poem a basic structure.

The picture – whether allegorical in intention or not – presented here is of a well-to-do family, neither aristocratic nor royal, which has achieved the prosperity and stability to which the peasant farmer of 10:1–22:16 aspired, and which is promised as a reward for decent, honest hard work in such proverbs as 28:19, 20; it is also far removed from the life depicted in chapters 1–9 and 22:17–24:22.

10. A good wife: see on 12:4, whose first line reads like a summary version of this poem. **who can find . . . ?**: this question can imply an impossibility (Ec. 7:24); but here, in view of 12:4, it presumably indicates rarity rather than impossibility. "Finding a wife" is used in a mundane sense in 18:22; the verb is also used of acquiring Wisdom in 1:28; 8:35; Job 28:12, 13. **far more precious than jewels**: a similar expression is used of Wisdom in 3:15. See on 3:13–18 for other similar passages.

11. gain: literally, "spoils" (*šālāl*); see on 16:19. This may refer to material wealth acquired by the wife through her industry and perspicacity, or may have a wider connotation. That this is a metaphor is recognized by many commentators including Gemser and Plöger, and also by *KB*³. Thomas (*VT* Suppl.3, 1955, pp. 291–2), however, rejected this interpretation and suggested the meaning "wool", and Driver "progeny", both citing supposed Arabic cognates; these suggestions, however, are speculative and unnecessary.

12. This verse probably refers to the commercial activities described in the following verses: such a wife always adds to her husband's wealth and sees that he never suffers losses. The verb (*gāmal*) is similarly used in 3:30b and 11:17a.

13. seeks: that is, takes trouble over acquiring, or "chooses" (so *REB*). **wool; flax**: for making clothes. It is not clear whether these materials are provided from the family farm or whether they are purchased from outside. **with willing hands**: or possibly "in the business of her hands" – that is, the work which she does with her hands is done competently.

14. afar is a relative term. This wife is unlike the peasant who lives from hand to mouth, as she has the means to import delicacies or luxury goods into her house like a merchant ship bringing imported goods from foreign countries. This casual allusion to foreign sea trade may suggest a late date for the poem.

15. food: despite McKane's statement that this meaning of *ṭerep* "cannot be justified", *RSV* is correct. Although the usual meaning of the word is "prey", it has this derived meaning in late works: Ps. 111:5; Mal. 3:10; Job 24:5. *RSV* is supported by many commentaries and by *KB*³ and *REB*, and the word was so understood by LXX. Kuhn's proposal to emend it to the rare word *ṭôraḥ*, "burden" is unnecessary. **provides**: perhaps better, "apportions" (*nātan*). **and tasks for her maidens**: this third line, similar to 27:27, may be a gloss.

16. Whatever may have been the legal status of women at various periods of Israelite history, there were no doubt always strong-minded and competent wives who took the initiative in matters concerning the family fortunes; compare Abigail in 1 Sam. 25. The wife depicted in this poem clearly acts with the full approval of her husband (compare v. 11). But it is she who buys a field after careful consideration (*zām*ᵉ*māh*, *RSV* **considers** – see on 30:32). **the fruit of her hands**: that is, she uses the profits from her commercial activities (vv. 18, 24) to extend the property. **she plants**: read Qere *nāṭ*ᵉ*ʿāh*.

17. Both lines of this verse speak of the vigour with which the wife sets about her work. To gird the loins is to tuck up the skirts of a garment with a belt in preparation for some activity (compare Exod. 12:11; 1 Kg. 18:46; 2 Kg. 4:29; Lk. 12:35). **with strength**: that is, energetically. **and makes her arms strong**: better, "summons the strength of her arms" (compare Am. 2:14; Nah. 2:1 [Heb. 2] for a similar use of this verb). *LXX* adds "for work".

18. Her lamp does not go out: this line probably means simply that she continues to work far into the night in order to increase her profits still more. It has been suggested that there is an allusion here to the use of **lamp** (*nēr*) as a symbol of prosperity and success; but in the three passages which refer to the "putting out" of the lamp of the wicked (13:9; 20:20; 24:20) the verb employed is a different one.

19. distaff (*kîšôr*); **spindle** (*pelek*): these words occur nowhere else in the Old Testament, and their precise meaning is not certain; but they are both objects used in spinning wool. The second occurs in Mishnaic Hebrew, but the contexts do not indicate whether a distaff or a spindle is meant.

20. The wife recognizes the same duty of generosity towards the poor as is advocated elsewhere in Proverbs. Although in general there is little sign of links between adjacent verses in this poem other than the alphabetic sequence in the initial letters, there is an additional, verbal, link here with v. 19 in the repetition of the phrase *yādehā šill^eḥāh* ("She puts her hands," v. 19; **She opens her hand**, v. 20) together with the use of the parallel word *kap*, also "hand", in v. 19b.

21. snow: compare 26:1. **scarlet** (*šānîm*): the reference is to garments or cloaks made of scarlet wool – luxury items. But since this does not seem to be relevant to keeping warm, some commentators have proposed that this word should be repointed as *š^enayim*, literally, "two" – that is, "double (garments)" or garments of double thickness. Both *LXX* and Vulg. understood it in this way. Dahood and Driver (on the basis of Ugaritic) together with McKane and Plöger, however, retain *MT*. McKane argues that "it is the quality of the clothes they wear which keeps them warm". It is true that the following verse is concerned with their quality, but the slight change of vocalization makes the better sense.

22. coverings (*marbaddîm*): see on 7:16. Although she does not disdain working with her hands, the wife's own clothes are of the finest imported material. **fine linen** or byssus was imported from Egypt. **purple** (*'argāmān*): a foreign word of unknown origin meaning wool or cloth dyed with a purple dye extracted from the murex, a shellfish found off the Phoenician coast. Like fine linen, it was exported as a luxury item throughout the ancient world. Compare the "purple and fine linen" of the rich man in Lk. 16:19.

23. Compare 12:4. There is no reason to suppose that the husband's reputation has anything to do directly with his or his wife's smart appearance. It is rather due to his wife's successful enhancement of the family's wealth that the **husband is known** – that is, is deferred to as a solid and influential citizen (compare the more detailed picture in Job 29). **in the gates**: see on 24:7. **land** (*'ereṣ*): although it was in the gates of the city that the **elders** met (compare Ru. 4:1, where the wealthy farmer Boaz takes his seat there), it is unlikely that *'ereṣ* here means "city" (Dahood). More probably it means "district" or "region" (so McKane, *REB*).

24. linen garments (*sādîn*): this is a foreign word, possibly of Egyptian origin. Although it occurs also in Jg. 14:12,13; Isa. 3:23, its meaning is uncertain. The commentaries render it in quite different ways, for example, shawl, sash, undergarment and linen. It is doubtful whether it is related to the English word "satin" (Gemser). **merchant** (*k^ena^{ca}nî*): not a Canaanite in the sense familiar from the rest of the Old Testament, but a – probably Phoenician – trader. This late use of the word is found only here and in Zech. 14:21; Job 41:6 (Heb. 40:30).

25. Frequently in the poetical texts of the Old Testament the figure of putting on clothing is used with the meaning of showing oneself in one's true colours or displaying one's true character – for example, righteousness, majesty, and also, as here, **Strength** (*'ōz*, compare Isa. 52:1) and **dignity** (*hādār*, Ps. 104:1; Job 40:10). It is in this sense that the wife is "clothed" with these abstract qualities. However, there is also an echo here of v. 22, where she is literally clothed in splendid garments. These characteristics show themselves in her appearance and bearing.

laughs at: see on 1:26. The wife feels secure in the prosperity which she has achieved for her family, and can afford to treat the future lightheartedly.

26. This verse is most naturally taken to mean that the wife instructs her own children, who are mentioned in v. 28 as blessing her (compare the mother as teacher in 1:8), though Toy thought that it refers to the instructions which she gives to her household servants (compare v. 27). The mention of **wisdom**, however, makes it possible to associate her with Wisdom herself, who appears as a teacher in the earlier chapters of the book, especially in chapter 8. **teaching of kindness**: that is, kindly or gentle teaching. But the phrase could also mean reliable or sound teaching.

27. She looks well to (*ṣôpiyyāh*): that is, supervises or keeps an eye on. The word is used in the same sense as in 15:3 (*RSV* "keeping watch on"). It is an unusual form of the feminine participle (see *GK* 75v); there is a similar form in 7:11 (*hōmiyyāh*, *RSV* "loud"). Wolters (1985, pp. 577–87) sees here a pun on the Greek *sophia*, "wisdom"; this would necessitate a very late date for the poem. **ways**: literally, "goings", that is, what goes on. **eat the bread of idleness**: that is, food not earned by labour.

28–31. The poem ends appropriately with praise: first the praise of the good wife's family is cited, and finally (v. 31) there is a general call to the readers to join in her praise.

28. rise up: a preliminary to making an important declaration (compare Mic. 6:1; Jer. 1:17; 1 Chr. 28:2; 2 Chr. 30:27). **call her blessed**: the verb is *'iššēr*, related to *'ašrê*, "Happy (is)" (3:13 etc.). It is a strong expression of approval as well as a recognition of good fortune (compare Job 29:11; Ps. 72:17; Mal. 3:12).

29. have done excellently: in Dt. 8:17 and Ezek. 28:4 this phrase (*'āśāh ḥayil*) means to acquire wealth. In Num. 24:18 and 1 Sam. 14:48, however, it means "to do valiant deeds" in war. Here it probably includes the first of these senses but also has a wider connotation. See on 12:4 (on *ḥayil*).

30. The point made in the first line of this verse is not that **Charm** and **beauty** are undesirable in a woman, but that they are **deceitful** and **vain** in the sense of being ephemeral. **a woman who fears the Lord**: it is strange that, after such an eulogy of a woman who relies completely on her own abilities, her piety should be mentioned only at the very end of the poem, where it lacks the force which it would have had if it had been introduced in v. 10. Some commentators have therefore suggested that the reference to the fear of Yahweh has been substituted by a later editor for some other attribute. LXX has a double reference: "for it is an intelligent woman that is blessed; and let her praise the fear of the Lord". Although the textual history behind this is not clear, it is possible that the Hebrew text originally had simply "an intelligent woman".

31. the fruit of her hands: that is, her achievements (the equivalent of **her works**. But **Give her** (*t*ᵉ*nû-lā*) is strange. Driver (*ETL* 26, 1950, p. 352) and Gemser suggested the repointing of the verb as *tannû*, "Recount" or "Celebrate" (compare Jg. 5:11; 11:40). See on 9:9. **praise her in the gates**: that is, in the hearing of all the people. For this use of "gate" compare Ru. 3:11, "all the gate of my people" – *RSV* "all my fellow townsmen".

GENERAL INDEX

INDEX OF AUTHORS

INDEX OF BIBLICAL REFERENCES

(excluding Proverbs)

JEREMIAH

LAMENTATIONS

EZEKIEL